Live Television Drama, 1946–1951

Live Television Drama, 1946–1951

by
WILLIAM HAWES

McFarland & Company, Inc., Publishers
Jefferson, North Carolina, and London

Library of Congress Cataloguing-in-Publication Data

Hawes, William, 1931–
    Live television drama, 1946–1951 / by William Hawes.
        p.   cm.
    Includes bibliographical references and index.
    ISBN 0-7864-0905-3 (softcover : 50# alkaline paper)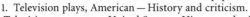
    1. Television plays, American — History and criticism.
    2. Television programs — United States — History and criticism.
    I. Title.
    PN1992.3.U5H385   2001
    812'.02509045 — dc21   00-51136

British Library cataloguing data are available

Cover image: © 2000 PhotoDisc

Manufactured in the United States of America

McFarland & Company, Inc., Publishers
  Box 611, Jefferson, North Carolina 28640
  www.mcfarlandpub.com

In loving memory of
Ella Margaret Hawes

Acknowledgments

Although this history is based mainly on data gathered over many years from network records and several libraries, as cited throughout the study, the author is deeply indebted to those who have provided correspondence, conversations, presentations, and interviews:

Eddie Albert, Tom C. Battin, John Behrens, Terry Benczik, Dick Block, Bert Briller, Herbert Brodkin, David Bruskin, Walter Coblenz, Aaron M. Cohen, Norman Corwin, Marc D'Alleyrand, Marc Daniels, Roy Danish, Robert L. Davis, Jr., Marilyn Dean, Jeanne Dembroski, Selise E. Eiseman, Horton Foote, Grace Voss Frederick, John Forsythe, William Fuller, John Furia, Lillian Gish, Claribel Baird Halstead, William Halstead, Kenneth A. Harwood, Catharine Heinz, Robert Herridge, Charlton Heston, Robert L. Hilliard, Marjorie Holyoak, Arthur Hungerford, Kim Hunter, Gwyniver Jones, Laura Kapnick, Jacqueline Kavanagh, William Lafferty, Robert J. Landry, Piper Laurie, Robert E. Lewine, Margaret Lynch, Delbert Mann, Mercedes McCambridge, Peter Miner, Worthington C. Miner, Florence Monroe, Alan J. Neuman, J. Paul Nickell, Agnes Nixon, Carole Parnes, Arthur Penn, Frank Pierson, Mary Kay Platte, Fred Rappoport, Margaret Miner Rawson, Gene Reynolds, Yvette Romero, Robert Saudek, George Schaefer, Franklin J. Schaffner, Rod Serling, David Shepard, Garry Simpson, Edward Stasheff, Lela Swift, John Tracy, David Victor, Gore Vidal, Melvin Wald, Edgar E. Willis, Shelley Winters, Robert Wise, William Work, Earl and Rhoda Wynn.

Delbert Mann and Walter Coblenz have been particularly generous with their time, advice, and industry prominence, and the late Alvin Guggenheim arranged for many celebrities to visit my classes.

I am indebted to the Columbia Broadcasting System, the National Broadcasting Company, the Directors Guild of America, the National Association of Broadcasters, and the BBC Written Archives Centre for use of their libraries, the National Endowment for the Humanities for a grant, and the University of Houston for leaves, research grants from the Office of Sponsored Programs, and for teaching two semesters in England. Most photographs have been provided by Photofest, New York, with the welcome assistance of Howard Mandelbaum.

My gratitude as always goes to William Kenneth Hawes, III, Robert E. Hawes, Nancy Hawes Wagner, and Michael Cloud for their encouragement, support, and love.

Contents

1

....

Experimental Television Drama, Origins to 1946

American television dramas number in the thousands. Many have achieved world prominence through syndication and a kind of immortality from preservation and reproduction that enables some programs and series to rank with the best-known cultural achievements of the 20th century. Despite this abundance and incredible recognition, American television drama remains relatively unstudied and unchallenged by rigorous scholarly publications, and so it is an excellent area for research.

The subject of this book is a unique era when television was "live," perished as it was broadcast, and would be remembered more for what it was not than for what it was. The live era of television drama—1946 to 1958—was an early, not a mature, period of achievement; it was an exciting period for creative and commercial accomplishment.

The mystique of "live" appearance has been passed on from previous generations. If an act was "live," it was "real," it was the genuine item. The person or the event materialized right before the viewer's eyes, proving the adage, "seeing is believing." So, the entertainment business throughout the 19th century promoted live acts in vaudeville, in circus sideshows, and in touring companies. The live and "in person" act sold the entertainer and the show. With moving pictures gaining prominence at the turn of the century, the work of entertainers of all kinds could be preserved on film. Performers did not look as good on film as they did in person; but film stocks quickly improved, and competition increased. The radio industry, for the most part, insisted on "live" shows, both "real-life" programs such as news and fictional presentations such as dramas. The preference for live productions generated by radio interests, where television was created and nurtured, lasted until about 1960. By then, film and videotape were widely accepted by the public and made financing expensive shows possible. Live television dramas disappeared, and the recorded era began. This is a history of the early part of the live era.

A "live" program is one in which the performers are in the studio or on location as the show is being broadcast. Whatever is said or done is telecast to viewers at the moment it happens, and that performance instantly perishes. During the live period a full season was 39 weeks before another program replaced it, usually in late spring or summer. Often anthologies were on trial, typically during the summer, with a contract commitment of 13 weeks or less. At the end of 13 weeks, if the show seemed promising, its option was picked up or renewed, usually for another 13 weeks.

The Big Picture

The history of television drama may be divided into four periods. The first American drama appeared in 1928; therefore, one could say the experimental period extends from its origin in 1928 to the 1947 debut of the first sustained anthology series.[1] The following decade, often referred to as the "golden age," is the decade of dramas that emanated mainly live from New York City (through 1951) and then from Los Angeles. If comparisons are useful, this period's equivalent in cinema history is 1907 — the beginning of D. W. Griffith's apprentice years — to 1918, encompassing the industry's move to Hollywood and into feature films. By 1958 the character of television dramas had shifted from apprenticeship to sophisticated anthologies to series, from New York to Los Angeles, and from live dramas to recording on film or videotape. This book focuses on the years when live drama on television came primarily from New York.

During the period 1958–1975, television drama frequently lost personnel to the film industry, wherein the newcomers from television generally continued to work. Some graduated to the loftier echelons of feature film. Middle class angst, common folks with strong personalities, characters involved in familiar problem-solving situations, actors whose lives on camera and off seemed like welcome neighbors, stunning or clever commercial messages that sold ordinary products or services as solutions to viewers' problems, imagined or real, were the stuff of television dramas. The movies, on the contrary, besides having locations of grandeur and scope, color and bigness, were still devoted to their stock-in-trade — the regal few, the beautiful, wealthy, powerful, and extremely wicked nobility in wildly romantic action that would require more stunt doubles and special effects to allow anthropomorphic characters, not ordinary human beings, to pursue their often naughty adventures that were inappropriate for living rooms.

A case could be made for a fourth period of television drama being from 1975 to 1995, noted for its acceptance of the human condition in facets of misery and glory, gowned and naked, with or without excuses. Media tolerance was the keynote. Long-standing European parameters of sexual acceptance merged with long-standing American fascination with violence. Such content was made available through worldwide dissemination everywhere, especially in homes, through the emerging technologies of the mid–1970s: satellites and cable television. This dissemination of dramas and information continues to force changes in content, because television is at its heart a medium of inclusion. Eventually, everyone would have to be included, would have a story to tell, or would identify with those told by others. The international appeal of television was not lost on the film industry that, during the 1980s, had its greatest profits come from computer-animated characters that minimized dialogue and maximized action, movement, spectacle, and music. How to maintain cultural differences and yet create stories with universal themes for worldwide consumption is a present and future challenge, as high-definition television and the Internet present perhaps the fifth period in drama's development beyond 2000.

Principally, this study examines the heritage of television drama in decades that, despite contemporary perceptions, were not long ago or far away.

In the 1920s, unstable mechanical scanners generated crude black-and-white images about the size of a baseball on receivers. During 1931–32, the Columbia Broadcasting System (CBS), using a mechanical process, tried out virtually every basic format, including dramatic sketches. Documenting this trial that ran over a year is difficult, but records may be boxed somewhere in the CBS archives. Vaudevillian and actress Grace Voss has recalled volunteering 15 minutes a week to do pantomimes and monologues, a few of which she wrote herself, in a six-by-eight foot space between the scanner and a blank screen and under "ghostly gray" lights. William Schudt was the energetic man in charge of experimenting at 485 Madison Avenue. Friends whom Voss invited to watch assured her television was never going anywhere.[2] In England, meanwhile, the British Broadcasting Corporation (BBC) telecast more frequent and complicated dramas.

From 1936, when the National Broadcasting Company (NBC) began telecasting experimental dramas to few viewers, to the 1939 New York World's Fair when dramas appeared regularly until the beginning of World War II, the supposition that the public would be interested in seeing Broadway on television was widely held by network administrators and critics. The belief that dramas successful on the Great White Way could be translated in terms that a huge, non-theater-oriented public would appreciate was, in retrospect, provincial. Television "theater" vanished at the end of the live period when the great mass audience basically rejected those adaptations in favor of characters in situations they recognized from everyday life, characters whom they could invite into their own homes, as the public had invited characters in radio's heyday. The details of these productions which established current procedures and the lives of production specialists who created them are relatively uninvestigated studies.

One such specialist is Garry Simpson. After graduating from Stanford University in 1938, Simpson accepted a scholarship to the Neighborhood Playhouse in New York City, where he pursued his ambitions as an actor and director. By 1940 he was director of studio productions for Scophony Television, Ltd., an English-based company operating in the United States and trying to get approval for its large-screen projection system. Before the year ended, Simpson had joined RCA's publicity division in Newark. As a theatrical director, he created short television demonstrations for department stores and for the RCA exhibit at the World's Fair, where the variety acts included the Kuklapolitan puppets. Later, Burr Tillstrom with Fran Allison would be on the network as *Kukla, Fran and Ollie.*

In 1941 Simpson moved to NBC, New York, as TV studio stage manager and director of special events. There he became involved in all phases of studio production. His list of "firsts" includes hiring the first IATSE (International Alliance of Theatrical Stage Employees) stage crew (and at a time when film comprised one-third of NBC's broadcast schedule) and, as film supervisor, selecting and renting all feature films. He directed mostly special events, such as boxing from the Jamaica Arena. After the bombing of Pearl Harbor, Simpson directed instructional television broadcasts to train area Civil Defense air-raid wardens. Then, on 12 May 1942, the FCC instigated wartime television regulations limiting transmission to four hours a week. As a result, Simpson and other experienced television personnel were recruited by the U.S. Navy and manufacturers of armaments to apply their expertise to the war effort.

In addition to NBC, General Electric staged various dramatic shows well into the 1940s. By November 1943 GE had constructed a large television studio using three cameras, anticipating the war's end. "The plant is a beaut. It is roughly about 70 feet long, 40 feet wide and 20 feet high. The walls and ceiling are sound proofed. The air-conditioning units work silently. Overhead there are 12 water-cooled mercury vapor lamps, each generating 3,000 watts of light and very, very little heat. Unlike other television studios, this plant is not a hot box."[3] GE has lots of early material, but like most companies it has not invested much in identifying photographs and detailing its activities beyond what Judy Dupuy did during the war.[4]

"Love Nest," starring Eddie Albert, Grace Bradt as "the Honeymooners," was on W2XBS (NBC), 21 September 1936. Courtesy of Eddie Albert.

So it goes with less impressive and infrequent productions elsewhere. Chicago and Los Angeles stations may be worthy of study, and the emergence of the DuMont studios may merit scholarly attention. The press carried reviews irregularly during this period, so there are some gaps. Those who witnessed these events are increasingly difficult to locate. Though researching this first generation of pioneers is taxing, documenting the lives, contributions, and significance of the individuals and corporations laboring through the birth of television drama is potentially worth the meticulous effort this would take. Not to be overlooked in this period are the works of journalists, writers, directors, and actors in radio and theater whose efforts formed the basis for much of what has become television drama.

Certainly the few war dramas would benefit from more consideration, and the attempt to transfer radio dramas to television merits another detailed investigation. There is a good deal of this information available, though radio and television materials sufficient for a thorough job are somewhat scattered. Adaptations from the stage were very popular, because they were easier to do than those from novels and short stories, and some of them were either out of copyright or low cost. Fees for anything and anyone who worked in television were minimal at the time. Television was not big business, so to a great extent that caused neglect in documenting activities at networks and stations. To this day, with rewards being few, there is no robust desire to delve into the archaeology of drama on television. But this point of view will surely change. To that end, this writer's previous book, *American Television Drama: The Experimental Years*, covers origins to 1946, followed herewith by the early period of live television drama, 1946 to 1951, including its preliminary transition to film.

The Literature

Most major bookstores show at a glance the relative abundance of film literature and the paucity of television information. The rough ratio of shelf space, for instance, may be 20:1. A closer look shows that a few genre publications such as ones on comedy or even drama with pictures, on science fiction such as *Star Trek*, and on soap operas occupy most of the shelf space. The many directors and actors who became movie celebrities are located in the film section. But studies in television drama are few. Fortunately, some playwrights have collected works with commentaries: Paddy Chayefsky, Reginald Rose, Rod Serling, JP Miller, Gore Vidal, and Horton Foote are among them. So far, individual dramas or dramatic series sponsored solely or by a variety of companies have not captured public interest to the extent that books on the subject are sought, purchased, and preserved. Although books on crime drama — television drama's initial productions — are more numerous than ever today, this genre is not studied with the same delicious excitement that the films of, say, Alfred Hitchcock stimulate. With the field over 70 years old, television drama, the vehicle for reexamining issues and changing people's minds, deserves more thoughtful attention.

Available Resources

Fundamental to the availability of materials is a willingness on the part of television companies to encourage study of television dramas. While some libraries exist at offices of networks and sponsors, the consistency of depositing materials has been jeopardized by lack of interest, poor storage methods, weak logs or records, small library staffs, limited storage space, and entangled legal complications in obtaining and using materials. Advertisers, in particular, have been overlooked as information sources and remain unrecognized for their contributions in nurturing early dramas. Legal restrictions have tended to increase, along with the expense of obtaining rights to publish photographs. Copyright to early items may be in limbo because of changes in company ownership. Some material such as the phonoscopes of television drama's earliest productions are yet to be found.

Libraries that deserve a visit are scattered all over the country. Donors have given their papers, in some cases, without any assurance that the library had the space or administrative capability of taking care of the material. Later, some donors have complained that the boxes of information they contributed were damaged or were not catalogued. Underfunded, many libraries have been given fine collections that they cannot properly handle. Into the 1980s the Television Information Office in New York centralized the principal information sources in a fine small library that enabled industry users to get references quickly. The Broadcast Pioneer Library in Washington, D.C., always had more material than it could manage in cramped quarters. Now the National Association of Broadcasters Library and Information Center in Washington, D.C., and Los Angeles libraries that concentrate on the film industry have important resources but often lack continuity for subjects. And none of the libraries outside of New York have much information on the first generation of television pioneers. The interest in public museums, such as the Museum of Television and Radio in New York, the Smithsonian Institution and the Newseum in Washington, D.C., cinema's museums of the Moving Image, and the American Advertising Museum in Portland, Oregon, indicate that the public is ready to know the details about television's history, but museums require scholarly investigation to support such cultural showcases. That research is lacking.

Research Techniques

Interviews, often on audiotape, and other projects of recent years have made an attempt to tell about television's history after World War II. The Directors Guild of America and the Academy of Television Arts and Sciences have collections of memoirs, some of which are published. Interviews are as good as the subjects are willing and able to make them. Remembrance plays tricks on even the most conscientious minds. The result may be a flawed narrative of what is remembered versus what the published record of the day seems to indicate. Retelling what it must have been like in another time, another place, is hazardous, and yet these recollections may be all we have. Therefore, scholars should prepare in detail for every important interview. Good preparation reinforces the subject's recollection without depending upon conversations relegated to videographies and reviews of known information.

Besides getting copyright clearances, identifying major individuals, preparing background notes for interviews, and locating principal libraries, an interviewer should have an unobtrusive recorder that can pick up the participant's voice from a few feet away, preferably without an obvious microphone. Equipment may impede an interview. More resistance may come from reluctant subjects who believe that some day they may write a book of their own. Usually, they do not, and so they should be encouraged to work in the moment. The potential for interviewing has a dynamic of its own. Each interviewee suggests other possible contacts. Time and money force one to speculate on what essential information an interviewee can provide. A prepared interviewer memorizes the questions and anticipates the probable answers; therefore, subtleties and new information are quickly noticed, if the interviewer listens carefully. For many famous people, a mutually respected intermediary is necessary to actually set a time to meet with them. Unfortunately, time is against scholars and interviewees for early television drama.

Another technique, perhaps the critical one, is to define the limitations of the work. A book is a synthesis of hours of interviews and, possibly, years of research. The author must target the research that must be accomplished to complete the project without straying into ancillary areas. Television drama can become a marvelous morass of enjoyment that never finds publication.

Future Study

From the end of World War II to the end of live television drama, a crystal ball materialized that envisioned the end of the century. Computers, television, audio and video tape, rocketry, color, widescreen, and greater sensory involvement were some of the inventions that would move television closer to the resolution and audio clarity of motion pictures and, thereby, would impact the future of television drama. The stories that led to these discoveries and the impact that television dramas have had in changing society suggest unlimited future areas of study. Cultural values, along with technology established in the 1940s (computers) and 1950s (magnetic tape), would be reassessed regularly throughout the latter half of the century. But important research showing how television dramas impact individuals and societies is just beginning.

Television drama is the most important form of television. A drama distills both the facts and the emotions of a situation into a succinct, understandable narrative. A drama may present the most troubling issues of the day and may suggest the options for solving these problems, projecting the temper and common sense of human behavior. A good drama has a universal theme that is recognized by all people; and yet, that theme may be presented in the narrow context of one cultural group. What does American television say to the world? What did the dramas of the late 1940s and 1950s say to viewers? What do they continue to say? Therein lies the fascination and complexity of future study. With widespread dissemination of television dramas, viewers become acquainted with world problems; with repetition, many viewers actually study in detail the positions and consequences of solving individual and collective concerns as they have been presented over the centuries. The result of such study can only bring greater enlightenment about the nature of human beings and their environment. The television drama, in part because there are so many on many different subjects, contributes an invaluable documentation of the truth and spirit of cultural heritage.

2

Postwar Television
Drama, 1946–1949

After a decade of mainly engineering experiments (1926–36), another five years of public programming demonstrations (1936–41), and the interruption of World War II (1941–45), television drama was ready once again for public viewing. On 1 July 1941 experimental stations became commercially licensed stations, and picture resolution standards increased from 405 lines in 1939 to 525 lines. Call letters of the experimental stations were changed: NBC's W2XBS became WNBT, CBS's W2XAB was WCBW, DuMont's W2XWV was WABD, in Los Angeles W6XAO changed to KTSL, W6XYZ became KTLA, and in Chicago W9XBK was WBKB. Anticipating the use of television as an advertising medium, by mid–1943 DuMont expanded its programming by one and one-half hours a week, and in November, General Electric completed a new television studio (as previously mentioned), and air conditioning and improved lighting became essential in all future construction.[1]

Though improving television facilities and programming seemed to be the principal activity during the war years, a love-hate relationship between the television and film industries was openly brewing. In 1944 plans were well underway concerning cooperative arrangements between Warner Bros. and Philco, Paramount and DuMont, 20th Century–Fox and General Electric. MGM was searching for a relationship with video while hiring radio writers, and RKO set up its own corporation for providing live or filmed packaged shows for television.[2] By contrast, in 1944 major film studio contracts for stars and new pictures included clauses that prohibited them from appearing on television.[3]

Personnel who gained even modest video experience during the war were promoted to significant responsibilities, facilities were being expanded and improved, and the struggle for distribution through chains and networks, already in progress unofficially, began officially in 1946, after the fledgling DuMont "network" claimed successful transmission of its programs from New York to Washington, DC.[4]

With television threatening business at the motion picture box office, just as radio promised to ruin vaudeville in the twenties, contractual prohibitions resulted in a rise of British and American silent films on the small screen. Temporarily, British films, especially those of Alexander Korda, and even silent films were aired on American television. When ABC-TV presented Rudolph Valentino in the silent classic *The Eagle* (1925), "It drew more excited response than any other film." This was not due to a renewed interest in silent films, but rather to the pre–Hays Office scenes of more direct lovemaking than viewers usually saw on television.[5]

After a decade of litigation, the U.S. government forced the motion picture companies that owned theaters to separate their filmmaking and distribution interests from their exhibition branches (U.S. v. Paramount Pictures, Inc., 1948). Ultimately, this gave rise to more independent producers, distributors, and exhibition companies, the release of major feature film libraries, and the use of movie stars on television. The first major film star to sign a television contract was Academy Award winner Ronald Colman.[6] When the Justice Department completed its antitrust fight against the Big Five film companies — Paramount Pictures, Warner Bros., 20th Century–Fox, Radio-Keith-Orpheum (RKO), and Metro-Goldwyn-Mayer (MGM) — in 1952, they agreed by consent decree to separate into two units: one for production and distribution and another for exhibition.[7]

During this brief interval, live television drama established itself (1946–52) and developed (1952–58). Major live dramatic program origination remained confined to the New York City area until the end of 1951, when American Telephone and Telegraph (AT&T) linked the East and West coasts. Simultaneously, huge investments were being made by the emerging television networks, headquartered in New York, that foreshadowed the future of television entertainment in Los Angeles.

Even though box office receipts for motion pictures had reached an all-time high, and the demand for radio receivers was unprecedented, 1946 held no guarantees for the future of television or television drama.[8] This was the year of transition from a wartime to a peacetime economy. Uncertainty caused extraordinary caution in business. Television looked promising, but public acceptance was untested. From 1946 to 1952 the television industry faced many problems. Some of the most complicated would take the Federal Communications Commission (FCC) four years to solve during a period in which new channel allocations were halted. The period was referred to as "The Freeze." In addition to providing a plan for allocating channels, selecting a suitable color system was necessary. Obvious postwar limitations had an even more immediate impact on television drama: personnel, matériel, facilities, distribution, advertising support, and programming content. Blacklisting also emerged as an insidious problem.

Personnel

By 1944 the turning point was reached in the war, and businesses began contemplating what they would do when it ended. NBC president Niles Trammel told the FCC that the television industry would create jobs for many thousands of men and women in radio manufacturing plants and studios. NBC was already interviewing returning veterans and conducting training courses. "There is reason to believe that television may offer even more new employment in the coming postwar period than sound broadcasting did after the last war."[9] Distinguished first generation pioneers at NBC, such as Thomas H. Hutchinson and Thomas Lyne Riley, and Gilbert Seldes at CBS, pursued other roles, and they no longer influenced network dramas.

Vice president John F. Royal and producer/directors Edward Sobol and Ernest Colling would continue at NBC for the next half dozen years, 1946–52, and pioneer Worthington Miner would continue to be the exception at CBS.

When the war ended, NBC had four principal producer/directors for dramas: Edward Sobol and Ernest S. Colling, who were experienced, and Ronald Oxford and Frederick H. Coe, the newcomers. Oxford joined NBC somewhat before Coe in 1945. So, on 12 May 1946, the highly praised Edward Sobol directed "Blithe Spirit" for NBC's Sunday night showcase, the *NBC Television Theatre*. Such work, a carryover from the previous decade, suggested what anthology television drama would become during the postwar years. Reviewer Joe Koehler wrote: "NBC is first in drama. That's not even open to question with Ed Sobol, rating every award that anybody could give out for producing straight legit entertainment from Broadway successes."[10] Ernest Colling, the other senior producer/director at NBC, was especially good at handling performers in crime or mystery scripts, but his productions on the whole received mixed reviews. *The Billboard* claimed that "Ronald Oxford and Fred Coe aren't at their best with story material and while Oxford had delivered acceptably on one or two assignments, he doesn't rate with his seniors, Colling and Sobol."[11]

In 1945, when William S. Paley returned from Europe, he expected his trusted friend Paul Kesten, a single man who had devoted his life to the company, to become CBS president, sharing responsibility by being in charge of daily operation. Kesten had severe arthritis that prevented his appointment, and Frank Stanton became president instead. A year earlier (4 May 1944) CBS had resumed live programming on WCBW and television operations in the Grand Central Terminal Building, 15 Vanderbilt Avenue, and by 1945 this facility was expanded.

Meanwhile, Kesten and Worthington Miner had become close associates, as CBS sought FCC acceptance by Dr. Peter Goldmark's mechanical color system as the industry standard. His color system, however, utilizing the very high frequency (VHF) range, proved to be difficult to sell, and it ultimately lost out to standards set down by the National Television System Committee (NTSC) that resembled NBC's compatible electronic color system.[12] As the outlook for a CBS color system wavered, Miner tumbled from director of television — with all the perks of a large office at Vanderbilt Avenue — to director of programming development, a meaningless title, and to a small office at the CBS building on 52nd Street.[13] Although the FCC's final decision on color was still pending, prospects for the CBS system were bleak. On 11 May 1947 CBS announced, in part for economic reasons, that it was abandoning live programming for an indefinite period; it was also curtailing its color television research. Instead, it would telecast films and remote pickups only.[14] Fifty-five staff employees were dropped from the payroll, including Ben Feiner, Jr., program director, Paul Belanger, director, and Jim McNaughton, the principal set designer. Virtually all of the CBS production staff was terminated. "In 1947 CBS-TV was a two-station network, and was programming less than an hour a day."[15]

The day this announcement was published in *Variety*, the competition, NBC, inaugurated the *Kraft Television Theatre*. That anthology, together with the incredible success of the 1947 World Series, showed that the small audience which was exposed to television avidly wanted more programming. CBS had to meet this challenge. Even so, radio experience was poor video training; producers, directors, and writers coming out of vaudeville, the movies, and the theater had a better chance of being successful on television. "Engineers still have much to improve in transmission and reception," *Newsweek* complained. "But the public wants its programs now. Consequently, video has not been allowed the privilege of developing its own writers, directors, producers and actors. With advertisers prodding them on, TV crews must turn out programs regardless of experience."[16]

Matériel

Raw materials needed to make television equipment, such as copper (so scarce that pennies were made of steel in 1942–43) were just being released to the civilian market. This caused critics to complain frequently about technical quality from obsolete equipment. "Most telecasters have been working with pre-war cameras, mike booms, lights and other technical studio and transmitter equipment which has tended to keep programming and operations at a low level.[17] Manufacturing ran behind demand. During the war when nearly everyone could find a job and make money, there was little in the way of consumer goods to spend it on. Afterward, improvements, many of them cars and household items, were highly prized. Many working-class people had money to spend on television sets as soon as they became available. Unlike after World War I, when radio in its early stages of development would take a decade to make its public impact, television manufacturers could already see the future in the past. They referred to television as radio with pictures.

The lack of matériel was evident soon again, just as color standards were being finalized for public use. This time the Office of Defense Mobilization asked manufacturers not to make color receivers and equipment during the Korean War emergency, 1951–52.[18] If color television had been authorized, some speculate that the period of black-and-white television might have ended then.

NBC Facilities

As a subsidiary of the Radio Corporation of America (RCA), an equipment-manufacturing company, NBC always had an advantage in new technology. Yet CBS, and later DuMont, were fierce competitors.

In order to improve its television demonstrations in the 1930s, NBC converted a sound recording studio in Rockefeller Center into Studio 3H. This would be the home of NBC's dramas for the next 12 years. Over the years 3H was acoustically treated and air conditioned. At the outset, an illumination of about 1,500-foot candles was required on the studio set for its Iconoscope cameras. This requirement was substantially reduced when RCA's Orthocon (1945) and Image Orthocon (IO) (1946) cameras replaced them.

For Studio 3H, updated in 1946, the principal source of illumination was 22 batteries of 12 500-watt lamps, all suspended from a pipe grid attached to the ceiling. Each battery of lamps was controllable as to direction, from a control platform or bridge in a corner of the studio near the control room. Lamps were turned off and on in groups of three. This overhead system was augmented by two arc and several incandescent floor units. Research was continuing on mercury vapor and fluorescent lamps. Telecasts originating from the studio, where lighting conditions were carefully maintained, generated a texture and quality of black-and-white picture that was unequalled. The new supersensitive IO cameras were portable, lightweight, and simple to operate, able to be quickly set up and put into operation. Although this was true by 1946 standards, the cameras were huge, awkward to operate, and bulky by later standards which utilized transistors and printed circuits. Nevertheless, in that day, the resolution of the black-and-white picture was impressive. The 3H control room, located twelve feet above the floor, had a glass observation partition with a neutral-density cellulose filter that made it possible to see the monitors distinctly, regardless of the brightness of the scene being staged below. Use of Studio 3H cost $500 per half hour with three hours of rehearsal time.

Close by, a television-film-scanning studio— 5F — had a projection room, a film vault, and a control room. The equipment consisted of two 35 mm projectors with sound heads, two 16 mm projectors with sound, and one still slide projector. The projection room included editing facilities. Although more compact, the film studio's control room functioned like the one in 3H.

On 22 April 1948 NBC announced the opening of "the world's most modern" studio and the largest one in Radio City, Studio 8G. Bragging rights were important at this time because DuMont and CBS had huge studios in various stages of completion. With 8G in operation, NBC could use more sequences shot on location by its two remote units, 1A and 1B.[19]

Meanwhile, NBC's Los Angeles facilities, begun in 1945 and located at Sunset Boulevard and Vine Street, were even more impressive. They occupied a building 370 feet long, 260 feet wide, and 45 feet high. It contained eight studios, each having its own foundation of concrete block fittings and 12-inch masonry walls. Air space between adjacent walls and cork and mastic compound construction maximized the sound proofing. Four of the studios could accommodate an audience of 340 persons.[20]

In April 1952 NBC constructed its main facilities on a 48-acre site in Burbank, California. By October the first program — a special presentation of *All Star Revue*— was telecast. NBC Burbank consisted of two studios with audience capacities of 500 persons each. Adjacent locations included carpentry shops, scenery painting, rehearsal and dressing rooms, control booths, lighting bridges overlooking the giant stages, and an electronic motion picture recording plant utilizing 35 mm films. By March 1953 what had started out as a film syndication area, the NBC Film Division, under the leadership of Robert W. Sarnoff, had become one of NBC's three major divisions.

During 1953–54, NBC was struggling to determine whether dominance in dramatic program origination should remain in New York or be relocated permanently to Los Angeles, whether dramas should be live or filmed, and whether distribution should continue in black and white or be in color. Location dominance was particularly worrisome in New York City.[21] On 9 September 1954, parallel investments in New York and Los Angeles were particularly evident. In New York, Mayor Robert Wagner dedicated the world's largest television studio as NBC's color production center at 1268 East 14th Street in Brooklyn. NBC paid $3.5 million to upgrade a former Warner Bros. sound stage, some 178 by 88 feet in size. Mayor Wagner said: "New York is the center of all the creative arts that go into television — writing, composing, producing, designing, acting and so on. New York is the logical home for television production. We want to keep it here." Executive Vice President Robert W. Sarnoff responded: "The studio expresses our conviction that New York must remain the television capital of America." Midtown theaters were being converted to color television studios: "Shows ordinarily originating in Hollywood and Chicago will come to New York for their color premiere."

As the New York studio was being dedicated, NBC's Television Center in Burbank was constructing its first color studio. Studio 2, Burbank, was 140 feet by 90 feet in area and 42 feet high. Complete with dressing rooms, as well as technical and storage space, it would be ready for use in early 1955.[22]

CBS Facilities

When CBS went on the air, programming a seven-day-a-week schedule in 1931–32 from its studio at 485 Madison Avenue, the estimated number of television receivers in the New York Metropolitan area was 7,500. "Along with ordering the Chrysler transmitter in 1937, CBS established that year its television program center in the Grand Central Terminal Building, to provide the first full-scale working model in this country of a complete television unit operating under typical conditions of actual daily production. The studio plant became a laboratory for the development of program and production techniques." The CBS program experiments lasted from 1933 until almost the end of the war. Little was live, and a drama of any kind was rare indeed. Then on 5 May 1944 CBS resumed live telecasting and encouraged a "working partnership" for those clients who were interested in testing, developing, and broadcasting commercial video programs.[23]

In February 1948 CBS president Frank Stanton announced that "the nation's largest television studio plant" was being constructed in New York. He was referring to the completion of the Grand Central Terminal Building, 15 Vanderbilt Avenue. The plant was comprised of three stories, with a basement and subbasement of fireproof brick, concrete, and steel construction. Eleven truck entrances, two elevators, and ramps allowed easy movement from railroad sidings below to upper floors. "Today CBS Television has 62 stations, from coast-to-coast, it averages about nine hours of programming daily, and there are over 17,000,000 television homes in the United States."[24]

Two years later CBS was engaged in rapid expansion in mid–Manhattan by leasing sites, such as Peace House at 109th Street and Fifth Avenue, renamed CBS-TV Studio 57, the Town Theatre at 55th and Ninth Avenue as Studio 58, the Mansfield Theatre on West 47th Street as Studio 59, and the Lincoln Square Theatre at 1947 Broadway as Studio 60. By September 1950, the total of CBS-TV studios in New York City increased to 13, and CBS planned to install a new transmitter on the 83rd floor of the Empire State Building. CBS expected to have 100 hours of television programming in the fall of 1951.

Simultaneously, radio and television studio space for KTTV, Inc., the Los Angeles Times–CBS television station, was leased from Capitol Records, Inc., 5515 Melrose Avenue in 1949. The top floors were for Studio A, a radio and television area, and for Studio B, a sound stage.[25] This was temporary housing, awaiting the construction on land known as Gilmore Island of CBS Television City, a giant complex at Beverly Boulevard and Fairfax Avenue, in Hollywood. Construction began in December 1950, and regular broadcasting coast to coast started with *My Friend Irma*, a comedy series, on 3 October 1952. Each of the initial four studios had 12,100 square feet of floor space and were as large as any Hollywood sound stage. Designed by CBS Creative Director William Golden, the administrative headquarters and studio facilities were geared for rapid production, featured movable walls, could accommodate an audience of 350 in each of two studios, and had a production capacity of about 28 hours of live television production a week or almost one-half of all 18 CBS-TV studios in New York.[26] By 1954 the "city within a city" had 19 weekly live broadcasts, had doubled its employees, and was a major tourist attraction.[27]

Distribution

The principal forms of distributing television programs in the mid-1940s were via broadcast signals sent from local television stations, point-to-point cable hook-ups, repeating performances by touring live actors, and shipping recorded programs. In 1946 only nine television stations were on the air. Within each city the distribution was limited to board rooms, engineering laboratories, and a few public locations. As early as 1940, however, signals from NBC's transmitter atop the Empire State Building were picked up via intermediate relay stations and rebroadcast in Schenectady by General Electric's WRGB and in Philadelphia by Philco Radio Corporation's WPTZ (1943). In 1941 NBC estimated 5,000 receivers in the New York area. During 1942–43, NBC installed 80 viewing posts to instruct 107,499 civilians how to be air-raid wardens through repeated programs. After the war, small repertory acting companies toured the East coast television stations repeating dramas live at each site. NBC executive producer Warren Wade suggested that perhaps television should bring back the dramatic stock and repertoire companies.[28]

"There were only 6,500 sets in use on Jan. 1, 1946," according to *Radio News*.[29] Yet that April 15th, DuMont Television formalized the first commercial "network" by sending dramatic and other fare from WABD, New York, to Washington, D.C. In about a year and one-half, by October 1947, eleven television stations were on the air linking 63,941 receivers in homes and 502,107 in bars and public gathering places, popular since television's inception, in four cities: New York, Philadelphia, Washington, D.C., and Schenectady. Sports, the most popular genre, claimed that an audience of nearly four million watched the 1947 World Series, according to a C. E. Hooper survey.[30] Drama came in second, according to *Television* magazine, with more and better plays in demand.[31]

As network affiliation emerged, the principal companies offered newsreels and theatrical features on film. In 1946 kinescope recording was put to use. It was the successor to phonoscope recording used ten years earlier. Instead of filming a scene directly in the studio, the kinescope process enabled highly sensitive motion picture film to record live television programs from the face of a television set in the studio. This method, though often poor in resolution, allowed fledgling networks to syndicate programs to stations not yet reached by coaxial cable or radio relay interconnections, such as new stations in Detroit and Milwaukee (1947). By 1948, 17 television stations were on the air. During the Freeze "108 VHF stations were operating in 63 markets across the country, according to testimony presented by Allen B. DuMont in 1954 before a Senate subcommittee chaired by Senator Charles Potter of Michigan. Of those markets, 40 had one station, and 11 had two. Eight cities had three stations, and only four had four or more. Of the markets with only one or two stations, all but three of those stations were owned by interests also having radio stations. Most of these TV outlets, DuMont indicated, were owned by CBS and NBC."[32] The DuMont network ceased operation on 15 September 1955. With interconnection coast to coast, NBC and CBS flourished. ABC-TV struggled throughout the fifties and sixties before it became a major network.

Advertising Support

NBC invited sponsors, advertising agencies, public officials, and media to view the first demonstrations in 1936 and to become involved with television production. Representatives came from General Foods, Philip Morris, Sealtest, General Motors, Bristol Myers, Young & Rubicam, Batten, Barton, Durstine & Osborne, J. Walter Thompson, the FCC, and other government organizations. They saw how commercial messages might be infused into comedy sketches. Some of these representatives became early experimenters, promoters, and sponsors of television dramas.

By the mid–1930s, advertising agencies were placing three-quarters of the radio advertising orders.[33] Large agencies were creating the ads and controlling the programs by hiring production companies to produce them. Often the agency took responsibility for engaging major talent and leasing facilities. The agency represented its client and delivered a complete "package," consisting of program content and commercials, to the radio network. The network usually sold air time and leased facilities. So long as the networks could deliver large audiences, this arrangement worked well. The advertising agencies took their income — about 15 percent — off the top of the gross cost of the package.

During the experimental years of broadcasting, prior to 1930 for radio and prior to the mid–1940s for television, the networks themselves devised the programs and sustained the costs. In the decades that followed, dominance in program development and ownership seesawed between networks and agencies. From 1930 to 1945 the networks, virtually by themselves, invested huge sums in the development of television programming. During this same period, the advertising agencies dominated radio programming. After World War II, the agencies expected to take over network television programming. The results were mixed, as the initial four prestige anthologies will illustrate.

The agencies were inclined to take over programming once the network had established itself as a viable advertising medium. Radio research in the 1930s, and refined techniques applied to television later, clearly indicated that both media were extraordinary sales tools. During World War II, the government had imposed a heavy excess-profits tax on wartime industries to discourage profiteering on war contracts. Advertising was excluded from that tax and was instead taxed at normal rates. Advertising, therefore, became a highly desirable bargain for prestige-conscious companies. Ordinarily, most advertising dollars would have gone into print media, but the war curtailed paper products, newsprint, and supplies. As a result, in 1943 advertisers turned to radio, making it the dominant advertising medium, absorbing nearly 40 percent of all national advertising dollars.[34] Thus, the radio business set a precedent for reaching vast numbers of consumers, who were forced to save their money during the war but would purchase new products, even expensive ones, as soon as they were available. Through their agencies, wealthy sponsors sought to gain public attention by means of the visual influence of television.

About one-fourth of the advertising on NBC and CBS radio networks was controlled by three agencies — Young & Rubicam, Dancer-Fitzgerald-Sample, and J. Walter Thompson.[35] They represented clients that wanted to sell products and promote company recognition and prestige. To meet the first requirement — mass sales — the radio advertisers had turned to music and variety programs. In the smaller percentage of dramatic shows, the soap opera serial, in which an incomplete story is told from day to day, was the most important type on network radio. For prestige, however, the radio networks took their cue from the theater and, in the late 1930s, began to present radio anthologies, stories completely told in a single program. Frequently, these stories were adaptations of famous works, but occasionally they were original works written especially for radio.

When NBC-TV's Warren Wade announced plans in 1946 to schedule 28 hours of programming over six days a week, in which Sunday was the principal showcase for drama, he was attempting to establish a viable, consistent television schedule.[36] NBC wanted to establish its own cooperative agreements with production sources such as the Dramatist's Guild of the Authors' League of America, which had worked out procedures to license plays to television; the Theatre Guild that was already sponsored on radio by United States Steel; and to strong financial backing from sponsors and advertising agencies in dramatic program development. At CBS, William Paley, who always had a keen eye for talent and a desire to keep programming in-house, was signing up creative people.

Even though heavily committed to radio drama, the J. Walter Thompson Agency expanded to television drama and gained substantial experience when it produced a series for Standard Brands (Lipton Tea, Chase and Sanborn Coffee). JWT clients invested $200,000 in a variety series on WNBT called *Hour Glass* (1946), consisting of 15-minute programs on Sundays and an hour telecast on Thursdays. The Thursday show often included a one-act play by a well-known writer. Then, in March 1947 after ten months on the air, *Hour Glass* was cancelled because of relatively few viewers, high production costs, and the belief that J. Walter Thompson and Standard Brands had gathered enough television experience for the present.[37]

In June 1947 the number of television advertisers was only 30, but a year later it had risen to 300.[38] The increase in advertisers forced the networks to reassess their available time on the air for spot announcements. An early sacrifice was the continuity of theatrical feature films. By September 1948, CBS announced its *Film Theater of the Air* would insert 60-second commercials during the picture.[39] "A sponsor won't buy a picture and wait an hour for sponsor identification ... We're establishing a precedent."[40] The ominous decision meant that sponsors of entire series, individual programs, or sales announcements would be interrupting dramatic program continuity.

Programming Content

During 1947 NBC directors Sobol, Colling, Coe, and Gordon Duff directed more than sixty dramas involving NBC, Theatre Guild, ANTA, Kraft, Borden, and their advertising agencies. At CBS, the first half of 1947 saw about a dozen short dramas, including an adaptation of radio's *The Whistler*. During the last half of the year — after the FCC turned down the first CBS bid to implement its color system — CBS did no live dramas. The pause was brief. In October 1947 CBS began to form a network and resume live production. Tony Miner made the canny observation that top acts from other forms of show business might not be successful on television, if they were not tuned to what he called "the mood of the home." The notion that elaborate radio or Broadway adaptations might not be that entertaining to viewers in the hinterlands would take a decade to appreciate.[41]

NBC Dramas

Unlike CBS, RCA through NBC was selling receivers, its color system, and programming. The prestigious Sunday prime-time drama was *NBC Television Theatre*, often sponsored by the Borden Company. On 27 April

"John Ferguson," starring Thomas Mitchell and Joyce Redman, was the premiere of *Theatre Guild*, on NBC-TV, 9 November 1947.

1947, an adaptation of Shakespeare's *Twelfth Night*, praised as "top drawer entertainment," boosted the recognition of Fred Coe, who directed the debut of *Kraft Television Theatre* a few nights later on 7 May.[42] *Kraft Television Theatre* would appear regularly midweek for the next 11 years. The one and one-half hour Sunday dramas would slowly improve under NBC's in-house nurturing, cooperating on Sunday, 9 November 1947, in a new series with the *Theatre Guild*. The premiere was an adaptation of the Theatre Guild's first financial success (1918), "John Ferguson," by St. John Ervine, with actors Thomas Mitchell and Joyce Redman. Edward Sobol directed it from Studio 3H and 5F.[43]

The process was described by Warren Caro, executive director of the Theatre Guild Television Division, who said that once the play was chosen and cleared, one of the Guild's administrative directors acted as producer, supervising production in collaboration with the NBC television director. They conferred about every aspect of the play: the outline, treatment, sets, special effects, and use of film. Pressures were intense. Often the teleplay was not ready until the last minute. Rehearsals, always too few, ran about nine days, with the first six days of dry runs without cameras in Theatre Guild rooms. "On Friday, Saturday, and Sunday preceding the broadcast, the company goes before the cameras and works in the actual set to be televised.[44] *The Late George Apley*, by John P. Marquand and George S. Kaufman, appeared as the December play in the monthly series. When the Theatre Guild and NBC presented the first play by George Bernard Shaw, *Great Catherine*, with an opulent St. Petersburg flavor built in Studio 8G for airing on 2 May 1948, it starred Gertrude Lawrence, with David Wayne and Joan McCracken. "Actress Lawrence could have claimed to be making, as well as re-creating history: ten years ago, in a telecast of *Susan and God*, she was the first big star to try television."[45]

As NBC connected other cities, theatrical companies, notably the American National Theatre and Academy (ANTA), began to provide scenes for Thursday's *Rehearsal in 3H* anthology, which frequently resembled a variety format. A formal debut of this cooperative effort, later retitled as *ANTA-NBC Television Playhouse*, debuted with *The Last of My Solid Gold Watches*, by Tennessee Williams on 4 December 1947. In this brief, flexible interval some thirty- to forty-minute scripts, including an original play by Noel Jordan called *Outside of Time* (11 January 1948), were designed to help playwrights through the professional production of one-acts. Adapting theatrical plays sometimes required eliminating language that was acceptable on the live stage. For a WBKB remote of *Night Without End* from Chicago's Eighth Street Theatre, adult language ("damns") and themes (illegitimate children) posed the question: Would a self-policing body or the FCC be required to clean up material?[46] When he adapted *The Front Page*, sprinkled with numerous "hells and damns," Edward Sobol came to the conclusion: "If in doubt, cut it out."[47] The list of categories, words, and even participants that would be eliminated from live television drama was just beginning.

In 1947 NBC changed from frequent short dramas shown in previous years to five in-house dramatic anthologies for which it had principal responsibility while seeking others to share it—*NBC Television Theatre, Rehearsal-3H, NBC-Theatre Guild, NBC-ANTA Playhouse,* and *Borden Theatre*. The *Kraft Television Theatre* was directed and staffed in-house for a few months before it was packaged entirely by J. Walter Thompson.

The following year the NBC network served New York, Schenectady, Philadelphia, Baltimore, and Washington, D.C. In Spring 1948 NBC returned to a historical interest — crime drama and the supersleuth, a flashback to the 1936 experiments featuring Sherlock Holmes. *Barney Blake, Police Reporter* was NBC's first regularly scheduled "mystery" drama. It ran

13 weeks, 22 April to 8 July 1948. In the debut episode, "Murder Me Twice," by Max Ehrlich, Blake (Gene O'Donnell) was a crime reporter for the *Courier-Journal*, working on a waterfront murder story. In the new want-ads department he meets Jennifer Allen (Judy Parrish), who helps him out. The live 9:30–10:00 P.M. telecast from 8G was produced by Wynn Wright and directed by Garry Simpson. It was sponsored by the American Tobacco Company (Lucky Strike) through N. W. Ayer & Son, Inc. For the second episode, "The Dark Cellar," by Max Ehrlich, radio actor Roc Rogers played a reluctant criminal who was forced by circumstances into a life of crime. The third program starred Clare Luce as a socialite murder victim who was strangled with the "E" string of a violin in Ehrlich's "E-String Murder."

On 1 September 1948, U.S. Tobacco had Martin Kane (William Gargan) meeting in Happy McMann's (Walter Kinsella) tobacco shop as a story location for *Martin Kane, Private Eye*, by Frank Wilson. Betty Furness appeared as Kitty Fenly in an early episode in the male-dominated series produced and directed by Edward Sutherland. The 10:00–10:30 P.M. half-hour, live nighttime series, already popular on radio, lasted five years and was eventually syndicated. One radio crime anthology wherein the characters changed each week was based on actual newspaper reporter accounts; *The Big Story* premiered on 16 September 1949. The American Tobacco Company also sponsored this anthology and gave awards to the real reporters whose stories were used as the basis for the dramas. The 9:30–10:00 P.M. dramas often told about sensational cases, and they became very popular, lasting eight years before going into syndication. In the real-life category was one of the few Chicago originations, *The Crisis*, telecast during the last quarter of 1949. A true story would be presented in interview form until near the crisis, which was then improvised by actors. The show was directed by Norman Felton, who would soon come to New York to direct *Robert Montgomery Presents*.

Noteworthy was *Chevrolet on Broadway*, also known as *Chevrolet Tele-Theatre*, which ran for two seasons (1948–50). This was a high-budget, live, half-hour series, 8:00–8:30 P.M. on Tuesdays. It featured top stars in some original scripts and adaptations. Its debut, 27 September 1948, was Richard Harrity's "Home Life of a Buffalo," the tale of a hoofer (John McQuade) and his family who refuse to believe that vaudeville is dead. The anthology was often produced by Owen Davis, Jr., and directed by Gordon Duff or Garry Simpson. For the 18 October 1948 show, "Whistle, Daughter, Whistle," by Ernest Kinoy, Gertrude Berg, author and star of radio's *The Goldbergs*, made her television debut. Academy Award winner James Dunn followed on 15 November in Lawrence DuPont's "No Shoes." The debut for Dunn concerned a wealthy trucking-company owner who expected his wife

William Gargan as *Martin Kane, Private Eye*, was on NBC-TV, September 1949–June 1954.

to deliver a boy to carry on the firm's name as "Cassidy and Son," but plans changed when she delivered a girl. That month, Academy Award winner Paul Muni recreated his 1929 film role of the condemned man in *The Valiant*, by Holworthy Hall and Robert Middlemass. In December, Edward Everett Horton appeared as a burglar looking for quality, not quantity, when he robs a couple in their home. A Paul Gallico story for *Cosmopolitan* was

Ben Grauer and blind journalist Victor Riesel prepared *The Big Story*, on NBC-TV, September 1949–June 1957.

adapted for Eddie Albert and Margo. Albert played a GI who believes a dog saved his life during the war. The couple bicker over his affection for the dog. Week after week, major stars were seen in stories by well-known writers whose plays, often adapted, began to form a reliable body of work repeated in other anthologies.

Summer relief for *Chevrolet on Broadway* was *Academy Theatre*, which

"Temporarily Purple" starred Nina Foch, for *Chevrolet Tele-Theatre*, on NBC-TV, 14 November 1949.

began on 25 July 1949 with Dan Totheroh's "The Stolen Prince," and ended on 12 September. Presenting *Academy Theatre*'s eight half-hour dramas was the handiwork of Curtis Canfield. His second play was Austin Strong's "Drums of Oude," a fine one-act play which just about everybody had done. Even so, Canfield's anthology was well received and in 1950, again as a summer replacement, he produced *Masterpiece Playhouse*. "What ordinarily takes a month or more to do in Hollywood is accomplished in a day in TV. A full thirty minutes of show is shot, edited, and exhibited in one day," commented veteran Victor McLeod, later producer of *Chevrolet Tele-Theatre*.

He stressed, however, that it took a great deal of teamwork. The major problem for a dramatic show was getting good material, McLeod said, citing a *Ladies' Home Journal* adaption, "The Door," by Jeb Stuart, as the kind of production suitable for the show. Don Ameche was the star on 28 November 1949.[48]

Another live half-hour anthology was *The Colgate Theatre*. Its first show on 3 January 1949 was "Fancy Meeting You Here," a *McCall's* story by Olga Moore, adapted by William Stuart. The "smooth" production was "tolerably well acted" by Betty Garde and Mary Wickes. *The Colgate Theatre* suffered from uneven scripts, according to producer-director Hal Keith. One of the dramas was another look at "Mr. and Mrs. North," an amusing couple who as amateur detectives solved crimes. The characters had been adapted to every medium: radio in 1942, television in 1946, the Broadway stage, and short stories. *Mr. and Mrs. North*, conceived by Richard and Frances Lockridge, finally did air as a television series from 1952 to 1954.

Having greater impact on the future of anthology drama was *Fireside Theatre*, premiering on 5 April 1949, as a half-hour live series. *Fireside Theatre*'s original concept was experimental, an attempt to try program ideas that might become a series. To start off, the cast played itself in fictional stories, and viewers were supposed to notify the network about their preferences. "Friend of the Family," for instance, starred "real life" couple Virginia Gilmore and Yul Brynner. The third program was totally different, however. It was a half hour from Leonard Sillman's annual Broadway revue, *New Faces*. Experimentation quickly proved undesirable for Proctor & Gamble's advertising objectives, and the sponsor signed a contract with General Television Enterprises, Inc. of Hollywood to supply 13 filmed programs for the 1949-50 season.[49] Within six months, *Fireside Theatre* was being cranked out as a filmed series on the Hal Roach lot, where the previous year Roach had spent $43 million dollars to convert his old film studio to meet the needs of television. *Fireside Theatre* posed important questions: Did the public really care whether a drama was live or on film? The answer was no, not if it was entertaining. The anthology proved to be very popular, comparatively economical, and it posed a persistent challenge to live drama, remaining on the air until 1963, well beyond the live era.

A potpourri of attempts were made in situation comedy in 1949. For instance, Grace and Paul Hartman, a well-known dance team, turned to suburban married life in *The Hartmans*, a contemporary comedy, debuting on 27 February for a year's stay. The 1940s radio series, *The Life of Riley*, came to video on 4 October 1949 with Jackie Gleason playing Chester A. Riley. After the first season ended, "a cross section of human behavior and

"Bless the Man" starred William Bishop and Joyce Holden, for *Fireside Theatre*, on NBC-TV, 8 September 1953.

emotion" called *Mr. Omn* temporarily filled in. Soon, *The Life of Riley* was revived with the original radio star, William Bendix, in the lead.

The oddities category included Robert L. Ripley's *Believe It Or Not*, based on his 1918 newspaper version of a carnival sideshow, which consisted of colored drawings and captions illustrating the bizarre in human beings and events. Presented as dramatic, true vignettes, Ripley hosted the

Jack LaRue in the signature scene for *Lights Out*, on NBC-TV, July 1949–September 1952.

show himself when it debuted on 1 March 1949. Despite his death, the anthology lasted until 28 September 1950.

Crime dramas included *The Clock*, based on its ABC radio predecessor (1946–48), airing its first episode on 16 May 1949. Although irregularly scheduled the first month, Fred Coe got it started, and Larry Schwab took over for a successful run. Another crime series was *Lights Out*, debuting 19 July 1949. *Lights Out*, origi-

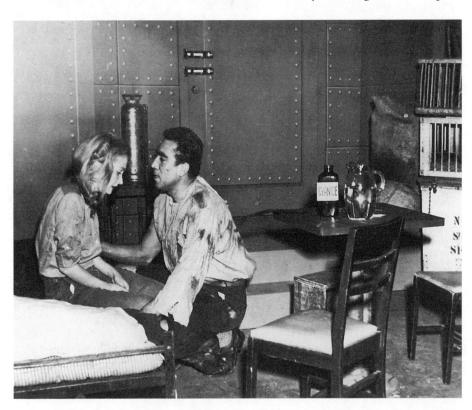

"The House of Dust" starred Nina Foch and Anthony Quinn, for *Lights Out*, on NBC-TV, 5 February 1951.

nally on radio in 1934, was transferred after Coe directed four telecasts in 1946. Horror, mystery, the supernatural, murder, and insanity were the basis of mostly live and original scary stories for both anthologies with guests stars such as Boris Karloff, Burgess Meredith, and Basil Rathbone. Courtroom reenactment was a long-time effort at bringing inexpensive realism to the video screen. Produced in collaboration with Phillips H. Lord, who gained fame as producer of radio's *Gangbusters* (1936), which was narrated for a time by Colonel H. Norman Schwarzkopf, and directed by Edward Sutherland, *The Black Robe*, a half-hour series, first appeared on 18 May 1949. It won favorable attention because it presented actual cases from New York City's night court, but the series failed to get a sponsor.

Carlton E. Morse created a soap opera called *Mixed Doubles*, which was about the struggles of newly married couples living next door to each other, for telecasting from 5 August to October 1949. After three months, he turned his attention to *One Man's Family*, the saga of a San Francisco banker and his family who lived in the suburbs. Beginning as a West Coast origination in 1932, this was radio's longest running serial drama. On television it lasted only three years, 1949–52.

CBS Dramas

At CBS, 1947 was a lean year for drama, as mentioned earlier, with few single attempts and one courtroom series converted from a 1946 variety format, *Judge for Yourself*. In April 1948, CBS promoted remote pick-ups with *Tonight on Broadway*, produced and directed by Martin Gosch. The show included interviews with stars and a scene or two from currently running plays. The opener was "Mister Roberts," starring Henry Fonda. It was broadcast live from the Alvin Theatre and sponsored by Lucky Strike cigarettes.[50] *Ford Theater* and *Studio One*, television versions of radio anthologies, debuted in the fall of 1948.

By 1949 CBS had five anthologies: *Ford Theater*, *Studio One*, *Suspense*, *Silver Theatre*, and *Theatre of Romance*. It also increased the number of series dramas, those with the same main characters each week. *The Silver Theatre*, hosted many years on radio by Conrad Nagel, came to television for several months on 3 October 1949. This anthology specialized in romance and had well-known stars in half-hour plays. Producer, director, script editor Frank Telford said he would use four cameras, integrate live and filmed action, and use symbolic props associated with the theme or major characters as a narrative device. The premiere was Burgess Meredith and Eva Gabor in "L'Amour the Merrier," an original romantic comedy by Sid Slon and Richard Steele. It also had original music and the long-time radio sponsor International Silver Company. *Theatre of Romance* (also known as *Romance*) debuted 3 November 1949 with a freely adapted modern-dress version of *Camille*, starring Ruth Ford as Marguerite Gautier. Other French names from the Alexandre Dumas novel, however, were changed: Armand Duval became Dillon Whitelaw.[51]

Front Page Theatre was a newspaper crime drama based on *The Front Page* (1928) by Ben Hecht and Charles MacArthur. CBS journalist John Daly, who reported the bombing of Pearl Harbor in 1941, gave some authenticity to the lead, Walter Burns; and Mark Roberts played Hildy Johnson during its five-month run beginning in September 1949. Real life often turned to fantasy in crime dramas, although the line frequently remained blurred. *Suspense*, an award-winning radio mainstay on CBS since 1942, debuted 1 March 1949. This half-hour, live anthology ran until 1954, mainly presenting popular New York stage and screen actors in horror stories with some change-of-pace variations. The *Suspense* formula was articulated by Leo Davis: "Real suspense comes out of the pressure of circumstance on

Rehearsal of "Roman Holiday," for *Suspense*, on CBS-TV, 21 February 1950.

character — not out of plot gimmicks or scenic effects. Our series should have central, understandable and sympathetic characters ... precipitated, if possible, by action, into taut physical or emotional dilemmas ... confronted not only by internal struggle but also by the exterior manifestation of the threat or the menace ... and forced to find in themselves the ability to act (with courage, morality, growth) and most of the time, to win (if not a big victory, a first small one)."[52] *Man Against Crime*, a half-hour mystery series, which began on 7 October 1949 starred Ralph Bellamy as Mike Barnett, "a shrewd, hard-hitting, fearless private detective who never carries a gun, preferring to pit his brain, and often his brawn, against formidable adversaries of the underworld."[53] This was another example of crime drama having strong appeal to cigarette manufacturers looking to attract male smokers with action characters. It was sponsored by Camel cigarettes through the William Esty agency.

CBS attempted three situation comedies. Gertrude Berg, who was author and star of *The Goldbergs* on radio for 20 years, as mentioned, transferred her half-hour show on 10 January 1949. The stories, concerning a poor Jewish family living in a Bronx apartment, were live until 1955–56, when the show went into syndication. "A very long time ago, I tried to set myself a rule; the life you lead yourself, the people you know and the things you have done are the only material a writer needs. The humbler the life, the greater meaning and appeal it will have," Berg said.[54] Worthington Miner produced the series; Walter Hart directed. *Mama*, starring Peggy Wood, had a 1910 San Francisco setting. The pleasant Norwegian family was based on *Mama's Bank Account*, by Kathryn Forbes. Ralph Nelson was producer/director, and General Foods sponsored it on 1 July 1949. "The first misadventure of Wesley, freckled, snub-nosed, 12-year-old prototype of the eternal American boy" debuted on Sunday, 8 May 1949. Written by the theater's Sam Taylor, the plots attempted to recapture the warmth and leisurely good humor of American family life. Tony Miner produced *Wesley* too, and with it, Franklin Schaffner, usually associated with current events programs, moved to situation comedy.[55]

DuMont Dramas

When it went into operation on 28 June 1942 over W2XWV, DuMont television was located on the forty-second floor of 515 Madison Avenue. The two studios for live and filmed shows were small, and it was not until 1945 that an audience participation studio was added. But "throughout World War II W2XWV telecast from five to ten hours a week — the only television station in the U.S. to maintain a regular program schedule."[56]

Aside from an occasional sketch such as the ones appearing opening night when DuMont began broadcasting from its new Wanamaker studio in New York, and its 1946 telecast of *Faraway Hill*, television's first soap opera, DuMont offered few dramas. In cooperation with the American Theatre Wing's training class, in 1947 WABD aired "All Men Are Created..." by Kitty Kirkbridge, produced by Harvey Marlowe. The satire showed discrimination in many aspects of life. It had a cast of 20 appearing in ten scenes and was sponsored by Mueller's Macaroni.[57] During 1947–48 three sitcoms were added, including *Mary Kay and Johnny*, debuting 18 November 1947. Written by Johnny Stearns, the married couple — she's the zany one, he's the stable one — who were also married in real life, had a baby, and this was written into the story line in 1948. The series was popular and transferred to NBC in 1950.

The DuMont network added two sitcoms in 1948, *The Growing Paynes* and *The Laytons*, starring black actress Amanda Randolph, who appeared in radio and television versions of *Amos 'n' Andy*. In 1949 DuMont had five crime dramas, including *Chicagoland Mystery Players*, a local crime drama that had only a few months on the network, but *The Plainclothes Man*, who was never seen on camera, became a DuMont success, lasting until September 1954. The subjective camera technique in this big-city drama has since been copied. Other efforts were a comedy, a romance, and an anthology for piloting new programs, *Program Playhouse*.

ABC Dramas

By 1949 the American Broadcasting Company, using facilities of other companies, had been on the air for only five months, but its main contribution, *Actor's Studio*, aired cutting-edge plays, winning a George Foster Peabody Award (1948) for "its uninhibited and brilliant pioneering in the field of television drama."[58] This half-hour anthology was produced by Actors Studio, Inc., the nonprofit training ground for professional actors, begun in New York in 1947 by Elia Kazan, Robert Lewis, and Cheryl Crawford, and made famous for its "method" acting under director Lee Strasberg. For its debut, 26 September 1948, Hume Cronyn directed his wife Jessica Tandy in Tennessee Williams's "taut one-act tour de force," *Portrait of a Madonna*, that was already doing well on tour. "I would not assert that *Portrait of a Madonna* was a better play, or better acted, or better directed than *Streetcar*. I do assert that it was different, that the viewer felt an impact and an intimacy which would have been denied him had he viewed the play from a seat in the theater," commented Charles Barry in *The Atlantic Monthly*. "The result was a vivid example of television's ability to make the viewer a participant in the drama, rather than an observer."[59]

Marlon Brando made his first television appearance in "I'm No Hero" on 9 January 1949. This was not happenstance. It illustrates the repertory nature of live television drama. Two years earlier, while scouting stage leads for *A Streetcar Named Desire* (1947), Elia Kazan sent Brando to Cape Cod to read for Margo Jones and Williams. Brando was an immediate hit with both Jones and Williams. Kazan also suggested that Williams see Tandy on tour. "It was instantly apparent to me Jessica was Blanche," Williams wrote in his *Memoirs*.[60]

Actor's Studio was a sustaining show; so money soon ran out for Producer Donald Davis to buy rights to well-known one-act plays. With variety claiming the big video audiences, Davis was advised to stick to melodrama and crime; instead, he chose to adapt short stories. He also ventured into the little-known area of television comedy. "This kind of amusement would, it seems, have to come from character rather than plot comedy. Moreover, in theory anyway, it's easier to tickle an audience of individuals if it can identify itself with the characters, and if the comic situation on which the story is based is one with which the audience is familiar."[61] Ring Lardner's "Zone of Quiet," adapted by David Shaw and directed by Alex Segal, told of a common man's experience confined to a hospital room. *Actor's Studio* had two seasons on ABC-TV. William Saroyan's "My Heart's in the Highlands" continued the spirit of *Actor's Studio* after it moved to CBS-TV for a few months in 1949–50.

Most crime dramas lasted only a few months — *Dick Tracy, Photocrime, Stand By For Crime, Mysteries of Chinatown, Treasury Men in Action*. It may be worth noting that Inspector Webb's sidekick in *Stand By For Crime*, Lt. Anthony Kidd, was played by Myron Wallace in his first network appearance; he is better known as journalist Mike Wallace. Sitcoms *Wren's Nest, The Ruggles*, and *That Wonderful Guy* did not last long either, but the latter debuting on 28 December 1949 gave Jack Lemmon as Harold, the valet to a theater critic (Neil Hamilton), a chance to meet his real-life wife-to-be Cynthia Stone, who played his girlfriend. They were married in 1950.

ABC's most popular show was *The Lone Ranger*, by George W. Trendle and Fran Striker, starring Clayton Moore and later John Hart as John Reid, with Jay Silverheels as Tonto. The series, filmed in Los Angeles, was often among the top 15 programs during its run from 15 September 1949 to 12 September 1957. After 1950 the number and scope of dramatic programs, discussed later, increased greatly.

"My Heart's in the Highlands" starred Butch Cavell, Russell Collins, John McQuade, for *Actor's Studio*, on CBS-TV, 6 December 1949.

Blacklisting

During the war the Union of Soviet Socialist Republics (U.S.S.R.) was an ally. After the war its Communist government was believed to be a threat to democracy. By 1947 President Harry S Truman attempted to contain the spread of communism in the world by means of his "Truman Doctrine," and at home he initiated loyalty oaths. These efforts encouraged concerns about the possible infiltration of communists into American life and government, resulting in a so-called "Red menace" that was reminiscent of the "Red scare" concerning Bolsheviks after World War I. Certain groups of self-appointed keepers of the public welfare were quick to seize upon the witch-hunting atmosphere, largely for their own gain. The destruction caused by blacklisting was on individual artists and not on the networks, motion picture companies, advertising agencies, or other large organizations. They may have decried the situation but worked around it.

For a while, communists seemed to be everywhere, including the entertainment industries. Broadcasting, film, and the arts were headline-getting targets. Beginning in fall 1947, the House Un-American Activities Committee investigated many in the entertainment business. Some Hollywood studio heads — Louis B. Mayer, Jack Warner, Walt Disney — and famous movie stars — Robert Taylor, Gary Cooper, Robert Montgomery, Ronald Reagan — appeared at one time or another before the committee, denying communist affiliation. The very idea of such an investigation repulsed many in the entertainment industries.[62] Ten well-known filmmakers refused to divulge their affiliations past or present, claiming that the committee's existence violated the Bill of Rights. They were cited in contempt of Congress and in 1948 were given the maximum sentence of a year in jail and a fine of $1,000. They became known as the Hollywood Ten: producer/director Herbert Biberman, director Edward Dmytryk, producer/writer Adrian Scott, and screenwriters Alvah Bessie, Lester Cole, Ring Lardner, Jr., John Howard Lawson, Albert Maltz, Samuel Ornitz, and Dalton Trumbo. Subsequently, some members of the film industry became defensive and started a list of individuals alleged in some way, often falsely or vaguely, to be linked to communism. Those blacklisted were prohibited from working. They were seldom told why they were blacklisted, yet there seemed to be no recourse for them.

"CBS became a special target of those on a Communist witch hunt. The spotlight shone brighter on CBS for another reason. Back in the late 1940s, Bill Paley had decided that CBS, and not the sponsors, theatrical producers, or ad agencies, should produce its own programs. There thus arose within the network a need for the very type of creative figure who would also be characterized as liberal and unconventional," said Robert Slater in *This Is CBS*.[63] The organizers hit at broadcasting's weakest point: the advertisers. Fearful of losing sales by creating controversy, advertisers pressured agencies so that threats of product boycotts would not occur. "With advertisers representing the broadcasting industry's source of income, no one in broadcasting would speak out against the practice or even admit it existed —

only persons who had been blacklisted themselves, and they were no longer in broadcasting."[64] Working conditions were monstrous. The unbelievable hysteria of the time was paralleled in Arthur Miller's courageous play *The Crucible* (1953).

American Business Consultants, a New York group, was active in publishing a newsletter called *Counterattack*, and in 1950 it issued *Red Channels: The Report of Communist Influence in Radio and Television*. The 215-page report implied that over 150 broadcast personalities were at least sympathetic to communism. Although it avoided direct accusations, those identified were accused by innuendo and association. Coincidently reenforcing the search for communists at home was America's involvement in the Korean conflict. Advertising and packaging agencies as well as networks assigned checkers to make sure that everyone associated with programs was acceptable to the blacklisters. Sometimes actors and writers could "confess" to wrongdoing, but often the veil of secrecy could not be penetrated.

At a time when radio stations and networks were either firing or refusing to hire writers and actors on the basis of the unsupported innuendoes contained in *Red Channels*, ABC's Robert Kintner and two of his associates were given a 1950 Peabody Award for refusing "to be stampeded into either action."[65] At CBS employees were asked to fill out a questionnaire to avoid accusations or pressures by outsiders. A clause was added to writers' contracts stating: "Artist agrees to conduct himself at all times with due regard to public morals and conventions." Critic Saul Carson complained: "He not only wears the network's collar; he wears its muzzle, too."[66]

In January 1950 Ed Sullivan had to write a letter which was distributed to the press, to the president of Kenyon & Eckhardt saying that he was bitterly opposed to communism and would oppose having *Toast of the Town* used as a political forum.[67] At NBC *The Aldrich Family* did not open with the fall season because Jean Muir, an actress of 20 years who played Henry's mother, was alleged to have belonged to organizations with communist leanings, according to *Red Channels*. Muir denied the allegations, but General Foods, which sold Jell-O through the program, said it avoided use of material and personalities who were, in its judgment, controversial. But Muir was paid for her 18-week contract.[68]

Carson applauded Jack Gould of *The New York Times*: "He set the pace for the opposition to the *Red Channels* mud-slinging mob when they ganged up on actors, writers, and directors by having Miss Jean Muir fired. Miss Muir did not get her job back, but Gould's forthright campaign gave courage to many broadcasters who weren't quite sure which way to turn. The *Red Channels* antipersonality bomb was a dud, thanks largely to Gould."[69] Yet, opposition to Gould's view was strong. Writing for *The Catholic World*,

William H. Shriver, Jr., took a different stance: "As for Jean Muir and her ilk, those listed in *Red Channels*, I've no patience, personally." He went on: "In these days, if you are not a Communist and are so accused, you should deny it; or if you made some mistakes of affiliating with shady organizations, you should be the first to admit your error, whenever and just as soon as you get the chance."[70] *Red Channels* or the committee at one point aired the names of more than 300 of the most talented persons in show business: Leonard Bernstein, Lloyd Bridges, Abe Burrows, Lee J. Cobb, Aaron Copland, Norman Corwin, Howard Duff, José Ferrer, Martin Gabel, John Garfield, Lee Grant, Dashiell Hammett, Lillian Hellman, Lena Horne, Langston Hughes, Burl Ives, Sam Jaffe, Garson Kamin, Burgess Meredith, Arthur Miller, Dorothy Parker, Larry Parks, Edward G. Robinson, Sam Wanamaker, and Orson Welles, among others. Gypsy Rose Lee and Hazel Scott pleaded innocent; radio's "Singing Lady," Irene Wicker, who attempted the move to television in 1946, lost her sponsor. Walter Bernstein who wrote for *Philco Television Playhouse* and Actress Judy Holliday were virtually unemployable. Philip Loeb, a director with the Theatre Guild and Group Theatre and who played Jake on *The Goldbergs*, committed suicide as the direct result of blacklisting.

In 1953 Senator Joseph McCarthy, a Wisconsin Republican, began an investigation of communism in the U.S. Army. Much of it was on television. The hearings lasted over a year. The corrupt tactics McCarthy used were revealed by Army counsel Joseph Welsh and the distinguished journalist Edward R. Murrow on his weekly CBS program, *See It Now* (9 March 1954). About the same time, some members of the American Federation of Television and Radio Artists (AFTRA) and the American Legion with advertiser connections formed Aware, Inc., a group that formalized the process for "clearing" performers whose background had been questioned. This anticommunist element was finally purged from these organizations in 1955 by a new group of independents. Blacklisting would be dealt a final blow by a well-known radio personality, John Henry Faulk. In the fall of 1957 Faulk found he was unemployed and unemployable. He sued Aware, accusing it of having caused the end of his radio sponsorship. With the financial aid of friends like Murrow and the legal skills of attorney Louis Nizer, Faulk won his libel case in 1962, and an appeal concerning his $3.5 million settlement was upheld. Thus, the blacklisting in this era slowly came to an end.

3

NBC Anthologies:
*Kraft Television
Theatre* and *Philco
Television Playhouse*

The foremost examples of dramatic anthologies at the National Broad-casting Company originating live from New York were the agency-produced *Kraft Television Theatre* (1947) and the in-house rival *Philco Television Play-house* (1948). At the outset, producers were the key figures: Stanley Quinn for *Kraft Television Theatre* and Fred Coe for *Philco Television Playhouse*. (And at CBS, Marc Daniels for *Ford Theater* and Worthington Miner for *Studio One*.) Usually, the producers adapted most of the plays and directed the first season. Then they hired other directors, but the recognition and responsibility for the success of the dramatic anthology remained with the producer.

Kraft Television Theatre

J. Walter Thompson (JWT), a major New York advertising agency, had been producing high-quality radio programs since its earliest days. Two of them were Robert L. Ripley's *Believe It Or Not* (1930), which dramatized weird events and the lives of unique people, and *Lux Radio Theatre* (1936–55), perhaps the most prestigious dramatic anthology of its day, which featured movie stars playing roles live in abridged versions of films recently in theaters. Movie and radio promoters realized the mutual value of this association. For television that was a different matter. After completing

Hour Glass (1946) for Standards Brands, JWT executive and radio vision-ary John Reber sought a one-hour dramatic series for television. The agency made a proposal to Lux, because it had the most experience in drama. Lux was not interested.

Another Thompson client, Kraft Foods Company, had an enormously successful series, *Kraft Music Hall*, that originally starred Al Jolson and Paul Whiteman's orchestra in 1934 and had moved to Los Angeles, where Bing Crosby hosted it for a decade, 1936–46. Then the *Music Hall* returned to New York. Kraft liked radio and trusted JWT enough to experiment with television. Kraft already optioned time on NBC's television schedule: 9:00 to 10:00 P.M., Thursdays, the same night as Standard Brands' variety series. Within two months after Standard Brands dropped *Hour Glass*, Kraft picked up its option; however, having a long-standing radio show on Thursdays, it moved the television series to Wednesdays, 7:30 to 8:30 P.M.

Kraft tried television as a corporate experiment, meaning that it could not use a regular advertising budget. So it created a budget for a rarely advertised gourmet item, MacLaren's Imperial Cheese. Many believed that only the wealthy would be watching expensive television sets and that this connoisseur item was appropriate. The cheese was plugged, but not dra-matized, between acts. "Well, we were only on in New York at that time and mostly in bars. I want to tell you that in four weeks, every MacLaren's package had disappeared from the shelves of gourmet shops in New York. The Kraft people got the message," Stanley Quinn recalled.[1] Miracle Whip and Velveeta, very popular products, were advertised immediately.

To originate a dramatic anthology for television required special expe-rience and talent. Reber chose Stanley Quinn for the job. Eager to get into radio after college in the 1930s, Quinn joined JWT. Briefly a messenger, he quickly moved into the radio department, which dispatched him to Holly-wood where the *Kraft Music Hall*, the *Chase and Sanborn Hour* with Char-lie McCarthy and Edgar Bergen, and the *Lux Radio Theatre* were among the huge successes attributed to the Thompson agency. Just as he was gain-ing confidence in writing and producing for prime-time radio, Quinn was sent to Schenectady, where General Electric needed assistance with its exper-imental television programming. JWT wanted GE's electric light bulb account, so it offered an experienced man from Hollywood, Stanley Quinn. In 1940 Quinn was appointed head of JWT's radio department in Sydney, Australia. By the time World War II was over, he had served in many capac-ities, including war correspondent in the South Pacific, and it looked like his postwar assignment would be as head of JWT Canada. However, his longtime boss and mentor John Reber gave the 32-year-old Quinn a different challenge — *Kraft Television Theatre*.

While Quinn cast and produced the anthology, Edmond Rice was hired to adapt the plays and to write the 90- and 120-second commercials. The first drama Rice selected was rejected by NBC Continuity Acceptance. NBC wanted to have more control over television than it had over radio programming. The key person was the director, the one who called the shots aloud, deciding what would be seen by the public; he worked with a technical director who physically punched the buttons that put the pictures on the air. NBC assigned Fred Coe as director and Al Protzman as technical director. This relationship between the network and the agencies caused tension for most of 1947. "In the beginning, only NBC staff directors were allowed to prepare shows for broadcast, but soon, the advertising agencies wanted to use their own staff directors. Most of these agency people were not experienced with TV production," Garry Simpson observed. "They may have been good stage directors, or radio directors, but they had to be exposed to the production techniques of a TV studio. Many came to observe, but when the neophytes attempted their first shows, NBC staff members were assigned to these shows to assist."[2]

For his second try, Rice adapted *Double Door*, by Eleanor McFadden, a 1933 Broadway success and a drama that NBC had telecast seven years earlier. *Variety* complained that the play was "the unfortunate selection of a dull, overly done, melodrama that has lost whatever merit it might once have possessed through the passage of time."[3] "Weeks of preparation were put into the first drama of the Kraft series," *The Televiser* reported. "The play, however, suffered from lack of direction — parts being high-schoolish."[4] Eleanor Wilson, as Victoria, the nervous, domineering head of the Van Brett household, headed a cast of veteran television performers: John Baragrey and Romola Robb as the romantic leads, along with John Stephen, Valerie Cossart, and Joseph Boley. Each week *Kraft Television Theatre* made a special effort to identify actors by their previous acting credits. The plays and properties were chosen for their appeal to a housewife because she was the most likely buyer of Kraft products: strong characters, good conflict, and intimate relationships told in closeups, with few interior sets and fewer exteriors that might appear unrealistic within the limitations of Studio 3H. The budget was about $3,000 to $4,000 a week.

Quinn produced 33 of the 35 productions in 1947. He would block the action and rehearse the actors, but Coe actually called the shots on air. In October the hazards of changing directors for the cast and the client came to a showdown. Quinn insisted that the show the client was paying for was in jeopardy. NBC's Vice President for Television John F. Royal reviewed the policy, and the network decided to permit "the agency's or client's producers to direct the show, whether in the studio or the field. In turn, NBC would provide a program director, a technical director and the necessary staff."[5] From then on, Quinn called his own shots, but NBC continued to use its staff director as a liaison to the inexperienced agency director. The NBC unit manager system had not been perfected, according to Garry Simpson, "so we staff members acted as liaisons with the agency people for ordering studio rehearsal time, equipment, sets, props, lighting effects, film or visual inserts, background music and titles. And during the studio rehearsal periods, we acted as assistants to help block to the equipment the programs in the studios. As soon as the agency directors learned the techniques, we staff members faded away. Finally, a Unit Manager Department was established and these NBC Unit Managers became the agency contacts for equipment and services."[6]

Eddie Mayehoff, a comedian with considerable television experience, headed *Kraft's* second show, "Merton of the Movies," by George S. Kaufman and Marc Connelly. The Puppets of Sganarelle and Martine helped to create the 7 August 1666 opening night atmosphere for Molière's *The Doctor in Spite of Himself*. On 9 July, the first commercial for Velveeta, a cheese product, was advertised between acts of Kaufman and Connelly's "To the Ladies." Ed Rice also announced that JWT would pay $100 for acceptable original teleplays. Well-known plays such as *Her Master's Voice*, *The Barker*, *There's Always Juliet*, and *A Doll's House*, mostly comedies, with occasional classics completed the hectic fall schedule.

By the time one Wednesday night drama went off the air, its successor had been selected and cast. Thursday morning conferences planned casting, script selection, and property clearance three weeks in advance. That afternoon Quinn had his first reading with the current week's cast. On Friday he cast the next show and worked out details for staging the present one with the set designer, usually NBC's Bob Wade. On Saturday actors used their books for blocking rehearsals. Sunday, Quinn read new plays at home, while actors finished learning their lines.

On Monday actors had to depend on discreet prompting. The set designer discussed the staging in the 45-foot by 90-foot studio, where much of the space had to be reserved for camera movement. NBC engineering did not allow camera operators to move pedestal cameras on the air. They had to be repositioned during breaks. Even with orthicon cameras, lighting remained intense, at least 800-foot candles per square inch for kinescoping. By Monday evening, Quinn knew which scenes were not going well, so he returned to the original version of the adaptation to correct the problem. Tuesday the staging was planned and the actors worked with props. By evening, camera operators had shot sheets and had some acquaintance of where they were to be positioned, although they did not actually have cameras.

Wednesday — the day of the show — was very busy. Cast and crew rehearsed on camera. Dress rehearsal usually came about an hour or two before airtime. To Quinn, the challenge was to prevent overrehearsing, so that the program retained the energy of a first-time performance as it went on the air. This was live; there was no second chance. "I always used everything the same on the dress [rehearsal] as on the air, because we had so many, many little problems that could go wrong on the dress. Anyway, all of a sudden, these actors would start playing — something would click and little known words would suddenly come easily and relationships would develop and all of a sudden they're playing a mile a minute."[7] Total rehearsal time amounted to about 26 hours, including five hours on camera.

At the end of 1947, Harry Herrmann joined the *Kraft Television Theatre* as an alternate director. Herrmann, Rice, and Quinn enjoyed the title "the unholy triumvirate."[8] Herrmann had joined the J. Walter Thompson agency four years earlier. Previously he had been in theater, along with a friend, Ed Pogenberg. When Pogenberg decided to become a theatrical producer and needed material for the love of his life, a promising young actress named Shirley Booth, Herrmann wrote enough to get her on Broadway and to get assignments for *Hour Glass*. Remembering his experience at *Kraft Theatre*, Herrmann once said: "We had to have one set in those days and few people in the cast. They got to be called 'kitchen dramas,' because they were all in the house in the kitchen or they were playing it in the parlor. We couldn't go outside and do any kind of set routines, until we got out of Studio 3H and went up to 8G [1948]. Up there we had a big studio. Then the new cameras came in with turret lenses, and we could get closeups without going down somebody's throat. And we could have sets, go from location to location, and give it more movement in space."[9]

For the thirty-fifth show that began the new year, 7 January 1948, *Kraft Television Theatre* moved to 9:00 P.M. An array of outstanding writers followed. *The Truth about Blayds* by A. A. Milne, featured Guy Spaull as William and Vaughn Taylor as Blayds, with veteran players Margaret Phillips, John Stephen, and Naomi Campbell. *Kraft's* first original television play, "Alternating Current" by Jack Roche, on 14 January, concerned a lawyer who wanted to get into politics. He was faced with a utility company and some preservationists who wanted the same land for different purposes. Ultimately, he switched his support to build a new Air Force base. Congressmen and utility executives found the drama particularly upsetting. Horton Foote's "Only the Heart," on 21 January, told about a Southern woman's search for love of family and friends. In "The Criminal Code," by Martin Flavin, a district attorney who sent a young boy to prison meets him again when the district attorney becomes a warden.

A 4 February adaptation of Sutton Vane's *Outward Bound* concerned strange passengers (Ralph Nelson, Vaughn Taylor, Charity Grace, Housely Stevens) on a mysterious voyage. Plays hereafter carried copyright notification: Kraft Foods Company, 1948. For "Spring Green" by Florence Ryerson and Colin Clements, on 11 February, Guy Spaull, Margaret Phillips, Vaughn Taylor, and Ralph Nelson were back. Susan Glaspell's "Alison's House," based partly on the life of poet Emily Dickinson, was 25 February. The 10 March production was "The Wind Is Ninety," a war-time fantasy by Ralph Nelson. Both John Stephen and Eleanor Wilson were praised for their performances in Owen Davis's "No Way Out," about the conflicting roles of a general practitioner and a research doctor. Casts for Oliver Goldsmith's classic *She Stoops to Conquer* and Ring Lardner and George S. Kaufman's *June Moon* doubled the typical cast size to ten, and included Ralph Nelson as Marlowe and Jack Albertson as Maxie. Sidney Howard's "The Silver Cord" and Philip Barry's "Foolish Notion" were in late spring.

By October, Scotland Yard searched for clues to several sudden deaths in "Criminal at Large," by Edgar Wallace. For S. N. Behrman's "Biography," John Forsythe, who was appearing on Broadway, made his Kraft debut. Customarily, Ed Herlihy announced the cast by listing least-known players and their credits first; he also began promoting upcoming shows. On 17 November, Jackie Cooper debuted as King Perivale in "The Ivory Door," by A. A. Milne. Now 27, the famous child star played a prince seeking the truth about everything, and so decided to go through the Ivory Door. On 24 November Vaughn Taylor, Ethel Griffies, and John Baragrey put on a "better than average" version of Emily Brontë's *Wuthering Heights*, while selling Kraft mayonnaise. For Christmas week, Sam Morgenstern conducted *Kraft Television Theatre's* musical rendition of "Hansel and Gretel," as its 85th television presentation.

Clare Kummer's comedy about a girl who gives up a promising operatic career for marriage, *Her Master's Voice*, was repeated on 2 February 1949, and John Cecil Holm's comedy about an old lady who bequeaths a ghost to a young girl in "Grammercy Ghost" starred Nancy Coleman on 9 February. For "The Flying Gerardos," by Kenyon Nicholson and Charles Robinson, 23 February, a vulgar line was changed: "As sure as God made green apples" to "Lord." On 9 March, Jack Lemmon and Patricia Kirkland had the leads for "The Arrival of Kitty," by Norman Lee Swarthout. Lemmon appeared again on 23 March when "Village Green," by Carl Allensworth, ran short but was saved by Maury Holland's excellent directing. The following week Stan Quinn did a difficult show particularly well. Sumner Locke Elliott's "Wicked Is the Wine" took place at the close of World War I in Australia, where two sisters — one insane — are in conflict.

"Bedelia" starred Julie Haydon, for *Kraft Television Theatre*, on NBC-TV, 31 August 1949.

Tom Ewell and Carl Reiner were new credits with *Kraft's* veteran group in "The Whole Town's Talking," by John Emerson and Anita Loos, telecast 20 April 1949. The story is about a small-town clerk romantically linked to a movie star by means of a photograph. Marie Baumer's "Little Brown Jug," which concerned blackmail by a witness to an accident, was produced by Tommy Ward and directed by Harry Herrmann.

By 1949 C. Maurice "Maury" Holland, a 43-year-old former vaudevillian, had become a producer/director. Kraft announced that it maintained a department where original and as yet unproduced scripts were read and, if found suitable, were adapted to the hour program. With few exceptions, Quinn and Holland alternated as producer/directors each week, hundreds of actors were on file, and rehearsals were continuous throughout the year.

An adaptation of *Bedelia* typified Kraft's dramas — less-well-known actors in interior sets — when it was aired on 31 August 1949. Still, Barre Lyndon's "The Man in Half Moon Street," about a couple's (John Newland,

Anne Jackson) experimentation with youth and living longer though in fear, was "one of its best" shows. It marked *Kraft Theatre's* return for a third season. A girl wooed by two ardent youths was the November plot for "In Love with Love," by Vincent Lawrence. Stanley Quinn directed Anne Francis and Maury Hill. On 7 December 1949, *Kraft Television Theatre* presented a cast of 28 in an "outstanding production" of Shakespeare's *The Comedy of Errors* for its 135th program. Everyone thought this added a touch of class.

Eric Hatch's "Kelly," about a GI in France who gets mixed up with a lady smuggling diamonds, on 25 January 1950, featured Mark Roberts as Kelly; and E. G. Marshall, John Newland and Flora Campbell had leads in "The Dark Tower," by Alexander Woollcott and George Kaufman, on 9 February. Joe Bates Smith's world premiere of "The Silent Room," on 15 February, told of a lonely old man and lost woman who find happiness despite "the meddling modern world." Washington's birthday saw Judson Laire as Washington and E. G. Marshall as Alcock in Maxwell Anderson's "Valley Forge." Mildred Natwick starred in "Ladies in Retirement," by Edward Percy and Reginald Denham, on 15 March.

In celebration of its 150th performance on 22 March 1950, the *Kraft Television Theatre* staged Robert E. Sherwood's 1928 play *The Queen's Husband* with veterans Mercer McLeod, Katherine Meskill, and Richard Purdy. Directed by Maury Holland, the plot concerns a monarch who outwits his domineering wife and the dictatorial prime minister by uniting with a communist labor coalition. It was also a precarious time for any association with communism. In the *Kraft* adaptation, however, *Time* complained there wasn't a communist in sight.[10]

By now, Maury Holland and Stanley Quinn were a pair that boasted about their well-oiled approach to drama. Each show cost about $6,000, paying a maximum of $250 to an actor and $500 per script to a writer. The average cost of some other anthologies had reached $20,000 a week. "We spend less time fooling around than any other show on the air," Holland claimed. Yet, as many agreed, the product was comparable with most summer stock productions. "We try to find a story of fairly simple people in an extraordinary emotional situation," said Quinn. The series appealing to "friends and bar watchers" was telecast to an audience of millions with little change from the original "beer-and-skittles diet," *Time* reported.[11]

"Every once and a while we'd do some Shakespeare, Galsworthy or something that was more challenging for us," Quinn said.[12] Such a challenge was presented on 5 April when the promising young actress Felicia Montealegre appeared as Nora in Ibsen's *A Doll's House*. Anne Francis was Dorothy for Elmer Rice's "Black Sheep," 26 April, and Augusta Dabney as

Margaret with Leslie Nielsen making an early appearance as Gregory in Joe Bates Smith's "The Fourth Step" was 3 May. The challenge to Stan Quinn for the third anniversary show on 10 May 1950 was *Macbeth*. Philip Hamburger wrote in *The New Yorker*: "Kraft gave Shakespeare an hour in which to show his stuff, and the Bard just couldn't make the grade." Uta Hagen was "the first Lady Macbeth in my experience to look like a sweater girl." Together with E. G. Marshall as Macbeth, "they sounded for the most part as though they felt a profound resentment against Shakespeare and all his works." In the witches' scene, "The Caldrons not only boiled and bubbled, they exploded several times, sending clouds of smoke into the night air. The witches, prancing about and shouting shrilly, were effective."[13]

Hamburger complained about "Good Housekeeping," by William McCleery, aired 14 June 1950. It was "a simple minded playlet relating how a college president is drafted to run for governor of his state and turn out the rascally politicians. There wasn't a human being in the crowd." "I cite 'Good Housekeeping' because one encounters fifty of its type for every 'Anything Can Happen,' [on *Philco Television Playhouse*, 18 June 1950] and as a result television drama, although it has learned to talk, still walks unsteadily."[14] On 30 August, Stan Quinn produced and Kirk Browning directed "The Detour," by Owen Davis, with a six-member cast. The next week Maury Holland directed 18 actors, as casts grew larger, in "The Last Trump." Mildred Dunnock starred in Irving Kaye Davis's "Last Stop" on 20 September, and Felicia Montealegre had another lead, along with John Newland, in "Michael and Mary," by A. A. Milne. Throughout the year various scripts were repeated. In the year's final show, 27 December 1950, E. G. Marshall was "Rip Van Winkle," from Washington Irving's collection that introduced the short story in 1820. Holland's production had a cast of 25.

On 31 January 1951, Ralph Meeker was in Harry Brown's "A Sound of Hunting." And in late February, *Kraft* presented Helen Jerome's adaptation of *Jane Eyre*, by Charlotte Brontë, in which "John Baragrey was a properly hedonistic, yet worthy — and eventually tragically redeemed — English gentleman," according to Robert Lewis Shayon in *The Saturday Review of Literature*.[15] But he wrote of "The Fortune Hunter," by Winchell Smith, on 21 February: "This tale was cut out of the slick, popular cloth of sentimentality.... A well-bred but poor young man [Jack Lemmon] sets out after a wealthy small-town heiress but falls for a Cinderella instead."[16] Holland was again in the director's chair for E. B. Ginty's "Of Famous Memory," featuring Nancy Marchand as Elizabeth and Leslie Nielsen as Dudley. On 11 April Cyril Ritchard, in his television debut, and Madge Elliott joined the lengthening list of well-known or promising new actors on *Kraft*

Television Theatre. They appeared in Henry Arthur Jones's "Mrs. Dane's Defense." Holland's "liaison" was John Rich for Booth Tarkington's "The Intimate Strangers," featuring Peggy Conklin, on 16 May, and for Quinn's "A Seacoast in Bohemia," by Ben Radin, on 6 June. July 18th brought Fielder Cook in as director of "Zone Four," featuring Richard Kiley. A cast of 35 was assembled for Eric Hatch's "Hour of Crisis" on 31 October 1951.

William H. Shriver, Jr., summarized *Kraft Television Theatre*'s progress: "Only occasionally are 'name' stars used on these presentations. But, good actors and actresses, true craftsmen of the trade, are always in evidence even down to minor roles. The writing is fine and the production capable and interesting. Week in and week out you can always expect good entertainment on this program. The Kraft Television Theatre is a fine example of what can be done by good, competent craftsmen honestly applying themselves to their art."[17]

By 1952 trends toward more expensive anthologies with celebrities, more original stories, and greater production values were evident, as Kraft's production costs rose to $17,500 per show. On 9 January Roddy McDowall appeared as Philip in George Kelly's "Philip Goes Forth," and Kraft celebrated its 250th program on 20 February 1952 with Hubert Henry Davies's "The Mollusc." The story was about a woman (Dortha Duckworth) who spent all her energy "sticking instead of moving" by declaring herself an invalid. Later in the year, a "highly satisfactory" production of Truman Capote's 1951 Broadway play, *The Grass Harp*, was aired on 17 September 1952. A spinster, played by Mildred Natwick, a young boy, and a black servant girl go into the woods to gather herbs for a secret formula labelled Gypsy Queen Dropsy Cure. Learning that a doctor wants to mass market the formula, the spinster climbs a tree in protest until the situation is resolved. "Often television actors, if they remember their lines at all, deliver them as though they were somewhat embarrassed to stand up and be heard in public, and for the most part they are right. If the *Kraft Theatre*'s presentation proved anything, it proved that television actors are critics, too, and that if they are handed lines of sensitivity and feeling, the odds are in favor of their delivering them with sensitivity and feeling."[18]

In a novel story on 28 January 1953 called "Duet," an expert pianist tells two beginners not to pursue piano as a career. In this "twisteroo," according to Hamburger writing for *The New Yorker*, the fellow who looked like a pianist turned to alcohol, while the other guy got a fine teacher and ended up playing in Carnegie Hall.[19] Kraft was so pleased with the return from its commercials on television it doubled the ante. "Beginning in mid–October, The Kraft Theatre will have a full hour on ABC television Thursday nights [9:30–10:30], in addition to its Wednesday night hour on

NBC, for a total of 104 plays a year instead of 52 and six directors instead of two."[20]

At John Reber's request, Quinn agreed to go to ABC, if he could choose the other two directors. Quinn chose his former assistant, Fielder Cook, and Fred Carney, Art Carney's brother. This left Maury Holland, Harry Herrmann, and Dick Dunlap at NBC-TV. The ABC-TV premiere, 26 November 1953, was R. C. Sheriff's *The White Carnation*, adapted by Frank D. Gilroy. In Gilroy's first video play were Ian Keith, Valerie Cossart, and Francis Compton.

"The Kraft TV Theater comes to you live from New York. The play is being performed at the moment you see it — living theater is your best television entertainment," *Time* reminded readers in March 1954. "The announcement read as each Kraft show comes on the air, dramatizes weekly the struggle for supremacy between live and filmed TV. It points up the fear of the TV networks, as well as that of the Manhattan producers of live shows, that they are about to be swallowed up by Hollywood. At first almost all television was live. Now one third of sponsored network shows are on film, and the percentage is growing."[21] On 5 May the *Kraft Television Theatre* presented Lewis Carroll's 19th century classic *Alice in Wonderland*, starring Edgar Bergen and Charlie McCarthy as narrators, and Robin Morgan as Alice, with an impressive list of New York actors. The "Drink Me" potion would reduce ventriloquist Bergen's size so he could follow Alice, but Charlie was already small enough. A few *Kraft* programs were in color; however, the entire series would not be in color for another two years.

Occasionally, the two anthologies would receive kudos and criticism in the same week. Jane Austen's *Emma*, starring Felicia Montealegre and Roddy McDowall on NBC on 24 November suffered from too many squealing women, fluttering around on tiptoes, and elfin men, while the next night at ABC *Kraft* had better luck with "Run for the Money," by Frank Gilroy, with Jamie Smith and Phyllis Love in the cast. It was "a drama that didn't begin to go to pieces until the final quarter hour."[22] In December Maury Holland attempted Alexandre Dumas's *Camille* at NBC. "Signe Hasso coughed and swooned appropriately as the lost lady of the camellias, but as her burning lover Jacques Bergerac (currently Ginger Rogers's husband) had scarcely as much animation as a wooden Indian and spoke his lines as if he learned them phonetically."[23] In 1955 Maury Holland was promoted to executive producer, a post he held until the anthology ended. George Roy Hill directed "Time of the Drought" for *Kraft* on ABC. "Ed Begley was brilliant as the cranky iconoclast who stuck to his principles in the face of overwhelming Christian charity and forgiveness on the part of his fellowmen, while Joe Maross made a believable young preacher who was

"Patterns" starred Everett Sloane, for *Kraft Television Theatre*, on NBC-TV, 12 January 1955.

both uncertain of and delighted by the results of prayer."[24] Again for ABC, Alberto Casella's "Death Takes a Holiday," featuring Joseph Wiseman as the Grim Reaper and Lelia Barry as the girl who falls in love with death was "the week's best video."[25]

The week's "surprise" was at NBC on 12 January 1955, when Fielder Cook directed Ed Begley, Richard Kiley, Everett Sloane, and a "superlative" cast in a wrenching story about a young executive who is being groomed to replace an old one in the corporate hierarchy. Rod Serling's "Patterns" is one of the best-remembered live television dramas. Serling said he didn't hope to write for movies: "I like TV fine, and I'll have it as long as it will have me."[26] "Patterns" was so highly praised that Serling said it took "Requiem for a Heavyweight" to assure him it was no "happy accident." Despite rave reviews, at week's end there was at least one strongly dissenting voice; *The Wall Street Journal* editorialized: "It is a strange thing if this is what playwrights, critics and the public generally think of as the true mood, atmosphere, and moral values of human beings in business. And if this is the general impression, it ought to send cold chills up to the upper executive reaches."[27] Playwrights and stars now enhanced *Kraft Theatre's* prestige, as Ossie Davis and Everett Sloane appeared in Eugene O'Neill's classic about the ruler of a small island who ruins his life through corruption: "The Emperor Jones" aired on 23 February 1955.

During the summer *Kraft Theatre* attempted Eugene O'Neill's 1918

"The Emperor Jones," starring Ossie Davis and Everett Sloane, for *Kraft Television Theatre*, was on NBC-TV, 23 February 1955.

play *The Straw*, about a consumptive Irish girl who falls in love with a writer who gets well and leaves the girl to waste away. Out of compassion he returns to give her hope. The stage play was bad, *Time* complained, but the television version that had a happy ending was even worse.[28] In "In the La Banza," by Sam Elkin, 20 July, a young boxer's talents are exploited too quickly by his greedy brother, and he is permanently injured. Robert Howard Lindsey's literate and perceptive play, *The Chess Game*, starred Melvyn Douglas as an old reprobate who adopted a boy headed for a life of crime. He wanted to pass on to the youngster that loneliness is worse than not belonging to anyone. The sharp point of the story fell to television's vices: the schematic, the facile, and the phony.[29] It played 31 August 1955.

To initiate the ninth season, the *Kraft Television Theatre* presented "The Diamond as Big as the Ritz," adapted from an F. Scott Fitzgerald fantasy. It was the 500th teleplay since 7 May 1947 and starred Lee Remick, Signe Hasso, and Elizabeth Montgomery. On 8 February 1956 Lee Tracy appeared in "Good Old Charley Faye," by David Karp, a well-written character role, but the play had "little to say," and suffered from an "implausible climax," according to the *Time* reviewer.[30] William Noble won $50,000 in a highly publicized playwrighting contest held by Kraft. His winning entry, *Snapfinger Creek*, featured Jo Van Fleet and Hope Lange on 22 February 1956.[31] That spring *Time* magazine attempted to settle the question about whether television drama is art: "In its long and lusty history, drama has never had as harsh a taskmaster as television, with its demands for a strong, simple story line, effective closeups, tight staging and split-second timing. Last week, with a brilliant series of first-rate plays, TV proved that, with all its demands, it is capable of producing a powerful and effective art form."[32] Using scarcely 200 actors to look like thousands, on 28 March 1956, George Roy Hill showed his mastery of television drama by directing live from NBC's new Brooklyn studios "A Night to Remember." Based on the Walter Lord account, the retelling of the collision of the *Titanic* with an iceberg in 1912 was a benchmark in live video drama. Hill moved six cameras through 40 sets, seven of which were built in duplicate so that one set could be flooded with water while the other remained dry to create a sinking effect. Claude Rains narrated the event.

During the mid–1950s, teen singers introduced songs on the series. Noteworthy is Gisele MacKenzie in 1955, and Ferlin Husky, Julius LaRosa, and Sal Mineo in 1957. After appearing in Paul Monash's "The Singin' Idol," 20-year-old Tommy Sands received numerous movie and network offers. Capitol Records said "Teen Age Crush," sung on the show, sold over 1.2 million copies. For *Kraft Television Theatre*'s tenth anniversary Sands starred again on 8 May 1957 in "Flesh and Blood," by Anthony Spinner.

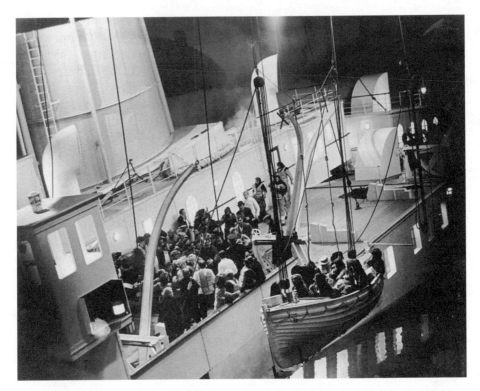

"A Night to Remember" aired for *Kraft Television Theatre*, on NBC-TV, 28 March 1956.

Sands now had a seven-year contract with 20th Century–Fox, made $10,000 a week at the Roxy Theatre, and got 2,000 fan letters a day.

By summer of that year, Maury Holland, an unassuming man, credited the longevity of the *Kraft Television Theatre* to the Kraft Foods Company. "Our sponsor," he told *Newsweek*, "is more understanding than others, allows us to make a certain number of mistakes. We're never made to feel uncomfortable, as though we're under a microscope. We're judged on overall performance rather than one show. As sponsors go, this is unique."[33]

Unlike most programs, *Kraft Television Theatre* never took a summer hiatus. It was off the air only on those occasions when it was preempted for a special program. The anthology ran over eleven years from 7 May 1947 to 17 September 1958. *TV Guide* wrote that it presented 650 out of nearly 19,000 scripts, that it starred or featured 3,955 actors and actresses in 6,750 roles, performing in 5,236 sets. Per program costs rose from $3,000 to $165,000.

For its last program on 4 June 1958, James P. Cavanagh adapted "The

Last of the Belles," an F. Scott Fitzgerald story with Jody McCrea, Roddy McDowall, and Janice Rule in the cast. Then, it lapsed into a summer anthology called *Kraft Mystery Theatre* that ran until October.

The *Kraft Television Theatre* was replaced by a video version of the *Kraft Music Hall*, a program familiar to radio listeners. In a letter to the author dated 28 July 1958, the Kraft Foods Company wrote:

> It is always a tremendous gamble in making such a selection. There are always a great many people concerned with the decision, including television program producers, network people, advertising agency people and of course people with the sponsoring corporation. We try to blend the best judgment of all those people and you may be sure decisions are reached only after very careful study. In selecting a television program, we try to find one which will prove entertaining to as many of our customers as we can. We have seriously considered giving up production of the Kraft Television Theatre, at least temporarily, for more than a year. During that time we have looked at every pilot film proposal and plan for network television shows we can find and have concluded that the new Milton Berle program Kraft will sponsor next year is the most outstanding show available.[34]

The program was not a success, however; therefore, the Berle show was dropped in May 1959. Instead, Kraft Foods signed a contract with singer Perry Como, who was to produce 66 one-hour color shows over NBC-TV within two years. The Como program cost Kraft $25 million, or more money than the company spent on live drama in the nearly 12-year history of the *Kraft Television Theatre*.[35]

Philco Television Playhouse

"This is the Broadway of television — WNBT, New York — The National Broadcasting Company, on Channel 4." It was 9:00 P.M. on 3 October 1948. "Every Sunday evening at this hour, the Philco Television Playhouse brings into your home the all-time hits of the American theatre, performed by the stars who made them famous," Bob Stanton announced.[36] "Philco Television Playhouse presents an Actors' Equity Television Production of 'Dinner at Eight' by George S. Kaufman and Edna Ferber, starring Peggy Wood, Dennis King, Mary Boland, Vicki Cummings, Philip Loeb, Matt Briggs, Jane Seymour, Royal Beal, Joyce Van Patten, and Judson Laire." Produced and directed by Fred Coe, it was a Music Corporation of America (MCA) package, represented by the Hutchins advertising agency.

The cooperative productions, budgeted at about $17,000 per episode, gave NBC the kind of control that 32-year-old Fred Coe was ready for. Frederick H. Coe was born in Alligator, Mississippi in 1914. His father, a lawyer, died before Coe knew him; his mother was a public health nurse. A loner by nature, he first showed interest in theater while attending Peabody Demonstration School in Nashville. He was also very active in community theater, spending six years with the Hillsboro Players, a youth group at Hillsboro Presbyterian Church, and a summer with the Lake Shore Players in Massachusetts. In 1935 while attending Peabody College, Coe became president of its drama group and planned a career in writing and directing. That same year local interests formed the Nashville Community Playhouse. Significantly, on this occasion Coe met Delbert Mann, who was six years younger, and they forged a common bond that made their lives inseparable.

Coe contributed to the Nashville Playhouse as a technician and actor, making his first appearance in *Double Door* by Elizabeth McFadden, which later was the debut production for *Kraft Television Theatre*. The Playhouse director, Fritz Kleibacker, recognized Coe's talent and dedication and aimed him toward his alma mater, Yale University. Coe attended Yale's Drama School from 1938 to 1940. He returned during summers, however, to the Nashville Community Playhouse, where he directed Shakespeare's *Julius Caesar* (1939), in modern dress, and *Twelfth Night* (1940) restaged for television in the late 1940s.

From 1940 to 1944 Coe was the director of the Town Theatre, Columbia, South Carolina. His military status was 4-F, so his career was not interrupted by the war. In 1945 he went to New York, where he was stage manager for *Bonanza*, by Ben Martin, but it closed before reaching Broadway. That year, he was hired as a director at NBC television. His initial assignment was three episodes of the children's program, *The Magic Ribbon*. Throughout the fall of 1945, Coe wrote and directed segments for *Hour Glass* and the *NBC Television Theatre*. Many of these programs were experimental, for NBC was mainly concerned with improving its signal reception by means of a new transmitter, better cameras, and better facilities. In 1946–47 he directed episodes of *Lights Out*, "Mr. and Mrs. North," a play that became a series, *ANTA-NBC Television Playhouse, Theatre Guild*, and *Kraft Television Theatre*.

During the "live" telecasts from Studio 8G, the *Philco Television Playhouse* dramas were kinescoped and distributed on film to other television stations. In the weeks after the "Dinner at Eight" premiere, Daphne du Maurier's *Rebecca* starred Bramwell Fletcher and Florence Reed, Elmer Rice's *Counsellor-at-Law* starred Paul Muni in his first telecast, and Bob Hilliard and Carl Sigman's musical revue *Angel in the Wings* starred Paul and Grace Hartman and the cast from the previous year's Broadway run at the Coronet Theatre.

On 31 October 1948 Fred Coe directed Elmer Rice's Pulitzer Prize-winning *Street Scene*, later described as one of the first American operas. It starred Betty Field and Erin O'Brien-Moore with an Actors' Equity cast. For an adaptation of Alexandre Dumas's *Camille*, on 14 November, Judith Evelyn headlined a cast of 32, with music conducted by Harry Sosnick. The "excellent" production, adapted by Samuel Taylor and directed by Coe, had ten and one-half hours on camera. On 28 November, Act I of A. B. Shiffrin's *I Like It Here*, on Broadway two years earlier, starred Bert Lytell. Between acts, announcer Bob Stanton welcomed Greenroom guest Paul Winchell, a ventriloquist, and his dummy Jerry Mahoney. Ruth Chatterton made her video debut in Edward Percy and Reginald Denham's "Suspect" on 5 December 1948.

A week later Edith Atwater debuted in "Parlor Story," a William McCleery comedy, with Dean Jagger. The production schedule for "Parlor Story" was typical. The cast was picked three weeks in advance of the show. Rehearsals began on 2 December and ran six to eight hours a day for one and one-half weeks. On 5 December music was set, cameras and sound were scheduled, costumes were checked, and scene construction was begun. By 8 December the cast was fitted. Commercials had to be ready by 9 December. The scenery was put up in Studio 8G the next day. December 11 and 12 were devoted to on-camera rehearsals and to the Sunday broadcast.[37]

Christmas week, *Philco Television Playhouse* offered Dennis King as Scrooge in a flawless production, according to the crew, of Charles Dickens's *A Christmas Carol*. Any show without technical errors was welcome relief to Coe and staff in a craft besieged with details and constantly endangered by failure. Afterward, however, NBC received many complaints from viewers who said they should have been told Bing Crosby's singing of "Silent Night" at the end of the program was on film, not live.

Several adaptations were by Samuel Taylor, including Edmund Rostand's *Cyrano de Bergerac* on 9 January 1949. It starred Jose Ferrer as Cyrano and Frances Reid as Roxanne, with a cast of 21. Perhaps one of the best shows to this time, it had some audio problems and provided one of the classic tales of live television. In the final garden scene when Roxanne learns that Cyrano had been writing the beautiful poetry, Fred Coe cued nuns to walk by: "Get the nuns in now, cue the nuns in. Get the god-damned nuns in there." This went out on the air.[38] In "Papa Is All," by Patterson Greene, on 16 January 1949, Ralph Nelson, Coe's assistant director, noted that a prop man was caught on camera. Camera tube problems arose on *Pride and Prejudice*, by Jane Austen. Assistant director Richard Goode noted that

"Ann Rutledge" starred Grace Kelly; "Pride's Castle" starred Anthony Quinn and Louise Allbritton; and "Cyrano de Bergerac" starred José Ferrer, for *Philco Television Playhouse*, on NBC-TV, 1949–50.

new tubes were "out of this world," but the old ones by comparison looked like "holy hell." On-the-job-training usually consisted of an employee entering as a production assistant, then going to floor director or manager in the studio, and moving into the control room as assistant director and then to, perhaps, director. In the busy days of increasing television programs, turnover was high and promotions could come fast if one demonstrated aptitude. Both Richard Goode and Ralph Nelson became directors.

"Dark Hammock" by Mary Orr and Reginald Denham, on 30 January 1949, like other shows, was prepared outside of NBC studios. Although on-air studio errors were unnoticeable, studio conditions had worsened. One of the four cameras was lost, resulting in Fred Coe quickly recomposing shots so that camera operators could compensate for the problem. For a production of Sidney Howard's "The Late Christopher Bean," Lillian Gish made her debut in "an excellent show" on 6 February. When her sister, Dorothy Gish, appeared the following week in "The Story of Mary Surratt," by John Patrick, Coe was concerned that the low-key lighting might make the kinescope too dark for affiliate station use. On 20 February, drawing upon his earlier theater experience, Coe and Samuel Taylor adapted *Twelfth Night* for a "smooth show."

On 6 March, Coe directed a "superb" showing of "The Druid Circle," by John Van Druten, with two members of the Broadway cast: Leo G. Carroll and Ethel Griffies. "He surrounded them with first-rate actors, placed them against Robert Wade sets that made them feel thoroughly at home, and played them naturally in front of cameras that knew where they were focusing and why." The reviewer lamented that television couldn't afford writers, a problem which he said was "still real and remains unsolved."[39] Hiring promising but unknown writers would become a mainstay of Coe's work for *Philco Television Playhouse*.

On 20 March Janet Blair and William Eythe starred in "Dinner at Antoine's." Though not a Broadway play, this "most satisfactory" telecast was adapted from Frances Parkington Keyes's novel. Camera rehearsals totaled 12 hours. In late March "Becky Sharp," based on William Thackeray's novel *Vanity Fair*, had numerous technical problems. On 10 April 1949 José Ferrer, heading a cast of 36, made a second appearance. Budd Schulberg's "What Makes Sammy Run" turned out to be *Philco's* most ambitious technical attempt to date. Although the production was somewhat more than Studio 8G could bear, assistant director Goode thought "as entertainment it was superb." Thus, Fred Coe ended the first season, consisting of 28 live dramas, for *Philco Television Playhouse*. Producing and directing the telecasts, usually adapted by Sam Carter and Sam Taylor, each Sunday night was "a burden that just about killed him," Delbert Mann once said.[40]

Replacement programs filled the Sunday period during the next several weeks. Initially, NBC presented "the premiere of *NBC Repertory Theatre*." Its first attraction was the popular fantasy "Mr. Mergenthwirker's Lobblies," by Nelson Bond and David Kent. (Coe directed it first on 22 September 1946.) Coe occasionally directed but mainly produced the programs while looking for two permanent directors for *Philco Playhouse*. Gordon Duff, Warren Wade, Garry Simpson, Victor McLeod, Ralph Nelson, and others took turns directing, although most of them already had their own series. NBC presented the 9 o'clock Sunday dramas under various titles and with various sponsors. The following week the series was called *NBC Drama Theatre* which Owen Davis, Jr., was to produce, until his sudden death in a boating accident. The first telecast, directed by Victor McLeod, was a repeat of "Burlesque," by George Manker Watters and Arthur Hopkins, and starred Bert Lahr. Next came *The Players Club*, a title Fred Coe used occasionally. It boasted the use of Edwin Booth's original prompt-book version of *Macbeth* when it was broadcast on 1 May 1949. The program featured Walter Hampden as Macbeth and Joyce Redman as Lady Macbeth.

On 8 May 1949, *Bedelia,* by Vera Caspary, was repeated for the *NBC Repertory Theatre,* the title most commonly used over the next two months. It was adapted and produced by Fred Coe but directed by Ralph Nelson, who said it was "an attempt at more experimentation and less complacency." The subsequent week Warren Wade took a turn at the Sunday experiment by presenting *Romeo and Juliet* in a new dramatic format called *Arena Theatre of the Air.* One Sunday NBC tried a double bill from the American Ballet Theatre, and the next, Gilbert and Sullivan's *The Mikado.* For the operetta Fred Coe served as producer and Gordon Duff directed the Gilbert and Sullivan Choral Society of New York.

By mid–1949 NBC's director of television production facilities Robert J. Wade described his work supervising 100 employees:

> Seven set designers [including *Philco*'s Otis Riggs] turn out blueprints for the five weekly dramatic programs and the diversified musical, comedy and variety shows; the settings are painted, stenciled and decorated by some 15 scenic artists, working in two and three shifts. A weekly allotment of 60 to 80 members of the Theatrical Protective Union, Local No. 1, build ... and operate shows emanating from NBC television studios situated in Radio City, the International Theatre at Columbus Circle, and former motion picture sound stages at the corner of 106th Street and Park Avenue.... Our largest dramatic productions, such as "Cyrano de Bergerac," "Pride and Prejudice," or "The Druid Circle," as well as the exacting demands of the Kraft and Chevrolet series, involve for each production seven to nine tons of scenery, which have to be built, painted or procured within two days.[41]

Finally, on 17 July, the program period was titled the *Philco Summer Playhouse.* Its premiere was "The Five Lives of Robert Gordon," by Nelson Bond. Melvyn Douglas had the lead, Coe produced, and Garry Simpson directed. Throughout July and August, Simpson and Gordon Duff alternated as directors. *You Touched Me,* by Tennessee Williams, brought Coe and Duff together again. The experienced and amiable Scotsman Gordon Duff seemed to get along well with the meticulous, sometimes volatile, and domineering Fred Coe. This team emerged as the second season began. Coe was involved in many projects, sometimes producing two or three series a week. Then, too, during the fall of 1949, NBC and CBS were engaged in a struggle over color standards. Coe had the responsibility of presenting NBC's color system to the FCC. While in Washington, D.C., he desperately needed someone he could rely on to carry out his expectations for *Philco Television Playhouse.* At times, Garry Simpson and Albert McCleery directed the series, but Coe was seeking consistency under his vision and relentless control. He needed an additional director to alternate with Gordon Duff.

Unlike the careful selection of strangers Tony Miner was putting together at *Studio One*, Fred Coe assembled his long-time friends and acquaintances from community theater and summer stock. No one illustrates this better than his choice for alternate director, Delbert Mann. As mentioned, the pair had met in 1935. Coe was always the mentor for his admirer, Mann, who had graduated from Vanderbilt University, where he developed a great interest in theater. He acted in Shakespeare's *Julius Caesar* and *Twelfth Night* at the Nashville Community Playhouse, where the productions were directed by Fred Coe. Because their interests were so similar, Mann kept in close contact with Coe and literally walked in Coe's footsteps. During World War II, Mann was a bomber pilot in Europe and saw a great deal of action. He has said the pressure in the pilot's seat in combat was great preparation for the pressure a director faced during a live telecast. After the war, he attended Yale, became director of the Town Theatre, Columbia, South Carolina, and, again through Coe's assistance, joined NBC.

Coe invited Mann to New York to meet Robert Sarnoff, who offered him a job as a floor manager. He began work on 15 June 1949. "After an indoctrination period of observing various shows, I was put on assignment as second floor manager on the simplest shows. I started throwing cues for such shows as *The Magic Chef*, a cooking show, *Kids A.C.* (Athletic Club), Tex Antoine, the weatherman, and *The Lady Next Door*, a children's story program. Finally, I graduated to *Mary Kay and Johnny*, one of the very first situation comedies, and on the *Three Flames*, a wild and far out show featuring three black musicians, I became a full-fledged floor manager."[42] On 25 August 1949 he got his first directing assignment for *Theatre of the Mind*, a series of sketches, written by Ralph Berton, and panel discussions to help viewers deal with emotional problems.

Keynoting the fall season, the *Philco Television Playhouse* announced that it would be adapting novels, such as Frank Yerby's *Pride's Castle*, starring Anthony Quinn and a large cast on 11 September 1949. The Hutchins agency had changed production companies, namely from MCA to Talent Associates, headed by Al Levy and David Susskind. Various producers and directors were used for two months, and fine writers continue to adapt well-known stories and plays. George Bernard Shaw already had some of his plays adapted for television, but when rights to *Cashel Byron's Profession* were sought, the 94-year-old Shaw returned a postcard reply: "My works are not available for the television. Television kills a living work commercially. Mine are all alive and growing. There are thousands of first-rate plays and books commercially dead. They are your natural prey.[43]

Meanwhile, Mann continued to learn his craft. When *The Life of Riley* began on 4 October 1949, it originated in Hollywood, but its commercials were done live in New York. To save the sponsor money, Mann learned how to pour a tempting glass of Schlitz beer without overflowing the brim. These commercials were directed by Kingman T. Moore, a former advertising man, who was also directing *Lights Out*. Moore willingly taught Mann, often his assistant, a great deal about television, this form of apprenticeship being common network practice.[44]

With the FCC color presentations nearing, Coe asked Mann to assist in the direction of an important *Philco Television Playhouse* drama, F. Scott Fitzgerald's *The Last Tycoon*. Coe asked Mann to do the preliminary directing so that he could add his finishing touches. To some directors this task may have seemed demeaning, but in fact, various shows, especially those packaged by advertising agencies, had dual directors. In any case, Mann was delighted for the opportunity. Joseph Liss adapted the story, and television veterans John Baragrey, Alfreda Wallace, and Leueen MacGrath, wife of George S. Kaufman, were cast. *The Last Tycoon* played to favorable reviews on 16 October 1949. Two weeks later Fred Coe produced David Shaw's adaptation of "Damion's Daughter," by Edwin Gilbert and starring Sidney Blackmer. Mann directed it, and then returned to *Lights Out* for his first major directing assignment, "Pengallen's Bell," starring Neva Patterson and adapted by Sumner Locke Elliott. At this point Coe offered Mann the chance to be alternating director for *Philco Playhouse*. With Coe as producer and Duff and Mann as directors, this was a combination that worked.[45]

When Gordon Duff did "Medical Meeting" in November, NBC Continuity Acceptance Department wrote him that it didn't want references to a man's lack of virility, the use of the Kinsey report in a "jocular" manner, brand names of liquor, or phrases like "He almost throws up" or a man asking his wife "for a making up roll in the hay." Coe and Duff took such constraints in stride.[46] Getting good material that would hold viewers was the main problem. Often, directors would have to suggest to writers ways to make a script more visual and language more realistic. No absolute picture emerges as to whether Coe assigned a certain type of script to directors, but comedies tended to end up on Duff's desk and dramas were given to Mann. The directors never made their own choices at *Philco Playhouse* and rarely at *Studio One*. This was in contrast to the way plays were chosen for *Ford Theater* or *Kraft Television Theatre*.

The two-week cycle for *Philco Television Playhouse* is best described in Delbert Mann's *Looking Back...at Live Television and Other Matters*.[47] By Monday the script had been assigned. On Tuesday and Wednesday casting and physical planning took place. On Thursday the entire cast, except for minor roles, had a first reading and character discussions. Schedules for costume fittings were established. The producer and director discussed potential problems and the running time of the show. Friday was a dry-run rehearsal with the writer present for changes and for preliminary blocking. Saturday and Sunday were homework days for everyone — actors learned lines, the director and writer did rewrites. The director also had to plot his shots and actor positions in his mind's eye and put them on the script. The second week usually had a first run-through on Wednesday, with actor notes from the director. Thursday's run-through was for the producer, technical director, lighting designer, and audio mixer. By now, the director had recorded all of the complex instructions onto a master script. As Coe watched the show being blocked for cameras in the studio, he demanded justification at that time for matters he disagreed with. Coe would nurture his actors and writers, but sessions with his directors were more traumatic. Sometimes the entire show was redone. Saturdays could be especially exhausting as each shot and detail was determined.

The agency's commercials were directed by Ira Skutch.[48] On Sunday mornings he rehearsed the television receiver and refrigerator spots that were to be aired live that evening. The drama was rehearsed and polished in a hectic romp with dress rehearsal, theoretically running nonstop, beginning at six o'clock. Final notes, changes, and details kept everyone tense. Then, "Fred's voice would be heard in the loudspeaker, 'Two minutes to air, pappy,' and I would double time up the stairs, hurl myself into the chair, and watch the second hand sweep up to nine o'clock, and we were on the air."[49] "Pappy," the father figure, was Coe's nickname and a term of endearment he extended to those he worked with closely. After the show, Coe and Mann had a brief postmortem at Hurley's, 6th Avenue and 49th Street. Mann had to catch the late commuter train for home so that the next day they could repeat the cycle.

Competition among anthologies intensified by the end of 1949. *Studio One* got very favorable attention from Paul Nickell's direction of *Julius Caesar* in modern dress, a Fred Coe standard. *Holiday*'s Harriet Van Horne wrote:

> The TV camera can not roam about as freely as does the Hollywood camera, nor can it be satisfied simply to photograph a play on stage. But already there are some distinguished dramatic shows, far and away the best one being *Studio One*. This is a full-hour Monday-evening program over CBS. The acting and directing are so good that even drama critics have been known to watch and applaud. *Studio One*'s hit of 1949 was *Julius Caesar* in modern dress, which the staid *New York Times* praised for two full Sunday columns and which has to be repeated by genuine public demand. Watching ancient Romans in tweed suits and trench coats struck an odd note at first, but one soon adjusted to it.[50]

Aesthetics at *Philco Playhouse* were jeopardized by NBC's engineering policy. Such limitations were not imposed upon those at CBS. For two decades NBC referred to dramas as engineering experiments; engineers had a great deal of influence over what cameras were capable of doing and how much lighting was required. While Tony Miner worked for a motion-picture look on the television screen, Coe's directors had to settle for more stringent technical conditions. For example, prior to the spring of 1950, a pedestal camera could not move on the air. The large, cumbersome cameras, operated by one rather strong person, could only move between shots, when the camera was not on the air. The skill needed for on-air camera movement provided a challenge that CBS operators were able to accept, and they provided smooth flowing shots that were highly praised by critics. Finally, during "The End Is Known," telecast 16 April 1950, NBC cameraman Jack Coffey proved in rehearsal that he had mastered on-air camera movement and that a straight dolly-in clearly enhanced the dramatic impact of the show.[51]

Because Fred Coe was himself a writer, producer, and director, he found it impossible to turn over total responsibility to his directors. Instead, he guided the directing tastes and strategies of those working for him, a trait common to producers who were once primarily involved with artistic decisions and then found themselves inundated with less attractive administrative decisions. Coe believed that a camera should never move without motivation, nor should a cut be made from one camera to another without reason. He liked the audience to be so absorbed with the emotional impact of the narrative and characters that viewers would not notice the camera cutting. He liked well-matched over-the-shoulder shots that did not obscure faces, and he preferred close-up shots to intensify the content and emotional level of the scene. Later camera theories have proved these notions may have worked for Coe, but many may not have been transferable to every directorial situation.

In any case, Fred Coe ran a tight ship. His temper and use of authority may have discouraged some from working with him but, as Tad Mosel once said, "Everyone adored Fred." Certainly many directors, writers, and actors learned the art of television under Coe's tutelage and attribute much of their success to him. Arthur Penn recalled that he was working as associate director on *The Colgate Comedy Hour* in California, when the call came: "Hi, pappy, wanna come to New York and direct some of these shows? You never saw anybody leave California so fast in your life...." Penn had been recommended by Vincent Donehue, who in 1950–51 directed some episodes of *The Quaker Oats Show* (also known as *The Gabby Hayes Show*). Penn was floor manager, and Horton Foote cowrote some scripts. This was an amusing early task for Donehue, Penn, and Foote. The Philco group was "unified around this man, Fred Coe, whose perception was these artists had to be protected," said Penn. "They had to be spared all of the nonsense that goes on in broadcasting, movies or the world of the theater, and somehow he managed to do that. So, we were able to develop these work relationships that were so intense, and so close, and so open that to this very day [1990] I have not experienced a body of collaborative work such as that."[52]

Luck plays a part in any person's life. Mann recalls his good fortune when he sought the lead for *Bethel Merriday*, by Sinclair Lewis and adapted by William Kendall Clarke. Aired 8 January 1950, the story was about a young, sincere, vulnerable, and attractive actress who is working in summer stock but trying to get her first important role. Coe steered Mann to Grace Kelly, whom Mann has described as "the most spectacularly beautiful girl I had ever seen." Grace Kelly at 21 was appearing as Raymond Massey's daughter in August Strindborg's 1887 play *The Father*. Besides playing Merriday, she starred as Ann Rutledge to Stephen Courtleigh's Lincoln, on the president's birthday. In Mann's view, Kelly was quick, hard working, totally professional, and very, very good.[53] The play was an expanded version of Norman Corwin's half-hour radio drama. "'Ann Rutledge' was not only a fitting tribute to the martyred President, it was also a commentary on what TV might receive from its better writers."[54] Joseph Liss used little from the Corwin work, but six years later Corwin wrote the Academy-Award-nominated screenplay *Lust for Life*, based on Irving Stone's novel about Vincent Van Gogh.[55]

"Vincent Van Gogh" was already the subject of a *Philco* drama by Hoffman Hays, aired on 5 March 1950, starring Everett Sloane. "I have a feeling that the Philco Television Playhouse authorities would have had less interest in Van Gogh if he had been just an immortal painter, rather than an immortal painter who happened to go insane. At any rate, they certainly made the most of the insanity."[56] Two months later Sloane was seen as an Austrian doctor, Ignaz Semmelweis. "Semmelweis," by Joseph Liss, with Felicia Montealegre as his wife, E. G. Marshall, and Guy Spaull was directed by Gordon Duff. "It was a sound job of writing — Liss has a respectful understanding of scientific work — and if the play failed, that was probably because the producing-directing team lacked the author's feeling for the subject."[57]

George and Helen Papashvily's *Anything Can Happen* was adapted by William Kendall Clarke. "All his characters retained a wholesome and colorful individuality — not a stereotype among them. His people talked the way people — Georgian or otherwise talk, and this alone put 'Anything Can Happen' in a special class."[58] It was the warm-hearted story of immigrants who try to preserve their distinctive way of life and at the same time adjust to their adopted home in America, where they welcome political freedom. "Hear My Heart Speak," by Charlotte Paul and adapted by Stephen de Baun, starred Charlton Heston and Olive Deering, on 25 June 1950. By the end of this season, according to A. C. Nielsen, the repertory-like company established *Philco Television Playhouse* as one of the Top Ten programs.

Masterpiece Playhouse, debuting on 23 July 1950, was the summer replacement. Jessica Tandy portrayed *Hedda Gabler* in the 1890 Ibsen classic, adapted by Hugh Kemp and directed by William Corrigan. "By modern standards, Ibsen's pedantic and studied style in 'Hedda' is not too exciting in any theatrical medium, and in television in particular it was much too garrulous, even when cut down to an hour's time," Jack Gould wrote in *The New York Times*. "With vehemence against women, it ran on and on, and only in the last few minutes did the screen come to life with people and not puppets."[59] Curtis Canfield, head of drama at Amherst and director of the Masquers, which had performed *Julius Caesar* at the Folger Shakespeare Library in Washington, D.C. in 1949, was a former NBC producer. He persuaded the network to do the dramas, budgeted at $10,000 each. "There's something pretty good about the classics; in spite of the fact they're spoiled for us at school," he said.[60] They provided some relief for Coe.

William Windom played *Richard III* in the second show, and Hurd Hatfield was in Richard Brinsley Sheridan's *The Rivals*. Luigi Pirandello's *Six Characters in Search of an Author*, starring Betty Field and Joseph Schildkraut, and Oscar Wilde's *The Importance of Being Earnest*, again with Hurd Hatfield, were among the other classic plays. Using an adaptation by Stephen de Baun, Coe and Mann presented Shakespeare's *Othello* with a cast of more than 20 on 27 August. "Under the searching eye of the television camera, and compressed into an hour's playing time, the TV Othello became a taut, single-minded study of the crack-up of the tormented Moor (played by Britain's Torin Thatcher) under the evil persistence of Iago (Alfred Ryder). Producer Fred Coe managed to fill, but not clutter, the TV screen with a swirl of movement, created a sense of space by letting his cameras poke down colonnaded halls and into drapery-hung apartments."[61]

The fall season of 1950 began with Maxwell Anderson's *High Tor* on 10 September. The video version of the award-winning play featured reliables Alfred Ryder and Felicia Montealegre. On 10 December *Bonanza* by Ben Martin, was adapted by Stephen de Baun and directed by Mann. A large cast of regulars performed it in front of Otis Riggs's Main Street, office of *The Weekly Argonaut*, and the Gold Eagle Saloon.

As with other anthologies, *Philco Television Playhouse* formed its own kind of repertory company. Although it had a large file of actors' names, it relied on a relatively small group of actors for whom some of the writers purposely wrote. Some were acquaintances from earlier days at school or in theater circles, and some had Southern backgrounds: A lanky, likable Alabamian well known in video circles, John Baragrey; a long-time friend and versatile actor who had spent time at the Town Theatre, Richard Goode; a writer, actor, and neighbor of Mann, Nelson Olmsted; one of television's earliest "stars," Vaughn Taylor; another Yale acquaintance, Ralph Longley; two actors from a decade ago at the Nashville Community Playhouse, Al Patterson and Frank Sutton; and the "cherished" E. G. Marshall were among those who appeared frequently. John Newland, Alfred Ryder, Alfreda Wallace, Betsy Blair, and Texan Larry Blyden were often employed. Otis Riggs, also from Yale, designed the settings.

The new year started with an original drama by William Kendall Clarke. "The Symbol," a biography of Jefferson Davis, president of the Confederacy, seemed to illustrate a tendency toward telling stories about the South. Aired 7 January 1951, the play, a favorite of Mann, starred John Baragrey as Davis and Ellen Cobb-Hill, also from Alabama, as his young wife. The role of the fiery South Carolinian Barnwell Rhett was played by E. G. Marshall. Coe disagreed with Mann's montage of the Civil War in Act II, but he later congratulated him for making the right decision despite Coe's objections. Act III dealt with Davis's return home with his second wife to face reconstruction. In February 1951, H. R. Hays wrote an original play, "Let Them Be Seacaptains," again starring E. G. Marshall and produced by the Coe/Mann team.

The most ambitious production to date, "The Great Escape," was directed by Gordon Duff on 28 January 1951. The cast numbered about 40 and included E. G. Marshall, Everett Sloane, Kurt Katch, and Horace Braham. Otis Riggs built a two-story set reaching to the ceiling of the studio, with underground tunnels and barbed wire fences. The highly praised production was adapted by Joseph Liss from a novel by Lieutenant Paul Brickall. About a month later, on 25 February, Gordon Duff directed "The Man Who Bought a Town," by Max Wilk.[62] "The pleasant conceit here was a former immigrant's rescue of a small town, which is condemned to oblivion by the removal of the town's only industry from the local factory. The immigrant's (Oscar Karlweiss) love for his town, his naive campaign to bring back the industry to the factory, the sterling qualities-in-crisis of the townspeople, the coming-to-recognition of the hard-boiled young executive — all were fairy tale; but Mr. Karlweiss's sensitive comic gifts rescued the show," claimed Robert Lewis Shayon.[63] On 11 March, handsome nine-year-old Brandon De Wilde and his father, Frederick, appeared in "No Medals on Pop," a teleplay by Henry K. Moritz. Young De Wilde had played nearly 500 performances of Carson McCullers's *The Member of the Wedding* on Broadway two years before. He had his own television series in 1953–54 and made outstanding movies such as *Shane* and *Hud*, prior to his death in a Denver traffic accident at age 30.

In March, Continuity Acceptance had Joseph Liss delete "damn" from Act II of "Bulletin 120," based on a U.S. Public Health Service report. In April, Fred Coe and Lillian Gish chatted on-camera leading into "The Birth of the Movies," a memoir about her working for silent film pioneer D. W. Griffith. Coe said: "The beginning of the movies must have been a wonderful and exciting time. We all felt that in working on this production." Gish replied: "I've been thinking how much this reminds me of the old Biograph studio. The bad lighting, the big cameras … everyone working under pressure and time."[64] On 17 June, David Swift and George Giroux, both in the U.S. Air Force Reserve, wrote "Operation Airlift," a large-scale production telling about the Berlin airlift. Mann found this drama particularly challenging because of its huge cast and complex scenes, especially one showing Templehof's runway and a cemetery in heavy fog, staged in Studio 8G. H. R. Hays wrote another original play, "I Want To March," for 15 July. It featured Katherine Meskill and the usual cast of professional New York players. Although Coe produced, Ira Skutch, who did the commercials, directed the drama.

During the 1951 season, *Philco* used professional New York actors and fine writers such as David Swift. Swift adapted Arthur Train's *Ephraim Tutt's Clean Hands*, featuring Parker Fennelly, on 12 August 1951. By summer, New York alone had 35 markets for original television scripts or adaptations. A writer received $750 to $1,500 for an original script and about $400 to $750 for an adaptation. Still, as Paddy Chayefsky complained, the most he ever made in one year was about $12,000. Topping the list of taboos were stories on sex, immorality, controversial religious subjects, or drunkenness presented in a favorable light. "These are the general restrictions but occasionally in case of *outstandingly* good scripts, they are broken. However, one unbroken rule is that there must be a moral lesson, just as in every story there should be a sympathetic character," Jay Caron warned in *The Writer*.[65]

David Swift had two original plays in succeeding weeks. "Requiem for a Model 'A'" was a *Philco* selection on 7 October 1951. It included another voice-over narration, just as in "Operation Airlift." His second venture was "October Story," starring Julie Harris and Leslie Nielsen. This play initiated on 14 October 1951 what was to be the alternate sponsor for *Philco Playhouse*—Goodyear. *Life* mentioned that "By building up its own stable of authors *Television Playhouse* (Sunday — NBC) has been able to present original plays in all its first five shows [of the fall season]. One of the best, 'October Story,' written by David Swift and directed by Delbert Mann, was distinguished both by the acting of Julie Harris ... [and] because settings such as Rockefeller Plaza were used. Miss Harris had to dart from the Plaza to the TV studio. She made the half block over and eight floors up in 90 seconds flat."[66]

Thus, in alternate weeks the anthology was called the *Goodyear Television Playhouse*, and arguably, more adventuresome material was introduced under the *Goodyear* aegis, in cooperation with Young and Rubicam. *Goodyear*'s second offering, 28 October 1951, was David Swift's third original drama, "The Copper," a funny script in which an odd fellow drives his superiors crazy and eventually goes to the electric chair, which malfunctions. It starred Wally Cox who, with Swift, would develop *Mr. Peepers*, a comedy series on NBC from 1952 to 1955.

By late 1951 the American Telephone and Telegraph Company had linked the East and West coasts via coaxial cable. Television programs could be sent and received in either direction. Television anthologies were now presented for the approval of a national audience, a mass diverse public of yet unknown preferences. In June 1952 Sylvester L. Weaver, Jr., at 41, was appointed vice president in charge of both radio and television networks. Weaver's background was in advertising before he came to NBC in 1949. He was immediately impressive with big programming concepts, such as *Your Show of Shows* and *Today*. Coe, who produced both of NBC's major Sunday night dramas, recognized Weaver's move toward bigness. To commemorate Pearl Harbor Day on 7 December 1952, *Goodyear Playhouse* presented "The Search," by David Shaw. Shaw updated a World War II air-sea rescue to a Korean War setting. Mann shot one-half of the action in a raft setting designed by Tom Jewett, but scores of other locations were also used to enhance a realistic effect.[67] By 1953, Fred Coe was executive producer of *Philco/Goodyear Television Playhouse*, *Mr. Peepers*, *First Person*, and *Bonino* with Enzio Pinza.

The debate that preoccupied the critical press as the *Goodyear Television Playhouse* began the fifth season months earlier on 14 September 1952 was whether — particularly with so many fine original dramas — television was emerging as a unique art form. Was television art? The case in point was the lead drama, "Holiday Song," by newcomer Paddy Chayefsky, who would become the best-known writer of live television dramas although not so well remembered in later decades. From late 1952 through 1955 this debate continued.

In Sumner Locke Elliott's "Elegy," on 25 January 1953, a poet (William Prince) writes an elegy on the death of his best friend (Charlton Heston) who is presumed to have died in Mexico. The friend blackmails the poet for half his earnings from writing the tribute. A cast-off girlfriend, played by Heston's wife, the "very talented actress" Lydia Clarke, plunged the blackmailer over an embankment. On 1 March 1953, Lillian Gish appeared. This time it was in Horton Foote's touching play about an elderly woman who wants to return to her roots and home, in *The Trip to Bountiful*. She is "a woman searching for her lost spirit," Gish wrote. *The Trip to Bountiful* was the first television film that the Museum of Modern Art requested for its archives.[68] It was soon followed on 5 April by Kim Stanley and Joanne Woodward in *A Young Lady of Property*, in which a young girl fantasizes about her inheritance. Foote's plays were noted for a dreamlike quality, strong character studies, especially of women, and Southern settings. Gore Vidal wrote in *Theatre Arts*: "He is allusive, delicate, elegiac, not unlike the early Tennessee Williams."[69] Produced by Fred Coe, many of Foote's plays were directed by Vincent J. "Vinnie" Donehue who had an especially keen understanding of Foote's small-town Texas characters. Donehue was another of Coe's friends from summer stock whom he helped to bring to NBC, where Donehue apprenticed and then became the third regular director of the Sunday anthologies. He was very thoughtful and personally well liked. Lillian Gish recalled how hard he tried to find the right script for her sister Dorothy's return to the stage. How quickly fortunes changed. It will be remembered that just two years earlier Donehue was producer/director of *The Gabby Hayes Show* for Quaker Oats. Its host/narrator was the loveable, toothless veteran of 200 movies, Gabby Hayes, who usually played the hero's sidekick. It is amusing to imagine Horton Foote as a story consultant to writer Jerome Coopersmith, with Arthur Penn as stage manager on this kiddie show. Foote's dramas also appeared: on 21 June, "Expectant Relations"; on 15 November, "John Turner Davis"; and 13 December 1953, "The Midnight Caller."

During the summer of 1953, N. Richard Nash adapted his 1948 Broadway play, *The Young and the Fair*, for *Goodyear Playhouse* on 26 July, and he wrote "The Rainmaker" initially for *Philco Television Playhouse* on 16 August. The former was restaged for another anthology, and the latter became a stage play and movie. While Fred Coe was on summer hiatus, David Susskind became producer.

Tad Mosel, a writer, was born in Steubenville, Ohio, in 1922, went into the Air Force at 18, graduated from Amherst College, worked at the Yale Drama School, and got a master's degree from Columbia University in 1953. Through his agent he contacted Susskind, and offered his first "personal" drama of a happening in everyday life to *Goodyear Playhouse*. David Susskind was encouraging and made numerous careful notes for revision of "Ernie Berger Is Fifty," prior to its 9 August telecast. This story concerned an average, hard-working guy (Ed Begley) who finds at age 50 that he is losing his success in business and the affection of his son. Mosel liked to deal with themes familiar to most people, often set in the Midwest. Perhaps better known for "Other People's Houses," produced by Susskind, Mosel remembered the evolution from what he originally envisioned to what his drama became after working with the actors, especially Eileen Heckart, and the production staff, "who worked so closely together and so much to the same purpose that the end result appeared to be a single creative effort."[70] The play, aired for *Philco Television Playhouse* on 30 August 1953,

"My Lost Saints," starred Eileen Heckart *(right)* and Lili Darvas *(left)*, for *Goodyear Television Playhouse*, on NBC-TV, 13 March 1954.

told the wrenching story of a woman (Eileen Heckart) who had to place her father (Joseph Sweeney) in a home for the elderly.

Tad Mosel was particularly fond of Fred Coe. "He believed that your work should go on as you wrote it," he mentioned to the author. "The play I told you about — the adultery-suicide play — I don't know what troubles he had with the sponsor. I'll bet he had a lot."[71] The drama was "The Haven," on 1 November 1953. Delbert Mann said it was "one of the best pieces I was ever privileged to work on." All efforts combined in an intricate mating dance that solved most of the problems convincingly. "Above all, I remember most vividly Heckie's [Eileen Heckert] brilliant performance for which she won a Sylvania Award." This was Mann's "high water-mark," after four years of directing 87 plays.[72]

As the sixth season began in the fall of 1953, staff changes took place. Arthur Penn, who was stationed at Fort Jackson while in the army, worked briefly at Town Theatre, and, encouraged by Coe to come to the network, was ready for increased responsibility. As soon as Gordon Duff turned his attention mainly to producing, Penn, having been through the ranks already, began directing for *Philco Playhouse*.

On 13 September, Robert Alan Aurthur's "The Baby," starring Eli Wallach, aired on *Philco Television Playhouse*. Aurthur's first work on television was described by *Variety* as good, if not distinguished. The baby in this initial script is 34 and still getting an allowance. Aurthur had become literary director for the *Playhouse* the previous February. An alumnus of the University of Pennsylvania, where he graduated with highest honors in journalism, a marine for over four years during World War II, and in charge of Armed Forces Radio in North China after the war, he had written extensively for magazines.[73] He would write several very successful scripts for television that were made into movies. Of "Spring Reunion," shown 11 April 1954 and starring Kevin McCarthy and Patricia Neal, the *Time* reviewer said: "The point (a father is not a substitute for a husband) was so trite that its dramatic impact was dissipated." It became a United Artists film in 1957.[74] For "Man on a Mountaintop," Aurthur's drama on *Philco* on 17 October, Arthur Penn directed and Gordon Duff produced. The story told about a shy prodigy who gives up his recognized abilities in science to wait tables so that he could blend in with ordinary people. "A Man Is Ten Feet Tall," starring Don Murray, Sidney Poitier, and Martin Balsam, was another award winner that became a movie, *Edge of Night* (1956), but "The Largest sum paid by Hollywood for a TV play, $100,000, was shelled out for a 'Television Playhouse' production, 'The Shadow of a Champ.'" This time, 20 March 1955, Aurthur told about a disenchanted sister (Lee Grant) who redirects the life of her brother while on a transatlantic voyage. Her brother (Eli Wallach) is a chum and part of the retinue of a world champion boxer (Jack Warden). The drama "as a whole failed to carry conviction," *Time* reported.[75]

On 19 December 1954 *Goodyear Playhouse* presented "Class of '58," by Louis Peterson, a 32-year-old black playwright. He had had a critical success about adolescence, *Take a Giant Step*, on Broadway a year earlier. The telecast told another story of a youth in misery because he is expelled from college just before Christmas vacation. "Jack Mullaney, as the boy stuffed to the ears with juvenile insolence and intolerance, struck occasional notes of bleak despair that were very moving. The ending was a shade too pat and Christmasy, but for most of its 60 minutes, *Class of '58* made an absorbing play."[76] Another East Texas writer, like Horton Foote and also from Yale, emerging from this rich period was JP Miller. His first play was *Old Tasselfoot*, starring E. G. Marshall on 25 April 1954. The cast for the second drama, *Somebody Special*, for *Philco Television Playhouse* on 6 June 1954,

"Shadow of a Champ" starred Lee Grant and Eli Wallach, for *Philco Television Playhouse*, on NBC-TV, 20 March 1955.

included Kim Stanley, Patty McCormick, and Harry Townes. It told about a woman married to a barber who thought her life might have been better if she had married her previous boyfriend. Miller also wrote *The Rabbit Trap*, which concerned a troubled relationship between a compulsive worker and the family he ignores. It was staged for *Goodyear Television Playhouse* on 13 February 1955, directed by Delbert Mann. Later, like many other television scripts, it was made into a movie.

Of all of the fine writers working for *Philco-Goodyear Playhouse*, Paddy Chayefsky's dramas seemed to best express the perception at the time that television might be a unique art form. Much of Chayefsky's "drama of the little man" was presented with great sensitivity by the Coe/Mann team. But his first work, "Holiday Song," about an aging cantor (Joseph Buloff) who has lost faith in God, was directed by Gordon Duff as the opening show of the fifth season for *Goodyear*, 14 September 1952, and again on 20 September 1953. Chayefsky thought that Buloff was too strong for the role but admitted he could not find five people to agree with him. Having great respect for Coe and his staff, Chayefsky felt most comfortable with Delbert Mann. "Delbert Mann is an extremely gifted director who has a precise affinity for my kind of writing and a sharp understanding of his own needs in conveying the values of the script to the actors and the cameramen."[77] "The Bachelor Party," on 11 October 1953, "The Mother" on 4 April 1954, and "Middle of the Night," on 19 September 1954 were among the intimate character studies by Chayefsky heralded by critics.

On 22 May 1955, when "The Catered Affair," directed by Robert Mulligan, was the *Goodyear Playhouse* choice, *Life* wrote: "Because Paddy Chayefsky is the most celebrated of the young TV playwrights, any new play he does draws a television audience as expectant and as critical as any attending a Broadway opening." "A Catered Affair" "was flawed in places, but it contained new evidence that Chayefsky [was] already a major theatrical talent."[78] "In the last year or so, television writers have learned that they can write 'intimate' dramas — 'intimate' meaning minutely detailed studies of small moments of life. Marty is a good example of this stage of progress. Now the word for television drama is depth, the digging under the surface of life for the more profound truths of human relationships."[79] Rod Steiger as Marty headed a distinguished cast that included Nancy Marchand, Esther Minciotti, Augusta Ciolli, Joe Mantell, Betsy Palmer, and Lee Philips. "Marty" was broadcast for *Philco Playhouse* on 24 May 1953. Marty, an ordinary guy, has difficulty finding a girlfriend whose values are more than skin deep. He also illustrates the normal homosexual tendencies young men have toward each other, as Chayefsky explained at length in the first collection of teleplays written by a single author.[80] In 1955, "Marty" was made into a motion picture after Delbert Mann agreed to direct it. Chayefsky greatly distrusted the film industry. Even so, *Marty* won Academy Awards for Best Screenplay, Best Actor (Ernest Borgnine), Best Director, and Best Picture — an unequalled moment in the history of television drama.

Coe developed a strong relationship with his writers. "Coe believes deeply in writers, and his belief, in turn, gives the writer a feeling of

"Marty" starred Rod Steiger and Nancy Marchand, for *Philco Television Play-house,* on NBC-TV, 24 May 1953.

confidence in himself, his talent, and his craft. The staff around Coe — Delbert Mann, Vincent Donehue, Arthur Penn, Gordon Duff, and Bill Nichols [who had become assistant producer by 1953] — all reflected and supported this belief," Horton Foote wrote in *Harrison, Texas.*[81] Gore Vidal's "The Death of Billy the Kid" starred Paul Newman and aired on *Philco* on 24 July 1955. Newman also starred in the film version, *The Left Handed Gun* (1958).

Perhaps the prolific Gore Vidal's best-known teleplay at the time was "Visit To a Small Planet," which aired on the *Goodyear Playhouse* May 1955. The weak plot found an alien, Kreton, played with delight by Cyril Ritchard, arriving during the second half of the 20th century rather than during the Civil War. Kreton had hoped to help the South win. The comedy, later on Broadway and filmed, was produced by Gordon Duff and directed by Jack Smight.[82]

Despite all of the respect Fred Coe and the *Philco/Goodyear Playhouse* had garnered over the years, with the *Playhouse* ranking eighth in Nielsen's Top Ten in February 1954, the anthologies had slipped by the end of the season. And some advertisers had complaints: "One week there'd be a story about a blind old lady in Texas and the next week a story about a blind young lady in Texas." *Time* reported: "This summer the *Playhouse* audience rating took a serious dip (usually it has been in or close to the Top Ten), and that, apparently, gave the ad men enough leverage to ease Coe's control of the show. Coe has been moved upstairs to the job of supervisor of production, Gordon Duff will replace him as producer."[83]

Simultaneously, Fred Coe produced several dramas for *Producer's Showcase*, beginning in 1954. This was RCA's 90-minute vehicle for promoting color television sets. The big budget shows, unlike *Philco/Goodyear Playhouse*, concentrated on sumptuous productions of well-known plays and stories. Among its splendid adaptations was Sir James M. Barrie's 1904 children's classic *Peter Pan*. Mary Martin starred as Peter and Cyril Ritchard as Captain Hook. Fred Coe produced the $450,000 showcase which aired 7 March 1955. Sponsored by Ford and RCA, *Producer's Showcase* ran for three seasons beginning in October 1954 to 1957. *Playwrights '56*, sponsored by Pontiac, gave Coe another chance to work with writers such as Foote, Mosel, and Vidal. However, it was dropped by June 1956 due to low ratings. Barely a year into a new contract, Coe announced he was leaving NBC because his talent was not being utilized.[84]

Meanwhile, *Philco/Goodyear Television Playhouse* continued until *The Alcoa Hour* premiered on 16 October 1955, starring Wendell Corey and Ann Todd in "The Black Wings," by Joseph Schull. By early 1956 Philco had phased out its sponsorship, but the Goodyear-Alcoa sponsorship continued. "NBC's *Alcoa Hour* made history by discovering a new way of treating the classic TV western story — writer Alvin Sapinsley put it in blank verse. Even more surprising: it worked. Franchot Tone, Lee Grant and Christopher Plummer played three tragic figures who end as corpses on a dusty street, while Boris Karloff leaned confidently into the camera as a one-man Greek chorus to give poetic expression to the eternal verities of life, death, and man's irreparable foolishness."[85] The live hour dramas sponsored by Goodyear and Alcoa ended in September 1957. They were immediately rescheduled, however, on Monday nights as half-hour filmed dramas and continued until 1960 under the series title, *A Turn of Fate.*

4

···

CBS Anthologies:
Ford Theater and
Studio One

Prompted by the swift competitive changes in television after World War II, the Columbia Broadcasting System, which had a long history of outstanding radio programs, quickly adapted them to television. Many of these radio programs, including Orson Welles's production of H. G. Wells's novel, *The War of the Worlds*, for *Mercury Theatre on the Air* on 30 October 1938 and *The Columbia Workshop*, originated from the grand Studio One on the 22nd floor at 485 Madison Avenue.[1] In 1947 *Studio One* aired as a one-hour radio anthology featuring adaptations with famous actors. That same year *Ford Theater* debuted on NBC radio Sunday afternoons at 5 o'clock. For its second season, 1948-49, *Ford Theater* moved to CBS as a weekly one-hour radio drama. Fletcher Markle, assisted by Robert J. Landry, was producer/director of both programs. Nine days after its CBS radio debut, *Ford Theater* appeared as a completely separate video anthology.

Ford Theater

Ford Theater offered a modified form of repertory theater featuring classic plays that were viewed live in New York, Philadelphia, Baltimore, Washington, D.C., Schenectady, and Richmond, and on kinescope recordings a week later in Detroit, Chicago, and Los Angeles. The Ford Motor Company and its agency, Kenyon & Eckhardt, Inc., were familiar with television drama through the agency's program series for the Borden Company, including the memorable production of *Twelfth Night* on NBC. The agency sought to extend the values of quality, sophistication, and "class" that its client represented. While the radio series lasted until 1 July 1949, the televised one-hour live anthology remained on the air for three seasons, 1948–51. After a season's absence, *Ford Theater* returned as a filmed half-hour drama, going off the air in 1957.

In searching for someone to head the series, Kenyon & Eckhardt ran across Marc Daniels. A genial man, Daniels loved to tell how he was directing summer stock when an agency representative told him about the anthology being planned that fall. Experienced in theater and recently discharged from the military service, he had a bachelor's degree from the University of Michigan and was teaching at the Academy of Dramatic Arts. Since he was a GI, he was entitled to take courses, so he enrolled in Harvey Marlowe's television class that was conducted in a small studio consisting of two camera chains that Marlowe had built. "They called me in and asked if I had any television experience, and I was able to quote my experience in Jamaica, New York, with this experimental station, and they allowed as how that was more than a lot of other people had at that point, I got the job of directing the *Ford Theater* for its first season on the air, which was one play a month, one hour show a month."[2] Garth Montgomery, a native of Malone, New York, had attended Columbia University and then went into radio-television advertising at Kenyon & Eckhardt. He became the *Ford Theater* producer.

Not only was everyone learning his craft, but the first show was telecast from the unfinished Studio 41, occupying the upper floors of the Grand Central Station Terminal Building that was entered from 15 Vanderbilt Avenue. At that point Studio 41 had only two walls. When the head of the agency asked to see the control room, expecting to see something similar to those in radio, all he could enter was a large enclosed plywood box partitioned off from the rest of the space. It contained switching equipment used in the field and four-by-six-inch monitors. Daniels had four cameras so that he could go from one scene to another continuously. Construction workers were hammering constantly, and the noise was driving the production people crazy.

For the premiere on 17 October 1948, the story was about actress Ruth Gordon growing up, called "Years Ago." Patricia Kirkland did an outstanding job repeating her stage role, but the warmth of the mother (Eva LeGallienne) and father (Raymond Massey) was not sufficiently conveyed by these two veteran actors. The father's role was initially offered to film star Louis Calhern, who said he had a bad tooth but probably was intimidated by live television. Daniels called Massey, whom he knew from summer stock. His wife answered. She said, "Well, television. What does it pay?" "Two thousand dollars," Daniels said. "Sure, he'll do it." Ford invested

Marc Daniels directed Fay Bainter in "Night Must Fall," for *Ford Theater*, on CBS-TV, 19 December 1948. Courtesy of Marc Daniels.

in each one-hour telecast somewhat more than, say, Kraft paid for four such programs per month.

While the first program was virtually lost between the premieres of *Philco Television Playhouse* and *Studio One*, and technical problems still persisted for the second broadcast on 21 November of "Joy to the World," starring Eddie Albert and Janet Blair, December's "Night Must Fall" finally came together. "It was a marvelous program, and we were getting along fine." Then, the boy (Oliver Thorndike), who carried a woman's head around in a hat box throughout the show and was about to kill the dear old lady (Fay Bainter), crossed to the mantle to get her some brandy. As Daniels panned with him, "I was horrified to find a stagehand leaning on the mantle, watching the show ... We were live of course; there wasn't anything you could do about it." Thorndike was "kind of marvelous."[3] He looked at the stagehand, shut it out of his mind, took the drink back, and gave it to Fay Bainter. Such errors could be edited out of the kinescope later.

Burgess Meredith portrayed Biff Grimes, a small-town dentist who still hated Hugo (Hume Cronyn), the fellow who stole his girl. Biff plots his revenge when Hugo has a toothache during a visit to the town. This comedy of life in the gay '90s, "One Sunday Afternoon," was penned by James Hagan and telecast on 16 May 1949. *Edward, My Son*, a Broadway play, was scheduled as the fourth production on 13 June. The cast was set and Daniels was well into rehearsals. Then, it was cancelled. Louis B. Mayer had complained to Henry Ford, of Ford Motor Company, that a telecast might hurt business for MGM's forthcoming movie. Ford agreed, and producer Montgomery and Daniels had to quickly find a substitute. They settled on another Broadway show that had just closed, *Light Up the Sky*, by Moss Hart. Barry Nelson and Glenn Anders flew back from California, the other actors were contacted, and it was ready to go in about four days. The biggest problem was cutting a two-hour play to 48 minutes.

Marc Daniels adapted most of the dramas for *Ford Theater* the first season. Sam Leve was in charge of sets, Cy Feuer provided the music, and Paul DuPont costumes. Nelson Case was the announcer.

On 7 October 1949 when the second season began with "Twentieth Century," a stage and screen farce by Ben Hecht and Charles MacArthur based on a play by Charles Milholland, the anthology became bimonthly. Paul Osborn adapted *On Borrowed Time*, by L. E. Watkins. Basil Rathbone played the somber Mr. Brink in the fantasy in which Death is chased up an apple tree by a boy and his grandfather (Walter Hampden). Judy Holliday starred as a night-club dancer who hides in a male college dormitory after witnessing a gang murder, for the 4 November choice, "She Loves Me Not." Max Wilk adapted this from Edward Hope's novel. A marriage in trouble because of a husband's preoccupation with his advertising business starred Faye Emerson and Lee Bowman in "Skylark," by Samson Raphaelson, for 18 November. Fay Bainter was the "Kind Lady," questioning her sanity when it is challenged by clever crooks, in her return appearance on 2 December. Peggy Ann Garner, June Lockhart, Meg Mundy, and Kim Hunter shared billing in Louisa May Alcott's 1869 Christmas favorite *Little Women*. Karl Malden and Will Hare were the male leads. Several of the 1949–50 adaptations were written by Ellis Marcus and Max Wilk. "The Farmer Takes a Wife," by Marc Connelly and Frank B. Elser, aired on 30 December 1949, was the story of a young farmer (Dane Clark) whose courtship is complicated by his girlfriend's inability to choose between life on the farm and the colorful life on the Erie Canal. Fortunately, Clark had done many movie fights, and so after choreographing them with Marc Daniels, Clark and the experienced Jabez Gray could gouge eyes and take punches that looked realistic.

At the beginning of 1950 Winston O'Keefe replaced Garth Montgomery as producer. O'Keefe, a graduate in theater from Northwestern University,

"The Barker," viewed from the control room, for *Ford Theater*, on CBS-TV, 13 January 1950. Courtesy of Marc Daniels.

was an actor and stage manager between 1935 and 1942 for 14 Broadway plays as well as director of various radio programs. After serving in the U.S. Army for four years, he founded a veterans' professional training program which had one of the first closed-circuit experimental workshops, and he was manager of the Washington (D.C.) Theatre Festival prior to coming to *Ford Theater*.[4]

The popular 1927 stage hit, *The Barker* by Kenyon Nicholson, was offered on 13 January 1950. The story illustrated a clash of wills between father (Lloyd Nolan) and son displayed against a colorful carnival background. The production was part of a trend toward more elaborate dramas that year. J. B. Priestley's comedy *Laburnum Grove*, adapted by Ted Mabley, brought Raymond Massey back to *Ford Theater*. The Broadway success, telecast 27 January 1950, concerned a quiet suburban Londoner who tries to get rid of his sponging relatives. Margaret Wycherly, Carol Goodner, and Richard Waring costarred in Edna Ferber and George S. Kaufman's *The Royal Family*, adapted by Norman Lessing. Another often repeated stage success, it told of a theatrical family in show business for generations, with the matriarch at 70 planning another tour.

Ford Theater had become so popular CBS-TV announced that when it returned in the fall it would appear weekly. Max Wilk readied "Uncle Harry," a 1942 hit by Thomas Job, for broadcasting on 24 February 1950. In the end Harry (Joseph Schildkraut), to everyone's disbelief, goes to jail for arranging the murder of one disagreeable sister and the hanging of another (Eva LeGallienne, Adelaide Klein). With no more room for a prison set, Wilk suggested it be done in the hallway with light and shadows for prison bars.[5] "Schildkraut was marvelous and loved this kind of work," Marc Daniels has commented. Because of the death of Jack Carson's father, Carson flew to Hollywood and then quickly returned to be in "Room Service," by George Abbott. With rehearsals already in progress he was about four days late. Two intensive weeks of rehearsals were normally needed. It was aired 10 March 1950.[6] In late fall 1949, *Actor's Studio* originally on ABC-TV in September 1948 for one season as a highly acclaimed half-hour anthology, moved to CBS-TV. After winning a George Foster Peabody award, in February 1950 *Actor's Studio* was lengthened, scheduled from 9:00 to 10:00 P.M. Fridays, and on 3 March it was retitled *The Play's the Thing*. *The Play's the Thing* was telecast in alternate weeks with *Ford Theater* through the summer.

The concerns and routine developed by Marc Daniels were aptly illustrated for the production of James M. Barrie's "Dear Brutus." The play was derived from a Shakespearean quotation in *Julius Caesar* that suggests people are molded less by circumstances than by qualities inherent in their characters. Stage and screen star Brian Aherne, making his video debut as Mr. Dearth, headed a group of weekend guests invited to visit a magic woods where they see what they would do if given a chance to relive their lives. To get it ready for airing on 24 March 1950, the cast met at Caravan Hall in mid–Manhattan, where a read-through and blocking began by painting set outlines on the floor. Daniels estimated it took him 72 hours of work at home to prepare for 60 hours of rehearsals. He used dummy cameras to line up shots based on blueprints of the sets. Four camera operators reported for mock performances before the rehearsals began in studio facilities. The use of full facilities cost Ford $1,200 an hour. On the ninth day set designer Leve and producer O'Keefe supervised set installation, and the day before the show actors reported in costume. One hundred employees worked about two weeks on each telecast. At this point *Ford Theater* cost $23,000 per program and was seen by an estimated 2.25 million people in 12 cities. "Aherne still looks back nostalgically to the simpler days of radio. 'It was all so easy,' he said wearily, 'at least for those of us who act.'"[7]

Barrie's *The Little Minister*, with Ian Keith and Frances Reid was an April 1950 selection. "Tom Drake [a movie star], as the Little Minister, gave as good a performance as I have seen on television," Philip Hamburger commented in *The New Yorker*. "Nancy Moore's adaptation was brisk, intelligent, and in the proper key; Marc Daniels' direction made exceptionally flexible use of the cameras; and Samuel Leve's sets were excellent."[8] Sheridan's 1771 classic, *The School for Scandal*, also adapted by Moore and aired on 21 April, had an expensive wardrobe budget. Most of the costumes were rented from Eaves, a big New York costume house, fitted and designed in the brief time available by Paul DuPont. Leueen MacGrath, who had become a reliable and versatile member of Daniels's informal repertory company, was Lady Teazle. *School for Scandal* was "an enormously complex production." In the beginning of the show was a kind of montage to introduce the time and the point of School for Scandal, which is that stories get exaggerated. Daniels remembered "that you start off with one story, but by the time it gets back to whoever started it, it is entirely different. So to do

"The School for Scandal" starred Richard Waring, Ian Keith, and Leueen Mac-Grath, for *Ford Theater*, on CBS-TV, 21 April 1950. Courtesy of Marc Daniels.

"Subway Express," telecast from subway barns in the Bronx, New York, for *Ford Theater*, on CBS-TV, 19 May 1950.

that, we had the whole studio set up with little vignette scenes. And as the camera went around to follow the story, the stagehands were striking those sets behind the camera. So that by the time we got all the way around, all of those [seven or eight] little in-sets had been struck — quietly — and we were able to go ahead with the play. They were all set in front of the main set, so to speak. It was kind of hairy, but it worked."[9] Oscar Wilde's *The Importance of Being Earnest* was scheduled, but it was never broadcast because of an engineers' strike just before it was moved into the studio.

As the second season came to an end, Daniels originated "Subway Express," a 21-year-old whodunit, from the car barns of New York's IRT subway division, located at 205th Street and Jerome Avenue in the Bronx. Trailer trucks hauled three tons of video equipment, including four camera chains and two tons of lighting facilities from the CBS Field Shop. Ian Keith, another of Daniels's favorite actors, headed a cast of 43 that had to rehearse at night so as not to interfere with the car barn's daytime activities. These unusual requirements raised the budget about $3,000 or $4,000.

"The majority of the action took place in the subway car where the murder took place, and just outside of it at a barn, where they took the [subway] car and detectives came to solve it." This was sent live by microwave downtown to CBS and recorded on kinescope. The most difficult moment came when they had to get a shot of the body on the ground — to examine it. Daniels had only four cameras, but five mounts. So, during a commercial break, he had one camera disconnected and then remounted in the tracks under the subway car. "This was a very big risk in taking a cable out of a camera in the middle of a show ... particularly in those days before solid state. You know they were all tubes."[10] "As an experiment it was a success," according to *Newsweek*. "But regular-location dramatic shows were still well into TV's future."[11]

The closing production on 30 June 1950 was Paul Osborn's *On Borrowed Time*. Daniels, who told *Theatre Arts* magazine that "the greatest single bar to art in television is the current practice of doing a play only once," used this opportunity to repeat a play with a new cast.[12] This fantasy is about a dying old man (Henry Hull) trying to keep his beloved grandson (Butch Cavell) from his straight-laced trouble maker aunt (Kathryn Grill) by keeping Death, in the form of Mr. Brink (Stanley Ridges), up an apple tree. Fantasies like this were also a preference of Winston O'Keefe: "What we need are strong, straight, logical dramatic issues. If a man is grappling with his problems, the camera can go right in and get it." He went on: "TV is fun, exciting, but its a real body eater. It's the first thing that's ever made me feel my years."[13] This was the end of the Winston O'Keefe–Marc Daniels supervision of *Ford Theater*. An entirely new staff would continue the anthology during the next season. Marc Daniels moved to Hollywood in late 1950, where he became director of the entire first season (38 episodes) of the filmed series, *I Love Lucy*.

That fall, for what would be the last year of live one-hour dramas on *Ford Theater*, Garth Montgomery, director of television at Kenyon & Eckhardt, Inc. and the original producer for *Ford Theater*, returned as executive producer. Franklin Schaffner, who was codirector of *Studio One*, assumed the directing responsibilities for what was announced months earlier as a weekly series.

The fall season began with Schaffner directing Lee Tracy in an adaptation of Herman Wouk's *The Traitor*. But the next week CBS introduced *Magnavox Theater*, on 15 September 1950, in the 9:00–10:00 P.M. time period. Garth Montgomery was also executive producer of this Kenyon & Eckhardt package that was directed in alternate weeks until the end of year by Carl Beier. The premiere for *Magnavox Theater* was an adaptation of Ferenc Molnar's "The Tale of the Wolf," starring Ilona Massey, a well-known

Hungarian-born actress. The story, translated from the original Hungarian by Barbara Tolnai, concerned a jealous man who was convinced that he could keep his wife's affection only by making her rich. John Wengraf and Steven Hill were cast as the male leads.[14]

Although the sponsorship alternated, high-caliber talent and plays continued to be the staple of the anthologies under Kenyon & Eckhardt guidance: Anna Lee in Nathaniel Hawthorne's *The Marble Faun*; Judith Evelyn in Patrick Hamilton's "Angel Street"; Victor Moore in Winchell Smith, Victor Mapes, and Frank Bacon's "Lightnin'"; Barry Fitzgerald in Lennox Robinson's "The White-Headed Boy"; Iris Mann in Lewis Carroll's *Alice in Wonderland*; and Richard Greene in George du Maurier's *Peter Ibbetson*. On 24 November 1950, for a *Magnavox Theater* presentation, CBS claimed that Alexandre Dumas's classic *The Three Musketeers* was the first hour-long drama filmed especially for television. It hinted at the direction *Ford Theater* would soon take. During the spring *Ford Theater* restaged Joseph Conrad's *Heart of Darkness*, starring Richard Carlson, and its season ended on 29 June 1951 with a repeat performance of Ernest Truex in "The Ghost Patrol."

After a season's absence, *Ford Theater* returned to television, this time on NBC, as a collection of half-hour films. The premiere, a video milestone, was a made-for-television movie produced at Columbia, the first major studio to do so. Mary McCall adapted a *Collier's* magazine story, "Life, Liberty and Orrin Dooley" that starred Will Rogers, Jr., and Marguerite Chapman. *Newsweek* claimed the difference between live and filmed production was "neither noticeable nor notable." But this reference failed to account for the move of the video industry to film and to Hollywood. Numerous stars, including Ronald Reagan and Nancy Davis who made their professional debuts together (5 February 1953), were lined up, along with nine writers already at work adapting stories from such sources as *The Saturday Evening Post*, *Cosmopolitan*, and *Popular Detective* for producer Jules Bricken. The anthology was directed by Robert Stevenson, James Neilson, and Leigh Jason. After four years, the show moved to ABC for its final season in 1957.

Studio One

By winter 1947 the competitive spirit was renewed at CBS. With most of the production staff having been fired the previous spring, Worthington C. "Tony" Miner was one of the few still on the payroll. Sitting in an office on 52nd Street with little to do, he was called upon to come up with different types of television programs that would compete favorably with NBC's *Texaco Star Theatre*, starring "Mr. Television" Milton Berle, a children's show, a situation comedy, and a dramatic anthology similar to *Philco Television Playhouse*. This was a tall order, even though Miner would not produce them all himself.

Miner was born in Buffalo, New York, in 1900. He served in the U.S. Army toward the end of World War I, graduated with Phi Beta Kappa honors from Yale in 1922, and spent another two years at Cambridge University. For the next several years he worked on Broadway, winning a Pulitzer Prize for *Both Your Houses*, and he was also a writer/director at RKO Pictures in 1933–34. He returned to directing on Broadway and became a member of the executive board of the Theatre Guild in 1937. Therefore, he was acquainted with everyone in entertainment in New York and Los Angeles, and he had experienced the uncertainties of the business. In late August 1939, having a family and a desire to be employed on a somewhat steady basis, he was considering redirecting his career. While he and his wife, actress Frances Fuller, were out for a drive with actress Ilka Chase and MCA executive Bill Murray, the car went into "a most ghastly skid." "There was understandably a moment of deadly silence, at which, and in a most casual tone, Bill Murray said: 'Tony, have you ever thought about going into television?'"[15] Destiny called. Within a week he had an agreement with CBS-TV head Gilbert Seldes and moved into the Grand Central Terminal Building, enabling him to thoroughly learn about prewar television efforts at the network.

Meanwhile, CBS radio thrived. William Paley took great pride in its programming and enjoyed the personalities that he, often personally, enticed to work for him. The long history of outstanding radio programs was quickly adapted to television. Miner recalled the meeting in which he suggested to President Frank Stanton and others that Ed Sullivan host a new variety series of promising young talents. This idea seemed stalled until Paley himself came into the room. He immediately inquired about what suggestions they had for competing with Berle. Miner explained his idea and that Sullivan's agent was inquiring about whether CBS might have a place for him. Paley liked the concept, and *Toast of the Town* with Ed Sullivan was aired 20 June 1948.[16] At first the critics complained about the dead-pan host or his odd collection of acts, but the show lasted for two decades. For the sitcom with a serious side, Miner had no difficulty in producing *The Goldbergs*, already on CBS radio, the work of Gertrude Berg. It premiered 10 January 1949. Miner's children's show, *Mr. I Magination*, debuting 29 May 1949, was played by children's author Paul Tripp and produced by Walter Hart.

CBS radio was famous for Orson Welles's version of "The War of the Worlds," also for *The Columbia Workshop*'s experimental plays in 1936 that featured some of the finest writers of the day seeking innovative ways to use radio. It also originated from Studio One located in the Madison Avenue headquarters. In 1947 *Studio One* was broadcast as an hour-long radio anthology featuring Vincent McConnor's adaptations of well-known plays with well-known actors. It was produced by Fletcher Markle and directed by Robert J. Landry. Landry told the author that they were so busy doing radio in those days, and with the recent firings at CBS television, they did not know whether television would last from one day to the next and paid little attention to it.[17]

Nevertheless, William Paley once again showed confidence in Miner, something which he greatly needed after being sidelined. Paley and Miner agreed that *Studio One* was a likely television conversion, in part because CBS already owned the title for what was to be a CBS in-house network program. Miner agreed to develop the series, provided that he could retain control over program content, thereby prohibiting other CBS executives from interfering with his judgment. Paley concurred; an administrative liaison was appointed to solve the few problems that arose.[18]

Miner always maintained great enthusiasm for the CBS "family" and had high regard for its leader, William S. Paley. Yet, after nearly a decade of dealing with close budgeting at CBS and the network's careful observation of what the public wanted to have for programming, Miner was well aware that *Studio One* would have to gain public support and critical prestige on a relatively low budget.

None of the four major dramatic anthologies in 1948—*Kraft, Ford, Philco,* or *Studio One*—had an exceptional debut. Fred Coe played it safest by offering *Dinner at Eight,* the 1932 Broadway hit by George S. Kaufman and Edna Ferber. Furthermore, *Studio One,* unlike the others, was sustaining. It had no sponsor.

For the premiere on 7 November 1948, Miner chose "The Storm" by McKnight Malmar. This genre of psychological melodrama, which Miner later claimed drew the best response and ratings for *Studio One,* was soundly criticized for leaving the audience dangling for lack of a solution.[19] Undaunted, Miner said he intended to open with a story that would give people something to talk about, a concept Hubbell Robinson would repeat years later.[20] Miner recognized that he would have to set the tone for *Studio One* by molding it himself— so he produced, adapted, and directed the first show. To finalize his control for the debut, he chose a long-time friend, actress Margaret Sullavan, as the star. Sullavan was well known for her delightful performances in films of the '30s and '40s (*The Little Shop Around the Corner, The Mortal Storm*). Recently she had turned her attention to the theater and was appearing in London in a revival of John Van Druten's 1943 hit, *The Voice of the Turtle*. The Miners knew Sullavan and Leland Hayward, her husband, a theatrical producer. Margaret and Fran, Miner's wife, were friends since being in the 1936 Broadway success *Stage Door*. The Miners lived at the Dakota, a huge apartment complex on the west side, and the Haywards resided on the east side of Central Park, where they would roller skate. Sullavan's London opening received poor reviews, so Miner's offer to star in the *Studio One* premiere was a welcome challenge. A major problem came up during rehearsal. For the last scenes, Sullavan had to react to a prerecorded voice-over-picture sequence. She started the scene and then fell apart emotionally. In her dressing room she confided that she was going deaf. Miner reassured her that the audio level would be adjusted and that she would be just fine.

Outwardly, Miner was a flamboyant showman in an old theatrical tradition that exhibited substantial self-confidence and occasional temperamental excess. But he was shrewd and conservative in his choices for *Studio One*. As producer, he kept tight control over the year's 44 shows. During the first season he said he wrote 39 of them, and upwards of 30 each year for the next three years. This took a lot of drudgery and exuberance. While he wanted to remain the producer/writer, he sought fresh young directing talent.

With few directors having much television experience on the East Coast in the late forties, those who were available were employed rather quickly. Typically, many of the possibles were educated in theater, hired in community theater, served in the military, and went back home to work in academia, local theater, or radio. Some had spent much of their life in the South. One such person was J. Paul Nickell. Soon after the war ended, Nickell was teaching English at North Carolina State University, Raleigh, which had an Army Air Corps program that provided a temporary deferment. Besides teaching, he was a frequent director at the Raleigh Little Theatre, and he liked to work in radio, where he and a friend decided to develop a children's series. While at the station one evening some soldiers came by, and Nickell invited them for spaghetti dinner. One of the soldiers—William Craig Smith—mentioned that he had been in something called "television."

After this, for a short time, Nickell was in the army himself. Upon his return, Smith invited him to WPTZ, the NBC affiliate in Philadelphia, to view on 23 March 1947 a Fred Coe drama called "Little Brown Jug," by Marie Baumer. Nickell recalled, "I was completely enthralled. And I said to Bill, when it was over, 'What is it? It isn't theater, it isn't film. What is it?' I was hooked right then and there."[21] Soon thereafter, he joined WPTZ as a cameraman and quickly worked his way up to director. After directing a miscellany of shows, he was allowed to direct "The Monkey's Paw," by W. W. Jacobs, "an old [1910] turkey of a one-act play."

In making its rounds from city to city, the Television Workshop of New York probably stopped at Philadelphia, where its actors accelerated his interest in television drama. Nickell went to New York to see how he could improve his video technique and sat in on a rehearsal for Gian Carlo Menotti's *The Medium*. Inspired by the stage production and not inhibited by legal restrictions imposed later, he combined the best talents he could get from New York and locally with clever inserts of the newly recorded album by the Broadway cast, directing *The Medium* from Philadelphia on 26 September 1948 for the fledgling NBC network.

Worthington Miner saw "The Medium" and called Nickell the next day. At lunch in New York, Miner claimed he'd seen Nickell's work for nine months and wanted him to direct a musical anthology until he realized he did not have enough money for it. Instead, "I directed the first show for *Studio One*, which was on every other week. The second show was a light comedy with John Conté called 'Let Me Do the Talking.' Paul and I directed it together."[22] The third show was "The Medium," which Nickell did alone on 12 December 1948.

Initially, *Studio One* appeared twice a month on Sundays. A Philip Morris spot preceded the program, and a Ronson lighter advertisement followed it. The eighth show on 6 March 1949 was William Shakespeare's *Julius Caesar*—in modern dress. Having already been seen—in modern dress—a decade earlier on the BBC (24 July 1938) and on NBC (15 March 1940) as television's first full-length Shakespeare adaptation, its appearance was not remarkable. As it happened, however, the *Studio One* version turned out to be a "superb" production. Saul Carlson's review for *The New Republic* stated,

> To Worthington Miner goes the chief credit for the Shakespeare hour, done in modern dress and acted with convincing fluidity by Robert Keith as Brutus, Philip Bourneuf as Marc Anthony and John O'Shaughnessy as Cassius. William Post, Jr., as Caesar, seemed embarrassed by reciting Elizabethan poetry in a storm trooper's shirt. But his weakness was lost in the large cast maneuvered with precision by Paul Nickell. Richard Rychtarik executed sensibly proportional sets which in their blandness and lack of attempt at phony "atmosphere," kept the focus on the actors. CBS had staged a contemporary morality piece, in which the villain was fascism.[23]

Jack Gould, the esteemed critic of *The New York Times* said: "Gould's 'honor roll' cites ... television's 'Studio One,' the production of Worthington

Miner. Its presentation of *Julius Caesar* in modern dress was one of the most stimulating and exciting theatrical experiences of the year, regardless of media, and the first work worthy of a place in television's permanent repertoire."[24] Thriving on such heady praise, *Julius Caesar* was repeated with the same cast within two months (1 May 1949).

When the anthology was viewed eleven days after the second viewing of *Julius Caesar*, *Studio One* was scheduled weekly at 10 o'clock Wednesdays, then moved to Mondays by fall 1949; significantly, the program was sponsored by the Westinghouse Electric Corporation, which paid $8,100 an episode. Soon Betty Furness would prove to be an outstanding spokesperson for the company, its products, and the anthology.

The first show for Westinghouse on 11 May had a decidedly commercial look with *The Glass Key*, by Dashiell Hammett. The 1931 novel and 1935 movie about a detective who saves a politician involved in a mysterious murder was adapted by Miner and directed by George Zachary, who began his radio career in the thirties as a writer for *Ellery Queen*, a master detective. Zachary's directing role was little more than a try-out as Miner sought a second director and relief for Paul Nickell. Comedies such as Ring Lardner and George S. Kaufman's *June Moon*, on 22 June, did not do so well, despite the presence of Glenda Farrell, Eva Marie Saint, and Jack Lemmon. Unexpectedly, Ivan Turgenev's *Smoke*, with Leueen MacGrath and Charlton Heston the previous week, was one of the most popular dramas. Miner's insistence on effective close ups, long shots for depth, blending of film and live action, and high technical polish gave the anthology favorable critical attention. The "pyrotechnic pageantry" of "The Battleship Bismarck," staged on 24 October 1949, was a benchmark moment. Miner adapted the Maurice Valency story about the sinking of the big Nazi ship, conceded to be the greatest single threat to Britain's lifeline in the Atlantic during the war.[25] The cast of 29 actors featured film star Paul Lukas as Captain Lindemann and Charlton Heston as Commander Schneider. The action was carefully staged in a small studio, where numerous explosions and gun shots clouded in lots of smoke punctuated fast, tense action directed by Paul Nickell.

Nickell would remain with *Studio One* eight and one-half years, longer than anyone else. His relationship with Miner was excellent. Only once, to Nickell's recollection, was he terribly upset with Miner. A film actress of the early thirties, Vivienne Segal, had the lead in "Here Is My Life," viewed on 28 May 1951. At age 54, "Vivienne was pulling out all the stops which she did very well, effectively, and I thought we were on the right track. But Tony felt, I guess, it was too sentimental. He didn't like the performance and changed it completely."[26] Week after week, regardless of the story,

"Julius Caesar," in modern dress, for *Studio One*, on CBS-TV, 6 March 1949.

Nickell focused on the actors, subtlely moving from one to the other. "I think probably a moving camera was the thing that I did possibly more than other directors. I always tried to motivate it. I always could give you a motivation at the time for doing it that way. This was the thing for me that separated television from film a great deal."[27]

Miner continued to look for an alternate director. He was impressed with the way 29-year-old Franklin Schaffner, already on the CBS staff in news and public affairs, shot a golden jubilee parade. So, he asked Schaffner to direct *Wesley*, a comedy series, which was never sold, before inviting him to direct *Studio One* during its second season in 1949. After Miner found Schaffner, he and Nickell alternated assignments. The collection of adaptations, which Schaffner referred to as "in public domain," was eclectic, just as Schaffner's later film choices would be wide ranging. In remembering *Studio One*, Schaffner commented that it was not built on a numbers game, when that kind of drama first started. "It was technically inept. It was restricted to very minimal budgets, and it was certainly restricted at least as directors by our own lack of experience. Having said that, we nonetheless found a very gratifying response in the highly limited audience."[28]

When Charlotte Brontë's *Jane Eyre*, which Schaffner directed, appeared on 12 December 1949, *Time* said: "Not all of Studio One's hour-long shows are as moving and well-integrated as was *Jane Eyre*; like all TV dramas the quality wavers up and down from week to week. But what makes Studio One outstanding in television is its invariable high technical polish."[29] Schaffner kept a kinescope of the program, starring Charlton Heston and Mary Sinclair. Years later he said, "I talked to Charlton Heston about it one time, and he said, 'Well, gee, you got a print of it. Why don't you bring it up to the house, and let's run the 16mm copy.' I said, 'Fine.' I wouldn't mind seeing it.'" About 20 people gathered, and Schaffner braced himself for what he thought would be a burst of laughter, because in those days one began with an establishing shot for background, usually a photograph, and moved in or out from it. Instead, the group was "enormously attentive." They were interested in the content, performances, and what a television drama looked like in the fifties.[30]

By January 1950 the complexity of *Studio One* was apparent. Most dramas were scheduled ten weeks in advance. Scripting, casting, set design and building, and the creation of special effects were in various stages of completion for at least two shows continually, one in its preliminary stages, the other in its final phase. Miner prepared the anthology in quarters; 13 dramas constituted a quarter. He was by now writing only one in four scripts and hiring freelance writers to do the other adaptations. The first draft was due ten weeks in advance.

One dependable writer, Joseph Liss, who adapted "The Dybbuk" (1 June 1949), was working on Rudyard Kipling's *The Light That Failed*. The story had two problems: The Lamp Division of Westinghouse refused to sponsor a drama about a faulty light, and the conclusion of the script depicted a lesbian theme. Miner was furious when he met with Joe Liss, who finally cooled him down. "Tony, baby, when did you last read 'The Light That Failed'? Read it, baby. Read it. I didn't add that lesbian angle. Kipling did. I just softened it a little." Liss was right.[31] The question of the play's title went all the way to William S. Paley himself, who stood by the program as scheduled, even though Westinghouse threatened to withdraw its sponsorship. Aired 10 October 1949, "The Light That Failed," starred Felicia Montealegre and Richard Hart.

For the 10 to 20 roles, a typical number for each play (although many dramas had a cast of 30 or more), about 500 performers auditioned each week. Robert Fryer, Miner's assistant, and Eleanor Kilgallen, CBS-TV casting director, proposed cast lists that Miner ultimately approved, the directors having no input in casting decisions. The final selection was made 13 days before airtime. The rehearsal cycle began the next day, followed by three days of blocking. More rehearsals were held in the hallways of CBS before the cast entered Studio 42 on Sunday, the day before the telecast, and Monday for ten and one-half hours of camera rehearsals.[32]

The theme for "The Willow Cabin," adapted from Pamela Frankau's novel by Sumner Locke Elliott, was taken from a line in Shakespeare's *Twelfth Night*. It describes a young girl (Priscilla Gillette) who dedicates her life to her lover (Charlton Heston) and becomes "a willow cabin at his gate." She is a successful actress who falls in love with a married doctor. The drama was telecast 27 February 1950. In May of 1950, Miner and Lois Jacoby did a literate job of adapting Henry James's *The Ambassadors*. They took major liberties with the plot, but Ilona Massey as The Countess was "a mature and fascinating woman," Robert Sterling as Chad Newsome revealed the character's severe dilemma, and Judson Laire as Lambert Strether "splendidly showed the heady effects of Paris upon a rock-ribbed New Englander."[33] Robert Lewis Shayon took exception to the plot changes, when *The Ambassadors* was repeated about a year later: "The Studio One ending had Chad go home to Woolet, the factory, and the right American sweetheart, while Lambert locked elbows with the Countess in a champaign toast. The switch was deliberate folklore, chauvinistic appeasement of Mom, the great goddess of American TV."[34]

Whether she was chosen as Christmas relief or for her undaunted service as Miner's assistant, Lela Swift was given the director's chair for a two-part production of *Little Women*, by Louisa May Alcott (18 and 25 December 1950). Mary Sinclair had the lead in Part I — "Meg's Story," and Nancy Marchand was the center of attention for Part II — "Jo's Story." Sumner Locke Elliott adapted the novel. Lela Swift would become an Emmy Award–winning director of the daytime soap opera *Ryan's Hope*; when contacted, she was inundated with features for an upcoming Olympics.

"Little Women," starred Mary Sinclair and Nancy Marchand, for *Studio One*, on CBS-TV, 18 December 1950.

The year 1951 began with Walter Slezak starring in a fast-moving comedy about a young couple's involvement in a fabulous antique deal called "Collector's Item." The play was adapted by Alvin Boretz and presented by the Miner/Nickell team. *Studio One* under Miner's tutelage provided experience for directors, writers, and numerous actors — Anne Bancroft (Anne Marno then), Charlton Heston, Grace Kelly, Don Murray, John Cassavetes, Yul Brynner, Felicia Montealegre, Maria Riva (Marlene Dietrich's daughter), and Mary Sinclair (George Abbott's wife) among them. Miner had begun to build an East Coast version of the Hollywood studio system, which developed talent. "Do not become overexposed early in your career" was one piece of advice Miner gave to young Heston. Looking toward Hollywood and his eventual place among movie superstars, Charlton Heston signed a seven-year contract with Hal Wallis that allowed him to return to perform on television. Years later, Heston referred to Miner and the live anthology period as a day gone by, "the like of which we'll never see again."[35] The list of critically acclaimed dramas under Miner's watchful eye began with "The Medium," "Julius Caesar," "The Dybbuk," "Smoke," "Battleship Bismarck," "The Ambassadors," "The Scarlet Letter," "Wuthering Heights," and "Trilby."

A 13-week series titled *Westinghouse Summer Theatre* made its debut on 18 June 1951 as *Studio One*'s summer replacement. Jerry Danzig and Montgomery Ford were producers, while John Peyser and Walter Hart alternated as directors. The opening show was a baseball comedy by Mel Goldberg, "Screwball," directed by Jack Donohue. Dick Foran played a one-time potential star baseball pitcher yearning for a comeback. His wife (Cloris Leachman) saw much more security in his occupation as an automobile mechanic. Former New York Yankees pitcher Vernon "Lefty" Gomez debuted as a scout for the big league. Other summer dramas were Hugh Pentecost's mystery "Lonely Boy"; Ferenc Molnar's "The Swan"; David Goodis's mystery "Nightfall"; and John Galsworthy's love story "The Apple Tree." Significantly, Donald Davis, with credits at ABC and connections with NBC, became the general supervisor of the series.

"The Idol of San Vittore" was the story of an ardent patriot who rekindles the morale of despondent Nazi prisoners during the winter of 1945. The role of General Andreas della Rovere was played by the story's author, Eduardo Ciannelli, and Maria Riva, a suffering patrician beauty, was the romantic interest. The adaptation was by Jane Hinton for the Miner/Nickell production. It was telecast 1 October 1951 as the first coast-to-coast full-hour drama to reach Hollywood from New York via AT&T's new cable connection.

"'Studio One' has an imaginative guide in Worthington Miner, who has already presented *The Taming of the Shrew* [June 1950] and *Coriolanus* [June 1951] in modern dress. Recently Mr. Miner did a costume version of *Macbeth* with only minor alterations necessary to make TV material out of Shakespeare's original. With a clear eye for what is important to the cameras, Mr. Miner came up with a play that caught the spirit and meaning of *Macbeth* within the program time of fifty-two minutes."[36] Charlton Heston played the part with tremendous enthusiasm and vitality, and Judith Evelyn was a woman of uncontrollable ambition and determination, as supple as tempered steel. Such compliments helped to elevate *Studio One* into the top ten programs on Hooper and Pulse rating surveys. By spring 1952 *Time* noted that *Studio One* had won more awards than any other dramatic program on television, "largely because of its professional competence and grown-up story-telling." Live television now cost *Studio One* $22,000, *Kraft Television Theatre* $17,500, and *Philco-Goodyear Playhouse* $28,000 per program.[37]

Still, the house of cards fell down, as dreaded, from time to time. One such occasion was on 25 February 1952, when Melvyn Douglas and Viveca Lindfors appeared in "Letter from an Unknown Woman." The disasters began as Douglas saw Lindfors on a Vienna street. Without warning, a wall began to billow out "like laundry in a high wind." Later, while waltzing in an intimate restaurant, they were abruptly doused with a thick flurry of snow; and the microphone boom, usually racked out on a long fishing rod-like pole, collided with an overhead metal lamp resulting in a noise so loud the actors momentarily looked up and forgot their lines. It was a night when everything went wrong, an assistant conceded.[38]

Perhaps this was a bizarre farewell to Worthington Miner, for about three weeks earlier (5 February), NBC had announced that Miner would be joining his rival. After being at CBS since 1939 and rising to the zenith of his career with the tremendously successful *Studio One*, Miner told the author he believed he deserved a salary increase. Up until this point, CBS had never paid him more than $750 a week. Sadly, the network was unwilling to meet his request. It looked to some as if NBC just wanted to buy out the competition. This was a wrenching move Miner did not want to make; as he told it, CBS was unwilling to compromise. So he left.[39] NBC's vice president in charge of the television network, Sylvester Weaver, announced that Miner would be producing a one-hour dramatic anthology for NBC in the fall. The move was unfortunate, as Miner related in retrospect: "I never had one rewarding, truly happy day at NBC. The shadow of the General [Sarnoff] was crass and joyless; the shadow of Bill Paley was sprinkled with sparks."[40]

Studio One's award-winning reputation was established. Its continuity continued to be preserved during the summer with *Studio One Summer Theatre*. It opened with "The Blonde Comes First" starring Lee Grant and Tom Helmore on 30 June and ended with "The Shadowy Third," starring Carmen Mathews, Geraldine Page, and Robert Pastene on 15 September 1952. Of the ten plays, five were restaged and recast.

As the fifth season for *Studio One* began, Donald Davis replaced Miner as the overall supervisor of the anthology. Davis, married to actress Dorothy Mathews who was named to assist him, was the son of Pulitzer prize winner Owen Davis (1874–1956). Early in his career, Owen Davis wrote many tragedies in verse but found there was no market for them. After that, it was said he wrote about 200 melodramas and became very popular. *Icebound* (1923) and other plays were often on experimental television. *Ethan Frome*, a video favorite, and *The Good Earth* were novels adapted with Donald Davis for the stage during the mid-thirties. They were also movies. Even though they did not write the screenplay, *The Good Earth* (1937) yielded an Oscar for its star Luise Rainer, and it is remembered for its outstanding special effects. Producing the highly acclaimed *Actor's Studio* for ABC, Davis had a background somewhat similar to Miner's, and he had been hired by CBS to produce *Studio One Summer Theatre* the previous year.

Davis looked after various aspects of three dramas at once. Paul Nickell and Franklin Schaffner alternated as directors, bringing together the work of some 160 technicians, artists, and actors for the weekly shows. Two or three weeks ahead of each performance, Richard Rychtarik, senior scenic designer, completed his basic floor plans which were then sent to Bill Mensching, who supervised the 49 carpenters and laborers that built as many as nine sets for a single show. Though broadcast in black and white, the "flats," or wall sections, were finished in colored water-based paints. Bob Jiras, head of makeup, had the responsibility of swiftly aging the actors while on the air as a story progressed. CBS had a huge property storage center in Manhattan and a staff resourceful in getting special items. A lighting director and three electricians were in charge of creating the atmosphere each play required. The CBS-TV Record Library, air conditioned and adjacent to the main studio, housed recorded music and sound effects that would be marked with cues and cleared for copyright. "On the day of the show [Monday], for the first time, all these far-flung and separate activities merge. They all come together under the coordinating supervision of producer Davis." *Studio One* was recorded live in CBS Studio 58, Ninth Avenue at 55th Street.[41]

The fall began with Nina Foch, Dick Foran, and Grace Kelly in "The Kill," on 22 September 1952. In addition to frequent players were Jack Palance in "Little Man, Big World," on 13 October, and Peggy Ann Garner and Frank Overton in "Plan for Escape," on 17 November. Except for his right hand, the lead character remained unseen in "I Am Jonathan Scrivener," on 1 December. Although this was not a new technique, it added novelty to the cast of favorite actors: John Forsythe, Maria Riva, John McQuade, Felicia Montealegre, and Everett Sloane. As the season began, CBS introduced "solid scenery" made of prefabricated masonite flats for a scene that takes place in a hotel. Television wall flats, like those used in the theater, were made of canvas stretched over a rectangular frame. They could contribute to the calamity already mentioned. This construction, painted in black and white for greater separation from actors, was supposed to add depth and authenticity to the setting. A conscious level of realism was well suited to director Paul Nickell, because cameras would be more mobile with greater freedom and fluidity of movement. The play was "The Square Peg," by George Malcolm-Smith, a comedy about a young personnel psychologist who is duped into streamlining the operations of a criminal combine. It starred Orson Bean and Hildy Parks.[42]

In February 1953 Fletcher Markle, the original producer of *Studio One* on radio, decided to make his acting debut in his own video production of "My Beloved Husband," adapted by Robert Wallsten from Philip Loraine's novel and directed by Franklin Schaffner. The story told of an unprincipled young man accused of murdering his wife who exacts ironic retribution after her death. Markle chose Mary Alice Moore and Ruth Warrick as the female leads. The series still sponsored by Westinghouse was represented by McCann-Erickson, Inc. In March, Margaret O'Brien, famous as a child star during the war, appeared with Everett Sloane in "A Breath of Air." In April, Markle and Nickell teamed up for Jackie Gleason's dramatic debut. Gleason was already a popular talent, having appeared on *The Cavalcade of Stars* for DuMont and, since the fall of 1952, in *The Jackie Gleason Show* on CBS. "The Laugh Maker," an original teleplay by A. J. Russell, presented "an enigma of personality and temperament — a man nobody knows," according to a CBS news release. "It is this mystery that a magazine writer attempts to unravel for a profile he is preparing on the comedian."[43]

"End of the Honeymoon," on 13 July 1953, starring John Kerr and Eva Marie Saint, was part of the summer fare. "Sentence of Death," on 17 August, included James Dean, Betsy Palmer, and Gene Lyons in the cast. Rudyard Kipling's *The Light That Failed*, which caused a major controversy during the second season, failed to keep its classic title when it was revived, because it was now called "The Gathering Night"; but *Studio One*'s premiere entry, "The Storm," restaged with Georgianna Johnson in the lead, retained its title, to close out the season on 14 September.

Adapted by British Playwright William P. Templeton, with assurances there would be no tampering with the ultimate blueprint of her late husband's work, George Orwell's *1984* starring Eddie Albert, Norma Crane, and Lorne Greene, opened the sixth season on 21 September 1953. "A grim, gruesome, humorless show, it was television at its best," *Time* reported. "*Studio One* did not flinch at an unhappy ending." Petty bureaucrat Winston Smith (Eddie Albert) groveled in a prison pit, was tortured into admitting that two and two equal five, came screaming out of a chamber of hungry rats, and admitted his fealty to Big Brother.[44] Nickell thought this was his most significant show.

Impressive as the keynote was, the season did not really gain momentum until after the first of the year. It was the initial scripts from Reginald Rose, Gore Vidal, and Rod Serling that brought new excitement to the long-running anthology.

Reginald Rose had been writing television scripts since 1951 while working as a copywriter for a small advertising agency. "Finally, in November 1953, with considerable urging on the part of Florence Britton, 'Studio

"1984" starred Eddie Albert, fourth from right, for *Studio One*, on CBS-TV, 21 September 1953.

One's' story editor, I wrote my first hour-long original drama, 'The Remarkable Incident at Carson Corners.' Not long after that the advertising business and I parted ways, both of us immeasurably brightened, and both probably the richer for it. Since then I have written some fourteen one-hour original plays for television … ," he wrote in *Six Television Plays*. "I have enjoyed myself thoroughly, spent a great deal of time with my wife and family, and managed to pay most of my bills by the tenth of the month."[45]

A schoolroom and a mock trial are the backdrop for Rose's inquiry into who is responsible for the death of a child in "The Remarkable Incident at Carson Corners," which aired 11 January 1954. As with *1984*, this was the work of producer Felix Jackson and, in Rose's words, "the brilliant and sensitive handling of a very complex script" by Paul Nickell. Franklin Schaffner directed "Thunder on Sycamore Street" on 15 March. Originally, Rose conceived the story about a black person moving into a white neighborhood, but he realized that this would be objectionable to networks having stations in the South. Therefore, he compromised and made the lead an ex-convict

"Twelve Angry Men," for *Studio One*, on CBS-TV, 20 September 1954.

who becomes the focus of mob action. Later, Rose learned: "Not one single person I spoke to felt that he was actually meant to be an ex-convict. This was extremely gratifying to me and made me feel that perhaps Thunder on Sycamore Street had more value in its various interpretations than it would have had had it simply presented the Negro problem."[46]

The only play that Rose based on his own experience was *Twelve Angry Men*. He had jury duty on a manslaughter case in New York's General Sessions Court. It occurred to him that the activity in a jury room deliberating a decision could be exciting and could comment on social responsibility, justice, and democracy in action. The result was the struggle between opposing points of view between a jury ready to hang the defendant (Franchot Tone) and the bland and believable juror who changes everyone's mind (Robert Cummings). Broadcast on 20 September 1954 through the efforts of producer Jackson and director Schaffner, *Twelve Angry Men* has been preserved as one of the benchmark moments in television drama. (In 1957, it became director Sidney Lumet's entry into film.) "An Almanac of Liberty," based on Supreme Court Justice William O. Douglas's book, enabled

Rose to write a drama for 8 November about townspeople who beat up a stranger looking for work. He supposedly has radical ideas that are protected by the Bill of Rights. Rose used time as a symbolic element in the sometimes mystical story. "When they repent, time, once again, moves ahead. Reginald Rose's expert script and a fine cast made Studio One the week's No. 1 entertainment."[47] With the McCarthy era at its peak, taking on controversial social issues was a courageous effort by the network, the advertising agency, and the sponsor. Perhaps Rose's best-known courtroom drama was yet to come: the 1957 *Studio One* two-part drama "The Defender."

By the time 27-year-old Gore Vidal had his first television script produced, he had already written seven novels, including two best sellers. Like his family, later he would run for public office. "Dark Possession," starring Geraldine Fitzgerald, Leslie Nielsen, and Barbara O'Neil, took place in 1911. The setting is an old Victorian house in New Hampshire, where three sisters find themselves in a web of fear and suspicion because of an anonymous letter writer. The story appeared on 15 February 1954. About a year later, 2 May 1955, Vidal's "Summer Pavilion" would star Charles Drake, Elizabeth Montgomery, and Miriam Hopkins. Both plays were subsequently restaged for *Matinee Theatre.*

Rod Serling's "The Strike," about a trapped patrol in Korea, aired 7 June 1954; "The Man Who Caught the Ball at Coogan's Bluff" starred Alan Young and Gisele MacKenzie on 28 November 1955; and "The Arena," about a junior senator who discovers a guilty secret involving his colleague, aired 9 April 1956. Serling, in his early thirties, went to Antioch College and was a paratrooper during World War II. He typically wrote for three or four hours in the morning and turned to other projects in the afternoon. He had written well over 100 teleplays, being awarded five Emmys. "I like movies as a change of pace, but TV is much more intimate. You're looking at people close up, physically and psychologically, and there aren't as many taboos," he told *Newsweek*, as he began to adapt his video hits to the movies (*Patterns*, 1956).[48] In 1959 he created and hosted *The Twilight Zone*, the science fiction series for which he is best remembered. Having written for radio early in his career, he said he had a special fondness for it when he was on a promotion tour for radio shortly before his untimely death in 1975.[49]

Twelve original television dramas were the center of attention during June and July 1954, as *Studio One Summer Theatre* came under Executive Producer Edgar Peterson. The first drama was "Fandango at War Bonnet," by Carey Wilbur. Set in an 1880s frontier town, one cowboy tries to save another from hanging. "Screwball," by Mel Goldberg, was the only repeated script. It was about an aging mechanic who had ambitions of becoming a big league pitcher. "The Small Door," by Irving Gaynor Neiman, concerned a recluse who is assumed to have a cache of money that another man, who has come to remove the gas meter, plans to get. "A Guest at the Embassy," by Jerome Ross, was based on a true story. A romantic triangle emerges when a young diplomat, who plans to be married, has a mysterious second woman show up claiming she is his lover. "Home Again, Home Again," by Elizabeth Hart, was about a woman who attempts unsuccessfully to become a Broadway actress. She returns home deeply depressed but finds a drama coach to help her adjust. Prominent stars — Darren McGavin, Jack Warden, Richard Kiley, Nina Foch, Janice Rule — headed the cast lists. Alex March, an actor and Air Corps veteran, was hired to carry out some of the producing tasks.

Reginald Rose's "Twelve Angry Men," previously discussed, was an important beginning for the seventh season, as was "An Almanac on Liberty" in November. Jackie Gleason, attempting drama once again, appeared in Carey Wilbur's "Short Cut" on 6 December 1954. Gleason, without resorting to comedy in any way, "gave a taut and convincing portrait of an unsavory politician."[50] Some new writers, Kathleen and Robert Howard Lindsay, had the eighth season opener, "Like Father, Like Son." It was the 318th hour-long drama, including summers, for *Studio One.* This original script involved a father (Ralph Bellamy) attempting to rear his son (Keenan Wynn) in his own image. Geraldine Fitzgerald had the mother's role. Paul Nickell directed it on 19 September 1955. William H. Brown, Jr., was added as a third director in the rotation. Later, the Lindsays wrote "My Son Johnny," starring Neva Patterson and Wendell Corey. Reginald Rose scripted "Three Empty Rooms," starring Steve Brodie, for 26 September 1955, and "Dino," starring Sal Mineo, on 2 January 1956. Mineo also played in the 1957 film version. Frank D. Gilroy wrote "A Likely Story," starring Eddie Bracken, for 3 October; Loring D. Mandel's "Shakedown Cruise" starred Richard Kiley and Lee Marvin on 7 November; and Paul Monash's "Blow Up at Cortland" featured Chester Morris.

Felix Jackson, an outstanding producer since the fall of 1953, continued to find fresh talent and approaches. Born in Hamburg, Germany, he spent his early life studying music and theater. He worked as a journalist and newspaper editor before he turned to the stage. Having gained musical theater experience in Berlin, in 1933 he moved to Budapest, where he wrote motion pictures for producer Joe Pasternak for the next three years. In 1937 he went to Hollywood to work on *100 Men and a Girl*, produced by Pasternak. It featured gifted teenager Deanna Durbin and maestro Leopold Stokowski. Several musicals under the Universal banner followed. In 1948 Jackson returned to New York and started writing for television, eventually being in charge of dramatic television for Young & Rubicam, Inc. The year 1952 found him supervising *Four Star Playhouse* in Hollywood and then returning to New York for *Studio One* the following year.

The 1953-54 season had 41 dramas; 1954-55 had 39. With many dramatic anthologies on television, the directors often worked for other series simultaneously. Paul Nickell began directing *The Best of Broadway* and *Climax!*, and he did one-performance specials for *Four Star Jubilee*, such as "Twentieth Century" and "A Bell for Adano" at CBS Television City in Hollywood. The procedure remained the same. He was assigned scripts and certain casts to work with by the producers who wrote comments while the production was in rehearsal. "Tony and I had the note session, Fletcher and I always had the note session, and Felix had a few notes." Nickell's objective was to bring his particular vision and style to whatever script was put on his desk.[51]

In 1955 Franklin Schaffner had another major task that reflected his news background and influenced his directing for *Studio One*. He spent six hours a week directing Edward R. Murrow's *Person to Person*, an interview program in which Murrow chatted with celebrities, seen at their homes, about their personal lives. Accordingly, Schaffner said, "The script and the actors should tell the story first. Then, the camera must 'report' what they're doing — what their talent is. It should tell what's going on as unobtrusively as possible, with the exception of certain visual punctuations that are necessary from time to time." Schaffner did not plot camera shots from a script in hand before rehearsals and before he met his actors. He developed characterizations with his actors and related them to the plot. As he did so, certain visual concepts emerged, but it was not until very late in the staging that he formed final visual concepts of the program. The formula consisting of ten days dry rehearsals before two days of in-studio camera rehearsals, including the on-air telecast, persisted.[52]

Robert Herridge was named producer of the *Westinghouse Summer Theatre* in 1957. Maximizing a low budget, Herridge had produced the experimental *Camera Three* since its inception on WCBS-TV in May 1953, winning among others a George Foster Peabody award. Critics cited the series as "one of the boldest, freshest programs yet devised for television" and as "an expression of that small and goodly company of producers, writers, technicians, actors and musicians who pump fresh blood into the channels of television." *Camera Three* was indeed a New Yorker's idea of video art. Herridge was convinced that television could be on a par with other art forms. "We need a theater everyone can go to — one everyone can enjoy … I'm looking for a theater to express honestly some fundamental truth about life, whether it be love, hatred, tyranny or whatever it is."[53] His first choice was his own adaptation of John Steinbeck's "The Flight." Its basic truth was that to become a man, a boy must accept the responsibilities and make the sacrifices of manhood. Herridge noted one problem with this play, that only one person was on camera during the last act. The 38-year-old Orange, New Jersey native planned to alternate serious and humorous stories by established and new writers. His second script was newcomer Richard de Roy's comic satire "Snap Your Fingers." For his third drama in the 13-week series, he adapted Conrad Aiken's "Mr. Arcularis," which was a metaphysical story about a man on an operating table who dreams of dying at sea but actually dies on the table. "Though thin and a bit arty," *Time* commented, "Mr. Arcularis was different and fascinating television fare."[54]

On 11 January 1957, CBS Television Executive Vice President in charge of network programs Hubbell Robinson, Jr., announced that *Studio One* would have a "new look," as Westinghouse Electric Corporation, through its agency, McCann-Erickson, Inc., was continuing its sponsorship.

> Our objectives for the "new" "Studio One" are to produce fresh and vigorous dramas, dynamic in concept, unhackneyed in treatment, and — to be "daring" in our themes. But always we will attempt to produce real stories about real people. Since "Studio One" first came to television in November, 1948, the series has received more honors and awards than any other program. It has started many young actors on the road to stardom and introduced to the public young writers and directors of major talent. For many years it has been accepted as the yardstick of good television drama. We want "Studio One" to continue to be a "talked about" program.[55]

The last line must have brought a smile to Worthington Miner, because a "talked about program" refers back to the 1948 *Studio One* debut.

"For a long time it was accepted as the yardstick of good TV drama. But in the past year, the big, full-hour productions have slipped in quality, also lost ground in the castings to *Robert Montgomery Presents*. Last week with an old but unproduced Fred Coe favorite, *The Five Dollar Bill*, *Studio One* lived up to CBS's high promise of a 'new look.'"[56] On vacation, a father (Hume Cronyn) tries to get a better understanding of his young son Ralph (Burt Brinckerhoff), who doesn't conform to a responsible mold like his brother. The Tad Mosel play, recognized as one of 1957's best, was produced by Gordon Duff and directed by Robert Mulligan for airing on 21 January 1957.

The next month's first original two-hour drama on television was presented on *Studio One*. "The Defender," written by the insightful Reginald Rose, showed a defense attorney (Ralph Bellamy) struggling to resolve his own inner conflict about his client's guilt. The client indicted for murder was played by Steve McQueen and the defense attorney's son by William Shatner, both in their mid-twenties. Martin Balsam was the prosecuting attorney. The drama, aired in two parts, 25 February and 4 March 1957, was produced by Herbert Brodkin and directed by Robert Mulligan. The story was the basis for a later series, *The Defenders* (1961–65).

With *Philco Television Playhouse* no longer in existence, some of its key talent was hired at *Studio One*. For 11 March, Vincent Donehue directed Abby Mann's "A Child Is Waiting." The story told of a successful career woman who tried to forget that her son was in a home for the retarded. On 25 March Robert Mulligan directed Horton Foote's "A Member of the Family." The story involved a wealthy elder brother who switches his interest from one nephew to another, causing suspicion and jealousy in the family. Norman Felton, who was ascending the ranks, was associate producer.

Foote grew up on a farm that the family had owned for three generations in Wharton, Texas, about 75 miles southeast of Houston. So it was a shock when he announced in 1930 that he was going to be an actor, studying in Dallas and at the Pasadena Playhouse in California. Soon he decided New York would be better for his acting and writing career. He found little success. With his wife, he even tried to establish a theater in Washington, D.C. About the same time his friend Vincent Donehue encouraged him to return to New York where he was directing the Gabby Hayes series, mentioned earlier. Donehue asked Foote to be a consultant. It wasn't much of a start, but it grew from there.[57] Like Chayefsky, he stuck to the characters he knew, those in small-town Texas, writing numerous plays in the late 1940s and 1950s. After the 1954 Broadway run of Foote's *The Traveling Lady*, its star, Kim Stanley, recreated the role for *Studio One* on 22 April 1957. Though pared down by 40 minutes, it lost little of its tenuous, dream-like quality. "As a homely, stammering drudge who is trying to reclaim her no-account husband just out of jail, Actress Stanley gave a sunlit performance. Like a hand picking up broken glass, she limned her character with tentative little twitches, awkward hesitations and mute expectancy." *Time* went on to complain about what had become commonplace, that her television work had slipped by the critics with little notice, as fewer and more selective reviews were published.[58]

Norman Felton, who at one time assisted on *Philco Playhouse*, became the producer of *Studio One Summer Theatre*. "We intend to present plays with a point of view — dramatic entertainment with something worthwhile to say." Felton introduced a new writer from Cape Girardeau, Missouri, who obtained a doctorate from the University of Wisconsin, Madison. Twenty-nine-year-old Jerry McNeely's first play, "The Staring Match," aired 17 June

1957. McNeely "deserved credit not only for an original fancy but for making his fable's dilemma both wonderstruck and plausible in the telling."[59] An important talent, McNeely would continue to write for television and teach at the university.

Studio One was in its final months live from New York. The opening show was a dramatization *about* the broadcast of H. G. Wells's "War of the Worlds." Desperately in need of material for his broadcast on Halloween 1938, Orson Welles and Howard Koch used a direct reporting style that claimed Martians really were invading New Jersey. "Let's make them believe it," Welles once said, not realizing the impact it might have. Listeners, switching frequencies capriciously, tuned in throughout various stages of the program. They had just begun to rely on radio for news, and many actually "believed" the Halloween hoax, resulting in widespread panic. Nelson Bond retold the event and recreated some scenes with Warren Beatty and Alexander Scourby in "The Night America Trembled," on 9 September 1957. Edward R. Murrow narrated the docudrama, but explanations and getting reactions from various groups could not create a sense of the original CBS broadcast. Though invited, Welles did not respond and was not mentioned. It was produced by Gordon Duff and directed by Tom Donovan. In October, Tad Mosel's "The Morning Face" told about a bored teacher who was looking for change in her life when she unexpectedly finds her integrity challenged. Again Duff produced, but Jack Smight directed. Also in October, Mayo Simon's "The Deaf Heart," starring Piper Laurie and William Shatner, proved to be a fresh drama on psychiatry. "Based on an actual case in Minneapolis, it was the story of girl who went psychosomatically deaf in emotional flight from her role as the ears of a deaf father, mother and brother."[60] On 4 November 1957 Franchot Tone played an octogenarian minister who with his wife sells everything so that they can retire to a home for the aged. The drama was John Vlahos's "A Bend in the Road."

On 11 October CBS announced that *Studio One* would be broadcast from the West Coast starting in January 1958. Executive Vice President Hubbell Robinson said that CBS Television and Westinghouse Electric Corporation had just signed a new two-year contract. Robinson said there were more stars in Hollywood, and CBS Television City could accommodate larger productions. Gordon Duff, previously with *Philco Playhouse*, had joined *Studio One* in December 1956, and Norman Felton, who had been the principal director for *Robert Montgomery Presents Your Lucky Strike Theatre* and various anthologies, frequently working with Herbert Brodkin, were chosen as producers of the live West Coast productions retitled *Studio One in Hollywood*. The premiere production on 6 January 1958 was "Brotherhood of the Bell," adapted by Dale Wasserman and Jack Balch from a novel by David Karp. It was a futuristic tale of a powerful, secret society's attempt to gain control of American government and business. It had a stellar cast: Cameron Mitchell, Tom Drake, John Baragrey, Joanne Dru, and Pat O'Brien. In Hollywood, *Studio One* lasted nine months.

5

···

The Competitors, 1950–1951

During 1950 and 1951 twenty-eight new anthologies appeared in the nighttime schedule. None improved upon the quality of content, production procedures, or legacy of the *Kraft Television Theatre, Philco-Goodyear Playhouse, Ford Theater,* or *Studio One.* The new entries did offer some innovations and variations in style and content. *Robert Montgomery Presents Your Lucky Strike Theatre* was the most highly touted. Robert Montgomery was a famous movie star, and his presence seemed to endorse the artistic value of the television medium and its relationship to the motion picture industry. Probably more by accident than design, *The Hallmark Hall of Fame* promised bigger and better, but fewer, dramas and musicals, which hinted at a coming trend. Genre anthologies continued to contribute impressively. Prestige dramas were developed by sponsors with deep commitment to television — the Schlitz playhouses and *Celanese Theatre,* and those hopeful efforts that lasted less than two seasons — *Billy Rose's Playbill* and the *Gruen Guild Playhouse.* The mystery/crime category was well represented by *Escape, The Trap, The Web, Danger, Sure as Fate,* and *Tales of Tomorrow.*

No long-lasting anthologies emerged in the romance genre. Added to *Silver Theatre* and *Theatre of Romance,* neither of which survived more than one season, was *Starlight Theatre,* half-hour romantic stories on CBS-TV, that began 2 April 1950 at 7:00–7:30 P.M. EST and ran for two seasons. True Boardman's story, "Second Concerto," for example, was adapted by Halsted Welles, produced by Robert Stevens, and directed by John Peyser. The most interesting aspect of the debut starring Barry Nelson was the subject: two young people trying to commit suicide, usually a taboo subject. *The Faith Baldwin Playhouse* tried to revive *Theatre of Romance,* but it failed after only one season. *Bigelow Theatre,* another CBS-TV half hour of comedy and romance, debuted on 10 December 1950. Filmed at the Jerry Fairbanks studios in Los Angeles, it combined film and television techniques that are noteworthy. "Several cameras are directed and monitored by a control room staff in exactly the same fashion as a live broadcast. The cameras, instead of picking up images to be sent over the air, record what they see on movie film."[1] Jack Gould assessed the Fairbanks product. The Fairbanks film "did produce a picture which often — though by no means always — was superior to a good deal of the newer films seen on the air. The images were more clearly defined than is the case with kinescope recordings and the lighting was better ... Neither the composition, texture nor detail which comes over with a 'live' show was present in the film, which for all its newness seemed old-fashioned... But in the last analysis there seemed to be no earthly reason to do the show by film when a much better and less expensive job could have been done 'live.'"[2]

Armstrong Circle Theatre was a unique documentary-drama combining fiction and fact into beguiling dramas that are today loosely to closely termed "based on" stories of real events; and *Cameo Theatre* was singular in style, mainly because of director Albert McCleery. In contrast, the dramatic anthologies that typically lasted were half-hour, packaged filmed programs and series shows, such as *I Love Lucy*, debuting 15 October 1951, as a Desilu production directed by Marc Daniels, remembered from *Ford Theater*. Increasingly, the public, according to the A. C. Neilsen Company, gave filmed shows high ratings.

Simultaneously, the British Broadcasting Corporation (BBC), a government agency, weighed in heavily with dramatic productions since its return to telecasting after the war in June 1946. An outline of the British efforts will be included here, because the British impact, though subtle, was more significant than often realized. Not only the Anglo heritage in literature and theater, but also the technical quality of productions and the performance of actors rather than personalities, would eventually bring an aura of sophistication and distinction to American television during the 1950s that would be passed along to appreciative audiences watching what in that period was called educational broadcasting.

Robert Montgomery Presents

Actor Robert Montgomery was born into a wealthy family in Beacon, New York, in 1904. He was raised among the privileged and attended exclusive schools. At age 16 his father died, leaving the family penniless. For a while Robert worked as a laborer before he moved to New York with the hope of becoming a writer. He found his handsome appearance, articulate voice, and sophisticated demeanor got him more work as an actor, making his stage debut in 1924. When sound film attracted everyone's imagination in 1929, he went to Hollywood as a contract player for MGM. Typecast as a leading man, he played opposite the glamorous leading ladies of the day. When World War II came along, he was an active participant, serving in the Pacific and in Europe on D-Day. After he left the service, he finished directing *They Were Expendable* (1945) when John Ford became ill. Next he directed and acted in an adaptation of Raymond Chandler's *Lady in the Lake* (1947), cleverly using a subjective camera technique that revealed him only briefly in the role of detective Philip Marlowe. Montgomery would continue to act less frequently. A conservative political activist, in 1947 Montgomery volunteered to testify as a friendly witness deploring communism before the House Un-American Activities Committee. He was associated with the 1948 Republican campaign and made his last film in England. In 1952 he was appointed communication consultant to President Dwight D. Eisenhower. So, with a certain political finesse, he represented a bridge between the television and film industries.

Meanwhile, the American Tobacco Company (Lucky Strike) which had sponsored *Tonight on Broadway*, from 6 April 1948 to 25 December 1949

"The Letter," starring Madeleine Carroll, was the premiere of *Robert Montgomery Presents Your Lucky Strike Theatre*, on NBC-TV, 30 January 1950.

and 26 half hours of *Your Show Time* on NBC from 21 January 1949 to 15 July 1949, receiving the first Emmy, began sponsoring *Robert Montgomery Presents Your Lucky Strike Theatre* on 30 January 1950. It competed directly with *Studio One* by airing one-half hour earlier on NBC, 9:30–10:30 P.M. EST, while *Studio One* aired on CBS 10:00–11:00 P.M. EST. For the premiere, the beautiful, ladylike British blonde, Madeleine Carroll, who retired from the movies the previous year, starred in a really safe bet, Somerset Maugham's "The Letter." (Maugham was about to have an entire anthology devoted to his work, *The Teller of Tales.*) *The Letter* was a memorable film for Bette Davis in 1940, who shot her lover without remorse, but "such emotional qualities as Maugham's overworked piece still possesses were brought to the fore by studied understatement. Montgomery and Felton [the director] were careful to put Miss Carroll through her role quietly."[3]

Montgomery claimed he was going "to experiment" on television, but to most critics he repeated the tried and true *Lux Radio Theatre* formula that, since the 1930s, was devoted to presenting stars in abridged motion picture scripts — and would soon do so again on 2 October 1950, when *Lux Video Theatre* had its premiere starring Joan Caulfield in an adaptation of Maxwell Anderson's play *Saturday's Children*, already filmed three times. This live CBS half hour was no competition, however, until *Lux* moved to NBC and Hollywood for a one-hour edition in 1954, debuting with "To Each His Own," an Oscar winner for Olivia de Havilland (1946). The two hour and 46-minute movie was cut by two-thirds in the telecast that starred Dorothy McGuire and was directed by Seymour "Buzz" Kulik.

The second drama for *Robert Montgomery Presents* was an adaptation of Christopher Morley's "Kitty Foyle," starring Jane Wyatt and Richard Derr. When the movie was released in 1940, Ginger Rogers won an Oscar for her role as a working girl involved in a tender romance. The swiftly paced television version also drew praise for its accomplished actors achieving "considerable charm and poignancy."[4] The choice on 10 April was Thornton Wilder's Pulitzer-Prize-winning Broadway play that became a 1940 screen debut for Martha Scott, *Our Town*. NBC and the National Association of Broadcast Engineers and Technicians (NABET) were experiencing strained relations to the extent that during rehearsal a cameraman, asked to dolly in for a close-up shot, kept dollying right past [Burgess] Meredith and into the wall because the technical director had not told him to stop. Consequently, the show was cancelled two hours before the telecast for insufficient rehearsals.[5] The network-union showdown was resolved, and "Our Town" was rescheduled a week later.

On 22 May 1950, "Rebecca," adapted from Daphne du Maurier's novel, suffered from a "monumentally incompetent script" and less than impressive acting by Barbara Bel Geddes as the second Mrs. de Winter, Peter Cook-son as Mr. de Winter, and Edith King as the obsessed housekeeper.[6] As yet, these prewar motion pictures were not released to television, but they were huge successes easily remembered by viewers and critics. Some recent film stories could not be released to television if the show was kinescoped. Alfred Hitchcock's 1940 film version of *Rebecca* won an Academy Award for Best Picture.

Philip Hamburger's main complaint was reserved for the six minutes of commercials. "L.S.M.F.T.—Lucky Strike Means Fine Tobacco" had become an unusually well-known slogan. "I look forward bleakly," Hamburger observed, "to the night when Hamlet, high on the lonely ramparts of Elsinore, spies the ghost of his father by the light of a Lucky. 'L.S.—M.F.T.,' the old man will mumble, to which his tortured son will no doubt reply, 'Let your own TASTE and THROAT be the judge, Father.'"[7] The first season ended on 19 June 1950 with Robert Montgomery playing opposite British actress Angela Lansbury in A. J. Cronin's "The Citadel." Cronin, a British novelist and doctor, had gained international fame from *The Stars Look Down* (1935). "The Citadel" involved a struggling doctor who neglected family and friends as he developed a medical practice aimed at wealthy patients. The fine 1938 U.S.–British film collaboration, directed by King Vidor, starred Englishman Robert Donat opposite American Rosalind Russell.

By fall 1950 Robert Montgomery was ensconced in spacious, immaculate offices at NBC, where he manipulated a six-person creative staff, and he sought a larger studio for his biweekly, one-hour anthology. The solution was Studio 8H, which had served for years as the home of Arturo Toscanini and the NBC Symphony Orchestra. The season began with Arthur Richman's "The Awful Truth," filmed for the third time in 1937 by Leo McCarey, who picked up an Oscar for directing. The screwy comedy about lovers who try to wreck each other's engagements starred Jane Wyatt and Lee Bowman, both of whom had appeared the previous spring. Montgomery, who claimed frequently that he would experiment with television, theorized that the motion picture industry grew large but failed to reach its potential in developing fully its social and political responsibility because of economics. Television, he thought, would meet these responsibilities, but at this point it was not apparent. In fact, he continued to complain about commercial encroachment long after the anthology ended. "It is well-rehearsed, well-acted, well-directed, well-produced. Only drawback is that it still isn't television. It's still a combination of films and theater and radio. Even so, it's pretty fine," William Shriver observed for *The Catholic World.*[8] As the seasons passed, *Robert Montgomery Presents* had to depend increasingly on content from media other than motion pictures. Although its cost per million viewers ran about $6.00, or about $35,000 a program, about the same as its rival *Studio One*, it did not climb to top ten rankings enjoyed by both *Studio One* and *Philco Playhouse* at year's end.

Helen Hayes's greatest triumph was in the title role for Laurence Housman's *Victoria Regina* on Broadway in 1935. For her television appearance on 15 January 1951, she was "completely ill at ease, if not bewildered, by the charade in which she found herself." The adaptation by Thomas W. Phipps concentrated on the Queen's earlier life, rather than the more memorable final phase. The "disaster" was made worse by persistent "Be happy, go Lucky" jingles that "made a mockery of the entire enterprise."[9] A few weeks later Robert Montgomery starred with June Duprez, the exotic princess in the 1940 British film *The Thief of Baghdad*, in an adaptation of F. Scott Fitzgerald's *The Last Tycoon*. Montgomery played a motion picture genius in search of love and studio power. "The TV adaptation respected the author's approach and — within the limitations of an hour's production with time out for the commercials — communicated it to video with taste and imagination."[10] On 21 May Nathaniel Hawthorne's *The House of the Seven Gables* had "a fine professional cast" consisting of Leslie Nielsen, longtime actor and writer Gene Lockhart, his daughter June Lockhart, known for *Lassie* (1955–64), and Richard Purdy.[11]

In April 1951 Maugham's *Teller of Tales*, now *Somerset Maugham Theatre*, moved to NBC and alternated with *Robert Montgomery Presents* as a one-hour production. The initial telecast for NBC starred Tom Helmore and Cloris Leachman in "Of Human Bondage," an adaptation of Maugham's 1916 novel by Theodore and Mathilde Ferro. As host, the 77-year-old novelist did a filmed opening and closing from his home on the French Riviera, a technique Montgomery would eventually adopt. "The basic transgression," complained Robert Lewis Shayon, "was the rape of the spirit and meaning of Maugham's novel.... We ask how was Maugham's tale honored or the entertainment of the audience enhanced by this fatuous distortion of the values of a fine novel to suit the hit-and-run hypocrisy of expedient mass-media assumptions?"[12]

The father-daughter act was repeated in the fall when Robert Montgomery and his daughter, Elizabeth, later remembered for *Bewitched* (1967–72), made her television debut. They appeared in "Top Secret" on 3 December 1951. To bring in the New Year and to celebrate the weekly appearance of his show and a new sponsor, the S. C. Johnson (wax) Company, Montgomery prevailed upon John O'Hara, who authored *Butterfield 8* in 1935, and — though claiming he had never seen a play on television and had no standards by which to judge his — consented to an hour of

"The Farmer's Hotel," originally an allegorical play but published as a short novel only weeks before. It starred Thomas Mitchell as the innkeeper and stuck closely to the novel.[13] "Cashel Byron's Profession," starring Charlton Heston and June Lockhart, was telecast the next week. Author George Bernard Shaw who claimed television was for commercially dead work — and none of his were dead — had died in 1950, and his estate had no problem with leasing the rights for airing on 14 January 1952.

Robert Montgomery not only hosted, produced, and occasionally acted in his dramatic anthology, he also had a regular news commentary series on radio, *A Citizen Views the News*. In April NBC announced that Montgomery was flying to Paris for a ten-day rest, and Robert Cummings would be his television substitute for "The Truth About Blayds," aired 28 April, that touted Edwardian costumes originally belonging to Cornelius Vanderbilt, owned by the Brooks Costume Company. By the time Montgomery returned and the political conventions were over in early July, he announced that the six summer shows would initiate a stock company in which John Newland, Margaret Hayes, and Vaughn Taylor would be seen regularly. He said he had been interested in forming such a company for a long time; however, such practice was already informally in place at other major anthologies. The summer line-up included James Thurber's *The Catbird Seat*, adapted by Robert J. Shaw and directed by Herbert Bayard Swope, Jr. for its debut on 14 July 1952. The cast included Newland, Hayes, and Taylor, who were seen in every program. Robert Shaw wrote an original script, "Nostradamus Berry," for the final show. Montgomery continued to host the series on film, while the dramas were telecast live.

The fourth season opener, airing 1 September 1952, was Denis Green's adaptation of "Unclouded Summer," by Alec Waugh. Its star was Signe Hasso, and it also featured Richard Kiley as the young American who goes abroad and falls in love with a married English noblewoman. The anthology was taken to task for stereotypes in "The Law Abiding," starring Chester Morris, shown on 8 September. The agent in the story, one critic observed, was nearly six feet tall and 190 pounds, with curly hair, unmarried but had 20/20 vision for women. The spy was some three inches shorter, only 150 pounds, past middle age, and wore dark-rimmed glasses with thick lenses. He looked like an absent-minded scholar.[14]

In early January 1953, Montgomery slipped on the ice near his Millbrook, New York home, dislocating his elbow and irritating a bone chip, resulting in shock, then contracting pneumonia. By summer, Elizabeth Montgomery had been added to the roster of the Robert Montgomery Players, and the schedule was extended to eight full-hour productions, beginning on 6 July with an adaptation of Richard O'Hare's *The Half-Millionaire*, by Irving Neiman. The story involved a man living at a boarding house (Vaughn Taylor) who discovered a murdered man surrounded by $500,000. Up next was an original farce, "Two of a Kind" by Theodore and Mathilde Ferro; more and more scripts were television originals. Montgomery hosted on film again, and Swope and Norman Felton directed in alternate weeks.

The fifth season began with an adaptation of Joan Transue's novel, *First Vice President,* by S. N. Savage on 31 August 1953 for *Robert Montgomery Presents the Johnson's Wax Program.* (This awkward title alternated with *Your Lucky Strike Theatre.*) The plot revealed a ruthless executive who was looking to succeed the retiring president of a prominent company at all costs; however, the outgoing president's family had other plans. Montgomery served as executive producer for Nepture Productions, which packaged the shows under the supervision of Joseph W. Bailey. Gerald Savoy replaced Herbert Swope as director for the Johnson's Wax programs, and Norman Felton continued to direct the Lucky Strike shows. For the second drama, Jackie Cooper appeared in a satire about a returning veteran who had a highly personal plan for world peace. "Private Purkey's Private Peace" was based on a character from H. I. Phillips's nationally syndicated column, "The Sun Dial." On 14 September 1953 "The Lost and Found" dealt with the rehabilitation of two children found in a concentration camp by an English social worker. "Breakdown," a melodrama by Patrick Nash telecast 5 October, told about a scientist working on a top secret weapon who suspects his wife and assistant have fallen in love. While the cast and writers for *Robert Montgomery Presents* were well known and capable, 1953–54 at *Studio One* and *Philco/Goodyear Playhouse* were peak years of illustrious achievement, displaying the work of the most promising writers and actors of the period.

Expanding his stock company concept, the titles of the anthologies changed to *Robert Montgomery Presents the American Tobacco Summer Theatre* or *The Johnson's Wax Summer Program.* John Newland, Elizabeth Montgomery, and Vaughn Taylor were back; newcomers included Jan Miner, Anne Seymour, and Cliff Robertson. In June 1954 Edwin Balmer's novel *In His Hands* was adapted by Agnes Eckhardt. The plot concerned a young doctor (Newland) who learns that the girl he loves (Miner) is dying of an incurable ailment. The story was a melodrama standard; the notion of television experiments seemed never to have taken hold with the agencies Batten, Barton, Durstine & Osborn for the American Tobacco Company or Needham, Louis and Brorby, Inc. for Johnson's wax.

By summer 1954 NBC boasted having *Lux Video Theatre* and *Lux Radio Theatre,* both sponsored by the Lever Brothers Company. The radio show was celebrating its 20th anniversary, and the half-hour television anthology

"A Child Is Born" starred Thomas Mitchell and Fay Bainter, for *Lux Video Theatre*, on CBS-TV, 25 December 1950.

had been seen since 1950. Dorothy McGuire, a major film star, and well connected in Hollywood — she and Gregory Peck, David O. Selznick, Jennifer Jones, and Mel Ferrer were founders of the La Jolla Playhouse and were enthusiastic supporters of live stage and live television — opened in a grand one-hour version of *Lux Video Theatre*, "To Each His Own," a big 1946 movie, mentioned elsewhere. The NBC debut was 10:00–11:00 P.M. EST on

26 August 1954. Hosting the Thursday dramas was British actor and Cambridge University graduate, James Mason, England's leading star and box office draw in the mid–1940s. This kind of glamour had faded from *Robert Montgomery Presents*, while Montgomery concentrated on his stock company of unknown young players and writers.[15]

With this competition, Montgomery's sixth season improved. Pulitzer Prize winner Robert E. Sherwood, who was paid $100,000 to write nine plays especially for NBC television, provided the opening drama, "Diary," on 20 September 1954. The stark drama told of a small-town girl (Janice Rule) who leaves her unhappy home for the city. She meets a young man of unsavory character (John Cassavetes), who extends to her the only warmth and understanding she has ever experienced. Norman Felton directed this production under the American Tobacco banner. James Sheldon was among the directors for the Johnson Wax program. Noel Gerson's original script had Jackie Cooper in "A Dream of Summer," which told about two young people who meet while on vacation. Thomas Phipps came up with a story about life in latter-day Germany, "The Wise Women," starring Signe Hasso on 4 October. Dobie Smith's Broadway play, *Autumn Crocus*, featured Julie Haydon on 11 October.

Victor Hugo's 1831 classic *The Hunchback of Notre Dame*, adapted by Alvin Sapinsley and telecast over two nights on 8 and 15 November 1954, starred Robert Ellenstein as Quasimodo, the deaf and deformed bell ringer, Scottish actress Celia Lipton as the dancing girl Esmeralda, and Bramwell Fletcher as the stern and calculating church deacon Frolio who desires her. Hurd Hatfield, Mary Sinclair, and Frederic Worlock were featured players. A two-part adaptation of Charles Dickens's *David Copperfield* in December followed the two-part production of *Great Expectations* the previous June. The story, dramatized by Doria Folliott, showed David's (Rex Thompson) early life of cruelty and exploitation in the first part, "The Search," and his finding a warm and genuine welcome from his aunt, in the second part, called "The Reward." It was designed to be a pleasing program, divided between the two sponsors, for Christmas viewing.

Surrounding himself with top writers and actors, Robert Montgomery took on the role of Don Birnam in an adaptation of Charles Reginald Jackson's novel about the devastating effects of alcohol, *The Lost Weekend*. It aired 7 February 1955. For this challenging character study of an alcoholic, Montgomery was supported by Walter Matthau as the bartender, Edward Andrews as his friend, and Leora Dana as his girl friend. The 1945 movie starring Ray Milland won Oscars for Best Actor, Best Director (Billy Wilder), Best Screenplay, and Best Picture. Montgomery starred again in F. Scott Fitzgerald's *The Great Gatsby*, adapted by Alvin Sapinsley and telecast 9 May 1955. Phyllis Kirk played Daisy; Lee Bowman, Gena Rowlands, and John Newland were also in the cast.

One of the highlights from the last two seasons, 1955–57 included "Woman in the Window" on 12 September 1955. The 1944 movie scenario by Nunnally Johnson made a highly suspenseful telecast about a man (Robert Preston) meeting the subject of an alluring painting (Maria Riva) and becoming involved in a murder and its investigation. Doria Folliott adapted about a dozen stage plays, film scripts, and other stories over two years. Her scenario for "Along Came Jones," a 1945 western about mistaking the good guy for the bad guy, starred Charlton Heston; Owen Criemp's Broadway comedy, "Southern Exposure," for the summer stock company aired on 30 July 1956; Betty McDonald's novel *Onions in the Stew*, starring Constance Bennett, got viewer approval on 17 September 1956; and the film scenario for "Sunset Boulevard," by Billy Wilder, Charles Brackett, and D. M. Marshman, Jr., had Mary Astor and Darren McGavin as its leads on 3 December 1956. Rod Alexander's play *The Grand Prize*, starring June Lockhart and John Newland, and Harry Kurnitz's Broadway show, *Reclining Figure*, starring Scott McKay and Sally Kemp, were both aired in February 1957.

Robert J. Shaw continued to be a frequent writer, with Sidney Blackmer in "Paper Town," on 10 October 1955 (directed by summer stock actor John Newland), "Three Men from Tomorrow" on 2 January 1956, "Don't Do Me Any Favors" on 30 April, "All Expenses Paid" on 21 May and Claudette Colbert making a rare appearance in his "After All These Years" telecast in September. James Cagney opened the final season with "Soldier from the Wars Returning" by Robert Wallace, Gian-Carlo Menotti's "Amahl and the Night Visitors" was restaged in December, and Shirley Yamaguchi appeared the following spring in Pearl Buck's *The Enemy*.

Writers Abby Mann and William Kendall Clarke were busy; and Robert E. Sherwood contributed another of his dramas especially written for television, "The Trial of Pontius Pilate," featuring Bruce Gordon and Maria Palmer, on 22 April 1957. Robert Montgomery narrated perhaps the biggest and most impressive production of the final season, "The Last Trip of the Hindenburg," a documentary-drama by Burton and James Benjamin that featured Gale Page on 1 October 1956 and was repeated on 10 June 1957. Two weeks later, *Robert Montgomery Presents* ended with Robert Wallace's "Faust '57" on 24 June 1957.

The Hallmark Hall of Fame

Hallmark Cards, Inc. began national radio sponsorship in 1938. Its unique selection had already been on CBS for some eight years, *Tony Wons' Scrapbook*. In romantic rich tones, Wons read poetry to a large, predominantly female, audience; and he told his listeners that they should look for the Hallmark crown on the back of greeting cards. Typically, many women often peeked under fine china cups and looked at the back of plates to determine their origin, age, and value by means of the craftsman's imprint. Soon, "When You Care Enough To Send The Very Best" became one of advertising's most enduring slogans.[16]

Drawing upon this symbol of regal English heritage, in September 1951 Hallmark sponsored weekly 15-minute interviews on CBS-TV featuring the daughter of Britain's distinguished statesman and wartime prime minister, Winston Churchill. *Hallmark Presents Sarah Churchill* enabled her to visit with prominent international guests. Then, on Christmas Eve 1951, Nelson Case announced: "The makers of Hallmark Cards — and the stores where you buy them — present the world premiere of the first opera written especially for television — Gian-Carlo Menotti's 'Amahl and the Night Visitors,' which will be performed tonight by a cast selected by Mr. Menotti, and under his direction." Commissioned by NBC-TV for its opera company, the cast included Chet Allen, Rosemary Kuhlman, Andrew McKinley, Leon Lishner, and David Aiken, a large chorus, and a 38-member orchestra.[17] Produced by Samuel Chotzinoff, directed by Kirk Browning, and billed as the first television "spectacular," the 9:30–10:30 P.M. EST telecast was a seminal moment for television and Hallmark. The production was repeated for Easter 1952 and the next three Christmases. The 1953 telecast was the network's first commercially sponsored program in color.

This benchmark program met the goals projected by Donal J. Hall, president of Hallmark Cards: "Properties are chosen for their *substance* as major dramatic events ... Every production must also lend *diversity* to the season, in order to give viewers a range of mood as well as important dramatic fare. The series had also sought to *inspire and delight*. And finally, the series has always hoped that its production be *permanent contributions* to the growth of the television medium as a whole."[18]

Immediately, in January 1952, the Churchill interviews were replaced by the *Hallmark Television Playhouse*, half-hour dramas hosted by Churchill and featuring stars of stage and screen. With the anthology's move to NBC-TV, the title was changed to *The Hallmark Hall of Fame*. Near the end of the second season of weekly dramas in which Sarah Churchill frequently acted, Hallmark once again offered an auspicious telecast: the first performance of *Hamlet*, the first two-hour teleplay, and the debut of Maurice Evans. *Hamlet* was presented on 26 April 1953, the date usually celebrated as William Shakespeare's birthday. Maurice Evans was one of the best-known Shakespearean actors of the day — along with Laurence Olivier and Orson Welles. Evans had a distinguished stage career in his native England and on Broadway, where in 1938 his stage production of *Hamlet* ran four hours.

In 1941 Evans became an American citizen and, as a U.S. Army major in charge of entertainment, he toured bases with his G.I. (Government Issue) version of "Hamlet." To trim it down to about 90 minutes, Mildred Alberg and Tom Sand had to omit entire characters (gravediggers) and soliloquies ("How all occasions do inform against me...."). Twelve minutes went for Hallmark commercials, but Hallmark was always flexible in this matter. Besides Evans, the swiftly moving story starred Ruth Chatterton as the Queen, Sarah Churchill as Ophelia, Joseph Schildkraut as the King, and Barry Jones as Polonius. Evans was very much a theater-oriented person, and so were those who worked with him in the service. They included George Schaefer, who staged the G.I. version and supervised the video transition. "The two-hour Hamlet production in '53 was black and white and out of a rather small studio up on 105th Street, but I think in its time it was the first time that Shakespeare of that length was presented to the total country."[19] Albert McCleery was executive producer and director of the $180,000 production requiring 80 tons of scenery, three weeks of rehearsal, and 28 actors. Roger Adams composed original music; Richard Sylbert created settings suggesting a 19th-century court that was military but decadent at the same time. Joyce C. Hall, the 60-year-old founder and chairman of Hallmark Cards, was pleased with the way the telecast wowed critics. Hall believed the public was ready for more adult viewing. From Memphis, Tennessee, *Newsweek* reported, however, that three viewers called in to thank the station for showing "Hamlet," "and 486 wanted to know what in the world was going on."[20] More people saw "Hamlet" in this single occasion than had seen it throughout history.

With the resumption of the third season, *The Hallmark Hall of Fame* was extended to one hour for its Sunday programs, 5:00–6:00 P.M., EST. It boasted that it would become the first 60-minute network dramatic anthology to be produced "live" from the West Coast.[21] The opener on 27 September 1953 starred Sarah Churchill in the "Queen's Way." This was a biography of Catherine Parr who, by outliving Henry VIII, was responsible for saving the lives of his children, including Elizabeth. It was written by Jennette and Francis Letton, authors of *The Young Elizabeth*, a current London stage hit.

Albert McCleery continued to utilize his theater-in-the-round or arena style technique developed for *Cameo Theatre*—breaking the proscenium arch by means of screen-filling closeups and moving cameras — for an adaptation of Thomas Wolfe's "Time and the River," aired 15 November 1953. Sarah Churchill returned as hostess-narrator, occasional star, and even as an actress in lesser roles.[22] Lamont Johnson, who began to appear quite often, was the son. Thomas Mitchell — Scarlett O'Hara's father in *Gone with the Wind* (1939), and one of early video's prominent stars — had the role of William Oliver Gant, with Sara Haden as his wife. "Actor Thomas Mitchell gave a memorable portrait of the old man" who, knowing that he had often lived badly, was now determined to die well. "The show was alive with crosscurrents of affection and hate, small tyranny and big-souled resignation, all set to the orchestration of Wolfe's sonorous words," *Time* wrote. Most *Hallmark* shows at this point were biographical playlets with upbeat endings perfectly suited for the television market. "If I do four or five popular hits," McCleery said, "then they'll let me do a serious show."[23] Significant dramas such as this one were restaged in part to conserve the budget. Herman Melville's *Moby Dick* starred Victor Jory as Ahab and Lamont Johnson as Ishmael on 16 May 1954. Lamont Johnson and Gloria Jean were in "John Paul Jones" on 4 July. Many stories were devoted to biographies of American heroes, historical or literary figures, and some contemporary personalities. "We believe we have material for an entertaining and, at the same time, inspiring series of dramatic programs that should interest a broad cross-section of television viewers," McCleery said.[24]

On 24 January 1954, George Schaefer began directing the Shakespearean plays that Albert McCleery produced. Schaefer stated,

> You develop your own style as you go along.... I started out not having come from film at all, [having] come strictly from the theater, and so my emphasis was on performing and composition, although I seemed to take very quickly to the advantages of the electronic cameras and have a very organized kind of a mind. [I play] a lot of contract bridge where you have all those little different 52 cards thrown around each hand in different formations, and you have to try to remember them all, so the trick of remembering the amount of things you had to remember on an electronic television show was not difficult for me. As with all of us, [you] learned as you went along. That was the great training ground for today's directors.[25]

The monarch Evans portrayed this time was King Richard II, and he adapted the script from Shakespeare's play. "This is the story of the 'playboy king' who believed he ruled by divine right and who was completely heedless of his personal responsibility to his people and his kingdom."[26] "Repeating his last year's triumph as a TV Hamlet, Evans brilliantly played Richard as a posturing, unsettled man, forever wavering between triumph and real despair," *Time* said.[27] He was supported by a cast of 37, including Sarah Churchill and Kent Smith. It was broadcast on Sunday from 4:00 until 6:00 P.M. The magnitude of the spectacle, built this time in the Brooklyn studio, ranged from a prison cell to 40-foot battlements of Berkeley Castle.

Hallmark's fourth season began with a one-hour biography of Alfred Nobel called "Dynamite," written by Harold Callen. Nobel (Wesley Addy) invented dynamite and then spent the rest of his life establishing awards for humanitarians contributing to world peace. The first Nobel Peace Prize went to Countess Bertha Kinsky, played by Osa Massen. Produced and directed by Albert McCleery, Hallmark and its agency, Foote, Cone, and Belding, were most comfortable with material about inspiring human beings and events. Foote, Cone, and Belding not only designed beautiful television commercials, but also produced attractive, informative printed materials detailing individual programs.[28]

For another afternoon of Shakespeare, 28 November 1954, *The Hallmark Hall of Fame* presented Maurice Evans in a two-hour colorcast of *Macbeth*. Evans once again produced, adapted, and starred in the live production. He played opposite Dame Judith Anderson as Lady Macbeth. The costars were recreating their 1941 stage success. The tragedy had a cast of 40 actors and was presented in two 50-minute acts that kept most of the original play intact. Director George Schaefer had three weeks of rehearsals before staging all of the Scottish pageantry, replete with tartans and plaids, against Macbeth's huge castle, designed by Otis Riggs in the Brooklyn studios. Lehman Engel composed an original score. "We have been extremely pleased with the reception given Mr. Evans' Shakespearean plays. We have received thousands of complimentary letters from viewers, and so has Mr. Evans. So many of them asked that we do 'Macbeth' next that it seemed a logical choice, especially in view of the great success Mr. Evans and Miss Anderson enjoyed with it in the theatre."[29] The 1953–54 season consisted of 21 one-hour dramas and 21 half-hour programs.

Maurice Evans continued to produce one Shakespearean play a year: *The Taming of the Shrew*, costarring Lilli Palmer, in 1956; *Twelfth Night*, costarring Rosemary Harris, in 1957; and *The Tempest* with an unforgettable cast: Richard Burton, Roddy McDowall, Lee Remick, Liam Redmond — in 1960. The cycle may have reached its high point in 1957 with *Twelfth Night*. Though starring Evans in a fine production directed by David Greene and adapted by William Nichols, it received *Hallmark's* lowest rating: 5.1.[30] In 1960, however, George Schaefer with his own company and raising money from Hallmark's $200,000 to $300,000 budget per show, Red Lion pictures, and other sources filmed *Macbeth* in England as a made-for-

"Macbeth" starred Maurice Evans and Judith Anderson, for *The Hallmark Hall of Fame*, on NBC-TV, 28 November 1954. Courtesy of George Schaefer.

television movie with a "brilliant" crew. This was, according to Schaefer, a first-of-a-kind effort for television and the only *Macbeth* to go into profitability through telecasts and syndication. The previous ones, including Welles's and later Roman Polansky's, were in the red.[31]

The fifth season commenced with a series of specials. The initial offering was another Sunday afternoon colorcast directed by George Schaefer from the Brooklyn studios on 23 October 1955. "They didn't have the control rooms then. We had to work through portable wagons outside."[32] The show was Lewis Carroll's *Alice in Wonderland* with Gillian Barber as Alice and Bobby Clark, a comic vaudevillian, as the Duchess, Gilbert and Sullivan star Martyn Green as the White Rabbit, Burr Tillstrom as the Mock Turtle and Puppeteer, Elsa Lanchester as the Red Queen, and Eva LeGallienne as the White Queen. Maurice Evans narrated.

As live dramatic anthologies reached their peak, George Schaefer expressed concerns about *The Hallmark Hall of Fame* program schedule: "On a one-shot basis I couldn't keep a staff together, and since an actor is so much at the mercy of technicians, I wouldn't venture onto the TV screen unless I know who was in charge of my destiny.... We are starting our season with familiar material, but because I feel it is important that new playwrights be given an opportunity to express themselves on television, we have reserved the right in our agreement with our sponsor, Hallmark, to do two original scripts."[33] In addition to the Lewis Carroll fantasy, 1955 specials included an adaptation of George Bernard Shaw's *The Devil's Disciple* on 20 November. It starred Evans, Ralph Bellamy, and Teresa Wright. Elmer Rice's "Dream Girl," starring Vivian Blaine and Hal March, followed on 11 December 1955. *Time* reviewed "The Cradle Song," 6 May 1956: "The play was dreamlike, but it was also sunlit with innocence and warmly acted by Judith Anderson, Evelyn Varden, Deirdre Owens and, particularly, by Ireland's Siobhan ... McKenna."[34]

Seven productions were telecast in 1957. Famous stars appeared in all of them. None was better known than Greer Garson, the quintessential British mother in MGM's *Mrs. Miniver* (1940). Garson, surrounded by Franchot Tone, Sidney Blackmer, and E. G. Marshall, made a rare appearance in Lillian Hellman's "The Little Foxes," which aired on 16 December 1956, and later in "The Invincible Mr. Disraeli" (1963). Robert E. Sherwood's "There Shall Be No Night" offered another rare appearance, that of Charles Boyer, costarring with Katharine Cornell. "As the hero's son, Bradford Dillman, 26, was tender and affecting, but in summing up his parents he also summed up what was wrong with the whole show: 'They are wonderful people, but they are unreal and they don't live in this country — in this time.'"[35] Sensitive to the changing times, Marc Connelly's *Green Pastures*, starring William Warfield, Eddie "Rochester" Anderson, and Earle Hyman with an all-black cast made numerous changes from the original 1930 Broadway stage hit:

> In the new edition, De Lawd becomes The Lord. He speaks grammatically now, no longer smokes 10¢ see-gars, is not addressed by irreverent gamblers any more as Liver Lips or even High Pockets; instead they call

him Preacher Man. According to a spokesman — the whole cast speaks with "a soft rural-type intonation" rather than the Negro dialect in Connelly's Pulitzer Prize–winning script. Nobody will wear a derby. Cain still slays Abel, but morals are tightened up all through Genesis, e.g., instead of getting high on his keg of whiskey, Noah just gets rosy.[36]

But it was 30-year-old Julie Harris, drawing Broadway applause in *The Member of the Wedding* (1950), who received the most attention now and in future years on *The Hallmark Hall of Fame*, beginning with Ferenc Molnar's "The Good Fairy" in 1956, followed by "The Lark," in 1957, based on the life of Joan of Arc. The versatile, able, and gifted Harris gave wrenching emotion-driven performances as Brigid Mary in "Little Moon of Alban," about a young woman trying to survive the 1920 Irish Revolution, and in "Johnny Belinda," about a violated deaf mute (both 1958), "A Doll's House" (1959), and later "Victoria Regina," "Pygmalion," and others. Aired 24 March 1958, "Little Moon of Alban," an original teleplay by James Costigan, brought Academy of Television Arts and Sciences, Sylvania, George Foster Peabody, and Christopher awards to Costigan, George Schaefer, and Julie Harris. "Victoria Regina" won Emmys for Harris and supporting actress Pamela Brown and also an Emmy award for Best Show of the Year.

Six specials were made each year from 1957 through 1959. By 1960 *The Hallmark Hall of Fame* had reaped scores of honors, as it has continued to do over the decades. In 1961 the National Academy of Television Arts and Sciences presented an unprecedented citation to Joyce C. Hall, founder and chairman of Hallmark Cards. He received the first special Emmy award given to a sponsor for the many enriching hours of entertainment on *The Hallmark Hall of Fame* and for his personal support of quality television.

The Schlitz Playhouses and Celanese Theatre

Taking advantage of coast-to-coast distribution, two fine dramatic anthologies were on the air in fall 1951: *The Pulitzer Prize Playhouse* and the *Celanese Theatre*. The concept for *Celanese Theatre* rallied around the importance of scripts adapted from stage plays, and *The Pulitzer Prize Playhouse* would presumably draw upon prize winners. *The Pulitzer Prize Playhouse* was in fact on the air as a one-hour live drama for the previous season before it alternated on Fridays over ABC.

Celanese Theatre emerged from the formation of the Playwrights' Repertory Theater of Television. Eugene O'Neill, Rachel Crothers, S. N. Behrman, Maxwell Anderson, John Van Druten, Elmer Rice, Paul Osborn, and the widows of Philip Barry and Sidney Howard were represented.

Robert E. Sherwood was not a member, but he was included. About 150 American plays were made available to an estimated 20 million viewers. Maxwell Anderson said that for the first time in television history "a group of plays will be presented exactly as the authors want them to be seen."[37]

A premise worth recalling at this point is that a playwright's manuscript written for the stage is considered literary art, like a novel, short story, or poem. The composition is sacred; therefore, neither its structure nor its words should be altered. A stage play is usually the work of one or maybe two authors who provide the genesis for the production that evolves. In theater, everyone tries to bring to life what the playwright had in mind. By contrast, in television or film the script is treated like an outline for a group project. Directors, leading actors, and several writers may contribute to the finished product that at best is only a collective version of what will make a successful media entity. The completed videotape, film, or live production is the artistic entity. So playwrights and novelists are justly fearful that works to which they sell the rights may be collectively rewritten. The final screen product may or may not resemble the original work.

Each playwright in the Playwrights' Repertory Theater of Television hoped to overcome any script problems by retaining the right to supervise the adaptation or write the adaptation himself. Hired adapters had to get final approval from the original playwright, which Anderson thought increased a sense of responsibility to the original work. Particularly irate at Hollywood, Anderson claimed that the movies "eviscerate" plays and "usually alter everything but the title, and then change that." Anderson's *Winterset* (1936) was made into a movie that utilized many in the original Broadway cast, and *Saturday's Children* was filmed in 1929 and 1940. Both plays were telecast on *Celanese Theatre*. "My wife says that when I saw *Birth of a Nation* I remarked that the medium would never come to anything. As far as I am concerned, it never has."[38] The authors got $2,000 in royalty payments and the privilege of supervision over the adaptation.

For its television premiere *Celanese Theatre* presented Eugene O'Neill's "Ah, Wilderness!" on 3 October 1951. The anthology was on ABC-TV alternate Wednesdays, 10–11 P.M. EST. This was, according to *Newsweek*, "the most professional hour ever seen in the new medium."[39] Roddy McDowall played the boy tackling the problems of adolescence at the turn of the century. Originally a stage play, O'Neill's only comedy was a big hit for MGM in 1935. For the second show on 17 October, Pamela Brown was flown in from London to appear in Rachel Crothers's play, *Susan and God*. "Miss Brown gave a fine performance as the fluttery and evangelistic heroine," *Life* wrote.[40] Gertrude Lawrence made video history when she did a single scene on NBC that was telecast in 1937. For John Van Druten's "Old Acquaintance," aired

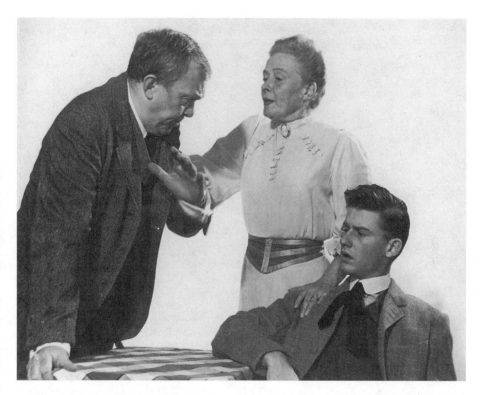

"Ah, Wilderness" starred Thomas Mitchell, Dorothy Peterson and Roddy McDowall, for the premiere of *Celanese Theatre*, on ABC-TV, 3 October 1951.

14 November, Edna Best and Ruth Chatterton had "two of the best female roles yet seen on television — old friends, both novelists, who spent their lives competing with one another."[41] This too was a fine 1943 movie with Bette Davis and Miriam Hopkins in the leads. Halfway through the season, *Celanese Theatre* showed a second O'Neill play, *Anna Christie*, on 23 January 1952. The story is a simple romance between a woman with a shady past, Anna (June Havoc), and her sweetheart seaman (Richard Burton). O'Neill's well-known stage profanity had to be eliminated for the tube. When Anna confessed her bitterness against all men in her life, she could not use the original line: "God damn 'em! I hate 'em!" *Anna Christie*, 1930, was MGM's choice for Greta Garbo's debut in talking pictures.

Time lamented the low rating of *Celanese Theatre* which was due partly because it was on the air at the same time as major boxing matches.[42] During the last half of the season the anthology was reduced to a half hour, playing on ABC from 10:00 until 10:30 P.M. EST. No doubt these changes and low ratings contributed to its demise on 25 June 1952, with Paul Osborn

"You Can't Take It with You," starring Charles Coburn and Ella Raines, for the premiere of *Pulitzer Prize Playhouse*, on ABC-TV, 6 October 1950.

and Lawrence Edward Watkin's play *On Borrowed Time*, starring Ralph Morgan and Mildred Dunnock.

The schedule of 20 outstanding plays on *Celanese Theatre* alternated with *Pulitzer Prize Playhouse*. In 1952 *The New Republic* claimed that they were "the season's two best dramatic series."[43] For the premiere of *The Pulitzer Prize Playhouse* on 6 October 1950, its sponsor, the Joseph Schlitz Brewing Company, brought 200 newspaper journalists to New York to view Charles Coburn and Ella Raines in "You Can't Take It with You," the Moss Hart–George S. Kaufman favorite. It was live on ABC from 9:00 until 10:00 P.M. EST. The Friday telecast proved to be "a smooth, professional lead-off for one of the most ambitious series of the year," according to *Newsweek*.[44] The ABC network acquired the rights from the Columbia University Graduate School of Journalism, which awards Pulitzer prizes, and leased them to Schlitz for the anthology, the assumption being that there were plenty of newspaper, play, and novel winners to provide the basis of an anthology. By the third telecast, on 27 October 1950, it was already apparent that not all selections were to be Pulitzer Prize winners. "The Late Christopher Bean," though a very fine program, was a case in point. It did not win the prize. Robert E. Sherwood's "The Queen's Husband" was a lot of fun but not much of a play. This 1928 comedy that had a short Broadway run told about King Eric VIII (Roland Young) who was beset with problems, among them his domineering wife (Edith King) and the leader of the opposition (Jonathan Harris). Felix Jackson adapted the script for Alex Segal to direct.

To open its second season on 19 December 1951, *The Pulitzer Prize Playhouse* alternated with *Celanese Theatre* on Wednesdays. Joseph Schrank adapted *The Skin of Our Teeth*, by Thornton Wilder. "The play was fitted so skillfully into the 50-minute straightjacket that it compared very well with the Broadway original."[45] Thomas Mitchell and Peggy Wood headed the Antrobus family as the Ice Age approached. Nina Foch, as Lilith, tangled with a prop camera and pulled the boom microphone into view for a few confidential words to viewers. That move did not work perfectly, but it was a refreshing attempt. The style of the Wilder fantasy leaned toward physically involving the audience; and so her action could allow some experimentation on television. Produced by Lawrence Carra and directed by Charles Dubin, with settings by Bob Bright, the host, a common role all of these anthologies seemed to require, was playwright Elmer Davies. *The Pulitzer Prize Playhouse*, which lasted for two seasons and over 50 telecasts, in 1950 was recognized by the Academy of Television Arts and Sciences as the best dramatic anthology.

The relationship of the two dramatic anthologies indicates that *The Pulitzer Prize Playhouse* as a live, one-hour program on ABC lasted one entire season, from October 1950 to June 1951. Then *Celanese Theatre* came on the air for the last quarter of 1951 as a live, one-hour drama. The anthologies alternated as half-hour dramas for the first six months of 1952.

At the same time the Joseph Schlitz Brewing Company sponsored the earlier anthologies, it sought yet another series. During the summer 1951, Schlitz sponsored 13 weeks of *Schlitz Film Firsts*, one-hour movies never shown before on television; in the fall Schlitz had *Saturday Playhouse*, a half-hour film series retitled *Schlitz Playhouse*. This evolution became *The Schlitz Playhouse of Stars*, and its focus was to be on famous celebrities. Felix Jackson was named executive producer. He planned to make major talent happy by tailoring his scripts especially for them and by paying them well. The first two stars were Helen Hayes and David Niven. Walter Hampden, Margaret Sullavan, Ronald Reagan, John Payne, and Rosalind Russell were soon to follow. The debut was 5 October 1951 from 9:00 until 10:00 P.M. on CBS-TV, during the period *The Pulitzer Prize Playhouse* was in hiatus on ABC-TV. Helen Hayes received $5,000 to appear in a light comedy, "Not a Chance," for the opener with David Niven. Rosalind Russell was so happy with her tailor-made script that, when she returned to Hollywood, it was expanded and a movie was made out of "Never Wave at a WAC," which was originally broadcast on 19 October 1951. The farce about a socialite who joined the Women's Army Corps, only to learn how difficult it was to conform to regulations, did become a motion picture the next year. Noel Coward's *Still Life*, a one-act play about lovers (Margaret Sullavan, Wendell Corey) who have an annual clandestine meeting in an English railroad station, was difficult to transpose to American sensitivities even in an expanded one-hour script. A variation on *Camille*, the essence of "One Is a Lonesome Number," which aired 23 November, was a more successful entry. A young husband and father (Charlton Heston) learns that he has an incurable disease. While he and his wife (June Lockhart) await his demise, he writes a book detailing his experience. According to *The Catholic World*, "Television did a masterful job of revitalizing the proceedings largely because of the thoughtful but essentially dry-eyed script." Robert Kass went on to praise the anthology: "This particular show was typical of the high standard of all the plays in this series. Each of them is marked by care and discrimination in writing, direction, sets, and performance."[46]

Schlitz came in for its share of complaints about commercials. For example, "There was a pantomime about a weary husband who had accompanied his wife to a fashion show. She turns to him for approval of a dress. He is gone — she finds him at the corner bar drinking Schlitz."[47]

In spring 1952 as the Schlitz company turned to half-hour formats, *Playhouse of Stars*, like *The Pulitzer Prize Playhouse*, was also shortened. Irene Dunne served as hostess for a few weeks. After the summer of 1953, the half-hour dramas were more frequently filmed. Yet *The Schlitz Playhouse of Stars* was on the air for almost eight years, October 1951–March 1959, offering opportunity, experience, and exposure to scores of aspiring hopefuls in entertainment.

The Mystery Genre

Seven dramatic anthologies specializing in mystery, horror, or science fiction originated on television from 1 January 1950 to 1 January 1952. They were *Escape*, *The Trap/Sure as Fate*, *The Web*, *Stage 13*, *Danger*, *The Gallery of Mme. Liu Tsong*, and *Tales of Tomorrow*. The scripts principally concerned mystery, suspense, horror, the unexplained, adventure, and usually involved crime. *Film noir*, a film genre depicting the often disastrous, predetermined fate of average individuals, had gained a good deal of popularity in the movies and was being tried on television. In 1950 CBS-TV was particularly active. Although it already had *Suspense* on Tuesdays and *Man Against Crime* as a Friday night staple, CBS-TV made several new attempts to find other programs of this type. Most of these programs were scheduled on weekdays, usually for a half-hour on Tuesdays. They were live and featured the upcoming group of professional actors in New York, the longer anthologies gradually depending more on stars.

Escape, transferring to video on 5 January 1950, was wonderful listening for sound-only fans who were "tired of the everyday grind" and wanted their imaginations to go on bizarre adventures; but it lasted barely three months. *Escape* began on CBS-TV, Thursdays from 9:00 until 9:30 P.M. EST, because the radio version was aired on Tuesdays. The premiere was an adaptation of Franklin Gregory's short story about a reporter who finds himself on an ice floe in the Arctic. "Rugged Journey" was adapted by Howard Rodman, produced and directed by Wyllis Cooper. Cooper's next show, *Stage 13*, referring to a superstitious number no sound stage would use, aired on CBS-TV, Wednesdays, 9:30–10:00 P.M. Its debut on April 19th, "Now You Know," by Philip Macdonald and adapted by Draper Lewis, told about the disappearance of patrons from a Third Avenue saloon. The unlucky anthology folded after seven weeks. Another attempt, *The Trap*, 29 April 1950, resembled a noir-like entry on Columbia. Scheduled Saturday nights from 9:00 until 10:00, the initial program was Patrick Quentin's "Puzzle for Fiends," adapted by Kelley Roos. Suffering from temporary amnesia, Peter Duluth (George Keane) is told by members of a strange family he is someone else, so that they can get access to a fortune. Franklin Heller was hired to produce the weekly shows with alternating units under the direction of Yul Brynner and Bryon Paul. *The Trap* made it through June, nine programs in all.

A summer replacement was needed for *Suspense* on CBS-TV; therefore, it agreed to a Mark Goodson–Bill Todman package, *The Web*, based on adaptations of stories by the Mystery Writers of America. Producer/director Franklin Heller was much luckier this time, with the second program sponsored by P. Lorillard Company for Embassy cigarettes and rescheduling planned for the fall. The characters in these half-hour dramas were caught in *The Web*, which was initiated on the Fourth of July 1950. Vincent Starrett's story of a juror who holds out for acquittal in a murder case, "The Twelfth Juror," was adapted by Charles Robinson. Jonathan Blake narrated the adventures. By 1952 the anthology won the Edgar Allan Poe award for excellence. In 1957 the format became half-hour dramas filmed in Hollywood.

In September 1950, with *The Web* and *Suspense* continuing for four or more seasons, *Danger* and *Sure as Fate* became regular shows. *The Trap*, retitled *Sure as Fate*, thematically tinged with the noir foreboding, had also debuted on July 4th and made a bid for permanence during the fall. Producer Jerry Danzig with directors Yul Brynner and Hal Gerson chose Ernest Borneman's "Tremolo," adapted by Mel Goldberg, as the opener. The hour-long melodramas lasted only a year.

The initial announcement for another entry was *Mystery Playhouse*, scheduled on CBS-TV, Tuesdays, 10:00–10:30 P.M. EDT. A convicted man (Dane Clark) trying to prove his innocence from his prison cell was the story line for Henry Norton's "The Black Door," adapted by Irving Elman for airing on 19 September. The producer was native New Yorker Martin Ritt, who had acted and directed on stage. He was teamed with Yul Brynner as director. Distinctive music was played by guitarist Tony Mattola, who would read the script in advance and score unusual ways his solo guitar could lend musical emphasis. The playhouse was sponsored by Block Drug Company, promoting Ammident Toothpaste. Within a week the show was retitled *Danger*. Soon produced by 32-year-old Charles Russell and 27-year-old Sidney Lumet, *Danger* gave them a chance to develop intimate stories about rough urban characters. "Danger is chiefly distinguished for fine camera work, the haunting theme music of Guitarist Tony Mottola, and a leaning toward psychological melodrama." Arnold Schulman's "Lady on the Rock" told the story of a man who mistakes affection and pity for love, only to find out later what people really thought of him. "One critic demanded that CBS send a kinescope to New York's Governor [Thomas E.] Dewey as Exhibit A in an argument for TV censorship."[48] After a year the innovative efforts in *Danger* were still being attacked by critics: "'Danger' is dedicated to scaring the very life out of those unfortunate enough to witness it, and it sets about this grisly and ignoble task by (1) manufacturing scripts a child of twelve would either disregard or set fire to, ... (2) presenting actors [who are weak], (3) emitting a succession of plunks from an electric guitar that are supposed to be ominous notes of death and fear; and (4) putting before the public sketches directed with such amateurishness and incompetence as to defy national description."[49] Ignoring critical opinion, the public watched *Danger* through five seasons and nearly 250 half-hour shows. Before the year ended, *Big Town*, essentially a newspaper crime adventure on radio since 1937, and *Charlie Wild, Private Detective*, the postwar successor to Sam Spade (CBS, 1946), appeared in half-hour formats on CBS-TV, along with other crime series.

Entries for 1951 in *The Galley of Mme. Liu Tsong*, starring Anna May Wong, a well-known film actress presenting stories of crime and intrigue, appeared briefly on DuMont television; and *Tales of Tomorrow* made a respectable debut on ABC-TV, 3 August 1951, and ran for two seasons as an early science fiction program. Science fiction, as futuristic space adventure, was in revival. Perhaps better served than adults were children with DuMont's *Captain Video and His Video Rangers* (1949–53) and the better financed *Tom Corbet, Space Cadet* (1950–56). On the silver screen *Destination Moon* (1950), the George Pal live-action seminal movie, depended on Academy Award winning painted special effects for space travel, still more than a half dozen years prior to the launch of Sputnik in 1957.

Experimental Theaters

Once commercial sponsorship of programs took over programming in the late 1940s, few anthologies could experiment significantly with the new medium. Before the war everything on television was an experiment, after the war little was an experiment. After producing a long list of dramas certain to be accepted by the public, some original dramas, few of which would be controversial, were produced. Sponsors, after all, did not want to offend anyone or have any of their products or services positioned unfavorably. In the late 1940s Albert McCleery came to NBC-TV hoping to try new ways to use the medium in drama. McCleery had diverse credentials. He spent a year and a half getting acquainted with the accepted routine by producing *Fireside Theatre*, which for him was largely a waste of time.

Typically, during the summer months, new program material was attempted, and on 16 May 1950 *Cameo Theatre* debuted with "It Takes a Thief," featuring Marjorie Gateson and Jack Hartley. McCleery, who gained some of his training from Gilmore Brown's Pasadena Playhouse in California, from writing for the movies (*The Lady Is Willing*, 1942), and from being head of Fordham University Theatre, was interested in attempting arena-style theater on television. Budgeted at $2,000 a program, *Cameo Theatre* gave him that opportunity. His aim was "to show that we can do things of delicacy and violence by using the arena theatre in television."[50] His work received a good deal of attention because critics were constantly complaining that the video medium was not being used in an innovative way. And he was at least doing something. "Cameo Theatre is making an honest attempt to break away from the tyranny of the proscenium arch and present television as theatre-in-the-round, and for that reason, if no other, it deserves attention," Philip Hamburger wrote in *The New Yorker*.[51]

Shirley Jackson's "The Lottery" on 16 June 1950 revealed McCleery's effort to "paint pictures with faces." In extreme tight shots, he tried to be "so close that you can see what the eye does and the heart does." Even those who supported this experiment thought such extreme closeups limited camera movement too much. One of the principal experimental playwrights at the time was William Saroyan, whose *People with the Light Coming Through Them* and *Hello, Out There* had been on prewar television. He was a practitioner of minimalist staging, so right for constructionist staging during the financially strapped Depression era. The seventh attempt on *Cameo Theatre* was Saroyan's "A Daughter to Think About," in his first play written especially for television. "He was evidently attempting to convey the conflicting emotions and deep, almost unbearable feelings that come over a man (Tod Andrew) and wife (Ruth Ford) when they decide to separate." Frequently, experiments did not work. This play was "one of those things Saroyan probably should have shown to no one but himself."[52]

When Jackson's "The Lottery" was repeated the following summer — tight closeups, lack of sets, few props, limited lighting — it exemplified a style McCleery would preserve and apply to his afternoon anthology, *Matinee Theatre* (1955–57). Its plot, however, concerned mob prejudice, involving an ancient practice of a town selecting one member by lot to be stoned to death. Such controversial themes were seldom scheduled. When not producing *The Hallmark Hall of Fame*, McCleery continued his experiments on *Cameo Theatre* mainly as a two- or three-month summer replacement in 1950, 1951, and 1953. A highlight was Henrik Ibsen's *Peer Gynt*, shown over three successive weeks in March 1952.

In late December 1951, CBS announced that it intended to resurrect its highly successful and experimental radio series *Columbia Workshop*, which had gone on the air 18 July 1936. The radio anthology was credited with bringing new ideas, techniques, and personalities to the medium. Norman Corwin, William Saroyan, Dorothy Parker, and Archibald MacLeish were among the promising writers, and Orson Welles, Max Wylie, William N. Robson, and Douglas Coulter were among the new production personnel. So, with the intention of providing "a proving ground for experiments in techniques, an area of encouragement for new writers and artists, and a foe of mental laziness," the *Columbia Television Workshop* made its debut on Sunday, 23 January 1952, from 4:00 until 4:30 P.M. EST.[53] Sidney Lumet was selected to direct Miguel de Cervantes's *Don Quixote*, adapted by Alvin Sapinsley. The second play, "Careless Love," was an original story about a member of a Dixieland jazz band, by John Gerstad and Norman Brooks. The 14 half-hours alternated the works of well-known writers with new material; but the new effort failed to achieve the lofty goals of the original *Columbia Workshop*.

"The Magnificent Gesture," starring Margaret Hayes and Brian Aherne, was the premiere of *Armstrong Circle Theatre*, on NBC-TV, 6 June 1950.

Armstrong Circle Theatre

The *Armstrong Circle Theatre* premiere on NBC-TV on Tuesday, 6 June 1950, was "The Magnificent Gesture," by James Garvin. Film actor Brian

Aherne had the lead. Most of the dramas would be produced by Hudson Faussett and directed by Garry Simpson. The half-hour format was lengthened to an hour in September 1955. Two years later it switched to CBS-TV as an hour drama, and it remained on the air until August 1963. The Armstrong Cork Company of Lancaster, Pennsylvania, and its agency Batten, Barton, Dustrine, and Osborn, Inc. wanted a cost-effective anthology that dealt with contemporary lives and problems that people were currently experiencing. *Armstrong Circle Theatre* claimed its original dramas were based on "indisputable fact" that blurred the line between the fictional drama and an actual documentary. Occasionally, light entertainment was mixed with dramas that had serious themes, such as racial intolerance and mental illness. At the outset the program cost about $8,000, but within 12 months that figure increased to $16,715. Yet, its more than five million viewers, who saw three commercials per program, cost just over $3.00 per million viewers, a low-end price for a dramatic anthology.[54]

During the initial period the perspective tended to favor fictional over factual stories. This was illustrated by *Armstrong Circle Theatre*'s first colorcast, even though most of the nation would see it in black and white. "Evening Star," written by Ed Roberts, Armstrong's story editor, and Anne Howard Bailey, his associate, spotlighted the return of a retired opera star (Jarmila Novotna) to sing on television. The diva is the essence of temperament and uncooperativeness because, as her producer learns, she lacks confidence in her ability to make good in the new medium. "The backstage story will give the home audience a behind-the-scenes view of the actual mechanics of a TV show in rehearsal, as the singer in the story prepares for her video debut." James Sheldon directed, and Hudson Faussett produced.[55]

This kind of simulated experience illustrated in a fictional dramatic format was the usual fare. Occasionally, the Armstrong Cork Company would try something entirely different, in what must have been a searching process for consistently acceptable program content. Frank De Felitta and Darrell Peter were called upon by Roberts and Bailey to write a half-hour opera. "Among the ten most inventive scripts bought and produced by 'Circle Theatre' in the two years it's been on the air, most of them were written by De Felitta," in the editors' opinion.[56] The original opera was "The Parrot," presented on 24 March 1953. The plot told of a bird that inherited a fortune and, with it, the hatred of envious relatives of the deceased eccentric. This too was a Faussett/Simpson production.

In 1955 as many dramas relocated to Los Angeles, *Armstrong Circle Theatre* remained in New York, extended its program to one hour, and turned to emphasizing factually based stories. The documentary-drama approach began on 15 February 1955 with "I Found Sixty Million Dollars," based on the true story of Charles A. Steen who, despite a declaration from the Atomic Energy Commission saying his land was barren, discovered a vast uranium reserve. Steen, played by Jackie Cooper, lived a classic rags-to-riches story. It was the ideal combination of fact presented in a fictional format. Seizing upon the value of showing true events and lives, the Armstrong Cork Company demanded stories that emphasized success over obstacles, understandable situations, and positive reasons for human motivation.[57]

When Talent Associates took over the production of *Armstrong Circle Theatre*, another dimension was added. Talent Associates, Inc. was formed in 1948 by David Susskind. Educated at the University of Wisconsin and Harvard, Susskind at 28 had already been a press agent at Warner Bros. and a talent agent for MCA. He was executive producer, and Robert Costello and William Corrigan were engaged as producer and director, respectively. Under Costello's guidance, dramas were structured to present possible solutions or hope for solving problems, a realm that departs from the tenets of documentary programs. In addition, for dramatic expediency, sometimes the activities of two or three persons actually involved in an event were composited into a single character who did not exist. As A. William Bluem observed in *Documentary in American Television*: "However authentic *Circle Theatre* might have been, as a form it was really neither fish nor fowl. On the one hand, its commitment to the faithful duplication of events and people limited its freedom as drama; on the other, the use of actors and theatrical conventions deprived it of any validity as documentary."[58] Four programs representative of these years were "Buried 2,000 Years: The Dead Sea Scrolls," by Irve Tunick; "Assignment: Junkie's Alley," by Mel Goldberg; "Thirty Days to Reconsider," by Robert Hirson; and "The Trial of Poznan," by Alvin Boretz.[59]

Certainly the fact that *Armstrong Circle Theatre* remained in New York presenting live dramas well after the other major dramatic anthologies had moved or ended entitles it to a singular recognition. Then, too, its impact was substantial. Viewers who were motivated to act on matters of adoption, divorce, or juvenile delinquency numbered in the thousands. More importantly, the concept of comingling factual content in reconstructed dramatic formats, while applying varying degrees of poetic license, has given rise to much of the revisionist history seen today in mass media.

Postwar British Drama

The Charter creating the British Broadcasting Corporation (BBC) was issued and the Postmaster General granted the Corporation a license for

ten years, beginning 1 January 1927. At the same time, NBC and CBS came
into existence. No commercial broadcasting companies were licensed in
England, however. The basic pattern in Britain was a monopoly, financed
by license fees on radio receivers and administered by an independent public corporation.[60] Experimentation in television rivals that of the United
States. In 1936 the first public service television programs in the world were
started by the BBC in Alexandra Palace. This activity parallels activity at
NBC and CBS. From 1936 to 1939, when the war abruptly ended telecasting, the BBC presented a total of just under 400 television dramas. From
1936 to 1942, when the war halted NBC operations, 153 television dramas
were shown. Rough estimates indicate that about 5,000 receivers were in
use in London and in New York at the time service was halted.[61]

When television was resumed in June 1946, an estimated 300,000 Lon-
doners watched television on about 20,000 licensed receivers.[62] Just as in
America, dramatic programming resumed with enthusiasm. The first task
of the BBC Television Service was to establish national coverage, and this
was essentially completed between 1952 and 1955, shortly after the
East–West Coast interconnection was completed in the United States. Distribution was in black and white; color remained experimental. The bulk
of the forty hours of programs transmitted each week originated from four
television studios at Lime Grove, Shepherd's Bush, and from the Television
Theatre nearby. The studio center had a substantial film department. In
1954 Parliament ended the BBC monopoly by establishing the Independent
Television Authority (ITA). Diversity from independent entertainment
competitors was a major trend in the 1950s in both countries. The close
relationship between Great Britain and the United States in dramatic content, talents, and techniques was substantial, as outlined here.

The BBC-TV mandate was to serve the diverse interests of the many
regions of the country as well as to provide programs of broad national
interest. On its sole program service the BBC telecast an average of ten dramas a month, not including repeats or musicals, each year: 1947—114,
1948—132, 1949—122, 1950—110, and 1951—117, for a total of 595 dramas.
They were generally shown at 8:00 to 10:00 P.M. and ran various lengths,
frequently one or two hours. Just as in the United States, Sunday evenings
had major dramatic productions, including large casts, a great deal of
scenery, and music. The BBC favored many dramas and authors who were
familiar in the United States: William Shakespeare, Somerset Maugham,
George Bernard Shaw, George S. Kaufman, Eugene O'Neill. English, American, and stories from the continent were, in general, evenly divided. BBC
attempted to develop some series and serials, and showed a Christmas nativity play as well as major productions of children's stories in December.

The year 1947 began with a major production of Henry J. Byron's 1860 "Cinderella," a musical shown at 8:30 P.M. on 2 January. Daphne du Maurier's *Rebecca*, also popular in the United States, featured 12 actors when telecast at 8:30 P.M. on Sunday, January 19. Du Maurier was the daughter of long-time British stage manager-actor, Sir Gerald du Maurier, whose play, *Trilby*, aired later that year. Natually English writers frequently held the spotlight: W. Somerset Maugham, J. B. Priestley, Welsh actor and dramatist Emlyn Williams, and Irish playwrights Sean O'Casey and George Bernard Shaw. Several Americans were selected too. Moss Hart and George S. Kaufman's *The Man Who Came to Dinner*, with a cast of 20, was presented on 23 March, and "You Can't Take It with You" on 18 May. Holworthy Hall and Robert Middlemass's one-act play, *The Valiant*, began at 9:10 and ran for 46 minutes on 27 March. Eugene O'Neill's *Mourning Becomes Electra* was performed over two weeks in March and April. Nelson Bond and David Kent's "Mr. Mergenthwirker's Lobblies," a favorite of NBC's Fred Coe, was on 4 May. Interestingly, Eleanor McFadden's "Double Door," featuring Ellen Pollock as Victoria Van Brett, appeared on 17 August about three months after its premiere for *Kraft Television Theatre*. T. S. Eliot, American by birth but English by adoption, had his 1935 play about the murder of Thomas à Beckett, *Murder in the Cathedral*, telecast in November 1947.

Continental playwrights were also popular. Anton Chekhov's *The Cherry Orchard* was in March, and during June, viewers saw Emlyn Williams's translation of Ivan Turgenev's *A Month in the Country*, Judith Gutherie's adaptation of Leonid Andreyev's "He Who Gets Slapped," and a 90-minute production of Luigi Pirandello's *Henry IV*.

Productions of classic English masters began appearing at mid-year. Christopher Marlowe's *The Tragical History of Doctor Faustus* was staged in a huge Sunday production with 35 actors just ten days before the first large Shakespearean production, *The Merchant of Venice*, on 1 July 1947. At month's end, *A Midsummer Night's Dream* was telecast from the Open Air Threatre, Regents Park, featuring Mary Honer as Puck among a cast of 25, including 12 fairy ballet dancers. Produced by Robert Atkins, the Open Air Theatre Orchestra was directed by Fosabel Watson. *Romeo and Juliet* with John Bailey as Romeo and Rosalie Crutchly as Juliet was presented by Michael Barry on 5 October. John Byron as "Hamlet," adapted by George More O'Ferrall, a director even more successful in television than film, was telecast in two parts on 7 and 14 December 1947. All in all, this partial schedule suggests a fierce level of postwar resilience despite being kept off the air for a month because of a fuel shortage.

As the major dramatic anthologies began to increase in America in

1948, BBC television increased its steady output, often selecting the same material as on U.S. television. Some of the plays were telecast remote from theaters, and frequently the same drama was repeated at a different time during the week or perhaps much later. Terence Rattigan's *The Winslow Boy* was picked up from the Intimate Theatre, Palmers Green, on 13 January 1948, Ronnie Winslow being played by Paul Jago. Elmer Rice's *The Adding Machine* was broadcast on Thursday, 15 January at 8:30 P.M. and rebroadcast the next day at 3:30 P.M. Margaret Lockwood headed a cast of 25 for George Bernard Shaw's *Pygmalion*; Margaret Leighton was seen in *Arms and the Man* in June; and a 4 o'clock scheduling of *Androcles and the Lion*, intended for children, was shown on 10 October 1948. Patrick Hamilton's turn-of-the-century mystery "Gaslight" was popular in both countries. In England, the Manninghams were played by Sebastian Shaw and Angela Baddeley, and John Turnbull was Sergeant Rough. Emily Brontë's *Wuthering Heights* with Kieron Moore and Katherine Blake appeared on Sunday, 7 March, from 8:30 to 9:40 P.M.; and Charlotte Brontë's *Jane Eyre*, adapted by Helen Jerome, the same version used in New York, starred Barbara Mullen as Jane and Reginald Tate as Mr. Rochester and was telecast on Sunday, 26 September 1948.

Typically, the next day's schedule and a sound-only recording of the news ended the day's telecast at about 11 o'clock. Irish plays such as John M. Synge's *In the Shadow of the Glen* and French plays like Jean Anouilh's *Antigone* received more attention in England, but John Galsworthy's *Loyalties*, and *An Inspector Calls* by J. B. Priestley, were favorites on both sides of the Atlantic. "The Breadwinner" was a May choice, "Home and Beauty" aired in July, "The Unattainable" viewed in August, and "The Circle," seen in September, illustrated Somerset Maugham's potential for a television anthology later seen in America. Noël Coward's first play was a one-act about struggling show-business performers, *Red Peppers* in July; and his *Blithe Spirit*, starring Frank Lawton, Marian Spencer, and Betty Ann Davies was in November. It, too, was often repeated in both countries. A. A. Milne's *The Truth about Blayds*, starring Henry Oscar as Blayds was on Friday, 6 August, and "The Dover Road" played on Sunday, 8 August 1948. "The Front Page," the Hecht-MacArthur newspaper story, was shown on 15 August, another Sunday. William Devlin as *King Lear*, along with other major Shakespearean plays, performed over two Sundays, 22 and 29 August. The year ended with a huge production on Christmas Day of Lewis Carroll's *Alice in Wonderland & Through the Looking-Glass*, adapted from the play by Herbert M. Prentice. Music frequently accompanied such productions, most of it recorded, but this time Alfred Reynolds conducted the orchestra provided by Eric Robinson.

Keynoting 1949's long list of impressive dramas was William Hodge's "The Trial of Madeleine Smith," a documentary-drama adapted by John Gough. Mary Morris was Madeleine. This reporting of an actual event in a fictional format precedes *Armstrong Circle Theatre*, which appeared in America the next year.

Dramas seen on BBC and New York networks at about the same time were: Oscar Wilde's *The Importance of Being Earnest*, on 2 January, starring William Fox as Algernon Moncrieff; Elmer Rice's "Counsellor-at-Law," broadcast 16 January; Sidney Howard's "The Silver Cord," starring Helen Haye, an English actress on the stage for 55 years, on 6 February; Shakespeare's *The Tragedy of Macbeth* with Stephen Murray in the lead on 20 February; Terence Rattigan's *The Browning Version* performed by the Phoenix Theatre Company on 30 May 1949; George Bernard Shaw's *The Devil's Disciple* with a cast of more than 50, half of whom were extras; and J. B. Priestley's "When We Are Married" as another July selection; A. A. Milne's "The Perfect Alibi" telecast on 6 August; Hubert Henry Davies's Edwardian comedy "The Mollusc" on 9 August; Agatha Christie's "Ten Little Niggers," retitled for its Broadway production as *Ten Little Indians* (1943), as the drama for 20 August; Cyril Campion's "Ladies in Waiting" repeated on 13 September; and J. B. Priestley's "Dangerous Corner" as a Sunday selection on 2 October.

For the Edgar Allan Poe Centenary, three plays were presented on Thursday, 6 October 1949. They were "The Cask of Amontillado," "Some Words with a Mummy," and "The Fall of the House of Usher." The short stories were adapted by Joan Maude and Michael Warre. Arthur Wing Pinero's "Trelawney of the Wells" was the 20 November selection; Rattigan's *The Winslow Boy* was repeated in December; and Thornton Wilder's *The Long Christmas Dinner* aired 27 December 1949, illustrating again the similar appeal of dramatic programming in Great Britain and the United States during the formative years of the live period.

During 1950 through 1951, unlike in the United States, the BBC Television Service did not turn to radio or motion picture scripts. Instead, it continued to adapt stage plays and classic literature, influencing particularly *Robert Montgomery Presents* and *The Hallmark Hall of Fame*. With increased transmission service, the BBC expected to cover 95 percent of the United Kingdom by the mid–1950s. It also planned expansion of its theatrical studio facilities, somewhat like the expansion plans for centralizing facilities in the United States, but instead of moving from one coast to another, the British were relocating across London from Alexandra Palace in North London to Shepherd's Bush (1960).[63]

The BBC television network would gain permanent access to the

American market with 15 productions of *The Age of Kings* (1961). The Shakespearean plays, beginning with the reign of Richard II and performed by the British Repertory Company which included Sean Connery, David Williams, and Noel Johnson, would sound the trumpets for National Educational Television's "Fourth Network" consisting of more than 50 affiliated stations. NET was the forerunner of the Public Broadcasting Service (PBS), where British productions have a major presence.

6

....

Summary/Conclusions: Will It Play in Peoria?

When World War II ended, New York City was the artistic and intellectual capital of the country. It had given birth to the entertainment industries, including moving pictures, radio, and television. By now, the public had an obsessive love affair with film and its creators and with radio programs that drew millions of faithful listeners to receivers. By 1946 the movies and radio had rewritten everything they could from the legitimate theater and print media. The voracious appetite of film and radio had devoured almost every suitable play, comedy, musical, book, and story. Radio provided huge amounts of original dramatic material and a great deal more in other genres — news, sports, variety — with which to feed its national audience. Importantly, radio and stage had reenforced the commitment to live entertainment. So when television reclaimed its place after the wartime hiatus, it devoured the content of earlier media at an alarming rate and presented it *live*.

For six short years, television was live from New York and promoted the concept that exists to this day: A live show is better than a prerecorded show, even if the public cannot tell the difference.

The public, starved for the good life that had eluded it for four years, wanted peace and prosperity. Television showed everyone how sweet life could be, as no other medium had done before. Television, moreover, was not elitist. The prognosticators were wrong. Television teased the average person — through materialistic commercials — suggesting that every viewer could have an abundant life. Neither film nor radio could repeat the promises of fulfillment that television revealed. Movies were attended for a few hours in the dark once or twice a week; radio had to be imagined through the mental and emotional constraints of the listener's own imagination. Television was effortless. Luxury was defined, and that luxury was

145

often wrapped around dramatic anthologies. The most delectable products were sold through stories, comedies, and musicals. The bigger the show, the better the commercials depicting irresistible products, and usually the bigger the public demand was for the products. Television advertising, subsidized by the government's decision not to tax it, spent huge sums on programming that enchanted the public with a long list of desirable products and services, accompanied night after night with dramatic programming.

While movies began to take on social issues with a hard, realistic, sometimes unpleasant, edge, and radio saw its programming content transferred to television, television presented in programming and commercials a wonderful life of delicious material existence for everyone, in a peaceful social setting earned by defeating the villains of war. In addition, televised dramas included respectful tributes to wartime heroes and events, such as the sinking of the battleship *Bismarck*. It was the right message for an American audience who believed hard work and sacrifice deserved rewards. Television showed that rewards were within easy reach. Some complaints were made that fictional dramatizations were frequently sanitized by sponsors, advertising agencies, and networks. This was, at the time, not that remarkable, for a cautious approach to programming blended in with the wartime necessities of restricted or manipulated information. The public was accustomed to exaggerated claims, and it was also wary of them.

During the six years after the war, the public was fascinated by the array of products coming into the marketplace. That was far more important. Television's dramatic theme that so often suited the American public had been articulated already by the popular 19th century English author and critic, John Ruskin, who wrote: "Whenever money is the principal object of life, it is both got ill and spent ill, and does harm both in the getting and the spending. When getting and spending happiness is our aim, life can be beautiful!" This quotation led into the CBS radio serial *Life Can Be Beautiful*, originating in 1938, and suggested the cultural mind-set still lingering during the postwar years.

It is little wonder, therefore, that the basis for so many dramas of the late 1940s and 1950s drew themes from the prewar years — and that today 1950s dramatic fare is looked upon with fond reverence as largely unrealistic, perhaps mythic. What is forgotten, or less well remembered, is that the uncertainties of the atomic age hovered over the country, the draft was still going on and would gain momentum as the Korean conflict approached, and the postwar economy was unstable. Back then, the public had suffered from the Great Depression followed by a great war, so its hopes were rather fundamental — a home, be it ever so humble, earned through hard work made possible by a good education. So what if, following the war, the public was not quite ready to clean up the rubble, much less take on a growing list of social ills? The public was tired of disaster. It wanted to put its feet up and be entertained. So, on television, "actuality" took a backseat, temporarily, to the promise of better things to come. Yes, judging from huge viewership, even government committees investigating crime and communism could be surprisingly entertaining.

Delayed Realism

World War II brought to an end the romance of what it meant to be American. Realism — facing the truth and dealing with it, as much of the world devastated by war had to— had not yet permeated Americans. It would take the turmoil of the next decades for that to happen. Meanwhile, American television dramas would be steeped in nostalgic adaptations and offered to the hinterland by New York television producers, who held Broadway dramas of the 1920s and 1930s in high esteem. The sheer novelty of television kept the public fascinated for several years. So long as dramas were mixed with various kinds of entertainment — variety, comedy, musicals, and sports — that viewers had grown so fond of to abate their anxieties of war, the old adaptations enjoyed a renaissance, despite censorship by network continuity acceptance offices. Prewar values were carried over to postwar dramas, in part, because the television business was risky enough for advertisers and networks that shared the cost of the new medium.

The Congregational Audience

The public had gathered for years around the radio to listen to and imagine what its sounds meant. At last, viewers gathered around television sets. It was a shared experience for the whole family and, in this period, often for neighbors who did not own a television receiver. This was a congregational experience enjoyed in the light of day and at night, widely discussed by the entire family and friends. It was a clearly different experience from going to the movies, where, though in the presence of a crowd, the viewer sat in the dark to enjoy what was mainly an experience in solitary voyeurism. The televiewer quickly became more interested in who was in the dramas than what the dramas were about. Viewers absorbed the actors and the commercial products in their daily lives. Actors brought to the viewer exciting vicarious experiences, and commercials brought a new awareness of technical progress. Quality was boldly trademarked, manu-facturers were trusted, and they sought prestige with confidence. The pub-lic demand for a good life made possible with peacetime prosperity was not about to be seriously jeopardized by an undercurrent of major national and international concerns that the average person chose to ignore.

As a result, television writers were forced to comply with this attitude. Network sponsors and continuity acceptance offices held the line, while producers considered it a real coup to have a drama that probed the tough issues that were on the horizon. Therefore, mainstream television drama largely consisted of adaptations of material already considered acceptable to viewers, in some cases having been broadcast prior to the war. Eventu-ally, the medium would have a larger and more diverse audience to please than had any previous entertainment medium. The complicated responsi-bility that would accompany its broad appeal could be delayed, at least for a while, by Dad playing the breadwinner and protector, Mom the home-maker and real intelligence behind the family, while their kids solved mod-est challenges as they and television were coming of age.

New Frontiers

Rocketry for satellites, computers, the challenge of frequency modu-lation (FM) to amplitude modulation (AM), revitalization of widescreen formats, a shift from black-and-white to color television, the invention of audio and video tape, electronic editing, and cable distribution were all in embryonic stages during this six-year period. But these could wait. Tele-vision itself was the new technology that the public could readily under-stand and appreciate, and it would become the means by which the other marvelous achievements would be revealed. Television itself would have the greatest impact on American culture during the latter half of the century.

Panning the Gold

The knowledge concerning dramatic production that had been accrued before the war, mainly at NBC, paved the way for remarkable success after the war. *Kraft Television Theatre* was the all-encompassing anthology. It was on the air for 11 years, it aired the most dramas, and it provided fine, yet relatively low cost, dramatic entertainment. It proved to be an out-standing training ground for veterans and newcomers alike. Over the years it had to be flexible in story content, searching for good adaptations and original material. It depended mainly on the consistency of producer/director Stanley Quinn, and later Maury Holland, to maintain the program's high level of quality, as well as the trust of the J. Walter Thompson agency and its sponsor Kraft Foods.

The *Philco/Goodyear Television Playhouse* combination was NBC's inhouse premier showcase that best expressed what the network had been trying to accomplish since 1936. Producer Fred Coe reaped the benefits of the previous decade and instilled his own vision by obtaining excellent writers, often with innovations for television drama, and by alternating directors, the highly experienced Gordon Duff and Coe protégé, Delbert Mann. Both understood Coe's objectives and were willing to carry them out. The *Playhouse*'s seven years on the air brought some of the finest moments in television drama.

At CBS, *Ford Theater* had the biggest budget per drama, but it was on the air less often. Director Marc Daniels had the theatrical background to make effective use of, mainly, stars and plays from Broadway. He experimented with a few elaborate productions on location around New York, thereby forcing other anthologies to be more keenly competitive. But *Ford Theater* lasted only four years as a live anthology. Then this agency package became an early producer of a half-hour filmed anthology that ran another five years. The success of these dramas produced in Hollywood and featuring movie talent was equally important in that it foreshadowed the future direction of anthologies.

Studio One provided yet another major television training center for both new and experienced talent. Though heavily into adaptations in the beginning, Worthington Miner's theatrical renaissance also extended to adaptations from print media. Having started on the stage and having spent time in Hollywood, he was all the more amenable to film techniques, encouraging his directors, Paul Nickell and Franklin Schaffner, to absorb the moving-camera style prevalent on the silver screen. Neither Miner nor *Studio One* were quite the same after he left in 1952, but the anthology continued to showcase talent for another six years.

These dramatic anthologies were all recognized for their attributes from time to time with awards and critical acclaim. They differed within the constraints of executive guidelines. The volume of work produced week after week is looked upon today with wonderment and respect. The other major dramatic anthology before 1952 was *Robert Montgomery Presents Your Lucky Strike Theatre*. Robert Montgomery was the only celebrity among these producers. He had earned his reputation as a handsome leading man on stage and screen. He understood the entertainment businesses, and he was personally very talented. He brought his acclaim and ability to the anthology, and he received strong network support. Some major film stars made their debuts on this anthology; nevertheless, the program concentrated on doing what was already being done, and it did this well. Robert Montgomery showed that a famous film star could be equally successful in television, and his executive abilities assuaged the political strains that were said to exist between the television and film industries. As this history indicates, however, the concerns faded as Hollywood found ways to merge with television. Robert Montgomery helped to promote harmony through the program and his political savvy.

All of the procedures for presenting television dramas had been established by 1952. The roles of networks, agencies, and producers were defined. Relationships with theatrical companies, rights-granting organizations, unions, and technicians were clarified. The producers chose properties and selected directors and principal cast. The directors set the schedule of dry-run readings, blocking, and precious on-camera time. Ten to 14 days for production became standard. The process for getting the scenery, lights, costumes, and untold tasks completed was extremely strenuous. Little wonder the harrowing experience was suitable for many returning veterans used to intense pressure.

Of the 12 major anthologies in existence in 1956, drama's peak year, only *Playhouse 90*, television's transition to the movies, was new and thriving. Of greater impact was what the public liked better, the half-hour and one-hour series formats which starred new faces who joined the family circle in homes across the nation — Molly Goldberg, Desi and Lucy, and a long list of actors who later became major motion picture stars. These personalities who seemed like "friends" the public cared about, or members of an extended family who viewers "knew," were welcomed week after week into homes. Television spread along both coasts after the war, reached the Midwest by 1950, and was linked coast to coast by 1951. As television spread north and south from AT&T's transcontinental link, Peoria, Illinois, got its first television station in 1953. Now television dramas would be appraised from the heartland.

The six years following the war encouraged three categories of actors: those established on television during the earlier decades, new talent being trained in New York, and those already famous from stage, radio, and film. While some radio actors were not suited to television, many major actors made the transition easily, though perhaps less visibly, and headlined television dramas. Numerous radio programs were adapted to television. Certainly Gertrude Berg as Molly Goldberg demonstrated that it was possible for a radio actor-writer to make this transition; William Bendix was memorable as Chester A. Riley; and Robert Casey as Henry Aldrich and numerous actors playing crime characters had respectable runs on television. Eddie Albert, Flora Campbell, Valerie Cossart, Stephen Courtleigh, Bramwell Fletcher, Jabez Gray, Vinton Hayworth, Leueen MacGrath, Mercer McLeod, John McQuade, Mary Patton, Margaret Phillips, Guy Spaull, Vaughn Taylor, and Philip Tonge were among those experienced actors who were on television before or during the war. They formed the cadre of dependable, inexpensive players who would be in leading roles one week and in supporting parts the next; they were the ones anthology producers could count on.

The excitement that television drama caused, however, came largely from new faces who were studying in professional schools, stock companies, and college drama departments, those who were yet to be discovered by television audiences. A few had sensational Broadway debuts, such as Brandon De Wilde in *The Member of the Wedding*, or other award recognition such as Jessica Tandy and Kim Hunter in *A Streetcar Named Desire*. Some older actors had their careers revitalized: Zero Mostel, Dean Jagger, E. G. Marshall, Ernest Truex, Robert Sterling, and cowboys William Boyd and Gabby Hayes. They enjoyed fame and fortune as television added new dimensions. But the majority of young performers were still waiting for opportunity in the wings or off-camera, and that's what live television gave them. As the demand grew, hundreds auditioned each week. At an early period in their careers were Warren Beatty, Janet Blair, Montgomery Clift, James Dean, Andrew Duggan, Faye Emerson, John Forsythe, Jackie Gleason, Julie Harris, Charlton Heston, Judy Holliday, Grace Kelly, Richard Kiley, Cloris Leachman, Jack Lemmon, Kevin McCarthy, Steve McQueen, Felicia Montealegre, Barry Nelson, John Newland, Leslie Nielsen, Eva Marie Saint, William Shatner, and Mary Sinclair, to mention a few. The Actors Studio, which had recently opened, trained a long list of talents involved in theater and television during these years, but whose ultimate showcase would be the movies.

Stars from stage and screen, who were not contractually prohibited, appeared in live dramas right away, among them: Judith Anderson, Fay Bainter, Freddie Bartholomew, Ralph Bellamy, Sidney Blackmer, Ronald Colman, Jackie Cooper, Hume Cronyn, Melvyn Douglas, Judith Evelyn, Jose Ferrer, Nina Foch, Lillian Gish, Rex Harrison, Edward Everett Horton, Marsha Hunt, Eva LeGallienne, Paul Lukas, Raymond Massey, Lon McCallister, Thomas Mitchell, Mildred Natwick, Lilli Palmer, and Basil Rathbone. These actors worked in all media. The debut of active major film stars — Madeleine Carroll, Brian Aherne — somewhat accelerated by producer/actor Robert Montgomery, at first was announced with fanfare as if some momentous decision had been made but, as the 1950s passed, their debuts, publicity notwithstanding, drew less attention.

Equally fascinating is the long and impressive list of producers, directors, and writers who were working in television during this apprentice period, learning the craft and gaining attention. Most of the early contributors remained with television throughout their careers. Some of the key figures in this first wave were Edward Sobol, Ernest Colling, Warren Wade, John F. Royal, Worthington Miner, Gilbert Seldes, Harvey Marlowe, and Bob Emery. Among the second postwar group of executives, producers, and directors were Kingman T. Moore, Victor McLeod, Alan J. Neuman, Garry Simpson, Hal Keith, Owen Davis, Jr., Donald Davis, Stanley Quinn, C. Maurice Holland, Gordon Duff, William McCleery, William Corrigan, and Paul Nickell. Although they may have continued to work throughout the 1950s, they remain best known for their distinguished efforts in early live television. Even Fred Coe (1914–1979), who produced some teleplays into films, such as *The Left-Handed Gun* (1958) and *The Miracle Worker* (1962), is best known as the mentor to many producer/directors through the *Philco/Goodyear Playhouse*. By contrast, Marc Daniels (1912–1989), who directed *Ford Television Theater* live, is better remembered for his filmed situation comedies, such as *I Love Lucy* (1951). George Schaefer (1920–1997), who made his mark with *The Hallmark Hall of Fame*, was also very proud of his filmed *Macbeth* (1963). And Alex Segal (1915–1977), who directed *Ransom* (1956) for his screen debut, is usually thought of as an award-winning director of live television dramas.

At lunch one day in the MGM commissary, Franklin Schaffner asked why some made it in Hollywood and others did not. There are as many explanations as there are individuals. An original teleplay that was adapted to the movies and became a big financial success was certainly a major part of it. Ambition, an intense interest in the film medium, and the point at which the person was in his career, including age and tap roots, were factors. Then, too, producers began to form their own small companies as the era of independent filmmakers began to bring new ideas and products outside of the great movie studios, and some had greater aptitude or stronger funding sources.

Frequently, long-lasting relationships between producers, directors, writers, and actors were established in the close proximity of New York's live studios. This mutual appreciation for talent and rapport led to important, sometimes seminal, films and telecasts. Ralph Nelson (1916–1987) is credited as actor, producer, or director for hundreds of television dramas, including Rod Serling's "Requiem for a Heavyweight" on television, which he used as his screen debut (1962). Franklin Schaffner (1920–1989), who started in news, began his eclectic film career with an adaptation of William Inge's play, *The Stripper* (1963) but returned to biographical drama for his

Academy Award winning *Patton* (1970). Delbert Mann's *Marty*, first on television in 1953, won Academy Awards for himself, screenwriter Paddy Chayefsky, and actor Ernest Borgnine after it became a 1955 movie. Sidney Lumet, whose work often depicts life on the streets of urban America, at the request of producer/actor Henry Fonda made his screen debut with *Twelve Angry Men* (1957), another adaptation from video. Arthur Penn, who first answered Fred Coe's call to direct *Philco Playhouse*, is undoubtedly better known for his seminal film *Bonnie and Clyde* (1967). Robert Mulligan's direction of Harper Lee's *To Kill a Mockingbird* (1962) enabled Gregory Peck and Horton Foote to win Academy Awards. These are only a few golden nuggets, so to speak, found in live television's rich mines.

Producers condensed all the literature that was fit to be seen, or so they thought, in those early days of what some have described as "public domain" television. Certainly, live television dramas gave viewers a quick study in Euro-American cultural heritage. In a single evening more people saw a Shakespearean play or an adaptation of a fine English novel, albeit condensed and sometimes changed, than had ever previously experienced the work in any form. Meanwhile, British productions paralleled those in the United States. The British created a distinct product in their own style, often more lavish than a similar adaptation in the United States, and they waited to find a proper entry into the American market. That unique opportunity came for them to reenforce their ties across the ocean. The "live" theatrical renaissance in New York and its British Broadcasting counterpart packaged programs for the well-educated, literate, and somewhat elitist populace that enjoyed complex and subtle dramas. These dramas, however, were slow to or failed to achieve sustained enthusiasm from mass audiences, as live television reached across the country. Educational television, which was beginning to appear and prosper, converted the famous three-foot bookshelf of classic works supposedly familiar to every educated person into an electronic précis generated from 1946 to 1952. American television drama's electronic versions of world literature would light up the screens of America, and through international outreach eventually those of the world, to impact all cultures far beyond the end of the century.

Notes

1. Experimental Television Drama, Origins to 1946

1. General Electric's WGY, Schenectady, New York, claims to have broadcast the first full-length drama on radio. It was "The Wolf," by Eugene Walter, presented by the Schenectady Players on 3 August 1922. The group became the WGY Players, and on 13 May 1924 they broadcast the first radio play over a "network" consisting of WGY, WJZ, New York, and WRC, Washington, D.C. On 11 September 1928, "The Queen's Messenger" by J. Hartley Manners became the first American television drama, with WGY providing the voice and its experimental W2XAF the video signals.

2. Grace Voss Frederick, interview by Nancy Hawes Wagner at Hopi House, Carefree, Maricopa County, Arizona, 22 June 1987.

3. Lou Frankel, "GE Fuels Future of Video with 'Showbiz' Telecast Plugs Neat, Talent Nifty," *The Billboard*, 13 November 1943, 12.

4. Judy Dupuy, *Television Show Business* (Schenectady, New York: General Electric, 1945).

2. Postwar Television Drama, 1946–1949

1. "Tele Increase Due May 5 When DuMont Tees Off Extra 90 Mins," *The Billboard*, 24 April 1943, 6; Lou Frankel, "GE Feels Future of Video, with 'Showbiz' Telecast Plugs Neat, Talent Nifty," *The Billboard*, 13 November 1943, 12.

2. "More Bosses for Video," *The Billboard*, 4 March 1944, 13; "Box Office's Job," *Business Week*, 17 June 1944, 94.

3. "Video Scaring Pic Biz," *The Billboard*, 29 April 1944, 3; *Time*, 17 May 1948, 91.

4. Transmission took place on 12 February 1946. In January 1947 the DuMont Network consisted of WABD, New York, WTTG, Washington, D.C., and WDTV, Pittsburgh. "DuMont Development Is Saga of Progress," *Television Daily* 12 April 1949, 21.

5. ABC-TV showed Rudolph Valentino films in 1948–49 with unexpected public interest. "The Busy Air," *Time*, 27 September 1948, 46. One reason was apparent a few months later: "Made before the days of the Hays Office, such old

films as *The Sheik* and *The Son of the Sheik* have a straight forward approach in their love scenes that shocks televiewers raised on tidied-up modern movies." *Time,* 7 March 1949, 68–69.

6. Ronald Coleman had agreed to narrate and act in 26 half-hour telefilms: 13 Charles Dickens and 13 Robert Louis Stevenson stories. *Time,* 21 June 1948, 77.

7. The "Big Five" film companies owned cinemas. "The Last Reel," *Time,* 18 February 1952, 102.

8. "In 1946 the American film business grossed $1.7 billion domestically, the peak box-office year in the 50-year history of the American film industry." Gerald Mast and Bruce Kawin, *A Short History of the Movies* (Boston, Mass.: Allyn and Bacon, 1996).

9. National Broadcasting Company, Annual Review, 1944–45, 33.

10. Joe Koehler, "Stem Shot Callers Tele-Rated," *The Billboard,* 15 June 1946, 19.

11. Ibid.

12. The FCC Freeze lasted from 29 September 1948 to 1 June 1952. The NTSC rules for color television were adopted on 17 December 1953. Sydney W. Head, *Broadcasting in America* (Boston, Mass.: Houghton Mifflin, 1972).

13. Worthington C. Miner, interview by author, Meurice Hotel, New York, August 1982.

14. "CBS Live Programming Ban Stirs Up Trade Queries; Effect Smalltown Operations Seen as Hurting Industry," *Variety,* 7 May 1947, 46.

15. Frank Stanton, "News From CBS," release, 17 February 1948.

16. "The Rise of Television," *Newsweek,* 20 December 1948, 50.

17. "Output of Sets, Color Ruling, Sponsors, '47 Tele Hurdles," *The Billboard,* 4 January 1947, 9.

18. Hyde, *Broadcasting in America,* 200.

19. *Newsweek,* 3 May 1948, 52.

20. "Seven Castles Serving the Nation," NBC, 1947.

21. With Sylvester L. Weaver as vice chairman of the NBC Board, NBC announced a series of experimental "color premieres" that would begin on 28 September 1953. "Color Television in Experimental NBC Network Broadcast...," *NBC Trade News,* 31 August 1953, 3.

22. "World's Largest TV Studio Dedicated as Production Center for NBC Color Television by New York's Mayor Wagner," *NBC Color Television News,* 10 September 1954, 2–3; "Construction of NBC's First West Coast Color Television Studio...," NBC news release, 7 April 1954.

23. "Tour of WCBW, CBS — Television," *Televiser,* November-December 1945, 14–15; Frank Stanton, *New from CBS,* 17 February 1948, 2.

24. Stanton, Ibid.

25. *News from CBS* (Claire Brown), 19 July 1949.

26. "This Is CBS Television City," Press Information, Television City, Hollywood, Calif., 15 November 1952.

27. "CBS Television City Today," *CBS Television Feature,* CBS Network, New York, 7 June 1954.

28. *The Billboard,* 12 April 1947, 14.

29. *Radio News,* December 1948, 47.

30. *The Billboard,* 11 October 1947, 3, 16, 18.

31. *Television,* January 1948, 12.

32. "The Death of the DuMont Network: A Real TV Whodunit," *Emmy Magazine*, July/August 1990, 100. Also, Gary Newton Hess, "An Historical Study of the DuMont Television Network" (Ph.D. dissertation, Evanston, Illinois: Northwestern University, 1960), 218.

33. Christopher H. Sterling and John M. Kittross, *Stay Tuned: A Concise History of American Broadcasting* (Belmont, Calif.: Wadsworth Publishing Company, 1978), 160.

34. Ibid., 211.

35. Ibid., 212.

36. "NBC Going Back on Six-Day Schedule," *Television*, April 1946, 24.

37. Sidney R. Lane, "Standard Brands' 'Hour Glass' Show," *Television*, October 1946, 12.

38. Saul Carson and Harold Wolff, "A Look at Television," *The New Republic*, 7 June 1948, 20.

39. "The Busy Air," *Time*, 27 September, 1948, 46.

40. Ibid.

41. "Top Acts from Other Showbiz Fields Flop in TV When Not Tuned to 'Mood of Home,'" *The Billboard*, 15 May 1947, 10.

42. *The Televiser*, May-June 1947, 36.

43. Saul Carson, "Radio: Theater on the Air," *The New Republic*, 24 November 1947, 37–38.

44. Warren Caro, "The Theatre Guild's Experience with Television," *The Televiser*, June 1948, 14.

45. "The Busy Air," *Time*, 10 May 1948, 85.

46. *The Billboard*, 10 May 1947, 14.

47. Edward Sobol, "Programming Primer," *Television*, September 1947, 21.

48. William I. Kaufman, ed., *The Best Television Plays of the Year* (New York: Merlin Press, 1950), 110. Includes "The Door."

49. "P&G Television," *Broadcasting-Telecasting*, 18 April 1949, 38; William Lafferty, "'No Attempt at Artiness, Profundity, or Significance': *Fireside Theatre* and the Economics of Early Television Drama," Conference paper, Dayton, Ohio: Wright State University, May 1986.

50. *News from CBS*, release, 2 April 1948; "Production News, 'Tonight on Broadway'—New Video Production," *The Televiser*, April 1948, 49.

51. CBS, press release (Claire Brown), 28 October 1949.

52. Leo Davis, "*SUSPENSE*," The Concept, A Half-Hour Film Series for CBS, 1949.

53. "Detective Story," CBS press release, 29 September 1949.

54. Kaufman, *Best Television Plays of the Year*, 166. Includes "The Goldbergs" (Composition Script).

55. "Meet Wesley," *CBS News*, 2 May 1949.

56. *Television Daily*, 12 April 1949, 23.

57. "Advertising," *Television*, July 1947, 29.

58. "Actor's Studio," CBS press release, 31 October 1949.

59. Charles C. Barry, "Tyrants of Television," *The Atlantic Monthly*, April 1949, 42.

60. Tennessee Williams, *Tennessee Williams: Memoirs* (Garden City, New York: Doubleday, 1983), 131–32.

61. Kaufman, *The Best Television Plays of the Year*, 79. Includes "Zone of Quiet" script.

62. *Legacy of the Hollywood Blacklist*, a documentary by Judy Chaikin. One Step Productions/KCET, Los Angeles/Community Television of Southern California, 1987.

63. Robert Slater, *This Is CBS: A Chronicle of 60 Years* (Englewood Cliffs, N.J.: Prentice Hall, 1988), 135–36.

64. Sterling and Kittross, *Stay Tuned*, 307.

65. *The Catholic World*, June 1951, 225–26.

66. Saul Carson, "Electronic Curtain," *The New Republic*, 19 June 1950, 22.

67. Slater, *This Is CBS*, 137.

68. Saul Carson, "The Aldrich Family," *The New Republic*, 25 December 1950, 21.

69. Ibid.

70. William H. Shriver, Jr., "Radio and Television," *The Catholic World*, November 1950, 144–46.

3. NBC Anthologies: Kraft Television Theatre and Philco Television Playhouse

1. Stanley Quinn, interview by Dana Ulloth, University of Connecticut, transcript, 31 July 1979, 28. Washington, D.C.: Broadcast Pioneers Library, National Association of Broadcasters.

2. Garry Simpson, letter to author, 10 March 1998.

3. *Variety*, 14 May 1947, 38.

4. "Kraft Tele Theater: 'Double Door,'" *The Televiser*, May-June, 1947, 36.

5. *Television*, November 1947, 27.

6. Garry Simpson, letter to author, op. cit.

7. Stanley Quinn, interview transcript, 32.

8. Harry Herrmann, interview by Dana Ulloth, University of Connecticut, transcript, 15 August 1979, 22. Washington, D.C.: Broadcast Pioneers Library, National Association of Broadcasters.

9. Ibid., 27.

10. "Radio and Television: The Common Touch," *Time*, 3 April 1950, 44.

11. Ibid.

12. Stanley Quinn, interview transcript, 29.

13. Philip Hamburger, "Television," *The New Yorker*, 27 May 1950, 92.

14. Philip Hamburger, "Television," *The New Yorker*, 1 July 1950, 53.

15. Robert Lewis Shayon, "Radio and Television," *The Saturday Review of Literature*, 24 March 1951, 28.

16. Ibid.

17. William H. Shriver, Jr., "Radio and Television," *The Catholic World*, June 1951, 226.

18. Philip Hamburger, "Television," *The New Yorker*, 4 October 1952, 116.

19. Philip Hamburger, "Television," *The New Yorker*, 7 February 1953, 74.

20. "Satisfied Customers," *Time*, 28 September 1953, 69.

21. "Film vs. Live Shows," *Time*, 29 March 1954, 77.

22. *Time*, 6 December 1954, 85.

23. *Time*, 13 December 1954, 36.

24. "The Week in Review," *Time*, 27 December 1954, 52.

25. "The Busy Air," *Time*, 10 January 1955, 49.

26. Quoted in *Time*, 24 January 1955, 39. Rod Serling repeated this view in an interview at his Houston, Texas, hotel, 16 March 1974.

27. Quoted in *Time*, 21 February, 1955, 64.

28. *Time*, 25 July 1955, 66.

29. *Time*, 12 September 1955, 79.

30. *Time*, 20 February 1956, 56.

31. William Noble, "Snapfinger Creek" in *Best Television Plays 1957*, Florence Britton, ed. (New York: Ballentine Books, 1957). Noble and James Leo Herlihy wrote *Blue Denim*, 1958, a successful Broadway play and feature film.

32. "The Week in Review," *Time*, 9 April 1956, 106.

33. "Live and Lively; Kraft Television Theater," *Newsweek*, 29 July 1957, 82.

34. Paul E. Chandler, public relations manager, Kraft Foods Company, letter to author, 28 July 1958.

35. "Show Business," *Time*, 16 March 1959, 65.

36. *WNBT Television Master Programs, Philco Television Playhouse*, 3 October 1948.

37. "The Rise of Television," *Newsweek*, 20 December 1948, 52.

38. Harry Herrmann, interview transcript, 31.

39. Saul Carson, "On the Air," *The New Republic*, 21 March 1949, 28.

40. Delbert Mann, interview by author at Mann's residence, Los Angeles, California, 10 November 1981.

41. Robert J. Wade, "Setting the Stage," *Theatre Arts*, June 1949, 43.

42. Delbert Mann, "Remembering," a 1200-page unpublished manuscript. Published as *Looking Back...at Live Television and Other Matters*, by Delbert Mann (Los Angeles, California: Directors Guild of America, 1998), 8.

43. "GBS vs. TV," *Newsweek*, 31 July 1950, 52.

44. Delbert Mann, interview, op. cit.

45. Ibid.

46. Dorothy McBride, NBC Continuity Acceptance, wrote Gordon Duff a memo on 11 November 1949: "We want to thank you and Fred for your wonderful cooperation."

47. Delbert Mann, "Remembering," 24–26.

48. Ira Skutch occasionally provided some relief by directing two or three dramas.

49. Delbert Mann, "Remembering," 29.

50. Harriet Van Horne, "Entertainment," *Holiday*, January 1950, 7–11.

51. Delbert Mann, "Remembering," 39.

52. Comments by Arthur Penn, Great Lakes Theater Festival, Cleveland, Ohio, 6 October 1990.

53. "A Remembrance of Pappy: Fred Coe —1914–1979," a program of tribute, Tennessee Performing Arts Center, Nashville, Tennessee, 8 September 1980.

54. Saul Carson, "On the Air," *The New Republic*, 27 February 1950, 23.

55. Norman Corwin, interview by author at Scottsdale Community College, Arizona, 12 February 1987. Corwin was perhaps radio's most distinguished dramatist. He said he did not remember seeing any of his work on television in the 1940s.

56. Philip Hamburger, "Television," *The New Yorker*, 18 March 1950, 82.

57. Saul Carson, "On the Air," *The New Republic*, 19 June 1950, 22.

58. Philip Hamburger, "Television," *The New Yorker*, 1 July 1950, 52–53.

59. Jack Gould, "Radio and Television in Review," *The New York Times*, 24 July 1950, 34.

60. "Noble Experiment," *Time*, 4 September 1950, 61.

61. Ibid.

62. Max Wilk, *The Golden Age of Television: Notes from the Survivors* (New York: Delacorte, 1976). Includes chapters on *Ford Television Theatre*, *Studio One*, *Mama*, *Suspense*, *The Web*, *Danger*, and *Philco Playhouse*.

63. Robert Lewis Shayon, "TV and Radio," *The Saturday Review of Literature*, 24 March 1951, 28.

64. *WNBT Television Master Programs*, *Philco Television Playhouse*, 22 April 1951.

65. Jay Caron, "Free-Lancing for Television," *The Writer*, July 1951, 220.

66. "The Play's the Thing on TV," *Life*, 12 November 1951, 108.

67. "Realism Is Keynote of 'Search,'" *NBC Feature*, press release, 25 November 1952, 1.

68. Lillian Gish with Ann Pinchot, *The Movies, Mr. Griffith, and Me* (Englewood Cliffs, New Jersey: Prentice-Hall, 1969), 362.

69. Gore Vidal, "Television Drama, Circa 1956," *Theatre Arts*, December 1956, 85.

70. Tad Mosel, *Other People's Houses* (New York: Simon and Schuster, 1956), 38.

71. Tad Mosel, interview at his residence by author, New York City, 9 August 1982.

72. Delbert Mann, "Remembering," 136.

73. "Robert Alan Aurthur," *NBC Trade News*, 3 February 1953.

74. "Radio and Television," *Time*, 12 September 1955, 79.

75. "The Week in Review," *Time*, 4 April 1955, 64.

76. "The Week in Review," *Time*, 27 December 1954, 52.

77. Paddy Chayefsky, *Television Plays* (New York: Simon and Schuster, 1955), xii.

78. "Bride in the Bronx," *Life*, 6 June 1955, 117–18.

79. Chayefsky, *Television Plays*, xii.

80. Ibid., 173–79.

81. Horton Foote, interview at his residence by author, Wharton, Texas, 19 June 1986; Horton Foote, *Harrison, Texas* (New York: Harcourt, Brace, 1956), vii–viii.

82. Gore Vidal, *Visit To a Small Planet* (Boston, Massachusetts: Little, Brown, 1956).

83. "Four Out of Top Five, Seven Out of Top Ten," *NBC Trade News*, 17 February 1954.

84. "The Week in Review," *Time*, 30 August 1954, 55.

85. "The Week in Review," *Time*, 30 April 1956, 91–92.

4. CBS Anthologies: Ford Theater and Studio One

1. Richard Goggin, transcript, AT #1333, Broadcast Pioneers Library, Washington, D.C., 29 April 1988.

2. Marc Daniels, interview at his residence by author, Studio City, California, 11 and 13 November 1981.

3. Ibid.

4. "Winston O'Keefe Takes Over as Producer of CBS-TV 'Ford Theater,'" CBS press release, 13 January 1950.

5. Max Wilk wrote many plays as well as *The Golden Age of Television: Notes from the Survivors* (New York: Delacorte, 1976).

6. CBS press release, 10 March 1950.

7. "Ford's TV 'Dear Brutus,'" *Newsweek*, 3 April 1950, 48–49.

8. Philip Hamburger, "Television," *The New Yorker*, 29 April 1950, 58.

9. Marc Daniels, interview, op. cit.

10. Ibid.

11. "Subway Special," *Newsweek*, 29 May 1950, 48.

12. Marc Daniels, "Always the First Time," *Theatre Arts*, February 1950, 46–48.

13. "Radio and Television. The Body Eater," *Time*, 28 May 1950, 60.

14. CBS press release, 6 September 1950.

15. Worthington C. Miner, "Look Back in Wonder," a manuscript transcribed from an interview by Franklin J. Schaffner, 1980, 235.

16. Worthington C. Miner, interview by author at the Meurice Hotel, New York, August 1982. *The Ed Sullivan Show* was first broadcast in 1931, when Sullivan was a columnist for the *New York Graphic*. That show was credited with the first appearances of Jack Benny, George M. Cohan, and Irving Berlin.

17. Robert J. Landry, interview in his *Variety* office by author, New York, 18 September 1981.

18. Worthington C. Miner, interview, op. cit.

19. "High Polish," *Time*, 26 December 1949, 43.

20. Miner, "Look Back in Wonder," 289.

21. Paul Nickell, interview at his residence by author, Chapel Hill, North Carolina, 29 July 1982, transcript, 2.

22. Miner, "Look Back in Wonder," 291; Paul Nickell, interview transcript, 6.

23. Saul Carson, "On the Air," *The New Republic*, 21 March 1949, 28.

24. Jack Gould, "The Honor Roll," *The New York Times*, 1 January 1950, 9.

25. Kaufman, *The Best Television Plays of the Year*, "The Battleship Bismarck," 257.

26. Paul Nickell, interview transcript, 11.

27. Ibid., 14.

28. Franklin Schaffner, interview in the Metro-Goldwyn-Mayer Commissary by author, Culver City, California, 16 November 1981. From the transcript, 7.

29. "High Polish," *Time*, 26 December 1949, 42.

30. Franklin Schaffner, interview transcript, 8.

31. Miner, "Look Back in Wonder," 303.

32. "Speaking of Television ... Putting on a Studio One Show Is a Ten-Week Job," CBS press release, 16 January 1950.

33. Philip Hamburger, "Television," *The New Yorker*, 27 May 1950, 92.

34. Robert Lewis Shayon, "TV and Radio," *The Saturday Review of Literature*, 24 March 1951, 28.

35. Worthington C. Miner, interview, op. cit.; Charlton Heston at Town & Country Cinema, Houston, Texas, 1982.

36. Robert Kass, "Film and Television," *The Catholic World*, December 1951, 224–25.

37. "Television Magazine's Network Program Report," *Television*, October 1952, 20–21.

38. "Snow Job," *Time*, 10 March 1952, 97.

39. Worthington C. Miner, interview, op. cit.

40. Miner, "Look Back in Wonder," op. cit.

41. "Each Production of CBS-TV's 'Studio One' Averages 10 Weeks of Grueling Preparation," *CBS Television Feature*, 17 September 1952, 3.

42. "CBS-TV's New 'Solid Scenery' Makes Its Debut...," *CBS News*, 22 September 1952.

43. "CBS-TV's Jackie Gleason in Dramatic Debut on 'Studio One,'" *CBS News*, 23 April 1953.

44. "Hour of Gloom," *Time*, 5 October 1953, 80.

45. Reginald Rose, *Six Television Plays* (New York: Simon Schuster, 1956), Foreword.

46. Ibid., 108.

47. "Radio & Television," *Time*, 22 November 1954, 54.

48. "Picking the Best," *Newsweek*, 12 December 1955, 108.

49. Rod Serling, op cit.

50. "The Tall Gambler," *Time*, 20 December 1954, 45.

51. Paul Nickell, interview transcript, 18.

52. "'Studio One': Franklin Schaffner's Camera 'Report' the Dramatic," *CBS Television Feature*, 26 April 1955.

53. "Robert Herridge Named Producer of 'Westinghouse Summer Theater,'" CBS press release, 15 February 1956.

54. "Radio & Television," *Time*, 2 July 1956, 60.

55. CBS press release, 11 January 1957.

56. "The Week in Review," *Time*, 4 February 1957, 65.

57. Horton Foote, interview, op. cit.

58. "One Hit, Four Errors," *Time*, 6 May 1957, 53.

59. "Key Critic," *Time*, 1 July 1957, 65.

60. "Radio & Television," *Time*, 4 November 1957, 57.

5. The Competitors: 1950–1952

1. "'Bigelow Theatre' Featuring Top Broadway and Hollywood Stars...," *CBS News* (Claire Bloom), 29 November 1950.

2. Jack Gould, "Programs in Review," *The New York Times*, 2 July 1950, 7.

3. Saul Carson, "On the Air," *The New Republic*, 13 February 1950, 28.

4. Philip Hamburger, "Television," *The New Yorker*, 18 March 1950, 95.

5. "Slowdown, Showdown," *Newsweek*, 24 April 1950, 55.

6. Philip Hamburger, "Television," *The New Yorker*, 10 June 1950, 70.

7. Ibid.

8. William H. Shriver, Jr., "Radio and Television," *The Catholic World*, December 1950, 224.

9. Philip Hamburger, "Television," *The New Yorker*, 3 February 1951, 3.

10. Robert Lewis Shayon, "TV and Radio," *The Saturday Review of Literature*, 24 March 1951, 28.

11. Philip Hamburger, "Television," *The New Yorker*, 2 June 1951, 84.

12. Robert Lewis Shayon, "TV and Radio," *The New Yorker*, 21 April 1951, 31.

13. "O'Hara's Hotel," *Newsweek*, 21 January 1952, 83.

14. Philip Hamburger, "Television," *The New Yorker*, 20 September 1952, 116–18.

15. "The Week in Review," *Time*, 6 September 1954, 58.

16. Hallmark Hall of Fame, press release, April 1968, 3–4.

17. *WNBT Television Master Programs*, 24 December 1951.

18. Hallmark Hall of Fame, press release, April 1968, 2.

19. George Schaefer, interview in his office by author, Century City, California, 10 November 1981.

20. "Greeting Card Hamlet," *Newsweek*, 11 May 1953, 69.

21. "'Hallmark Hall of Fame' Starting New Season, Is Expanded To Full-Hour Format, Originating in Hollywood," *NBC Trade News*, 11 September 1953.

22. "Sarah Churchill Returns as Hostess in New 'Hallmark Hall of Fame,'" *NBC Trade News*, 19 August 1953.

23. "Beautiful Words," *Time*, 7 December 1953, 96.

24. Ibid.

25. George Schaefer, interview, op. cit.

26. "Maurice Evans To Re-create His Most Famous Role...," *NBC Trade News*, 25 November 1953, 2.

27. "Horses, Ships, & Kings," *Time*, 1 February 1954, 59.

28. "It looks so very simple on the screen," Foote, Cone and Belding, 1966.

29. "Maurice Evans and Judith Anderson To Star in 2-Hour Colorcast...," *NBC Trade News*, 27 September 1954, 2.

30. "Television & Radio," *Time*, 30 December 1957, 38.

31. George Schaefer, interview, op. cit.

32. Ibid.

33. Byron Bentley, "No Time for Playwrights," *Theatre Arts*, December 1955, 96.

34. "The Week in Review," *Time*, 21 May 1956, 89.

35. "Television & Radio," *Time*, 1 April 1957, 40.

36. "Television & Radio," *Time*, 21 October 1957, 58.

37. "Plays and People," *Newsweek*, 15 October 1951, 51.

38. Ibid.

39. Ibid.

40. "The Play's the Thing on TV," *Life*, 12 November 1951, 106.

41. Robert Kass, "Film and TV," *The Catholic World*, January 1952, 306.

42. "Drama for an Hour," *Time*, 5 May 1952, 88.

43. Saul Carson, "On the Air," *The New Republic*, 21 January 1952, 22.

44. "Biggest Week," *Newsweek*, 16 October 1950, 54.

45. Saul Carson, "On the Air," *The New Republic*, 7 January 1952, 21.

46. Robert Kass, "Film and TV," *The Catholic World*, January 1952, 307.

47. Ibid., 306.

48. "Experiment in Realism," *Time*, 31 December 1951, 47.

49. Philip Hamburger, "Television," *The New Yorker*, 6 September 1952, 63.

50. "Delicacy & Violence," *Time*, 26 June 1950, 49.

51. Philip Hamburger, "Television," *The New Yorker*, 22 July 1950, 46.

52. Ibid.

53. "'Columbia Television Workshop' Makes Debut Jan. 13...," *CBS News*, 27 December 1951.

54. *Television*, December 1950, 8.

55. "Jamila Novotna Starred in First Colorcast of 'Armstrong Circle Theatre' on Feb. 23," *NBC Color Television News*, 12 February 1954.

56. "'The Parrot,' Original Opera on Circle Theatre...," *NBC News Feature*, 17 March 1953.

57. Myron Berkely Shaw, "A Descriptive Analysis of the Documentary Drama Program: Armstrong Circle Theatre, 1955–1961," Ph.D dissertation, University of Michigan, 1962.

58. A. William Bluem, *Documentary in American Television* (New York: Hastings House, 1965), 193.

59. *The Best of Armstrong Circle Theatre*, adapted by Trudy and Irving Settel (New York: The Citadel Press, 1959); Kaufman, *Best Television Plays 1957*.

60. Walter B. Emery, *National and International Systems of Broadcasting: Their History Operation and Control* (East Lansing, Mich.: Michigan State University Press, 1969).

61. William Hawes, *American Television Drama: The Experimental Years* (University, Alabama: The University of Alabama Press, 1986), 30.

62. *BBC Handbook* (London: British Broadcasting Corporation Broadcasting House, 1955), 26–27.

63. Principal source: *BBC Programmes as Broadcast*, 1947–1952.

Appendix A

BBC Television Dramas Relevant to American Television, 1946–1951

1946

7 June 1946 — 2:30p Official reopening of the BBC London Television Service. Programming includes music, ballet, variety, films, and dramas.

  8:43–10:10 "The Importance of Being Earnest," by Oscar Wilde. *Cast:* Robert Eddison, Mackenzie Ward, David Horne, Dorothy Hyson, Margaret Rutherford. Presented by George More O'Ferrall.

11 June 1946— 8:30 "Dangerous Corner," by J. B. Priestley. *Cast:* Lydia Sherwood, Judy Campbell, Joy Shelton, Ivan Samson, D. A. Clarke-Smith.

23 June 1946— 8:30 "Saint Joan," Part I, by George Bernard Shaw. *Cast:* Basil Langston, Anne Casson. Presented by George More O'Ferrall.

30 June 1946— 8:38 "Saint Joan," Part II.

July 1946— 8:45 "The Ringer," by Edgar Wallace. *Cast:* Wallace Douglas, Edmund Williard. Presented by Royston Morley.

July 1946— 8:30 "Anna Christie," by Eugene O'Neill. *Cast:* Monica McGrath, Frank Foster. Presented by Fred O'Donovan.

24 July 1946— 2:30 "A Midsummer Night's Dream," by William Shakespeare. From Open Air Theatre, Regents Park. Presented by Harold Cox.

15 September 1946— 8:38 "The Corn Is Green," by Emlyn Williams. *Cast:* Kenneth Evans, Judith Fellows. Presented by John Glyn-Jones.

16 September 1946— 8:30 "All God's Chillun Got Wings," by Eugene O'Neill. *Cast:* Robert Adams, Connie Smith. Presented by Eric Fawcett.

27 September 1946— 8:30–10:01 "Jane Eyre," by Charlotte Brontë, adapted by Helen Jerome. *Cast:* Mary Mackenzie, Anthony Hawtrey. Presented by Howard Clayton.

6 October 1946— 8:30 "Candida," by George Bernard Shaw. *Cast:* Angela Baddeley. Presented by Fred O'Donovan.

3 November 1946— 8:54 "Androcles and the Lion," by George Bernard Shaw. *Cast:* Victor Woolf, Andrew Leigh, Pauline Letts. Presented by Desmond Davis.

21 **December 1946**— 9:15 "Alice in Wonderland," by Lewis Carroll, dramatized by Clemence Dane. *Cast:* Vivian Pickles. Presented by George More O'Ferrall.

22 **December 1946**— 8:30 "Arms and the Man," by George Bernard Shaw. *Cast:* Rosemary Scott, Netta Westcott, Andre Morell. Presented by Harold Clayton.

1947

5 **January 1947**— 8:41 "Rope," by Patrick Hamilton. Presented by Stephen Harrison.

6 **January 1947**— 6:46 "Jack and the Beanstalk," Part 1, from the Grand Theatre, Croydon.

19 **January 1947**— 8:30 "Rebecca," by Daphne du Maurier. *Cast:* Michael Hordern, Dorothy Gordon, Dorothy Black.

6 **February 1947**— 8:30–21:57 "The Two Mrs. Carrolls," by Martin Vale. Presented by Ian Atkins.

9 **February 1947**— 8:49–22:01 "Cry Havoc," by Allan R. Kenward. Presented by George More O'Ferrall.

11 **March 1947**— 8:30–8:35 "Outward Bound," by Sutton Vane. *Cast:* Oliver Johnston, Ralda Herring, Don MacAlister. Presented by Joel O'Brien.

13 **March 1947**— 8:41–22:05 "Laburnum Grove," by J. B. Priestley. *Cast:* Wilfred Hyde-White, Terry Randall. Presented by Ian Atkins.

20 **March 1947**— 8:20 "The Cherry Orchard," by Anton Tchekhov, translated by S. S. Koteliansky. *Cast:* Marian Spencer, Irmgard Spoliansky, Jack Livesey, Sebastian Cabot, Oliver Johnston, Margot Van Der Burgh.

23 **March 1947**— 8:30–22:15 "The Man Who Came to Dinner," by Moss Hart and George S. Kaufman. *Cast:* Janet Morrison, Jean St. Clair, Frank Pettingell. Presented by Joel O'Brien.

27 **March 1947**— 9:09–9:56 "The Valiant," by Holworthy Hall and Robert Middlemass. *Cast:* Andrew Osborn, Rene Ray. Presented by Joel O'Brien.

30 **March 1947**— 8:36–10:22 "Mourning Becomes Electra," Part I, by Eugene O'Neill. *Cast:* Mary Newcomb, Ralph Michael, Basil C. Langton, Marjorie Mars. Presented by Royston Morley.

4 **April 1947**— 8:30 "Everyman." *Cast:* Andre Morell, Margaret Leighton.

10 **April 1947**— 8:30 "Mourning Becomes Electra," Part II.

4 **May 1947**— 8:30 "Mr. Mergenthwirker's Lobblies," by Nelson Bond and David Kent. *Cast:* MacDonald Parke, Presented by Eric Fawcett.

18 **May 1947**— 8:30 "You Can't Take It With You," by Moss Hart and George S. Kaufman. *Cast:* Bessie Love. Presented by Joel O'Brien.

8 **June 1947**— 8:30 "A Month in the Country," by Ivan Turgenev, translated by Emlyn Williams. *Cast:* Winifred Oughton, Leo de Pokorny.

17 **June 1947**— 8:30–9:56 "Henry IV," by Luigi Pirandello, translated by Edward Storer. *Cast:* Ralph Michael. Presented by Royston Morley.

19 **June 1947**— 8:30–9:59 "He Who Gets Slapped," by Leonid Andreyev, translated by Judith Gutherie. Presented by Jan Bussell.

22 **June 1947**— 8:41 "The Tragical History of Doctor Faustus," by Christopher Marlowe, *Cast:* David King-Wood, Hugh Griffith. Presented by Stephen Harrison.

24 **June 1947**— 8:30–10:10 "The Bad Man," by Porter Emerson Browne. *Cast:* Robert Ayres, Charles Irwin, Ben Williams, Carla Lehmann, Charles Farrell, Charles Rolfe, Zena Foster, Richard Molinas, Leo de Pokorny. Presented by Eric Fawcett.

27 June 1947 — 7:15 "The Family Upstairs," by Harry Delf, from the Intimate Theatre, Palmers Green.

1 July 1947 — 8:31–10:07 "The Merchant of Venice," by William Shakespeare. *Cast:* Abraham Sofaer, Margaretta Scott. Presented by George More O'Ferrall.

20 July 1947 — 8:30–21:57 "The Cradle Song," by Gregario and Maria Martinez Sierra, translated by John Garret Underhill. Presented by Harold Clayton.

24 July 1947 — 8:30 "Gaslight," by Patrick Hamilton. *Cast:* Anthony Ireland, Catherine Lacey, Milton Rosmer. Presented by Stephen Harrison.

28 July 1947 — 7:30 "A Midsummer Night's Dream," Part I, from the Open Air Theatre, Regents Park.

17 August 1947 — 8:30 "Double Door," by Elizabeth McFadden. *Cast:* Ellen Pollock. Presented by Joel O'Brien.

28 August 1947 — 8:30 "Quality Street," by James M. Barrie.

5 October 1947 — 8:30 "Romeo and Juliet," by William Shakespeare. *Cast:* John Bailey, Rosalie Crutchley. Presented by Michael Barry.

11 October 1947 — 9:49 "The Round Dozen," by W. Somerset Maugham, adapted by Gilbert Thomas. Presented by Ian Atkins.

19 October 1947 — 8:31 "The Infernal Machine," by Jean Cocteau, translated by Carl Wildman. Presented by Royston Morley.

23 October 1947 — 8:32 "Trilby," by George du Maurier, dramatized by Paul M. Potter. *Cast:* Sally Rogers.

26 October 1947 — 9:36–10:07 "End of the Beginning," by Sean O'Casey. Presented by Kenneth Buckley.

6 November 1947 — 8:31 "Sweeney Todd, the Demon Barber of Fleet Street," by George Diblin Pitt, adapted by John Glyn-Jones. *Cast:* Valentine Dyall. Presented by Glyn-Jones.

20 November 1947 — 9:01 "Victoria Regina," by Laurence Housman.

7 December 1947 — 8:30 "Hamlet," Part I, by William Shakespeare, adapted by George More O'Ferrall. *Cast:* John Byron, Sebastian Shaw, Arthur Wontner, Margaret Rawlings, Muriel Pavlow. Presented by George More O'Ferrall.

14 December 1947 — 8:30 "Hamlet," Part II, by William Shakespeare. Presented by George More O'Ferrall.

1948

8 January 1948 — 8:30–22:01 "A Woman of No Importance," by Oscar Wilde. *Cast:* Angela Braddeley. Presented by Stephen Harrison.

13 January 1948 — 7:00–10:29 "The Winslow Boy," by Terence Rattigan, from the Intimate Theatre, Palmers Green. Produced by J. Grant Anderson. Presented by Campbell Logan.

15 January 1948 — 8:30 "The Adding Machine," by Elmer Rice. Presented by Eric Fawcett.

8 February 1948 — 8:00 "Pygmalion," by George Bernard Shaw. *Cast:* Margaret Lockwood, Gordon Harker, Ralph Michael.

12 February 1948 — 8:30 "Gaslight," by Patrick Hamilton. *Cast:* Sebastian Shaw, Angela Baddeley, John Turnbull.

7 March 1948 — 8:30 "Wuthering Heights," by Emily Brontë, adapted by George More O'Ferrall. *Cast:* Kieron Moore, Katherine Blake. Presented by O'Ferrall.

17 March 1948 — 9:44 "The Shadow of the Glen," by John M. Synge.

2 May 1948 — 8:30 "Loyalties," by John Galsworthy, adapted by John Glyn-Jones. Presented by Glyn-Jones.

4 May 1948 — 8:31 "An Inspector Calls," by J. B. Priestley. *Cast:* George Hayes, Julian Mitchell, Mary Merrall, Joy Shelton.

1 June 1948 — 8:30 "The Guardsman," by Ferenc Molnar, translated by Grace I. Colbron and Hans Bartsch. Presented by Stephen Harrison.

6 June 1948 — 8:55 "The Breadwinner," by W. Somerset Maugham, adapted by John Glyn-Jones. *Cast:* Nicholas Hannen, Joyce Barbour. Presented by Glyn-Jones.

13 June 1948 — 8:36 "Berkeley Square," by John L. Balderston.

20 June 1948 — 8:30 "Arms and the Man," by George Bernard Shaw. *Cast:* Margaret Leighton, Cyril Raymond. Presented by Harold Clayton.

27 June 1948 — 8:30 "Volpone," by Ben Johnson. *Cast:* Cecil Trouncer, Alan Wheatley. Presented by Stephen Harrison.

4 July 1948 — 8:30 "Home and Beauty," by W. Somerset Maugham.

7 July 1948 — 9:28 "Red Peppers," by Noël Coward. *Cast:* Patricia Burke, Graham Payn. Presented by Michael Mills.

11 July 1948 — 8:30 "Mourning Becomes Electra," Part I, repeated.

15 July 1948 — 8:32 "Mourning Becomes Electra," Part II, repeated.

6 August 1948 — 8:37 "The Truth about Blayds," by A. A. Milne. *Cast:* Henry Oscar, Avice Landone.

8 August 1948 — 8:31 "The Dover Road," by A. A. Milne. *Cast:* George Bishop, Richard Hurndall, Iris Russell.

15 August 1948 — 8:30 "Front Page," by Ben Hecht and Charles MacArthur. *Cast:* Sidney James, Marjorie Gordon. Presented by Joel O'Brien.

22 August 1948 — 8:30 "King Lear," Part I, by William Shakespeare. *Cast:* William Devlin, Alan Wheatley, Robert Sansom, Henry Oscar. Presented by Royston Morley and Douglas Allen.

29 August 1948 — 8:30 "King Lear," Part II, by William Shakespeare.

31 August 1948 — 8:30 "The Unattainable," by W. Somerset Maugham. Presented by Stephen Harrison.

12 September 1948 — 8:30 "The Circle," by W. Somerset Maugham. Presented by Campbell Logan.

26 September 1948 — 8:30 "Jane Eyre," by Charlotte Brontë, dramatized by Helen Jerome, adapted by Harold Clayton. *Cast:* Barbara Mullen, Reginald Tate. Presented by Clayton.

10 October 1948 — 4:00–5:16 "Androcles and the Lion," by George Bernard Shaw. Presented by Jan Bussell.

14 November 1948 — 8:30 "The Rivals," by Richard Brinsley Sheridan.

16 November 1948 — 8:30 "Blithe Spirit," by Noël Coward. *Cast:* Frank Lawton, Marian Spencer, Betty Ann Davies, Beryl Measer. Presented by George More O'Ferrall.

30 December 1948 — 3:00 "Alice in Wonderland," by Lewis Carroll, adapted by Herbert M. Prentice. *Cast:* Margaret Barton.

1949

2 January 1949 — 8:30 "The Importance of Being Earnest," by Oscar Wilde. *Cast:* William Fox, Anthony Ireland, Edith Evans, Joan Greenwood. Presented by Harold Clayton.

16 January 1949 — 8:30 "Counsellor-at-Law," by Elmer Rice. Presented by Eric Fawcett.

24 January 1949 — 9:39 "The Merchant of Venice," (Trial Scene). Presented by Desmond Davis.

6 February 1949 — 8:31 "The Silver Cord," by Sidney Howard. *Cast:* Helen Haye.

20 February 1949 — 8:30 "The Tragedy of Macbeth," by William Shakespeare. *Cast:* Stephen Anthony, Ruth Lodge.

23 February 1949 — 8:30 "The Linden Tree," J. B. Priestley. Presented by Kevin Sheldon.

2 May 1949 — 7:01 "She Stoops to Conquer," by Oliver Goldsmith. From The Arts Theatre. Presented by Campbell Logan.

8 May 1949 — 8:31 "Whiteoaks," by Mazo de la Roche. Presented by Douglas Allen.

30 May 1949 — 9:19 "The Browning Version," by Terence Rattigan. *Cast:* The Phoenix Theatre Company. Presented by Campbell Logan.

10 June 1949 — 8:46 "Witness for the Prosecution," by Agatha Christie, adapted by Sidney W. Budd.

10 July 1949 — 8:31 "When We Are Married," by J. B. Priestley. Presented by John Glyn-Jones.

26 July 1949 — 8:12 "The Devil's Disciple," by George Bernard Shaw.

6 August 1949 — 8:31 "The Perfect Alibi," by A. A. Milne. *Cast:* Denis Gordon, Honor Shepherd. Presented by Joel O'Brien.

9 August 1949 — 9:05 "The Mollusc," by Hubert Henry Davies. *Cast:* Vivienne Bennett, Patrick Waddington. Presented by Campbell Logan.

20 August 1949 — 8:31 "Ten Little Niggers," by Agatha Christie.

30 August 1949 — 8:31 "Mr. Mergenthwirker's Lobblies," by Nelson Bond and David Kent. Produced by Eric Fawcett.

13 September 1949 — 8:30 "Ladies in Waiting," by Cyril Campion. *Cast:* Rosalie Crutchley, Tonia Heldreth, Anne Rawsthorne. Produced by Joy Harington.

2 October 1949 — 8:30 "Dangerous Corner," J. B. Priestley. *Cast:* Helen Shingler, Greta Gynt, Mary Lincoln, Jen Wright, Jack Livesey. Presented by Joel O'Brien.

6 October 1949 — 9:39 "Edgar Allan Poe Centenary," includes "The Cask of Amontillado," "Some Words with a Mummy," and "The Fall of the House of Usher," adapted and devised by Joan Maude and Michael Ware.

18 October 1949 — 8:31 "Antigone," by Jean Anouilh, adapted by Lewis Galantiere. *Cast:* Irene Worth. Presented by Harold Clayton.

11 November 1949 — 8:30 "Pagliacci," a drama in two acts with words and music by R. Leoncavallo.

15 November 1949 — 8:31 "The Silver Box," by John Galsworthy.

20 November 1949 — 8:57 "Trelawney of the Wells," by Arthur Wing Pinero. Produced by Michael Barry.

4 December 1949 — 8:35 "The Duchess of Malfi," by John Webster. *Cast:* Irene Worth, David King-Wood. Produced by Stephen Harrison.

18 December 1949 — 8:30 "The Winslow Boy," by Terence Rattigan. Presented by Royston Morley.

27 December 1949 — 8:31 "The Long Christmas Dinner," by Thornton Wilder. *Cast:* Barbara Kelly, Guy Kingsley Poynter, Natalie Lynn, Henry Worthington. Produced by Kevin Sheldon.

1950

2 January 1950— 5:32 "Little Women," Part III, by Louisa May Alcott. *Cast:* Sheila Shand Gibbs, Jane Hardie, Norah Gaussen, Susan Stephen, Barbara Everest, Anita Dolster, David Jacobs, Wensley Pithey.

8 January 1950— 8:31 "Rope," by Patrick Hamilton. *Cast:* Alan Wheatley, David Markham, Peter Wyngarde, Noel Howlett, Peter George, Shelagh Fraser, George de Warfaz. Produced by Christian Simpson.

9 January 1950— 8:45 "Twelfth Night," by William Shakespeare. *Cast:* Terence Morgan, Michael Redington, Robert Sansom, John Biggerstaff, Michael Legan, Stuart Latham, Donald Tandy. Produced by Harold Clayton.

   9:26 "Pagliacci," by R. Leoncavallo, adapted by E. R. Weatherley. *Cast:* Arthur Sevent, Eugenie Castle, Morgan Davies, Eric Whitley, John Cameron.

29 January 1950— 8:31 "Trespass," by Emlyn Williams. *Cast:* Robert Westwell, Daphne Arthur.

5 February 1950— 8:31 "The Scarlet Pimpernel," by Baroness Orczy and Montague Barstowe. Produced by Fred O'Donovan.

2 March 1950— 8:31 "Thérèse Raquin," by Émil Zola. *Cast:* Brian Oulton, David Greene, Sonia Dresdel, Nancy Price.

5 March 1950— 8:32 "The Seagull," Anton Tchekov, translated by George Calderon. *Cast:* Norman Claridge, Tatiana Lieven, Allan Jeayes, George Keen, Luise Rainer, Michael Rose, Nora Gordon.

8 March 1950— 8:31 "Othello," by William Shakespeare, French adaptation by Georges Neveux. *Cast:* Aime Clariond, Jean Debucourt, Rennee Faure, from the Comedie Francaise. Presented by Eric Fawcett.

12 March 1950— 8:31 "The Lady's Not for Burning," by Christopher Fry. From the Globe Theatre production directed by John Gielgud. *Cast:* Richard Burton, Alec Clunes, Carol Marsh, David Evans, Nora Nicholas, Richard Leech. Produced by George More O'Ferrall.

17 March 1950—10:02 "Hello Out There," by William Saroyan. *Cast:* James Schmitt, Varvara Pitoeff, John Lawrence, Jane Lawrence. Produced by Eric Fawcett.

21 March 1950— 8:31 "The Man of Destiny," by George Bernard Shaw. *Cast:* Valerie Hobson, Hugh Burden, Percy Walsh, Bryan Coleman. Produced by Campbell Logan.

26 March 1950— 8:01 "Miss Mabel," by R. C. Sherriff. *Cast:* Mary Jerrold, W. E. Holloway, Josephine Middleton. Produced by Kevin Sheldon.

30 March 1950— 8:31 "Miss Dot," by W. Somerset Maugham. *Cast:* Sonia Dresdel, Jack Allen, Alan Wheatley, Fabia Drake, June Moir, John Neville. Produced by Stephen Harrison.

2 April 1950— 8:31 "Hobson's Choice," by Harold Brighouse. *Cast:* Sonia Williams, Belle Chrystall, Sylvia Clarke, Alan Bromley, Edgar K. Bruce. Produced by Eric Fawcett.

18 April 1950— 8:44 "The First Mrs. Fraser," by St. John Ervine. *Cast:* Mary Ellis, D. A. Clarke-Smith, D. Anthony, E. Summerfield. Presented by Harold Clayton.

23 April 1950— 8:31 "The Tragedy of Othello," by William Shakespeare. *Cast:* Andre Morell, Stephen Murray, Joan Hopkins, Margaretta Scott, Laurence Harvey. Produced by George More O'Ferrall.

25 April 1950— 8:32 "The Twelve Pound Look," by J. M. Barrie. *Cast:* Ivan Samson, Iris Baker, Belle Chrystall. Produced by Campbell Logan.

2 May 1950— 8:47 "The Master Builder," by Henrik Ibsen, translated by Edmund Gosse and William Archer. *Cast:* Roger Liversey, Catherine Lacey, Adina Manlova. Presented by Royston Morley.

14 May 1950— 8:31 "Third Cousin," by Vera Mathews. *Cast:* Sybil Baker, Shelley Lynn, Arthur Hill, Harry Towb. Presented by Eric Fawcett.

11 June 1950— 8:01 "The Admiral Crichton," by J. M. Barrie. *Cast:* Raymond Huntley, Joan Hopkins. Produced by Royston Morley.

25 June 1950— 8:44 "Justice," by John Galsworthy. *Cast:* Anthony Shaw, Derek Elphinstone, Henry Oscar, Richard Attenborough, Edward Evans. Presented by Harold Clayton.

16 July 1950— 9:12 "The Ivory Tower," by William Templeton. *Cast:* Francis Lister, Iris Baker, Elizabeth Henson. Presented by Campbell Logan.

17 July 1950— 9:03 "Frankie and Johnnie," based on the American ballad. *Cast:* Robert Beatty, Marion Harris. Presented by Christian Simpson.

1 August 1950— 8:31 "Bright Shadow," by J. B. Priestley. *Cast:* Brian Worth, Norman Pierce, Helen Shingler. Presented by Harold Clayton.

3 September 1950— 8:01 "Vanity Fair," by William Thackeray, adapted by Constance Cox. *Cast:* Edna Morris, Glyn Lawson, Peter Bull, Tom Gill, Jeanette Tregarthen, Belle Chrystall.

12 September 1950— 8:01 "The Marquise," by Noël Coward. *Cast:* Angela Baddeley, Wyndam Goldie, John Wyse, Judith Stott, Richard Bebb, Denis Gordon. Presented by Stephen Harrison.

15 October 1950— 8:25 "The Million Pound Note," by Mark Twain, adapted by Rex Rienits. *Cast:* Arthur Hill, Denys Blakelock, Erik Chitty, Peggy Simpson. Presented by Stephen Harrison.

22 October 1950— 8:19 "Strife," by John Galsworthy. *Cast:* Julian Mitchell. Produced by Michael Barry.

29 October 1950— 8:01 "Richard II," by William Shakespeare. *Cast:* Alan Wheatley. Produced by Royston Morley.

5 November 1950— 8:16 "The Little Minister," by J. M. Barrie. *Cast:* Jack Stewart, Willoughby Gray, Norman Macowan, Alan Gordon, Keith Faulkner, Emrys Jones. Produced by Douglas Allen.

14 November 1950— 8:31 "The Strange Case of Dr. Jekyll and Mr. Hyde," by Robert Louis Stevenson, adapted by John Keir Cross. *Cast:* Alan Judd, Desmond Llewlyn, Jack Livesey, Patrick MacNee. Presented by Fred O'Donovan.

19 November 1950— 8:15 "Time and the Conways," by J. B. Priestley. *Cast:* Barbara Everest, Eric Berry, Helen Shingler. Produced by Harold Clayton.

3 December 1950— 8:01 "An Enemy of the People," by Henrik Ibsen, adapted by W. P. Rilla. *Cast:* Edward Chapman, Alan Blakelock, Hector Ross, Douglas Jefferies, Andre Morell, Barbara Couper.

25 December 1950— 9:20 "A Christmas Carol," by Charles Dickens, adapted by Eric Fawcett. *Cast:* MacDonald Hobley, Bransby Williams, Robert Cawdron, W. E. Halloway, Arthur Hambling, Julian d'Albie, Thomas Moore. Produced by Eric Fawcett.

26 December 1950— 8:02 "Cinderella." *Cast:* Sally Ann Howes.

31 December 1950— 8:33 "Candida," by George Bernard Shaw. *Cast:* Helen Shingler, Patrick Barr, Brian Nissen. Alexis France, James Dale, Gordon Whiting. Produced by Royston Morley.

1951

14 January 1951— 8:31 "The Scarlet Pimpernel," by Baroness Orczy and Montague Barstowe. *Cast:* Michael Brennan, Ivan Craig.

21 January 1951— 8:30 "David Garrick," by Constance Cox and Donald Wolfit. *Cast:* Donald Wolfit. Produced by Stephen Harrison.

4 February 1951— 8:31 "Counsellor-at-Law," by Elmer Rice. *Cast:* Tucker McGuire, Peter Mendoza, Clara Meisels, Bennett O'Loghlen, Madeleine Burgess. Produced by Eric Fawcett.

11 February 1951— 8:32 "The Skin Game," by John Galsworthy. *Cast:* Arthur Wontner, Arthur Young, Barbara Couper, Helen Shingler, Philip Dale, Diane Watts. Produced by Barry Learoyd.

25 February 1951— 8:15 "Julius Caesar," by William Shakespeare. *Cast:* Walter Hudd, Richard Bebb, Anthony Hawtrey, Eric Berry, Patrick Barr, Clement McCallin, Michael Brennan, Tom Colmer, Peter Bathurst, John Gatrell, Edmund Purdom. Produced by Stephen Harrison.

4 March 1951— 8:30 "Dinner at Eight," by George S. Kaufman and Edna Ferber. *Cast:* Jessie Royce Landis, Elaine Dundy, Cecil Brock, Percy Marmont, Jane Barrett, Robert Marsden, Wynne Clar. Produced by Eric Fawcett.

13 March 1951— 8:27 "The Sacred Flame," by W. Somerset Maugham. *Cast:* Laurence Hardy, Kenneth Mackintosh, Mary Jerrold, Mary Kerridge, Fenella Scott. Produced by Matthew Forsyth.

3 April 1951— 8:01 "The Golden Door," by Sylvia Regan. *Cast:* Neil Landor, Elizabeth Goodman, Fred Berger, June Rodney, Leonard Sachs, John Levitt, Stella Richman. Produced by Eric Fawcett.

8 April 1951— 8:32 "Caesar's Wife," by W. Somerset Maugham. *Cast:* Marjorie Manning, Joan Marion, Veronica Hurst, Michael Nightingale, John Longden, Brian Nissen, Barbara Couper, John Kyde. Produced by Harold Clayton.

17 April 1951— 5:00 "A Midsummer Night's Dream," by William Shakespeare, adapted by Robert and Ian Atkins. *Cast:* Robert Atkins, Frederick Piper, Dudley Jones, Leslie Crowther. Produced by Joy Harington.

22 April 1951— 8:31 "The Life of Henry Vth," by William Shakespeare. *Cast:* Clement McCallin, Varvara Pitoeff, Marius Goring, Claf Pooley, Norman Claridge, Oliver Burt. Produced by Royston Morley.

6 May 1951— 7:44 "St. Joan," by George Bernard Shaw. *Cast:* Michael O'Halloran, Humphrey Morton, Constance Cummings, Hilton Bowden, Elwyn Brook-Jones, Felix Felton, Sonia Moray, Bryan Johnson, Richard Warner, Heron Carvic, Alan Wheatley. Produced by Kevin Sheldon.

8 May 1951— 5:39 "Treasure Island," Episode 2, by Robert Louis Stevenson, adapted by Joy Harington. *Cast:* Bernard Miles, John Quayle, Howell Davis. Produced by Joy Harington. 8:01 "The Bishop Misbehaves," by Frederick Jackson. *Cast:* Alan Gura, Ronald Howard, Rona Anderson, Campbell Singer, Joan Young. Produced by Matthew Forsyth.

10 May 1951— 5:00 "The Tempest," by William Shakespeare. *Cast:* Godfrey Kenton, Knyaston Reeves, Robert Marsden. Produced by Rex Tucker.

20 May 1951— 8:30 "The Petrified Forest," by Robert E. Sherwood. *Cast:* Douglas Montgomery, Jane Barrett, Robert Ayres, Gerald Lawson, Gerald Metcalfe, Alan Keith, Charles Irwin, MacDonald Parke, Doris Nolan, Sydney Keith, Anna Korda. Produced by Royston Morley.

27 May 1951— 8:25 "The Amazing Dr. Clitterhouse," by Barre Lyndon. *Cast:* Helen Cherry, Hugh Sinclair, Jack Lambert, Richard Caldicot, Charles Farrell, Susan Shaw. Produced by Harold Clayton.

28 May 1951— 8:15 "The Consul," by Gian-Carlo Menotti. *Cast:* Russell George, Patricia Neway, Marie Powers, Leon Lishner, Francis Monachin, Gloria Lane. Produced by Eric Fawcett.

3 June 1951— 8:22 "The Way of the World," by William Congreve. *Cast:* Sonia Dresdel, Griffith Jones, Alan Wheatley, Margaretta Scott, Agnes Lauchlan, Nancy Nevinson, Heron Carvic, Elwyn Brook-Jones, Robert Brown. Produced by Stephen Harrison.

12 June 1951— 8:01 "The Telephone," by Gian-Carlo Menotti. *Cast:* Eric Shelling, Elizabeth Boyd. Presented by Christian Simpson.

17 June 1951— 8:49 "Dear Brutus," by J. M. Barrie. *Cast:* Douglas Hurn, Judy Campbell, Kathleen Crawley, Mary Jerrold, Patricia Field, June Moir. Presented by Kenneth Sheldon.

3 July 1951— 8:30 "There's Always Juliet," by John Van Druten. *Cast:* Margaret Johnston, Robert Beatty, Beatrice Varley, John Robinson. Presented by Leonard Brett.

22 July 1951— 8:15 "The Doctor's Dilemma," by George Bernard Shaw. *Cast:* Leslie Phillips, Kathleen Boutall, John Robinson, Karel Stepanek, Eugene Leahy, Knyaston Reeves, Arthur Young, Michael Hitchman, Rachel Gurney, David Markham. Presented by Fred O'Donovan.

29 July 1951— 8:15 "The Final Test," by Terence Rattigan. *Cast:* Patrick Barr, John Witty, Harold Siddons, Campbell Singer, James Dale, Jane Barrett. Produced by Royston Morley.

1 August 1951— 7:38 "The Happy Prince," by Oscar Wilde. *Cast:* Jan Bussell, Ann Hogarth, Jack Whitehead. Presented by Philip Bate.

21 August 1951— 8:01 "Whiteoaks," by Mazo de la Roche. *Cast:* Nancy Price, Margery Bryce, Julian d'Albie. Produced by Douglas Allen.

26 August 1951— 8:15 "Claudia," by Rose Franken. *Cast:* Renee Kelly, Patrick Barr, Ann Walford, Rolf Carston, Catherina Ferraz. Presented by Eric Fawcett.

28 August 1951— 8:01 "Androcles and the Lion," by George Bernard Shaw. *Cast:* Toke Townley, Lionel Hale, Nora Loos, Basil Cunard, Michael Gough, Margaret Johnston. Presented by Desmond Davis.

1 September 1951— 8:01 "Treasure Island," Part II, by Robert Louis Stevenson, adapted by Joy Harington. *Cast:* Anthony Quinn, Valentine Dyall, Peter Hawkins, Howell Davies, John Quayle, Robert Marsden. Presented by Joy Harington.

2 September 1951— 8:15 "Treasure of Pelican," by J. B. Priestley. *Cast:* Basil Sydney, Julien Mitchell, Clive Morton, Roger Snowdown, Barbara Couper. Produced by Harold Clayton.

8 September 1951— 8:01 "Treasure Island," Part III, by Robert Louis Stevenson, adapted by Joy Harington. *Cast:* Peter Hawkins, Derek Birch, Tony Quinn, John Quayle, Robert Crawdon, Valentine Dyall. Presented by Joy Harington.

15 September 1951— 8:01 "Treasure Island," Part IV, by Robert Louis Stevenson. Presented by Joy Harington.

22 September 1951— 8:16 "Treasure Island," Part V, by Robert Louis Stevenson. Presented by Joy Harington.

23 September 1951— 8:14 "The Little Foxes," by Lillian Hellman. *Cast:* Eileen Hurlie, Hugh Williams, George Coulouris, Nora Nicholson, Walter Crisham. Presented by Stanley Haynes.

2 October 1951— 8:37 "The Whiteheaded Boy," by Lennox Robinson. *Cast:* Peggy Hayes, Denis O'Dea, James Kenny, Belle Johnston, Joan Plunkett, Siobhan McKenna, Liam Gannon, Doreen Keogh, Carroll O'Conner. Presented by Fred O'Donovan.

14 October 1951— 9:01 "The Barretts of Wimpole Street," by Rudolf Bosier. *Cast:* Arnold Ridley, Pauline Jameson, Eileen Beldon, Patricia Marmont, Betty Cooper, Michael Rodington, John Fabian, Griffith Jones. Produced by Harold Clayton.

20 October 1951— 8:01 "The Empty House," by Arthur Conan Doyle, adapted by C. A. Lejeune, for *Sherlock Holmes*, No. 1. *Cast:* Alan Wheatley, Raymond Francis, Bill Owen, Iris Vandeleur, Eric Maturin. Presented by Ian Atkins.

28 October 1951— 8:53 "Escape," by John Galsworthy. *Cast:* Hugh Burdon, Anna Turner, Brian Hayes, Alan Rolfe, Alexander Field, Arthur Hambling, Adrianne Allan, Christopher Steele. Presented by Campbell Logan.

2 November 1951— 8:01 "The Dying Detective," by Arthur Conan Doyle, adapted by C. A. Lejeune, for *Sherlock Holmes*, No. 3. *Cast:* Alan Wheatley, Raymond Francis, Bill Owen, Iris Vandeleur. Presented by Ian Atkins.

17 November 1951— 8:01 "The Reigate Squires," by Arthur Conan Doyle, adapted by C. A. Lejeune, for *Sherlock Holmes*, No. 4. *Cast:* Alan Wheatley, Raymond Francis, Iris Vandeleur. Presented by Ian Atkins.

24 November 1951— 8:01 "The Red-Handed League," by Arthur Conan Doyle, adapted by C. A. Lejeune, for *Sherlock Holmes*, No. 5. *Cast:* Alan Wheatley, Raymond Francis, Bill Owen, Sebastian Cabot. Presented by Ian Atkins.

1 December 1951— 8:01 "The Second Strain," by Arthur Conan Doyle, adapted by C. A. Lejeune, for *Sherlock Holmes*, No. 6. *Cast:* Alan Wheatley, Raymond Francis. Presented by Ian Atkins.

2 December 1951— 8:14 "Eden End," by J. B. Priestley. *Cast:* David Aylmer, Dorothy Dewhurst, Rachel Gurney, Julian Mitchell, Helen Shingler, Jack Allan, Peter Cushing. Presented by Harold Clayton.

16 December 1951— 8:33 "A Sleep of Prisoners," by Christopher Fry. *Cast:* John Slater, Robin Lloyd, Andrew Leigh, Peter Williams. Produced by W. P. Rilla.

22 December 1951— 8:53 "Cinderella," from the Hippodrome, Dudley. *Cast:* Viki Emra, Roy Jefferies, Joan Burden, George Moon.

25 December 1951— 9:11 "When We Are Married," by J. B. Priestley. *Cast:* Gabrielle Daye, Peter Cushing, Edna Morris, Julia Braddock, Lewis Wilson, Frank Pettingell, Jack Howarth, Eileen Draycott. Produced by Fred O'Donovan.

30 December 1951— 8:16 "Sire de Maletroit's Door," by Robert Louis Stevenson, adapted by Winston Clewes. *Cast:* Alan Wheatley, Josephine Griffin, Robin Lloyd, Geoffrey Barrie, Julian Bream, John Heller. Presented by Dennis Vance.

Principal Source: *BBC Programming as Broadcast*, 1946–1951.

Appendix B
CBS Television Dramas, 1946–1951*

1946

4 January 1946— 8:42–9:02 *You Be the Judge*, dramas of famous criminal cases. *Cast:* Edward Stasheff.

8 January 1946— *Tales to Remember*, narrated episodes. *Director:* Rudy Bretz. *Cast:* Milton Bacon.

22 January 1946— *Tales to Remember*.

30 January 1946— 8:31–8:56 "Sorry, Wrong Number," by Lucille Fletcher. *Director:* Frances Buss (originally John Houseman). *Cast:* Mildred Natwick.

1 February 1946— *Tales to Remember*.

5 February 1946— *You Be the Judge*.

12 February 1946— 7:55–8:00 "Gettysburg Address," an original sketch by Samuel Taylor. *Director:* Cledge Roberts. *Cast:* Raymond Massey, John Cromwell.

15 February 1946— 8:30–8:46p *Tales by Hoff*, a series of bedtime stories told with drawings. [Not listed hereafter.]

21 February 1946— *You Be the Judge*.

9 May 1946— *Tales to Remember*.

19 May 1946— "Kaleidoscope." *You Be the Judge*.

26 May 1946— *Tales to Remember*.

9 June 1946— *You Be the Judge*.

16 June 1946— *Tales to Remember*.

23 June 1946— *You Be the Judge*.

4 July 1946— 8:59–9:16 "Prudence Indeed."

7 July 1946— *You Be the Judge*.

21 July 1946— *You Be the Judge*.

4 August 1946— *You Be the Judge*.

29 August 1946— *Improvisation*.

3 October 1946— *You Be the Judge*.

10 October 1946— *Improvisation*.

12 December 1946— *You Be the Judge*.

*This list includes dramas and drama-related programs from 1946 to 1951.

1947

2 January 1947 — 9:04–9:28 *Judge for Yourself*, variety, later logged as courtroom drama.

3 January 1947 — 11:30–11:45 Documentary.

16 January 1947 — 9:03–9:27 "Delivery Guaranteed," adapted from the radio series, *The Whistler*, by Gordon Minter. *Director:* Steve Marvin. *Cast:* Anne Burr, Robert Bolger, Maxin Stewart, Tom McMorrow, John James.

23 January 1947 — 8:45–9:15 "Case of the Twice Murdered Man," courtroom drama, for *Judge for Yourself*.

31 January 1947 — 8:53–9:19 Dramatic show.

6 February 1947 — 9:00–9:30 "The Case of the Midnight Murder," for *Judge for Yourself*.

13 February 1947 — 9:00–9:30 "Till Death Do Us Part," for *Judge for Yourself*. *Cast:* Naomi Campbell, Stiano Braggiotti, Marga Ann Deighton.

27 February 1947 — 9:00–9:30 "The Keenest Edge," for *Judge for Yourself*.

13 March 1947 — 9:01–9:26 "The Experiment of Dr. Bronson."

27 March 1947 — 9:06–9:33 "Too Little To Live On," suspense drama.

3 April 1947 — 9:03 "The Case of the Frightened Operator," for *Judge for Yourself*.

10 April 1947 — 9:06–9:33 "Fumed Oak," by Noël Coward. *Cast:* Haila Stoddard, Vaughn Taylor.

20 April 1947 — 8:17–8:29 "The Ways of Innocence."

24 April 1947 — 9:03–9:30 *Judge for Yourself*.

1 May 1947 — 9:05–9:30 "Too Little to Live On."

22 May 1947 — 8:35 "What Price Crime," on film.

June–Dec. 1947 — Numerous 30-minute feature films including some dramas are often sponsored by Lucky Strike Cigarettes. No live dramas.

1948

January 1948 — *Kit Carson*, a western filmed series.

8 February 1948 — 8:25–9:34 Dramatic show, a remote pick up. *Cast:* Madison Square Boys' Club.

22 February 1948 — 8:00–8:29 "Three Men from Surabachi," remote.

February–March 1948 — 1:00–12:00 The program schedule lists no dramas. Some programs are remote. Most are sustaining; about three per day are commercial. Frequent sponsors are Ford Motor Company, General Foods, Pepsi Cola, American Tobacco, Walco Sales Company, Monarch Corporation, Pioneer Scientific Corporation, Bulova Watch.

6 April 1948 — 7:00–7:38 "Mr. Roberts," scenes/interviews from the Alvin Theatre, for *Tonight on Broadway* debut. *Producer/Director:* Martin A. Gosch. *Cast:* Henry Fonda. Sponsor: American Tobacco Company (Lucky Strike Cigarettes).

13 April 1948 — 7:00 "The Heiress," by Ruth and Augustus Goetz, from the Biltmore Theatre, for *Tonight on Broadway*.

    8:02–9:02 *Kitty O'Dare, Detective*, feature film.

14 April 1948 — 8:33–9:37 *Charlie Chan and the Chinese Cat*, a film.

20 April 1948— 7:00 "High Button Shoes," a musical from the Shubert Theatre, for *Tonight on Broadway*.

27 April 1948— 7:00 "Strange Bedfellows," from the Moresco Theatre, for *Tonight on Broadway*.

4 May 1948— 7:00 "Make Mine Manhattan," from the Broadhurst Theatre, for *Tonight on Broadway*.

11 May 1948— 7:00–7:29 "The Play's the Thing," by Ferenc Molnar, from the Booth Theatre, for *Tonight on Broadway*. Sponsor: Bulova Watch.

18 May 1948— 7:00–7:29 "For Love Or Money," from the Henry Miller Theatre, for *Tonight on Broadway*.
  8:00–9:59 *Criminal Investigator*, a feature film.

25 May 1948— 7:00 "Look Ma, I'm Dancing," from the Adelphi Theatre, for *Tonight on Broadway*.

June–July 1948— Programming is often remote sports and political conventions. "Local routing" (i.e., network) included WCBS-TV, New York, WCAU-TV, Philadelphia, WMAR-TV, Baltimore, WMAL-TV, Washington, D.C., WNAC-TV, Boston.

8 July 1948— 9:00–9:29 *Headline Story*, on film.

17 August 1948— 7:16–8:10 "The Mad Monster," for *Film Theater*.

20 August 1948— 8:30–8:56 "The Panther's Claw," for *Film Theater*.

23 August 1948— 8:15–9:47 "Vampire Bat," for *Film Theater*.

25 August 1948— 9:00–10:13 "One Thrilling Night, for *Film Theater*.

29 August 1948— 7:46–8:46 "I Demand Payment," for *Film Theater*, interrupted by relatively uncommon "announcements."

30 August 1948— 8:45–9:51 "Chasing Trouble," for *Film Theater*.

31 August 1948— 8:00–8:54 "Billy the Kid in Texas," for *Film Theater*.

1 September 1948— 9:00–9:41 "Gang Bullets," for *Film Theater*.

3 September 1948— 9:00–9:51 "Behind Green Lights," for *Film Theater of the Air*, new title for local film series.

5 September 1948— 7:46–8:56 "Criminals Within," for *Film Theater of the Air*.

6 September 1948— 8:45–9:54 "Devil Bat," for *Film Theater of the Air*.

7 September 1948— 8:00–8:58 "Rolling Westward," for *Film Theater of the Air*.

8 September 1948— 9:00–9:53 "The Crusader," for *Film Theater of the Air*.

9 September 1948— 9:00–10:26 *Second Chorus*, a feature film.

10 September 1948— 8:45–9:44 "What a Man," for *Film Theater of the Air*.

12 September 1948— 8:23–8:52 "Charlie Chan in Secret Service," for *Film Theater of the Air*.

September–October 1948— Feature film theaters continue six nights a week or wherever needed. Films are repeated.

8 October 1948—10:00–10:29 Remote from the Old Knick Playhouse. Announcement sponsored by American Tobacco Company.

10 October 1948— 7:15–8:49 *Jack London*, Parts I & II, a feature film with sponsored announcements.

17 October 1948— 7:31–8:28 "Years Ago," by Ruth Gordon, for *Ford Theater* [later *The Ford Television Theatre*] debut. Producers: Garth Montgomery, Ellis Sard. *Director:* Marc Daniels. *Cast:* Patricia Kirkland, Raymond Massey, Eva Le Gallienne, Logan Ramsey, Virginia Gorski, Jennifer Bunker, Judith Cargill, Richard Taber, Seth Arnold, Cy Feuer.

24 October 1948— 7:15 *Film Theater*.

26 October 1948 — 7:00–7:15 "The Roar of the Rails," sketches about the history of trains. Sponsor: A. C. Gilbert Company (American Flyer trains).

31 October 1948 — 7:15–8:22 "Becky Sharp," for *Film Theater.*

7 November 1948 — 7:31–8:29 "The Storm," by McKnight Malmar, adapted by Worthington Miner, for *Studio One* debut. *Producer/Director:* Worthington Miner. *Cast:* Margaret Sullavan, Dean Jagger. Sponsor spots precede (Philip Morris) and follow (Ronson Lighter) the drama.

11 November 1948 — 8:31–9:37 "Dragnet," for *Film Theater.*

14 November 1948 — 7:15–8:29 "Nothing Sacred," for *Film Theater.*

21 November 1948 — 7:31–8:29 "Joy to the World," by Alan Scott and George Haight, for *Ford Theater. Director:* Marc Daniels. *Cast:* Eddie Albert, Janet Blair, Philip Coolidge, Myron McCormick, Florida Friebus, Arthur Henderson, Jack Hartley.

25 November 1948 — 11:07–12:12a "Little Men," for *Film Theater,* begins morning feature films.

28 November 1948 — 7:31–8:29 "Let Me Do the Talking," for *Studio One. Producer:* Worthington Miner. *Directors:* Miner and Paul Nickell. *Cast:* John Conté, Susan Douglas.

5 December 1948 — 7:16–8:26 "Dixie Jamboree," for *Film Theater.*

12 December 1948 — 7:31–8:29 "The Medium," by Gian-Carlo Menotti, for *Studio One. Producer:* Worthington Miner. *Director:* Paul Nickell. *Cast:* Marie Powers, Leo Coleman, Beverly Dame.

19 December 1948 — 7:30–8:29 "Night Must Fall," by Emlyn Williams, for *Ford Theater. Director:* Marc Daniels. *Cast:* Fay Bainter, Oliver Thorndike, Howard St. John, Mildred Dunnock, Cloris Leachman.

25 December 1948 — 9:00–10:12 "Silver Skates," for *Film Theater.*

26 December 1948 — 7:30 "Not So Long Ago," by Joseph Liss, for *Studio One. Producer:* Worthington Miner. *Cast:* Katherine Bard, Karl Weber, Jerome Thor.

1949

2 January 1949 — 5:30–6:29 "Raiders of the West," film.
     7:15–8:25 *Film Theater.* Sponsors: Philip Morris, Ronson Lighters.

3 January 1949 — 9:00–9:54 "Girls' Town," for *Film Theater.* Sponsor: Liggett & Myers.

4 January 1949 — 8:00–8:58 "Navajo Kid," for *Film Theater.*

9 January 1949 — 7:30–8:30 "The Outward Room," by Millen Brand, for *Studio One. Producer/Director:* Worthington Miner. *Cast:* Ruth Ford, Bramwell Fletcher, John Forsythe. Sponsor: Liggett & Myers.

10 January 1949 — 8:00–8:29 *The Goldbergs,* a situation comedy by Gertrude Berg, debuts. *Producer:* Worthington Miner. *Director:* Walter Hart. *Cast:* Gertrude Berg, Philip Loeb.
     9:00–9:52 "City Without Men," for *Film Theater.*

11 January 1949 — 8:00–8:58 "Journey Together," for *Film Theater.*

14 January 1949 — 9:51–10:56 "Silent Witness," for *Film Theater.*

16 January 1949 — 7:30–8:30 "The Man Who Came to Dinner," by George S. Kaufman and Moss Hart, for *Ford Theater. Director:* Marc Daniels. *Cast:* Edward Everett Horton, Vicki Cummings, Judy Parrish, Kevin McCarthy, Mary Wickes, Zero Mostel, Rex O'Malley.

17 January 1949 — 8:00 *The Goldbergs.*

18 January 1949— 8:00–8:59 *Cross Question* [later *They Stand Accused*] extemporaneous courtroom drama from WGN-TV, Chicago, debuts on network.

20 January 1949— 9:00–10:02 "Lighthouse," for *Film Theater.*

21 January 1949— 9:51–10:51 "Arson Squad," for *Film Theater.*

22 January 1949— 8:30–9:39 "Larceny at Heart," for *Film Theater.*

23 January 1949— 7:00–8:23 "Three Is a Family," for *Film Theater.*

24 January 1949— 8:00 *The Goldbergs.*

25 January 1949— 8:00–8:59 *Cross Question.*

27 January 1949— 9:00–10:00 *Film Theater of the Air.*

28 January 1949— 9:50–10:59 "I Accuse My Past," for *Film Theater.*

30 January 1949— 7:30 "Blind Alley," by James Warwick, for *Studio One. Cast:* Bramwell Fletcher, Jerome Thor.

31 January 1949— 8:00 *The Goldbergs.*

1 February 1949— 8:00 *Cross Question.*

4 February 1949— 9:50–10:50 "Danger Chaser," for *Film Theater.*

7 February 1949— 8:00 *The Goldbergs.*

8 February 1949— 8:00 *Cross Question.*

13 February 1949— 7:30 "The Silver Cord," by Sidney Howard, for *Ford Theater. Director:* Marc Daniels. *Cast:* Mady Christians, Meg Mundy.

14 February 1949— 8:00 *The Goldbergs.*

15 February 1949— 8:00 *Cross Question.*

20 February 1949— 7:30 "Holiday," by Philip Barry, for *Studio One. Cast:* Valerie Bettis.

21 February 1949— 8:00 *The Goldbergs.*

22 February 1949— 8:00 *Cross Question.*

26 February 1949— 7:45–7:59 "Horrors of the Bat," for *Film Theater.*

28 February 1949— 8:00 *The Goldbergs.*

29 February 1949— 8:00 *Cross Question.*

1 March 1949— 9:30–9:59 "Revenge," by Cornell Woolrich, for the *Suspense* debut. *Director:* Robert Stevens. *Cast:* Eddie Albert, Margo. Sponsor: Electric Auto-Lite.

2 March 1949— 9:00–9:29 *Mary Kay and Johnny,* a situation comedy transferred from NBC, debuts. Writer: Johnny Stearns. *Cast:* Mary Kay and Johnny Stearns. Sponsor: Whitehall Pharmaceutical Company.

6 March 1949— 7:30 "Julius Caesar," by William Shakespeare, adapted by Worthington Miner, for *Studio One. Director:* Paul Nickell. *Cast:* William Post, Jr., Robert Keith, Joe Silver, Vaughn Taylor, Emmett Rogers, John O'Shaughnessy, Philip Bourneuf, Ruth Ford. Sponsor: Philip Morris spot preceded the telecast.

7 March 1949— 8:00 *The Goldbergs.*

8 March 1949— 8:00 *Cross Question.*

9 March 1949— 9:00 *Mary Kay and Johnny.*

10 March 1949— 9:30–10:35 *Theater of the Air.*

11 March 1949— 9:30–10:37 *Theater of the Air.*

13 March 1949— 7:30 "Outward Bound," by Sutton Vane, *Ford Theater. Director:* Marc Daniels. *Cast:* Lillian Gish, Freddie Bartholomew, Mary Boland, Richard Hart.

14 March 1949— 8:00 *The Goldbergs.*

15 March 1949— 8:00 *Cross Question.*

    9:30 "Suspicion," for *Suspense. Cast:* Ernest Truex, Sylvia Field, Viola Roche.

16 March 1949—9:00 *Mary Kay and Johnny.*
18 March 1949—9:30–10:29 "It Happened in Paris," for *Film Theater.*
19 March 1949—7:00–7:29 Western film.
20 March 1949—7:30 "Berkeley Square," by John L. Balderston and J. C. Squire, for *Studio One. Cast:* Leureen McGrath, William Prince, Leslie Woods.
21 March 1949—8:00 *The Goldbergs.*
22 March 1949—8:00 *Cross Question.*
23 March 1949—9:00 *Mary Kay and Johnny.*
24 March 1949—9:00–10:04 *Film Theater.*
25 March 1949—9:29–11:54 *Premier Playhouse,* a filmed anthology, debuts. Sponsor: American Tobacco Company.
25 March 1949—8:00–9:01 *Film Theater.*
27 March 1949—7:00–7:59 "I'm from Arkansas," for *Film Theater.*
     9:00–9:59 "Secret Mission," for *Film Theater.*
28 March 1949—8:00 *The Goldbergs.*
29 March 1949—8:00 *Cross Question.*
     9:30 "Cabin B-13," by John Dickson Carr, for *Suspense. Cast:* Charles Korvin, Eleanor Lynn.
30 March 1949—9:00 *Mary Kay and Johnny.*
3 April 1949—7:30 "Redemption," by Leo Tolstoy, for *Studio One. Cast:* Richard Hart, Joan Wetmore.
     9:00–9:59 *Film Theater.*
4 April 1949—8:00 *The Goldbergs.*
5 April 1949—8:00 *Cross Question,* commentary later drama.
     9:30 "The Man Upstairs," for *Suspense. Cast:* Anthony Ross, Mildred Natwick.
6 April 1949—9:00 *Mary Kay and Johnny.*
7 April 1949—9:00–10:10 *Film Theater of the Air.*
8 April 1949—9:30–10:48 *Premier Playhouse.*
10 April 1949—7:00–7:59 *Film Theater.*
     9:00–9:59 *Film Theater.*
11 April 1949—9:00–9:59 "Arsenic and Old Lace," by Joseph Kesseiring, for *Ford Theater. Cast:* Boris Karloff, Josephine Hull, Anthony Ross.
12 April 1949—8:00 *Cross Question.*
     9:30 "After Dinner Story," for *Suspense. Cast:* Otto Kruger.
13 April 1949—9:00 *Mary Kay and Johnny.*
14 April 1949—9:30–10:30 *Film Theater.*
15 April 1949—9:30 *Premier Playhouse.*
16 April 1949—8:00–8:59 *Film Theater.*
17 April 1949—7:30 "The Moment of Truth," by Storm Jameson, for *Studio One. Cast:* Leo G. Carroll.
18 April 1949—9:30 *The Goldbergs.*
19 April 1949—8:00 *Cross Question,* a drama.
     9:30 "The Creeper," by Joseph Ruscoll, adapted by Frank Gabrielson, for *Suspense. Cast:* Nina Foch, Anthony Ross, Edgar Stehli.
20 April 1949—9:00 *Mary Kay and Johnny.*
22 April 1949—9:30 *Premier Playhouse.*
23 April 1949—8:00–8:59 *Film Theater of the Air.*
24 April 1949—7:00–7:59 "Dear Octopus," for *Film Theater.*
25 April 1949—9:30 *The Goldbergs.*

26 April 1949— 8:00 *Cross Question.*
9:30 "A Night at an Inn," by Lord Dunsany, adapted by Halsted Welles for *Suspense. Cast:* Boris Karloff, Jack Manning, Anthony Ross, Joan Stanley, Barry McCallum.
27 April 1949— 9:00 *Mary Kay and Johnny.*
28 April 1949— 9:00–9:30 *Film Theater.*
29 April 1949— 9:00–10:00 *Film Theater of the Air.*
30 April 1949— 8:00–9:15 *Film Theater of the Air.*
9:45–10:47 *Burman Victory*, a documentary.
1 May 1949— 7:00–7:59 "Julius Caesar," by William Shakespeare, originally presented 6 March, for *Studio One.*
2 May 1949— 9:30 *The Goldbergs.*
3 May 1949— 9:30 "Dead Ernest," by Merwin Gerard and Seelag Lester, adapted by Mary Orr and Reginald Denham, for *Suspense. Cast:* Tod Andrews, Margaret Phillips, Will Hare, Joshua Shelley.
4 May 1949— 9:00 *Mary Kay and Johnny.*
5 May 1949— 9:00–9:29 *Crime Reporter*, a CBS film.
7 May 1949— 8:30–9:52 *Film Theater of the Air.*
8 May 1949— 7:30–7:59 *Wesley*, a situation comedy, debuts. Producer: Worthington Miner. *Director:* Franklin Schaffner. *Cast:* Donald Devlin, Frankie Thomas, Sr., Mona Thomas.
9 May 1949— 9:30 *The Goldbergs.*
10 May 1949— 9:30 "Post Mortem," by Cornell Woolrich, adapted by Frank Gabrielson, for *Suspense. Cast:* Peggy Conklin, Sidney Blackmer, Richard Coogan, Julian Noe, Darren Dublin, Harry Laskos.
11 May 1949— 9:00 *Mary Kay and Johnny.*
10:00–10:59 "The Glass Key," by Dashiell Hammett, adapted by Worthington Miner, for *Studio One. Director:* George Zachary. *Cast:* Don Briggs, Lawrence Fletcher, Jean Carlson. Sponsor: Westinghouse Electric Company.
13 May 1949— 9:30–10:50 *Premier Playhouse.*
15 May 1949— 7:30 *Wesley.*
16 May 1949— 9:00–9:59 "One Sunday Afternoon," by James Hagen, for *Ford Theater. Cast:* Burgess Meredith, Hume Cronyn, Francesca Brunning.
17 May 1949— 8:00–8:59 *Film Theater of the Air.*
9:30 "The Monkey's Paw," by W. W. Jacobs, adapted by Frank Gabrielson, for *Suspense. Cast:* Boris Karloff, Mildred Natwick.
18 May 1949— 9:00 *Mary Kay and Johnny.*
10:00 "Shadow and Substance," by Paul Vincent Carroll, adapted by Worthington Miner, for *Studio One. Cast:* Leo G. Carroll, Margaret Phillips.
20 May 1949— 9:30–11:03 *Premier Playhouse.*
22 May 1949— 7:30 *Wesley.*
23 May 1949— 9:30 *The Goldbergs.*
24 May 1949— 8:00–8:59 *Film Theater of the Air.*
9:30 "Murder Through the Looking Glass," by Craig Rice, adapted by Mary Orr and Reginald Denham, for *Suspense. Cast:* William Prince, Ruth Madison, Peter Von Zernick.
25 May 1949— 9:00 *Mary Kay and Johnny.*
10:00 "Flowers from a Stranger," by Dorothea Carousso, for *Studio One. Cast:* John Conté, Felicia Montealegre, Yul Brynner.

28 May 1949— 8:30–9:37 *Film Theater of the Air.*
29 May 1949— 7:30 *Wesley.*
30 May 1949— 9:30 *The Goldbergs.*
31 May 1949— 9:30 "The Door's on the Thirteenth Floor," by Marie Rodell, adapted by Edward Mabley, for *Suspense. Cast:* Louisa Horton, Robert Sterling, Anthony Ross.
1 June 1949— 9:00 *Mary Kay and Johnny.*
    10:00 "The Dybbuk," by S. Ansky, adapted by Joseph Liss, for *Studio One. Director:* Paul Nickell. *Cast:* Arnold Moss, Mary Sinclair, James Lamphier.
4 June 1949— 8:30–9:42 *Film Theater of the Air.*
5 June 1949— 7:30 *Wesley.*
6 June 1949— 9:30 *The Goldbergs.*
7 June 1949— 8:00–8:59 *Film Theater.*
    9:30 "The Yellow Scarf," by Thomas Burke, adapted by Halsted Welles, for *Suspense. Cast:* Boris Karloff.
8 June 1949—10:00 "Boy Meets Girl," by Samuel and Bella Spewack, adapted by Walter Hart, for *Studio One. Cast:* Hume Cronyn, Michael Harvey, William Post, Jr., Sarah O'Connell.
12 June 1949— 7:30 *Wesley.*
13 June 1949— 9:00 "Light Up the Sky," by Moss Hart, for *Ford Theater. Director:* Marc Daniels. *Cast:* Barry Nelson, Glenn Anders.
14 June 1949— 8:00–8:59 *Film Theater.*
    9:30 "Help Wanted," by Stanley Ellin, adapted by Mary Orr and Reginald Denham, for *Suspense. Cast:* Otto Kruger, Peggy French, Ruth McDevitt, George Matthews.
15 June 1949—10:00 "Smoke," by Ivan Turgenev, adapted by Worthington Miner, for *Studio One. Cast:* Leueen MacGrath, Charlton Heston, Mary Sinclair, Josephine Brown, Guy Spaull.
17 June 1949— 9:30 *Premier Playhouse.*
18 June 1949— 8:00–8:59 *Film Theater of the Air.*
20 June 1949— 9:30 *The Goldbergs.*
21 June 1949— 9:30 "Stolen Empire," by James Sheean, adapted Halsted Welles, for *Suspense. Cast:* Kenneth Lynch, Carol Goodner.
22 June 1949— 9:00 *CBS Film Theater.*
    10:00 "June Moon," by Ring Lardner and George S. Kaufman, adapted by Gerald Goode, for *Studio One. Cast:* Glenda Farrell, Edward Andrews, Eva Marie Saint, Jack Lemmon.
24 June 1949— 8:30–9:51 *Premier Playhouse.*
25 June 1949— 8:30 *Film Theater.*
26 June 1949— 9:00–9:59 *Film Theater.*
27 June 1949— 9:30 *The Goldbergs.*
28 June 1949— 8:00–8:59 *Film Theater.*
    9:30 "The Hands of Mr. Ottermole," by Thomas Burke, adapted by Frank Gabrielson, for *Suspense. Cast:* Ralph Bell.
29 June 1949— 9:00 *CBS Film Theater.*
    10:00 "The Shadowy Third," by Ellen Glasgow, for *Studio One. Cast:* Margaret Phillips, Helmut Dantine, Sandra Ann Wigginton, Frances Fuller.
1 July 1949— 8:00–8:29 *Mama,* based on *Mama's Bank Account,* by Kathryn Forbes, debuts. *Director:* Ralph Nelson. *Cast:* Peggy Wood, Judson Laire. Sponsor: General Foods.

9:30 *Premier Playhouse.*

2 July 1949— 8:59–9:49 *Film Theater of the Air.*

3 July 1949— 9:00–9:59 *Film Theater.*

5 July 1949— 8:00–8:59 *Film Theater.*

6 July 1949— 9:00–9:31 *Armchair Detective,* a series of criminal cases solved by an audience, debuts. *Cast:* John Milton Kennedy, H. Allen Smith.

7 July 1949— 9:00–9:29 *Film Theater.*

8 July 1949— 8:00 *Mama.*

9 July 1949— 8:49–10:36 *Film Theater.*

10 July 1949— 9:00–9:59 *Film Theater of the Air.*

12 July 1949— 8:00–8:59 *Film Theater.*

13 July 1949— 9:00 *Armchair Detective.*

15 July 1949— 8:00 *Mama.*

16 July 1949— 8:50–10:18 "Julius Caesar," for *Film Theater of the Air.*

17 July 1949— 8:00–8:59 *Film Theater of the Air.*

19 July 1949— 8:00–8:59 *Film Theater.*

9:30 *Wesley,* returns.

20 July 1949— 9:00 *Armchair Detective.*

21 July 1949— 9:00–10:08 *Film Theater.*

22 July 1949— 8:00 *Mama.*

23 July 1949— 8:30–10:03 *Film Theater.*

26 July 1949— 8:00–8:59 *Film Theater.*

9:30 *Wesley.*

27 July 1949— 9:00 *Armchair Detective.*

28 July 1949— 9:00–10:14 *Film Theater.*

29 July 1949— 8:00 *Mama.*

30 July 1949— 8:52–10:11 *Premier Playhouse.*

10:12–11:12 *Film Theater of the Air.*

31 July 1949— 9:00–9:59 *Film Theater of the Air.*

2 August 1949— 9:30 *Wesley.*

3 August 1949— 9:00 *Armchair Detective.*

4 August 1949— 9:00–10:07 *Film Theater.*

5 August 1949— 8:00 *Mama.*

6 August 1949— 8:58–9:48 *Premier Playhouse.*

7 August 1949— 9:00–9:59 *Film Theater.*

8 August 1949—7:55–7:59 *Ruthie on the Phone,* a sketch, runs until November. Sponsor: Philip Morris. [Not listed hereafter.]

9 August 1949— 8:00–8:59 *Film Theater of the Air.*

9:30 *Wesley.*

10 August 1949— 9:00 *Armchair Detective.*

11 August 1949— 9:00–9:59 *CBS Film Theater.*

12 August 1949— 8:00 *Mama.*

13 August 1949— 8:30–10:13 *Film Theater.*

14 August 1949— 9:00–9:59 *Film Theater of the Air.*

16 August 1949— 8:00 *Wesley.*

17 August 1949— 9:00 *Armchair Detective.*

18 August 1949— 9:00–10:02 *CBS Film Theater.*

19 August 1949— 8:00 *Mama.*

8:30–8:59 *CBS Film Theater.*

20 August 1949— 8:30–10:14 *Film Theater of the Air.*
21 August 1949— 9:00–9:59 *Film Theater of the Air.*
23 August 1949— 8:00 *Wesley.*
24 August 1949— 9:00 *Armchair Detective.*
25 August 1949— 9:00–10:04 "Bombs Over Burma," for *Film Theater.*
26 August 1949— 8:00 *Mama.*
27 August 1949— 8:57–10:01 *Premier Playhouse.*
28 August 1949— 7:00–7:29 Film Featurette.
    9:30–9:59 Film Featurette.
29 August 1949— 9:30 *The Goldbergs* returns.
30 August 1949— 8:00 *Wesley.*
    9:30–10:35 *Film Theater of the Air.*
31 August 1949— 9:00 *Armchair Detective.*
2 September 1949— 8:00 *Mama.*
    8:30–9:29 *Film Theater.*
3 September 1949— 8:49–10:11 *Premier Playhouse.*
4 September 1949— 8:59–9:59 *Film Theater.*
5 September 1949— 9:30 *The Goldbergs.*
6 September 1949— 8:00–8:59 *Film Theater of the Air.*
    9:30 "Lunch Box," by Larry Malone, adapted by Turner Bullock, Frank Gabriel-
    son, for *Suspense* return. *Cast:* Lon McAllister, Abe Vigoda.
7 September 1949— 9:00 *Armchair Detective.*
9 September 1949— 8:00 *Mama.*
    8:41–9:58 *Bulova Film Theater.*
10 September 1949— 9:00 *Premier Playhouse.*
11 September 1949— 9:00 *Film Theater of the Air.*
12 September 1949— 9:30 *The Goldbergs.*
    10:00 "Kyra Zelas," by Stanley J. Weinbaum, adapted by Worthington Miner,
    for *Studio One* return. *Cast:* Felicia Montealegre, Richard Hart, Mercedes
    McCambridge.
13 September 1949— 9:30 "Collector's Item," by Robert Stevens, adapted by Doris
    Frankel, for *Suspense. Cast:* Lon McAllister.
14 September 1949— 9:00 *Armchair Detective.*
    9:50–10:59 "Black Eyes," for *Film Theater.*
15 September 1949— 9:00–9:59 *Film Theater.*
16 September 1949— 8:00 *Mama.*
    8:52–9:57 *Film Theater of the Air.*
17 September 1949— 9:00 *Premier Playhouse.*
18 September 1949— 9:00–9:59 *Film Theater.*
19 September 1949— 9:30 *The Goldbergs.*
    10:00 "The Rival Dummy," by Ben Hecht, adapted by Worthington Miner and
    David Opatoshu, for *Studio One. Cast:* Paul Lukas, Anne Francis.
20 September 1949— 9:30 "Dr. Jekyll and Mr. Hyde," by Robert Louis Stevenson,
    adapted by Halsted Welles, for *Suspense. Cast:* Ralph Bell.
21 September 1949— 9:00 *Armchair Detective.*
    10:00–10:59 *Film Theater.*
22 September 1949— 9:00–9:59 *Film Theater of the Air.*
23 September 1949— 8:00 *Mama.*
    8:54–9:58 *Film Theater.*

26 September 1949— 9:30 *The Goldbergs.*

10:00 "The Outward Room," by Millen Brand, adapted by Joseph Liss, for *Studio One. Cast:* Ruth Ford, Bramwell Fletcher, Charlton Heston.

27 September 1949— 9:30 "The Comic Strip Murder," by Fred Methot, adapted by Turner Bullock, Frank Gabrielson, for *Suspense. Cast:* Lilli Palmer, Rex Harrison.

28 September 1949— 9:00 *Armchair Detective.*

10:00–10:59 *Film Theater.*

29 September 1949— 9:00–9:58 *CBS Presents Film Theater of the Air.*

30 September 1949— 8:00 *Mama.*

1 October 1949— 8:50–10:11 *Film Theater.*

2 October 1949— 7:00 "Lend an Ear," for *Tonight on Broadway* return.

3 October 1949— 8:00–8:29 "L'Amour the Merrier," for *Silver Theatre* debut. *Cast:* Eva Gabor, Burgess Meredith, Conrad Nagel. Sponsor: International Silver Company.

9:30 *The Goldbergs.*

10:00 "Mrs. Moonlight," by Benn Levy, adapted by William Jayme, for *Studio One. Cast:* Katherine Bard, James MacCall, Una O'Conner.

4 October 1949— 8:00–8:59 *Film Theater of the Air.*

9:30 "Doctor Violet," by Halsted Welles, for *Suspense. Cast:* Hume Cronyn, Evelyn Varden.

6 October 1949— 8:00–8:29 *Front Page Film Theatre* debuts.

9:30–10:39 *Film Theater.*

7 October 1949— 8:00 *Mama.*

8:30–8:59 *The Man Against Crime* debuts. *Director:* Paul Nickell. *Cast:* Ralph Bellamy, Frank Lovejoy. Sponsor: R. J. Reynolds Tobacco Company.

9:00 "Twentieth Century," by Ben Hecht and Charles MacArthur, for *Ford Theater* return. *Director:* Marc Daniels. *Cast:* Fredric March, Lilli Palmer.

8 October 1949— 9:00 *Premier Playhouse.*

9 October 1949— 7:00 "Twelfth Night," by William Shakespeare, from the Empire Theatre, for *Tonight on Broadway.*

10 October 1949— 8:00 "'Til Death Do Us Part," for *Silver Theatre. Cast:* John Loder, Faye Emerson.

9:30 *The Goldbergs.*

10:00 "The Light That Failed," by Rudyard Kipling, adapted by Gerald Goode, for *Studio One. Cast:* Felicia Montealegre, Richard Hart.

11 October 1949— 8:00–8:59 "A Chump from Oxford," for *Film Theater.*

9:30 "The Cask of Amontillado," by Edgar Allan Poe, adapted by Halsted Welles, for *Suspense. Cast:* Bela Lugosi.

13 October 1949— 8:00–8:29 *Front Page Film Theatre.* Documentaries.

14 October 1949— 8:00 *Mama.*

8:30 *The Man Against Crime.*

15 October 1949— 8:49–10:00 *Film Theater of the Air.*

16 October 1949— 7:00 "Twelfth Night," repeats for *Tonight on Broadway.*

17 October 1949— 8:00 "Rhapsody in Discord," for *Silver Theatre. Cast:* Paul Lukas, Kim Hunter.

9:30 *The Goldbergs.*

10:00 "The Storm," by McKnight Malmar, adapted by Worthington Miner, for *Studio One.* Repeat of debut with new cast: Marsha Hunt, John Rodney, Dean Harens.

18 October 1949— 8:00–8:59 *Film Theatre of the Air.*
9:30 "The Serpent Ring," by Louis Pollock, adapted by John Gearon, for *Suspense. Cast:* Joan Wetmore, Steven Hill, Peter Von Zernick, Ray Walston, Royal Dano.

20 October 1949— 8:00–8:29 *Front Page Film Theatre.*

21 October 1949— 8:00 *Mama.*
8:30 *The Man Against Crime.*
9:00–9:59 "On Borrowed Time," by L. E. Watkins, adapted by Paul Osborn, for *Ford Theater on the Air. Cast:* Basil Rathbone, Walter Hampden.

22 October 1949— 9:00 *Film Theater of the Air.*

23 October 1949— 7:00 Revue from Lou Walter's Latin Quarter for *Tonight on Broadway.*

24 October 1949— 8:00 "School for Love," for *Silver Theatre. Cast:* John Payne.
9:30 *The Goldbergs.*
10:00 "Battleship Bismarck," by Maurice Valency, adapted by Worthington Miner, for *Studio One. Director:* Paul Nickell. *Cast:* Paul Lukas, Charlton Heston, Vaughn Taylor.

25 October 1949— 8:00–8:59 *Film Theater of the Air.*
9:30 "The Murderer," by Joel Townsley Rogers, adapted by Joseph Hayes, for *Suspense. Cast:* Jeffrey Lynn.

27 October 1949— 8:00–8:29 *Front Page Film Theatre.*
9:31–10:30 *Film Theater.*

28 October 1949— 8:00 *Mama.*
8:30 *The Man Against Crime.*

29 October 1949— 9:00 *Premier Playhouse.*

30 October 1949— 7:00 "Howdy Mr. Ice of 1950," from the Center Theatre, for *Tonight on Broadway.*

31 October 1949— 8:00 "The Farewell Supper," for *Silver Theatre. Cast:* Charles Korvin, Leonore Aubert, Myron McCormick.
9:30 *The Goldbergs.*
10:00 "Concerning a Woman of Sin," by Ben Hecht, adapted by Gerald Goode, for *Studio One. Cast:* Iris Mann, E. G. Marshall, Hildy Parks, James McCall, Dean Hearns.

1 November 1949— 9:00–9:29 "The Return to Kansas City," for *Actor's Studio* debut on CBS. *Cast:* Kim Hunter, Elliott Sullivan.
9:30 "Black Passage," by Robert Louis Stevenson, adapted by Halsted Welles, for *Suspense. Cast:* William Prince, Stella Adler, Mary Sinclair, Carlos Montalban, Peter Fernandez.

3 November 1949— 8:00–8:29 *Front Page Film Theatre.*
8:30–8:59 "Camille," by Alexandre Dumas, for *Theatre of Romance,* debut. *Cast:* Ruth Ford.
9:30–10:07 *Film Theatre.*

4 November 1949— 8:00 *Mama.*
8:30 *The Man Against Crime.*
9:00 "She Loves Me Not," by Edward Hope, adapted by Max Wilk, for *Ford Theater. Cast:* Judy Holliday.

5 November 1949— 8:30–9:29 "Silent Passenger," for *Film Theater.*

6 November 1949— 7:00 Revue from Havana Madrid night club for *Tonight on Broadway.*

7 November 1949— 8:00 "Patient Unknown," for *Silver Theatre. Cast:* John Baragrey, Felicia Montealegre.
    9:30 *The Goldbergs.*
    10:00 "The Husband," by Natalie A. Scott, adapted by Worthington Miner, for *Studio One. Cast:* Margaret Phillips, Robert Favart.

8 November 1949— 8:00–8:30 Film Featurette.
    9:00 "O'Halloran's Luck," for *Actor's Studio. Cast:* George Reeves, Cloris Leachman.
    9:30 "Suspicion," by Billy Rose, adapted by Joseph Liss, for *Suspense. Cast:* Meg Mundy, Edgar Stehli, Russell Collins, Charlton Heston.

10 November 1949— 8:00–8:29 *Front Page Film Theatre.*
    9:30–10:52 *Film Theater.*

11 November 1949— 8:00 *Mama.*
    8:30 *The Man Against Crime.*

12 November 1949— 8:47–10:03 *Film Theater.*

13 November 1949— 7:00 "Regina," from the 44th Street Theatre, for *Tonight on Broadway.*

14 November 1949— 8:00 "Don't Give Up the Ship," for *Silver Theatre. Cast:* Louise Allbritton, Henry Morgan.
    9:30 *The Goldbergs.*
    10:00 "Two Sharp Knives," by Dashiell Hammett, adapted by Worthington Miner, for *Studio One. Cast:* Stanley Ridges, Hildy Parks.

15 November 1949— 8:00–8:59 *Film Theater of the Air.*
    9:00 "The Frame-Up," for *Actor's Studio. Cast:* Joshua Shelley, Cloris Leachman.
    9:30 "The Thin Edge of Violence," by William O'Farrell, for *Suspense. Cast:* George Reeves, Leonore Aubert, Emily Lawrence.

17 November 1949— 8:00–8:29 *Front Page Film Theatre.*
    8:30–8:59 "Sometime, Every Summertime," for *Theatre of Romance. Cast:* Mary Sinclair.

18 November 1949— 8:00 *Mama.*
    8:30 *The Man Against Crime.*
    9:00 "Skylark," by Samson Raphaelson, for *Ford Theater. Cast:* Faye Emerson, Lee Bowman.

19 November 1949— 8:30–9:52 *Film Theater.*

20 November 1949— 7:00–7:29 "Montserrat," from the Fulton Theatre, for *Tonight on Broadway.*

21 November 1949— 8:00 "Silent as the Grave," for *Silver Theatre. Cast:* Marsha Hunt, George Reeves.
    9:30 *The Goldbergs.*
    10:00 "Of Human Bondage," by W. Somerset Maugham, for *Studio One. Cast:* Charlton Heston, Felicia Montealegre.

22 November 1949— 8:00–8:59 *Film Theater of the Air.*
    9:00 "The Three Strangers," for *Actor's Studio. Cast:* John Randolph, Steven Hill.
    9:30 "The Third One," by Arthur Heinemann, for *Suspense. Cast:* Iris Mann, Theodore Newton, Margaret Phillips.

24 November 1949— 8:00–8:29 *Front Page Film Theatre.*
    8:30–8:59 *Theatre of Romance.*

25 November 1949— 8:00 *Mama.*
    8:30 *The Man Against Crime.*

26 November 1949—*Premier Playhouse.*

27 November 1949— 7:00 "Yes, M'Lord," from the Booth Theatre, for *Tonight on Broadway.*

28 November 1949— 8:00 "Much Ado About Something," for *Silver Theatre. Cast:* Jean Pugsley, Laurence Hugo.

  9:30 *The Goldbergs.*

  10:00 "At Mrs. Beam's," by C. K. Monro, adapted by Charles S. Monroe, for *Studio One. Cast:* Eva Gabor, John Baragrey, Mildred Natwick, Cathleen Cordell.

29 November 1949— 8:00–8:49 *Film Theater of the Air.*

  9:00 "The Thousand Dollar Bill," for *Actor's Studio. Cast:* Don Hanmer, Nancy Franklin.

  9:30 "The Man in the House," by Leslie Edgby, adapted by Joseph Liss, for *Suspense. Cast:* Alan Baxter, Boyd Crawford, Kim Hunter.

1 December 1949— 8:00–8:29 *Front Page Film Theatre.*

  8:30–8:59 "The M. P. and the Mouse," for *Theatre of Romance. Cast:* Susan Douglas.

  10:08–11:05 *Film Theater.* Sponsor: Pall Mall.

2 December 1949— 8:00 *Mama.*

  8:30 *The Man Against Crime.*

  9:00 "Kind Lady," by Edward Chodorov, for *Ford Theater. Cast:* Fay Bainter, Joseph Schildkraut.

3 December 1949— 8:30–9:58 *Film Theater of the Air.*

4 December 1949— 7:00 "Texas Li'l Darlin'," from the Mark Hellinger Theatre, for *Tonight on Broadway.*

5 December 1949— 8:00 "Star Over Bridgeport," for *Silver Theatre. Cast:* Richard Hart.

  9:30 *The Goldbergs.*

  10:00 "Henry IV," by Luigi Pirandello, adapted by Maurice Valency, for *Studio One. Cast:* Richard Purdy, Catherine Willard, Berry Kroeger, Virginia McMahon.

6 December 1949— 8:00–8:59 *Film Theater of the Air.*

  9:00 "My Heart's in the Highlands," by William Saroyan, for *Actor's Studio. Cast:* John McQuade, Butch Cavell.

  9:30 "The Scar," for *Suspense. Cast:* Edgar Stehli.

8 December 1949— 8:00–8:29 *Front Page Film Theatre.*

  9:35–10:44 *Film Theater.*

9 December 1949— 8:00 *Mama.*

  8:30 *The Man Against Crime.*

10 December 1949— 8:30–9:59 *Film Theater of the Air.* Sponsor: spot announcements by various companies.

11 December 1949— 7:00 "The Closing Door," from the Empire Theatre, for *Tonight on Broadway.*

12 December 1949— 8:00 "Strange Rebound," for *Silver Theatre. Cast:* Vicki Cummings.

  9:30 *The Goldbergs.*

  10:00 "Jane Eyre," by Charlotte Brontë, adapted by Worthington Miner, for *Studio One. Director:* Franklin Schaffner. *Cast:* Mary Sinclair, Charlton Heston, Viola Roache.

13 December 1949— 8:00–8:59 *Film Theater of the Air.*

9:00 "The Midway," for *Actor's Studio. Cast:* Ann Shepherd, George Reeves.

9:30 "The Gray Helmet," by Robert Carse, adapted by Halsted Welles, for *Suspense. Cast:* Jack Lemmon, Mort Stevens, Bernard Kates.

15 December 1949— 8:00–8:29 *Front Page Film Theatre.*

8:30–8:59 "Michael and Mary," by A. A. Milne, for *Theatre of Romance. Cast:* Jean Gillespie.

9:35–10:47 *Film Theater.*

16 December 1949— 8:00 *Mama.*

8:30 *The Man Against Crime.*

9:00 "Little Women," by Louisa May Alcott, for *Ford Theater. Director:* Marc Daniels. *Cast:* Kim Hunter, June Lockhart, Patricia Kirkland, Meg Mundy, Karl Malden.

17 December 1949— 8:31–9:55 *Film Theater of the Air.*

18 December 1949— 7:00 "Sleeping Beauty," from *Howdy Mr. Ice of 1950,* for *Tonight on Broadway.*

19 December 1949— 8:00 "The Guilding Star," for *Silver Theatre. Cast:* Clem Bevans.

9:30 *The Goldbergs.*

10:00 "Mary Poppins," by Pamela L. Travers, adapted by Worthington Miner, for *Studio One. Cast:* Mary Wickes, E. G. Marshall, Tommy Rettig, Valerie Cossart, Iris Mann.

20 December 1949— 8:00–8:59 *Film Theater of the Air.*

9:00 "A Child Is Born," by Stephen Vincent Benét, for *Actor's Studio. Cast:* Jean Muir.

9:30 "The Seeker and the Sought," by Marie Baumer, adapted by Halsted Welles, for *Suspense. Cast:* Philip Loeb, Grace Valentine, Eileen Heckart, Joseph Holland.

22 December 1949— 8:00 *Front Page Film Theatre.*

9:30–10:44 *Film Theater of the Air.*

23 December 1949— 8:00 *Mama.*

8:30 *The Man Against Crime.*

24 December 1949— 8:30–10:00 *Film Theater of the Air.*

25 December 1949— 7:00 Variety from CBS studio for final *Tonight on Broadway.* Producer: Barry Wood. *Cast:* Robert Q. Lewis.

26 December 1949— 8:00 "Four Callers," for *Silver Theatre. Cast:* Donald Buka.

9:30 *The Goldbergs.*

10:00 "The Inner Light, by Dr. Hugo Caergo, adapted by Joseph Liss, for *Studio One. Cast:* Margaret Phillips, Richard Purdy.

27 December 1949— 8:00–8:59 *Film Theater of the Air.*

9:00 "Country Full of Sweden," for *Actor's Studio. Cast:* Dorothy Sands, E. G. Marshall, Elliott Sullivan.

9:30 "The Case of Lady Sannox," by Arthur Conan Doyle, adapted by Robert Wallsten, for *Suspense. Cast:* Berry Kroeger, Stella Adler, Henry Brandon.

29 December 1949— 8:00–8:29 *Front Page Film Theatre.*

8:30–8:59 "The Afternoon of a Faun," for *Theatre of Romance. Cast:* Steven Hill, Bethel Leslie, Cara Williams.

9:30 *Film Theater of the Air.*

30 December 1949— 8:00 *Mama.*

8:30 *The Man Against Crime.*

9:00 "The Farmer Takes a Wife," by Marc Connelly and Frank Ball Elser, for *Ford Theater. Cast:* Dane Clark, Geraldine Brooks.
31 December 1949— 8:30–10:00 *Film Theater of the Air.*

1950

2 January 1950— 8:00 "The First Snow of 1950," for *Silver Theatre. Cast:* Conrad Nigel, Joyce Mathews, George Reeves.
9:30 *The Goldbergs.*
10:00 "Riviera," by Ferenc Molnar, adapted by Worthington Miner, for *Studio One. Cast:* Dolly Haas, David Opatoshu, Tonio Selwart.
3 January 1950— 8:00–8:59 *Film Theater of the Air.*
9:00 "Hannah," for *Actor's Studio. Cast:* Frances Ingalls, Eva Condon.
9:30 "Morning Boat to Africa," for *Suspense. Cast:* Nina Foch.
5 January 1950— 8:00–8:29 *Front Page Film Theatre.*
9:30 *Film Theater of the Air.*
6 January 1950— 8:00 *Mama.*
8:30 *The Man Against Crime.*
9 January 1950— 8:00 "Papa Romani," for *Silver Theatre. Cast:* Chico Marx, William Frawley, Margaret Hamilton.
9:30 *The Goldbergs.*
10:00 "Beyond Reason," by Devery Freeman, adapted by Worthington Miner, for *Studio One. Cast:* Mary Sinclair, Stanley Ridges, Richard Derr, Haila Stoddard.
10 January 1950— 8:00–8:59 *Film Theatre of the Air.*
9:00 "An Ingenue of the Sierras," for *Actor's Studio. Cast:* Elliott Sullivan, Nancy Franklin.
9:30 "The Bomber Command," for *Suspense. Cast:* Susan Douglas, George Reeves.
12 January 1950— 8:00–8:30 *Front Page Film Theatre.*
10:00–11:07 *Film Theater.*
13 January 1950— 8:00 *Mama.*
8:30 *The Man Against Crime.*
9:00 "The Barker," by Kenyon Nicholson, for *Ford Theater. Cast:* Lloyd Nolan, Eileen Eckhart, William Redfield, Jean Carson.
14 January 1950— 8:30–10:00 *Film Theater of the Air.*
15 January 1950— 7:00–7:30 *The Girls,* situation comedy, based on *Our Hearts Were Young and Gay,* by Cornelia Otis Skinner and Emily Kimbrough, debuts.
16 January 1950— 8:00 "Happy Marriage," for *Silver Theatre. Cast:* Carol Bruce.
9:30 *The Goldbergs.*
10:00 "Give Us Our Dream," by Arthemise Goertz, adapted by Worthington Miner, for *Studio One. Cast:* Josephine Hull, Marie Powers, Charlotte Keane, Butterfly McQueen.
17 January 1950— 8:00–8:59 *Film Theater of the Air.*
9:00 "The Little Wife," by William Marik, adapted by David Shaw, for *Actor's Studio. Cast:* Mary McLeod, George Keane.
9:30 "Summer Storm," for *Suspense. Cast:* E. G. Marshall, Jackie Diamond.
19 January 1950— 8:00–8:30 *Front Page Film Theatre.*
9:00–9:30 *Escape,* debut. *Producer/Director:* Wyllis Cooper.

20 January 1950— 8:00 *Mama*.

8:30 *The Man Against Crime*.

21 January 1950—10:00 "Court Is in Session," for *Film Theater of the Air*.

22 January 1950— 7:00 *The Girls*.

23 January 1950— 8:00 "The Great Nikoli," for *Silver Theatre*. *Cast:* Mikhail Rasumny, Peter Capell.

8:30 *The Goldbergs*.

10:00 "The Rockingham Tea Set," by Virginia Douglass Dawson, adapted by Worthington Miner and Matthau Horlib, for *Studio One*. *Cast:* Louise Allbritton, Judson Laire, Grace Kelly, Katherine Emmett, Catherine Willard.

24 January 1950— 8:00–8:27 "Shadows of Suspicion," for *Film Theater*.

9:00 "The Timid Guy," for *Actor's Studio*. *Cast:* Philip Truex, Patricia Kirkland, Henry Jones.

9:30 "The Horizontal Man," for *Suspense*. *Cast:* Mildred Natwick.

26 January 1950— 8:00–8:29 *Front Page Film Theatre*.

9:00 *Escape*.

10:00–10:59 "Court Is in Session," for *Film Theater of the Air*.

27 January 1950— 8:00 *Mama*.

8:30 *The Man Against Crime*.

9:00 "Laburnum Grove," by J. B. Priestley, for *Ford Theater*. *Cast:* Raymond Massey, Valerie and Ernest Cossart.

29 January 1950— 7:00 *The Girls*.

30 January 1950— 8:00 "Never Hit a Pigeon," for *Silver Theatre*. *Cast:* Gene Anton, Jr., Jo Anne Dolan.

9:30 *The Goldbergs*.

10:00 "Father and the Angels," by William Manners, adapted by David Shaw, for *Studio One*. *Cast:* Stanley Ridges.

31 January 1950— 8:00–8:59 *Film Theater of the Air*.

9:00 "Joe McSween's Atomic Machine," for *Actor's Studio*. *Cast:* Conrad Janis, Nancy Franklin.

9:30 "The Distant Island," for *Suspense*. *Cast:* Patricia Kirkland.

2 February 1950— 9:00 *Escape*.

3 February 1950— 8:00 *Mama*.

8:30 *The Man Against Crime*.

9:00–9:59 "Telas, the King," for *Actor's Studio*. *Cast:* Susan Douglas, Robert Pastene.

4 February 1950—10:00–11:37 *Film Theater of the Air*.

5 February 1950— 7:00 *The Girls*.

6 February 1950— 8:00 "The Late Mr. Beasley," for *Silver Theatre*. *Cast:* Donald Curtis.

9:30 *The Goldbergs*.

10:00 "The Loud Red Patrick," by Ruth McKenny and John Boruff, adapted by Worthington Miner, for *Studio One*. *Cast:* Dick Foran, Peg Hillias, Joy Geffen.

7 February 1950— 8:00 *Film Theater of the Air*.

9:00–9:29 *Stage Door*, based on George S. Kaufman and Edna Ferber's play, debuts. *Cast:* Louise Allbritton, Scott McKay.

9:30 "Escape This Night," for *Suspense*. *Cast:* Donald Buka, Robert Harris, Peter Capell.

9 February 1950— 9:00 *Escape*.

    9:45–9:58 *Film Theater of the Air.*

10 February 1950— 8:00 *Mama.*

    8:30 *The Man Against Crime.*

    9:00 "The Royal Family," by George S. Kaufman and Edna Ferber, for *Ford Theater of the Air. Cast:* Margaret Wycherly, Carol Goodner, Richard Waring.

11 February 1950—10:00–11:26 *Film Theater of the Air.*

12 February 1950— 7:00 *The Girls.*

13 February 1950— 8:00 "Gaudy Lady," for *Silver Theatre. Cast:* Glenda Farrell.

    9:30 *The Goldbergs.*

    10:00 "Flowers from a Stranger," by Dorothea Carousso, for *Studio One. Cast:* Felicia Montealegre, Yul Brynner.

14 February 1950— 9:00 *Stage Door.*

    9:30 "The Suicide Club," by Robert Louis Stevenson, for *Suspense. Cast:* Donald Buka, Ralph Clanton.

16 February 1950— 9:00 *Escape.*

17 February 1950— 8:00 *Mama.*

    8:30 *The Man Against Crime.*

    9:00 "Mr. Mummery's Suspicion," for *Actor's Studio. Cast:* George Keane, Ann Shaw.

18 February 1950—10:00 *Film Theater of the Air.*

19 February 1950— 7:00 *The Girls.*

20 February 1950— 8:00 "My Brother's Keeper," for *Silver Theatre,* first time on film. *Cast:* Ward Bond, Glenn Corbett, Beverly Tyler.

    9:30 *The Goldbergs.*

    10:00 "The Wisdom Tooth," by Marc Connelly, for *Studio One. Cast:* Jack Lemmon, Barbara Bolton.

21 February 1950— 9:00 *Stage Door.*

    9:30 "Roman Holiday," for *Suspense. Cast:* Leslie Nielsen, Jack Simond.

23 February 1950— 9:00 *Escape.*

24 February 1950— 8:00 *Mama.*

    8:30 *The Man Against Crime.*

    9:00 "Uncle Harry," by Thomas Job, for *Ford Theater. Cast:* Joseph Schildkraut, Eva le Gallienne.

25 February 1950—10:00 *Film Theater of the Air.*

26 February 1950— 7:00 *The Girls.*

27 February 1950— 8:00 "For Richer, for Poorer," for *Silver Theatre. Cast:* Geraldine Brooks, Richard Derr.

    9:30 *The Goldbergs.*

    10:00 "The Willow Cabin," by Pamela Frankau, for *Studio One. Cast:* Priscilla Gillette, Charlton Heston.

28 February 1950— 9:00 *Stage Door.*

    9:30 "The Man Who Talked in His Sleep," for *Suspense. Cast:* Edith Atwater, Donald Briggs.

2 March 1950— 9:00 *Escape.*

3 March 1950— 8:00 *Mama.*

    8:30 *The Man Against Crime.*

    9:00–9:59 "The Apple Tree," by John Galsworthy, for *The Play's the Thing,* debut. *Cast:* John Merivale, Patricia Kirkland, Grace Kelly.

4 March 1950—10:00 *Film Theater of the Air.*

5 March 1950—7:00 *The Girls.*

6 March 1950—8:00 "Lucky Pierre," for *Silver Theatre. Cast:* George Ripka, Skip Homeier, Ben Gross.

9:30 *The Goldbergs.*

10:00 "The Dreams of Jasper Hornby," by Kevin Mullin, for *Studio One. Cast:* David Wayne, Doris Rich, Tom Carney, Alan Stevenson.

7 March 1950—9:00 *Stage Door.*

9:30 "The Ledge," for *Suspense. Cast:* Dick Foran, E. G. Marshall.

9 March 1950—9:00 *Escape.*

10 March 1950—8:00 *Mama.*

8:30 *The Man Against Crime.*

9:00 "Room Service," by John Murray and Alvin Boretz, for *Ford Theater. Cast:* Jack Carson, Hume Cronyn.

11 March 1950—10:00 *Film Theater of the Air.*

12 March 1950—7:00 *The Girls.*

13 March 1950—8:00 "Quiet Neighborhood," for *Silver Theatre. Cast:* Nancy Coleman.

9:30 *The Goldbergs.*

10:00 "The Dusty Godmother," by Michael Foster, for *Studio One. Cast:* Mac-Donald Carey, Mary Sinclair, Laura Weber.

14 March 1950—9:00 *Stage Door.*

9:30 "The Parcel," for *Suspense. Cast:* Conrad Janis, Ann Thomas.

16 March 1950—9:00 *Escape.*

17 March 1950—8:00 *Mama.*

8:30 *The Man Against Crime.*

9:00–9:59 "The Pink Hussar," for *The Play's the Thing. Cast:* Joseph Buloff, George Keane, Leonore Aubert.

18 March 1950—10:00 *Film Theater of the Air.*

19 March 1950—7:00 *The Girls.*

20 March 1950—8:00 "Concerning the Soul of Felicity," for *Silver Theatre. Cast:* Ilka Chase.

9:30 *The Goldbergs.*

10:00 "The Survivors," by Irwin Shaw and Peter Viertel, for *Studio One. Cast:* Leslie Nielsen, Donald Curtis, Stanley Ridges.

21 March 1950—9:00 *Stage Door.*

9:30 "The Old Man's Badge," for *Suspense. Cast:* Barry Nelson, Steven Hill.

23 March 1950—9:00 *Escape.*

24 March 1950—8:00 *Mama.*

8:30 *The Man Against Crime.*

9:00 "Dear Brutus," by James M. Barrie, for *Ford Theater. Cast:* Brian Aherne, Mary Malone, Valerie Cossart, Ralph Riggs.

25 March 1950—10:00 *Film Theater.*

26 March 1950—7:00 *The Girls.*

27 March 1950—8:00 "The Howland Fling," for *Silver Theatre. Cast:* Carol Goodner, Vinton Hayworth.

9:30 *The Goldbergs.*

10:00 "A Passenger to Bali," by Ellis St. John, for *Studio One. Cast:* Berry Kroeger, Francis Compton, E. G. Marshall, Colin Keith-Johnston.

28 March 1950—9:00 *Stage Door.*

9:30 "The Second Class Passenger," for *Suspense. Cast:* Leslie Nielsen, Monica Boyer, Alfreda Wallace.

30 March 1950— 9:00 *Escape.*

31 March 1950— 8:00 *Mama.*

    8:30 *The Man Against Crime.*

    9:00 "The Salt of the Earth," for *The Play's the Thing. Cast:* Ann Shepherd, Robert Pastene.

1 April 1950—10:00 *Film Theater.*

2 April 1950— 7:00–7:29 "Second Concerto," for *Starlight Theatre,* debut. *Cast:* Meg Mundy, Barry Nelson.

3 April 1950— 8:00 "Coals of Fire," for *Silver Theatre. Cast:* Carol Thurston, Vinton Hayworth.

    9:30 *The Goldbergs.*

    10:00 "The Scarlet Letter," by Nathaniel Hawthorne, for *Studio One. Cast:* Mary Sinclair, John Baragrey, Richard Purdy.

4 April 1950— 9:30 "One Thousand Dollars to One for Your Money," for *Suspense. Cast:* Tom Drake, Carol Williams, Betty Garde, Paul Stewart.

7 April 1950— 8:00 *Mama.*

    8:30 *The Man Against Crime.*

    9:00 "The Little Minister," by James M. Barrie, for *Ford Theater. Cast:* Tom Drake, Frances Reid, Ian Keith, Rhoderick Walker.

8 April 1950—10:00 *Film Theater.*

9 April 1950— 7:00 "Night Before Sailing," for *Starlight Theatre. Cast:* Valerie Cossart, Mildred Natwick, Lawrence Fletcher.

10 April 1950— 8:00 "Minor Incident," for *Silver Theatre. Cast:* Nancy Kelly, Donald Woods.

    9:30 *The Goldbergs.*

    10:00 "Walk the Dark Streets," by William Krasner, for *Studio One. Cast:* Franchot Tone, Sally Gracie, Patricia Ferris.

11 April 1950— 8:00–8:59 *Film Theater of the Air.*

    9:30 "Steely, Steely Eyes," for *Suspense. Cast:* Betty Garde.

14 April 1950— 8:00 *Mama.*

    8:30 *The Man Against Crime.*

    9:00 "Sanctuary in Paris," for *The Play's the Thing. Cast:* Elliott Sullivan, Joan Chandler.

15 April 1950—*Premier Playhouse.*

16 April 1950— 7:00 "The M. P. and the Mouse," for *Starlight Theatre. Cast:* Susan Douglas, William Prince.

17 April 1950— 8:00 "Double Feature," for *Silver Theatre. Cast:* Don DeFore, Diana Lynn. 9:30 *The Goldbergs.*

    10:00 "Torrents of Spring," by Ivan Turgenev, for *Studio One. Cast:* Louise Allbritton, John Baragrey.

18 April 1950— 8:00–8:59 *Film Theater of the Air.*

    9:30 "Murder at the Mardi Gras," for *Suspense. Cast:* Hume Cronyn, Tom Drake.

19 April 1950— 9:30–9:59 *Stage 13,* debut. Producer/Director: Wyllis Cooper.

21 April 1950— 8:00 *Mama.*

    8:30 *The Man Against Crime.*

    9:00 "The School for Scandal," by Richard Brinsley Sheridan, for *Ford Theater. Cast:* Leueen MacGrath, Margalo Gillmore, Ian Keith, Philip Bourneuf.

22 April 1950—*Premier Playhouse*.

23 April 1950—7:00 "White Mail," for *Starlight Theatre*. *Cast:* Margaret Phillips, George Reeves.

24 April 1950—8:00 "Bad Guy," for *Silver Theatre*. *Cast:* Lee Bowman, John Archer, Barbara Lawrence.

9:30 *The Goldbergs*.

10:00 "The Horse's Mouth," by Joyce Cary, for *Studio One*. *Cast:* Burgess Meredith.

25 April 1950—8:00–8:59 *Film Theater of the Air*.

9:30 "The Gentleman from America," for *Suspense*. *Cast:* Barry Nelson.

26 April 1950—9:30 *Stage 13*.

28 April 1950—8:00 *Mama*.

8:30 *The Man Against Crime*.

9:00 "Screwball," for *The Play's the Thing*. *Cast:* Jack Gilford, Lee Grant.

29 April 1950—9:00–9:59 "Puzzle for Friends," for *The Trap*, debut. *Cast:* George Keane, Jean Carson, Vera Allen, Joseph De Santis.

10:00–11:30 *Film Theater*.

30 April 1950—7:00 "The Sire de Maletroit's Door," by Robert Louis Stevenson, for *Starlight Theatre*. *Cast:* Douglas Watson, Mary Sinclair.

1 May 1950—8:00 "The First Hundred Years," for *Silver Theatre*. *Cast:* Barbara Whiting, William Frawley, Jimmy Lydon, Allene Roberts.

9:30 *The Goldbergs*.

10:00 "Miracle in the Rain," by Ben Hecht, for *Studio One*. *Cast:* Jeffrey Lynn, Joy Geffen, Eleanor Wilson.

2 May 1950—8:00–8:59 *Film Theater of the Air*.

9:30 "Death of a Dummy," for *Suspense*. *Cast:* Conrad Janis.

3 May 1950—9:30 "Midsummer's Eve," for *Stage 13*. *Cast:* Pat O'Malley, Richard MacMurray, Emily Barnes.

5 May 1950—8:00 *Mama*.

8:30 *The Main Against Crime*.

9:00 "Father Malachy's Miracle," for *Ford Theater*. *Cast:* Ernest Truex.

6 May 1950—9:00 "Lonely Boy," for *The Trap*. *Cast:* Wright King, Howard Wierum, Dorothy Sands.

10:00 *Premier Playhouse*.

7 May 1950—7:00 "The Song the Soldiers Sang," for *Starlight Theatre*. *Cast:* Scott McKay.

8 May 1950—8:00 "Lady with Ideas," for *Silver Theatre*. *Cast:* Pamela Britton, Gig Young, Mikhail Rasumny.

9:30 *The Goldbergs*.

10:00 "A Wreath of Roses," by Charles S. Monroe, for *Studio One*. *Cast:* Conrad Nagel, Charles Korvin, Margaret Phillips.

9 May 1950—8:00–8:59 *Film Theater of the Air*.

9:30 "Red Wine," for *Suspense*. *Cast:* Tom Drake, Hume Cronyn.

10 May 1950—9:30 "Never Murder Your Grandfather," for *Stage 13*. *Cast:* Leslie Nielsen, Barbara Bolton.

12 May 1950—8:00 *Mama*.

8:30 *The Man Against Crime*.

9:00 "Alison's House," by Susan Glaspell, for *The Play's the Thing*. *Cast:* Flora Campbell.

13 May 1950— 9:00 "The Last Thing I Do," for *The Trap*. *Cast:* Richard Purdy, Robert Pastene, John D. Seymour.
   10:00 *Premier Playhouse*.
14 May 1950— 7:00 "The Roman Kid," by Paul Gallico, for *Starlight Theatre*. *Cast:* Barry Nelson, Joan Chandler.
15 May 1950— 8:00 "Papa Romani," for *Silver Theatre*, repeat.
   9:30 *The Goldbergs*.
   10:00 "The Ambassadors," by Henry James for *Studio One*. *Cast:* Ilona Massey.
16 May 1950— 8:00–8:59 *Film Theater of the Air*.
   9:30 "One and One's a Lonesome," for *Suspense*. *Cast:* Nina Foch, Scott McKay, Meg Mundy, Robert Emhardt.
17 May 1950— 9:30 "Permission to Kill," for *Stage 13*. *Cast:* Alice Reinheart.
19 May 1950— 8:00 *Mama*.
   8:30 *The Main Against Crime*.
   9:00 "Subway Express," by Eva May Flint and Martha Madison, for *Ford Theater*. *Cast:* Ian Keith, Mary Mason, Richard Newton.
20 May 1950— 9:00 "Stan, the Killer," for *The Trap*. *Cast:* E. G. Marshall, Herbert Berghoff, Michael Ozep.
   10:00 *Premier Playhouse*.
21 May 1950— 7:00 "Her Son," for *Starlight Theatre*. *Cast:* Oliver Thorndike, Mildred Natwick, Neil Hamilton.
22 May 1950— 8:00 "Wedding Anniversary," for *Silver Theatre*. *Cast:* Virginia Bruce, Rita Leroy, Louis Jean Heydt.
   9:30 *The Goldbergs*.
   10:00 "The Room Upstairs," by Mildred Davis, for *Studio One*. *Cast:* Valerie Bettis, Mary Sinclair.
23 May 1950— 8:00–8:50 *Film Theater of the Air*.
   9:30 "Photo Finish," for *Suspense*. *Cast:* Ralph Clanton, Eileen Heckart.
24 May 1950— 9:30 "The Last Man," for *Stage 13*. *Cast:* Vinton Hayworth.
26 May 1950— 8:00 *Mama*.
   8:30 *The Man Against Crime*.
   9:00 "The Token," for *The Play's the Thing*. *Cast:* Grace Kelly, Mark Roberts.
27 May 1950— 9:00 "Sentence of Death," for *The Trap*. *Cast:* Leslie Nielsen, Kim Stanley, George Reeves, Joseph Boland.
   10:00 *Premier Playhouse*.
28 May 1950— 7:00 "The Juggler," for *Starlight Theatre*. *Cast:* Betty Garde, Barry Nelson, Judy Parrish.
29 May 1950— 8:00 "Close-Up," for *Silver Theatre*. *Cast:* Ann Dvorak, Donald Woods.
   9:30 *The Goldbergs*.
   10:00 "The Man Who Had Influence," by Don Mankiewicz, for *Studio One*. *Cast:* Robert Sterling.
30 May 1950— 8:00–8:59 *Film Theater of the Air*.
   9:30 "Listen, Listen," for *Suspense*. *Cast:* Mildred Natwick.
31 May 1950— 9:30 "Now You See Him," for *Stage 13*. *Cast:* Dennis Harrison.
   10:00 *Film Theater*.
2 June 1950— 8:00 *Mama*.
   8:30 *The Man Against Crime*.
   9:00 "The Shining Hour," by Keith Winter, for *Ford Theater*. *Cast:* Lois Wheeler, Margaret Lindsay, Richard Derr.

3 June 1950— 9:00 "Chocolate Cobweb," for *The Trap*. *Cast:* Nancy Franklin, Peter Brandon, Luella Gear.

10:00 *Premier Playhouse*.

4 June 1950— 7:00 "The Winner and the Champion," for *Starlight Theatre*. *Cast:* Virginia Gilmore, Mark Roberts.

5 June 1950— 8:00 "Walt and Lavinia," for *Silver Theatre*. *Cast:* Don DeFore, Diana Lynn.

9:30 *The Goldbergs*.

10:00 "The Taming of the Shrew," by William Shakespeare, for *Studio One*. *Cast:* Lisa Kirk, Charlton Heston.

6 June 1950— 8:00–8:59 *Film Theater of the Air*.

9:30 "Black Bronze," for *Suspense*. *Cast:* Franchot Tone, Joan Diener.

7 June 1950— 9:30 *Stage 13*.

10:00–10:59 *Film Theater*.

9 June 1950— 8:30 *The Man Against Crime*.

9:00 "The Swan," by Ferenc Molnar, for *The Play's the Thing*. *Cast:* Grace Kelly, George Keane, Alfred Ryder.

10 June 1950— 9:00 "The Man They Acquitted," for *The Trap*. *Cast:* Torin Thatcher.

10:00 "Winter Carnival," for *Film Theater*.

11 June 1950— 7:00 "Verna," for *Starlight Theatre*. *Cast:* Don Matthews, Bernie Kates, Dulcy Jordan.

12 June 1950— 8:00 "Double Feature," for *Silver Theatre*.

10:00 "Zone Four," by Fielder Cook, for *Studio One*. *Cast:* Mary Sinclair, Leslie Nielsen, Judson Laire.

13 June 1950— 8:00–8:54 *Film Theater of the Air*.

14 June 1950— 10:00–10:59 *Film Theater of the Air*.

16 June 1950— 8:30 *The Man Against Crime*.

9:00–9:59 *Film Theater of the Air*.

17 June 1950— 9:00 "Three Blind Mice," for *The Trap*. *Cast:* Augusta Dabney, John Newland, Bertha Belmore.

10:00–11:26 "The Kansan," for *Film Theater*.

18 June 1950— 7:00 "The Witch of Woonsapucket," for *Starlight Theatre*. *Cast:* Mary Malone, Conrad Janis.

19 June 1950— 8:00 "Bad Guy," for *Silver Theatre*, repeat.

9:30 *The Goldbergs*.

10:00 "There Was a Crooked Man," by Guy Pierce Jones and Constance Bridges Jones, adapted by Kelly Roos, for *Studio One*. *Cast:* Robert Sterling, Charles Korvin, Richard Purdy, Virginia Graham.

20 June 1950— 8:00–8:59 *Film Theater of the Air*.

9:30 "I'm No Hero," for *Suspense*. *Cast:* Hume Cronyn, Mark Roberts.

21 June 1950— 9:30 "You Have Been Warned," for *Stage 13*. *Cast:* James Monks, Jane White.

10:00 "House of Secrets," for *Film Theater*.

23 June 1950— 8:30 *The Man Against Crime*.

9:00 "The Good Companions," by J. B. Priestly, for *The Play's the Thing*. *Cast:* Edith Atwater, Nancy Franklin, James Noble.

24 June 1950— 9:00 "The Dark Corner," for *The Trap*. *Cast:* Frieda Altman, Warren Stevens, Mary MacLeod, Elliott Sullivan.

10:00 *Premier Playhouse*.

25 June 1950 — 7:00 "The Afternoon of a Faun," for *Starlight Theatre. Cast:* Donald Buka.

26 June 1950 — 8:00 "My Heart's in the Highlands," by William Saroyan, for *Silver Theatre. Cast:* Howard Da Silva, Byron Folgar, Tommy Pihl.

　　9:30 *The Goldbergs.*

　　10:00 "My Granny Van," by George Sessions Perry, for *Studio One. Cast:* Mildred Natwick.

27 June 1950 — 8:00–8:59 *Film Theater of the Air.*

　　9:30 "Wisteria," for *Suspense. Cast:* Conrad Janis, Marjorie Gateson.

28 June 1950 — 9:30 "No More Wishes," for *Studio 13. Cast:* Donald Briggs, Lucille Patton, Phil Sterling.

　　10:00–10:59 "The Ghost and the Guest," for *Film Theater.*

29 June 1950 — 10:30–11:00 *Film Theater.*

30 June 1950 — 8:30 *The Man Against Crime.*

　　9:00 "On Borrowed Time," by Paul Osborn, for *Ford Theater. Cast:* Henry Hull.

1 July 1950 — 10:00 *Premier Playhouse.*

3 July 1950 — 8:00–8:30 "Much Ado About Spring," for *Starlight Theatre. Cast:* Ernest Truex, Sylvia Field.

4 July 1950 — 8:00–8:59 *Sure as Fate*, debut.

　　9:30–9:59 "The Last Juror," for *The Web*, debut. *Cast:* Robert Pastene, John Shay.

5 July 1950 — 9:30–10:59 "The Isle of Forgotten Sins," for *Film Theater.*

7 July 1950 — 8:30–8:59 *Detective's Wife* returns. *Cast:* Donald Curtis, Lynn Bari.

8 July 1950 — 9:00–10:45 *Film Theater.*

10 July 1950 — 8:00 "The Last Kiss," for *Starlight Theatre. Cast:* Mary Sinclair, John McQuade.

11 July 1950 — 8:00 *Sure as Fate.*

　　9:30 "The Orderly Mr. Appleby," for *The Web. Cast:* Jonathan Harris, Selena Royal, Harold Wiernum.

12 July 1950 — Feature Film.

14 July 1950 — 8:30 *Detective's Wife.*

15 July 1950 — 9:01–10:30 *Premier Playhouse.*

16 July 1950 — 10:00–11:23 *Film Theater of the Air.*

17 July 1950 — 9:45–10:58 *Film Theater.*

18 July 1950 — 8:00–8:59 *Film Theater.*

　　9:30 "The Memory of Murder," for *The Web. Cast:* Warren Stevens.

19 July 1950 — 9:31–10:28 *Film Theater.*

20 July 1950 — 9:00–9:29 "The Great Nonentity," for *Starlight Theatre. Cast:* Arnold Stang, George Reeves, Cliff Hall, Cara Williams.

　　9:45–10:59 *Film Theater of the Air.*

21 July 1950 — 8:30 *Detective's Wife.*

22 July 1950 — *Premier Playhouse.*

23 July 1950 — 7:00–7:29 *The Gene Autry Show*, a filmed western, debuts. *Cast:* Gene Autry, Pat Buttram. [It continued until 1956, but is not listed hereafter.]

　　10:00–11:16 *Film Theater.*

24 July 1950 — 9:46–10:59 *Film Theater of the Air.*

25 July 1950 — 8:00–8:59 *Film Theater of the Air.*

　　9:30 "Solo to Singapore," for *The Web. Cast:* Guy Spaull, Robert Chrisholm, Berry Kroeger.

26 July 1950— 9:30–10:59 "Thursday's Child," for *Film Theater of the Air.*

27 July 1950— 9:00 "Three Hours Between Planes," by F. Scott Fitzgerald, for *Starlight Theatre. Cast:* Virginia Gilmore, Alfred Ryder.

9:45 *Film Theater of the Air.*

28 July 1950— 8:30 *Detective's Wife.*

29 July 1950— 9:00 *Premier Playhouse.*

30 July 1950—10:00 "Queen of Broadway," for *Film Theater.*

31 July 1950— 9:45 *Film Theater of the Air.*

1 August 1950— 8:00–8:59 "Scattergood Survives a Murder," for *Film Theater.*

9:30 "Help Wanted," for *The Web. Cast:* Howard Wierum, Peggy French, Robert Downing.

2 August 1950— 9:30 "Secrets of the Loch," for *Film Theater of the Air.*

3 August 1950— 9:00 "Passing Fancy," for *Starlight Theatre. Cast:* Warren Stevens, Olive Deering, James Little.

9:45 "Jive Junction," for *Film Theater of the Air.*

4 August 1950— 8:00–8:29 *Mama,* returns.

8:30–8:59 *Detective's Wife.*

5 August 1950— 9:01–10:44 "Stagecoach," for *Premier Playhouse.*

6 August 1950—10:00–11:12 "My Son, the Hero," for *Film Theater.*

7 August 1950— 9:46 *Film Theater of the Air.*

8 August 1950— 9:30 "Heaven Ran Last," for *The Web. Cast:* John McQuade.

9 August 1950— 9:30 *Film Theater of the Air.*

10 August 1950— 9:00 "The Poet Takes a Wife," for *Starlight Theater. Cast:* Hiram Sherman, Jane Hoffman.

9:46–10:59 "The Contender," for *Film Theater of the Air.*

11 August 1950— 8:00 *Mama.*

8:30 *Detective's Wife.*

12 August 1950— 9:01–10:30 "The Silver Queen," for *Premier Playhouse.*

13 August 1950—10:00 "Of Mice and Men," for *Film Theater.*

14 August 1950— 9:46 "The Yanks are Coming," for *Film Theater.*

15 August 1950— 8:00–8:59 *Film Theater of the Air.*

9:30 "Home for Christmas," for *The Web. Cast:* Leslie Nielsen, George Reeves, Millicent Brower.

16 August 1950— 9:30 "High Command," for *Film Theater of the Air.*

17 August 1950— 9:00 "Forgotten Melody," for *Starlight Theatre. Cast:* Felicia Montealegre.

9:46 *Film Theater of the Air.*

18 August 1950— 8:00 *Mama.*

8:30 *Detective's Wife.*

19 August 1950— 9:01 "House Across the Bay," for *Premier Playhouse.*

20 August 1950—10:00 "Hangmen Also Die," for *Film Theater.*

21 August 1950— 9:46 "Behind Prison Walls," for *Film Theater.*

22 August 1950— 8:00–8:58 "The Black Raven," for *Film Theater of the Air.*

9:30 "Man in the Velvet Hat," for *The Web. Cast:* Vinton Hayworth, Morton Stevens, Randolph Justice Watson.

23 August 1950— 9:30 "It Happened in Paris," for *Film Theater of the Air.*

24 August 1950— 9:00 "Fumble," for *Starlight Theatre. Cast:* Conrad Janis, Gloria Strook, Joshua Shelley.

9:31–10:45 *Film Theater.*

25 August 1950— 8:00 *Mama.*
8:30 *Detective's Wife.*
26 August 1950— 9:01 *Premier Playhouse.*
27 August 1950—10:00 *Film Theater of the Air.*
28 August 1950—10:00–10:59 "Zone Four," by Fielder Cook, replaces "The Other Father," by Laura Z. Hobson, for *Studio One* return.
29 August 1950— 8:00–8:59 *Film Theater of the Air.*
9:30–9:59 "Poison," for *Suspense* return. *Cast:* Arnold Moss.
30 August 1950— 9:30 "Key Witness," for *The Web. Cast:* Diana Douglas, Richard MacMurray, Charles Mendrick.
10:00–10:54 *Film Theater of the Air.*
31 August 1950— 9:00 "The Philanderer," for *Starlight Theatre. Cast:* Ernest Truex, Sylvia Field.
9:31–10:36 "The Girl from Monterey," for *Film Theater.*
1 September 1950— 8:00 *Mama.*
8:30 *Detective's Wife.*
2 September 1950— 9:00–10:24 "I Married a Witch," for *Premier Playhouse.*
3 September 1950—10:00 *Film Theater of the Air.*
4 September 1950—10:00 "Look Homeward, Hayseed," by John Ed Pearce, for *Studio One. Cast:* Tom Avera, Janet Ward, Jane Seymour.
5 September 1950— 8:00–8:59 "Nightfall," for *Sure As Fate. Cast:* John McQuade.
9:30 "A Pocket Full of Murder," for *Suspense. Cast:* Steven Hill, Barry Nelson.
6 September 1950— 9:30 "Dark Cross Roads," for *The Web. Cast:* Colin Keith-Johnston, Richard Frazier, Eva Thomas.
10:00 *Film Theater of the Air.*
7 September 1950— 9:00 "The Face Is Familiar — But," for *Starlight Theatre. Cast:* Barbara Whiting, Joshua Shelley.
10:30–10:59 *Crime Reporter.*
8 September 1950— 8:00 *Mama.*
8:30 *Detective's Wife.*
9:00 "The Traitor," by Herman Wouk, for *Ford Theater* season debut. Director: Franklin Schaffner. *Cast:* Lee Tracy, Barbara Ames, Walter Hampden.
9 September 1950— 9:00 "Crystal Ballroom," for *Premier Playhouse.*
10 September 1950—10:00 *Film Theater of the Air.*
11 September 1950—10:00 "Mist," by Rita Weiman, for *Studio One. Cast:* Tamara Geva, Stanley Ridges, Sally Chamberlin.
12 September 1950— 8:00 "Child's Play," for *Sure As Fate. Cast:* Victor Jory, Robert Lantin.
9:30 "Edge of Panic," for *Suspense. Cast:* Patrick McVey, Louisa Horton, Haila Stoddard.
13 September 1950— 9:30 "Talk of the Town," for *The Web. Cast:* Don Hanmer, George Reeves. 10:00 *Film Theater of the Air.*
14 September 1950— 9:00 *Starlight Theatre.*
10:30–10:59 "Cassandra Club," for *Film Theatre.*
15 September 1950— 8:00 *Mama.*
8:30 *Detective's Wife.*
9:00–9:59 "The Tale of the Wolf," by Ferenc Molnar, for *Magnavox Theatre*, debut. *Producer:* Garth Montgomery. *Director:* Carl Beier. *Cast:* Ilona Massey, John Wengraf, Steven Hill. Sponsor: Magnavox Corporation.

16 September 1950— 9:00 *Premier Playhouse.*

17 September 1950—10:00 *Film Theater of the Air.*

18 September 1950—10:00 "Trilby," by George duMaurier, for *Studio One. Cast:* Arnold Moss, Priscilla Gillette.

19 September 1950— 8:00 "Run from the Sun," for *Sure As Fate. Cast:* Robert Cummings, Jean Gillespie.

    9:30 "Dark Shadows," for *Suspense. Cast:* William Redfield, Robert Harris.

    10:00–10:29 *Mystery Playhouse/Danger.* Sponsor: Block Drug Company.

20 September 1950— 9:30 "Murder's Challenge," for *The Web. Cast:* E. G. Marshall, Ralph Bell.

    10:00 *Film Theater of the Air.*

21 September 1950— 9:00 *Starlight Theatre.*

    10:00–10:59 "A Double-Dyed Deceiver," for *The Nash Airflyte Theatre* debut. *Producer/Director:* Marc Daniels. *Cast:* Van Heflin, John Payne, Ralph Riggs, Ian Keith, William Gaxton.

22 September 1950— 8:00 *Mama.*

    8:30 *Detective's Wife.*

    9:00 "The Married Look," for *Ford Theater. Cast:* Paul Kelly, Lois Wilson, Betsy Blair.

23 September 1950— 9:00–9:59 *Premier Playhouse.*

25 September 1950— 9:30–9:59 *The Goldbergs* returns. Sponsor: General Foods.

    10:00 "Away from It All," by Val Gielgud, for *Studio One. Cast:* Kevin McCarthy, Haila Stoddard, Richard Purdy.

26 September 1950— 8:00 "Mary Had a Little Lad," for *Sure As Fate. Cast:* Felicia Montealegre, Douglas Watson.

    9:30 "Six to One," for *Suspense. Cast:* Edith Atwater.

    10:00 *Mystery Playhouse/Danger.*

27 September 1950— 9:30 "The Witness," for *The Web. Cast:* Richard Kollnar.

28 September 1950— 9:00 *Starlight Theatre.*

    10:30 "Borrowed Memory," for *The Nash Airflyte Theatre. Cast:* Ruth Hussey, Torin Thatcher, Chester Stratton.

29 September 1950— 8:00 *Mama.*

    8:30 *Detective's Wife.*

    9:00 "The Fog," by John Willard, for *Magnavox Theatre. Cast:* Francis L. Sullivan, Jack Manning, Peter Hobbs.

30 September 1950— 9:00 *Premier Playhouse.*

2 October 1950— 8:00–8:29 "Saturday's Children," by Maxwell Anderson, for *The Lux Video Theatre*, debut. *Cast:* Joan Caulfield, Dean Harens, John Ericson. Sponsor: Lever Bros.

    9:30 *The Goldbergs.*

    10:00 "The Passionate Pilgrim," by Charles Terrott, for *Studio One. Cast:* Leureen MacGrath, Richard Hart.

3 October 1950— 8:00 "Beyond Reason," for *Sure as Fate. Cast:* Haila Stoddard, Joseph Boland, Peggy French.

    9:30 "The Monkey's Paw," by W. W. Jacobs, for *Suspense. Cast:* Mildred Natwick, Stanley Ridges.

    10:00–10:29 "The Fearful One," by Saki, for *Danger* debut. *Producers:* Martin Ritt, Charles Russell, William Dozier. *Cast:* Iris Mann, Nan McFarland, John Shellie.

4 October 1950— 9:00 *Starlight Theatre.*
9:30 "Blessed Are the Meek," for *The Web. Cast:* Jonathan Harris, Robert Harris, Morton Stevens, Peter Capell, Adelaide Klein.
5 October 1950— 9:30–9:59 *Big Town*, debut. *Producers:* Lloyd and Jack Gross, Charles Robinson. *Director:* David Rich. *Cast:* Patrick McVey, Margaret Hayes. Sponsor: Lever Bros.
10:30 "Portrait of Lydia," for *The Nash Airflyte Theatre. Cast:* David Niven, Mary Beth Hughes.
6 October 1950— 8:00 *Mama.*
8:30–8:59 *The Man Against Crime*, returns. Sponsor: R. J. Reynolds.
9:00 "The Marble Faun," by Nathaniel Hawthorne, for *Ford Theater. Cast:* Anna Lee, Alan Shayne, Sally Chamberlin.
9 October 1950— 8:00 "Rosalind," for *The Lux Video Theatre. Cast:* Luise Rainer.
9:30 *The Goldbergs.*
10:00 "Spectre of Alexander Wolff," by Gaito Gazdanov, for *Studio One. Cast:* Joan Chandler, Leslie Nielsen, Murvyn Vye.
10 October 1950— 8:00–8:59 "Biography," by S. N. Behrman, for *The Prudential Family Playhouse*, debut. Producer: Donald Davis. *Cast:* Gertrude Lawrence, Kevin McCarthy, Hiram Sherman.
9:30 "Criminal's Mark," for *Suspense. Cast:* Catherine McLeod, Richard Kiley, Joseph Wiseman.
10:00 "Dressing Up," for *Danger. Cast:* Lee Grant.
11 October 1950— 9:00 *Starlight Theatre.*
9:30 "The Dark Curtain," for *The Web. Cast:* Haila Stoddard, John Newland.
12 October 1950— 8:00 *The George Burns and Gracie Allen Show*, a situation comedy, debuts. *Cast:* George Burns, Gracie Allen, Bea Benaderet, Hal March. Sponsor: Carnation Milk.
9:30 *Big Town.*
10:30 "The Boor," for *The Nash Airflyte Theatre. Cast:* Fredric March.
13 October 1950— 8:00 *Mama.*
8:30 *The Man Against Crime.*
9:00 "Strange Harbor," for *Magnavox Theatre. Cast:* Geraldine Brooks, Dane Clark.
16 October 1950— 8:00 "Shadow on the Heart," for *The Lux Video Theatre. Cast:* Veronica Lake.
9:30 *The Goldbergs.*
10:00 "Good for Thirty Days," by Richard Stern, for *Studio One. Cast:* Stanley Ridges, Sally Chamberlin, Helen Fortesque.
17 October 1950— 8:00 "The Vanishing Lady," for *Sure as Fate. Cast:* Kim Stanley, Jeff Morrow.
9:30 "The Man Who Would Be King," by Rudyard Kipling, for *Suspense. Cast:* Francis L. Sullivan.
10:30 "The Green and Gold String," for *Danger. Cast:* Lee Tracy.
18 October 1950— 9:00–9:30 "The Creative Impulse," by W. Somerset Maugham, for *Teller of Tales* debut. *Cast:* Mildred Natwick, Alan Bunce, Sylvia Field, Chester Stratton, Somerset Maugham as Host.
9:30 "Never Say Die," for *The Web. Cast:* Richard Carlyle.
19 October 1950— 9:30 *Big Town.*
10:30 "The Box Supper," for *The Nash Airflyte Theatre. Cast:* Maguerite Piazza, Dorothy Peterson.

20 October 1950—8:00 *Mama.*
    8:30 *The Man Against Crime.*
    9:00 "Angel Street," by Patrick Hamilton, for *Ford Theater. Cast:* Judith Evelyn.
23 October 1950—6:45–6:59 *Space Cadet* debuts. Later it is a half-hour series, *Tom Corbett, Space Cadet.* Sponsor: Kellogg Company. [Not listed hereafter.]
    8:00 "The Valiant," for *The Lux Video Theatre. Cast:* Nina Foch, Zachary Scott.
    9:30 *The Goldbergs.*
    10:00 "The Road to Jericho," by Elmer Davis, for *Studio One. Cast:* Lydia Clarke, Richard Carlson, John Newland, Ann Shoemaker.
24 October 1950—8:00 "Dodsworth," by Sinclair Lewis, for *The Prudential Family Playhouse. Cast:* Ruth Chatterton, Walter Abel.
    9:30 "Breakdown," by Francis Cockrell and Louis Pollock, for *Suspense. Cast:* Ellen Violett, Don Briggs.
    10:00 "See No Evil," for *Danger. Cast:* Leo Penn, Nancy Franklin.
25 October 1950—9:00 "McKintosh," for *Teller of Tales. Cast:* Torin Thatcher, Francis L. Sullivan, Richard Malek.
    9:30 "Journey by Night," for *The Web. Cast:* Richard Webb, Richard Kiley, Marilyn Monk.
26 October 1950—8:00 *The George Burns and Gracie Allen Show.*
    9:30 *Big Town.*
    10:30 "Municipal Report," for *The Nash Airflyte Theatre. Cast:* Herbert Marshall.
27 October 1950—8:00 *Mama.*
    8:30 *The Man Against Crime.*
    9:00 "Lightnin'," by Winchell Smith, Victor Mapes, and Frank Bacon, for *Magnavox Theatre. Cast:* Leslie Nielsen, Jean Gillespie, Victor Moore.
30 October 1950—8:00 "Mine to Have," for *The Lux Video Theatre. Cast:* Nina Foch, Andrew Duggan.
    9:30 *The Goldbergs.*
    10:00 "Wuthering Heights," by Emily Brontë, for *Studio One. Cast:* Charlton Heston, Mary Sinclair.
31 October 1950—8:00 "Three Blind Mice," for *Sure as Fate. Cast:* John McQuade.
    9:30 "Halloween Hold-Up," for *Suspense. Cast:* Conrad Janis.
    10:00 "The Liquor Glass," for *Danger. Cast:* Fay Bainter.
1 November 1950—9:00 "Winter Cruise," for *Teller of Tales. Cast:* Adrienne Allen.
    9:30 "Mirror of Delusion," for *The Web. Cast:* Grace Kelly, Mary Stuart, Hugh Franklin.
2 November 1950—9:30 *Big Town.*
    10:30 "The Cut Glass Bowl," for *The Nash Airflyte Theatre. Cast:* Martha Scott.
3 November 1950—8:00 *Mama.*
    8:30 *The Man Against Crime.*
    9:00 "Heart of Darkness," by Joseph Conrad, for *Ford Theater. Cast:* Richard Carlson.
6 November 1950—8:00 "The Wonderful Night," for *The Lux Video Theatre. Cast:* Angela Lansbury, Glenn Langen, Cliff Hall.
    9:30 *The Goldbergs.*
    10:00 "The Blond Comes First," by Aben Kandel, for *Studio One. Cast:* Lee Bowman, Virginia Fraser.
7 November 1950—8:00 "Call It a Day," by Dodie Smith, for *The Prudential Family Playhouse. Cast:* Peggy Ann Garner, John Loder, Kay Francis, John McQuade.

9:30 "Nightmare," for *Suspense. Cast:* Richard Kiley, Berry Kroeger.

10:00 "Witness for the Prosecution," by Agatha Christie, for *Danger. Cast:* Sarah Churchill.

8 November 1950— 9:00 "The Unconquered," for *Somerset Maugham Theatre.* [New title for *Teller of Tales.*] *Cast:* Rex Williams, Olive Deering. Sponsor: Bymart & Company.

9:30 "Fit to Kill," for *The Web. Cast:* Conrad Janis. [Program distribution changes from specific designations such as L-local to "network."]

9 November 1950— 8:00 *The George Burns and Gracie Allen Show.*

9:30 *Big Town.*

10:30 "I Won't Take a Minute," for *The Nash Airflyte Theatre. Cast:* Dane Clark.

10 November 1950— 8:00 *Mama.*

8:30 *The Man Against Crime.*

9:00 "Father, Dear Father," for *Magnavox Theatre. Cast:* Edward Everett Horton, Kim Stanley, Leora Thatcher.

13 November 1950— 8:00 "Gallant Lady," for *The Lux Video Theatre. Cast:* Ruth Hussey, Herbert Rudley, John Stephen.

9:30 *The Goldbergs.*

10:00 "The Last Cruise," by Commander William J. Lederer, for *Studio One. Cast:* Leslie Nielsen, Don Dickinson, Richard Webb.

14 November 1950— 8:00 "Ten Days to Spring," for *Sure as Fate. Cast:* Sara Anderson, Theodore Newton.

9:30 "The Brush-Off," for *Suspense. Cast:* Leslie Nielsen, Mary Sinclair.

10:00 "The Man in the Cage," for *Danger. Cast:* Joseph Anthony.

15 November 1950— 9:00 "Episode," for *Somerset Maugham Theatre. Cast:* Grace Kelly, Leo Penn.

9:30 "The Boy," for *The Web. Cast:* Jane Seymour, Joey Walsh.

16 November 1950— 8:00–8:29 "Welcome Home," for *Starlight Theatre,* return. *Cast:* Nancy Kelly, Robert Webber, Dorothy Rohr.

9:20 *Big Town.*

10:30 "Suppressed Desires," for *The Nash Airflyte Theatre. Cast:* Lee Bowman, Meg Mundy.

17 November 1950— 8:00 *Mama.*

8:30 *The Man Against Crime.*

9:00 "The Whiteheaded Boy," by Lennox Robinson, for *Ford Theater. Cast:* Barry Fitzgerald, Biff McQuire, Mildred Natwick, Elinor Randel.

20 November 1950— 8:00 "Goodnight, Please," for *The Lux Video Theatre. Cast:* Franchot Tone.

9:30 *The Goldbergs.*

10:00 "The Floor of Heaven," by Sylvia Chatfield, for *Studio One. Cast:* Glenn Langan, Mabel Taliaferro.

21 November 1950— 8:00 "Three Men on a Horse," by John Cecil Holm and George Abbott, for *The Prudential Family Playhouse. Cast:* Hiram Sherman.

9:30 "The Death Cards," for *Suspense. Cast:* Francis L. Sullivan.

10:00 "Borderline Affair," for *Danger. Cast:* Iris Mann.

22 November 1950— 9:00 "Lord Mountdrago," for *Somerset Maugham Theatre. Cast:* Luis Van Rooten, Arnold Moss.

9:30 "The Amateur," for *The Web. Cast:* Murvyn Vye.

23 November 1950— 8:00 *The George Burns and Gracie Allen Show.*

9:30 *Big Town.*

10:30 "The Doll in the Pink Silk Dress," for *The Nash Airflyte Theatre. Cast:* Ann Rutherford, Otto Kruger.

24 November 1950— 8:00 *Mama.*

8:30 *The Man Against Crime.*

9:00 "The Three Musketeers," by Alexandre Dumas, *Magnavox Theatre. Cast:* Charles Lang, Robert Clarke, John Hubbard, Lyn Thomas, Mel Archer, Kristine Miller. [First one-hour film made for television.]

27 November 1950— 8:00 "The Token," for *The Lux Video Theatre. Cast:* Wanda Hendrix, Dean Harens, June Dayton.

9:30 *The Goldbergs.*

10:00 "Shadow of a Man," by May Sarton, for *Studio One. Cast:* Ilona Massey, John Van Dreelen, Berry Kroeger, Judson Laire.

28 November 1950— 8:00 "The Dancing Doll," for *Sure as Fate. Cast:* Arlene Francis, Haila Stoddard, John Newland, James Nolan.

9:30 "The Hands of Mr. Ottermole," by Thomas Burke, for *Suspense. Cast:* Lawrence Fletcher, Robert Emhardt.

10:00 "Taste of Ashes," for *Danger. Cast:* Rod Steiger, Mary Patton, Joseph Anthony.

29 November 1950— 9:00 "The String of Beads," for *Somerset Maugham Theatre. Cast:* Anna Lee, John Van Dreelen.

9:30 "The Creeper," for *The Web. Cast:* Mary K. Wells, Gene Lyons, Robert Nelson, Natalie Priest.

30 November 1950— 8:00 "Before You Came Along," for *Starlight Theatre. Cast:* Wendy Barrie, Frank Albertson.

9:30 *Big Town.*

10:30 "Trail by Jury," by Gilbert and Sullivan, for *The Nash Airflyte Theatre. Cast:* Ralph Riggs, Patricia Morison, Donald Clark.

1 December 1950— 8:00 *Mama.*

8:30 *The Man Against Crime.*

9:00 "Another Darling," for *Ford Theater. Cast:* Patricia Crowley, Jack Ewing.

4 December 1950— 2:30–2:45 *First Hundred Years,* debut of daily serial. *Producer:* Hoyt Allen. *Director:* Everett Gannon. *Cast:* Jimmy Lydon, Anne Sargent. Sponsor: Procter & Gamble. Not listed hereafter.

8:00 "To Thine Own Self," for *The Lux Video Theatre. Cast:* Melvyn Douglas.

9:30 *The Goldbergs.*

10:00 "Letter from Cairo," by James Robbins Miller, for *Studio One. Cast:* Charlton Heston, Anne Marno.

5 December 1950— 8:00 "The Barretts of Wimpole Street," by Rudolph Besier, for *The Prudential Family Playhouse. Cast:* Helen Hayes, Bethel Leslie, Gene Lockhart, Robert Pastene.

9:30 "The Guy from Nowhere," for *Suspense. Cast:* Barry Nelson, Catherine McLeod, Lawrence Fletcher.

10:00 "Another Man's Poison," for *Danger. Cast:* John Newland.

10:30–10:59 *Tales of the Black Cat,* a local series. Sponsor: Ford Dealers.

6 December 1950— 9:00 "Force of Circumstance," for *Somerset Maugham Theatre. Cast:* Virginia Gilmore, Dennis Harrison.

9:30 "The Deadly Friend," for *The Web. Cast:* Richard Purdy, E. G. Marshall, Raymond Bramley, Jimsey Sommers.

7 December 1950— 8:00 *The George Burns and Gracie Allen Show.*
9:30 *Big Town.*
10:30 "The Case of the Missing Lady," for *The Nash Airflyte Theatre. Cast:* Ronald Reagan.

8 December 1950— 8:00 *Mama.*
8:30 *The Man Against Crime.*
9:00 "The Hurricane at Pilgrim Hill," for *Magnavox Theatre. Cast:* Cecil Kellaway, Virginia Grey, Clem Bevans, Leslye Banning.

10 December 1950— 6:00–6:29 *Bigelow Theatre,* filmed dramas, debut.

11 December 1950— 8:00 "The Lovely Menace," for *The Lux Video Theatre. Cast:* Walter Abel, Mercedes McCambridge.
9:30 *The Goldbergs.*
10:00 "Mary Lou," by Catherine Turney, for *Studio One. Cast:* Mildred Natwick, Laura Weber.

12 December 1950— 8:00 "Nightfall," for *Sure as Fate. Cast:* E. G. Marshall, Augusta Dabney, Chester Stratton.
9:30 "The Mallet," for *Suspense. Cast:* Walter Slezak, Pamela Gordon, Claire Williams, Victor Beecroft.
10:00 "The Hungry Woman," for *Danger. Cast:* Marsha Hunt.
10:30 *Tales of the Black Cat.*

13 December 1950— 9:00 "The Round Dozen," for *Somerset Maugham Theatre. Cast:* Mildred Dunnock, Pat O'Malley.
9:30 "Fifty Dollars Reward," for *The Web. Cast:* Dennis Harrison, Jean Gillespie.

14 December 1950— 8:00 *Starlight Theatre.*
9:30 *Big Town.*
10:30 "The Windfall," for *The Nash Airflyte Theatre. Cast:* Peggy Conklin, Gene Lockhart.

15 December 1950— 8:00 *Mama.*
8:30 *The Man Against Crime.*
9:00 "Alice in Wonderland," by Lewis Carroll, for *Ford Theater. Cast:* Iris Mann, Richard Waring, Tiny Shrimp, Lervi Operti.

17 December 1950— 6:00 *Bigelow Theatre.*

18 December 1950— 8:00 "Down Bayou DuBac," for *The Lux Video Theatre. Cast:* Lon McAllister, Diana Lynn.
9:30 *The Goldbergs.*
10:00 "Little Women," Part One, by Louisa May Alcott, for *Studio One. Director:* Lela Swift. *Cast:* Nancy Marchand, Mary Sinclair, June Dayton, Lois Hall, Una O'Conner, John Baragrey, Berry Kroeger, Richard Purdy.

19 December 1950— 8:00 "Over Twenty-One," by Ruth Gordon, for *The Prudential Family Playhouse. Cast:* Ruth Gordon, Paul Stewart.
9:30 "Dancing Dan's Christmas," for *Suspense. Cast:* Wally Cox.
10:00 "The Sergeant and the Doll," for *Danger. Cast:* Laura Weber, James Westerfield.
10:30 *Tales of the Black Cat.*

20 December 1950— 9:00 "Footprints in the Jungle," for *Somerset Maugham Theatre. Cast:* Dennis Hoey, Ronald Alexander, Patricia Wheel.
9:30 "The Friendly Hearts," for *The Web. Cast:* Mildred Dunnock.

21 December 1950— 8:00 *The George Burns and Gracie Allen Show.*
9:30 *Big Town.*

10:30 "Molly Morgan," for *The Nash Airflyte Theatre*. *Cast:* Barbara Bel Geddes, Jane Seymour, James Broderick.

22 December 1950— 8:00 *Mama.*

8:30 *The Man Against Crime.*

9:00–9:29 *Charlie Wild, Private Detective. Producers:* Carlo De'Angelo, Herbert Brodkin. *Director:* Leonard Valenta. *Cast:* John McQuade, Cloris Leachman. Sponsor: Wildroot Company.

9:30–9:59 *The Lone Ranger*, a feature film.

24 December 1950— 6:00 *Bigelow Theatre.*

25 December 1950— 8:00 "A Child Is Born," by Stephen Vincent Benét, for *The Lux Video Theatre. Cast:* Thomas Mitchell, Fay Bainter.

9:30 *The Goldbergs.*

10:00 "Little Women," Part Two, for *Studio One.*

26 December 1950— 8:00 "Tremolo," for *Sure as Fate. Cast:* John McQuade, Mary Patton, Luella Gear.

9:30 "The Tip," for *Suspense. Cast:* Felicia Montealegre, Stanley Ridges.

10:00 "Surprise for the Boys," for *Danger. Cast:* Henry Burke Jones, John McGovern, Joseph Julian.

10:30 *Tales of the Black Cat.*

27 December 1950— 9:00 "Virtue," for *Somerset Maugham Theatre. Cast:* John Merivale, Ruth Madison.

9:30 "Stone Cold Dead," for *The Web. Cast:* John Carradine, Catherine McLeod, Richard Webb.

28 December 1950— 8:00 *Starlight Theatre.*

9:30 *Big Town.*

10:30 "The Kind Mr. Smith," for *The Nash Airflyte Theatre. Cast:* Basil Rathbone, Bethel Leslie, Vinton Hayworth.

29 December 1950— 8:00 *I Remember Mama.* [Formerly *Mama.*]

8:30 *The Man Against Crime.*

9:00 "Cause for Suspicion," for *Ford Theater. Cast:* Glen Langan, Dean Harens, Louisa Horton.

31 December 1950— 6:00 *Bigalow Theatre.*

1951

1 January 1951— 2:30–2:44 *First Hundred Years*, daily serial. [Not listed hereafter.]

8:00–8:29 "A Well-Remembered Voice," for *The Lux Video Theatre. Cast:* Brian Aherne.

9:30–9:59 *The Goldbergs.*

10:00–10:59 "Collector's Item," by Lillian Day and Alfred Golden, for *Studio One. Cast:* Walter Slezak.

2 January 1951— 8:00–8:59 "Burlesque," by George Manker Watters and Arthur Hopkins, for *The Prudential Family Playhouse. Cast:* Donald Curtis, Haila Stoddard, Bert Lahr, Carol Stone.

9:30–9:59 "Death in the River," for *Suspense.*

10:00–10:29 "Charles Markham, Antique Dealer," for *Danger. Cast:* Jerome Thor.

10:30–10:59 *Tales of the Black Cat.*

3 January 1951— 9:00–9:29 "The Treasure," for *Somerset Maugham Theatre. Cast:* Tom Helmore, Beatrice Straight.

9:30–9:59 "Dark Legacy," for *The Web. Cast:* Charles Korvin, Kathleen Comegys, James McDonald, Audra Lindley.

4 January 1951— 8:00–8:29 *The George Burns and Gracie Allen Show.*
9:30–9:59 *Big Town.*
10:30–10:59 "Waltz Dream," for *The Nash Airflyte Theatre. Cast:* Kitty Carlisle, Jimmy Carroll, Marsha Van Dyke.

5 January 1951— 8:00–8:29 *I Remember Mama.*
8:30–8:59 *The Man Against Crime.*
9:00–9:29 *Charlie Wild, Private Detective.*

7 January 1951— 6:00–6:29 *Bigelow Theatre.*

8 January 1951— 8:00 "The Purple Doorknob," for *The Lux Video Theatre. Cast:* Josephine Hull.
9:30 *The Goldbergs.*
10:00 "England Made Me," by Graham Greene, for *Studio One. Cast:* Richard Waring, Joan Wetmore.

9 January 1951— 8:00–8:59 "Macbeth," by William Shakespeare, for *Sure as Fate. Cast:* John Carradine, Judith Evelyn.
9:30 "Tough Cop," for *Suspense. Cast:* Barry Nelson, Katherine Bard.
10:00 "Footfalls," for *Danger. Cast:* Walter Slezak, Henry Jones.
10:30 *Tales of the Black Cat.*

10 January 1951— 9:00 "The Man from Glasgow," for *Somerset Maugham Theatre. Cast:* Jessica Tandy, Robert Harris.
9:30 "The Man Who Had No Friends," for *The Web. Cast:* Haila Stoddard, Steve Elliot.

11 January 1951— 8:00–8:59 "Relatively Speaking," for *Starlight Theatre. Cast:* Melvyn Douglas.
9:30 *Big Town.*
10:30 "The Lipstick," for *The Nash Airflyte Theatre. Cast:* Kitty Carlisle, Robert Pastene, Donald Curtis, Jimmy Carroll, Jane Wyatt.

12 January 1951— 8:00 *I Remember Mama.*
8:30 *The Man Against Crime.*
9:00 *Look* magazine awards, for *Ford Theater.*

14 January 1951— 6:00 *Bigelow Theatre.*

15 January 1951— 8:00 "Purple and Fine Linen," for *The Lux Video Theatre. Cast:* Ilona Massey, Basil Rathbone.
9:30 *The Goldbergs.*
10:00 "Track of the Cat," by Van Tilburg Clark, for *Studio One. Cast:* Stanley Ridges, Jane Seymour.

16 January 1951— 8:00 "Skylark," by Samson Raphaelson, for *The Prudential Family Playhouse. Cast:* Donald Curtis, Haila Stoddard, Donald Cook, John McQuade, Gertrude Lawrence.
9:30 "The Fool's Heart," for *Suspense. Cast:* Henry Hull.
10:00 "Appointment with Death," for *Danger. Cast:* Dean Harens, Jerome Thor.
10:30 *Tales of the Black Cat.*

17 January 1951— 9:00 "The Vessel of Wrath," for *Somerset Maugham Theatre. Cast:* Martha Scott, Bramwell Fletcher.
9:30 "Essence of Strawberry," for *The Web. Cast:* Michael O'Halloran, Leslie Pave, Sally Gracie.

18 January 1951— 8:00 *The George Burns and Gracie Allen Show.*

9:30 *Big Town.*

10:30 "Pot o' Gold," for *The Nash Airflyte Theatre. Cast:* Richard Arlen, Joan Blondell.

19 January 1951— 8:00 *I Remember Mama.*

8:30 *The Man Against Crime.*

9:00 *Charlie Wild, Private Detective.*

21 January 1951— 6:00 *Bigelow Theatre.*

22 January 1951— 8:00 "Manhattan Pastorale," for *The Lux Video Theatre. Cast:* Teresa Wright.

9:30 *The Goldbergs.*

10:00 "The Trial of John Peter Zenger," by Irve Tunick, for *Studio One. Cast:* Judson Laire.

23 January 1951— 8:00 "Distinguished Gathering," for *Sure as Fate.*

9:30 "Dead Fall," for *Suspense. Cast:* Barry Nelson.

10:00 "The Ghost Is Your Heart," for *Danger. Cast:* Frank Albertson.

10:30 *Tales of the Black Cat.*

24 January 1951— 9:00 "Honolulu," for *Somerset Maugham Theatre. Cast:* Luther Adler, Roberta Haines.

9:30 "You Killed Elizabeth," for *The Web. Cast:* Leslie Nielsen, Jerome Thor.

25 January 1951— 3:15–3:29 *Bride and Groom,* daily serial, debut. [Not listed hereafter.]

8:00 "Be Nice to Mr. Campbell," for *Starlight Theatre. Cast:* Jean Parker, Frank McHugh, Augusta Dabney.

9:30 *Big Town.*

10:30 "The Case of the Calico Dog," for *The Nash Airflyte Theatre. Cast:* Nina Foch, Barbara Rollins, Lucille Watson.

26 January 1951— 8:00 *I Remember Mama.*

8:30 *The Man Against Crime.*

9:00 "Final Copy," for *Ford Theater. Cast:* Anna Minot, Robert Sterling.

28 January 1951— 6:00 *Bigelow Theatre.*

29 January 1951— 8:00 "The Shiny People," for *The Lux Video Theatre. Cast:* Robert Cummings.

9:30 *The Goldbergs.*

10:00 "Public Servant," for *Studio One. Cast:* Hume Cronyn, Sally Chamberlin.

30 January 1951— 8:00 "Icebound," by Owen Davis, for *The Prudential Family Playhouse. Cast:* Jessica Tandy, Kevin McCarthy.

9:30 "The Rose Garden," for *Suspense. Cast:* Mildred Natwick, Estelle Winwood.

10:00 "The Anniversary," for *Danger. Cast:* Kim Stanley.

10:30 *Tales of the Black Cat.*

31 January 1951— 9:00 "Partners," for *Somerset Maugham Theatre. Cast:* Dane Clark, Anthony Quinn, Perry Bruskin.

9:30 "The Crisis of Dirk Diamond," for *The Web. Cast:* Alfred Ryder, Robert Emhardt.

1 February 1951— 8:00 *The George Burns and Gracie Allen Show.*

9:30 *Big Town.*

10:30 "The Crisis," for *The Nash Airflyte Theatre. Cast:* Laraine Day.

2 February 1951— 8:00 *I Remember Mama.*

8:30 *The Man Against Crime.*

9:00 *Charlie Wild, Private Detective.*

4 February 1951 — 6:00 *Bigelow Theatre.*

5 February 1951 — 8:00 "The Choir Rehearsal," for *The Lux Video Theatre. Cast:* Martha Scott, Robert Sterling.

9:30 *The Goldbergs.*

10:00 "The Target," by Rita Weiman, for *Studio One. Cast:* Henry Daniell.

6 February 1951 — 8:00 "The Devil Takes a Bride," for *Sure as Fate. Cast:* Leslie Nielsen, Lawrence Fletcher.

9:30 "Night Break," for *Suspense. Cast:* E. G. Marshall, Anne Marno, Jane Seymour.

10:00 "Ask Me Another," for *Danger. Cast:* Wally Cox, Philip Leeds.

10:30 *Tales of the Black Cat.*

7 February 1951 — 9:00 "The Romantic Young Lady," for *Somerset Maugham Theatre. Cast:* Joan Chandler, Art Smith.

9:30 "The Wallet," for *The Web. Cast:* Joey Walsh, John Marley.

8 February 1951 — 8:00 "Julie," for *Starlight Theatre. Cast:* Eve Arden.

9:30 *Big Town.*

10:30 "Peggy," for *The Nash Airflyte Theatre. Cast:* Joan Bennett, Katherine Alexander.

9 February 1951 — 8:00 *I Remember Mama.*

8:30 *The Man Against Crime.*

9:00 "Spring Again," by Isobel Leighton and Bertram Bloch, for *Ford Theater. Cast:* Dorothy Gish, Walter Hampden.

11 February 1951 — 6:00 *Bigelow Theatre.*

12 February 1951 — 8:00 "Abe Lincoln in Illinois," by Robert E. Sherwood, for *The Lux Video Theatre. Cast:* Raymond Massey, Muriel Kirkland, Frank Tweddell.

9:30 *The Goldbergs.*

10:00 "None but My Foe," by David Duncan, for *Studio One. Cast:* John Forsythe.

13 February 1951 — 8:00 "Berkeley Square," by John Balderston, for *The Prudential Family Playhouse. Cast:* Grace Kelly, Richard Greene, Rosalind Ivan, Mary Scott.

9:30 "Double Entry," for *Suspense. Cast:* Virginia Gilmore, Robert Emhardt.

10:00 "The Net Draws Tight," for *Danger. Cast:* E. G. Marshall, Wright King.

10:30 *Tales of the Black Cat.*

14 February 1951 — 9:00 "The Dream," for *Somerset Maugham Theatre. Cast:* Joan Bennett, Francis Lederer.

9:30 "Thread of Life," for *The Web. Cast:* Meg Mundy, Herbert Rudley.

15 February 1951 — 8:00 *The George Burns and Gracie Allen Show.*

9:30 *Big Town.*

10:30 "Pearls Are a Nuisance," for *The Nash Airflyte Theatre. Cast:* Dane Clark, Constance Dowling, Lionel Stander.

16 February 1951 — 8:00 *I Remember Mama.*

8:30 *The Man Against Crime.*

9:00 *Charlie Wild, Private Detective.*

18 February 1951 — 6:00 *Bigelow Theatre.*

19 February 1951 — 8:00 "To the Lovely Margaret," for *The Lux Video Theatre. Cast:* Margaret O'Brien, Skip Homeier.

9:30 *The Goldbergs.*

10:00 "The Way Things Are," by Josephine Lawrence, for *Studio One. Cast:* Barbara Baxley, Richard Carlyle.

20 February 1951— 8:00 "The Rabbit," for *Sure as Fate. Cast:* Maria Riva, Martin Brooks.
9:30 "The Victims," for *Suspense. Cast:* Eileen Heckart, Stanley Ridges.
10:00 "The Corpse and Tighe O'Kane, for *Danger. Cast:* Pat O'Malley, Don Hanmer.
10:30 *Tales of the Black Cat.*
21 February 1951— 9:00 "The People You Meet," for *Somerset Maugham Theatre. Cast:* John Conté, Howard Freeman, Laura Pierpont.
9:30 "For Laura," for *The Web. Cast:* Don Briggs, Will Hare, Barbara Joyce.
22 February 1951— 8:00 "The Magic Wire," for *Starlight Theatre. Cast:* Geraldine Brooks, Leslie Nielsen, Frank Sylvern.
9:30 *Big Town.*
10:30 "A Kiss for Mr. Lincoln," for *The Nash Airflyte Theatre. Cast:* Richard Greene.
23 February 1951— 8:00 *I Remember Mama.*
8:30 *The Man Against Crime.*
9:00 "The Golden Mouth," for *Ford Theater. Cast:* John Forsythe, Anne Marno, Henry Hull, Gerald Mohr, Virginia Gilmore.
25 February 1951— 6:00 *Bigelow Theatre.*
26 February 1951— 8:00 "The Irish Drifter," for *The Lux Video Theatre. Cast:* Pat O'Brien, Jonathan Marlowe.
9:30 *The Goldbergs.*
10:00 "The Ambassadors," by Henry James, for *Studio One. Cast:* Ilona Massey, Robert Sterling, Judson Laire.
27 February 1951— 8:00 "The Ruggles of Red Gap," by Harry Leon Wilson, for *The Prudential Family Playhouse. Cast:* Cyril Ritchard, Glenda Farrell, Walter Abel.
9:30 "Margin for Safety," for *Suspense. Cast:* Denholm Elliott, Francis Bethencourt.
10:00 "Will You Walk Into My Parlor," for *Danger. Cast:* Geraldine Brooke, Joseph Anthony, Laurence Hugo.
28 February 1951— 9:00 "The Outstation," for *Somerset Maugham Theatre. Cast:* Otto Kruger, Edith Atwater, Stefan Schnabel, Joyce Matthews.
9:30 "Star Witness," for *The Web. Cast:* Katherine Bard, Clark Gordon, Charles Mendrick.
1 March 1951— 8:00 *The George Burns and Gracie Allen Show.*
9:30 *Big Town.*
10:30 "Scandalous Conduct," for *The Nash Airflyte Theatre.*
2 March 1951— 8:00 *I Remember Mama.*
8:30 *The Man Against Crime.*
9:00 *Charlie Wild, Private Detective.*
4 March 1951— 6:00 *Bigelow Theatre.*
5 March 1951— 8:00 "Not Guilty — Of Much," for *The Lux Video Theatre. Cast:* Dane Clark, Bonita Granville.
9:30 *The Goldbergs.*
10:00 "One Pair of Hands," by Monica Stevens, for *Studio One. Cast:* Mildred Natwick, Denholm Elliott, Catherine McLeod.
6 March 1951— 8:00 "One in a Million," for *Sure as Fate. Cast:* Joseph Schildkraut.
9:30 "Dr. Jekyll and Mr. Hyde," by Robert Louis Stevenson, for *Suspense. Cast:* Basil Rathbone.

10:00 "The Night of March Fifteenth," for *Danger. Cast:* Tom Ewell.

10:30 *Tales of the Black Cat.*

7 March 1951— 9:00 "The Back of Beyond," for *Somerset Maugham Theatre.*

9:30 "The Shadowy Men," for *The Web. Cast:* E. G. Marshall, Audra Lindley, Viola Roche.

8 March 1951— 8:00 "Miss Buell," for *Starlight Theatre. Cast:* Judith Evelyn, Patricia Peardon, Lonnie Chapman.

9:30 *Big Town.*

10:30 "The Fiddling Fool," for *The Nash Airflyte Theatre. Cast:* Parker Fennelly, Nathan Milstein.

9 March 1951— 8:00 *I Remember Mama.*

8:30 *The Man Against Crime.*

9:00 "The Ghost Patrol," for *Ford Theater. Cast:* Ernest Truex, Jane Seymour, Dennis Harrison.

11 March 1951— 6:00 *Bigelow Theatre.*

12 March 1951— 8:00 "Long Distance," for *The Lux Video Theatre. Cast:* Miriam Hopkins, Lila Lee.

9:30 *The Goldbergs.*

10:00 "A Chill on the Wind," by Edward Gibbons, for *Studio One. Cast:* John Conté, Beatrice Straight, Reba Tassell, Sally Chamberlin, Richard Purdy.

13 March 1951— 8:00 "One Sunday Afternoon," by James Hagen, for *The Prudential Family Playhouse. Cast:* Richard Carlson, Virginia Gilmore, June Lockhart.

9:30 "On a Country Road," for *Suspense. Cast:* John Forsythe, Mary Sinclair, Mildred Natwick.

10:00 "Mr. John Nobody," for *Danger. Cast:* David Opatoshu.

10:30 *Tales of the Black Cat.*

14 March 1951— 9:00 "Halfway to Broadway," for *Somerset Maugham Theatre. Cast:* William Prince, Katherine Bard.

9:30 "Finders Keepers," for *The Web. Cast:* Russell Hardy.

15 March 1951— 8:00 *The George Burns and Gracie Allen Show.* 9:30 *Big Town.*

10:30 "The Professor's Punch," for *The Nash Airflyte Theatre. Cast:* John Beal.

16 March 1951— 8:00 *I Remember Mama.*

8:30 *The Man Against Crime.*

9:00 *Charlie Wild, Private Detective.*

18 March 1951— 6:00 *Bigelow Theatre.*

19 March 1951— 8:00 "No Shoes," for *The Lux Video Theatre. Cast:* Jack Carson.

9:30 *The Goldbergs.*

10:00 "Hangman's House," by Donn Byrne, for *Studio One. Cast:* Jessica Tandy, Kevin McCarthy.

20 March 1951— 8:00 "Errand for Noonan," for *Sure as Fate.* Cast Jerome Thor, Dickie Moore, Teddy Wilson.

9:30 "Telephone Call," for *Suspense. Cast:* Russell Collins, Eileen Heckart, Robert Emhardt.

10:00 "Nightmare," for *Danger. Cast:* Dane Clark, Tony Mottola.

10:30 *Tales of the Black Cat.*

21 March 1951— 9:00 "The Luncheon," for *Somerset Maugham Theatre. Cast:* Robert Cummings.

9:30 "Incident in a Blizzard," for *The Web. Cast:* Robert Pastene, Alfreda Wallace, Lynn Loring.

22 March 1951— 8:00 "Flaxen-Haired Mannequin," for *Starlight Theatre. Cast:* Margaret Hayes, Gil Lamb, Fred Stewart, Julie Bennett.
9:30 *Big Town.*
23 March 1951— 8:00 *I Remember Mama.*
8:30 *The Man Against Crime.*
9:00 "Heart of Darkness," by Joseph Conrad, for *Ford Theater. Cast:* Richard Carlson.
25 March 1951— 6:00 *Bigelow Theatre.*
26 March 1951— 8:00 "The Treasure Trove," for *The Lux Video Theatre. Cast:* Barbara Britton, Bruce Cabot, Dick Foran.
9:30 *The Goldbergs.*
10:00 "The Case of Karen Smith," by Viola Brothers Shore, for *Studio One. Cast:* Felicia Montealegre, Leslie Nielsen.
27 March 1951— 8:00 "The Bishop Misbehaves," by Frederick Jackson, for *The Prudential Family Playhouse. Cast:* Lillian Gish, Walter Hampden.
9:30 "The Three of Silence," for *Suspense. Cast:* Walter Slezak, Betty Garde.
10:00 "Head Print," for *Danger. Cast:* Leo G. Carroll.
10:30 *Tales of the Black Cat.*
28 March 1951— 9:00 "End of Flight," for *Somerset Maugham Theatre. Cast:* Signe Hasso, Alfred Ryder.
9:30 "The Great Diamond Discovery," for *The Web.* Guy Sorel, Robert Allen.
29 March 1951— 8:00 *The George Burns and Gracie Allen Show.*
9:30 *Big Town.*
30 March 1951— 8:00 *I Remember Mama.*
8:30 *The Man Against Crime.*
9:00 *Charlie Wild, Private Detective.*
1 April 1951— 6:00 *Bigelow Theatre.*
2 April 1951— 6:00 *Bigelow Theatre.*
8:00 "The Old Lady Shows Her Medals," by James M. Barrie, for *The Lux Video Theatre. Cast:* Robert Preston, Margaret Wycherly.
9:30 *The Goldbergs.*
10:00 "Wintertime," by Jan Valtin, for *Studio One. Cast:* Patrick Knowles, Anne Marno.
3 April 1951— 8:00 "The Guinea Pigs," for *Sure as Fate. Cast:* Marsha Hunt, Dane Clark.
9:30 "Go Home Dead Man," for *Suspense. Cast:* Jackie Cooper.
10:00 "The Undefeated," for *Danger. Cast:* Walter Slezak.
10:30 *Tales of the Black Cat.*
4 April 1951— 9:00 *Charlie Wild, Private Detective.*
9:30 "Guardian Angel," for *The Web. Cast:* John Stephens, Jerome Thor, Edith King.
5 April 1951— 8:00 "Season for Marriage," for *Starlight Theatre. Cast:* Coleen Gray, Charles Korvin, William Prince.
9:30 *Big Town.*
6 April 1951— 8:00 *I Remember Mama.*
8:30 *The Man Against Crime.*
9:00 "Ticket to Oblivion," for *Ford Theater. Cast:* Signe Hasso, Anthony Quinn.
8 April 1951— 6:00 *Bigelow Theatre.*

9 April 1951— 8:00 "Column Item," for *The Lux Video Theatre*. *Cast:* Laraine Day.
9:30 *The Goldbergs*.
10:00 "Shake the Stars Down," by Pamela Frankau, for *Studio One*. *Cast:* Beverly Whitney, Richard McMurray.
10 April 1951— 9:30 "The Foggy Night Visitor," for *Suspense*. *Cast:* Leslie Neilsen, Cloris Leachman.
10:00 "The Undertaker Calls," for *Danger*. *Cast:* Chester Morris.
11 April 1951— 9:00 *Charlie Wild, Private Detective*.
9:30 "Mr. Fish," for *The Web*. *Cast:* Roland Winters, Bert Conway, Preston Hanson.
12 April 1951— 8:00 *The George Burns and Gracie Allen Show*.
9:30 *Big Town*.
13 April 1951— 8:00 *I Remember Mama*.
8:30 *The Man Against Crime*.
15 April 1951— 6:00 *Bigelow Theatre*.
16 April 1951— 8:00 "Heritage of Wimpole Street," for *The Lux Video Theatre*. *Cast:* Walter Hampden, Patricia Wheel, Judson Ross.
9:30 *The Goldbergs*.
10:00 "Strait and Narrow," by Geoffrey Cotterell, for *Studio One*. *Cast:* Patrick Knowles, Judith Evelyn.
17 April 1951— 8:00–8:59 *Film Theatre*.
9:30 "The Juice Man," for *Suspense*. *Cast:* Cloris Leachman.
10:00 "The Great Gibson Bequest," for *Danger*. *Cast:* Franchot Tone.
10:30 *Tales of the Black Cat*.
18 April 1951— 9:00 *Charlie Wild, Private Detective*.
9:30 "The Dream," for *The Web*. *Cast:* Wesley Addy, Lawrence Fletcher.
19 April 1951— 8:00–8:29 "The Magnificent Faker," for *Starlight Theatre*. *Cast:* Dorothy Gish.
9:30 *Big Town*.
10:30–10:49 *Casey, Crime Photographer*, debuts. Sponsor: Carter Products.
20 April 1951— 8:00 *I Remember Mama*.
8:30 *The Man Against Crime*.
9:00 "The Touchstone," for *Ford Theater*. *Cast:* Margaret Sullavan, Paul McGrath, Jerome Cowan.
22 April 1951— 6:00 *Bigelow Theatre*.
23 April 1951— 8:00 "Hit and Run," for *The Lux Video Theatre*. *Cast:* Edmond O'Brien.
9:30 *The Goldbergs*.
10:00 "The Happy Housewife," by Hedda Rosten, for *Studio One*. *Cast:* John Forsythe, June Dayton.
24 April 1951— 8:00–8:59 *Film Theater*.
9:30 "The Meeting," for *Suspense*. *Cast:* Jackie Cooper, Mildred Natwick, Wally Cox.
10:00 "Blue," for *Danger*. *Cast:* Anthony Quinn, Coleen Gray.
10:30 *Tales of the Black Cat*.
25 April 1951— 9:00 *Charlie Wild, Private Detective*.
9:30 "The Kid's Last Fight," for *The Web*. *Cast:* Russell Hardie, Cliff Hall, Howard Smith.
26 April 1951— 8:00 *The George Burns and Gracie Allen Show*.

9:30 *Big Town.*

27 April 1951 — 8:00 *I Remember Mama.*

8:30 *The Man Against Crime.*

29 April 1951 — 6:00 *Bigelow Theatre.*

30 April 1951 — 8:00 "The Speech," for *The Lux Video Theatre. Cast:* Fredric March, Florence Eldridge.

9:30 *The Goldbergs.*

10:00 "Portrait of Rembrandt," by Irve Tunick, for *Studio One. Cast:* Berry Kroeger, Maria Riva, Judson Laire.

1 May 1951 — 8:00–8:59 *Film Theater of the Air.*

9:30 "No Friend Like an Old Friend," for *Suspense. Cast:* Judith Evelyn, Ruth Ford, Tom Helmore.

10:00 "The Killer Scarf," for *Danger. Cast:* Anne Marno, Gregory Morton.

10:30 *Tales of the Black Cat.*

2 May 1951 — 9:00 *Charlie Wild, Private Detective.*

9:30 "Solid Gold," for *The Web. Cast:* Clay Clement, Polly Rowles.

3 May 1951 — 8:00 "I Guess There Are Other Girls," for *Starlight Theatre. Cast:* Wally Cox.

9:30 *Big Town.*

10:30 *Casey, Crime Photographer.*

4 May 1951 — 8:00 *I Remember Mama.*

8:30 *The Man Against Crime.*

9:00 "Dead on the Vine," for *Ford Theater. Cast:* Margaret Phillips, William Prince, John Alexander, Faith Brook.

6 May 1951 — 6:00 *Bigelow Theatre.*

7 May 1951 — 8:00 "The Sire de Maletroit's Door," by Robert Louis Stevenson, for *The Lux Video Theatre. Cast:* Richard Greene, Coleen Gray.

9:30 *The Goldbergs.*

10:00 "No Tears for Hilda," by Andrew Garve, for *Studio One. Cast:* John Forsythe, Don Dickinson, Patsy Bruder, Howard Smith, Mary Sinclair.

8 May 1951 — 8:00–8:59 *Film Theater of the Air.*

9:30 "Murder in the Ring," for *Suspense. Cast:* Don Briggs, Hiram Sherman, Audrey Christie.

10:00 "The Eye Witness Who Couldn't See," for *Danger. Cast:* June Dayton, John Sylvester.

10:30 *Tales of the Black Cat.*

9 May 1951 — 9:00 *Charlie Wild, Private Detective.*

9:30 "Trojan Horse," for *The Web. Cast:* Jerome Thor, Joseph Anthony.

10 May 1951 — 8:00 *The George Burns and Gracie Allen Show.*

9:30 *Big Town.*

11 May 1951 — 8:00 *I Remember Mama.*

8:30 *The Man Against Crime.*

13 May 1951 — 6:00 *Bigelow Theatre.*

14 May 1951 — 8:00 "Local Storm," for *The Lux Video Theatre. Cast:* Betty Field.

9:30 *The Goldbergs.*

10:00 "The Old Foolishness," by Paul Vincent Carroll, for *Studio One. Cast:* Dick Foran.

15 May 1951 — 8:00–8:59 *Film Theater of the Air.*

9:30 "Too Hot to Live," for *Suspense. Cast:* Billy Redfield, Olive Deering.

10:00 "The Mirror," for *Danger. Cast:* Judith Evelyn.

10:30 *Tales of the Black Cat.*

16 May 1951—9:00 *Charlie Wild, Private Detective.*

9:30 "The Judas Bullet," for *The Web. Cast:* Mary Sinclair, Lawrence Fletcher, Marc Daniels.

17 May 1951—8:00 "Bernice Bobs Her Hair," by F. Scott Fitzgerald, for *Starlight Theatre. Cast:* Mary Sinclair, Anita Loos, Julie Harris.

9:30 *Big Town.*

10:30 *Casey, Crime Photographer.*

18 May 1951—8:00 *I Remember Mama.*

8:30 *The Man Against Crime.*

9:00 "Peter Ibbetson," by George du Maurier, for *Ford Theater. Cast:* Richard Greene, Stella Andrew, Anna Lee, Iris Mann, Ivan Simpson.

20 May 1951—6:00 *Bigelow Theatre.*

21 May 1951—8:00 "Wild Geese," for *The Lux Video Theatre. Cast:* Evelyn Keyes.

9:30 *The Goldbergs.*

10:00 "A Chance for Happiness," by James Ronald for *Studio One. Cast:* Maria Riva, Murray Matheson.

22 May 1951—8:00–8:59 *Film Theater of the Air.*

9:30 "Escape This Night," for *Suspense. Cast:* Judith Evelyn, Theo Goetz.

10:00 "A Clear Case of Suicide," for *Danger. Cast:* John Forsythe, Joan Bennett.

10:30 *Tales of the Black Cat.*

23 May 1951—9:00 *Charlie Wild, Private Detective.*

9:30 "A Stitch in Time," for *The Web. Cast:* Henry Jones, Audrey Christie, Herbert Rudley.

24 May 1951—8:00 *The George Burns and Gracie Allen Show.*

9:30 *Big Town.*

10:30 *Casey, Crime Photographer.*

25 May 1951—8:00 *I Remember Mama.*

8:30 *The Man Against Crime.*

27 May 1951—6:00 *Bigelow Theatre.*

28 May 1951—8:00 "Sweet Sorrow," for *The Lux Video Theatre. Cast:* Jeffrey Lynn, Sarah Churchill.

9:30 *The Goldbergs.*

10:00 "Here Is My Life," by Rita Weiman, for *Studio One. Cast:* Vivienne Segal, Judson Laire.

29 May 1951—8:00–8:59 *Film Theater.*

9:30 "Vamp Till Dead," for *Suspense. Cast:* Mary Sinclair.

10:00 "The Trumpet of Doom," for *Danger. Cast:* Maria Riva, Bobby Sherwood, Teddy Wilson.

30 May 1951—9:00 *Charlie Wild, Private Detective.*

31 May 1951—8:00 "The Come-Back," for *Starlight Theatre. Cast:* Glenda Farrell, Nils Asther, Melville Cooper.

9:30 *Big Town.* 10:30 *Casey, Crime Photographer.*

1 June 1951—8:00 *I Remember Mama.*

8:30 *The Man Against Crime.*

9:00 "Three in a Room," for *Ford Theater. Cast:* Judith Evelyn, Louisa Horton, Patricia Kirkland.

3 June 1951—6:00 *Bigelow Theatre.*

4 June 1951— 8:00 "Consider the Lillies," for *The Lux Video Theatre*. *Cast:* Kay Francis.

9:30 *The Goldbergs*.

10:00 "Shield for Murder," by William P. McGivern, for *Studio One*. *Cast:* Kevin McCarthy, Marcia Henderson, James Nolan.

5 June 1951— 8:00–8:59 *Film Theater*.

9:30 "The Call," for *Suspense*. *Cast:* Cloris Leachman, Billy Redfield, Lawrence Fletcher, Paul Langton.

10:00 "The Fatal Step," for *Danger*. *Cast:* Ann Shepherd, Paul Mann, Anne Jackson, Mickey Knox, Sylvia Davis.

6 June 1951— 9:00 *Charlie Wild, Private Detective*.

9:30 "All the Way Home," for *The Web*. *Cast:* Alfreda Wallace, Jane Seymour, John Randolph.

7 June 1951— 8:00 *The George Burns and Gracie Allen Show*.

9:30 *Big Town*.

10:00–10:29 *Racket Squad*, a crime series, returns on film. *Cast:* Reed Hadley.

10:30 *Casey, Crime Photographer*.

8 June 1951— 8:00 *I Remember Mama*.

8:30 *The Man Against Crime*.

9 June 1951— 8:00–8:59 *Budweiser Summer Theatre*, debut on film.

11 June 1951— 8:00 "Weather for Today," for *The Lux Video Theatre*. *Cast:* Lee Bowman, Lynn Bari.

9:30 *The Goldbergs*.

10:00 "Coriolanus," by William Shakespeare, for *Studio One*. *Cast:* Richard Greene, Judith Evelyn.

12 June 1951— 8:00–8:59 *Film Theater*.

9:30 "De Mortius," by John Collier, for *Suspense*. *Cast:* Olive Deering, Walter Slezak.

10:00 "Operation Murder," for *Danger*. *Cast:* Maria Riva, Jerome Thor.

13 June 1951— 9:00 *Charlie Wild, Private Detective*.

9:30 "Checkmate," for *The Web*. *Cast:* Neva Patterson, Jerome Cowan, John Newland.

14 June 1951— 8:00 "The Fascinating Mr. Hogan," for *Starlight Theatre*. *Cast:* Jackie Cooper.

9:30 *Big Town*.

10:30 *Casey, Crime Photographer*.

15 June 1951— 8:00 *I Remember Mama*.

8:30 *The Man Against Crime*.

9:00 "Night Over London," for *Ford Theater*. *Cast:* Stella Andrew, Hugh Reilly.

16 June 1951— 8:00 *Budweiser Summer Theatre*.

18 June 1951— 8:00 "Inside Story," for *The Lux Video Theatre*. *Cast:* Robert Sterling, Lola Albright.

9:30 *The Goldbergs*.

10:00 "Screwball," by Mel Goldberg, for *Westinghouse Summer Theatre*, debut. *Cast:* Dick Foran, Cloris Leachman.

19 June 1951— 8:00–8:59 *Film Theater*.

9:30 "A Killing in Abilene," for *Suspense*. *Cast:* William Prince.

10:00 "The Knave of Diamonds," for *Danger*. *Cast:* Walter Slezak, Roger Dekoven.

20 June 1951— 9:00 *Charlie Wild, Private Detective*.

9:30 "Wanted, Someone Innocent," for *The Web*. *Cast:* Anna Lee, Diana Olsen, Peter Pagan.

21 June 1951— 8:00 *The George Burns and Gracie Allen Show*.
    9:30 *Big Town*.
    10:00 *Racket Squad*.
    10:30 *Casey, Crime Photographer*.

22 June 1951— 8:00 *I Remember Mama*.
    8:30 *The Man Against Crime*.

23 June 1951— 8:00 *Budweiser Summer Theatre*.

25 June 1951— 8:00 "The Promise," for *The Lux Video Theatre*. *Cast:* Vincent Price.
    10:00 "The Lonely Boy," by Hugh Pentecost, for *Westinghouse Summer Theatre*.
    Cast: Mary Sinclair, Jerome Cowan, Wright King.

26 June 1951— 8:00–8:59 *Film Theater*.
    9:30 "The Greatest Crime," a documentary, for *Suspense*. *Cast:* Walter Slezak.
    10:00 "Marley's Ghost," for *Danger*. *Cast:* Rita Gam, Joseph Anthony.

27 June 1951— 9:00 *Charlie Wild, Private Detective*.
    9:30 "No Escape," for *The Web*. *Cast:* Richard Kiley, Judy Parrish.

28 June 1951— 8:00 "Three Hours Between Planes," for *Starlight Theatre*. *Cast:* Virginia Gilmore, John Forsythe.
    9:30 *Big Town*.
    10:30 *Casey, Crime Photographer*.

29 June 1951— 8:00 *I Remember Mama*.
    8:30 *The Man Against Crime*.
    9:00 "The Ghost Patrol," for *Ford Theatre*. *Cast:* Ernest Truex.

30 June 1951— 8:00 *Budweiser Summer Theatre*.

2 July 1951—10:00 "The Swan," by Ferenc Molnar, for *Westinghouse Summer Theatre*. *Cast:* Maria Riva, Alfred Ryder, John Newland.

3 July 1951— 8:00–8:59 *Film Theater*.
    9:30 "Blood on the Trumpet," for *Suspense*. *Cast:* Cloris Leachman, John Forsythe, Virginia Gibson.
    10:00 "The Paper Box Kid," by Mark Hellinger, for *Danger*. *Cast:* Martin Ritt.

4 July 1951— 9:30 "Old Jim's Second Woman," for *The Web*.

5 July 1951— 8:00 *The George Burns and Gracie Allen Show*.
    9:30 *Big Town*.
    10:00 *Racket Squad*.
    10:30 *Casey, Crime Photographer*.

6 July 1951— 8:00 *I Remember Mama*.
    8:30 *The Man Against Crime*.
    9:00 "Jungle Patrol," for *Film Firsts*, debut. Sponsor: Schlitz Brewing Company.

7 July 1951— 8:00 *Budweiser Summer Theatre*.

9 July 1951—10:00 "Nightfall," by David Goodis, for *Westinghouse Summer Theatre*. *Cast:* John McQuade, Margaret Hayes, Herbert Rudley.

10 July 1951— 8:00–8:59 *Film Theater*.
    9:30 "Tent on the Beach," for *Suspense*. *Cast:* Eileen Heckart, Paul Langton.
    10:00 "Criminal at Large," by Edgar Wallace, for *Danger*. *Cast:* Bobby Santon, George Matthews.

11 July 1951— 9:30 "The Man in the Goldfish Bowl," for *The Web*.

12 July 1951— 6:30–7:30 *The Early Show*, on film.
    8:00 "The Big Head," for *Starlight Theatre*. *Cast:* Dulcie Moore.

9:30 *Big Town.*
10:30 *Casey, Crime Photographer.*
13 July 1951— 8:00 *I Remember Mama.*
8:30 *The Man Against Crime.*
9:00–9:59 "Gay Intruders," for *Film Firsts.*
10:00–10:29 *Corliss Archer*, debut on film.
10:30–11:00 *Emotion*, local series.
11:10–12:23 "The Red Desert," for *Film Theater.*
14 July 1951— 8:00 *Budweiser Summer Theatre.*
16 July 1951—10:00 "The Apple Tree," by John Galsworthy, for *Westinghouse Summer Theatre. Cast:* Lucy Vines, John Heldabrand, William Whitman.
17 July 1951— 8:00–8:59 "Dual Alibi," for *Film Theater.*
9:30 "Wisteria Cottage," for *Suspense. Cast:* Billy Redfield, Marjorie Gateson.
10:00 "Mr. Lupescu," for *Danger.*
18 July 1951— 9:30 "Breakup," for *The Web. Cast:* Dan Briggs, James Nolan, Billy Greene.
19 July 1951— 6:30–7:30 *The Early Show.*
8:00 *The George Burns and Gracie Allen Show.*
8:30–8:59 *Amos 'n' Andy*, debut on film. *Cast:* Alvin Childress, Spencer Williams, Jr. Sponsor: Blatz Beer.
9:30 *Big Town.*
10:30 *Casey, Crime Photographer.*
20 July 1951— 8:00 *I Remember Mama.*
8:30 *The Man Against Crime.*
9:00 *Film Firsts.*
10:30–10:59 *Hollywood Opening Night*, debut, on film. Sponsor: Pearson Pharmaceutical Company.
21 July 1951— 8:00 *Budweiser Summer Theatre.*
23 July 1951—10:00 "Tremolo," by Ernest Borneman, for *Westinghouse Summer Theatre. Cast:* Haila Stoddard, Dick Foran.
24 July 1951— 6:30–7:30 *The Early Show.*
9:30 "The Incident at Story Point," for *Suspense. Cast:* Donald Buka, Russell Hardie, Rusty Lane.
10:00 "Sparrow Cup," for *Danger. Cast:* Jack Lemmon, Robert Morse.
25 July 1951— 9:30 "Wolf Cry," for *The Web.*
26 July 1951— 6:30–7:30 *The Early Show.*
8:00 "In a Military Manner," for *Starlight Theatre. Cast:* John Forsythe, Alfred Ryder.
8:30 *Amos 'n' Andy.*
9:30 *Big Town.*
10:00 *Racket Squad.*
10:30 *Casey, Crime Photographer.*
11:00 *The Late Show*, on film.
27 July 1951— 8:00 *I Remember Mama.*
8:30 *The Man Against Crime.*
10:00 *Corliss Archer.*
11:00 *The Late Show.*
28 July 1951— 6:00 *Budweiser Summer Theatre.*
11:00 *The Late Show*, on film.

30 July 1951—10:00 "At Mrs. Beam's," for *Westinghouse Summer Theatre*. *Cast:* Eva Gabor, Jean Adair, Una O'Conner.
31 July 1951—9:30 "A Vision of Death," for *Suspense*. *Cast:* Henry Hull, Jerome Cowan.
   10:00 "Death Gambles," for *Danger*. *Cast:* Henry Jones, Frieda Altman.
1 August 1951—9:30 "According to Regulations," for *The Web*.
2 August 1951—8:00 *The George Burns and Gracie Allen Show*.
   8:30 *Amos 'n' Andy*.
   9:30 *Big Town*.
   10:00 *Racket Squad*.
   10:30 *Casey, Crime Photographer*.
   11:00 *The Late Show*.
3 August 1951—*The Early Show*.
   8:30 *The Man Against Crime*.
   9:00 *Film Firsts*.
   10:30 *Hollywood Opening Night*.
4 August 1951—6:00 *Budweiser Summer Theatre*.
6 August 1951—*The Early Show*.
   10:00 "The Pink Hussar," by Ben Hecht, for *Westinghouse Summer Theatre*. *Cast:* Ludwig Donath, Scott McKay, Howard Freeman.
   11:00 *The Late Show*.
7 August 1951—6:30–7:30 *The Early Show*.
   8:00–8:59 *CBS Presents Film Theatre*.
   9:30 "Killers of the City," for *Suspense*. *Cast:* Conrad Janis.
   10:00 "Goodbye, Hannah," for *Danger*. *Cast:* Paul Langton, John Randolph.
   11:00 *The Late Show*.
8 August 1951—*The Early Show*.
   9:30 "Murder for a Friend," for *The Web*.
   The Late Show.
9 August 1951—8:00 "With Baited Breath," for *Starlight Theatre*. *Cast:* Henry Hull.
   8:30 *Amos 'n' Andy*.
   9:30 *Big Town*.
   10:30 *Casey, Crime Photographer*.
   11:00 *The Late Show*.
10 August 1951—8:30 *The Man Against Crime*.
   9:00 *Film Firsts*.
   10:00 *Corliss Archer*.
   10:30 *Hollywood Opening Night*.
   11:00 *The Late Show*.
11 August 1951—6:00 *Budweiser Summer Theatre*.
   The Late Show.
12 August 1951—*The Late Show*.
13 August 1951—*The Early Show*.
   10:00 "The Rabbit," by Morton Grant, for *Westinghouse Summer Theatre*. *Cast:* Richard Purdy, Maria Riva.
   The Late Show.
14 August 1951—6:30–7:30 *The Early Show*.
   8:00–8:59 *CBS Presents Film Theatre*.
   9:30 "Death Sabre," for *Suspense*. *Cast:* Felicia Montealegre, Leslie Nielsen.

10:00 "Murderer's Face," for *Danger. Cast:* Robert Pastene, Ann Marno.
11:00 *The Late Show.*
15 August 1951—*The Early Show.*
9:30 "The Edge of Error," for *The Web. Cast:* Paul Langton, Robert Emhardt,
Beverly Whitney.
The Late Show.
16 August 1951— 8:00 *The George Burns and Gracie Allen Show.*
8:30 *Amos 'n' Andy.*
9:30 *Big Town.*
10:30 *Casey, Crime Photographer.*
11:00 *The Late Show.*
17 August 1951— 8:30 *The Man Against Crime.*
9:00 *Film Firsts.*
10:30 *Hollywood Opening Night.*
11:00 *The Late Show.*
18 August 1951— 6:00 *Budweiser Summer Theatre.*
The Late Show.
19 August 1951—*The Late Show.*
20 August 1951—*The Early Show.*
10:00 "Run from the Sun," by William H. Krasner, for *Westinghouse Summer
Theatre. Cast:* Marc Daniels, Gaby Rodgers.
The Late Show.
21 August 1951—*The Early Show.*
8:00–8:59 *Film Theater of the Air.*
9:30 "This Is Your Confession," Part One, for *Suspense. Cast:* William Bishop,
Eva Gabor, Sidney Blackmer.
10:00 "Motive for Murder," for *Danger. Cast:* Richard Kiley, Judy Parrish.
The Late Show.
22 August 1951—*The Early Show.*
9:30 "The Dishonorable Thief," for *The Web. Cast:* Henry Jones, Eileen Heckart.
The Late Show.
23 August 1951—*The Early Show.*
8:00 "Lunch at Disalvo's," for *Starlight Theatre. Cast:* Franchot Tone, Donald
Curtis.
8:30 *Amos 'n' Andy.*
9:30 *Big Town.*
10:00 *Racket Squad.*
10:30 *Casey, Crime Photographer.*
11:00 *The Late Show.*
24 August 1951—*The Early Show.*
8:00 *The Man Against Crime.*
9:00 *Film Firsts.*
10:00 *Corliss Archer.*
10:30 *Hollywood Opening Night.*
11:00 *The Late Show.*
25 August 1951— 8:00 *Budweiser Summer Theatre.*
The Late Show.
11:19–1:06 *The Late Late Show.*
26 August 1951—*The Late Show.*

27 August 1951—*The Early Show*.
    8:00–8:29 "The Pacing Goose," for *The Lux Video Theatre*. *Cast:* Celeste Holm.
    10:00 "Summer Had Better Be Good," for *Westinghouse Summer Theatre*. *Cast:*
William Eythe, Katherine Bard.
    The Late Show.
28 August 1951—*The Early Show*.
    8:00–8:59 *Film Theater of the Air*.
    9:30 "This Is Your Confession," Part Two, for *Suspense*.
    10:00 "Madman of Midville," for *Danger*. *Cast:* Walter Slezak, Everett Sloane.
    The Late Show.
29 August 1951—*The Early Show*.
    9:30 "Too Late to Run," for *The Web*. *Cast:* Judy Parrish, Russell Hardie.
    The Late Show.
30 August 1951—*The Early Show*.
    8:00 *The George Burns and Gracie Allen Show*.
    8:30 *Amos 'n' Andy*.
    9:30 *Big Town*.
    10:00 *Racket Squad*.
    10:30 *Casey, Crime Photographer*.
    11:00 *The Late Show*.
31 August 1951—*The Early Show*.
    8:30 *The Man Against Crime*.
    9:00 *Film Firsts*.
    10:30 *Hollywood Opening Night*.
    11:00 *The Late Show*.
1 September 1951— 8:00 *Budweiser Summer Theatre*.
    The Late Show.
    The Late Late Show.
2 September 1951—*The Late Show*.
3 September 1951—12:00–12:15 *The Egg and I*, daily serial, debuts.
    12:30–12:45 *Search for Tomorrow*, daily serial, debuts. [Not listed hereafter.]
    The Early Show.
    8:00 "Forever Walking Free," for *The Lux Video Theatre*. *Cast:* Wendell Cory.
    10:00 "Mr. Mummery's Suspicion," for *Westinghouse Summer Theatre*. *Cast:*
Roland Young, Faith Brook, Francis Compton.
    The Late Show.
4 September 1951—*The Early Show*.
    8:00–8:59 *Film Theater of the Air*.
    9:30 "This Way Out," for *Suspense*. *Cast:* Jean Parker, Richard Coogan.
    10:00 "Death among the Relics," for *Danger*. *Cast:* Joey Walsh, Edward Binns.
    The Late Show.
5 September 1951—*The Early Show*.
    9:30 "The Practical Joke," for *The Web*. *Cast:* Maria Riva, Anthony Ross.
6 September 1951—*The Early Show*.
    8:00 "Act of God Notwithstanding," for *Starlight Theatre*. *Cast:* Chester Morris.
    8:30 *Amos 'n' Andy*.
    9:30 *Big Town*.
    10:00 *Racket Squad*.

10:30 *Casey, Crime Photographer.*
11:00 *The Late Show.*
7 September 1951—*The Early Show.*
8:30 *The Man Against Crime.*
8 September 1951—*The Late Show.*
The Late Late Show.
9:00 *Film Firsts.*
9 September 1951—*The Late Show.*
10 September 1951—*The Early Show.*
8:00 "It's a Promise," for *The Lux Video Theatre. Cast:* Laraine Day.
10:00 "The Guinea Pig," for *Westinghouse Summer Theatre. Cast:* Richard Kiley, Ruth Ford, Jack O'Brien.
The Late Show.
11 September 1951—*The Early Show.*
8:00–8:59 *Film Theater of the Air.*
9:30 "Strange for a Killer," for *Suspense. Cast:* John Forsythe, Anthony Ross.
10:00 "In the La Banza," for *Danger. Cast:* Jack Warden.
The Late Show.
12 September 1951—*The Early Show.*
9:30 "Hand in Glove," for *The Web. Cast:* Donald Buka, Bertha Belmore.
The Late Show.
13 September 1951—*The Early Show.*
8:00 *The George Burns and Gracie Allen Show.*
8:30 *Amos 'n' Andy.*
9:30 *Big Town.*
10:00 *Racquet Squad.*
10:30 *Casey, Crime Photographer.*
11:00 *The Late Show.*
14 September 1951—*The Early Show.*
8:00 *The Man Against Crime.*
9:00 *Film Firsts.*
10:30 *Hollywood Opening Night.*
11:00 *The Late Show.*
15 September 1951—*The Late Show.*
The Late Late Show.
16 September 1951—*The Late Show.*
17 September 1951—*The Early Show.*
8:00 "A Family Affair," for *The Lux Video Theatre. Cast:* Roland Young, Lorna Lynn.
10:00 "The Angelic Avengers," by Pierre Andrezel, for *Studio One* return. *Cast:* Mary Sinclair, Maria Riva, Richard Purdy, Murray Matheson.
11:00 *The Late Show.*
18 September 1951—*The Early Show.*
9:00 *Crime Syndicated*, documentaries, debut. *Producer:* Jerry Danzig. *Director:* John Peyser. Sponsor: Shick.
9:30 "Merryman's Murder," for *Suspense. Cast:* Red Buttons.
10:00 "The Fourth Concession," for *Danger. Cast:* Harold Vermilyea, Stephen Elliott.
The Late Show.

19 September 1951—*The Early Show.*
9:30 "The Contradictory Case," for *The Web. Cast:* Jack Grimes, Rita Lynn, Marc Kramer, Donald Curtis.
The Late Show.
20 September 1951—*The Early Show.*
8:00 "The Gravy Train," for *Starlight Theatre. Cast:* Dane Clark, Elinor Lynn, Loring Smith.
8:30 *Amos 'n' Andy.*
9:30 *Big Town.*
10:00 *Racket Squad.*
10:30 *Casey, Crime Photographer.*
11:00 *The Late Show.*
21 September 1951—*The Early Show.*
8:00 *I Remember Mama,* returns.
8:30 *The Man Against Crime.*
9:00 *Film Firsts.*
10:30 *Hollywood Opening Night.*
11:00 *The Late Show.*
The Late Late Show.
22 September 1951—*The Late Show.*
The Late Late Show.
23 September 1951—*The Late Show.*
24 September 1951—*The Early Show.*
8:00 "A Matter of Life," for *The Lux Video Theatre. Cast:* Edmond O'Brien.
10:00 "The Little Black Bag," by Samuel R. Golding, for *Studio One. Cast:* Harry Townes, Howard St. John.
11:00 *The Late Show.*
25 September 1951—*The Early Show.*
9:00 *Crime Syndicated.*
9:30 "Doctor Anonymous," for *Suspense. Cast:* Walter Slezak, Josephine Brown.
10:00 "Love Comes to Miss Lucy," for *Danger. Cast:* Maria Riva.
The Late Show.
26 September 1951—*The Early Show.*
9:30 "The Customs of the Country," for *The Web. Cast:* Peter Cookson, Ann Marno, Joseph Anthony, Gene Gross.
The Late Show.
27 September 1951—*The Early Show.*
8:00 *The George Burns and Gracie Allen Show.*
8:30 *Amos 'n' Andy.*
9:30 *Big Town.*
10:00 *Racket Squad.*
10:30 *Casey, Crime Photographer.*
11:00 *The Late Show.*
28 September 1951—*The Early Show.*
8:00 *I Remember Mama.*
8:30 *The Man Against Crime.*
9:00 *Film Firsts.*
10:30 *Hollywood Opening Night.*
11:00 *The Late Show.*

The Late Late Show.
29 September 1951—*The Late Show.*
The Late Late Show.
30 September 1951—*The Late Show.*
1 October 1951—*The Early Show.*
    8:00 "Grandma Was an Actress," for *The Lux Video Theatre. Cast:* Josephine Hull.
    9:00 *Racket Squad,* new time.
    10:00 "The Idol of San Vittore," by Endro Montanelli, for *Studio One. Cast:* Eduardo Ciannelli, Maria Riva.
The Late Show.
2 October 1951—*The Early Show.*
    9:00 *Crime Syndicated.*
    9:30 "Santa Fe Fight," for *Suspense. Cast:* Charlton Heston, Margaret Phillips.
    10:00 "Free Zoo," for *Danger. Cast:* Gene Lyons, Judy Parrish.
The Late Show.
3 October 1951—*The Early Show.*
    9:30 "All the Way to the Moon," for *The Web. Cast:* Henry Jones, Eleanor Wilson, James Gregory.
The Late Show.
4 October 1951—*The Early Show.*
    8:00 *Starlight Theatre.*
    8:30 *Amos 'n' Andy.*
    9:30 *Big Town.*
    10:30 *Casey, Crime Photographer.*
The Late Show.
5 October 1951—*The Early Show.*
    8:00 *I Remember Mama.*
    8:30 *The Man Against Crime.*
    9:00–9:59 "Not a Chance," debut on film, for *The Schlitz Playhouse of the Stars. Cast:* Helen Hayes, David Niven.
    10:30 *Hollywood Opening Night.*
The Late Show.
The Late Late Show.
6 October 1951—*The Late Show.*
The Late Late Show.
7 October 1951—*The Late Show.*
8 October 1951—*The Early Show.*
    8:00 "Route Nineteen," for *The Lux Video Theatre. Cast:* Dennis O'Keefe, Charlton Heston, Robert Stack, Vanessa Brown.
    9:00 *Racket Squad.*
    10:00 "Mighty Like a Rogue," by Dan Keene, for *Studio One. Cast:* Tom Ewell, Nita Talbot, Joshua Shelley.
The Late Show.
9 October 1951—*The Early Show.*
    9:30 "High Street," for *Suspense. Cast:* Mary Sinclair, Mildred Natwick.
    10:00 "Sleep and Tell," for *Danger. Cast:* Maria Riva, Marc Kramer, Paul Langton.
The Late Show.
10 October 1951—*The Early Show.*

9:30 "Volcano," for *The Web. Cast:* Alfred Ryder, Oliver Thorndike, Lois Wheeler, Russell Hardie.
The Late Show.

11 October 1951—*The Early Show.*
8:00 *The George Burns and Gracie Allen Show.*
8:30 *Amos 'n' Andy.*
9:30 *Big town.*
10:30 *Casey, Crime Photographer.*
The Late Show.

12 October 1951—*The Early Show.*
8:00 *I Remember Mama.*
8:30 *The Man Against Crime.*
9:00 "The Name Is Bellingham," for *The Schlitz Playhouse of the Stars. Cast:* John Payne, Romney Brent.
10:30 *Hollywood Opening Night.*
11:00 *The Late Show.*
The Late Late Show.

13 October 1951—*The Late Show.*
The Late Late Show.

14 October 1951—*The Late Show.*

15 October 1951—*The Early Show.*
8:00 "Cafe Ami," for *The Lux Video Theatre. Cast:* Robert Preston, Maria Riva.
9:00 *I Love Lucy*, debut. Executive Producer: Desi Arnaz. Producer: Jess Oppenheimer. Director: Marc Daniels. *Cast:* Lucille Ball, Desi Arnaz. Sponsor: Philip Morris Cigarettes.
10:00 "Colonel Judas," by Derwent Davis, for *Studio One. Cast:* Anthony Dawson, Iris Jensen.
The Late Show.

16 October 1951—*The Early Show.*
9:00 *Crime Syndicated.*
9:30 "The Fifth Dummy," for *Suspense. Cast:* Francis L. Sullivan.
10:00 "Inherit Murder," for *Danger. Cast:* Anthony Ross, Paul Langton, Rita Gam.
The Late Show.

17 October 1951—*The Early Show.*
9:30 "The House Guests," for *The Web. Cast:* Marc Cramer, Lenka Peterson.
The Late Show.

18 October 1951—*The Early Show.*
8:00 *Starlight Theatre.*
8:30 *Amos 'n' Andy.*
9:30 *Big Town.*
10:30 *Casey, Crime Photographer.*
The Late Show.

19 October 1951—*The Early Show.*
8:00 *I Remember Mama.*
8:30 *The Man Against Crime.*
9:00 "Never Wave at a WAC," for *The Schlitz Playhouse of the Stars. Cast:* Rosalind Russell.
10:30 *Hollywood Opening Night.*
The Late Show.

The Late Late Show.

20 October 1951— *The Late Show.*

The Late Late Show.

21 October 1951— *The Late Show.*

22 October 1951— *The Early Show.*

8:00 "The Twinkle in Her Eye," for *The Lux Video Theatre. Cast:* Diana Lynn, Dick Foran.

9:00 *I Love Lucy.*

10:00 "Macbeth," by William Shakespeare, for *Studio One. Cast:* Charlton Heston.

The Late Show.

23 October 1951— 9:00 *Crime Syndicated.*

9:30 "The Train from Czechoslovakia," for *Suspense. Cast:* Maria Riva, Richard Kiley.

10:00 "Final Rejection," for *Danger. Cast:* Ernest Truex.

The Late Show.

24 October 1951— 4:40–5:30 *Film Theater of the Air.*

The Early Show.

9:30 "Beyond the Sea of Death," for *The Web. Cast:* Richard Purdy, Katherine Bard, Ann Shoemaker.

The Late Show.

25 October 1951— *Film Theater of the Air.*

The Early Show.

8:00 *The George Burns and Gracie Allen Show.*

9:30 *Big Town.*

10:00 *Racket Squad*, time change.

10:30 *Casey, Crime Photographer.*

The Late Show.

26 October 1951— *Film Theater of the Air.*

The Early Show.

8:00 *I Remember Mama.*

8:30 *The Man Against Crime.*

9:00 "Still Life," for *The Schlitz Playhouse of the Stars. Cast:* Margaret Sullavan, Wendell Cory.

10:30 *Hollywood Opening Night.*

The Late Show.

27 October 1951— *The Late Show.*

The Late Late Show.

29 October 1951— *Film Theater of the Air.*

The Early Show.

8:00 "The Doctor's Wife," for *The Lux Video Theatre. Cast:* June Lockhart.

9:00 *I Love Lucy.*

10:00 "They Served the Muses," by Kressman Taylor, for *Studio One. Cast:* Frances Fuller, Patricia Gillette, Noel Leslie.

The Late Show.

30 October 1951— *Film Theater of the Air.*

The Early Show.

9:00 *Crime Syndicated*, now logged as talk.

9:30 "Court Day," for *Suspense. Cast:* Richard Coogan, Parker Fennelly, Steve Holland.

10:00 "Deadline," for *Danger. Cast:* Richard Kiley, Joseph Anthony.
The Late Show.
31 October 1951—*The Early Show.*
9:30 "A Man Dies," for *The Web. Cast:* Reba Tassell, Jerome Cowan.
The Late Show.
1 November 1951—*The Early Show.*
8:30 *Amos 'n' Andy.*
9:30 *Big Town.*
10:00 *Racket Squad.*
10:30 *Casey, Crime Photographer.*
The Late Show.
2 November 1951—*The Early Show.*
8:00 *I Remember Mama.*
8:30 *The Man Against Crime.*
9:00 "The Lucky Touch," for *The Schlitz Playhouse of the Stars. Cast:* Helen Hayes.
10:30 *Hollywood Opening Night.*
The Late Show.
The Late Late Show.
3 November 1951—*The Late Show.*
The Late Late Show.
4 November 1951—*The Late Show.*
5 November 1951—*The Early Show.*
8:00 "Confession," for *The Lux Video Theatre. Cast:* Thomas Mitchell.
9:00 *I Love Lucy.*
10:00 "The Hero," by Irving Lewis, for *Studio One. Cast:* Paul Hartman, Patricia Collinge.
The Late Show.
6 November 1951— 6:30–7:29 *The Early Show.*
9:00 *Crime Syndicated.*
9:30 "Moonfleet," Part One, for *Suspense. Cast:* John Baragrey, Jackie Diamond, Edgar Stehli.
10:00 "High Wire, High Steel," for *Danger. Cast:* James Westerfield, Steven Hill.
The Late Show.
7 November 1951—*The Early Show.*
9:30 "He Was Asking for You," for *The Web. Cast:* Patricia Wheel.
The Late Show.
8 November 1951—*The Early Show.*
8:00 *The George Burns and Gracie Allen Show.*
8:30 *Amos 'n' Andy.*
9:30 *Big Town.*
10:00 *Racket Squad.*
10:30 *Casey, Crime Photographer.*
The Late Show.
9 November 1951—*The Early Show.*
8:00 *I Remember Mama.*
8:30 *The Man Against Crime.*
9:00 "Decision and Daniel Webster," for *The Schlitz Playhouse of the Stars. Cast:* Walter Hampden, Matt Briggs, Charles Dingle.
10:30 *Hollywood Opening Night.*

The Late Show.
The Late Late Show.
10 November 1951—*The Late Show.*
The Late Late Show.
11 November 1951—*The Late Show.*
12 November 1951—*The Early Show.*
8:00 "No Will of His Own," for *The Lux Video Theatre. Cast:* Binnie Barnes, Gene Lockhart.
9:00 *I Love Lucy.*
10:00 "A Bolt of Lightning," by Irve Tunick, for *Studio One. Cast:* Charlton Heston.
The Late Show.
13 November 1951—*The Early Show.*
9:00 *Crime Syndicated.*
9:30 "Moonfleet," Part Two, for *Suspense.*
10:00 "Death Beat," for *Danger.*
The Late Show.
14 November 1951—*The Early Show.*
9:30 "Golden Secret," for *The Web. Cast:* John Carradine, Tamara Geva.
The Late Show.
15 November 1951—*The Early Show.*
8:30 *Amos 'n' Andy.*
9:30 *Big Town.*
10:00 *Racket Squad.*
10:30 *Casey, Crime Photographer.*
The Late Show.
16 November 1951—*The Early Show.*
8:00 *I Remember Mama.*
8:30 *The Man Against Crime.*
9:00 "The Memoirs of Aimee Durant," for *The Schlitz Playhouse of the Stars. Cast:* Diana Lynn.
10:30 *Hollywood Opening Night.*
The Late Show.
The Late Late Show.
17 November 1951—*The Late Show.*
The Late Late Show.
18 November 1951—*The Late Show.*
19 November 1951—*The Early Show.*
8:00 "Stolen Years," for *The Lux Video Theatre. Cast:* Lola Albright, Richard Greene, Robert Sterling, Francis L. Sullivan.
9:00 *I Love Lucy.*
10:00 "The King in Yellow," by Raymond Chandler, for *Studio One. Cast:* Carol Bruce, Jack Palance, Jack Lambert, Leonard Sues.
The Late Show.
20 November 1951— 9:00 *Crime Syndicated.*
9:30 "Frisco Payoff," for *Suspense. Cast:* Anthony Ross, Paul Langton.
10:00 "The Killer Instinct," for *Danger. Cast:* Martin Ritt.
The Late Show.
21 November 1951—*The Early Show.*

9:30 "Danger in the Shadows," for *The Web*.
The Late Show.
22 November 1951—*The Early Show*.
8:00 *The George Burns and Gracie Allen Show*.
8:30 *Amos 'n' Andy*.
9:30 *Big Town*.
10:00 *Racket Squad*.
10:30 *Casey, Crime Photographer*.
The Late Show.
23 November 1951—*The Early Show*.
8:00 *I Remember Mama*.
8:30 *The Man Against Crime*.
9:00 "One Is a Lonesome Number," for *The Schlitz Playhouse of the Stars*. *Cast:* Charlton Heston, June Lockhart.
10:30 *Hollywood Opening Night*.
The Late Show.
24 November 1951—*The Late Show*.
The Late Late Show.
25 November 1951—*The Late Show*.
26 November 1951—*The Early Show*.
8:00 "Dames Are Poison," for *The Lux Video Theatre*. *Cast:* Nina Foch, William Eythe.
9:00 *I Love Lucy*.
10:00 "The Dangerous Years," by Basil Beyea and Leo Davis, for *Studio One*. *Cast:* Maria Riva, Frances Fuller, Harry Townes.
The Late Show.
27 November 1951—*The Early Show*.
9:00 *Crime Syndicated*.
9:30 "Mikki," for *Suspense*. *Cast:* Joan Chandler, Brandon Peters.
10:00 "The Friend Who Killed," for *Danger*.
The Late Show.
28 November 1951—*The Early Show*.
9:30 "Shine, Mister," for *The Web*.
The Late Show.
29 November 1951—*The Early Show*.
8:30 *Amos 'n' Andy*.
9:30 *Big Town*.
10:00 *Racket Squad*.
10:30 *Casey, Crime Photographer*.
The Late Show.
30 November 1951—*The Early Show*.
8:00 *I Remember Mama*.
8:30 *The Man Against Crime*.
9:00 "Two Living and One Dead," for *The Schlitz Playhouse of the Stars*. *Cast:* Fay Bainter, Walter Hampden.
10:30 *Hollywood Opening Night*.
The Late Show.
1 December 1951—*The Late Show*.
The Late Late Show.

2 December 1951—*The Late Show.*
The Late Late Show.
3 December 1951—*The Early Show.*
8:00 "Tin Badge," for *The Lux Video Theatre. Cast:* Pat O'Brien.
9:00 *I Love Lucy.*
10:00 "Mutiny on the Nicolette," by James Norman, for *Studio One. Cast:* Boris Karloff.
The Late Show.
4 December 1951—*The Early Show.*
9:00 *Crime Syndicated.*
9:30 "The Man Without a Face," for *Suspense. Cast:* Judith Evelyn, Douglas Watson, Henry James.
10:00 "The Captain Has Bad Dreams," for *Danger. Cast:* Joseph Anthony.
The Late Show.
The Late Late Show.
5 December 1951—*The Early Show.*
9:30 "St. Petersburg Dilemma," for *The Web. Cast:* Jerome Cowan.
The Late Show.
The Late Late Show.
6 December 1951—*The Early Show.*
8:00 *The George Burns and Gracie Allen Show.*
8:30 *Amos 'n' Andy.*
9:30 *Big Town.*
10:00 *Racket Squad.*
10:30 *Casey, Crime Photographer.*
The Late Show.
The Late Late Show.
7 December 1951—*The Early Show.*
8:00 *I Remember Mama.*
8:30 *The Man Against Crime.*
9:00 "The Nymph and the Lamp," for *The Schlitz Playhouse of the Stars. Cast:* Robert Preston, Margaret Sullavan.
10:30 *Hollywood Opening Night.*
The Late Show.
8 December 1951—*The Late Show.*
The Late Late Show.
9 December 1951—*The Late Show.*
The Late Late Show.
10 December 1951—*The Early Show.*
8:00 "Second Sight," for *The Lux Video Theatre. Cast:* Celeste Holm.
9:00 *I Love Lucy.*
10:00 "The Legend of Jenny Lind," for Irve Tunick, for *Studio One. Cast:* Thomas Mitchell, Priscilla Gillette.
The Late Show.
11 December 1951—*The Early Show.*
9:00 *Crime Syndicated.*
9:30 "Meditation in Mexico," for *Suspense.*
10:00 "The Face of Fear," for *Danger.*
The Late Show.

12 December 1951—*The Early Show.*
    9:30 "The Package," for *The Web.*
    The Late Show.
13 December 1951—*The Early Show.*
    8:30 *Amos 'n' Andy.*
    9:30 *Big Town.*
    10:00 *Racket Squad.*
    10:30 *Casey, Crime Photographer.*
    The Late Show.
14 December 1951—*The Early Show.*
    8:00 *I Remember Mama.*
    8:30 *The Man Against Crime.*
    9:00 "Exit," for *The Schlitz Playhouse of the Stars. Cast:* John Payne, Coleen Gray.
    10:30 *Hollywood Opening Night.*
    The Late Show.
15 December 1951—*The Late Show.*
    The Late Late Show.
16 December 1951—*The Late Show.*
    The Late Late Show.
17 December 1951—*The Early Show.*
    8:00 "The Blues Street," for *The Lux Video Theatre. Cast:* Veronica Lake, Roddy McDowall.
    9:00 *I Love Lucy.*
    10:00 "The Innocence of Pastor Muller," for *Studio One. Cast:* Maria Riva, Walter Slezak.
    The Late Show.
18 December 1951—*The Early Show.*
    9:00 *Crime Syndicated.*
    9:30 "Pier 17," for *Suspense.*
    10:00 "The Lady on the Rock," for *Danger. Cast:* Don Hanmer, Olive Deering.
19 December 1951—*The Early Show.*
    9:30 "The Man Who Was Always Right," for *The Web. Cast:* Joseph Anthony, Jackie Diamond.
    The Late Show.
    The Late Late Show.
20 December 1951—*The Early Show.*
    8:00 *The George Burns and Gracie Allen Show.*
    8:30 *Amos 'n' Andy.*
    9:30 *Big Town.*
    10:00 *Racket Squad.*
    10:30 *Casey, Crime Photographer.*
    The Late Show.
    The Late Late Show.
21 December 1951—*The Early Show.*
    8:00 *I Remember Mama.*
    8:30 *The Man Against Crime.*
    9:00 "Dark Fleece," for *The Schlitz Playhouse of the Stars. Cast:* Helen Hayes, Anthony Quinn, Carmen Mathews.

10:30 *Hollywood Opening Night.*
The Late Show.
22 December 1951 — *The Late Show.*
The Late Late Show.
23 December 1951 — *The Late Show.*
The Late Late Show.
24 December 1951 — *The Early Show.*
8:00 "A Child Is Born," by Stephen Vincent Benét, for *The Lux Video Theatre.* *Cast:* Thomas Mitchell, Fay Bainter.
9:00 *I Love Lucy.*
10:00 "The Little Princess," by Frances Hodgson Burnett, for *Studio One. Cast:* Iris Mann, Henry Stephenson, Rita Vale.
The Late Show.
25 December 1951 — *The Early Show.*
9:00 *Crime Syndicated.*
9:30 "The Lonely Place," for *Danger. Cast:* Robin Morgan, Boris Karloff, Judith Evelyn.
10:00 "Passage for Christmas," for *Danger. Cast:* Mary Sinclair, Joseph Anthony.
The Late Show.
26 December 1951 — *The Early Show.*
9:30 "Model Murder," for *The Web. Cast:* John Baragrey, Whit Bissell.
The Late Show.
The Late Late Show.
27 December 1951 — *The Early Show.*
8:30 *Amos 'n' Andy.*
9:30 *Big Town.*
10:00 *Racket Squad.*
10:30 *Casey, Crime Photographer.*
The Late Show.
The Late Late Show.
28 December 1951 — *The Early Show.*
8:00 *I Remember Mama.*
8:30 *The Man Against Crime.*
9:00 "Girl in a Million," for *The Schlitz Playhouse of the Stars. Cast:* Joan Caulfield, John Forsythe.
10:30 *Hollywood Opening Night.*
The Late Show.
29 December 1951 — *The Late Show.*
The Late Late Show.
30 December 1951 — *The Late Show.*
The Late Late Show.
31 December 1951 — *The Early Show.*
8:00 "The Jest of Hahalaba," for *The Lux Video Theatre. Cast:* Boris Karloff.
9:00 *I Love Lucy.*
10:00 "The Paris Feeling," by Paul Hogan, for *Studio One. Cast:* Wright King, Ann Gillis.
Principal source: *CBS Television Master Control Log* and the *CBS Technical Operations Master Control Log,* 1946–1951.

Appendix C
NBC Television Dramas, 1946–1951*

1946

3 January 1946— 7:41–8:04 "Peter Stuyvesant," adapted by William Basil Courtney, for *The Chronicles of America*. Producer: Yale University Press Film Service. Director: Frank Tuttle. *Cast:* William Calhoun.

6 January 1946— 8:00–9:39 "Dark Hammock," adapted by Mary Orr and Reginald Denham.

10 January 1946—"The Gateway to the West," for *The Chronicles of America*.

13 January 1946—"The First Year," by Frank Craven.

17 January 1946—"Wolfe and Montcalm," for *The Chronicles of America*.

20 January 1946—"Angel Street," by Patrick Hamilton. Director: Ernest Colling. *Cast:* Judith Evelyn, Henry Daniell, Cecil Humfryes.

24 January 1946—"On the Eve of the Revolution," for *The Chronicles of America*.

27 January 1946—"The Game of Chess," by Kenneth Sawyer Goodman.

30 January 1946—"Children of Ol' Man River," by Walter Richards. Director: Warren Wade.

31 January 1946—"The Declaration of Independence," for *The Chronicles of America*.

3 February 1946—"Children of Ol' Man River" repeats.

7 February 1946—"Yorktown," for *The Chronicles of America*.

10 February 1946—"Abe Lincoln in Illinois," Act III, by Robert E. Sherwood. Producer/Director: Edward Sobol. *Cast:* Stephen Courtleigh.

14 February 1946—"Vincennes," for *The Chronicles of America*.

17 February 1946— 8:30–9:15 "Laughter in Paris," an original teleplay by Richard P. McDonagh. Producer: Fred Coe. *Cast:* Frank Lea Short.

21 February 1946— 7:32–8:20 "The Pioneer Woman" and "Daniel Boone," for *The Chronicles of America*.

24 February 1946— 8:00–9:03 "Knockout," by J. C. and Elliott Nugent.

28 February 1946—"Alexander Hamilton" and "Dixie," for *The Chronicles of America*.

This list includes dramas and drama-related programs from 1946 to 1951.

235

1 March 1946—WNBT went off the air to install a new transmitter on the Empire State Building, to switch to Channel 4, and to conduct Image Orthicon demonstrations directed by Garry Simpson.

9 March 1946—*Hour Glass*, a variety series that includes some dramas, debuts. Includes "Moonshine," by Arthur Hopkins. *Cast:* Paul Douglas. Sponsor: Standard Brands.

12 May 1946—"Blithe Spirit," by Noël Coward, adapted by Edward Sobol, for *NBC Television Theatre.* Producer: Sobol. *Cast:* Philip Tonge, Leonora Corbett, Carol Goodner, Estelle Winwood.

19 May 1946—"Mr. and Mrs. North," by Frances and Richard Lockridge, adapted by Owen Davis, Jr. *Cast:* John McQuade, Maxine Stuart.

26 May 1946—"The Bad Man," by Porter Emerson Browne, adapted by Ernest Colling. *Cast:* Peter Capell.

2 June 1946—"The Flattering World," by George Kelly, adapted by Edward Sobol. *Cast:* Edward Kreisler, Louise Campbell, Enid Markey, Joyce Van Patten, Adam Handley.

9 June 1946—"Enter Madame," by Gilda Varesi and Dolly Byrne. *Cast:* Carol Goodner, John Graham.

16 June 1946—"The Strangest Feeling," by John Kirkpatrick, adapted by Ernest Colling.

23 June 1946—"Tea," by William G. B. Carson.

30 June 1946—"First Person Singular," Episode 1, by Wyllis Cooper, adapted by Fred Coe, for *Lights Out.*

1 July 1946—"A Tooth for Paul Revere," by Stephen Vincent Benét, adapted by Fred Baron, for *Hour Glass. Cast:* William Post, Jr.

7 July 1946— 8:45–10:12 "Seven Keys to Baldpate," by George M. Cohan, adapted by Ernest Colling. *Cast:* Vinton Hayworth.

9 July 1946— 8:00–9:00 "Jim Bramble Meets the Folks," for *Hour Glass.*

14 July 1946— 8:56–9:28 "The Weak Spot," by George Kelly. Director: Edward Sobol. *Cast:* Lillian Foster, Maxine Stuart, John Harvey.

17 July 1946—"The Servant Problem," for *Hour Glass. Cast:* Hope Emerson.

21 July 1946— 8:49–9:27 "The Home Life of a Buffalo," by Richard Harrity. Director: Fred Coe. *Cast:* John McQuade, Virginia Smith, Mickey Carroll.

25 July 1946—"Two Men on a Merry-Go-Round," by Arthur Purcell, for *Hour Glass.*

1 August 1946—"The Finger of God," by Percival Wilde, for *Hour Glass. Cast:* Vinton Hayworth.

4 August 1946—"The Show Off," by George Kelly. Producer: Edward Sobol. *Cast:* Lillian Foster.

8 August 1946—"Jim Bramble and the Bank Robber," by Howard Rodman, for *Hour Glass.*

11 August 1946—"Something in the Wind," Episode 2, adapted by Fred Coe, for *Lights Out.* Director: Coe.

15 August 1946—"Western Night," by Robert Finch and Betty Smith, for *Hour Glass.*

22 August 1946—"Cinderella Married," by Rachel Field, for *Hour Glass.*

1 September 1946—"De Mortius," Episode 3, by John Collier, adapted by Fred Coe, for *Lights Out.* Producer: Coe. *Cast:* John Loder.

8 September 1946—"The Clod," by Lewis Beach.

12 September 1946 — 8:00–8:57 "The Witless Witness," by Lon D. Hollister for *Tender Leaf Tea Hour*. Director: Fred Coe.

15 September 1946 — "The Lady and the Law," by George W. Cronyn, adapted by Edward Sobol.

22 September 1946 — "Mr. Mergenthwirker's Lobblies," by Nelson Bond and David Kent. Producer/Director: Fred Coe. *Cast:* Vaughn Taylor.

29 September 1946 — "The Walrus and the Carpenter," by Noël Langley. Director: Ernest Colling.

6 October 1946 — "The Curtain Rises," by Benjamin M. Kaye, adapted by Edward Sobol.

13 October 1946 — "The Brave Man with a Cord," Episode 4, by Peter Strand and Rudolph Bernstein, adapted by Fred Coe, for *Lights Out*.

20 October 1946 — "Heartbeat," Part 1, by Cornell Woolrich, adapted by Ernest Colling. *Cast:* Vinton Hayworth, Peter Capell, Virginia Smith.

27 October 1946 — "Dr. Death," Part 2, by Cornell Woolrich, adapted by Ernest Colling.

10 November 1946 — 8:44–9:30 "The Last War," by Nell Grant, adapted by E. S. Mills, Jr., and Fred Coe.

22 December 1946 — "A Poem for Christmas." Producer: American Theatre Wing's Television Workshop.

1947

5 January 1947 — 8:56–9:13 "Boy Wanted," an original teleplay based on *No Shoes*, by Lawrence DuPont, for *NBC Television Theatre*. Director: Edward Sobol. *Cast:* George Mathews, Vinton Hayworth, Doreen Lang, Hugh Rennie.

19 January 1947 — 8:45–9:15 "Thinking Aloud," by Emlyn Williams, adapted by Fred Coe. *Cast:* Carol Goodner, Bramwell Fletcher.

26 January 1947 — 8:42–9:06 "A Marriage Proposal," by Anton Chekhov, adapted by Hilmar Baukhage and Barrett H. Clark, for *NBC Television Theatre*. *Cast:* Norman Rose, Boris Cameron, Noel Mills. Sponsors: NBC and American Theatre Wing.

9 February 1947 — 8:55–9:12 "Abe Lincoln in Illinois," by Robert E. Sherwood, adapted by Edward Sobol. *Cast:* Stephen Courtleigh, Mary Michael, W. O. MacWatters, Philip Coolidge. Sponsors: NBC and American Theatre Wing.

23 February 1947 — 9:05–9:50 "Miracle in the Rain," by Ben Hecht, adapted by Fred Coe. Sponsor: Borden.

2 March 1947 — 8:51–9:14 "Where There's a Will," by Ira Richards. Director: Fred Coe. *Cast:* Mary Patton, Carol Goodner, Cyrilla Dorn, Alexander Clark.

9 March 1947 — 8:34–9:46 "Feathers in a Gale." Director: Fred Coe. *Cast:* Mary Stuart, Allan Hall, Ben Lackland, Ed Mannery.

13 March 1947 — "The Experiment of Dr. Bronson."

16 March 1947 — 8:36–9:07 "The Florist Shop," by Winifred Hawkridge, adapted by Fred Coe, for *NBC Television Theatre*. *Cast:* Ben Lackland, Bruno Wick, Nydia Westman. Sponsor: Borden.

23 March 1947 — 8:33–9:41 "Little Brown Jug," by Marie Baumer, adapted by Ernest Colling. *Cast:* Katherine Alexander, Alexander Kirkland, Vaughn Taylor, John Drew Devereaux, Margaret Hayes.

30 March 1947 — 8:53–9:44 "Orchids for Margaret," by Pearl and Thatcher Allred, adapted by Edward Sobol, for *NBC Television Theatre*. *Cast:* Beverly Bayne, Joy Geffen, Charles Francis, Jan Powers, Richard Malloy.

20 April 1947 — 8:38–9:15 "A Gentleman Never Tells," a psychological thriller.

27 April 1947 — 8:27–9:41 "Twelfth Night," by William Shakespeare, adapted by Fred Coe, for *NBC Television Theatre*. Producer: Coe. Sponsor: Borden.

7 May 1947 — 7:30–8:30 "Double Door," by Elizabeth McFadden, adapted by Edmond Rice, for the debut of *Kraft Television Theatre*. Producer: Stanley Quinn. Director: Fred Coe (NBC), Quinn (JWT). *Cast:* Eleanor Wilson, John Baragrey, Romola Robb, John Stephen, Valerie Cossart, Ed Herlihy. Settings: Robert Wade. Sponsor: Kraft Foods Company. Agency: J. Walter Thompson.

14 May 1947 — "Merton of the Movies," by George S. Kaufman and Marc Connelly, for *Kraft Television Theatre*. *Cast:* Eddie Mayehoff, Patricia Englund.

21 May 1947 — "The Doctor in Spite of Himself," by Molière, for *Kraft Television Theatre*. *Cast:* William Lynn.

23 May 1947 — "Welcome, Jeremiah!" adapted from *Esquire*, for *NBC Television Theatre*. *Cast:* Vinton Hayworth, John McQuade, Vaughn Taylor. Sponsor: Borden.

28 May 1947 — "Her Master's Voice," by Clare Kummer, for *Kraft Television Theatre*.

4 June 1947 — "The Barker," by J. Kenyon Nicholson, for *Kraft Television Theatre*.

11 June 1947 — "There's Always Juliet," by John Van Druten, for *Kraft Television Theatre*.

18 June 1947 — "A Doll's House," by Henrik Ibsen, for *Kraft Television Theatre*.

25 June 1947 — "I Like It Here," by A. B. Shiffrin, adapted by Samuel Taylor, for *Kraft Television Theatre*.

2 July 1947 — "You and I," by Philip Barry, for *Kraft Television Theatre*.

9 July 1947 — "To the Ladies," by George S. Kaufman and Marc Connelly, for *Kraft Television Theatre*. *Cast:* Jay Meredith, John Conway, Walter Armitage.

16 July 1947 — "Consider Lily," by Stanley Kauffman, for *Kraft Television Theatre*. *Cast:* Ruth Yorke, Vaughn Taylor, Andrea Wallace.

23 July 1947 — "Papa Is All," by Patterson Greene, for *Kraft Television Theatre*. *Cast:* Stefan Schnabel, Marie Kenney, Don Keefer, Inge Adams.

27 July 1947 — 9:00–9:30 "A Dangerous Man," by Lawrence Williams, adapted by Fred Coe, for *The Borden Show* [aka *The Borden Theatre*]. *Cast:* The Borden Players. Agency: Kenyon & Eckhardt, Inc.

30 July 1947 — "Interference," by Roland Pertwee and Harold Dearden, for *Kraft Television Theatre*. Director: Ernest Colling.

6 August 1947 — 7:30–8:30 "The Man Who Married a Dumb Wife," by Anantole France, for *Kraft Television Theatre*. *Cast:* Mercer McLeod, Inge Adams.

8:30 "Write Me a Love Scene," by Florence Ryerson and Colin Clements, for *In the Kelvinator Kitchen*. Producer: Edward Sobol.

13 August 1947 — "Laburnum Grove," by J. B. Priestley, for *Kraft Television Theatre*. Director: Ernest Colling. *Cast:* Vaughn Taylor.

20 August 1947 — "The First Year," by Frank Craven, for *Kraft Television Theatre*. *Cast:* Helen Parrish, Jack Manning, Richard Keith, Katherine Hall, Jane Hix, Earl Gilbert, Virginia Smith, Bernard Randall, Arthur Franz, Dick Loring, Tommy Tucker.

24 August 1947 — 9:00 "A Scotch Dilemma," by Glenn Wilson, for *The Borden The-*

atre. Director: Fred Coe. *Cast:* Frank Thomas, Barbara Morrison, Dorothy Beattie, Vaughn Taylor.

27 August 1947—"Yes and No," by Kenneth Horne, for *Kraft Television Theatre.* *Cast:* Margaret Phillips, Warren Parker, Richard Newton, Isham Constable, Sylvia Davis.

3 September 1947—"Mr. Pim Passes By," by A. A. Milne, for *Kraft Television Theatre.* *Cast:* Isham Constable, Flora Campbell, Vaughn Taylor, Judy Blake.

7 September 1947—9:00 "Ethel's Cabin," a play with music, for *The Borden Theatre.* *Cast:* Ethel Waters.

10 September 1947—"Craig's Wife," by George Kelly, for *Kraft Television Theatre.* *Cast:* Grace Keddy, Lorence Kerr, Jo Anne Dolan, Nicholas Saunders, John Seymour, Patricia Quinn O'Hara.

17 September 1947—"Murder Without Crime," by J. Lee Thompson for *Kraft Television Theatre.* *Cast:* Warren Parker, Guy Spaull, Mary Dudley, Cathleen Cordell.

21 September 1947—"This Time Next Year," by Fred Coe, for *The Borden Theatre.* *Cast:* Jay Jackson.

24 September 1947—"Suspect," by Edward Percy and Reginald Denham, for *Kraft Television Theatre.* Director: Ernest Colling. *Cast:* Philippa Bevans, Philip Foster, J. W. Austin, Marga Ann Deighton, Cynthia Latham, Ogden Miles, Hildy Parks.

1 October 1947—"Payment Deferred," adapted by Jeffrey Dell, for *Kraft Television Theatre.* *Cast:* Mercer McLeod, Michael Blair.

8 October 1947—"January Thaw," by Bellamy Partridge, adapted by William Roos, for *Kraft Television Theatre.* *Cast:* Vaughn Taylor, Valerie Cossart, Warren Parker, Virginia Sale.

15 October 1947—"Thérèse," by Émile Zola, adapted by Thomas Job, for *Kraft Television Theatre.* *Cast:* Thomas Palmer, John Baragrey, Lucille Patton, Sidney Arnold, Mary Young.

22 October 1947—"The Man Who Changed His Name," by Edgar Wallace, for *Kraft Television Theatre.* *Cast:* Claude Horton, Patricia Jenkins, John Steven, Frank Thomas, Byron Russell.

26 October 1947—*NBC Television Theatre* was a variety show.

29 October 1947—"Blind Alley," by James Warwick, for *Kraft Television Theatre.* Director: Ernest Colling. *Cast:* Gordon Mills, Robert Burr.

5 November 1947—"On Stage," for *Kraft Television Theatre.* Director: Ernest Colling.

9 November 1947—8:30–9:53 "John Ferguson," by St. John Ervine, for *Theatre Guild* debut. Director: Edward Sobol. *Cast:* Thomas Mitchell, Joyce Redman, Barry McCullen, Vaughn Taylor. Sponsors: NBC and Theatre Guild.

12 November 1947—"Ladies in Retirement," for *Kraft Television Theatre.* *Cast:* Eda Heinemann, Marjorie Maude, Earl Hammond.

19 November 1947—"But Not Goodbye," by George Seaton, for *Kraft Television Theatre.* *Cast:* Ralph Bunker, Warren Parker, Charity Grace, Hildy Parks, Don Keefer, Nicholas Saunders.

23 November 1947—8:32 *Rehearsal-3H,* a variety show, includes "Romeo and Juliet," Act II, Scene 2. Directors: Fred Coe and Gordon Duff. *Cast:* Mary Alice Moore, William Kendall Clarke, John McQuade, Eddie Mayehoff.

26 November 1947—"The Curtain Rises," by Benjamin M. Kaye, for *Kraft Television Theatre.* *Cast:* John Stephen, Margaret Phillips.

3 December 1947—"Parlor Story," by William McCleery, for *Kraft Television*

Theatre. Cast: Florence Campbell, Gene O'Donnell, Don Keefer, Eva Marie Saint, Susan Thorne, Jack Orrison, Eileen Heckart, Gordon Peters, Ed Reichert.

4 December 1947— 9:14–9:55 "The Last of My Solid Gold Watches," by Tennessee Williams. Director: Fred Coe. *Cast:* John Stuart Dudley, Luther L. Henderson, Robert Morgan. Sponsors: NBC, American National Theater and Academy (ANTA).

7 December 1947— 8:30–10:00 "The Late George Apley," by John P. Marquand and George S. Kaufman, for *Theatre Guild.* Directors: Edward Sobol (NBC), Paul Crabtree (TG). Art Direction: Otis Riggs. *Cast:* Leo G. Carroll, Janet Beecher, Reynolds Evans, Margaret Phillips, William David, Archie Smith, Ellen Cobb Hill.

10 December 1947—"The Importance of Being Earnest," by Oscar Wilde, for *Kraft Television Theatre. Cast:* Margaret Phillips, John Stephen, Romola Robb, Anna Russell, Elliot Reid, Guy Spaull, Sylvia Davis, Michael Blair.

14 December 1947— 8:00–8:30 "The Purple Doorknob," by Walter Pritchard Eaton. Producer: Owen Davis Jr. Directors: Fred Coe (NBC), Richard Harrity (ANTA). *Cast:* Judith Evelyn, Ethel Griffies, Raymond Massey. Sponsors: NBC, ANTA.

17 December 1947—"Holiday," by Philip Barry, for *Kraft Television Theatre. Cast:* Margaret Phillips, Patricia Jenkins, Walter Brooke, Don Keefer, John Seymour.

20 December 1947—*Campus Hoop-La,* a variety series, includes a scene from "The Taming of the Shrew," by William Shakespeare.

21 December 1947— 8:30–9:30 "The End of the Beginning," by Sean O'Casey, for *NBC Television Theatre. Cast:* Frank Thomas, Vaughn Taylor. Sponsors: NBC, ANTA.

24 December 1947—"Reverie," by Percival Wilde, and "The Desert Shall Rejoice," by Robert Finch, a nativity sequence, for *Kraft Television Theatre.*

28 December 1947—*Rehearsal-3H.* Director: Fred Coe.

31 December 1947—"Respectfully Yours," by Peggy L. Amson, for *Kraft Television Theatre. Cast:* Nicholas Saunders, Grace Keddy, Alan Stevenson, Ralph Bunker, Hildy Parks, John Seymour, Marie Carroll, William Beach, Jane Bennett Hix.

1948

1 January 1948—"Julius Caesar," ACT III, Scene 2, by William Shakespeare, for *Rehearsal in 3-H. Cast:* William Post, Jr., Stephen Courtleigh.

4 January 1948— 8:41–9:12 "The Game of Chess," by Kenneth Sawyer Goodman, for *Rehearsal in 3-H. Cast:* Richard Goode, John Graham, William Post, Jr., Robert Davis.

7 January 1948— 9:00–9:59 (new time) "The Truth about Blayds," by A. A. Milne, for *Kraft Television Theatre. Cast:* Vaughn Taylor, Margaret Phillips, Guy Spaull, John Stephen, Naomi Campbell.

11 January 1948— 8:39–9:10 "Outside of Time," an original teleplay by Noël Jordan, for ANTA-NBC *Television Playhouse.* Producer: Owen Davis, Jr., and Richard Harrity. Director: Fred Coe. *Cast:* Peter Cookson, Mary Alice Moore, Noel Leslie, Viola Fayne, Leona Powers.

14 January 1948—"Alternating Current," an original teleplay by Jack Roche, for *Kraft Television Theatre.*

18 January 1948— 8:40–8:59 "Time of Night," by Jack Foster, adapted by Fred Coe, for *Rehearsal in 3-H. Cast:* John McQuade.

21 January 1948 — "Only the Heart," by Horton Foote, for *Kraft Television Theatre.* *Cast:* Maribeth Aurelius, Robert Healy, Joan Stanley, Ruth Yorke, Richard Keith.

25 January 1948 — 8:00–9:05 "Angel Street," by Patrick Hamilton, for *Theatre Guild.* Producer/Director: Edward Sobol. *Cast:* Walter Abel.

28 January 1948 — "The Criminal Code," by Martin Flavin, for *Kraft Television Theatre.* *Cast:* Bram Nossen, Don Keefer, Ellen Cobb Hill.

1 February 1948 — 8:40–9:09 "The Bachelor Queen," by Lawton Campbell, for ANTA-NBC *Television Playhouse.* Producer/Director: Fred Coe. *Cast:* Judith Evelyn, Peter Cookson, Ivan Simpson, Howard St. John.

4 February 1948 — "Outward Bound," by Sutton Vane, for *Kraft Television Theatre.* *Cast:* Ralph Nelson, Vaughn Taylor, Charity Grace, Housely Stevens.

8 February 1948 — 8:40–9:01 "Nor Long Remember," by Harold Hoffman, for ANTA-NBC *Television Playhouse.* Producer: Fred Coe. *Cast:* Stephen Courtleigh.

11 February 1948 — "Spring Green," by Florence Ryerson and Colin Clements, for *Kraft Television Theatre.* *Cast:* Ralph Nelson, Housely Stevens, Charity Grace, Katherine Meskill, Vaughn Taylor, John Stanton, Margaret Phillips, Guy Spaull, Mel Brandt.

15 February 1948 — 8:40 "First Person Singular," by Wyllis Cooper, adapted by Frederick Coe, for ANTA-NBC *Television Playhouse.* Producer/Director: Coe. Stage Manager: Gordon Duff. Set Designer: Otis Riggs. Costume Designer: Elwell.

18 February 1948 — "Apple of His Eye," by Kenyon Nicholson and Charles Robinson, for *Kraft Television Theatre.*

22 February 1948 — 8:00–9:14 "Mornings at Seven," by Paul Osborn, adapted by Frederick Coe, for *Theatre Guild.* Producer: Coe. *Cast:* Hiram Sherman, Enid Markey.

25 February 1948 — "Alison's House," by Susan Glaspell, for *Kraft Television Theatre.* *Cast:* Edward Harvey, Grace Keddy, Marga Ann Deighton, Blair Davies, Maribeth Aurelius, James Dodson, Ogden Miles, Joy Geffen, Maxine Flood.

29 February 1948 — 8:40–9:09 "The Weak Spot," by George Kelly, for ANTA-NBC *Television Playhouse.* Producer: Edward Sobol. *Cast:* Lillian Foster, Maxine Stuart, John Harvey.

3 March 1948 — "Counsellor-at-Law," by Elmer Rice, for *Kraft Television Theatre.* *Cast:* Adele Longmire, Paul Hammond, Pat Harrington, Virginia Robinson.

7 March 1948 — 8:40–9:09 "Introduction," by Edward Peple, adapted by Fred Coe, for ANTA-NBC *Television Playhouse.* *Cast:* Howard St. John, Oliver Thorndike, Pamela Conroy.

10 March 1948 — "The Wind Is Ninety," by Ralph Nelson, for *Kraft Television Theatre.* *Cast:* Grace Keddy, Grant Calhoun, David Frank, John Hudson, Sidney Bassler, Henry Barnard, Charity Grace, James Atkin.

14 March 1948 — 8:40 "Brilliant Performance," by Marjorie Allen, adapted by Frederick Coe, for ANTA-NBC *Television Playhouse.* Producer: Coe.

17 March 1948 — "No Way Out," by Owen Davis, for *Kraft Television Theatre.* *Cast:* John Stephen, Andrea Wallace, Joy Geffen, John Seymour, Emory Richardson, Eleanor Wilson, Muriel Hutchinson.

21 March 1948 — 8:40 *Rehearsal-3-H* is now variety.

24 March 1948 — "Captain Applejack," by Walter Hackett, for *Kraft Television Theatre.* *Cast:* Byron Russell, Leonard Trolley, Wilma Drake, Leonard Elliott, Cherry Hardy, Peggy Sanford.

28 March 1948— 8:00–9:08 "Stage Door," by George S. Kaufman and Edna Ferber, for *Theatre Guild*. Producer: Edward Sobol. *Cast:* Louisa Horton.

31 March 1948—"She Stoops to Conquer," by Oliver Goldsmith, for *Kraft Television Theatre*. *Cast:* Margaret Phillips, Ralph Nelson, Katherine Meskill, Vaughn Taylor, Everett Gammon, Margaret Draper, John Richards, Mercer McLeod, Leonard Bell.

4 April 1948— 8:40–9:09 "Dear Departed," by Stanley Hurghten, for ANTA-NBC *Television Playhouse*. *Cast:* Frank Thomas, Ben Lackland, Jimsey Sommers.

7 April 1948—"June Moon," by Ring Lardner and George S. Kaufman, for *Kraft Television Theatre*. *Cast:* Claire Stuart, Nicholas Saunders, Jo Anne Dolan, Don Keefer, Hildy Parks, Jack Albertson, Joan Morgan, Bert Thorn.

11 April 1948— 8:48–9:09 "Jealousy Scene from Othello," by William Shakespeare, for ANTA-NBC *Television Playhouse*.

14 April 1948—"Barchester Towers," by Anthony Trollopes, adapted by Thomas Job, for *Kraft Television Theatre*. *Cast:* Flora Campbell, Housely Stevens, Vaughn Taylor.

21 April 1948—"The Silver Cord," by Sidney Howard, for *Kraft Television Theatre*. *Cast:* Grace Keddy, Nicholas Saunders, Don Keefer, Hildy Parks.

22 April 1948— 9:30–10:00 "Murder Me Twice," by Max Ehrlich, for debut of *Barney Blake, Police Reporter*. Producer: Wynn Wright. Director: Garry Simpson. *Cast:* Gene O'Donnell, Judy Parrish. Sponsor: American Tobacco Company (Lucky Strike Cigarettes). Agency: N. W. Ayer & Son, Incorporated.

25 April 1948— 8:30–8:50 "Boy Wanted," by Lawrence DuPont, adapted by Edward Sobol, for ANTA-NBC *Television Playhouse*. *Cast:* Vinton Hayworth, George Mathews, Doreen Lang.

28 April 1948—"Louder Please," by Norman Krasna, for *Kraft Television Theatre*. *Cast:* Virginia Gilmore, Bert Thorne, Pat Harrington, Andrea Wallace.

29 April 1948—"Chicken Charlie," by Sally Milgrim, for *Barney Blake, Police Reporter*.

2 May 1948— 8:30–9:20 "Great Catherine," by George Bernard Shaw, for *Theatre Guild*. Producer/Director: Fred Coe. Assistant Producer: Gordon Duff. *Cast:* Gertrude Lawrence, David Wayne, Joan McCracken.

5 May 1948—"The Royal Family," by George S. Kaufman and Edna Ferber, for *Kraft Television Theatre*. *Cast:* Guy Spaull, Hildy Parks, Bess Winburn, Ethel Owen, Nicholas Saunders, John Seymour, Robert Burr, Malcolm Beggs.

6 May 1948—"E-String Murder," by Max Ehrlich, for *Barney Blake, Police Reporter*.

9 May 1948— 8:30–9:09 "Tea," by William G. B. Carson, for *Sunday Varieties*. Producer/Director: Edward Sobol. *Cast:* Viola Frayne, Howard St. John.

12 May 1948—"Broken Dishes," by Martin Flavin, for *Kraft Television Theatre*. *Cast:* John Shellie, Katherine Hall, Betty Caulfield, Bill Terry, Carroll Ashburn, Alan MacAteer, Rica Martens, Nancy Davis, Klock Ryder, Robert Lieb.

13 May 1948—"Lillies for Lucas," for *Barney Blake, Police Reporter*.

16 May 1948— 8:30–9:00 "The Wine Glass," by A. A. Milne, adapted by Fred Coe, for *NBC Television Theatre*.

19 May 1948—"Minick," by George S. Kaufman and Edna Ferber, for *Kraft Television Theatre*. *Cast:* Ralph Bunker, Robert Allen, Flora Campbell, Janet Fox, Lucille Dodge, Edward Holmes, G. Swayne Gordon, Owen Coll, Jane Bennett-Hix, Elizabeth Watts, Leora Thatcher.

20 May 1948—"The Case of the Corpse Who Came to Dinner," for *Barney Blake, Police Reporter*.

26 May 1948—"Riddle Me This," by Daniel N. Ruben, for *Kraft Television Theatre.* *Cast:* Richard Kiley, Frank Thomas, Kathleen Maguire, Virginia Smith, Phil Sterling, Mary Best.

27 May 1948—"Matrimony Is Murder," for *Barney Blake, Police Reporter.*

30 May 1948— 8:30–9:30 "Mr. Mergenthwirker's Lobblies," by Nelson Bond and David Kent, for NBC *Television Presents.* Producer/Director: Fred Coe.

2 June 1948—"The Torchbearers," by George Kelly, for *Kraft Television Theatre.* *Cast:* Harold Stone, Maude Wallace, Carlton Carpenter, Connie Lembcke, Klock Ryder, Bud Gammon, Danny Webb, Sylvia Davis, Warren Parker, Valerie Cossart, Adelaide Klein.

3 June 1948—"The Case of the Curious Corpse," for *Barney Blake, Police Reporter.*

6 June 1948— 8:40–9:50 "Our Town," by Thornton Wilder, adapted by Eric Barner, for *Theatre Guild.* Producer/Director: Fred Coe. *Cast:* Raymond Massey, Billy Redfield, Olive Stacey, Helen Carew, Howard Smith, Jane Seymour, Frank Thomas.

9 June 1948—"The Fourth Wall," by A. A. Milne, for *Kraft Television Theatre. Cast:* Ben Lackland, Leonard Trolley, J. W. Austin, Jane Lloyd Jones, Elliot Reid, Vaughn Taylor, Margaret Phillips, Philip Tonge.

10 June 1948—"Never Use Bullets," for *Barney Blake, Police Reporter.*

13 June 1948—"The Miniature Mikado," Act I, for *NBC Television Presents.* Producer/Director: Fred Coe. *Cast:* The National Savoyards with Bob Harter as Mikado.

16 June 1948—"Applesauce," by Barry Conners, for *Kraft Television Theatre. Cast:* Myrtle Ferguson, Malcolm Biggs, Hildy Parks, Ty Perry, Charity Grace, Klock Ryder, Earl Wrightson.

17 June 1948—"The Dark Cellar," for *Barney Blake, Police Reporter.*

23 June 1948—"Foolish Notion," by Philip Barry, for *Kraft Television Theatre.* Preempted due to political conventions.

30 June 1948—"Foolish Notion," by Philip Barry, for *Kraft Television Theatre. Cast:* Eleanore Swayne, Katherine Meskill, Edith Bell, Jimsey Sommers, Bess Winburn, Grant Calhoun, John Stephen.

1 July 1948—"Farewell to Mrs. Forest," for *Barney Blake, Police Reporter.*

7 July 1948—"The Show Off," by George Kelly, for *Kraft Television Theatre. Cast:* Alan Bunce, Nancy Sheridan, Janet Tyler, Earl Gilbert, Helen MacKellar, Peter Dane, Henry Gurvey, Nicholas Saunders.

8 July 1948—"And So to Death," by Alvin Boretz, for *Barney Blake, Police Reporter.*

18 July 1948— 9:00–9:30 "The Fisherman," by Jonathan Tree, for *NBC Television Playhouse.* Producer/Director: Fred Coe. *Cast:* Vaughn Taylor, Frank Thomas.

21 July 1948—"Berkeley Square," by John L. Balderston, for *Kraft Television Theatre. Cast:* Ralph Nelson, Joan Stanley, Margaret Phillips, Leon Shaw, Leonard Trolley, Louise Prussing, Humphrey Davis, Michael Blair.

22 July 1948—*Barney Blake* is preempted.

25 July 1948— 9:00 "Suppressed Desires," by Susan Glaspell, NBC *Television Audition.* Producer/Director: Edward Padula. Sponsor: Admiral Radio and Television Corporation.

28 July 1948—"Green Cars Go East," by Paul Vincent Carroll, for *Kraft Television Theatre. Cast:* Edith Shayne, Swayne Gordon, Peter Dane, Charles Dayton, Tony Burger, Justine Johnson, Craig Kelly, Janet Tyler, James Dobson, Jane Bennett-Hix, John Boyd, Myrtle Ferguson.

1 August 1948— 9:00–9:27 "Henry, the Fifth," by William Shakespeare for *NBC Television Playhouse*. Producer/Director: Garry Simpson. *Cast:* Sam Wanamaker, Rita Colton, Margit Forssen.

4 August 1948—"Theater," by Somerset Maugham, for *Kraft Television Theatre*. *Cast:* Sara Burton, Blaine Cordner, Lex Richards.

8 August 1948— 9:01–9:29 "The Fourth Mrs. Phillips," by Carl Glick, for *Show Shop*. Director: Carroll O'Meare. *Cast:* Jean Darling, John Graham, Virginia Smith, Charles Purcell.

11 August 1948—"The Tenth Man," by Somerset Maugham, for *Kraft Television Theatre*. *Cast:* Roy Irving, Margaret Phillips, Sidney Arnold, Noel Leslie, Vaughn Taylor, John Stephen, Byron Russell, Ralph Sumpter.

15 August 1948— 9:00–9:30 "The Game of Chess," by Kenneth Sawyer Goodman, for *The Players*. Producer/Director: Fred Coe. *Cast:* William Post, Jr., John Graham.

18 August 1948—"The Whiteheaded Boy," by Lennox Robinson, for *Kraft Television Theatre*. *Cast:* Pat Harrington, Grania O'Malley, Somer Alberg, Charity Grace, Andrea Wallace, Jane Bennett-Hix, Michael Sadlier, John McLiam.

25 August 1948—"Poor Audrey," by George Kelly, for *Kraft Television Theatre*.

1 September 1948—"Icebound," by Owen Davis, for *Kraft Television Theatre*. *Cast:* John Hudson, Mary James, June Walker, Marjorie Brown, Vaughn Taylor, Robert Lieb, Gertrude Beach, Edwin Bruce, Gene Leonard.

8 September 1948—"Poor Little Me," by Katherine Hilliker and H. H. Campbell, for *Kraft Television Theatre*. Producer/Director: Alan J. Neuman. *Cast:* Betty Ann Nyman, John Stephen, Katherine Meskill, Gloria Strook.

15 September 1948—"Lady Frederick," by Somerset Maugham, for *Kraft Television Theatre*. *Cast:* Erin O'Brien, Geoffrey Lumb, William Whitman, Oliver Thorndike, Louise Prussing, Richard Deane, Lenore Gellar.

19 September 1948— 9:01–9:28 "Heavens to Betsy," for *The Players*. Producer/Director: Fred Coe.

22 September 1948—"Her Husband's Wife," by A. E. Thomas, for *Kraft Television Theatre*. *Cast:* Valerie Cossart, Charles Campbell, Carl Ziegler, Romola Robb, Ralph Bunker.

27 September 1948— 8:00–8:29 "The Home Life of a Buffalo," by Richard Harrity, for debut of *Chevrolet on Broadway*. Producer/Director: Ira Skutch. *Cast:* John McQuade, Virginia Smith, Ernest Truex, Sylvia Field, Kevin Mathews.

29 September 1948—"Great Day," by Leslie Storm, for *Kraft Television Theatre*. *Cast:* Katherine Meskill, Philippa Bevans, Maury Hill, Anna Minot, Jean Cameron, Leona Powers, John Moore, Diane de Brett, Madeleine King.

3 October 1948— 9:00–9:59 "Dinner at Eight," by George S. Kaufman and Edna Ferber, for *Philco Television Playhouse* debut. Producer: Actors' Equity Television. Director: Fred Coe. *Cast:* Peggy Wood, Dennis King, Mary Boland, Vicki Cummings, Philip Loeb, Matt Briggs, Jane Seymour, Royal Beal, Joyce Van Patten, Judson Laire, Bob Stanton.

4 October 1948—"Mirage in Manhattan," by Lawrence DuPont, for *Chevrolet on Broadway*. Producer/Director: Garry Simpson. *Cast:* Jessie Royce Landis, Eric Rhodes, Helene Reynolds, Alan Stevenson, Russell Arms, Will Geer.

6 October 1948—"The Twin Diamonds," for *Kraft Television Theatre*. *Cast:* Richard Kiley, Eileen Heckart, Charles Champbell, A. J. Herbert, Cherry Hardy, Ralph Smiley, Michael Blair.

10 October 1948—7:00–7:19 *Mary Kay and Johnny* premieres. Producer/Director: Garry Simpson. *Cast:* Mary Kay Stearns, Howard Thomas.
    9:19–9:59 "Rebecca," by Daphne du Maurier, for *Philco Television Playhouse.* Producer/Director: Fred Coe. *Cast:* Florence Reed, Bramwell Fletcher, Mary Anderson.

11 October 1948—"Thinking Aloud," Emlyn Williams, adapted by Fred Coe, for *Chevrolet on Broadway.* Producer/Director: Gordon Duff. *Cast:* Dean Jagger, Judith Evelyn, Vaughn Taylor, Jack Shea.

13 October 1948—"The Truth Game," by Ivor Novello, for *Kraft Television Theatre.* *Cast:* Joyce Hayward, Joel Thomas, Valerie Cossart, Byron Russell, Cherry Hardy.

17 October 1948—7:00 *Mary Kay and Johnny.*
    9:00 "Counsellor-at Law," by Elmer Rice, for *Philco Television Playhouse.* Producer/Director: Fred Coe. *Cast:* Paul Muni.

18 October 1948—"Whistle, Daughter, Whistle," by Ernest Kinoy, for *Chevrolet on Broadway.* *Cast:* Gertrude Berg, Minerva Pius, Lenore Lonergan, John Harvey.

20 October 1948—"Criminal-at-Large," by Edgar Wallace, for *Kraft Television Theatre.* *Cast:* Thomas Palmer, Olive Reeves, William Hendrek, Alfreda Wallace, Philip Dakin, Lawrence Fletcher, Humphrey Davis, Gordon Mills.

24 October 1948—7:00 *Mary Kay and Johnny.*
    9:00 "Angel in the Wings," a revue by Bob Hilliard and Carl Sigman, adapted by Hank Ladd, for *Philco Television Playhouse.* Producer/Director: Fred Coe. *Cast:* Paul and Grace Hartman.

25 October 1948—"His Master's Affairs," by Victor McLeod, for *Chevrolet on Broadway.* Producer/Director: Gordon Duff. *Cast:* Arthur Treacher, Mischa Auer, Judy Parrish, Mickey Carroll, Jerry Housner.

27 October 1948—"Biography," by S. N. Behrman, for *Kraft Television Theatre.* *Cast:* Virginia Gilmore, Gene O'Donnell, John Forsythe, Rusty Arden, Kirk Brown, Ilse Marvenga, Louis Borell.

31 October 1948—7:00 *Mary Kay and Johnny.*
    9:00 "Street Scene," by Elmer Rice, for *Philco Television Playhouse.* Producer/Director: Fred Coe. *Cast:* Bert Lytell, Betty Field, Erin O'Brien.

1 November 1948—"The Purple Doorknob," by Walter Pritchard Eaton, for *Chevrolet on Broadway.* Producer/Director: Garry Simpson. *Cast:* Faye Emerson, Ethel Griffies, Joanna Ross.

3 November 1948—"Old Lady Robbins," by Albert G. Miller, for *Kraft Television Theatre.* *Cast:* Ethel Owen, Martin Miller, Betty Ann Nyman, Nicholas Saunders, Grace Keddy, James Dobson, Louis Lytton, Owen Coll.

7 November 1948—7:00 *Mary Kay and Johnny.*
    9:00 "This Thing Called Love," for *Philco Television Playhouse.* Producer/Director: Fred Coe. *Cast:* Ralph Bellamy, Ann Lee, Peggy Conklin, Ernest Cossart.

8 November 1948—"A Study in Triangles," by True Boardman, for *Chevrolet on Broadway.* Producer/Director: Gordon Duff. *Cast:* Gloria Holden, Richard Waring, Erni Arneson, Alexander Clark, Mary Best.

10 November 1948—"The Detour," by Owen Davis, for *Kraft Television Theatre.* *Cast:* Curtis Cooksey, Isabel Price, Henry Beckman, Joan Stanley, David Orrick, Madeleine Clive.

14 November 1948—7:00 *Mary Kay and Johnny.*
    9:00 "Camille," by Alexandre Dumas, son, adapted as a musical by Samuel

Taylor, for *Philco Television Playhouse. Cast:* Judith Evelyn as Camille with a 32-member cast.

15 November 1948—"No Shoes," for *Chevrolet Tele-Theatre* [aka *Chevrolet on Broadway*]. Producer/Director: Garry Simpson. *Cast:* James Dunn, Vinton Hayworth, John Kane, Helene Reynolds, Robert Bolger, Marion Weeks, Andrea Wallace.

17 November 1948—"The Ivory Door," by A. A. Milne, for *Kraft Television Theatre. Cast:* Jackie Cooper, Owen Tolbert, Frank M. Thomas, Sr., Jerome Collamore, James Van Dyke, Jackie Diamond, Patricia Jenkins, Neil Harrison, Richard Hamilton, Edith Bell Heyman.

21 November 1948—7:00 *Mary Kay and Johnny.*
9:00 "An Inspector Calls," by J. B. Priestley, for *Philco Television Playhouse.* Producer/Director: Fred Coe. *Cast:* Walter Abel, George Coulouris.

22 November 1948—"The Flattering World," by George Kelly, adapted by Edward Sobol, for *Chevrolet Tele-Theatre.* Producer/Director: Gordon Duff. *Cast:* Zazu Pitts, John Carradine.

24 November 1948—"Wuthering Heights," by Emily Brontë, for *Kraft Television Theatre. Cast:* John Baragrey, Louisa Horton, Ethel Griffies, Alfreda Wallace, Lex Richards, Vaughn Taylor.

28 November 1948—6:00–6:59 "Twilight on the Trail," for *Hopalong Cassidy,* a Western film series, debut. *Cast:* William Boyd. [Not listed hereafter.]
7:00 *Mary Kay and Johnny.*
9:00 "I Like It Here," Act I, by A. B. Shiffrin, adapted by Samuel Taylor, for *Philco Television Playhouse. Cast:* Bert Lytell, Oscar Karlweiss.

29 November 1948—"The Valiant," by Holworthy Hall and Robert Middlemass, adapted by Hobart Douglas Skidmore, for *Chevrolet Tele-Theatre.* Producer/Director: Garry Simpson. *Cast:* Paul Muni, Curtis Cooksey, Whitford Kane, Augusta Dabney.

1 December 1948—"The Dover Road," by A. A. Milne, for *Kraft Television Theatre. Cast:* Geoffrey Lumb, Neva Patterson, Valerie Cossart, Owen Talbert-Hewitt, Gage Clarke, John Stephen.

5 December 1948—7:00 *Mary Kay and Johnny.*
9:00 "Suspect," by Edward Percy and Reginald Denham, for *Philco Television Playhouse.* Producer/Director: Fred Coe. *Cast:* Ruth Chatterton, Bramwell Fletcher.

6 December 1948—"Close Quarters," by Catherine McDonald, for *Chevrolet Tele-Theatre.* Producer/Director: Gordon Duff. *Cast:* Barry Nelson, Louisa Horton, Marjorie Gateson, Sidney Blackmer, Eva Marie Saint, Dean Hearns.

8 December 1948—"The Flashing Stream," by Charles Morgan, for *Kraft Television Theatre. Cast:* Richard Kendrick, Gwen Anderson, Robin Craven, Lorna Kent, John Bryant, Derrick Lynn-Thomas, Alexander Clark, Edward Cooper, Fairfax Burgher.

12 December 1948—7:00 *Mary Kay and Johnny.*
9:00 "Parlor Story," by William McCleery, for *Philco Television Playhouse.* Producer/Director: Fred Coe. *Cast:* Edith Atwater, Dean Jagger.

13 December 1948—"Sham," by Frank E. Thompkins, for *Chevrolet Tele-Theatre.* Producer/Director: Garry Simpson. *Cast:* Edward Everett Horton, Natalie Schafer, John Kane, Howard St. John.

15 December 1948—"The Old Soak," by Don Marquis, for *Kraft Television Theatre.*

Cast: Guy Kibbee, Edith Shayne, Jack Orrison, Curtis Cooksey, Janet Taylor, Richard Kiley, Joe E. Marks, Linda Carlow.

19 December 1948—7:00 *Mary Kay and Johnny.*

9:00 "A Christmas Carol," by Charles Dickens, for *Philco Television Playhouse. Cast:* Dennis King.

20 December 1948—"A Simple Matter of Faith," by Ann Dixon, adapted by Carl Allensworth, for *Chevrolet Tele-Theatre.* Producer/Director: Gordon Duff. *Cast:* Frank Conroy, Katherine Meskill, Vinton Hayworth, Frank Tweddell, Walter Brooke, Iris Mann, Vaughn Taylor.

22 December 1948—"Hansel and Gretel," by Engelbert Humperdinck, for *Kraft Television Theatre.* Conductor: Sam Morgenstern. *Cast:* Florence Forsberz, William McLockin, Marian Selef.

26 December 1948—7:00 *Mary Kay and Johnny.*

9:00 "The Old Lady Shows Her Medals," by James M. Barrie, adapted by Samuel Taylor, for *Philco Television Playhouse. Cast:* Lucille Watson, Cameron Mitchell.

27 December 1948—"Who Is Your Judge?" by Paul Gallico, for *Chevrolet Tele-Theatre. Cast:* Margo, Eddie Albert, Frank Thomas, Susan Harris.

29 December 1948—"Meet the Prince," by A. A. Milne, for *Kraft Television Theatre. Cast:* Howard St. John, Wauna Paul, Neva Patterson, Robin Craven, Philippa Bevans, Ivy Bethune, Roland von Weber, Marjorie Brown, Robert Hookey.

1949

2 January 1949—5:30 *Hopalong Cassidy* continues on film throughout 1949. William Boyd is promoted as television's Number One Western actor. [Not listed hereafter.]

7:00 *Mary Kay and Johnny.*

9:00 "Ramshackle Inn," by George Batson, for *Philco Television Playhouse.* Producer/Director: Fred Coe. *Cast:* ZaSu Pitts.

3 January 1949—7:00–7:30 *The Monohans*, a situation comedy. Producer/Director: Mark Hawley.

8:00 "The Mayor and the Manicure," by George Ade, for *Chevrolet Tele-Theatre.* Producer/Director: Garry Simpson. *Cast:* Guy Kibbee, Glenda Farrell, Walter Starkey, John McQuade, Gloria Patrice, Eric Burtis.

9:00 "Fancy Meeting You Here," by Olga Moore, adapted by William Stuart, for the debut of *The Colgate Theatre.* Producer/Director: Hal Keith. (The pilot was directed by Garry Simpson on 19 November 1948.) *Cast:* Betty Garde, Mary Wickes, Eva Condon, Nancy Marchand, Peggy Van Fleet, Brooks West. Sponsor: Colgate-Palmolive Peat Company.

5 January 1949—9:00 "To Catch the Wind," by Riza Royce, for *Kraft Television Theatre. Cast:* Noel Leslie, John Conway, Joan Stanley, Walter Kinsella, Mark Roberts, Audrey Ridgewell.

9 January 1949—7:00 *Mary Kay and Johnny.*

9:00 "Cyrano De Bergerac," by Edmund Rostand, adapted by Samuel Taylor, for *Philco Television Playhouse.* Producer/Director: Fred Coe. *Cast:* Jose Ferrer, Frances Reid, Robert Carroll, Paula Lawrence, Ernest Graves, John McQuade, Hildy Parks, Vincent J. Donehue, Paul Wilson.

10 January 1949—7:00 *The Monohans.*

8:00 "Goodbye to the Lazy K," an original drama by Robert Finch, for *Chevrolet on Broadway.* Producer/Director: Garry Simpson. *Cast:* Buddy Ebsen, Betty Caulfield, Tom Scott, Charles McClelland, Dennis Harrison.

9:00 "The Haunting Year," by Betty Hodgson, adapted by William Stuart, for *The Colgate Theatre.* Producer/Director: Hal Keith. *Cast:* Peggy Conklin, Alexander Kirkland, Neva Patterson, Howard Wendell, Lawrence Tibbett, Edward Forbes.

12 January 1949—"Miranda," by Peter Blackmore, for *Kraft Television Theatre. Cast:* Beverly Roberts, Richard Kendrick, Betty Ann Nyman.

16 January 1949— 7:00 *Mary Kay and Johnny.*

9:00 "Papa Is All," by Patterson Greene, for *Philco Television Playhouse.* Producer/Director: Fred Coe. *Cast:* Mady Christians, Carl Benton Reid.

17 January 1949— 8:00 "Jinxed," by George Mosel, for *Chevrolet on Broadway.* Producer/Director: Gordon Duff. *Cast:* Jackie Cooper, Mary Anderson, Ralph Theadore, Jesse White, Vaughn Taylor.

9:00 "Murder by Choice," for *The Colgate Theatre.* Producer/Director: Hal Keith. *Cast:* Myrtle Tannehill, Augusta Dabney, William Neil, Eddie Hyans.

19 January 1949— 9:00 "Duet for Two Hands," by Mary Hayley Bell, *Kraft Television Theatre. Cast:* Valerie Cossart, Louisa Horton, Guy Spaull, Rhoderick Walker.

23 January 1949— 7:00 *Mary Kay and Johnny.*

9:00 "Pride and Prejudice," by Jane Austen, adapted by Samuel Taylor, for *Philco Television Playhouse.* Producer/Director: Fred Coe. *Cast:* Madge Evans, John Baragrey, Viola Roache, Louis Hector, Elizabeth Bennett.

24 January 1949— 6:30 *Meet the Monohans.*

8:30 "Trapeze," by Hector Chevigny, for *Chevrolet on Broadway.* Director: Garry Simpson. *Cast:* Luise Rainer, Charles Korvin, Clay Clement, King Calder, Tod Andrews.

9:00 "Ring Once for Central," an original story and adaptation by Carl Allensworth, for *The Colgate Theatre.* Producer/Director: Hal Keith.

26 January 1949— 9:00 "There's Always Juliet," by John Van Druten, for *Kraft Television Theatre. Cast:* Margery Maude, Huntington Watts, Lex Richards, Gwen Anderson.

30 January 1949— 7:00 *Mary Kay and Johnny.*

9:00 "Dark Hammock," by Mary Orr and Reginald Denham, for *Philco Television Playhouse.* Producer/Director: Fred Coe. *Cast:* Peggy Wood, Sidney Blackmer, Mary Wickes, Mary Orr.

31 January 1949— 8:30 "All's Fair," by Lawrence DuPont, for *Chevrolet on Broadway.* Producer/Director: Gordon Duff, *Cast:* Mary Boland, Roland Young, Patricia Kirkland, Georgette Harvey, Kevin McCarthy.

9:00 "A Husband's Rights," by Eleanor Gilchrist for *The Colgate Theatre. Cast:* Ian Keith, Melba Rae, John Harvey, Jean Arden Cobb, Philippa Bevans.

2 February 1949— 9:00 "Her Master's Voice," by Clare Kummer, for *Kraft Television Theatre. Cast:* Augusta Dabney, Valerie Cossart, Fairfax Burgher, Cherry Hardy, Jackie Diamond, Susan Harris, Ethel Owen, Philip Truex.

6 February 1949— 7:00 *Mary Kay and Johnny.*

9:00 "The Late Christopher Bean," by Sidney Howard, adapted by Samuel Taylor, for *Philco Television Playhouse. Cast:* Lillian Gish debuts; Bert Lytell.

7 February 1949— 8:30 "Expert Opinion," by True Boardman, for *Chevrolet on Broadway.* Producer/Director: Garry Simpson. *Cast:* Dennis King, Boris Karloff, Vicki Cummings, Frank Thomas, Ivan Simpson, Clyde Waddell, John Graham.

9:00 "Tough Kid," by Morgan Lewis, adapted by William Stuart, for *The Colgate Theatre*. Producer/Director: Hal Keith. *Cast:* Carl Benton Reid, Lon McAllister, Jeanne Shepherd, Richard Astor.

9 February 1949— 9:00 "Grammercy Ghost," a new comedy by John Cecil Holm, for *Kraft Television Theatre*. *Cast:* Nancy Coleman, William Van Sleet, Richard Hamilton, Eugene Francis, Kittie Cosgriff, Fredd Wayne, Humphrey Davis, Ivan Simpson, Curtis Cooksey.

13 February 1949— 7:00 *Mary Kay and Johnny*.

9:00 "The Story of Mary Surratt," by John Patrick, for *Philco Television Playhouse*. Producer/Director: Fred Coe. Music: Harry Sosnick. *Cast:* Dorothy Gish, Kent Smith.

14 February 1949— 8:30 "Miracle in the Rain," by Ben Hecht, for *Chevrolet on Broadway*. Producer: Owen Davis, Jr. Director: Gordon Duff. *Cast:* Mary Anderson, John Dall, Viola Trayne, Lee Harris, Jesse White.

9:00 "Anything But Love," by Gertrude Schweitzer, adapted by William Stuart, for *The Colgate Theatre*. Producer/Director: Hal Keith. *Cast:* Joy Geffen, Herbert Evers, Si Vario, Dorothy Beattie, Alexander Ivo, Don Pardo.

16 February 1949— 9:00 "Room Service," by John Murray and Alvin Boretz, for *Kraft Television Theatre*. Producer/Director: Jack Caldwell. *Cast:* Warren Parker, Dudley Sadler, Gage Clark, Joe Silver, Jean Sincere, Charles Penman, Charles Mayer, Donald MacDonald, Humphrey Davis, Owen Coll.

20 February 1949— 7:00 *Mary Kay and Johnny*.

9:00 "Twelfth Night," by William Shakespeare, adapted by Fred Coe and Samuel Taylor, for *Philco Television Playhouse*. Producer/Director: Fred Coe. *Cast:* Marsha Hunt, John Carradine, Frances Reid, Vaughn Taylor, Richard Goode.

21 February 1949— 8:30 "Suppressed Desires," by Susan Glaspell, for *Chevrolet on Broadway*. Producer: Owen Davis, Jr. Director: Garry Simpson. *Cast:* Ernest Truex, Ilka Chase, Valerie Cossart, George Matthews, E. A. Krumschmidt.

9:00 "The Girl," by Edward Peple, adapted by William Stuart, for *The Colgate Theatre*. Case: Guy Spaull, Tod Andrews, Jean Carson.

23 February 1949— 9:00 "The Flying Gerardos," by Kenyon Nicholson and Charles Robinson, for *Kraft Television Theatre*. *Cast:* Lucille Fenton, Hugh Reilly, Barbara Meyer, Winfield Hoeny, William Thunhurst, Susan Thorne.

27 February 1949— 7:00 *Mary Kay and Johnny*.

7:30–7:59 *The Hartmans*, a situation comedy, debuts. Producer/Director: Garry Simpson. *Cast:* Grace and Paul Hartman.

9:00 "St. Helena," by R. C. Sherriff and Jeanne de Casalie, for *Philco Television Playhouse*. Producer/Director: Fred Coe. *Cast:* Dennis King.

28 February 1949— 8:30 "Heat Lightning," by Robert F. Carroll, for *Chevrolet on Broadway*. Producer: Owen Davis, Jr. Director: Gordon Duff. *Cast:* Elizabeth Bergner, Dean Jagger, Philip Huston, Andrew Duggan, Robert Bolger, John Acair, Wayne Howard.

9:00 "Security," by Alex Rackowe and William Clarke, for *The Colgate Theatre*. *Cast:* Augusta Dabney, Paul Park, Mort Stevens; Bob Warren.

1 March 1949— 9:30 *Believe It or Not*, a variety/drama series by Robert L. Ripley, debuts. Producer/Director: Victor McLeod. Sponsor: Motorola.

2 March 1949— 9:00 "A Bill of Divorcement," by Clemence Dane, for *Kraft Television Theatre*.

6 March 1949— 7:00 *Mary Kay and Johnny*. 7:30 *The Hartmans*.

9:00 "The Druid Circle," by John Van Druten, for *Philco Television Playhouse*. Producer/Director: Fred Coe. *Cast:* Leo G. Carroll, Ethel Griffies.

7 March 1949—8:30 "Mr. Bell's Creation," by Stanley Richards for *Chevrolet on Broadway*. Producer: Owen Davis Jr. Director: Garry Simpson. *Cast:* Janet Blair, Romney Brent, Ann Thomas, Harry Bannister, Robert White, Philippa Bevans, David Forsythe, Marjorie Anderson.

9:00 "The Florist Shop," by Winifred Hawkridge, adapted by Charles Campbell, for *The Colgate Theatre*. Producer/Director: Hal Keith. *Cast:* Ruth Gilbert, David Orrick, Donald MacDonald, Ivan MacDonald, Peggy Conklin.

8 March 1949—9:30 *Believe It or Not*.

9 March 1949—9:00 "The Arrival of Kitty," by Norman Lee Swarthout, for *Kraft Television Theatre*. *Cast:* Jack Lemmon, Patricia Kirkland, Malcolm Beggs, Dorothy Elder, Gage Clarke, Maud Scheerer, Dort Clark, Harry Sothern.

13 March 1949—7:00 *Mary Kay and Johnny*.

7:30 *The Hartmans*.

9:00 "Quality Street," by James M. Barrie, for *Philco Television Playhouse*. *Cast:* Alfred Drake, Marsha Hunt.

14 March 1949—8:30 "Londonderry Air," by Rachel Field, for *Chevrolet on Broadway*. Producer/Director: Gordon Duff. *Cast:* Nanette Fabray, John Conté, Eva Condon, Iggie Wolfington.

9:00 "Addison's Lad," by Beulah Marie Dix, adapted by William Stuart, for *The Colgate Theatre*. Producer/Director: Hal Keith. *Cast:* William Whitman, Louis Hector, J. W. Austin, Neil Fitzgerald, Francis Compton, Anthony Kemble Cooper, Bob Warren.

15 March 1949—9:30 *Believe It or Not*.

16 March 1949—9:00 "Consider Lily," by Stanley Kauffman, for *Kraft Television Theatre*. *Cast:* Margaret Phillips, Ann Donaldson, Ron Randall.

20 March 1949—7:00 *Mary Kay and Johnny*.

7:30 *The Hartmans*.

9:00 "Dinner at Antoine's," by Florence Parkinson Keyes, for *Philco Television Playhouse*. *Cast:* Janet Blair, William Eythe.

21 March 1949—8:30 "Smart Guy," by Hector Chevigny, for *Chevrolet on Broadway*. Producer/Director: Garry Simpson. *Cast:* Nancy Coleman, Alan Baxter, John Forsythe, Virginia Smith, Philip Foster.

9:00 "Right of Way," by Howard Buermann, adapted by William Stuart, for *The Colgate Theatre*. Producer/Director: Hal Keith. *Cast:* Bill Story, Ralph Riggs, Andrew Duggan, Jeanne Shepherd, Anthony Blair, Calvin Thomas.

22 March 1949—9:30 *Believe It or Not*.

23 March 1949—9:00 "Village Green," by Carl Allensworth, for *Kraft Television Theatre*. Director: Maury Holland. *Cast:* Dianne de Brett, Jack Orrison, David Orrick, Jack Lemmon, Harrison Down, Reynolds Evans, Vaughn Taylor, Mark Roberts, Jean Gillespie, Helen Carew, Carl Benton Reid.

27 March 1949—7:00 *Mary Kay and Johnny*.

7:30 *The Hartmans*.

9:00 "Becky Sharp," by William Thackeray, adapted by Samuel Taylor, for *Philco Television Playhouse*. *Cast:* Clare Luce, Francis Bethencourt.

28 March 1949—8:30 "The Managers," by Joseph C. Lincoln, for *Chevrolet on Broadway*. Producer/Director: Gordon Duff. *Cast:* Victor Moore, Guy Kibbee, Judy Parrish, John Harvey, Howard Blaine, Bill Story.

9:00 "Sunday Punch," by Jerome Barry, adapted William Stuart, for *The Colgate Theatre*. Producer/Director: Hal Keith. *Cast:* Phil Arthur, Phillip Huston, Iggie Wolfington, Joseph Allen, Jr.

29 March 1949— 9:30 *Believe It or Not*.

30 March 1949— 9:00 "Wicked Is the Wine," by Sumner Locke Elliott, for *Kraft Television Theatre*. Producer: Tom Ward. Director: Stanley Quinn. *Cast:* Margaret Phillips, Joan Stanley, Ron Randall, Janet Fox, Bryan Herbert, Michael Everett, John Hamilton, Margery Maude, Byron Russell.

3 April 1949— 3:30–5:15 "The Tragedy of Julius Caesar," by William Shakespeare, adapted by Curtis Canfield. Producer: Owen Davis, Jr. Director: Garry Simpson. *Cast:* Amherst College Masquers. A WNBW remote from The Folger Shakespeare Library, Washington, D.C. Sponsor: Esso Standard Oil Company.

7:30 *The Hartmans*.

9:00 "And Never Been Kissed," by Sylvia Dee, adapted by Samuel Taylor, for *Philco Television Playhouse*. Producer/Director: Fred Coe. *Cast:* Patricia Kirkland, William Redfield, Muriel Kirkland, Ben Lackland, Arthur Anderson, Sylvia Lane, Peter Fernandez, Edith Fellows, Lenka Peterson.

4 April 1949— 8:30 "Goodnight, Please," by James L. Daggert, for *Chevrolet on Broadway*. Producer: Owen Davis, Jr. Director: Gordon Duff. *Cast:* Edward Everett Horton, Natalie Schafer, Philip Tonge, Elinor Randel, Howard St. John, Ivan Simpson, Ann Sullivan.

9:00 "Sugar and Spice," by Florence Ryerson and Colin Clements, adapted by Robert Wetzel for *The Colgate Theatre*. Producer/Director: Hal Keith.

5 April 1949— 9:00–9:29 "Friend of the Family," for *Fireside Theatre* debut. Producer/ Director: Lawrence Schwab, Jr. *Cast:* Virginia Gilmore, Yul Brynner, Peter Barry, Win Elliot.

9:30 *Believe It or Not*.

6 April 1949— 9:00 "As Husbands Go," by Rachel Crothers, for *Kraft Television Theatre*. *Cast:* Lawrence Fletcher, Ruth Matteson, Roderick Walker, Paula Trueman, Betty Ann Nyman, Tonio Selwart, Anne Ives.

10 April 1949— 7:30 *The Hartmans*.

9:00 "What Makes Sammy Run?" by Budd Schulberg, adapted by Samuel Carter, for *Philco Television Playhouse*. *Cast:* José Ferrer.

11 April 1949— 8:30 "The Twelve Pound Look," by James M. Barrie, for *Chevrolet on Broadway*. Producer: Owen Davis, Jr. Director: Gordon Duff. *Cast:* Margaret Sullavan, Ralph Forbes, Valerie Cossart, Byron Russell.

9:00 "Fairly Won," by Barbara Corrigan, adapted by William Stuart, for *The Colgate Theatre*. Producer Director: Hal Keith. *Cast:* Margaret Wycherly.

12 April 1949— 9:00 "Ghost Story," by John Meshan and Thomas W. Phipps, for *Fireside Theatre*. Producer: Larry Corcoran. Director: Robert Elwyn. *Cast:* Eda Heinemann, Ethel Remey, Dorthea Jackson.

9:30 *Believe It or Not*.

13 April 1949— 9:00 "Miracle at Chickerton," by Peter Barry, for *Kraft Television Theatre*. *Cast:* Gage Clarke, Natalie Schafer, William Lee, Frank Baxter, Barbara Meyer, Grania O'Malley, Humphrey Davis, Dwight Marfield, Alan Macateer.

17 April 1949— 7:30 *The Hartmans*.

9:00 "Mr. Mergenthwirker's Lobblies," by Nelson Bond and David Kent, for *NBC Repertory Theatre* debut. Producer: Fred Coe. Director: Ralph Nelson. *Cast:* Vaughn Taylor, Vinton Hayworth, John McQuade.

18 April 1949— 8:30 "Everybody Loves My Baby," by Max Schulman, for *Chevrolet on Broadway*. Producer: Owen Davis, Jr. Director: Garry Simpson. *Cast:* Jane Withers, Richard Noyes, Harry Bannister.

    9:00 "Just for Tonight," by True Boardman, for *The Colgate Theatre*. Producer/Director: Hal Keith. *Cast:* Neva Patterson, Patricia Shay, John Forsythe.

19 April 1949— 9:00 "New Faces," a revue by Leonard Sillman, for *Fireside Theatre*. Producer/Director: Lawrence Schwab, Jr.

    9:30 *Believe It or Not.*

20 April 1949—"The Whole Town's Talking," by John Emerson and Anita Loos, for *Kraft Television Theatre*. *Cast:* Lawrence Fletcher, Valerie Cossart, Jane Bennett-Hix, Carl Reiner, Cynthia Stone, Andrea Wallace, Timothy Lynn Kearse, Tom Ewell.

24 April 1949— 7:30 *The Hartmans.*

    9:00–9:59 "Burlesque," by George Manker Watters and Arthur Hopkins, for *NBC Drama Theatre* debut. Producer: Owen Davis, Jr. Director: Victor McLeod. *Cast:* Bert Lahr, Vicki Cummings, Ann Thomas.

25 April 1949— 8:30 "Tommy Malone Comes Home," by True Boardman, for *Chevrolet on Broadway*. Producer/Director: Gordon Duff. *Cast:* James Dunn, Margaret Wycherly, Virginia Gilmore, Theodore Newton, Patrick Malone, Edward Waglin.

    9:00 "Mistress Sims Inherits," by William Kendall Clarke, for *The Colgate Theatre*. Producer: Owens Davis, Jr. Director: Hal Keith. *Cast:* Mabel Taliaferro.

26 April 1949— 9:00 *Fireside Theatre* was variety.

    9:30 *Believe It or Not.*

27 April 1949—"Green Stockings," by A. E. W. Mason, for *Kraft Television Theatre*. Producer: Tom Ward. Director: Stanley Quinn. *Cast:* Ruth Matteson, Joseph Allen, Jr., William Jeffrey, Cynthia Lathum, Tom Vize, June Dayton, Edwin Mills, Joan Webster, Emory Richardson, John Adair.

1 May 1949—"Macbeth," by William Shakespeare, adapted from Edwin Booth's Prompt book, for *NBC Repertory Theatre*. Director: Garry Simpson. *Cast:* The Players' Club. *Cast:* Walter Hampden, Joyce Redman, Walter Abel, Leo G. Carroll.

2 May 1949— 8:30 "The Suicide Club," by Robert Louis Stevenson, for *Chevrolet on Broadway*. Producer: Owen Davis, Jr. Director: Gordon Duff. *Cast:* Frances L. Sullivan, Bramwell Fletcher, Oliver Thorndike.

    9:00 "Tin Can Skipper," by Jacland Marmur, adapted by William Stuart, for *The Colgate Theatre*. Producer: Owen Davis, Jr. Director: Hal Keith.

3 May 1949— 9:00 "Meet My Sister," a musical by Felix Jackson, for *Fireside Theatre*. Producer: Felix Jackson. *Cast:* Betty and Jane Kean.

    9:30 *Believe It or Not.*

4 May 1949— 9:00 "Adam and Eva," by George Middleton and Guy Bolton, for *Kraft Television Theatre*. *Cast:* Carl Benton Reid, Mark Roberts, Patricia White.

8 May 1949— 7:30 *The Hartmans.*

    9:00 "Bedelia," by Vera Caspary, adapted by Fred Coe, for *NBC Repertory Theatre*. Producer: Fred Coe. Director: Ralph Nelson. *Cast:* Francis Reed, Philip Dorneuf.

9 May 1949— 8:00 "A Passenger to Bali," by Ellis St. John, for *Chevrolet on Broadway*. Producer: Owen Davis, Jr. Director: Garry Simpson. *Cast:* Boris Karloff, Vicki Cummings, Stanley Ridges, E. A. Krumschmidt.

8:30 *The Jackie Gleason Show.*

9:00 "Lady, Look Out," by Ruth Rankin Lawson, adapted by Mortimer Frankel, for *The Colgate Theatre.* Producer: Owen Davis, Jr. Director: Hal Keith. *Cast:* Natalie Schafer, David Orrick, Cloris Leachman, Philip Truex.

10 May 1949—9:00 "Time Bomb," for *Fireside Theatre.* Producer: Frank Wisbar. Director: Lawrence Schwab, Jr. *Cast:* Jack Mitschum, Robert Bice, Robert Stevenson, Allan Wells, Christine Cooper, Michael Barrett.

9:30 *Believe It or Not.*

11 May 1949—9:00 "The Oath of Hippocrates," an original play by M. V. Heberden, for *Kraft Television Theatre. Cast:* Guy Spaull, Dean Harens, Felicia Montealegre.

15 May 1949—7:30 *The Hartmans.*

9:00 "Romeo and Juliet," by William Shakespeare for *NBC Repertory Theatre* (aka *Arena Theatre of the Air*). Producer/Director: Warren Wade. *Cast:* Kevin McCarthy, Patricia Breslin.

16 May 1949—8:00 "Manhattan Mary," by Samuel Taylor and Russell Beggs, for *Chevrolet on Broadway.* Producer/Director: Victor McLeod. *Cast:* Mitzi Green.

8:30 "The Clock," Episode 1, by Laurence Klee, for *The Clock* debut. Producer: Fred Coe. Director: Hal Keith. *Cast:* William David, Louisa Norton, Owen Coll.

9:00 "First Dance," for *The Colgate Theatre.*

17 May 1949—9:00 *Fireside Theatre* reviewed old movies.

9:30 *Believe It or Not.*

18 May 1949—8:30 *The Black Robe,* a recreation of court cases and an NBC–Phillips H. Lord series, debuts. Producer/Director: Edward Sutherland. *Cast:* "Ordinary people."

9:00 "Big Hearted Herbert," by Sophia Kerr and Anna Steese Richardson, for *Kraft Television Theatre.*

23 May 1949—8:00 "The Uncertain Hour," by Kathleen Norris, adapted by Samuel Carter, for *Chevrolet on Broadway.* Producer: Owen Davis, Jr. Director: Gordon Duff. *Cast:* Fay Bainter, Hume Cronyn.

8:30 *The Clock.* Producer/Director: Fred Coe.

9:00 "First Dance," adapted by William Stuart, for *The Colgate Theatre.*

24 May 1949—9:00 "Make a Wish," a concept by John Nelson, for *Fireside Theatre.* Viewers' wishes are filmed in Hollywood. *Cast:* Nelson Case.

9:30 *Believe It or Not.*

25 May 1949—8:30 *The Black Robe.*

9:00 "Autumn Fire," by Thomas C. Murray, for *Kraft Television Theatre. Cast:* Frank Baxter, Martin Lewis, Andrea Wallace.

29 May 1949—9:00 "The Mikado," by W. S. Gilbert and Arthur Sullivan, adapted by Samuel Carter for *NBC Repertory Theatre.* Producer: Fred Coe. Director: Gordon Duff. *Cast:* Gilbert and Sullivan Choral Society of New York.

30 May 1949—8:30 "Long Lost Brother," by Gordon Walker, for *Chevrolet on Broadway.* Producer: Owen Davis, Jr. Director: Garry Simpson. *Cast:* John Carradine. [*The Clock* was not aired.]

9:00 "Entrapment," by Thomas Walsh, adapted by William Stuart, for *The Colgate Theatre.* Producer/Director: Hal Keith. *Cast:* John Howard, Royal Dano, Peggy Carnegie, Karen Stevens, Henry Hamilton, Doug Rutherford, Richard Barrows.

31 May 1949—9:00 "The Birthday Murder," by Alfred Bester, for *Fireside Theatre.* Producer: Charles Eastman.

9:30 *Believe It or Not*. *Cast:* Robert L. Ripley died on 27 May. Bugs Baer replaced him.

1 June 1949 — 8:30 *The Black Robe*.

9:00 "The Elephant Shepherd," for *Kraft Television Theatre*. *Cast:* Neil Hamilton, Madelaine Smith, Vernon Smith.

5 June 1949 — 9:00 "This Time Next Year," adapted from "This Time Next Week," for *NBC Repertory Theatre*. Producer: Fred Coe. Director: Gary Simpson. *Cast:* Diana Kemble, Frank Daren, Catherine McDonald, Bob Davis, James Rafferty, Martin Greene, Frederic De Wilde, Nancy Franklin.

6 June 1949 — 8:00 "Johnny Cartwright's Camera," by Nelson Bond, for *Chevrolet on Broadway*. Producer: Gordon Duff. *Cast:* Lee Tracy, John O'Hara, Iggie Wolfington, Maurice Manson, Betty George.

8:30 *The Clock* is substituted with a film due to technical difficulties.

9:00 *The Colgate Theatre* was a variety program.

7 June 1949 — 9:00 "Feature Story," for *Fireside Theatre*. Executive Producer: Harry Salzman. *Cast:* Dwight Weist. Sponsor: Procter & Gamble.

9:30 *Believe It or Not*.

8 June 1949 — 8:30 *The Black Robe*.

9:00 "Payment Deferred," by C. S. Forester, adapted by Jeffrey Dell, for *Kraft Television Theatre*. Producer: Tom Ward. Director: Stanley Quinn. *Cast:* Mercer McLeod, Grace Carney, Cloris Leachman, Vilma Kurer, Vaughn Taylor, Richard Deane, Michael Blair.

12 June 1949 — 9:00 "It Pays to Advertise," by Roi Cooper Megrue and Walter Hackett, adapted by Samuel Carter for *NBC Repertory Theatre*. Producer/Director: Victor McLeod. *Cast:* Frank Albertson, Jean Sincere.

13 June 1949 — 8:00 "Weather Ahead," by William Devlin, for *Chevrolet on Broadway*. Producer: Victor McLeod. Director: Garry Simpson. *Cast:* Brian Donlevy, Jesse White.

8:30 "The Wives," for *The Clock*. Producer/Director: Lawrence Schwab, Jr.

9:00 "Applesauce of Thousands," by Laurie Hillyer, adapted by Robert Wallsten, for *The Colgate Theatre*. Producer/Director: Hal Keith.

14 June 1949 — 9:00 *Fireside Theatre* was a dance program.

9:30 *Believe It or Not*.

15 June 1949 — 8:30 *The Black Robe*.

9:00 "Little Brown Jug," by Marie Baumer, for *Kraft Television Theatre*. Producer: Tom Ward. Director: Harry Herrmann. *Cast:* John Stephen, John Harvey, Malcolm Lee Brown, Gwen Anderson, Katherine Anderson, Vaughn Taylor.

19 June 1949 — "Summer Formal," variety for *NBC Repertory Theatre*.

20 June 1949 — 8:00 "The Heritage of Wimpole Street," by Robert Knipe, adapted by Ethel Frank, for *Chevrolet on Broadway*. Producer: Victor McLeod. Director: Gordon Duff. *Cast:* Emily Lawrence, Valerie Cossart, Leo G. Carroll.

8:30 "Passage for Two," for *The Clock*. Producer/Director: Lawrence Schwab, Jr.

9:00 "Home Town," by William Stuart, for *The Colgate Theatre*. Director: Garry Simpson. *Cast:* Louise Allbritton, Daniel Reed, Grant Gordon, Mary Dallas, Theodore Newton, Leo Eadia.

21 June 1949 — 9:00 "The Stronger," with Geraldine Fitzgerald, and "A Terribly Strange Bed," by Wilkie Collins, with Richard Greene, for *Fireside Theatre*.

9:30 *Believe It or Not*.

22 June 1949 — 8:30 *The Black Robe*.

9:00 "Pink String and Sealing Wax," by Roland Pertwee, for *Kraft Television Theatre. Cast:* Leslie Barrie, Peter Fernandez, Cloris Leachman, Jean Gillespie, Elizabeth Ross, Bonnie Baken, Viola Frayne, Michael Blair.

26 June 1949—"Jenny Kissed Me," by Jean Kerr, adapted Howard Richardson and William Berney, for *NBC Repertory Theatre. Cast:* Leo G. Carroll, Elinor Randel.

27 June 1949— 8:00 "Half Hour," by James M. Barrie, adapted by Samuel Carter, for *Chevrolet on Broadway.* Producer: Victor McLeod. Director: Garry Simpson. *Cast:* Nina Foch, John Conté, D. A. Clarke-Smith.

8:30 "The Loft Case," adapted by Bob Wald, for *The Clock.* Producer/Director: Fred Coe.

9:00 "All Things Come Home," an original teleplay, by True Boardman, for *The Colgate Theatre. Cast:* Neil Hamilton, Phil Arthur, Merle Madden.

28 June 1949— 9:00 "Father," for *Fireside Theatre. Cast:* Harry Bannister, June Walker.

9:30 *Believe It or Not.*

29 June 1949— 8:30 *The Black Robe.*

9:00 "Baby Mine," by Margaret Mayo, for *Kraft Television Theatre. Cast:* Warren Parker, Kyle MacDonnell.

3 July 1949—"Dark of the Moon," by Howard Richardson and William Berney, for *NBC Repertory Theatre.* Producer: Warren Wade. *Cast:* Carol Stone, Richard Hart.

4 July 1949— 8:00 "Lesson for Eddie," by Robert Finch adapted by Samuel Carter, for *Chevrolet on Broadway.* Producer: Gordon Duff. Director: Victor McLeod. *Cast:* Charles Ruggles, Betty Ann Nyman, Frank Tweddell, James Dobson.

8:30 "A Man Called Fletcher," for *The Clock.* Producer: Fred Coe. Director: Lawrence Schwab, Jr.

9:00 "Mr. and Mrs. North," by Frances and Richard Lockridge, adapted from the radio series, for *The Colgate Theatre.* Director: Duane McKinney.

5 July 1949—*Fireside Theatre* was preempted for the debut of *Hobby Lobby.*

6 July 1949— 9:00 "Within the Law," by Bayard Veiller, for *Kraft Television Theatre. Cast:* Patricia Jenkins, Maury Hill, Malcolm Beggs, John Stephen, Gage Clark, Earl Hammond, Polly Cole, Michael Everett, Rosetta Lenoire, Jack Orrison.

10:00 *Believe It or Not.*

10 July 1949— 9:00 "For Love or Money," by F. Hugh Herbert, adapted by Ethel Frank, for *NBC Repertory Theatre.* Producer: Warren Wade. Director: Duane McKinney. *Cast:* William Post, Jr., Janet Blake.

11 July 1949— 8:00 "The Castle of Mr. Simpson," by John Kirkpatrick, adapted by Samuel Carter, for *Chevrolet on Broadway.* Producer: Victor McLeod. Director: Hal Keith. *Cast:* Curtis Cooksey, Irene Rich, Melba Rae, Virginia Gilmore, Sally Moffett, Jimmy Goodwin, David Orrick, Ernest Graves, Lizalotta Valecca.

8:30 "Roulette Wheel," by Lawrence Klee, adapted by Bob Wald, for *The Clock.* Producer: Fred Coe. Director: Lawrence Schwab, Jr. *Cast:* Dan Morgan, Vaughn Taylor, Timothy Kearse.

9:00 *The Colgate Theatre* originates from Chicago.

12 July 1949—*Fireside Theatre* is preempted for a *Lights Out* promotion.

13 July 1949— 8:30 *The Black Robe.*

9:00 "A Young Man's Fancy," by Harry Thurschwell and Alfred Golden, for *Kraft Television Theatre. Cast:* Andrew Sanders, Martin Miller, Walter Butterworth,

Richard Leone, Herbert Evers, Peggy McCay, Dennis Harrison, Sally Chamberlin, Humphrey Davis, Lee Carney, Myrtle Ferguson.
    10:00 *Believe It or Not.*
14 July 1949— 8:30 *Mary Kay and Johnny.*
    9:30 *Theatre of the Mind.*
17 July 1949— 9:00 "The Five Lives of Robert Gordon," by Nelson Bond, for the
debut of *Philco Summer Playhouse.* Producer: Fred Coe. Director: Garry Simpson. *Cast:* Melvyn Douglas.
18 July 1949— 8:00 "The Wine Glass," by A. A. Milne, adapted by Samuel Carter,
for *Chevrolet on Broadway.* Producer: Victor McLeod. Director: Gordon Duff.
Cast: Alan Mowbray, Douglas Smith, Philip Tonge, John Moore, Martha Linden,
Peter Pagan, Richard Fraser, Cherry Hardy, Byron Russell, Frank Darren.
    8:30 An original story by Lawrence Klee, adapted by Ivan Reiner, for *The Clock.*
Producer: Fred Coe. *Cast:* Jimmy Dobson, Eva Marie Saint, Guy Sorel.
    9:00 "Vic and Sade," by Paul Rhymer, a comedy serial, debuts from Chicago
for *The Colgate Theatre.*
19 July 1949— 9:00–9:30 "Episode One," *Lights Out,* a suspense anthology created
by Wyllis Cooper for radio, debuts. Producer: Fred Coe. Director: Kingman T.
Moore. *Cast:* Frances Reid, Phil Arthur, Anita Anton, Gladys Clark. Sponsor:
Admiral.
20 July 1949— 9:00 "The Curtain Rises," by Benjamin M. Kaye, for *Kraft Televi-*
sion Theatre. Cast: Nancy Coleman, Lex Richards, Guy Spaull, William Thunhurst, Richard Hamilton, Peggy French.
    10:00 *Believe It or Not.*
21 July 1949— 8:30 *Mary Kay and Johnny.*
    9:30 *Theatre of the Mind.*
24 July 1949—"You Touched Me!" by Tennessee Williams, adapted by Samuel
Carter, for *Philco Summer Playhouse.* Director: Gordon Duff. *Cast:* Dennis King,
Mary McLeod, William Prince, Margaret Bannerman, Neil Fitzgerald, Elizabeth
Eustis.
25 July 1949— 8:00–8:29 "The Stolen Prince," by Dan Totheroh, for *Academy The-*
atre debut. *Cast:* Shirley Dale, Ivan MacDonald, Collins Bain.
    8:30 *The Clock.*
    9:00 "Vic and Sade," for *The Colgate Theatre.*
26 July 1949—"Episode Two," for *Lights Out.* Producer: Fred Coe. Director: Kingman T. Moore. *Cast:* William Post, Jr., Mary Patton, Eva Marie Saint.
27 July 1949— 8:30 *The Black Robe.*
    9:00 "Time for Elizabeth," by Norman Krasna and Groucho Marx, for *Kraft Tele-*
vision Theatre. Cast: John Seymour, Maurice Manson.
    10:00 *Believe It or Not.*
28 July 1949— 8:30 *Mary Kay and Johnny.*
    9:30 *Theatre of the Mind.*
31 July 1949— 9:00 "The Fourth Wall," by A. A. Milne, adapted by Samuel Carter,
for *Philco Summer Playhouse.* Producer: Fred Coe. Director: Garry Simpson.
Cast: Frances Reid, D. A. Clarke-Smith, Philip Tonge, Peter Pagan, Maurice
Franklin, Phil Teed, Alexander Campbell, Louise Prussing, Frank Darren.
1 August 1949— 8:00 "Mr. Lincoln's Whiskers," by Adrian Scott, for *Academy The-*
atre. Producer: Curtis Canfield. Director: Mark Hawley.
    8:30 "The Dentist," for *The Clock.* Producer: Fred Coe. Director: Lawrence

Schwab, Jr. *Cast:* John Beal, John Randolph, Jean Carson, Ann Summers, Roy Fant, Iggie Wolfington, Jim Boles, Laurence Duggan, Larry Semon.

9:00 "Expert Opinion," by True Boardman, for *The Colgate Theatre* originating from New York. *Cast:* Richard Hart.

2 August 1949— 9:00 "Episode Three," for *Lights Out.* Producer: Fred Coe. Director: Kingman T. Moore.

3 August 1949— 8:30 *The Black Robe.*

9:00 "Heaven and Charing Cross," by Aubrey Danvers-Walker, for *Kraft Television Theatre.* Producer: Tom Ward. Director: Stanley Quinn. *Cast:* Una O'Connor.

10:00 *Believe It or Not.*

4 August 1949— 8:30 *Mary Kay and Johnny.*

9:30 *Theatre of the Mind.*

5 August 1949— 9:30–10:00 *Mixed Doubles*, a situation comedy, by Carlton E. Morse, debuts. Producer/Director: Carlton E. Morse. *Cast:* Billy Idelson, Ada Coleman, Eddie Firestone.

7 August 1949— 9:00 "Enter Madame," by Gilda Varesi and Dolly Byrne, for *Philco Summer Playhouse.* Producer: Fred Coe. Director: Gordon Duff. *Cast:* Carol Goodner, Philip Bourneuf.

8 August 1949— 8:00 "The Drums of Oude," by Austin Strong, for *Academy Theatre.* Producer: Curtis Canfield. Director: Mark Hawley. *Cast:* Richard Newton, Emily Lawrence, Peter Pagan.

8:30 *Jack and Jill*, a film.

9:00 "Expert Opinion," was repeated for *The Clock.* Producer/Director: Hal Keith.

9 August 1949— 9:00 "The Crater," by Sumner Locke Elliot, adapted by Ethel Frank, for *Lights Out.* Director: Kingman T. Moore.

10 August 1949— 8:30–8:59 *The Clock* at a new time.

9:00 "The Misleading Lady," by Charles W. Goddard and Paul Dickey, for *Kraft Television Theatre. Cast:* Patricia Jenkins, Mark Roberts, Vaughn Taylor, Fredd Wayne, Walter Klavun, Eugene Francise, Sally Pearse, Richard McCracken.

10:00 *Believe It or Not.*

11 August 1949— 8:30 *Mary Kay and Johnny.*

9:30 *Theatre of the Mind.*

12 August 1949— 9:30 *Mixed Doubles.*

14 August 1949— 9:00 "A Murder Has Been Arranged," by Emlyn Williams, adapted by Ethel Frank, for *Philco Summer Playhouse.* Producer: Fred Coe. Director: Garry Simpson. *Cast:* Donald Cook, Louisa Horton, Bill Terry, Adelaide Klein, Nancy Sheridan, Russell Gaige, Mercedes Gilbert, Diane de Brett, Scott Tennyson, Jay Jackson.

15 August 1949— 8:00 "In the Shadow of the Glen," by John M. Synge, for *Academy Theatre.* Producer: Curtis Canfield. Director: Mark Hawley. *Cast:* Anne Jackson, Barry McCullen, Paul Anderson, Peter Wynn.

8:30 *The Black Robe.*

9:00 "The Key in the Lock," by Howard Goldman, adapted by Jack Bentkover, for *The Colgate Theatre.* Producer/Director: Hal Keith.

16 August 1949—*Lights Out.* Producer: Fred Coe. Director: Kingman T. Moore.

17 August 1949— 8:30 The Bank Vault," adapted by Bob Wald, for *The Clock.* Producer: Fred Coe. Director: William Corrigan.

9:00 "Mr. Pim Passes By," A. A. Milne, for *Kraft Television Theatre.* Producer:

Tom Ward. Director: Stanley Quinn. *Cast:* Valerie Cossart, Geoffrey Lumb, Rex O'Malley, Barbara Meyer, Richard Deane, Louise Prussing.

10:00 *Believe It or Not.*

18 August 1949— 8:30 *Mary Kay and Johnny.*

9:30 *Theatre of the Mind.*

19 August 1949— 9:30 *Mixed Doubles.*

21 August 1949— 9:00 "Pretty Little Parlor," by Claiborne Foster, adapted by Ethel Frank, for *Philco Summer Playhouse.* Producer: Fred Coe. Director: Garry Simpson. *Cast:* Martha Linden, Betty Furness, Alexander Campbell, Peggy McCay, Paul Parks, Homer Smith, Charles McClelland, William Windom.

22 August 1949— 8:00 "Such Things Only Happen in Books," and "Love and How to Cure It," both by Thornton Wilder, for *Academy Theatre.* Producer: Curtis Canfield. Director: Mark Hawley.

9:00 "What Price Story," by Max Brand, adapted by William Stuart, for *The Colgate Theatre.*

23 August 1949— 9:00 "The Housekeeper," by Nelson Bond, adapted by Bob Wald, for *Lights Out.* Producer: Fred Coe. Director: Kingman T. Moore.

24 August 1949— 8:30 "Uncle Amos," adapted by Bob Wald, for *The Clock.* Producer: Fred Coe. Director: Lawrence Schwab, Jr.

9:00 "Where the Dear Antelope Play," by William Rogers, for *Kraft Television Theatre. Cast:* Mary Young, Joyce Van Patten, Ruth Hammond, Charles Nolte, Hunter Gardner, Gage Clark, Helen Hatch, Edith Meiser, Emory Richardson, Elizabeth Eustis, Jay Presson.

10:00 *Believe It or Not.*

25 August 1949— 8:30 *Mary Kay and Johnny.*

9:00–9:29 "My Name Is Wilma," a sketch by Ralph Berton, for *Theatre of the Mind* debut. Director: Delbert Mann.

26 August 1949— 9:30 *Mixed Doubles.*

28 August 1949— 9:00 "Three Cornered Moon," by Gertrude Tonkonogy, for *Philco Summer Playhouse.* Producer: Fred Coe. *Cast:* Nina Foch, Kurt Richards.

29 August 1949— 8:00 "Summer Goes to the Diamond O," by Robert Finch, for *Academy Theatre.* Producer: Curtis Canfield. Director: Mark Hawley. *Cast:* Mark Roberts, Jack Davis, Robert Bolger.

8:30 *The Black Robe.*

9:00 "Old Flame," by William Stuart, for *The Colgate Theatre.* Producer/Director: Hal Keith. *Cast:* John Boeuff, Sally Moffet, Lou McGuire, Dennis Bohea, Herbert Evers, Wyrley Birch, Ben Hammer.

30 August 1949— 9:00 *Lights Out.* Producer: Ernest Walling. Director: Kingman T. Moore.

31 August 1949— 8:30 *The Clock.* Producer: Fred Coe. Director: William Corrigan.

9:00 "Bedelia," by Vera Caspary, for *Kraft Television Theatre. Cast:* Julie Haydon, Jim Davidson, John Newland, Edwin Jerome, Sally Chamberlin, Velma Royton, Frances Tannehill, Grace Carney, Helen Warren.

10:00 *Believe It or Not.*

1 September 1949— 8:30 *Mary Kay and Johnny.*

9:00 *Theatre of the Mind.* Director: Alan J. Neuman.

10:00–10:30 *Martin Kane, Private Eye,* by Frank Wilson debuts. Producer: Tom Ward. Director: Edward Sutherland. *Cast:* William Gargan, Steven Gethers, Betty Furness, Harry Bannister, Jeanne Shepherd, Walter Kinsella.

2 September 1949 — 8:00 *Hopalong Cassidy* was moved to prime time and continues.
9:30 *Mixed Doubles.*
4 September 1949 — 9:00 "What Every Woman Knows," by James M. Barrie, for
Philco Summer Playhouse. Cast: Margaret Phillips, Wesley Addy, Rex Evans, Paula
Laurence, Horace Graham.
5 September 1949 — 8:00 "Aria da Capo," by Edna St. Vincent Millay, for *Academy
Theatre.* Producer: Curtis Canfield. Director: Mark Hawley.
   9:00 "My Wife Is a Liar," by George S. Albee, for *The Colgate Theatre. Cast:* William Post, Jr., Frank Thomas, Erin O'Brien, John Mailey, David Orrick, John Shay.
6 September 1949 — 9:00 "Germelshausen" and "Smooth Fingers," for *Fireside Theatre* return. Director: Stan Parlan. Sponsor: Procter & Gamble.
7 September 1949 — 8:30 "Madame Pompadour," adapted by Evelyn Goodman, for
The Clock. Director: Lawrence Schwab, Jr.
   9:00 "Respectfully Yours," by Peggy Lamson, for *Kraft Television Theatre. Cast:*
Flora Campbell, Chester Stratton, Gage Clark, Jay Presson, Dorothy Francis, Mercer McLeod, John Rodney, Betty Ann Nyman, Michael Blair.
   10:00 *Martin Kane, Private Eye.*
8 September 1949 — 8:30 *Mary Kay and Johnny.*
   9:00 "Big Brother," an original drama by Ralph Berton, for *Theatre of the Mind.*
Director: Alan J. Neuman. *Cast:* Jonathan Marlowe, Mark K. Wells.
   10:00 *Martin Kane, Private Eye.*
9 September 1949 — 9:30 *Mixed Doubles.*
11 September 1949 — 9:00 "Pride's Castle," by Frank Yerby, adapted by Samuel
Carter, for return of *Philco Television Playhouse.* Producer: Fred Coe. Director:
Gordon Duff. *Cast:* Anthony Quinn, Catherine McLeod, Louise Allbritton, Boyd
Crawford, Loring Smith, Clyde Waddell, Bethel Leslie, Jack Lemmon, Patrick
Malone.
12 September 1949 — 8:00 "The Sisters McIntosh," by Richard Corson, for *Academy Theatre.* Producer: Curtis Canfield. Director: Mark Hawley.
   9:00 "Perkins Finds $3,400,000," by Phillip Wylie, adapted by Robert Wallsten,
for *The Colgate Theatre. Cast:* Romney Brent, Calvin Thomas, Philip Houston,
Ed Hyans, Leiter Carr.
   9:30 *The Black Robe.*
13 September 1949 — 9:00 "The Four Fifteen Express" and "Charlotte Corday," for
Fireside Theatre. Director: Stan Parlan.
14 September 1949 — 8:30 "Wrong Woman Mad," adapted by Stephen de Baun, for
The Clock. Producer: Edward Walling. Director: William Corrigan. *Cast:* Adam
Stewart.
   9:00 "Little Darling," by Eric Hatch, for *Kraft Television Theatre. Cast:* Tom
Bickley, Marilyn Monk, Nancy Ross, Patricia Pope, Frederic De Wilde, Gene
Fuller, Jack Orrison.
   10:00 *Believe It or Not.*
15 September 1949 — 8:30 *Mary Kay and Johnny.*
   9:00 *Theatre of the Mind.* Director: Alan J. Neuman. *Cast:* Harvey Dunn, Peg
Mayo, Henry Chavell.
   10:00 *Martin Kane, Private Eye.*
16 September 1949 — 9:30–10:00 *The Big Story,* a documentary-drama anthology
based on newspaper stories, debuts. Producer: Alan Scott. Sponsor: American
Tobacco Company (Pall Mall Cigarettes).

17 September 1949— 8:30 *Mixed Doubles.*

18 September 1949— 9:00 "The Little Sister," by Raymond Chandler, adapted by Samuel Carter, for *Philco Television Playhouse.* Producer/Director: Albert McCleery. *Cast:* William Eythe, Arthur O'Connell, Calvin Thomas, Jean Carson, Lola Montez, Pat Breslin.

19 September 1949— 8:00 "Leo and Sagittarius," by Jack Bentkover, for *Chevrolet Tele-Theatre* return. Producer: Victor McLeod. Director: Garry Simpson. *Cast:* Vicki Cummings, Bert Lytell, Marjorie Gateson, Enid Markey.

  9:00 "The Loan," for *The Colgate Theatre.* Producer/Director: Hal Keith. *Cast:* Tom Ewell, Billy Lynn, Fay Sappington, Harry Bannister, Jerome Shaw, Norma Jane Marlowe, Eva Condon, Jay MacDougal.

  9:30 *The Black Robe.*

20 September 1949— 9:00 "Vain Glory" and "Out of the River," for *Fireside Theatre.*

21 September 1949— 8:30 "The Medium," for *The Clock.* Producer: Ernest Walling. Director: Lawrence Schwab, Jr.

  9:00 "The Man in Half Moon Street," by Barre Lyndon, for *Kraft Television Theatre. Cast:* John Newland, Mercer McLeod, Anne Jackson.

  10:00 *Believe It or Not.* Director: Alan J. Neuman.

22 September 1949— 8:30 *Mary Kay and Johnny.*

  10:00 *Martin Kane, Private Eye.*

23 September 1949— 9:00 *Lights Out.* Producer: Ernest Walling. Director: Kingman T. Moore.

24 September 1949— 8:30 *Mixed Doubles.*

25 September 1949— 9:00 "The Lonely," for *Philco Television Playhouse.* Producer: Fred Coe. *Cast:* William Prince, Kim Hunter.

26 September 1949— 8:00 "Her Majesty the King," by Florence Ryerson and Colin Clements, for *Chevrolet Tele-Theatre.* Producer: Victor McLeod. Director: Barry Bernard. *Cast:* Ethel Griffies, Henry Stephenson, Barry McCollum, Elaine Williams.

  9:00 "The Contest," Episode 2, for *The Colgate Theatre.* Producer/Director: Hal Keith. *Cast:* Tom Ewell, William Lynn, Donald Rose, Jerome Shaw, Fay Sappington, Henry Bannister, Norma Jane Marlowe.

  10:00 *The Black Robe.*

27 September 1949— 9:00 "The Postmistress of Laurel Run" and "The Spy," for *Fireside Theatre.*

28 September 1949— 8:30 *The Clock.* Producer: Ernest Walling. Director: William Corrigan. *Cast:* Treva Frazee, George Reeves, Rosita Moreno.

  9:00 "The Climax," by Jacques Duval, for *Kraft Television Theatre. Cast:* John Arthur.

  10:00 *Believe It or Not.*

29 September 1949— 8:30 *Mary Kay and Johnny.*

  10:00 *Martin Kane, Private Eye.*

30 September 1949— 9:30 *The Big Story.*

1 October 1949— 9:30 *Mixed Doubles.*

2 October 1949— 7:30–8:00 *The Aldrich Family,* a situation comedy from radio by Clifford Goldsmith, debuts. Producer: Duane McKinney. Director: Edwin Duerr. *Cast:* Robert Casey, Jackie Kelk, House Jameson, Lois Wilson, Alan Manson, Mary Patton, Faye Roop.

  8:00 *Believe It or Not.*

9:00 "The Queen Bee," by Edna Lee, adapted by Samuel Carter, for *Philco Television Playhouse*. Producer: Robert Salter. Director: Albert McCleery. *Cast:* Clare Luce, Paul McGrath, Margaret Phillips, Nelson Case, William Post, Jr., Sara Anderson, Ruth Saville, Margaret Barker, Sigrid Olsen, Stefan Olsen, Alex March.

3 October 1949— 8:00 "The Unguarded Moment," by Ernest Lehman, adapted by Eleanor Tarshis and Harry W. Junkin, for *Chevrolet Tele-Theatre*. Producer: Victor McLeod. Director: Garry Simpson. *Cast:* Paul Lukas, Valerie Bettis.

9:00 "Picture of the Bride," by Hal Thompson, adapted by William Stuart, for *The Colgate Theatre*. *Cast:* Nancy Coleman, A. J. Herbert, Roberta Bellenger, Dean Harens.

9:30 *The Black Robe*.

4 October 1949— 9:00 "Like Money in the Bank" and "Magic Skin," for *Fireside Theatre*.

9:30 *The Life of Riley*, a situation comedy from radio by Irving Brecher now filmed in Hollywood, debuts. Producer: Stan Parlan. Director: Edward Stevens. *Cast:* Jackie Gleason, Rosemary DeCamp, Lanny Rees, Gloria Winters, Sid Tomack, John Brown.

5 October 1949— 8:00–8:30 *The Crisis*, dramas of real cases, debuts.

8:30 *The Clock*.

9:00 "The Apple of His Eye," by Kenyon Nicholson and Charles Robinson, for *Kraft Television Theatre*. *Cast:* Lawrence Fletcher, Pamela Rivers, Vaughn Taylor, Helen Stenborg, Dorrit Kelton, Myrtle Ferguson, Norma Jane Marlowe, Charles Robinson.

6 October 1949— 8:00–8:30 "Walter Fortune," by Howard De Silva, for *Hollywood Premiere Theatre*, debut on film. Producer: Edward Stevens.

8:30 *Mary Kay and Johnny*.

10:00 *Martin Kane, Private Eye*.

8 October 1949— 8:30 *Mixed Doubles*.

9 October 1949— 7:30 *The Aldrich Family*.

8:00 *Believe It or Not*.

9:00 "Something's Got to Give," by Marion Hargrove, adapted by Samuel Carter, for *Philco Television Playhouse*. *Cast:* John Beal, Haila Stoddard.

10 October 1949— 8:00 "Leave It to Mother," by Milton J. Kramer, for *Chevrolet Tele-Theatre*. Producer: Barry Bernard. Director: Victor McLeod. *Cast:* Irene Rich, Ralph Locke, Mary Malone, James Stephens, Douglas Gregory.

9:00 "Grandma, Born Alice," by Sylvia C. Berger, for *The Colgate Theatre*. Director: Hal Keith. *Cast:* Kathleen Comegys, Anna Minot, Mort Stevens, Ameria Barleon, Kate McComb.

9:30 *The Black Robe*.

11 October 1949— 9:00 "Scream in the Night" and "Troubled Harbor," for *Fireside Theatre*.

9:30 *The Life of Riley*.

12 October 1949— 8:00 *Crisis*, now remote from Chicago. [Not listed hereafter.]

8:30 "The Prisoners," adapted by Bill Berns, for *The Clock*. Producer: Ernest Walling. Director: Lawrence Schwab, Jr.

9:00 "Your Friendly Nabors," by Joe Bates Smith, for *Kraft Television Theatre*. *Cast:* Valerie Cossart, Warren Parker, Phil Sterling, Enid Markey, Gene Fuller, Nancy Ross, Lawrence Fletcher.

13 October 1949— 8:30 *Mary Kay and Johnny*.

10:00 *Martin Kane, Private Eye.*
14 October 1949— 9:30 *The Big Story.*
15 October 1949— 8:30 *Mixed Doubles.*
16 October 1949— 7:30 *The Aldrich Family.*
    8:30 "Retaliation," by William Stuart, for *The Colgate Theatre.* Producer/Director: Hal Keith. *Cast:* Edwin Cooper, Oliver Thorndike, Margaret Phillips, Nancy Millard, Herschell Bentley.
    9:00 "The Last Tycoon," by F. Scott Fitzgerald, adapted by Joseph Liss, for *Philco Television Playhouse.* Producer: Fred Coe. Directors: Coe and Delbert Mann. *Cast:* Leueen MacGrath, John Baragrey.
17 October 1949— 8:00 "Operation Coral," by Stewart Pierce Brown, for *Chevrolet Tele-Theatre.* Director: Garry Simpson. *Cast:* Dane Clark, Frank Albertson, Cameron Mitchell.
    9:30 *The Black Robe.*
18 October 1949— 9:00 "Banker, Bandit and Blonde" and "The Wall," for *Fireside Theatre.*
    9:30 *The Life of Riley.*
19 October 1949— 8:30 "Payment on Time," adapted by Stephen de Baun, for *The Clock.* Producer: Ernest Walling. Director: William Corrigan. *Cast:* Gavin Gordon, Roland Hogue, Matt Busch.
    9:00 "Accidently Yours," by Pauline Williams Snapp, for *Kraft Television Theatre.* *Cast:* Valerie Cossart, Mercer McLeod, Betty de Cormier, Jack Lemmon, Treva Frazee, Edith Gresham, Reynolds Evans, Gage Clark, James Daly, Cloris Leachman.
20 October 1949— 8:00 "A Doctor's Patience" and "Hey Sweeney," for *Hollywood Premiere Theatre.*
    8:30 *Mary Kay and Johnny.*
    10:00 *Martin Kane, Private Eye.*
21 October 1949— 9:30 *Believe It or Not.*
22 October 1949— 8:30 *Mixed Doubles.*
23 October 1949— 7:30 *The Aldrich Family.*
    8:30 "Young Stacey," by William Kendall Clarke, for *The Colgate Theatre.* Producer: Hal Keith. *Cast:* Norma Jane Marlowe, Joan Castle, Dean Norton, Ella Houston.
    9:00 "Because of the Lockwoods," by Dorothy Whipple, adapted by Samuel Carter, for *Philco Television Playhouse.* Producer: Fred Coe. Director: Gordon Duff. *Cast:* June Dayton, Bramwell Fletcher, Marjorie Gateson, Mary Lou Hennessy, Drake Thorton, Thomas Rogers, Leni Stengel, Alan Manson.
24 October 1949— 8:00 "Birthday Party," by Shirl Hendrix, adapted by Eleanor Tarshis, for *Chevrolet Tele-Theatre.* *Cast:* Henry Hull, John Beal.
    9:00 *The Black Robe.* *Cast:* Blanche Yurka.
25 October 1949— 9:00 "Heartbeat" and "Mardi Gras," for *Fireside Theatre.*
    9:30 *The Life of Riley.*
26 October 1949— 8:30 *The Clock.* *Cast:* Brook Brian, William Thunhirst, Dan Morgan, Edward Ashley, John Boruff, Larry Semon.
    9:00 "To Dream Again," by Veronica Haigh, for *Kraft Television Theatre.* *Cast:* Lauren Gilbert, Janet DeGore, Leon Shaw, Robert Craven, Velma Royton.
27 October 1949— 8:30 *Mary Kay and Johnny.*
    10:00 *Martin Kane, Private Eye.*

28 October 1949— 9:30 *The Big Story.*
29 October 1949— 8:30 *Mixed Doubles.*
30 October 1949— 7:30 *The Aldrich Family.*
   8:30 "The Old Lady Shows Her Medals," by James M. Barrie, adapted by William Kendall Clarke, for *The Colgate Theatre. Cast:* Florence Reed, Mabel Taylor, Daisy Bellmore, Eva Condon, John Baragrey, Norman Barre.
   9:00 "Damion's Daughter," by Edwin Gilbert, adapted by David Shaw, for *Philco Television Playhouse.* Producer: Fred Coe. *Cast:* Sidney Blackmer, Hildy Parks, John McQuade.
31 October 1949— 8:00 "Witness for the Prosecution," by Agatha Christie, adapted by Eleanor Tarshis, for *Chevrolet Tele-Theatre.* Producer: Victor McLeod. Director: Garry Simpson. *Cast:* Nicholas Saunders, Felicia Montealegre, Walter Abel, Hilda Vaughn, Victor Sutherland, Paul Lilly, Clifford Sales.
   9:00 *The Black Robe.*
1 November 1949— 9:00 "Checkmate" and "Solange," for *Fireside Theatre.*
   9:30 *The Life of Riley.*
   11:00 "52nd Street," a documentary-drama remote from the Sixth Avenue subway, for *City at Midnight* debut. Producer: W. O. Horbach. Director: Alan J. Neuman. *Cast:* Richard MacMurray, Viola Harris, Phil Carter, Harold McGee, Grant Gordon, Ted Field, Olga Cornett.
2 November 1949— 8:30 *The Clock.*
   9:00 "Whistling in the Dark," for *Kraft Television Theatre. Cast:* Jack Lemmon, Rosemary Rice.
3 November 1949— 8:00 *Hollywood Premiere Theatre* is cancelled.
   8:30 *Mary Kay and Johnny.*
   10:00 *Martin Kane, Private Eye.*
4 November 1949— 8:00–8:30 *One Man's Family*, by Carlton E. Morse, a radio serial, debuts. Producer: Morse. Director: Clark Jones. *Cast:* Anthony Smythe, Russell Thorson, Billy Idelson, Marjorie Gates, Bert Lytell, Roger Tuttle.
   9:30 *Believe It or Not.*
6 November 1949— 7:30 *The Aldrich Family.*
   8:30 "Remember the Day," by Philco Higley and Philip Dunning, adapted by Ann Selby, for *The Colgate Theatre.*
   9:00 "The House of the Seven Gables," by Nathaniel Hawthorne, adapted by Samuel Carter, for *Philco Television Playhouse.* Producer: Fred Coe. Director: Gordon Duff. *Cast:* Peter Cookson, Carl Benton Reid, Mary Alice Moore, Helen Carew, Joan Chandler.
7 November 1949— 8:00 "His Name Is Jason," by Joseph Cochran, for *Chevrolet Tele-Theatre.* Producer: Victor McLeod. Director: Barry Bernard. *Cast:* Margo, Jonathan Harris, Dora Clement, Jason Johnson, Sid Cassel, Norma Jane Marlowe.
   9:00 "Conqueror's Island," by Nelson Bond, for *Lights Out* return. Producer: Ernest Walling. Director: Kingman T. Moore. *Cast:* Richard Derr, Mercer McLeod, Vinton Hayworth, Sara Benham, Jack LaRue.
8 November 1949— 9:00 "Night Owl" and "Another Road," for *Fireside Theatre.*
   9:30 *The Life of Riley.*
   11:00 *City at Midnight* was preempted for election returns.
9 November 1949— 8:30 "The Hitchhiker," by Bob Wald, for *The Clock.* Producer: Ernest Walling. Director: Lawrence Schwab, Jr. *Cast:* Anne Ives, John O'Hara, Parker McCormick, Wyrley Birch, Bill Berns, Alexander Marshall.

9:00 "Happy Ending," by Joe Bates Smith, for *Kraft Television Theatre. Cast:* June Dayton, Jack Davis, Isabel Price, Emily Rose, Jim Davidson, Florence Robinson.

10 November 1949— 8:30 *Mary Kay and Johnny.*

10:00 *Martin Kane, Private Eye.*

11 November 1949— 8:00 *One Man's Family.*

9:30 *The Big Story.*

13 November 1949— 7:30 *The Aldrich Family.*

8:30 "O'Brien," by William Brandon, adapted by William Stuart, for *The Colgate Theatre.*

9:00 "The Promise," by Mildred Cram, adapted by Samuel Taylor, for *Philco Television Playhouse. Cast:* William Eythe, Kim Hunter.

14 November 1949— 8:00 "Temporarily Purple," by Ernest Kinoy, for *Chevrolet Tele-Theatre.* Director: Garry Simpson. *Cast:* John Conté, Nina Foch.

9:00 "Pengallen's Bell," by Sumner Locke Elliott, for *Lights Out.* Director: Delbert Mann. *Cast:* Neva Patterson, Alan Frank, Grant Gordon, Al Patterson.

15 November 1949— 9:00 "Stagecoach Driver MacLean" and "Cowboy's Lament," for *Fireside Theatre.*

11:00 *City at Midnight* originates from Pier 27, Brooklyn. Director: Doug Rogers. *Cast:* Rod Steiger, Victor Sutherland, Treva Frazee, Ralph Camazzo, Joe Foley, Frank Tweddell, William Turner, Ray Pisoni.

16 November 1949— 8:30 "The Web," by George Batson and Richard McCracken, for *The Clock. Cast:* Oliver Thorndike, Alfreda Wallace.

9:00 "The Happiest Years," by Thomas Coby and William Roerick, for *Kraft Television Theatre.* Director: Maury Holland. *Cast:* James Daly, Hildy Parks.

17 November 1949— 8:00 "Paging Mr. Holloway," remote from Chicago for *Hollywood Premiere Theatre.* Producer: Jack Haskin.

8:30 *Mary Kay and Johnny.*

10:00 *Martin Kane, Private Eye.*

18 November 1949— 8:00 *One Man's Family.*

9:30 *The Black Robe.*

20 November 1949— 7:30 *The Aldrich Family.*

8:30 "New Item," by Albert G. Miller, adapted by William Kendall Clarke, for *The Colgate Theatre.*

9:00 "Medical Meeting," for *Philco Television Playhouse.* Producer: Fred Coe. Director: Gordon Duff. *Cast:* Frances Reid, Philip Bourneuf, Ben Lackland, Katherine Meskill, John Newland, John McQuade.

21 November 1949— 8:00 "Have a Heart," by Helen and Al Martin, for *Chevrolet Tele-Theatre.* Producer: Victor McLeod. Director: Barry Bernard. *Cast:* Miriam Hopkins, Donald Curtis, Wayne Howell.

9:00 "The Fall of the House of Usher," by Edgar Allen Poe, for *Lights Out. Cast:* Helmut Dantine, Pamela Conroy, Stephen Courtleigh, Oswald Marshall.

22 November 1949— 9:00 *Fireside Theatre.*

9:30 *The Life of Riley.*

11:00 *City at Midnight,* remote from Jackson Avenue, Queens. *Cast:* Eddie Hyans, Frank Reynolds, Norman Shelby, Edward Holmes, Bob Davis, Leonard Bell.

23 November 1949— 8:30 "Reverse," by Lawrence Klee, adapted by Michael Blair, for *The Clock.* Producer: Ernest Walling. Director: Lawrence Schwab, Jr. *Cast:* Bramwell Fletcher, Sherry Bennett, John McQuade.

9:00 "In Love with Love," by Vincent Lawrence, for *Kraft Television Theatre*. Director: Stanley Quinn. *Cast:* Anne Francis, Maury Hill.

24 November 1949— 8:00 *Mary Kay and Johnny*.

10:00 *Martin Kane, Private Eye*.

25 November 1949— 8:00 *One Man's Family*.

9:30 *The Big Story*.

26 November 1949—10:00 *The Black Robe*.

27 November 1949— 7:30 *The Aldrich Family*.

8:30 "Daughters Are Different," for *The Colgate Theatre*.

9:00 "The Wonderful Mrs. Ingram," by Harlan Ware, adapted by David Shaw, for *Philco Television Playhouse*. Producer: Fred Coe. Director: Delbert Mann. *Cast:* Carol Goodner, Stephen Courtleigh, Nydia Westman.

28 November 1949— 8:00 "The Door," by Jeb Stuart, for *Chevrolet Tele-Theatre*. Director: Garry Simpson. *Cast:* Don Ameche, Tom Pedi, Grace Valentine, Dennis Harrison.

9:00 "I Dreamt I Died," for *Lights Out*. *Cast:* Alfreda Wallace, Philip Truex, Karen Stevens, Ross Martin.

29 November 1949— 9:00 "The Room" and "Epilogue," for *Fireside Theatre*.

9:30 *The Life of Riley*.

11:00 *City at Midnight*, a drama from the YMCA on 63rd Street by Ken Hart. Director: Doug Rogers.

30 November 1949— 8:30 "Cousin Maria," for *The Clock*. *Cast:* Vilma Kurer, Ann Summers, John Shay.

9:00 "Seen but Not Heard," by Martin Berkeley, for *Kraft Television Theatre*. *Cast:* Jean Gillespie, Eleanor Wilson, Lawrence Fletcher, George Reeves.

1 December 1949— 8:30 *Mary Kay and Johnny*.

10:00 *Martin Kane, Private Eye*.

2 December 1949— 8:00 *One Man's Family*.

9:30 *TV Detective*, remote from Washington, D. C. *Cast:* A subjective camera was the Detective as the audience solved the crime.

3 December 1949—10:00 *The Black Robe*.

4 December 1949— 7:30 *The Aldrich Family*.

8:30 "Company for Dinner," by Florence Jane Soman, adapted by William Stuart, for *The Colgate Theatre*.

9:00 "Mist on the Water," by F. L. Green, adapted by Joseph Liss, for *Philco Television Playhouse*. Producer: Fred Coe. Director: Gordon Duff. *Cast:* Torin Thatcher, Margaret Phillips, Anne Jackson, Dan Morgan.

5 December 1949— 8:00 "At Night All Cats Are Gray," by Robert Garland, for *Chevrolet Tele-Theatre*. *Cast:* Basil Rathbone, Pamela Conroy, John Moore.

9:00 "Something in the Wind," by Fred Coe, adapted by Ethel Frank, for *Lights Out*. Producer: Ernest Walling. Director: Kingman T. Moore. *Cast:* John Graham.

6 December 1949— 9:00 "Sealed Orders" and "Battle Scene," for *Fireside Theatre*.

9:30 *The Life of Riley*.

7 December 1949— 8:00 "Manic at Large," by Lawrence Klee, adapted by David Hughes, for *The Clock*.

9:00 "The Comedy of Errors," by William Shakespeare, for *Kraft Television Theatre*. Producer: Bill Warwick. *Cast:* Stewart Bradley, James Daly, Harry Townes, Kurt Richards.

8 December 1949— 8:00 *Portrait of America*, drama from Chicago, debuts.

8:30 *Mary Kay and Johnny.*
10:00 *Martin Kane, Private Eye.*
9 December 1949— 8:00 *One Man's Family.*
9:30 *The Big Story.*
10 December 1949—10:00 *The Black Robe.*
11 December 1949— 7:30 *The Aldrich Family.*
8:30 "A Trip to Czardis," by Edwin Granberry, adapted by Elizabeth and James Hart, for *The Colgate Theatre. Cast:* Butch Cavell, Norma Jane Marlowe.
9:00 "The Beautiful Bequest," by Eric Hatch, adapted by Samuel Taylor, for *Philco Television Playhouse.* Producer: Fred Coe. Director: Delbert Mann. *Cast:* Loring Smith, Eli Wallach, Joan Castle.
12 December 1949— 8:00 "Desert Incident," by Maurice Richlin, for *Chevrolet Tele-Theatre. Cast:* Guy Kibbee, Iggie Wolfington.
9:00 "Justice Lies Waiting," for *Lights Out. Cast:* Mercer McLeod, Lawrence Fletcher.
13 December 1949— 9:00 "The Human Touch" and "The Pardoner's Tale," for *Fireside Theatre.*
9:30 *The Life of Riley.*
14 December 1949— 8:30 "Lease of Death," adapted by Joseph Ruscoll, for *The Clock.* Director: William Corrigan. *Cast:* Oliver Thorndike, Adelaide Klein, Robert Pastene, Teena Starr, Larry Semon.
9:00 "The Nantucket Legend," for *Kraft Television Theatre. Cast:* Vaughn Taylor, Philip Faversham, Myrtle Ferguson, Edith Gresham, Brook Byron, Jane Alexander, Gage Clark, William Lynn, William Lee, Donald Keyes, Dort Clark, Eileen Poe, Sara Floyd, Robert Leseur, George Nesbitt.
15 December 1949— 8:00 *Portrait of America.*
8:30 *Mary Kay and Johnny.*
10:00 *Martin Kane, Private Eye.*
16 December 1949— 8:00 *One Man's Family.* 9:30 *TV Detective.*
17 December 1949—10:00 *The Black Robe.*
18 December 1949— 7:30 *The Aldrich Family.*
8:30 "The Pearls," by Philip Wylie, adapted by Robert L. Acker, for *The Colgate Theatre. Cast:* Reynolds Evans, Mary K. Wells, Donald Buka, Jane Kane, Morton Stevens, Mary McAlister, Adelaide Hensel, James Holden.
9:00 "The Strange Christmas Dinner," by Margaret Cousins, adapted by Fred Coe and Joseph Liss, for *Philco Television Playhouse. Cast:* Melvyn Douglas, Vaughn Taylor.
19 December 1949— 8:00 "The Priceless Gift," by Victor McLeod, for *Chevrolet Tele-Theatre.* Director: Barry Bernard. *Cast:* Lee Tracy, Mercedes Gilbert, Mary Patton, Maurice Franklin.
9:00 "The Elevator," by George and Betty Lefferts, for *Lights Out. Cast:* Jack Hartley, Helene Dumas.
20 December 1949— 9:00 "The Doll" and "The Bet," for *Fireside Theatre.*
9:30 *The Life of Riley.*
21 December 1949— 8:30 "Romance," by Lawrence Klee, adapted by Stephen de Baun, for *The Clock.* Producer: Ernest Walling. Director: William Corrigan. *Cast:* Pamela Rivers, Philip Faversham.
9:00 "The Grove," by Winchell Smith, for *Kraft Television Theatre. Cast:* Margaret Phillips, Dennis Harrison.

22 December 1949— 8:00 *Portrait of America.*
8:30 *Mary Kay and Johnny.*
10:00 *Martin Kane, Private Eye.*
23 December 1949— 8:00 *One Man's Family.*
9:30 *The Big Story.*
24 December 1949—10:00 *The Black Robe.*
10:30 "Nativity" (aka "According to Joseph"), by Merrick McCarthy, adapted by Fred Coe. Producer: Coe. Director: Richard Goode. *Cast:* Mary Patton, William Post, Jr., Betty O'Leary, Jo Anne Paul, Jim Sheridan, Vaughn Taylor.
25 December 1949— 5:00 *A Christmas Carol,* a feature film.
7:30 *The Aldrich Family.*
8:30 "Blessed Are They," by True Boardman, for *The Colgate Theatre.*
9:00 "In Beauty Like the Night," for *Philco Television Playhouse.* Producer: Fred Coe. Director: Delbert Mann. *Cast:* Alfred Ryder, Mary Alice Moore, Mercer McLeod.
26 December 1949— 8:00 "I Cover Times Square," by Harold Huber, for *Chevrolet Tele-Theatre.* Producer: Huber. Director: Garry Simpson. *Cast:* Jean Carson, Frank Albertson, Louis Sorin.
9:00 "The Man Who Couldn't Lose," for *Lights Out. Cast:* Dean Harens, Alfreda Wallace.
27 December 1949— 9:00 "The Gamblers" and "Threshold," for *Fireside Theatre.*
9:30 *The Life of Riley.*
28 December 1949— 8:30 "Mark Wade, D.A.," by Lawrence Klee, adapted by David Hughes, for *The Clock.* Producer: Ernest Walling. Director: Lawrence Schwab, Jr. *Cast:* William Post, Jr.
9:00 "New Brooms," by Frank Craven, for *Kraft Television Theatre. Cast:* William Lee, William Hare, Frances Waller, June Dayton.
29 December 1949— 8:00 *Portrait of America.*
8:30 *Mary Kay and Johnny.*
10:00 *Martin Kane, Private Eye.*
30 December 1949— 8:00 *One Man's Family.*
9:30 *TV Detective.*

1950

1 January 1950— 7:30 *The Aldrich Family.*
8:30 "I'll Marry You Later," by Katherine Brush, adapted by Robert Wallsten, for *The Colgate Theatre.* Director: Melville Burke. *Cast:* Bobby Sherwood, Roberta Janay, Andrea Mann, Walter Flaven, Donald Keyes.
9:00 "Little Boy Lost," by Marguerita Laskin, adapted by Joseph Liss for *Philco Television Playhouse.* Producer: Fred Coe. Director: Gordon Duff. *Cast:* John Newland, Alfreda Wallace, Maurice Cavell.
2 January 1950— 8:00 "Hart to Heart," for *Chevrolet Tele-Theatre.* Director: Barry Bernard. *Cast:* Louise Allbritton, Dick Foran, Roscoe Karns.
9:00 "The Riverman," by Jack Barefield, for *Lights Out.* Producer: Ernest Walling. Director: Kingman T. Moore, *Cast:* Athena Larde, Elizabeth Moore, Henry Brandon, Eddie Garr, Lamont Johnson.
3 January 1950— 9:00 "Dinner for Three" and "The Vampire," for *Fireside Theatre.*
9:30 *The Life of Riley.*

4 January 1950— 8:00 "Murder in Duplicate," by Robert L. Ripley, for *Believe It or Not* returns as a dramatic anthology. *Cast:* Naomi Campbell, Hazel Wallace, A. J. Herbert, Byron Russell, Frank Gallup.

8:30 "The Firebug," adapted by Patrick Whitehead, for *The Clock. Cast:* Helen Harvey, Phil Arthur, Priscilla Towers, Jack Albertson.

9:00 "That Naborly Feeling," by Joe Bates Smith, for *Kraft Television Theatre.* Producer: Bill Warwick. *Cast:* Valerie Cossart, Warren Parker, Enid Markey, Philip Tonge, Leona Powers, Bernard Burke, Lorna Lynn.

5 January 1950— 8:00 *The Black Robe,* a cross section of life that appears before a night court judge. Producer: Phillips H. Lord.

10:00 *Martin Lane, Private Eye,* original story by Finis Farr and Joel Sayre. Producer/Director: Edward Sutherland. *Cast:* William Gargan, Walter Kinsella, Merle McHugh, Donald Buka, Jack Hartley, Therese Hunter, Tom Ward, Maurice Fitzgerald, Fred Hillebrand.

6 January 1950— 8:00 *One Man's Family.*

9:30 *The Big Story.*

7 January 1950— 9:00 *Mary Kay and Johnny,* new time.

8 January 1950— 7:30 *The Aldrich Family.*

8:30 "Second Generation," for *The Colgate Theatre. Cast:* Neva Patterson, Carroll Ashburn, Dean Harens, Pat Breslin.

9:00 "Bethel Merriday," by Sinclair Lewis, adapted by William Kendall Clarke, for *Philco Television Playhouse.* Producer: Fred Coe. Director: Delbert Mann. *Cast:* Grace Kelly, Oliver Thorndike.

9 January 1950— 8:00 "Midnight Flight," by Norman Anthony, for *Chevrolet Tele-Theatre.* Producer: Victor McLeod. Director: Garry Simpson. *Cast:* Barry Nelson, Ferdi Hoffmann, Sylvia Stone, Guy Spaull, Melba Rae, Don Kennedy, Milton Herman, Douglas Gregory, Frank Daren.

9:00 "Judgment Reversed," by Frederick H. Frey, adapted by Bob Wald, for *Lights Out.* Producer: Ernest Walling. Director: Hal Keith. *Cast:* King Calder, Nancy Coleman, Ralph Riggs, Bernard Nedell, Tom McElhaney, John Farrell, Humphrey Davis, James Rafferty.

10 January 1950— 9:00 "The Devil and Tom Walker," by Washington Irving, and "Rendezvous," for *Fireside Theatre.*

9:30 *The Life of Riley.*

11 January 1950— 8:00 "The Voice of Obsession," for *Believe It or Not.* Director: Tom Ward. *Cast:* Hildy Parks, John Hudson, Grace Kelly.

8:30 "The Book Seller," by Lawrence Klee, adapted by Bob Wald, for *The Clock.* Producer: Ernest Walling. Director: William Corrigan. *Cast:* Philippa Bevans, Jason Johnson, Theodore Marcuse, Iggie Wolfington.

9:00 "As Husbands Go," by Rachel Crothers, for *Kraft Television Theatre. Cast:* Mary Alice Moore, Donald Briggs.

12 January 1950— 8:00 *The Black Robe.*

10:00 *Martin Kane, Private Eye.*

13 January 1950— 8:00 *One Man's Family.*

14 January 1950— 9:00 *Mary Kay and Johnny.*

15 January 1950— 7:30 *The Aldrich Family.*

8:30 "Bert's Wedding," by William Ford Manley, for *The Colgate Theatre. Cast:* Parker Fennelly.

9:00 "Murder at the Stork Club," by Vera Caspary, for *Philco Television Play-*

house. Cast: Franchot Tone, Ruth Matteson, Mary Orr, Valerie Cossart, Maurice Burke, Elliott Sullivan, Calvin Thomas, Hearld Bromley, Sherman Billingsley.

16 January 1950— 8:00 "The Chirp of the Cricket," by Joseph Cochran, for *Chevrolet Tele-Theatre. Cast:* Noel Leslie, Dennis Harrison, Mercedes McCambridge.

9:00 "The Green Dress," by Katherine Gregg, for *Lights Out.* Producer: George McGarrett. Director: Kingman T. Moore. *Cast:* Robert Pastene, Lynn Salisbury, Mercedes Gilbert, Candy Montgomery.

17 January 1950— 9:00 "The Golden Ball" and "Just Three Words," for *Fireside Theatre.*

9:30 *The Life of Riley.*

18 January 1950— 8:00 "The Masked Madonna," for *Believe It or Not.*

8:30 "Who Is This Man?" by Joseph and Janet Ruscoll, *The Clock.* Producer: Ernest Walling. Director: Lawrence Schwab, Jr. *Cast:* Dora Clement, Elizabeth Ross, Dean Harens.

9:00 "The Vinegar Tree," by Paul Osborn, for *Kraft Television Theatre. Cast:* Raymond Bramley, Bess Winburn, Edmon Ryan.

19 January 1950— 8:00 *The Black Robe.*

10:00 *Martin Kane, Private Eye.*

20 January 1950— 8:00 *One Man's Family.*

9:30 *The Big Story,* from *The Toledo Blade. Cast:* Melba Rae, James Little, Walter Greaza, Milton Herman, Ed Beck, Charles Randall.

21 January 1950— 9:00 *Mary Kay and Johnny.*

22 January 1950— 7:30 *The Aldrich Family.*

8:30 "Two for a Penny," by Carol Warner Gluck, for *The Colgate Theatre. Cast:* Neva Patterson, William Post, Jr., Norma Jane Marlowe, Charles Crane, Alyce Mace, Calvin Thomas, Clyde M. Waddell, A. H. Van Buren.

9:00 "The Marriages," by Henry James, adapted by H. R. Hays, for *Philco Television Playhouse.* Director: Delbert Mann. *Cast:* Henry Daniell, Margaret Phillips, Carol Goodner.

23 January 1950— 8:00 "The Final Bell," by Frank Alexander, for *Chevrolet Tele-Theatre. Cast:* Romola Robb, Charles Taylor, Bobby Barr, Charles Jordan, Ed Wagner, Canada Lee, Harry Bellaver, Greg Haggerty.

9:00 "The Devil to Pay," by Elizabeth Evans, for *Lights Out.* Producer: George McGarrett. Director: Hal Keith. *Cast:* Alfreda Wallace, Arnold Moss.

24 January 1950— 9:00 "Confession," with John Warburton, and "Reprieve" for *Fireside Theatre.*

9:30 *The Life of Riley.*

25 January 1950— 8:00 "Voice of Destiny," for *Believe It or Not.* Producer: Tom Ward. *Cast:* Patricia Jenkins.

8:30 "Dig Your Own Grave," by Joseph and Janet for *The Clock. Cast:* David Kerman, Parker McCormick.

9:00 "Kelly," by Eric Hatch, for *Kraft Television Theatre.* Producer: Bill Warwick. *Cast:* Mark Roberts, Anne Francis, E. G. Marshall, George Reeves, Emil Tremont, Yvonne Rudie, Barbara Cook, Lawrence Fletcher.

26 January 1950— 8:00 *The Black Robe.*

8:30 *One Man's Family,* new time.

10:00 *Martin Kane, Private Kane.*

28 January 1950— 9:00 *Mary Kay and Johnny.*

29 January 1950— 8:30 "Abby, Her Farm," by Margaret Buell Wilder, for *The Colgate Theatre. Cast:* Jimsey Sommers, Joan Castle, John Newland, Jackie Diamond.

9:00 "Uncle Dynamite," by P. G. Wodehouse, adapted by David Shaw, for *Philco Television Playhouse*. Producer: Fred Coe. Director: Gordon Duff. *Cast:* Arthur Treacher.

30 January 1950— 8:00 "The Million Dollar Question," by Sheldon Reynolds, for *Chevrolet Tele-Theatre*. *Cast:* Faye Emerson, Frank Albertson.

9:00 "Reservations for Four," by Martin Ryerson, for *Lights Out*. Producer: George McGarrett. Director: Kingman T. Moore, *Cast:* Mercer McLeod, Dean Harens.

9:30 "The Letter," by W. Somerset Maugham, adapted by Felix Jackson, for *Robert Montgomery Presents Your Lucky Strike Theatre* debut. *Cast:* Madeleine Carroll, Theodore Newton, William Post, Jr., Howard Wierum.

31 January 1950— 9:00 "Of Thee I Love" and "Double Jeopardy," for *Fireside Theatre*.

9:30 *The Life of Riley*.

1 February 1950— 8:00 "Wheels of Chance," for *Believe It or Not*. *Cast:* Ann Sorg, Henry Hart, Maurice Manson.

8:30 "The Cat," by Lawrence Klee, adapted by Michael Blair, for *The Clock*. Producer: Herbert Swope, Jr. Director: Lawrence Schwab, Jr. *Cast:* Beverly Roberts, Richard Purdy.

9:00 "The Old Ladies," by Rodney Ackland, for *Kraft Television Theatre*. *Cast:* Mildred Natwick, Katherine Meskill, Doris Rich.

2 February 1950— 8:00 *The Black Robe*.

8:30 *One Man's Family*.

10:00 *Martin Kane, Private Eye*.

3 February 1950— 9:30 *The Big Story*.

4 February 1950— 9:00 *Mary Kay and Johnny*.

5 February 1950— 7:30 *The Aldrich Family*.

8:30 "The Trap," by Lynn Shubert, for *The Colgate Theatre*. Director: Melville Burke. *Cast:* Oliver Thorndike, Mary K. Wells, Bernard Nedell, Paul Davis, John Marley.

9:00 "The Sudden Guest," by Christopher LaFarge, adapted by Joseph Liss, for *Philco Television Playhouse*. Producer: Fred Coe. Director: Delbert Mann. *Cast:* John Baragrey, Jean Muir.

6 February 1950— 8:00 "The Wine of Oropolo," by John E. Hasty, for *Chevrolet Tele-Theatre*. *Cast:* Victor Jory, Clarence Derivent, Jack Arthur, Helen Choate.

9:00 "Dead Pigeon," by John and Helen Boruff, for *Lights Out*. Producer: George McGarrett. Director: Hal Keith. *Cast:* John Boruff, Philip Coolidge, Joel Ashley, Florida Friebus.

7 February 1950— 9:00 "The Imp in the Bottle" and "The Stronger," with Geraldine Fitzgerald, for *Fireside Theatre*.

9:30 *The Life of Riley*.

8 February 1950— 8:00 "The Man Without a Country," by Edward Everett Hale, for *Believe It or Not*. *Cast:* John Stephens, Anne Francis.

8:30 "William and Mary," by Frank Phares, for *The Clock*. *Cast:* Byron Russell, Helen Kingstead, Wyrley Birch, Maurice Manson, Olive Blakeney.

9:00 "The Dark Tower," by Alexander Woolcott and George S. Kaufman, for *Kraft Television Theatre*. *Cast:* E. G. Marshall, Flora Campbell, John Newland, John McQuade, Mildred Natwick, Mercer McLeod, Katherine Squire, King Calder, Marilyn Sable, Dick Camp.

9 February 1950— 8:00 *The Black Robe.*

8:30 *One Man's Family.*

10:00 *Martin Kane, Private Eye.*

11 February 1950— 9:00 *Mary Kay and Johnny.*

12 February 1950— 7:30 *The Aldrich Family.*

8:30 "The Brave and Early Fallen," for *The Colgate Theatre. Cast:* Royal Dane, Butch Cavell, Jonathan Marlowe, Muriel Kirkland, John Drew Devereaux, Lulu King.

9:00 "Ann Rutledge," by Norman Corwin, Adapted by Joseph Liss, for *Philco Television Playhouse. Cast:* Stephen Courtleigh, Grace Kelly, John McQuade, William Adams, James Gannon.

13 February 1950— 8:00 "The Hoosier Schoolmaster," adapted by Edward Eggleston, for *Chevrolet Tele-Theatre. Cast:* Wesley Addy, Emily Barnes, Forrest Tucker.

9:00 "The Invisible Staircase," by Reginald Denham and Mary Orr, for *Lights Out. Cast:* Clarence and Elfrida Derwent.

9:30 "Kitty Foyle," by Christopher Morley, adapted by Robert Cenedella, for *Robert Montgomery Presents.* Producer: Robert Montgomery. Director: Norman Felton. *Cast:* Jane Wyatt, Richard Derr, Farrell Pelly, Peter Cookson.

14 February 1950— 9:00 "The Shot" and "The Bed by the Window," for *Fireside Theatre.*

9:30 *The Life of Riley.*

15 February 1950— 8:00 "The Case of the Missing Model," for *Believe It or Not. Cast:* Charles Summers, Barbara Joyce.

8:30 "Bury Her Deep," by Robert Arthur and David Kogan, for *The Clock.* Producer: Herbert Swope, Jr. Director: Lawrence Schwab, Jr. *Cast:* Arnold Moss, Berry Kroeger, Alan Bunce, Carol Matthews, Palmer Ward, Frank Baxter.

9:00 "The Silent Room," an original play by Joe Bates Smith, for *Kraft Television Theatre. Cast:* Neva Patterson, Thomas Nello.

16 February 1950— 8:00 *The Black Robe.*

8:30 *One Man's Family.*

10:00 *Martin Kane, Private Eye.*

17 February 1950— 9:30 *The Big Story,* from *The New Orleans Item.*

18 February 1950— 9:00 *Mary Kay and Johnny.*

19 February 1950— 7:30 *The Aldrich Family.*

8:30 "The Karpoldi Letter," by George and Gertrude Fass, for *The Colgate Theatre. Cast:* Theodore Goetz, William Neil, Henry Richards, Leonard Bell, E. A. Krumschmidt, Vilma Kurer, Boris Marshalov, Walter Brooke.

9:00 "A Letter to Mr. Priest," by Margaret Cousins, adapted by Nelson Olmsted, for *Philco Television Playhouse.* Producer: Fred Coe. Director: Delbert Mann. *Cast:* Nelson Olmsted, Leora Dana.

20 February 1950— 8:00 "Once to Every Boy," by Stanley Richards, for *Chevrolet Tele-Theatre.* Director: Garry Simpson. *Cast:* Howard Smith, Peggy Ann Garner, Carmen Mathews, Enid Markey, Billy James.

9:00 "Graven Image," for *Lights Out. Cast:* Dean Harens, Patricia Jenkins, John Glendinning.

9:30 *Menasha the Magnificent,* a new comedy debuts. Director: Alan J. Neuman. *Cast:* Menasha Skulnik.

21 February 1950— 9:00 "The Spy," and "Another Road," for *Fireside Theatre.*

9:30 *The Life of Riley.*

22 February 1950— 8:00 "The Diamond Eye," for *Believe It or Not. Cast:* William Keane, Hi Enzel.

8:30 "The Take," by Lawrence Klee, adapted by Edgar Marvin, for *The Clock.* Producer: Herbert Swope, Jr. Director: William Corrigan, *Cast:* Gene Barry, Dulcy Jordan, Peter Capell.

9:00 "Valley Forge," by Maxwell Anderson, for *Kraft Television Theatre.* Producer/Director: Bill Warwick. *Cast:* Judson Laire, E. G. Marshall, Vaughn Taylor, Neil O'Malley, John Stephen, Louis Beachner, Peter Griffith, Henry Hart, Edward Bryce, Nicholas Saunders, Curtis Cooksey, Philip Carlyle, Maurice Mason, Charles Penman.

23 February 1950— 8:00 *The Black Robe.*

8:30 *One Man's Family.*

10:00 *Martin Kane, Private Eye.*

25 February 1950— 7:30 *Mary Kay and Johnny.*

26 February 1950— 7:30 *The Aldrich Family.*

8:30 "The Long Young Dreams," by Katharine Brush, adapted by Robert Wallsten, for *The Colgate Theatre.* Director: Melville Burke. Assistant Director: John Lynch. *Cast:* Richard McMurray, Dean Harens, Pam Duncan, Alfreda Wallace, Lulu King, James Goodwin, Richard Cleary, John MacDougall.

9:00 "Hometown," by Cleveland Amory, adapted by William Kendall Clarke, for *Philco Television Playhouse. Cast:* Faye Emerson, Barry Nelson, Vinton Hayworth, Betty Caulfield, Leona Powers, Larry Fletcher, Philippa Bevans, Eileen Heckart, Lorenzo Fuller, Billy Greene, Ann Lincoln.

27 February 1950— 8:00 "Three Smart Girls," by Peter Barry, for *Chevrolet Tele-Theatre.* Producer: Victor McLeod. Director: Barry Bernard. *Cast:* Charles Winninger, Isobel Elsom, Sally Moffett, Pat Breslin, Pat Crowley, Lee Goodman, Arthur Edwards, James Coates.

9:00 "Portrait of a Man" (aka "Dead Man"), for *Lights Out. Cast:* Richard Fraser, Horace Braham.

9:30 "The Male Animal," by James Thurber and Elliott Nugent, adapted by Robert J. Shaw, for *Robert Montgomery Presents. Cast:* Martha Scott, Elliott Nugent, Tommy Turner.

28 February 1950— 9:00 "The Stronger," with Geraldine Fitzgerald, and "A Terribly Strange Bed," for *Fireside Theatre.*

9:30 *The Life of Riley.*

1 March 1950— 8:00 "Journey Through Darkness," for *Believe It or Not.* Producer/Director: Donald S. Hillman. *Cast:* Anna Minot, George Reeves.

8:30 "Woman in the Road," by George Bateson and Richard McCracken, for *The Clock.* Producer: Herbert Swope, Jr. Director: Lawrence Schwab, Jr. *Cast:* Mildred Natwick, Joy Reese, Bob Smith.

9:00 "Miss Moonlight," by Benn Levy, for *Kraft Television Theatre.* Producer/Director: Bill Warwick. *Cast:* Mary Sinclair, E. G. Marshall.

2 March 1950— 8:00 *The Black Robe.*

8:30 *One Man's Family.*

10:00 *Martin Kane, Private Eye.*

3 March 1950— 9:30 *The Big Story,* from *The Houston Press.*

4 March 1950— 9:30 *Mary Kay and Johnny.*

5 March 1950— 7:30 *The Aldrich Family.*

8:30 "Neither a Borrower," an original drama by Mary Orr and Richard

Denham, for *The Colgate Theatre. Cast:* Marcella Manners, Audrey Ames, Kitty Hawk, Betty McCleary, Kileen Stuart, Dorothea Craig.

    9:00 "Vincent Van Gogh," by H. R. Hays, for *Philco Television Playhouse.* Director: Delbert Mann. *Cast:* Everett Sloane, Chester Stratton.

6 March 1950— 8:00 "Queen of Spades," by Aleksandr Pushkin, adapted by Michael Sayers, for *Chevrolet Tele-Theatre.* Producer: Victor McLeod. *Cast:* Basil Rathbone, Margaret Wycherly, Felicia Montealegre.

    9:00 "The Strange Case of John Kingman," for *Lights Out. Cast:* John Newland, Richard Purdy.

7 March 1950— 9:00 "Germelshausen" and "Sealed Orders," for *Fireside Theatre.*

    9:30 *The Life of Riley.*

8 March 1950— 8:00 "Murder to Come," for *Believe It or Not. Cast:* Vicki Marsden.

    8:30 "Graveyard Shift," by James Lee, for *The Clock. Cast:* Tom Drake.

    9:00 "The Nineteenth Hole," by Frank Craven, for *Kraft Television Theatre. Cast:* Alan Stevenson, Enid Markey, Hildy Parks.

9 March 1950— 8:00 *The Black Robe.*

    8:30 *One Man's Family.*

    10:00 *Martin Kane, Private Eye.*

11 March 1950— 7:30 *Mary Kay and Johnny.*

12 March 1950— 7:30 *The Aldrich Family.*

    8:30 "Always a Knife in the Back," by George Bradshaw, adapted by Doris Frankel, for *The Colgate Theatre. Cast:* John Drew Devereaux, Blair Davies, Vicki Cummings, June Dayton, John Regan, John Kane.

    9:00 "The Uncertain Molly Collicutt," by Booth Tarkington, adapted by William Kendall Clarke, for *Philco Television Playhouse.* Producer: Fred Coe. Director: Gordon Duff. *Cast:* Lilli Palmer, Philip Bourneuf, Ben Lackland.

13 March 1950— 8:00 "The Man Who Ordered Apple Pie," by Guy de Vry, adapted by Margaret Buell Wilder, for *Chevrolet Tele-Theatre. Cast:* Guy Kibbee.

    9:00 "The Emerald Lavalier," by Douglass Parkhirst, for *Lights Out.* Director: Kingman T. Moore. *Cast:* Felicia Montealegre, Theodore Newton.

    9:30 "The Egg and I," by Betty MacDonald, adapted by Gaynor Neiman, for *Robert Montgomery Presents. Cast:* June Havoc, Barry Nelson, Vaughn Taylor.

14 March 1950— 9:00 "The General's Coast" and "Vain Glory," for *Fireside Theatre.*

    9:30 *The Life of Riley.*

15 March 1950— 8:00 "Cross of Valor," for *Believe It or Not. Cast:* Leonard Ceeley, Frederick Bradlee.

    8:30 "What Makes a Murder," adapted by Thomas W. Phipps, for *The Clock. Cast:* Dennis Harrison, Arthur McCormick.

    9:00 "Ladies in Retirement," by Edward Percy and Reginald Denham, for *Kraft Television Theatre. Cast:* Mildred Natwick, Jean Cameron, Marga Ann Deighton, Richard Newton, Cherry Hardy, Brook Byron, Philippa Bevans.

16 March 1950— 8:00 *The Black Robe.*

    8:30 *One Man's Family.*

    10:00 *Martin Kane, Private Eye.*

17 March 1950— 9:30 *The Big Story.*

19 March 1950— 7:30 *The Aldrich Family.*

    8:30 "Blackmail," adapted by Evelyn Goodman, for *The Colgate Theatre.* Director: Melville Burke. *Cast:* William Post, Jr., Cynthia Carlin, Virginia Gilmore, Maurice Manson, Wendell K. Phillips, Victor Sutherland.

9:00 "The Trial of Steven Kent," by Josephine Bentham, adapted by Nelson Olmsted, for *Philco Television Playhouse*. *Cast:* John Newland, Richard Sanders, Alfreda Wallace, Richard Frazier.

20 March 1950— 8:00 "The Walking Stick," by Michael Sayers, for *Chevrolet Tele-Theatre*. Producer: Victor McLeod. Director: Garry Simpson. *Cast:* Rex Harrison, Dennis Hoey, Eileen Peel, Una O'Connor, Douglas Chandler, Byron Russell.

8:00 *The Black Robe*.

8:30 *One Man's Family*.

10:00 *Martin Kane, Private Eye*.

26 March 1950— 7:30 *The Aldrich Family*.

8:30 "The Green Bush," by William Kendall Clarke, for *The Colgate Theatre*. *Cast:* Robert Feyti, Eleanor Lynn, Jonathan Marlowe.

9:00 "The Second Oldest Profession," by Robert Sylvester, adapted by Joseph Liss, for *Philco Television Playhouse*. Producer: Fred Coe. Director: Gordon Duff. *Cast:* Felicia Montealegre, William Prince, Victor Jory.

27 March 1950— 8:00 "The Great Emptiness," by Joseph Cochran, for *Chevrolet Tele-Theatre*. Producer: Victor McLeod. *Cast:* Dick Foran, Peggy Badey.

9:00 "Mary, Mary Quite Contrary," by Clifford Kraus, adapted by James Lee, for *Lights Out*. Director: Kingman T. Moore. *Cast:* John McQuade, Carol Ohmart, George Englund.

9:30 "Ride the Pink Horse," by Felton Cabasin, adapted by Robert Cenedella, for *Robert Montgomery Presents*. *Cast:* Robert Montgomery, Thomas Gomez, Susan Douglas, Vaughn Taylor.

28 March 1950— 9:00 "The Bunker," for *Fireside Theatre*. *Cast:* Dick Wessel, Jack Mitchum.

9:30 *The Life of Riley*.

29 March 1950— 8:00 "The Frightened City," for *Believe It or Not*. *Cast:* Patricia Benoit, Barbara Bolton, Wesley Addy.

8:30 "Open the Door for Murder," by John Shaw, adapted by Elinor Tarshis, for *The Clock*. Director: William Corrigan. *Cast:* Paul McGrath, Don Tobin, Frank Daly, Bram Nossen, Ann Summers, Mara McCullagh, Bob Lauritzen, Margaret Kirkwood.

9:00 "The Copperhead," by Augustus Thomas, for *Kraft Television Theatre*. *Cast:* John Shellie, Flora Campbell, Doris Rich, James Coots, Phil Faversham, Arthur Jaret, John Starke, Robert Lynn, James Gannon, Michael Dreyfuss, Nelson Olmsted, Jane Compton, Dan Morgan, Kay Strozzi.

30 March 1950— 8:00 *The Black Robe*.

8:30 *One Man's Family*.

10:00 *Martin Kane, Private Eye*.

31 March 1950— 9:30 *The Big Story*.

2 April 1950— 7:30 *The Aldrich Family*.

8:30 "Burden of Guilt," by John and Ward Hawkins, adapted by William Kendall Clarke, for *The Colgate Theatre*.

9:00 "Nocturne," by Frank Swinnerton, adapted by William Kendall Clarke, for *Philco Television Playhouse*. Producer: Fred Coe. Director: Delbert Mann. *Cast:* Leora Dana, Cloris Leachman.

3 April 1950— 8:00 "Voice in the Night" (aka "Death Comes by Night"), by Leonard Levinson, for *Chevrolet Tele-Theatre*. *Cast:* Arlene Whelan, Don Hanmer, Sherry O'Neil, Dorothy Frances, Dort Clark.

9:00 "The Queen Is Dead," for *Lights Out. Cast:* Lynn Bari, Mildred Natwick, Una O'Connor, Dorothy Steele, Keith Masters.

4 April 1950— 9:00 "Operation Mona Lisa," for *Fireside Theatre. Cast:* Ralph Byrd, Marion Martin.

9:30 *Mr. Omn,* a drama of a cross section of human behavior and emotion, replaces *The Life of Riley.* Executive Producer: Sylvester Weaver. Producer: Peter Barnum. Director: Dory Rodgers. *Cast:* Beatrice Thompkins, Susan Harris, Barbara Bolton.

5 April 1950— 8:00 "The Bandit of Ballingry Ridge," for *Believe It or Not.*

8:30 *The Clock.*

9:00 "A Doll's House," by Henrik Ibsen, for *Kraft Television Theatre. Cast:* Felicia Montealegre, Theodore Newton, Joan Wetmore, John Newland, Geoffrey Lumb, Alice Yourman.

6 April 1950— 8:00 *Deadline,* two extempore dramas from Studebaker Theatre in Chicago, debuts. *Cast:* Anne Jefferies, Gerry Kay, Robert White.

8:30 *One Man's Family.*

10:00 *Martin Kane, Private Eye.*

7 April 1950— 9:30 *The Clock.*

9 April 1950— 7:30 *The Aldrich Family.*

8:30 "Motive for Murder," by John and Ward Hawkins, adapted by Jack Bentover, for *The Colgate Theatre. Cast:* John Baragrey.

9:00 "Dirty Eddie," by Ludwig Bemelmans, adapted by David Shaw, for *Philco Television Playhouse.* Producer: Fred Coe. Director: Gordon Duff. *Cast:* John Buckmaster, Joseph Buloff, Judy Parrish, Vinton Hayworth, Frank Thomas, Kathleen Comegys, James MacCall.

10 April 1950— 8:00 "Once a Gentleman," by Betty Wright, for *Chevrolet Tele-Theatre. Cast:* Kathleen Phelan, Victor Varconi, Milton Frome, Joe Downing.

9:00 "The Faithful Heart," by Douglas Parkhirst, for *Lights Out.* Producer: Herbert Swope, Jr. Director: Kingman T. Moore. *Cast:* Liam Sullivan, Anne Francis, Dorothy Francis, James O'Neill, John Hamilton, Riza Royce, Frank Gallop.

9:30 *The Adventures of Martin Eden,* a 16mm film, replaced "Our Town," for *Robert Montgomery Presents.*

11 April 1950— 9:00 "The Web," for *Fireside Theatre.*

9:30 *Mr. Omn.*

12 April 1950— 8:00 "The Bloodhound and the Burglar," for *Believe It or Not.*

9:00 "The Lucky Finger," by Lennox Robinson, for *Kraft Television Theatre.* Producer/Director: Lew Brown. *Cast:* Lois Holmes, Eleanor Wilson, Dan Morgan, E. G. Marshall, Nelson Olmsted, William Sheidy, Mildred Clinton, Louise Prussing, Kirk Brown, Robert McQuade, Byron Russell.

13 April 1950— 8:00 *Studs' Place,* a neighborhood hangout where characters express their views from Chicago, returns. It was a variety show originally telecast on 26 November 1949. *Cast:* Studs Terkel, Beverly Younger, Jonathan Hole, William Stracke, Louis Sorin.

8:30 *One Man's Family.*

10:00 *Martin Kane, Private Eye.*

14 April 1950— 9:00 *The Big Story,* from *The San Antonio Light.*

16 April 1950— 7:30 *The Aldrich Family.*

8:30 "Double Entry," by John G. Fuller and Jack Bentkover, for *The Colgate Theatre.*

9:00 "The End Is Known," by Geoffrey Holiday Hall, adapted by Joseph Liss, for *Philco Television Playhouse.* Producer: Fred Coe. Director: Delbert Mann. *Cast:* Kent Smith, Jack Warden, Wilson, Cara Williams, Adalaide Klein, Warren Stevens, Nicholas Saunders, Al Patterson, Anna Minot, Bill Gibberson.

17 April 1950— 8:00 "The Bone for the Shadow," by Marcia Harris, for *Chevrolet Tele-Theatre.* Producer: Victor McLeod. Director: Garry Simpson. *Cast:* Flora Campbell, Roberta Janay, John Loder, James Noble, Victor Sutherland, Florence Tompkins.

9:00 "A Toast to Sergeant Farnsworth," by Harry Muheim, for *Lights Out. Cast:* Bill Terry, Earl Dawson, John Marley, Heywood Hale Braun, Ross Martin.

9:30 "Our Town," by Thornton Wilder, for *Robert Montgomery Presents.* Producer: Montgomery. Director: Norman Felton. *Cast:* Burgess Meredith, Dean Harens, Dudley Sadler, Jean Gillespie, Leona Powers, John McGowan.

18 April 1950— 9:00 "No Strings Attached," for *Fireside Theatre.*

9:30 *Mr. Omn.*

19 April 1950— 8:00 *Believe It or Not.*

9:00 "Make Way for Lucia," by John Van Druten, for *Kraft Television Theatre. Cast:* Doris Dalton, Geoffrey Lumb, Philippa Bevans, Leslie Barrie, Cherry Hardy, Oswald Marshall, Kay Strozzi, Edward Harvey, Giuseppe Sterni.

20 April 1950— 8:00 *Studs' Place.*

8:30 *One Man's Family.*

10:00 *Martin Kane, Private Eye.*

23 April 1950— 7:30 *The Aldrich Family.*

8:30 "The Witness to the Crime," by George and Gertrude Fass, for *The Colgate Theatre.*

9:00 "The Man in the Black Hat," by Michael Fessier, adapted by Nelson Olmsted, for *Philco Television Playhouse.* Producer: Fred Coe. Director: Gordon Duff.

24 April 1950— 8:00 "The Californian's Tale," by Mark Twain, for *Chevrolet Tele-Theatre.* Producer: Fred Coe. Director: Alan J. Neuman. *Cast:* Edgar Stenli, Dean Harens, E. G. Marshall, Daniel Reed, Patricia Ferris, Butch Cavell, John Becker, Eddie Hyans, Mac Ceppos.

9:00 "The Man Who Couldn't Remember," by Betty Lefferts, adapted by George Lefferts, for *Lights Out. Cast:* Beverly Lawrence, Tom Walsh, Jim Davidson.

9:30 "Phantom Lady," for *Robert Montgomery Presents. Cast:* Ella Raines.

25 April 1950— 9:00 "Boys Will Be Men," for *Fireside Theatre.*

9:30 "The Lovesick Robber," by Thomas W. Phipps and Herbert Swope, Jr., for *Cads and Scoundrels and Charming Ladies,* debut. *Cast:* George Englund, Grace Kelly, Francis Bethencourt, Miriam Goldina, Lotte Stravisky.

26 April 1950— 8:00 "The Pointing Finger," for *Believe It or Not.*

9:00 "The Black Sheep," by Elmer Rice, for *Kraft Television Theatre. Cast:* Richard McMurray, Eileen Heckart, Anne Francis, Ethel Remey, Howard Erskine, Patricia Hosley, Allison Prescott, Ruth Hammond.

27 April 1950— 8:00 *Studs' Place.*

8:30 *One Man's Family.*

10:00 *Martin Kane, Private Eye.*

28 April 1950— 9:30 *The Big Story.*

30 April 1950— 7:30 *The Aldrich Family.*

8:30 "The Law Beaters," for *The Colgate Theatre.*

9:00 "The American," by Henry James, adapted by Joseph Cochran, for *Philco*

Television Playhouse. Producer: Fred Coe. Director: Gordon Duff. *Cast:* John Newland, Alfred Ryder, Neva Patterson, Blaine Cordner, Augusta Roeland.

1 May 1950— 8:00 "Introduction," by Edward Peple, adapted by Fred Coe, for *Chevrolet Tele-Theatre.* Producer: Coe. Director: Garry Simpson. *Cast:* Philip Bourneuf, Frances Reid, William Prince.

9:00 *Lights Out.*

2 May 1950— 9:00 "Operation Mona Lisa," for *Fireside Theatre.*

3 May 1950— 8:00 "Murder Makes the Headlines," for *Believe It or Not.*

9:00 "The Fourth Step," by Joe Bates Smith, for *Kraft Television Theatre. Cast:* Augusta Dabney, Matt Briggs, Leslie Nielsen, Emmett Vogan, Roy Fant, Janet Tyler, Joseph Boland, James Coots, John C. Becher, John Shellie.

4 May 1950— 8:00 *Studs' Place.*

8:30 *One Man's Family.*

10:00 *Martin Kane, Private Eye.*

5 May 1950— 9:30 "Voyage West," by Elinor Tarshis, for *The Clock.* Director: Lawrence Schwab, Jr. *Cast:* Berry Kroeger, Walter Brooke, Grey Robbins, William Crane, John Moore.

7 May 1950— 7:30 *The Aldrich Family.*

8:30 "The Suitable Present," by Rachael Thornton, adapted by John Haggart, for *The Colgate Theatre.*

9:00 "The Feast," by Margaret Kennedy, for *Philco Television Playhouse. Cast:* Margaret Wycherly, Mildred Natwick, Louis Hector, Colin Keith-Johnston.

8 May 1950— 8:00 "Welcome Jeremiah," by Harold Heifer, adapted by Fred Coe, for *Chevrolet Tele-Theatre.*

9:00 "The Silent Voice," by Douglass Parkhirst, for *Lights Out.*

9:30 "Pitfall," by Robert MacCauley, for *Robert Montgomery Presents. Cast:* Lee Bowman, Nancy Coleman, Charles Meredith, Jean Carson, Dorothy Collins, Gordon B. Clarke, Philip Gordon, Ray Morgan.

9 May 1950— 9:00 "The Parasol," for *Fireside Theatre. Cast:* Frances Ford, Jack Mitchum.

9:30 "The Hired Boy," for *Downbeat.* Producer: Richard Berger. Director: Lawrence Schwab, Jr. *Cast:* Iggie Woffington, James Dobson.

10 May 1950— 8:00 "Mystery of the Missing Guests," for *Believe It or Not.*

9:00 "Macbeth," by William Shakespeare, for *Kraft Television Theatre.* Producer: Stanley Quinn. Director: Lew Brown. *Cast:* E. G. Marshall, Uta Hagen, Chester Stratton, Philip Carlyle.

11 May 1950— 8:00 *Studs' Place.*

8:30 *One Man's Family.*

10:00 *Martin Kane, Private Eye.*

12 May 1950— 9:30 *The Big Story.*

14 May 1950— 7:30 *The Aldrich Family.*

8:30 "Revenge by Proxy," by Jack Bentkover and Tom Everitt, for *The Colgate Theatre.*

9:00 "Brat Farrar," by Josephine Tay, adapted by Norman Rosten, for *Philco Television Playhouse.* Director: Gordon Duff. *Cast:* John Newland, John Baragrey, Augusta Dabney, Francis Compton, Oliver Thorndike, Margery Maude, Laura Weber.

15 May 1950— 8:00 "The Sun," by John Galsworthy, adapted by Stephen de Baun, for *Chevrolet Tele-Theatre.* Producer: Fred Coe. Director: Garry Simpson. *Cast:*

John Buckmaster, Torin Thatcher, Frank Darren, Cara Williams, Edwin Taylor.
9:00 "The House That Time Forgot," by Sigmund Miller, for *Lights Out*. Producer: Herbert Swope, Jr. Director: William Corrigan. *Cast:* Jack Manning, Jeff Morrow, Byron Russell.
16 May 1950— 9:00 "The Hired Girl," for *Fireside Theatre*. *Cast:* Shirley Jones, James Anderson.
9:30 "It Takes a Thief," by Arthur Miller, adapted by Norman Rosten, for *Cameo Theatre* debut. Producer: Ernest Walling. Director: Albert McCleery. *Cast:* Marjorie Gateson, Jack Hartley, Robert Bolger.
17 May 1950— 8:30 *One Man's Family*, new time.
9:00 "Storm in a Teacup," by Bruno Frank London, for *Kraft Television Theatre*. Producer: Maury Holland. Director: Lew Brown. *Cast:* Andrea Wallace, George Reeves, Doris Rich, Neil O'Malley, Ivan Simpson.
18 May 1950— 8:00 "The Bodark Tree," for *Believe It or Not*.
8:45 *Studs' Place*.
10:00 *Martin Kane, Private Eye*.
19 May 1950— 9:30 "Just a Minute," by Milton Subotsky and Phyllis Coe, for *The Clock*. *Cast:* Helmut Dantine, Bruce Hall.
21 May 1950— 7:30 *The Aldrich Family*.
5:30 "Chance of Murder," by Cornell Woolrich, adapted Neil Bent, for *The Colgate Theatre*.
9:00 "The Charmed Circle," by Peggy Lamson, adapted by William Kendall Clarke, for *Philco Television Playhouse*. Producer: Fred Coe. Director: Delbert Mann. *Cast:* Alfred Ryder, Betsy Blair, Jo Ann Rauls, Herbert Evers, Helen Carson, Ralph Riggs, Larry Blyden.
22 May 1950— 8:00 "Highly Recommended," by Saki, adapted by Thomas W. Phipps, for *Chevrolet Tele-Theatre*. Producer: Fred Coe. Director: Alan J. Neuman. *Cast:* Mary Wickes, Philip Tonge, Dora Clement, Francis Compton, Joe E. Marks, Lynn Bari, Bobby Nick, Robert Chisholm, Helen Donaldson, Helen Auerbach, Jane Murray.
9:00 "Rendezvous," by William Welch, for *Lights Out*. *Cast:* Inge Adams, Richard McMurray, Winfield Hoeny.
9:30 "Rebecca," by Daphne du Maurier, for *Robert Montgomery Presents*. *Cast:* Barbara Bel Geddes, Peter Cookson.
23 May 1950— 9:00 "Big Ben," for *Fireside Theatre*.
9:30 "The Great Merlini," by Clayton Rawson, adapted by Jack Bentkover. Producer/Director: Curtis Canfield. *Cast:* Chester Morris, Mary K. Wells, Kirk Brown, Alfreda Wallace, John Englund, Bill Terry, Wyrley Birch, Patricia Wheel, Bram Nessen.
24 May 1950— 8:30 *One Man's Family*.
9:00 "The House Beautiful," by Channing Pollock, for *Kraft Television Theatre*.
25 May 1950— 8:00 *Believe It or Not*.
8:30 *Studs' Place*.
10:00 *Martin Kane, Private Eye*.
26 May 1950— 9:30 *The Big Story*.
28 May 1950— 7:30 *The Aldrich Family*.
8:30 "South Wind," by Theodore Tinsley, adapted by William Kendall Clarke, for *The Colgate Theatre*. *Cast:* William Post, Jr.

9:00 "Semmelweis," by Joseph Liss, for *Philco Television Playhouse.* Producer: Fred Coe. Director: Gordon Duff. *Cast:* Everett Sloane, Felicia Montealegre, Guy Spaull, Robert H. Harris, Anna Minot.

29 May 1950— 8:00 "Letter to Edith," by Faith Baldwin, adapted by Nelson Olmsted, for *Chevrolet Tele-Theatre.* Producer: Fred Coe. Director: Vincent J. Donehue. *Cast:* Nelson Olmsted, Alfreda Wallace, Sandra Ann Wigginton.

9:00 "How Love Came to Professor Guildea," by Robert Hichens, adapted by James Lee, for *Lights Out.* Producer: Herbert Swope, Jr. Director: Kingman T. Moore. *Cast:* Arnold Moss, Brandon Peters, Frank Daly.

30 May 1950— 9:00 "The Man Without a Country," for *Fireside Theatre.*

9:30 "The Door," by Harry Junkin, adapted by Ethel Frank and Richard Goode, for *Cameo Theatre.* Director: Albert McCleery. *Cast:* Richard Carlyle, Pat Breslin, Alexander Campbell, Winfield Hoeny.

31 May 1950— 8:30 *One Man's Family.*

9:00 "The Luck of Guldeford," by Edward Percy and Reginald Denham, for *Kraft Television Theatre.* Producer: Maury Holland. Director: Lew Brown. *Cast:* Leslie Nielsen, Betsy Blair, William Brower, Peter Griffith, Judith Jordan, Alice Thorsell, Leon Maricle, Reynolds Evans, Robert Blackburn, Kenn Mileston, Frank Daren, Harry Bergman.

1 June 1950— 8:00 "Passage to Zermatt," for *Believe It or Not.*

8:30 *Studs' Place.*

10:00 *Martin Kane, Private Eye.*

2 June 1950— 9:30 "I Keep Forgetting," Neil Brant, for *The Clock. Cast:* Donald Curtis, Philip Coolidge, Augusta Dabney, Earl Rowe, Lorraine Pressler, Marilyn Clark, Al Thaler.

4 June 1950— 7:30 *The Aldrich Family.*

8:30 "I've Got What It Takes," by Kevin Mullin, for *The Colgate Theatre. Cast:* Cameron Mitchell.

9:00 "Sense and Sensibility," by Jane Austen, for *Philco Television Playhouse.* Producer: Fred Coe. Director: Delbert Mann. *Cast:* Madge Evans, Cloris Leachman, Dora Clement, John Stephen, Josephine Brown, John Baragrey, Laurence Hugo, Chester Stratton, Patricia Hosley, Cherry Hardy.

5 June 1950— 8:00 "The Brave Man with a Cord," by Peter Strand and Rudolph Bernstein, for *Chevrolet Tele-Theatre.* Producer: Fred Coe. Director: Alan J. Neuman. *Cast:* John Newland, William Post, Jr., Mary Patton, Somer Alberg, Billy James.

9:00 "The Heart of Jonathan O'Rourke," by A. J. Russell, for *Lights Out.* Producer: Herbert Swope, Jr. Director: William Corrigan.

9:30 "Champion," by Carl Foreman, for *Robert Montgomery Presents.* Producer: Montgomery. Director: Norman Felton, *Cast:* Vicki Cummings, Richard Kiley, Herbert Dudley, Warren Stewart, Brook Byron, Bill Martel, Sidney Smith, Helen Harrelson, Speed Riggs, Dorothy Collins, Robert Lieb.

6 June 1950— 9:00 "The Human Touch" and "The Assassin," for *Fireside Theatre.*

9:30–10:00 "The Magnificent Gesture," by James Garvin, for *Armstrong Circle Theatre* debut. Producer: Hudson Faussett. Director: Garry Simpson. *Cast:* Brian Aherne, Roland Hogue, Ronald Dawson, Elizabeth Ross, Helene Seamon, Gene Barry, Richard Shankland, Matt Briggs, Margaret Hayes.

7 June 1950— 8:30 "Manhattan Footsteps," by Raphael Hayes, adapted by Ethel Frank, for *Cameo Theatre.* Producer/Director: Albert McCleery. *Cast:* Sam Wanamaker.

9:00 "The Doctor in Spite of Himself," by Molière, for *Kraft Television Theatre*. Director: Lew Brown.

8 June 1950 — 8:00 "Death Call the Tune," for *Believe It or Not*.

8:30 *Studs' Place*.

10:00 *Martin Kane, Private Eye*.

9 June 1950 — 9:30 *The Big Story*.

11 June 1950 — 7:30 *The Aldrich Family*.

8:30 "Hotel of the Three Kings," adapted by Margaret Miller, for *The Colgate Theatre*.

9:00 "The Bump on Brannigan's Head," by Myles Connolly, for *Philco Television Playhouse*. Producer: Fred Coe. Director: Gordon Duff. *Cast:* Pat O'Malley, Vinton Hayworth, Dean Harens, Leona Powers, Betty Caulfield, Ralph Riggs, Ruth McDevitt, Michael Strong.

12 June 1950 — 8:00 "The Way I Feel," by Jeff Brown, adapted by William Kendall Clarke, for *Chevrolet Tele-Theatre*. Producer: Fred Coe. Director: Vincent J. Donehue. *Cast:* Biff McGuire, Ellen Cobb Hill, Don Lackland, Edith King, Byron Russell, Bill Story.

9:00 "The Determined Lady," by Harry Muheim for *Lights Out*. *Cast:* Ethel Griffies, Donald Foster, Robert Eckles, Gene Blakely, Lee Nugent, Fred Barron.

13 June 1950 — 9:00 "Dinner for Three" and "Devil's Due," for *Fireside Theatre*.

9:30 "The Jackpot," by Ira Avery and Cameron Hawley, for *Armstrong Circle Theatre*. Producer: Hudson Faussett. Director: Hal Keith. *Cast:* Stuart Erwin, Jason Johnson, Alexander Campbell, Lionel Wilson, Ann Summers, George Haggerty.

14 June 1950 — 8:30 "The Lottery," by Shirley Jackson, adapted by Ethel Frank and Ellen Violett, for *Cameo Theatre*. Producer/Director: Albert McCleery. *Cast:* Andrew Duggan, Helen Wagner, Don Kennedy, Humphrey Davis.

9:00 "Good Housekeeping," by William McCleery, for *Kraft Television Theatre*. *Cast:* Jack Arthur, Nelson Olmsted, Anne Francis, Arthur Walsh, Valerie Cossart.

15 June 1950 — 8:00 "The Rose of Vengence," for *Believe It or Not*. *Cast:* Louis Hector, Faith Brook, Ernest Graves, J. W. Austin, Tiger Andrews, David Stewart.

8:30 *Studs' Place*.

10:00 *Martin Kane, Private Eye*.

16 June 1950 — 9:30 "The Caller," by Meyer Labin, adapted by Stephen de Baun, for *The Clock*. Director: Lawrence Schwab, Jr. *Cast:* Dan Morgan, Eva Marie Saint, Henry Beckman, Brook Byron, Pitt Herbert, Arthur Hanson, Joyce Randolph, Winfield Hoeny, George Charles, Mary Mace, Kurt Katch.

18 June 1950 — 7:30 *The Aldrich Family*.

8:30 "The Hands of the Enemy," by Richard Booth and John Colford, adapted by Jack Bentkover, for *The Colgate Theatre*.

9:00 "Anything Can Happen," by George and Helen Papashvily, adapted by William Kendall Clarke, for *Philco Television Playhouse*. Producer: Fred Coe. Director: Delbert Mann. *Cast:* Joseph Buloff, Barbara Bulgakov, George Renavent, Enid Pulver, Nicholas Saunders.

19 June 1950 — 8:00 "The Fisherman," by Jonathan Tree, for *Chevrolet Tele-Theatre*. Producer: Fred Coe. Director: Alan J. Neuman. *Cast:* Dennis Hoey, Dort Clark, Daniel Reed, Betty Caulfield, Gene Barry, Pearl Chertok.

9:00 "A Child Is Crying," by John J. MacDonald, adapted by Ernest Kinoy, for *Lights Out*. Producer: Herbert Swope, Jr. Director: William Corrigan. *Cast:* David

Cole, Frank M. Thomas, Leslie Nielsen, Mary Stuart MacDonald, Florence Robinson, Sam Alexander, Martin Brandt, Jason Johnson.

9:30 "The Citadel," adapted by Richard Morrison, for *Robert Montgomery Presents. Cast:* Robert Montgomery, Angela Lansbury, Anna Lee, Alexander Clark, Byron Russell, Graham Velsey, Dorothy Collins, Bob Stanton, Doris Deane, Richard Abbott.

20 June 1950— 9:00 "The Courting of Belle" and "Rendezvous," for *Fireside Theatre.*

9:30 "Only This Night," by Ira Avery, for *Armstrong Circle Theatre. Cast:* Nina Foch, Donald Curtis, Kathleen Comegys, Richard Hamilton.

21 June 1950— 8:30 "Weep for the Heart," by James Truex, for *Cameo Theatre. Cast:* Ernest Truex.

9:00 "Noah," by Andre Obey, for *Kraft Television Theatre. Cast:* Vaughn Taylor, Doris Rich, Harry Kingston, Stewart Bradley, Jean Pugsley, William Allen, Jean Pearson, Charles Nolte, Joy Reese.

22 June 1950— 8:00 *Believe It or Not.*

8:30 *Studs' Place.*

10:00 *Martin Kane, Private Eye.*

23 June 1950— 9:30 *The Big Story.*

25 June 1950— 7:30 *The Aldrich Family.*

8:30 *The Colgate Theatre.*

9:00 "Hearing My Heart Speak," by Charlotte Paul, adapted by Stephen de Baun, for *Philco Television Playhouse.* Producer: Fred Coe. Director: Gordon Duff. *Cast:* Charlton Heston, Olive Deering, Jane Seymour, Frank Maxwell, John Seymour, Ellen Cobb Hill, Robert McQuade, Wallace Rooney, Ronald Smith.

26 June 1950— 8:00 "The Veranda," by Alexander Kirkland, for *Chevrolet Tele-Theatre.* Producer: Fred Coe. Director: Vincent J. Donehue. *Cast:* Nydia Westman, Hiram Johnson, Jonathan Harris, Victor Sutherland, Leslie Nielsen, Charlotte Keane, Dulcy Jordan, Anne Ives, Nell Harrison.

9:00 "Encore," by Douglass Parkhirst, for *Lights Out.* Producer: Herbert Swope, Jr. Director: Kingman T. Moore. *Cast:* Don Hanmer, Adelaide Klein, Denise Alexander, Heywood Hale Braun, Reginald Mason.

27 June 1950— 9:00 "The Bar," for *Fireside Theatre.*

9:30 "The Chair," by Elaine Ryan for *Armstrong Circle Theatre. Cast:* Lucille Watson, Ralph Riggs, John Boruff, Frank Daren, Vaughn Taylor, Wells Richardson, Helen Donaldson, Mardette Richards, Clifford Sales, Richard Case.

28 June 1950— 8:30 "A Daughter to Think About," an original play by William Saroyan, for *Cameo Theatre* debut. Producer/Director: Albert McCleery.

9:00 "The Wind Is Ninety," by Ralph Nelson, for *Kraft Television Theatre.* Producer: Maury Holland. Director: William Harbach. *Cast:* George Reeves, Nancy Coleman, Kathleen Comegys, John Shellie, Harry Townes, Jonathan Marlowe, Richard Wigginton, Keith Russell, Herbie Walsh, Donald Duerr.

29 June 1950— 8:00 "The Bleeding Heart," for *Believe It or Not.*

8:30 *Studs' Place.*

10:00 *Martin Kane, Private Eye.*

30 June 1950— 9:00 "Someone Must Die," by Bob Wald, for *The Clock. Cast:* Vinton Hayworth, Ann Summers, Peter Capell, Richard Webb, Frank Thomas, Craig Shepard, Ava Noring, Richard Lacovra.

2 July 1950— 8:30 "The Stronger," with Geraldine Fitzgerald, Valerie Bettis, and "Gloria," for *Double Bill,* an anthology debut.

9:00 "The Reluctant Landlord," by Scott Corbett, adapted by Joseph Liss, for *Philco Television Playhouse*. Producer: Fred Coe. Director: Delbert Mann. *Cast:* Hume Cronyn, Haila Stoddard.

3 July 1950—8:00 *Menasha the Magnificent*, a comedy by Matt Brooks and Louis Quinn. Producer: Martin Goodman. Director: Alan J. Neuman. *Cast:* Menasha Skulnik.

9:00 "I Dreamt I Died," for *Lights Out. Cast:* Alfreda Wallace, Robert McMurray, Rita Lynn.

4 July 1950—8:00 *Cinema Playhouse*, feature films, debuts.

9:00 *Lights, Camera, Action*, debuts Hollywood dramas on the East Coast.

9:30 "The Skyrocket," by Cameron Hawley, for *Armstrong Circle Theatre. Cast:* Ed Begley, Jane Seymour, James Stephens, Dorothy Steele, Andrew Duggan.

5 July 1950—8:30 "Correction," by C. L. Hutchings, adapted by Ethel Frank, for *Cameo Theatre*. Producer/Director: Albert McCleery. *Cast:* Wesley Addy, Phil Faversham, Joey Walsh, William Windom, Jane Murray, Anita Weble, John Adair.

9:00 "Jeannie," by Aimee Stewart, for *Kraft Television Theatre*. Producer: Stanley Quinn. Director: William Harbach.

6 July 1950—8:00 "A Million Dollar Corpse," for *Believe It or Not*.

8:30 *Studs' Place*.

10:00 *Martin Kane, Private Eye* is replaced.

7 July 1950—9:30 *The Big Story*.

9 July 1950—9:00 "The Tentacles," by Dana Lyon, adapted by H. R. Hays, for *Philco Television Playhouse* season end. Producer: Fred Coe. Director: Gordon Duff. *Cast:* Alfreda Wallace, Warren Stevens, John Seymour, Margery Maude, E. G. Marshall, Ethel Remey.

10 July 1950—8:00 *Menasha the Magnificent*.

11 July 1950—9:30 "Local Stop," by James Garvin, for *Armstrong Circle Theatre*. Producer: Hudson Faussett. Director: Hal Keith. *Cast:* Vaughn Taylor, Jed Prouty, David Burke, Jimsey Sommers.

12 July 1950—8:30 "The Clinic," by Ted Key, adapted by Ethel Frank, for *Cameo Theatre*. Producer: Albert McCleery. Director: Grey Lockwood. *Cast:* Lee Tracy, Frank Daren, Sylvia Cole.

9:00 "Murder on the Nile," by Agatha Christie, for *Kraft Television Theatre*. Producer: William Harbach. Director: Cal Kuhl. *Cast:* Guy Spaull, Patricia Wheel, Lex Richards, Andrea Wallace, Theo Goetz, Lili Valenty, Cherry Hardy, David Stewart, Stewart Nedd.

13 July 1950—8:00 "Double Jeopardy," for *Believe It or Not*.

8:30 *Studs' Place*.

14 July 1950—9:30 "A Grave Plot," by Robert Arthur and David Kogan, adapted by John L. Gerstad, for *The Clock*. Producer/Director: Lawrence Schwab, Jr. *Cast:* John Boruff, Sara Anderson, Leslie Nielsen, Joy Reese, Peggy Harrison, Beeman Lord.

17 July 1950—8:00 *Menasha the Magnificent*.

9:00 "The Devil to Pay," by Elizabeth Evans, for *Lights Out*. Producer: Gordon Duff. Director: William Corrigan. *Cast:* Theodore Marcuse, Jonathan Harris, Grace Kelly, Anthony Burr, William Beach.

18 July 1950—9:30 "The Bald Spot," by Bob Duncan, for *Armstrong Circle Theatre. Cast:* Johnny Stearns, Helen Marey, Richard Wigginton, Norma Jean, Joy Reese.

19 July 1950—8:30 "The Canon's Curtains," by Seamus de Faoite, adapted by Ethel

Frank, for *The NBC Cameo Theatre.* Producer/Director: Albert McCleery. *Cast:* Ernest Truex, Joseph O'Brien, Peggy MacKay, Lynn Thatcher, Grania O'Malley. 9:00 "Accent on Youth," by Samson Raphaelson, for *Kraft Television Theatre.* *Cast:* Melville Ruick, Steven Gaye, Marilyn Erskine, Verne Collett, Robert Chrisholm, Pat Englund, Roland von Weber, Louise Prussing, Moultrie Patten, Charles Nolte.

20 July 1950— 8:00 "The Well of Despair," for *Believe It or Not.* 8:30 *Studs' Place.*

21 July 1950— 9:30 *The Big Story.*

23 July 1950— 9:00 "Hedda Gabler," by Henrik Ibsen, adapted by Hugh Kemp, for *NBC Masterworks Theatre* (aka *Masterpiece Playhouse*) debut. *Cast:* Jessica Tandy, Walter Abel, Kent Smith, Margaret Phillips, Helen Louise Riggs, Gordon B. Clarke.

24 July 1950— 8:00 *Menasha the Magnificent.*

25 July 1950— 9:30 "The Rocking Horse," by Doris Halman, for *Armstrong Circle Theatre.* *Cast:* Don Kennedy, Evelyn Varden, Marilyn Monk, Julian Noe, Emily Barnes.

26 July 1950— 8:30 "The Line of Duty," by Guy de Vry, for *Cameo Theatre.* Producer/Director: Albert McCleery. *Cast:* William Post, Jr., James Little, Douglas Kennedy, Ed Begley, Richard McMurray, Robert Grenier, Jane Murray. 9:00 "Mr. Barry's Etchings," by Walter Bullock and Daniel Hicker, for *Kraft Television Theatre.* *Cast:* John Shellie, Dorrit Kelton, Jim Davidson, Peggy McCay, Dan Morgan, Bess Winburn, Lucille Fenton, Arthur Hanson, Ted Jacques, Richard Shankland, Richard Wigginton, Edna Hernly.

27 July 1950— 8:00 "Murder with a Payoff," for *Believe It or Not.* 8:30 *Studs' Place.*

28 July 1950— 9:30 "Jump, Elbert, Jump," by Eleanor Beeson, for *The Clock.* Producer/Director: Lawrence Schwab, Jr. *Cast:* Oliver Thorndike, Berry Kroeger, Riza Royce, Lola Montez, John O'Hare, Ed Peck, Dulcy Jordan, Clark Gordon, Lorenzo Fuller.

29 July 1950— 7:30 *One Man's Family* debuts as a "new" series. *Cast:* Bert Lytell, Marjorie Gateson, Eva Marie Saint.

30 July 1950— 9:00 "The Tragedy of King Richard the Third," by William Shakespeare, adapted by Ethel Frank, for *Masterpiece Playhouse.* Producer: Albert McCleery. *Cast:* William Windom, Kurt Richards, Hugh Williams, William Post, Jr., Douglas Watson, Grant Gordon, Richard Goode, Nella Richardson.

31 July 1950— 8:00 *Menasha the Magnificent.* 9:00 "The Strange Case of John Kingman," by Murray Leinster, adapted by Ernest Kinoy, for *Lights Out.* Producer: Gordon Duff. Director: Grey Lockwood. *Cast:* Oliver Cliff, John Boruff, Philip Coolidge, Calvin Thomas, Dan Morgan, Frank Darren, Larry Sherman.

1 August 1950— 9:30 "The Big Day," by Dennis Conover, for *Armstrong Circle Theatre.* *Cast:* Jeffery Mcendrick, Louise Labaree, Grace Valentine, Pat Crowley, Sally Moffett, Mimi Strongan, Frank Nellis.

2 August 1950— 8:30 "Googan," by Ben Radin, adapted by Ethel Frank for *Cameo Theatre.* Producer/Director: Albert McCleery. *Cast:* John Harvey, Judy Parrish. 9:00 "January Thaw," by Bellamy Partridge, adapted by William Roos, for *Kraft Television Theatre.* *Cast:* Valerie Cossart, Nelson Olmsted, Vaughn Taylor, Leona Powers, Robert Barr, Barbara Rucik, Susan Harris, Don Murray.

3 August 1950 — 8:00 "Loser Take All," for *Believe It or Not*.
   8:30 *Studs' Place*.
4 August 1950 — 9:30 *The Big Story*.
5 August 1950 — 7:30 *One Man's Family*.
6 August 1950 — 9:00 "The Rivals," by Richard Brinsley Sheridan, for *Masterpiece Playhouse*. Producer: Curtis Canfield. Director: William Corrigan. *Cast:* Mary Boland, Ralph Forbes, Hurd Hatfield, Diana Douglas, Jonathan Harris, Richard Newton, Melba Rae, Pat O'Malley, John Gerstad.
7 August 1950 — 8:00 *Menasha the Magnificent*.
8 August 1950 — 9:30 "Man of Action," by Jerome Rose, for *Armstrong Circle Theatre*. Producer: Hudson Faussett. Director: Hal Keith. *Cast:* Daniel Reed, Alan Bunce, Katherine Anderson, Richard Wigginton, Jonathan Marlowe, Bill Tree, Bill Perrot, Cliff Hall.
9 August 1950 — 8:30 "Triumph of Justice," for *Armstrong Circle Theatre*.
   9:00 "Feathers in a Gale," by Pauline Jamerson and Reginald Lawrence, for *Kraft Television Theatre*.
10 August 1950 — 8:00 "The Ghosty Will," for *Believe It or Not*.
   8:30 *Studs' Place*.
11 August 1950 — 9:30 "The Checked Suit," by Richard McCracken and George Batson, for *The Clock*. *Cast:* Ann Lee Emaline, Leon Tokaytan, Leonard Bell, Dehl Berti, Pat Malone, Jason Johnson.
12 August 1950 — 7:30 *One Man's Family*, by Carlton E. Morse. Producer: Edgar C. Kahn. Director: Richard Clemmer.
13 August 1950 — 9:00 "Six Characters in Search of an Author," by Luigi Pirandello, adapted by Ernest Kinoy, for *Masterpiece Playhouse*. Producer: Caroline Burke. Director: Charles Polacheck. *Cast:* Betty Freed, Joseph Schildkraut, Paula Trumas, Don Appell, Vinton Hayworth.
14 August 1950 — 8:00 *Menasha the Magnificent*.
   9:00 "The Queen Is Dead," by Mildred Arthur, adapted by Eric Arthur, for *Lights Out*. Producer: Herbert Swope, Jr. Director: Grey Lockwood. *Cast:* Mildred Natwick, Una O'Conner, Leora Thatcher, Dorothy Steele, Denise Alexander, Ruth Masters.
15 August 1950 — 9:30 "Ring Around My Finger," by Doris Halman, for *Armstrong Circle Theatre*. *Cast:* Patricia Wheel, John Harvey, Joann Dolan, Lucille Paton, J. C. Dunne, Jeffrey O'Malley.
16 August 1950 — 8:30 "A Point of View," by Ruth Woodman and Turner Bullock, for *Cameo Theatre*. *Cast:* William Post, Jr., Viola Frayne, Tom Walsh, Leon Maricle, John Seymour, Richard Abbott, Larry Robbins, Betty McCabe, Roger Tuttle.
   9:00 "September Tide," by Daphne du Maurier, for *Kraft Television Theatre*. Director: William Harbach.
17 August 1950 — 8:00 "Corpus Delicti," for *Believe It or Not*.
   8:30 *Studs' Place*.
18 August 1950 — 9:30 *The Big Story*.
19 August 1950 — 7:30 *One Man's Family*.
20 August 1950 — 9:00 "The Importance of Being Earnest," by Oscar Wilde, adapted by Hugh Kemp, for *Masterpiece Playhouse*. Producer: Curtis Canfield. Director: William Corrigan. *Cast:* Hurd Hatfield, John Buckmaster, Margaret Phillips, Breck Byron, Bertha Belmore, Hazel James, Dayton Luis, Byron Russell, Huntington Watts.

21 August 1950— 8:00 *Menasha the Magnificent.*

9:00 "The Heart of Jonathan O'Rourke," by A. J. Russell, for *Lights Out.* Producer: Herbert Swope, Jr. Director: Lawrence Schwab, Jr. *Cast:* Peter Capell, Alfreda Wallace, William David, James O'Neill.

22 August 1950— 8:00 *The Uncertain Feeling,* a film for NBC *Cinema Playhouse.*

9:30 "Remember, Remember," for *Armstrong Circle Theatre. Cast:* Don McLeland, Valerie Cossart.

23 August 1950— 8:30 "Saralee and the Children," by Ellen McCracken, adapted by Ethel Frank, for *Cameo Theatre. Cast:* Mildred Natwick, Alexander Campbell, Lee Graham, Sigrid Olsen, Bobby Nick, Stan Martin, Susan Harris, Susan Gray, Stefan Olsen.

9:00 "The First Mrs. Fraser," by St. John Ervine, for *Kraft Television Theatre.* Producer: Maury Holland. Director: William Harbach. *Cast:* Dorothy Peterson, Evan Thomas, Lex Richards, E. G. Marshall, Andrea Wallace, Byron Russell, Reginald Wilson, Dermot McNamara, Hartney Arthur, Eileen Page.

24 August 1950— 8:00 *Believe It or Not.*

8:30 *Studs' Place* is replaced.

25 August 1950— 9:30 "Rumble in Manhattan," by George and Gertrude Fass, for *The Clock.* Producer: Herbert Swope, Jr. Director: Lawrence Schwab, Jr. *Cast:* Vito Christy, Natalie Norwick, Miriel Landers, Dennis Harrison, E. W. Swackhammer, Frank Thomas, Jr., Marion Nobel, Irving Winters.

26 August 1950— 7:30 *One Man's Family.*

27 August 1950— 9:00 "Othello," by William Shakespeare, adapted by Stephen de Baun, for *Masterpiece Playhouse.* Producer: Fred Coe. Director: Delbert Mann. *Cast:* Torin Thatcher, Alfred Ryder, Olive Deering, George Keane, John Seymour, Muriel Hutchinson.

28 August 1950— 8:00 *Menasha the Magnificent.*

9:00 *Lights Out.* Producer: Herbert Swope, Jr. Director: William Corrigan. *Cast:* Ella Raines, George Reeves, Rosalind Ivan, Horace McMahon, Mabel Taylor, Richard Wigginton.

29 August 1950— 8:00 *Cinema Playhouse.*

9:00 "Polly," for a "grand reopening" of *Fireside Theatre. Cast:* Ann Savage, Cora Witherspoon.

9:30 "Blaze of Glory," by Jerome Ross, for *Armstrong Circle Theatre. Cast:* Mary Patton, Judson Pratt, Reed Brown, Jr., Dort Clark, Murray Jordan.

30 August 1950— 8:30 "Ringside Seat," by Jerome Ross, for *Cameo Theatre. Cast:* John Farrell, Dan Matthews, Margaret Hayes, Dan Kennedy, Harold Grau, Denise Norris, Jane Murray, Ted Jacques, David Allen, Frank Dana, Barry Cahill, Bill Coleman, Ronald Cusack, Benny Kane, Terry Green, Edgar Pitkin, Chip Cipella.

9:00 "The Detour," by Owen Davis, for *Kraft Television Theatre.* Producer: Stanley Quinn.

31 August 1950— 8:00 "The Blood Call," for *Believe It or Not.* Producer/Director: Fielder Cook.

10:00 *Martin Kane, Private Eye* (aka *Martin Kane, Private Investigator*) returns. Producer: Edward Sutherland. *Cast:* William Gargan.

1 September 1950— 9:30 *The Big Story.*

2 September 1950— 7:30 *One Man's Family.*

3 September 1950— 7:30 *The Aldrich Family* returns. Producer: R. Papp. *Cast:* Richard Tyler, Nancy Carrol, House Jameson, Jack Kelk.

9:00 "Uncle Vanya," by Anton Chekhov, adapted by Philip Ninis, for *Masterpiece Playhouse*. Producer: Curtis Canfield. Director: Gordon Duff. *Cast:* Walter Abel, Boris Karloff, Eva Gabor, Leora Dana, Eda Heinemann, Isobel Elsom, Tod Andrews.

4 September 1950— 8:00 *Menasha the Magnificent*.

9:00 *Lights Out*. *Cast:* Ed Begley, Tom Drake, Jeanne Shepherd, Ralph Riggs, Leora Thatcher, Wells Richardson, Wyrley Birch, Philip Robinson.

5 September 1950— 8:00 *Cinema Playhouse*.

9:00 "Stopover," by David Boehm, for *Fireside Theatre*. Producer/Director: Frank Wisbar.

9:30 "First Formal," by James Garvin and Bob Duncan, for *Armstrong Circle Theatre*. *Cast:* Ruth Matteson, Victor Jory, Jane Sutherland, Edwin Bruce, Tom Reynolds, Martin Miller.

6 September 1950— 8:30 "The Black Doll," for NBC *Mystery Film* substitutes for *Cameo Theatre*.

9:00 "The Last Trump," for *Kraft Television Theatre*. Producer: Maury Holland.

10:30 "Beauty Is a Joy," a film for *Stars Over Hollywood* debut.

7 September 1950— 8:00 *Believe It or Not*.

10:00 *Martin Kane, Private Eye*.

8 September 1950— 9:30 "Prescription for Death," for *The Clock*. Producer: Herbert Swope, Jr. Director: Grey Lockwood. *Cast:* Leslie Nielsen, Maggi MacNamara, Helen Donaldson, Phil Sterling, Julie Bennett, John Farrell.

9 September 1950— 7:30 *One Man's Family*.

10 September 1950— 7:30 *The Aldrich Family*.

9:00 "High Tor," by Maxwell Anderson, for *Philco Television Playhouse* return. Producer: Fred Coe. Director: Delbert Mann. *Cast:* William Ryder, Felicia Montealegre, Gloria Strook, Edgar Strenli, Maurice Mauson, Vinton Hayworth, Leo Penn, Michael Dreyfuss, Nicholas Saunders, John Randolph, Ben Irvine, Edward Cullen.

11 September 1950— 8:00 *Menasha the Magnificent*.

9:00 "The Dark Corner," by A. J. Russell, for *Lights Out*. *Cast:* Alan Marshall, Cloris Leachman, John Newland, Joe E. Marks, Alan Bunce.

9:30 "The Awful Truth," adapted by Don Ettlinger, for *Robert Montgomery Presents* return. *Cast:* Lee Bowman, Jane Wyatt, Donald Curtis, Eda Heinemann, Maxine Stuart, Helda Haynes, Maurice Burke.

12 September 1950— 9:00 "Leatherheart," with Irene Vernon, Wilton Graff, for *Fireside Theatre*.

9:30 "The Oddest Song," by Philip W. Foster, for *Armstrong Circle Theatre*. *Cast:* Ross Martin, Theo Goetz, Olga Fabian, Gregory Merton.

13 September 1950— 8:30 NBC *Mystery Film*.

9:00 "The Big Doorstep," by Frances Goodrich and Albert Hackett, for *Kraft Television Theatre*. Producer: Maury Holland.

10:30 *Stars Over Hollywood*.

14 September 1950— 8:00 *Believe It or Not* is replaced.

10:00 *Martin Kane, Private Eye*.

15 September 1950— 9:30 *The Big Story*.

16 September 1950— 7:30 *One Man's Family*.

17 September 1950— 7:30 *The Aldrich Family*.

9:00 "The Long Run," by Jerry Weidman, adapted by William Kendall Clarke,

Philco Television Playhouse. Producer: Fred Coe. Director: Gordon Duff. *Cast:* Vicki Cummings, Francis Lederer, Augusta Dabney, Maurice Burke, Francis Compton, Margaret Barker.

18 September 1950 — 8:00 *Menasha the Magnificent* is replaced.

9:00 "The Leopard Lady," by Dorothy L. Sayers, adapted by James Lee, for *Lights Out.* Producer: Herbert Swope, Jr. Director: William Corrigan. *Cast:* Boris Karloff, Jo Huntley Wright, Ronald Long, Sid Cassel, Martin Brandt, Byron Russell, Al Thaler, Laurie Douglas, Bobby Nick, A. J. Herbert, Doug Gregory, Helen Falvey.

9:30 NBC *Cinema Playhouse.*

19 September 1950 — 9:00 "Incident in the Rain," with Irene Vernon, for *Fireside Theatre.*

9:30 "That Other Woman," by Dennis Conover, for *Armstrong Circle Theatre.* *Cast:* Louise Allbritton, Glenn Langan, Beverly Whitney, Amanda Randolph.

20 September 1950 — 8:30 "The Paper Sack," by Norman Zeno, adapted by Ethel Frank, for *Cameo Theatre.* Producer: Albert McCleery. *Cast:* Dennis Harrison, Pat Malone, John Marley, Pat O'Malley, James Little, John Gerstad, Tom Heaphy, Robert Bolger, Harry Kingston, John Harvey.

9:00 "The Last Stop," by Irving Kaye Davis, for *Kraft Television Theatre.* *Cast:* Mildred Dunnock, Isabel Price, Vaughn Taylor, Josephine Brown, Eda Heinemann, Enid Markey, Neil Harrison, Grania O'Malley, David Orrick, Barbara Townsend.

10:30 *Stars Over Hollywood.*

21 September 1950 — 8:00 "The Dead Will Speak," for *Believe It or Not.*

10:00 *Martin Kane, Private Eye.*

22 September 1950 — 9:30 "The Morning After," by Eugene Paul, for *The Clock.* Producer: Herbert Swope, Jr. Director: Grey Lockwood. *Cast:* Raymond Massey, Mady Christians, Donald Foster, Helen Falvey.

23 September 1950 — 7:30 *One Man's Family.*

24 September 1950 — 7:30 *The Aldrich Family.*

9:00 "Dear Guest and Ghost," by Sylvia Dee, adapted by Alexander Kirkland, for *Philco Television Playhouse.* Producer: Fred Coe.

25 September 1950 — 9:00 "Sisters of Shadow," by George Batson and Richard McCracken, for *Lights Out.* Producer: Herbert Swope, Jr. Director: William Corrigan. *Cast:* William Eythe, Priscilla Towers, Elinor Randel, Francois Grimard, Stan Ross, Jason Johnson.

9:30 "The Big Sleep," by Raymond Chandler, adapted by Richard Morrison, for *Robert Montgomery Presents.* *Cast:* Robert Montgomery, Zachary Scott.

26 September 1950 — 9:00 "Andy's Old Man," for *Fireside Theatre.*

9:30 "The Elopement," by Harold Jaediker Taub, for *Armstrong Circle Theatre.* *Cast:* Robert Allen, Betty Caulfield, Biff McGuire, Patricia Hamick, John Haffen.

27 September 1950 — 8:30 "Murder Is a Matter of Opinion," by Jules Archer, for *Cameo Theatre.* Freddie Bartholomew, William Windom, Jane Sutherland, Harry Kingston, J. W. Austin, Don Briggs, William Kent, Harold Grau, Pat Breslin, Winfield Hoeny, Tom Reynolds, Henry Bernard, Irene Lund, Patsie de Sousa, John Heisler, Barry Cahill, Carol Windom, Jane Murray.

9:00 "The Green Pack," by Edgar Wallace, for *Kraft Television Theatre.* *Cast:* James Daly, Mercer McLeod, Diana Douglas, Phil Houston, Paul Kirk, Dayton Lummis, Eleanor Wilson, William Kee, Dorothy Graham.

10:30 *Stars Over Hollywood*.
28 September 1950— 8:00 "Homicide," for *Believe It or Not*.
10:00 *Martin Kane, Private Eye*.
29 September 1950— 9:30 *The Big Story*.
30 September 1950— 7:30 *One Man's Family*.
1 October 1950— 7:30 *The Aldrich Family*.
9:00 "The Touch of a Stranger," by Whitfield Cook, adapted by Joseph Liss, for *Philco Television Playhouse*. Producer: Fred Coe. Director: Delbert Mann. *Cast:* Leslie Nielsen, Ally Lewis, John Boruff, Gloria Strook, Philip Foster, Bert Conway, Richard Morningstar, Charles Mendick, Alan Shayne, Olive Deering, E. G. Marshall, Jack Warden, Doris Rich, Melba Rae, Bill Gibberson, Leo Penn, Will Hare, James Rafferty.
2 October 1950— 9:00 "The Posthumous Dead," by Richard Seff and Harvey Pack, for *Lights Out*. Producer: Herbert Swope, Jr. Director: William Corrigan. *Cast:* Ed Begley, Biff Elliott, Arthur Hanson, Ken Renard, Blair Davies, Leonard Sherer, Roland Hague.
3 October 1950— 9:00 "International Incident," for *Fireside Theatre*.
9:30 "The Roundup," by Ruth Woodman, for *Armstrong Circle Theatre*. Producer: Hudson Faussett. Director: Hal Keith. *Cast:* Zachary Scott, Klock Ryder, Jeanne Shepherd, James Maloney, William Free, Dudley Sadler, J. Y. Yen.
4 October 1950— 8:00 *Four Star Revue* replaces *Cameo Theatre*.
9:00 "I Like It Here," by A. B. Shiffrin, for *Kraft Television Theatre*. *Cast:* Anne Francis.
10:30 "Some Small Nobility," for *Stars Over Hollywood*.
5 October 1950— 8:00 *Believe It or Not* is replaced.
10:00 *Martin Kane, Private Eye*.
6 October 1950— 9:30 "The Joke," by Ben Radin, for *The Clock*. Producer: Herbert Swope, Jr. Director: Grey Lockwood. *Cast:* James Daly, Harold McGee, Ian Keith, Diana Douglas, George Englund, Helen Kingstead, John Gerstad.
7 October 1950— 7:30 *One Man's Family*.
8 October 1950— 7:30 *The Aldrich Family*.
9:00 "The Vine That Grew on 50th Street," by Charles Robbins, adapted by Nelson Olmsted, for *Philco Television Playhouse*. Director: Gordon Duff. *Cast:* William Farnum, Nelson Olmsted, Bethel Leslie, Florida Friebus, Frank Maxwell, Arthur Malone, Peggy Finch, Henry Jones, Dorothy Sands.
9 October 1950— 9:00 "Just What Happened," by Gelett Burges, adapted by R. N. Brant, for *Lights Out*. *Cast:* John Howard, Richard Purdy, Rita Lynn, Lilia Heston, Allen Stevenson.
9:30 "Arrowsmith," by Sinclair Lewis, for *Robert Montgomery Presents*. Producer: Robert Montgomery. Director: Norman Felton. *Cast:* Van Heflin, June Dayton, Bruno Wick, Robert Chisholm, Edward Cullen, Humphrey Davis, Anthony Kemble Cooper, Klock Ryder.
10 October 1950— 9:00 "Lucy and the Stranger," an original comedy, for *Fireside Theatre*. Producer/Director: Edward Stevens. *Cast:* Margaret Lambert.
9:30 "Give and Take," by Lawrence and Virginia Dugan, for *Armstrong Circle Theatre*. Producer: Hudson Faussett. Director: Hal Keith. *Cast:* Frank Albertson, Richard S. Bishop, Harriet E. MacGibbon, Joanna Douglas, Peggy Wagner, Arthur Storch, Seth Arnold, Martin Ruby, Nelson Case, Kay Campbell.
11 October 1950— 9:00 "The Great Broxopp," by A. A. Milne, for *Kraft Television*

Theatre. Producer: Stanley Quinn. Director: Dick Dunlap. *Cast:* Rex O'Malley, Philip Tonge, Irene Sutherland, Michael Dreyfuss, Edith Brock, Chester Stratton.

10:30 "Rock Against the Sea," for *Stars Over Hollywood.*

12 October 1950—10:00 *Martin Kane, Private Eye.*

13 October 1950— 9:30 *The Big Story.*

14 October 1950— 7:30 *One Man's Family.*

15 October 1950— 7:30 *The Aldrich Family.*

9:00 "A Husband for Mama," by Louis Paul, for *Philco Television Playhouse.* Producer: Fred Coe. Director: Delbert Mann. *Cast:* Muriel Kirkland, Betty Caulfield, Vinton Hayworth, Conrad Janis, Laura Weber, Biff McGuire, Billy M. Greene, Tom Reynolds, Peggy Bruskin.

16 October 1950— 9:00 "The Thing Upstairs," by James Lee and Thomas W. Phipps, for *Lights Out.* Producer: Herbert Swope, Jr. Director: William Corrigan. *Cast:* Florence Reed, Fred Bartholomew, Peggy Nelson, Dayton Lummis, Robert Ober.

17 October 1950— 9:00 "Hope Chest," by Frieda Innescourt and Mary Sinclair, for *Fireside Theatre.*

9:30 "The Penalty," by William Welch, for *Armstrong Circle Theatre. Cast:* Donald Woods, Mary Alice Moore, John Conway, Reginald Mason, Russ Brown, Charles Mendick, Henry Silva.

18 October 1950— 9:00 "Old Lady Robbins," by Albert G. Miller, for *Kraft Television Theatre.* Producer: Maury Holland. *Cast:* Enid Markey, Augusta Dabney.

10:30 "Texas Parson," for *Stars Over Hollywood.*

19 October 1950—10:00 *Martin Kane, Private Eye.*

20 October 1950— 9:30 "Vengeance," by Honore de Balzac, adapted by Milton Subotsky and Phyllis Coe, for *The Clock.* Producer: Herbert Swope, Jr. Director: Grey Lockwood. *Cast:* Torin Thatcher, Grace Kelly, Lotte Stavisky, Earl Gilbert, Richard Dana, Philip Robinson, Rick Shanklin, Marion Leeds, W. A. Coleman.

21 October 1950— 7:30 *One Man's Family.*

22 October 1950— 9:00 "Portrait in Smoke," by Bill Ballinger, adapted by Mary Orr and Reginald Denham, for *Philco Television Playhouse.* Producer: Fred Coe. Director: Gordon Duff. *Cast:* Shepperd Strudwick, Olive Deering, Lawrence Fletcher, Daniel Red, Herbert Rudley, Vaughn Taylor, James Daly.

23 October 1950— 9:00 "The Skeptics," by Elizabeth Evans and Paul Ellwood, for *Lights Out.* Producer: Herbert Swope, Jr. Director: Lawrence Schwab, Jr. *Cast:* Leo G. Carroll, Faith Brook, Frank Daly, Bruno Wick, Richard Fraser, Ernestine McClenden, Bartle Doyle, Isabella Hoopes, Eunice Anderson.

9:30 "The Petrified Forest," by Robert E. Sherwood, adapted by Adrian Spies, for *Robert Montgomery Presents.* Producer: Robert Montgomery. Director: Norman Felton. *Cast:* Robert Montgomery, Joan Lorring, Herbert Rudley, Glenn Denning, Ralph Riggs, Morton Stevens, Slim Thompson, Kitty Kelly, Jack Bittner, Jack Vaughan, Jason Johnson.

24 October 1950— 9:00 "Amber Gods," for *Fireside Theatre. Cast:* Mary Sinclair.

9:30 "Time of Their Lives," by Ruth Woodman, for *Armstrong Circle Theatre.* Producer: Hudson Faussett. Director: Hal Keith. *Cast:* Frank Thomas, Marian Randolph, Mary Finney, Joyce Van Patten, Tom King, Chris Gaye.

25 October 1950— 9:00 "Truant in Park Lane," by James Parish, for *Kraft Television Theatre.* Producer: Stanley Quinn. *Cast:* Blanche Yurka, Dan Morgan.

10:30 "Showdown," for *Stars Over Hollywood.*

26 October 1950—10:00 *Martin Kane, Private Eye.*
27 October 1950— 9:30 *The Big Story,* from *The Denver Post.*
28 October 1950— 7:30 *One Man's Family.*
29 October 1950— 7:30 *The Aldrich Family.*
　9:00 "The Gambler," by Fyodor Dostoevsky, adapted by Joseph Liss, for *Philco Television Playhouse.* Producer: Fred Coe. Director: Delbert Mann. *Cast:* Ethel Griffies, Alfred Ryder, Philip Coolidge, Anne Crawford, Maurice Burke, Sam Alexander.
30 October 1950— 9:00 "The Martian Eyes," by Henry Kuttner, adapted by George Lefferts, for *Lights Out.* Producer: Herbert Swope, Jr. Director: Lawrence Schwab, Jr. *Cast:* Burgess Meredith, David Lewis, Gavin Gordon, Pat O'Malley, Bill Hellenger.
31 October 1950— 9:00 "Mother's Mutiny," for *Fireside Theatre.*
　9:30 "Man and Wife," by Doris Halman, for *Armstrong Circle Theatre.* Producer: Hudson Faussett. Director: Garry Simpson. *Cast:* Paul McGrath, Augusta Roeland, Tonio Selwart, Cara Williams, Tony Bickley, Jeraldine Dworak, Jean Arden Cobb, Virginia Smith.
1 November 1950— 9:00 "Dolphin's Reach," by R. H. Benson, for *Kraft Television Theatre. Cast:* Mercer McLeod, Carmen Mathews, Enid Pulver, Stefan Schnabel.
　10:30 "A Model Young Lady," for *Stars Over Hollywood.*
2 November 1950—10:00 *Martin Kane, Private Eye.*
3 November 1950— 9:30 "The Brief Case," for *The Clock.* Producer: George Wolfe. Director: Grey Lockwood. *Cast:* Somer Alberg, Bruno Wick, Martin Green, Dennis Harrison, Jim McMahon, Milton Herman, Jane Compton, Harold Grau, Metro Wells, Heywood Hale Braun, Kirk Brown, Lucille Rogers.
4 November 1950— 7:30 *One Man's Family.*
5 November 1950— 7:30 *The Aldrich Family.*
　9:00 "The Power Devil," by Eustace Cockrell and Herbert Dolmas, adapted by William Kendall Clarke, for *Philco Television Playhouse.* Producer: Fred Coe. Director: Gordon Duff. *Cast:* Kevin McCarthy, Augusta Dabney, Walter Brooke, John Seymour, Carroll Ashburn, Roland Wood, Wallace Rooney, Adelaide Bean.
6 November 1950— 8:30 "The Half-Pint Flask," by Dubose Heyward, adapted by Milton Subotsky and Phyllis Coe, for *Lights Out.* Producer: Herbert Swope, Jr. Director: Lawrence Schwab, Jr. *Cast:* John Carradine, Kent Smith, Douglass Parkhirst, Orville Philips, Sandy Saunders.
　9:30 "The Seventh Veil," adapted by Sarett and Herbert Rudley, for *Robert Montgomery Presents.* Director: Norman Felton. *Cast:* Robert Montgomery, Elliot Reid, Elizabeth Eustis, Lili Valenty, Nina Hanson, Walter Palm, Dennis Hoey, Leueen MacGrath.
7 November 1950— 9:00 "Judas," for *Fireside Theatre. Cast:* Ann Savage, Gertrude Michael, George Wallace.
　9:30 "Person to Person," by Leonard T. Holton and James Garvin. Producer: Hudson Faussett. Director: Hal Keith. *Cast:* Laurence Hugo, Gloria Strook, Dorothy Francis, Earl Dawson, George Jason, Bartle Doyle.
8 November 1950— 9:00 "Sixteen," by Aimee and Philip Stuart, for *Kraft Television Theatre.* Producer: Stanley Quinn. *Cast:* Anna Lee, Patricia Crowley, Donald Curtis.
　10:30 "Midnight," for *Stars Over Hollywood. Cast:* Herb Patterson, Gloria Sanders.

9 November 1950—10:00 *Martin Kane, Private Eye.*

10 November 1950— 9:30 *The Big Story.*

11 November 1950— 7:30 *One Man's Family.*

12 November 1950— 7:30 *The Aldrich Family.*

9:00 "The Men Who Got Away with It," by Bernice Carey, adapted by Alexander Kirkland, for *Philco Television Playhouse.* Producer: Fred Coe. Director: Delbert Mann. *Cast:* Francis L. Sullivan, Donald Woods, Barbara Robbins, Margaret Hayes, Richard Sanders, Bernard Nedell, Carol Lee, Fred Beir, Norman W. Bernhardt, Wells Richardson, Frank Sanderford, Charles Bang.

13 November 1950— 9:00 "The Waxwork," by A. M. Burrage, adapted by Nelson Olmsted, for *Lights Out. Cast:* John Beal, Mark Stone, Tom Reynolds, Harry Hugenot, Roy Irving, Edwin Taylor, Nelson Olmsted.

14 November 1950— 9:00 "Party Line," for *Fireside Theatre. Cast:* Ginny Jackson, Gertrude Michael, Walter Grail, Don Beddoe.

9:30 "The Best Trip Ever," by Frederic Manley, for *Armstrong Circle Theatre. Cast:* Elizabeth Patterson, Enid Markey, Alexander Campbell, John O'Hare, Stanley Nelson.

15 November 1950— 9:00 "The Romantic Age," by A. A. Milne, for *Kraft Television Theatre. Cast:* Bethel Leslie, Dean Harens.

10:30 "This Little Pig Cried," for *Stars Over Hollywood. Cast:* Frances Rafferty, Robert Rockwell.

16 November 1950—10:00 *Martin Kane, Private Eye.*

17 November 1950— 9:30 "The Ninth Life," by Sidney E. Porcelain and Donald Wood Gibson, for *The Clock.* Producer: Herbert Swope, Jr. Director: Grey Lockwood. *Cast:* Ian Keith, John Newland, Margaret Hayes, Andrew Duggan, John Gerstad.

18 November 1950— 7:30 *One Man's Family.*

19 November 1950— 7:30 *The Aldrich Family.*

9:00 "I Am Still Alive," by Edward Hope, adapted by David Shaw, for *Philco Television Playhouse.* Producer: Fred Coe. Director: Gordon Duff. *Cast:* Haila Stoddard, Howard Smith, Walter Brooke, Mary Welch, Joshua Shelley, Les Tremayne, Lenny Brenan, Raymond Bramley, John Conner.

20 November 1950— 9:00 "Dr. Heidegger's Experiment," by Nathaniel Hawthorne, for *Lights Out.* Producer: Herbert Swope, Jr. Director: Lawrence Schwab, Jr. *Cast:* Billie Burke, Gene Lockhart, Halliwell Hobbes, Tom Poston, Claire Kirby, Jack Ewing.

9:30 "The Canterville Ghost," by Oscar Wilde, for *Robert Montgomery Presents. Cast:* Robert Montgomery, Margaret O'Brien, Cecil Parker, Maurice Manson, Valerie Cossart, Allison Prescott, Lex Richards, Byron Russell, Phoebe MacKay, Basil Howes, George Kluge.

21 November 1950— 9:00 "The Love of Mike," for *Fireside Theatre. Cast:* Irene Vernon, Anthony Caruso.

9:30 "The Perfect Type," by J. Carver Olds, for *Armstrong Circle Theatre.* Producer: Hudson Faussett. *Cast:* Richard Derr, Augusta Dabney, Romney Brent, Ruth Ford, Barbara White.

22 November 1950— 9:00 "The Romantic Young Lady," by G. Martin Sierra, for *Kraft Television Theatre. Cast:* Betty Caulfield, Ethel Griffies, E. G. Marshall.

10:30 "Winter Love," for *Stars Over Hollywood. Cast:* Ellen Corby, Art Smith.

23 November 1950—10:00 *Martin Kane, Private Eye.*

24 November 1950— 9:30 *The Big Story*.

25 November 1950— 7:30 *One Man's Family*.

26 November 1950— 7:30 *The Aldrich Family*.

9:00 "Torch for a Dark Journey," by Lionel Shapiro, adapted by Max Wilk, for *Philco Television Playhouse*. Producer: Fred Coe. Director: Delbert Mann. *Cast:* Richard Webb, Felicia Montealegre, Edgar Stehli, Bramwell Fletcher, Loring Smith, Robert H. Harris, Louis Sorin.

27 November 1950— 9:00 "The Mule Man," by George Lefferts, for *Lights Out*. Producer: Herbert Swope, Jr. Director: Lawrence Schwab, Jr. *Cast:* Charles Korvin, Peter Capell, Leon Askin, Melba Rae, James O'Neil, Remo Pisani, Sye Lamont, Henry Silva.

28 November 1950— 9:00 "Three Strangers," for *Fireside Theatre*. *Cast:* John Call, Myron Healey, George Calhoun, Kay Lee, George Clancy.

9:30 "Anything but Love," for *Armstrong Circle Theatre*. Producer: Hudson Faussett. Director: Garry Simpson. *Cast:* Julie Haydon, Karl Malden, Jean Castro, Charles Mendick, William Free, Maurice Burke, Edward Bushman, Sandy Sanders.

29 November 1950— 9:00 "Windows," by John Galsworthy, for *Kraft Television Theatre*. Producer: Maury Holland. *Cast:* Valerie Cossart, Lex Richards, Mercer McLeod, Joyce Sullivan.

10:30 "Landing at Daybreak," for *Stars Over Hollywood*. *Cast:* Anita Louise, Marsha Van Dyke, Ray Montgomery.

30 November 1950—10:00 *Martin Kane, Private Eye*.

1 December 1950— 9:30 "The Old Woman," by Ira Levin, for *The Clock*. Producer: Herbert Swope, Jr. Director: Grey Lockwood. *Cast:* Ethel Griffies, Olive Deering, Moultrie Patten, John Seymour.

2 December 1950— 7:30 *One Man's Family*.

3 December 1950— 7:30 *The Aldrich Family*.

9:00 "Wacky, the Small Boy," by Fred Schwed, Jr., adapted by William Kendall Clarke, for *Philco Television Playhouse*. Producer: Fred Coe. Director: Gordon Duff. *Cast:* Bill Goodwin, Flora Campbell, Aline MacMahon, Butch Cavell, Billy Nevard, Sonny Cavell, Joey Walsh, John Kenny, Adelaide Bean.

4 December 1950— 9:00 "Beware This Woman," by Grace Amundson, adapted by Douglas Wood Gibson, for *Lights Out*. Producer: Herbert Swope, Jr. Director: Lawrence Schwab, Jr. *Cast:* Veronica Lake, Glenn Denning, Daniel Reed, Paul Andor, Phoebe McKay, Beth Elliott.

9:30 "The Philadelphia Story," by Philip Barry, adapted by Don Ettlinger, for *Robert Montgomery Presents*. Producer: Montgomery. Director: Norman Felton. *Cast:* Robert Montgomery, Barbara Bel Geddes, Richard Derr, Judy Parrish, Leslie Nielsen, James Van Dyke, Madeleine Clive, Louis Holister, John Craven, Richard Abbott, Peggy Nelson, Riza Royce, Edward Lindemann.

5 December 1950— 9:00 "The Green Convertible," for *Fireside Theatre*. *Cast:* Frances Dee, Gertrude Michael, John Warburton, Joan Miller, Dabbs Greer.

9:30 "Happy Ending," for *Armstrong Circle Theatre*. Producer: Hudson Faussett. Director: Hal Keith. *Cast:* Otto Kruger, Cathleen Cordell, Mark Roberts, Janet Fox, Brandon Peters, Barbara Cook, Helen Gillette, Stuart Nedd.

6 December 1950— 9:00 "Short Story," by Robert Morley, for *Kraft Television Theatre*. Director: Stanley Quinn. *Cast:* Bramwell Fletcher, Viola Keats, Jane Sutherland.

10:30 "Small Town Story," by Ross Ford, for *Stars Over Hollywood*. *Cast:* Alan Mowbray.

7 December 1950—10:00 *Martin Kane, Private Eye*.

8 December 1950—9:30 *The Big Story*.

9 December 1950—7:30 *One Man's Family*.

10 December 1950—7:30 *The Aldrich Family*.

9:00 "Bonanza," by Ben Martin, adapted by Stephen de Baun. Producer: Fred Coe. Director: Delbert Mann. *Cast:* Stanley Ridges, Alfreda Wallace, William Kemp, Dan Morgan, Johnny Stewart, Anne Ives, Frank Tweddell, Doug Rutherford.

11 December 1950—9:00 "Masque," by Hal Hackady, for *Lights Out*. *Cast:* Estelle Winwood, Gar Moore, Mary Stuart, Lynn Salisbury.

12 December 1950—9:00 "The Case of Marina Goodwin," for *Fireside Theatre*. *Cast:* Mary Sinclair, Edgar Barrier, Wilton Graff.

9:30 "Green Eyes," for *Armstrong Circle Theatre*. Producer: Hudson Faussett. Director: Garry Simpson. *Cast:* Judith Evelyn, Tom Helmore, Joyce Mathews, Wyrley Birch, Lili Valenty.

13 December 1950—9:00 "Michael and Mary," by A. A. Milne, for *Kraft Television Theatre*. Producer: Maury Holland. *Cast:* Felicia Montealegre, John Newland, Anne Francis, Peter Fernandez, Harry Townes, Mark Stone.

10:30 "My Rival Is a Fiddle," for *Stars Over Hollywood*. *Cast:* Hans Conreid, Maria Palmer.

14 December 1950—10:00 *Martin Kane, Private Eye*.

15 December 1950—9:30 "The Last Tomorrow," by A. J. Russell, for *The Clock*. Producer: Herbert Swope, Jr. Director: Grey Lockwood. *Cast:* Cloris Leachman, Richard Kiley, Nelson Olmsted, Frank M. Thomas, Sr., Mary Corbett.

16 December 1950—7:30 *One Man's Family*.

17 December 1950—7:30 *The Aldrich Family*.

9:00 "Decoy" (aka "A Nice Clean Job"), by William Fay, adapted by Abram S. Ginnes, for *Philco Television Playhouse*. Producer: Fred Coe. Director: Gordon Duff. *Cast:* John McQuade, Harold Vermilyea, William Lee, Dulcy Jordan, Lou Polan, Harry Landers, James Daly, Heywood Hale Broun, Helen Donaldson, Ronald Smyth.

18 December 1950—9:00 "The Men on the Mountain," by Harry Muheim, for *Lights Out*. Producer: Herbert Swope, Jr. Director: Lawrence Schwab, Jr. *Cast:* Lee Tracy, Stewart Brock, Biff Elliott, Verne Collett, William Free.

9:30 "Mrs. Mike," by Benedict and Nancy Freedman, adapted by Thomas W. Phipps, for *Robert Montgomery Presents*. Producer: Robert Montgomery. Director: Norman Felton. *Cast:* Barbara Britton, Glen Langan, Bill Martel, Joseph McInerney, Margarita Warwick, Ann Dere, Jimsey Sommers.

19 December 1950—9:00 "Miggles," for *Fireside Theatre*. *Cast:* Mary Sinclair, Hugh O'Brian, Grant Calhoun.

9:30 "The Diet," adapted by Don Ettlinger, for *Armstrong Circle Theatre*. Director: Garry Simpson. *Cast:* Lois Wilson, Lawrence Fletcher, Belle Flower.

20 December 1950—9:00 "Village Green," by Carl Allensworth, for *Kraft Television Theatre*. Director: Stanley Quinn. *Cast:* Raymond Van Sickle, Leona Powers, Donald McKee, Wendy Drew, Glenn Denning, Ronald Woods, Brandon Peters, Alan MacAteer, Nancy Pollack, Robert Lieb.

21 December 1950—10:00 *Martin Kane, Private Eye*.

22 December 1950—9:30 *The Big Story.*
23 December 1950—7:30 *One Man's Family.*
24 December 1950—7:30 *The Aldrich Family.*
   9:00 "The Pupil," by Henry James, adapted by Stephen de Baun. Producer: Fred Coe. Director: Delbert Mann. *Cast:* John Newland, Judson Rees, Viola Roache, Neil Fitzgerald.
25 December 1950—9:00 "Jaspar," by Edward Maybly, for *Lights Out. Cast:* Johnny Johnston, Janis Carter, Meg Mundy, Howard Freman.
26 December 1950—9:00 "No Children, No Dogs," for *Fireside Theatre. Cast:* Irene Vernon, Warren Douglas.
   9:30 "Christopher Beach," by Leslie Scott, for *Armstrong Circle Theatre.* Producer: Hudson Faussett. Director: Harvey Marlowe. *Cast:* Barbara Britton, Nydia Westman, Tyler Carpenter, Nancy Pollock.
27 December 1950—9:00 "Rip Van Winkle," by Washington Irving, for *Kraft Television Theatre.* Director: Maury Holland. *Cast:* E. G. Marshall.
   10:30 "Never Trust a Redhead," for *Stars Over Hollywood. Cast:* Herb Patterson, Sandra Dorn.
28 December 1950—10:00 *Martin Kane, Private Eye.*
29 December 1950—9:30 "The New Year Caper," by A. J. Russell, for *The Clock.* Producer: Herbert Swope, Jr. Director: Grey Lockwood. *Cast:* John Van Dreelen, Patricia Wheel, Frank Stevens.
30 December 1950—7:30 *One Man's Family.*
31 December 1950—7:30 *The Aldrich Family.*
   9:00 "Leaf Out of a Book," by Margaret Cousins, adapted by Stephen de Baun, for *Philco Television Playhouse.* Producer: Fred Coe. Director: Gordon Duff. *Cast:* Vicki Cummings, Grace Kelly, Lauren Gilbert, Dorothy Elder, Claudia Morgan, Gordon Peters, Maxine Stuart.

1951

1 January 1951—9:00 "The Haunted Skyscraper," an original drama by Ferrin Fraser, for *Lights Out.* Producer: Herbert Swope, Jr. Director: Lawrence Schwab, Jr. *Cast:* Felicia Montealegre, Virginia Gilmore, Don Dickinson, Ralph Sumpter, Frank Marth, Sandra Ann Wigginton, Richard Wigginton.
   9:30 "Kiss and Tell," by F. Hugh Herbert, adapted by Irving Gaynor Neiman, for *Robert Montgomery Presents.* Producer: Robert Montgomery. Director: Norman Felton. *Cast:* Robert Montgomery, Betty Caulfield, Walter Abel, Anne Seymour, William Windom, Charles Mullen, Herbie Walsh, Ann Sorg, Grace Keddy, Walter Kavun, Joseph Boland, Tom Reynolds, Charlotte Knight.
2 January 1951—9:00 "Flight Thirteen," for *Fireside Theatre. Cast:* Walter Coy, Patricia Dane, Dorothy Bruce.
   9:30 "That Man Is Mine," for *Armstrong Circle Theatre.* Producer: Hudson Faussett. Director: Garry Simpson. *Cast:* Margaret Lindsay, Philip Reed, Kathleen McLean, Betty Wragge, Regina Jourin, Denise Alexander.
3 January 1951—9:00 "Paper Moon," by Peggy Phillips, for *Kraft Television Theatre.* Producer: Stanley Quinn. Director: Dick Dunlap. *Cast:* Francis Robinson, Richard Kiley, Amy Douglas, Loretta Deye, Nelson Olmsted, Fred Beir, Beulah Bryant.
   10:30 "My Nephew Norell," for *Stars Over Hollywood. Cast:* Harold Peary.

4 January 1951 — 10:00 *Martin Kane, Private Eye.*

5 January 1951 — 9:30 *The Big Story.*

6 January 1951 — 7:30 *One Man's Family.*

7 January 1951 — 7:30 *The Aldrich Family.*

9:00 "The Symbol" (Jefferson Davis), adapted by William Kendall Clarke, for *Philco Television Playhouse.* Producer: Fred Coe. Director: Delbert Mann. *Cast:* John Baragrey, Leslie Woods, Ellen Cobb Hill, E. G. Marshall, John D. Seymour, Van Prince, Victor Sutherland, Scott Moore, Harold McGee, Norma Jane Marlowe, Jonathan Marlowe.

8 January 1951 — 9:00 "The Bird of Time," by A. J. Russell, for *Lights Out. Cast:* Jessica Tandy, David Lewis, Julie Bennett.

9 January 1951 — 9:00 "Neutral Corner," for *Fireside Theatre. Cast:* George Wallace, Peter Brocco, Anthony Caruso.

9:30 "Rooftop," by Eli Cantor and Leslie Scott, for *Armstrong Circle Theatre.* Producer: Hudson Faussett. Director: Harvey Marlowe. *Cast:* Ann Shoemaker, Jean Pearson, Biff McGuire, Liam Sullivan, Frank Tweddell.

10 January 1951 — 9:00 "Kelly," by Eric Hatch, for *Kraft Television Theatre.* Producer: Maury Holland. Director: Dick Dunlap. *Cast:* Olive Deering, Mark Roberts, E. G. Marshall.

10:30 "The Ace of Spades," for *Stars Over Hollywood. Cast:* Leon Ames.

11 January 1951 — 10:00 *Martin Kane: Private Eye.*

12 January 1951 — 9:30 "A Dream for Susan," by Thomas W. Phipps and Robert Shackleton, for *The Clock.* Producer: Herbert Swope, Jr. Director: Grey Lockwood. *Cast:* Arlene Francis, Laura Weber, Michael Harvey, Regina Jarvis, Ben Lackland, Phil Sterling.

14 January 1951 — 7:30 *The Aldrich Family.*

9:00 "The Lost Diplomat," by Oscar Schisgall, adapted by Mary Orr and Reginald Denham, for *Philco Television Playhouse.* Producer: Fred Coe. Director: Gordon Duff. *Cast:* Scott McKay, Frances Reid, Donald Foster, Arny Freeman, Roger Dekoven, Mary Alice Moore, Maxine Stuart, Bruce Gordon.

15 January 1951 — 9:00 "The Bottle Imp," by Robert Louis Stevenson, adapted by Richard E. Davis, for *Lights Out. Cast:* Eugene Ruyman, Glenn Langan, Donald Buka, Joan Chandler, Naomi Ray, Francis Bethencourt, Ravol de Lyon, Norman Rose.

9:30 "Victoria Regina," by Laurence Housman, adapted by Thomas W. Phipps, for *Robert Montgomery Presents. Cast:* Helen Hayes, Kent Smith, Robert Harris, Alexander Clark, Olga Fabian.

16 January 1951 — 9:00 "Crime in the Night," for *Fireside Theatre. Cast:* Malcolm Keane, Lester Matthews.

9:30 "The Younger Generation," by William Noble, for *Armstrong Circle Theatre.* Producer: Hudson Faussett. Director: Garry Simpson. *Cast:* Loring Smith, Geraldine Wall, Pat Gaye, Jackie Diamond, Roger Sullivan.

17 January 1951 — 9:00 "The Best Years," by Raymond Van Sickle, for *Kraft Television Theatre.* Producer: Stanley Quinn. Director: Dick Dunlap. *Cast:* Augusta Dabney, Dorothy Sands, Leslie Nielsen, Sylvia Davis, Bonnie Baken, Raymond Van Sickle, John D. Seymour.

10:30 "Yang Yin and Mrs. Wiswell," for *Stars Over Hollywood. Cast:* Adele Jergens, Helen Parrish.

18 January 1951 — 10:00 *Martin Kane, Private Eye.*

19 January 1951— 9:30 *The Big Story.*

20 January 1951— 7:30 *One Man's Family.*

21 January 1951— 7:30 *The Aldrich Family.*

9:00 "Confession," by Gertrude Schweitzer, adapted by David Shaw, for *Philco Television Playhouse.* Producer: Fred Coe. Director: Delbert Mann. *Cast:* John Ireland, Neva Patterson, John Sylvester, Nelson Olmsted, Anne Ives, Robert Simon, James Van Dyk, Ken Rockefeller, Thomas Heaphy, Douglas MacLean, Hollis Mitchell.

22 January 1951— 9:00 "For Release Today," for *Lights Out. Cast:* K. T. Stevens, Herbert Rudley, Vinton Hayworth, Guy Sorel, Romola Robb, William Turner, Shirley Grayson.

23 January 1951— 9:00 "Looking Through," for *Fireside Theatre. Cast:* Irene Vernon, Edgar Barrier.

9:30 "Silver Service," for *Armstrong Circle Theatre.* Producer: Hudson Faussett. Director: Charles Harrell. *Cast:* Geraldine Brooks, John Archer, Alan Manson, Dorothy Eaton.

24 January 1951— 9:00 "Spring Green," by Florence Ryerson and Colin Clements, for *Kraft Television Theatre. Cast:* Herbert Nelson, Flora Conrad, Janis Campbell, Helene Seamon.

10:30 "Moon on Wires," for *Stars Over Hollywood. Cast:* Dorothy Patrick.

25 January 1951— 10:00 *Martin Kane, Private Eye.*

26 January 1951— 9:30 "Whenever I'm Alone," by Joseph Anthony, for *The Clock.* Producer: Herbert Swope, Jr. Director: Grey Lockwood. *Cast:* Charles Korvin, Louisa Horton, Henry Hart.

27 January 1951— 7:30 *One Man's Family.*

28 January 1951— 7:30 *The Aldrich Family.*

9:00 "The Great Escape," by Lt. Paul Brickall, adapted by Joseph Liss, for *Philco Television Playhouse.* Producer: Fred Coe. Director: Gordon Duff. *Cast:* Horace Braham, Kurt Katch, E. G. Marshall, Oliver Thorndike, Robert H. Harris, Frank Maxwell, Vaughn Taylor, John Van Dreelen, Boris Marshalov, John C. Becher.

29 January 1951— 9:00 "The Masque of the Red Death," by Edgar Allan Poe, adapted by Hal C. Hackady, for *Lights Out. Cast:* Hurd Hatfield, Berry Kroeger, Monica Lang, Claude Hoyton.

9:30 "Quicksand," adapted by Richard Morrison, for *Robert Montgomery Presents. Cast:* Skip Homeier, Claire Kirby, Martin Newman, Harry Worth, Cara Williams, Norman Keats, Roc Rogers, Frank Stephens, Kathleen Bolton, Charles Jordan, Billy Greene, Lester Lonergan, Jr., James MacDonald, Tom Ahearne, Donnell O'Brien, Michael Wyler, Hal Alexander, Gerald Hilton, Frank Rowan, Arthur Edwards, Bethell Long, A. Redman Walck, Frank Thomas.

30 January 1951— 9:00 "A Child in the House," for *Fireside Theatre. Cast:* Frances Dee.

9:30 "Those Wonderful People," by Joe Venable and Leslie Scott, for *Armstrong Circle Theatre.* Producer: Hudson Faussett. Director: Garry Simpson. *Cast:* James Van Dyk, Bess Johnson, Paul Ford, Laurie Lambert, Cameron Prud'homme.

31 January 1951— 9:00 "A Sound of Hunting," by Harry Brown, for *Kraft Television Theatre.* Producer: Stanley Quinn. Director: Dick Dunlap. *Cast:* Ralph Meeker, Joseph Di Reda, Biff Elliott.

10:30 "Cutie Pie," for *Stars Over Hollywood. Cast:* Carol Matthews.

1 February 1951— 10:00 *Martin Kane, Private Eye.*

2 February 1951— 9:30 *The Big Story,* from *The Odgen Standard Examiner.* Producer/Director: Charles Skinner.

3 February 1951— 7:30 *One Man's Family.*

4 February 1951— 7:30 *The Aldrich Family.*

9:00 "A Matter of Life and Death," by John and Ward Hawkins, adapted by Abram S. Ginnes, for *Philco Television Playhouse.* Producer: Fred Coe. Director: Delbert Mann. *Cast:* Cloris Leachman, Pat O'Malley, John Ericson, Kathleen Comegys, Herbert Nelson, Marian Winters, Tom Reynolds, Salem Ludwig, Bartle Doyle, Hal Carrier, Harold Grau.

5 February 1951— 9:00 "The House of Dust," by A. J. Russell, for *Lights Out. Cast:* Nina Foch, Anthony Quinn.

6 February 1951— 9:00 "The Hottest Day of the Year," for *Fireside Theatre. Cast:* James Anderson, Carol Matthews, Sheilah Watson.

9:30 "Superhighway," by Jerome Ross and James Garvin, for *Armstrong Circle Theatre.* Producer: Hudson Faussett. Director: Charles Harrell. *Cast:* Ed Begley, Richard Hamilton, Richard Carlyle, Allen Stevenson, Vincent Berg, Richard S. Bishop.

7 February 1951— 9:00 "The End of the Line" (changed from "The Glass Mountain") by Bruce Kimes, for *Kraft Television Theatre.* Producer: Maury Holland. Assistant: John Rich. *Cast:* Blanche Yurka, Belle Flower, John Stephen, Robert Pastene, Patricia Wheel, Mabel Paige, Jay Jackson.

10:30 "The Return of Van Sickle," for *Stars Over Hollywood. Cast:* Cliff Arquette.

8 February 1951—10:00 *Martin Kane, Private Eye.*

9 February 1951— 9:00 "Runaway," by A. J. Russell, for *The Clock.* Producer: Herbert Swope, Jr. Director: Grey Lockwood. *Cast:* Peter Capell, Martin Newman, John Boyd, Adelaide Klein, Louis Sorin, John Drew Colt.

10 February 1951— 7:30 *One Man's Family.*

11 February 1951— 7:30 *The Aldrich Family.*

9:00 "Kitty Doone," by Aben Kandel, adapted by Joan Crowley, for *Philco Television Playhouse.* Producer: Fred Coe. Director: Gordon Duff. *Cast:* Valerie Bettis, Edmon Ryan, Harry Worth, David White, Russell Dennis, Viola Roache, Brandon Peters, Nina Varela, Irving Winters, Carl Green.

12 February 1951— 9:00 "Death Takes a Curtain Call," by Frank Daly, for *Lights Out.* Producer: Herbert Swope, Jr. Director: Richard Eastland. *Cast:* Otto Kruger, Alan Bunce, Frank Daly, Anna Karen.

9:30 "A Star Is Born," by William A. Wellman and Robert Carson, for *Robert Montgomery Presents.* Producer: Montgomery/Felton. Director: Dan Lounsbury. *Cast:* Kathleen Crowley, Conrad Nagel, Howard St. John, George Petrie, Harry Sheppard, Nelson Olmsted, William Bush, Rosemary Murphy, Blake Ritter.

13 February 1951— 9:00 "Substance of His House," for *Fireside Theatre. Cast:* Jimmy Hickman, Lillian Albertson, Jack Daly.

9:30 "A Different World," for *Armstrong Circle Theatre. Cast:* Joan Chandler, Tom Avera.

14 February 1951— 9:00 "Engaged," by W. S. Gilbert, for *Kraft Television Theatre.* Producer: Stanley Quinn. Director: Dick Dunlap. *Cast:* Louis Edmonds, Jean Gillespie, Lloyd Bochner, Elizabeth Ross, Dan Morgan.

10:30 "Hand on My Shoulder," for *Stars Over Hollywood. Cast:* Frank Jenks.

15 February 1951—10:00 *Martin Kane, Private Eye.*

16 February 1951— 9:30 *The Big Story.*

17 February 1951— 7:30 *One Man's Family*.

18 February 1951— 7:30 *The Aldrich Family*.

9:00 "Let Them Be Seacaptains," an original play by H. R. Hays, for *Philco Television Playhouse*. Producer: Fred Coe. Director: Delbert Mann. *Cast:* E. G. Marshall, Anne Crawford, Florida Friebus, Charles Taylor, David Lewis, Harold McGee, Nicholas Saunders, Ken Rockefeller, Ruth Hope.

19 February 1951— 9:00 "Strange Legacy," by Marcia Harris, for *Lights Out*. Producer: Herbert Swope, Jr. Director: Lawrence Schwab, Jr. *Cast:* Robert Stack, Margaret Hayes, Henry Hart, Joseph Sweeney, Philip Huston, Walter Kohler.

20 February 1951— 9:00 "Going Home," for *Fireside Theatre*. *Cast:* Hugh O'Brian, Dabbs Greer, Noreen Nash.

9:30 "That Simmon's Girl," by Turner Bullock, for *Armstrong Circle Theatre*. Producer: Hudson Faussett. Director: Charles Harrell, *Cast:* Bonita Granville, Robert Pastene, Elizabeth Watts, Sally Gracie, Harry Tyler, Bobby Nick, Mary Loane.

21 February 1951— 9:00 "The Fortune Hunter," by Winchell Smith, for *Kraft Television Theatre*. Producer: Maury Holland. Director: Dick Dunlap. *Cast:* Jack Lemmon, Margot Moser.

10:30 "Son of the Rock," for *Stars Over Hollywood*. *Cast:* Ellen Corby, Stanley Andrews, John Qualen.

22 February 1951—10:00 *Martin Kane, Private Eye*.

23 February 1951— 9:30 "An Accident on Canigou," by Ben Radin, for *The Clock*. Producer: Herbert Swope, Jr. Director: Grey Lockwood. *Cast:* Richard Carlyle, Richard Kiley, Monty Banks, Jr.

24 February 1951— 7:30 *One Man's Family*.

25 February 1951— 7:30 *The Aldrich Family*.

9:00 "The Man Who Bought a Town," by Max Wilk, for *Philco Television Playhouse*. Producer: Fred Coe. Director: Gordon Duff. *Cast:* Oscar Homolka, Karl Weiss, Vinton Hayworth, Catherine Balfour, Bert Conway, Dorothy Sands.

26 February 1951— 9:00 "The Dispossessed," for *Lights Out*. *Cast:* Jeffrey Lynn, Stefan Schnabel, June Dayton, John Graham, Alfred Hopson, Doris Belack.

9:30 "The Last Tycoon," by F. Scott Fitzgerald, for *Robert Montgomery Presents*. Director: Dan Lounsbury. *Cast:* Robert Montgomery, June Duprez, Judy Parrish, Louis Hector, Robert Harris, John Griggs, Richard Kendrick.

27 February 1951— 9:00 "Copy Boy," for *Fireside Theatre*. *Cast:* Bob Ellis, Hunter Gardner, David Bruce, John Warburton.

9:30 "Twenty One Days," by Ira Avery, for *Armstrong Circle Theatre*. Producer: Hudson Faussett. Director: Garry Simpson. *Cast:* Skip Homeier, Lola Albright, Joan Morgan, Bob Shawley, Allan Tower, Harrison Dowd, William Turner.

28 February 1951— 9:00 "Jane Eyre," by Charlotte Brontë, adapted by Helen Jerome, for *Kraft Television Theatre*. Producer: Stanley Quinn. Director: Dick Dunlap. *Cast:* Kathleen Crowley, John Baragrey, Peggy Nelson, Amy Douglas, John Stephen, Shirley Dale Moore, Rhoderick Walker, Alan Shayne, Rica Martens.

10:30 "Autumn Flames," for *Stars Over Hollywood*. *Cast:* Maria Palmer, Onslow Stevens.

1 March 1951—10:00 *Martin Kane, Private Eye*.

2 March 1951— 9:30 *The Big Story*.

3 March 1951— 7:30 *One Man's Family*.

4 March 1951— 7:30 *The Aldrich Family*.

5 March 1951— 9:00 "The Man with the Astrakhan Hat," for *Lights Out*. Producer: Herbert Swope, Jr. *Cast:* Paul Stewart, Peter Capell, Ross Martin, Theodore Goetz, Jason Johnson, James Bender, Willis Pinkett, John Gerstad.

6 March 1951— 9:00 "Malachi's Cove," for *Fireside Theatre*. *Cast:* Tony McMillon, Sally Owen, Wilfred Walters.

    9:30 "The Partnership," by Doris Halman, for *Armstrong Circle Theatre*. Director: Charles Harrell. *Cast:* Lucille Watson, John Newland, Bruno Nick, Harry Sheppard, Glenn Denning, Ethel Remey, Lita Dal Porto, Barbara Pond.

7 March 1951— 9:00 "Delicate Story," by Ferenc Molnar, for *Kraft Television Theatre*. Producer: Maury Holland. Director: Dick Dunlap. *Cast:* Felicia Montealegre, Nelson Olmsted, John Ericson, Dan Morgan, Gene Leonard, Cricket Skilling, Noel Leslie, Clarence Nordstrom.

    10:30 "When the Devil Is Sick," for *Stars Over Hollywood*. *Cast:* Larry Blake, Dorothy Adams.

8 March 1951—10:00 *Martin Kane, Private Eye*.

9 March 1951— 9:30 *The Big Story*.

10 March 1951— 7:30 *One Man's Family*.

11 March 1951— 7:30 *The Aldrich Family*.

    9:00 "No Medals for Pop," by Henry K. Moritz, for *Philco Television Playhouse*. Producer: Fred Coe. Director: Delbert Mann. *Cast:* Brandon De Wilde, Frederic de Wilde, Ellen Cobb Hill, Rod Steiger, Hal Currier, Joe Fallon.

12 March 1951— 9:00 "Leda's Portrait," by Ira Levin, for *Lights Out*. *Cast:* John Emery, Felicia Montealegre, George Reeves.

    9:30 "The Young at Heart," by Ida A. R. Wylie, adapted by Gilbert Seldes, for *Robert Montgomery Presents*. *Cast:* Alan Mowbray, Adrienne Allen, Dorothy Sands, Joyce Linden, Rhoderick Walker, Valerie Cardew, Elizabeth Eustis, Richard Fraser.

13 March 1951— 9:00 "Shifting Sands," for *Fireside Theatre*. *Cast:* Hugh O'Brian, Gertrude Michael.

    9:30 "The Patcher-Upper," by John G. Fuller, for *Armstrong Circle Theatre*. *Cast:* Vinton Hayworth, Judy Parrish, Richard Derr, Neva Patterson, Pat Pearson, John O'Hare, Beulah Bryant.

14 March 1951— 9:00 "On Stage," by Benjamin Kaye, for *Kraft Television Theatre*. Producer: Stanley Quinn. Director: Dick Dunlap. *Cast:* E. G. Marshall, Vaughn Taylor, Richard Ahearne, Stewart Bradley, Raymond Bramley, Paul Lipson, Dan Morgan, Ed Herlihy.

    10:30 "Prison Doctor," for *Stars Over Hollywood*. *Cast:* Cameron Mitchell, Raymond Burr.

15 March 1951—10:00 *Martin Kane, Private Eye*.

16 March 1951— 9:30 *The Big Story*.

17 March 1951— 7:30 *One Man's Family*.

18 March 1951— 7:30 *The Aldrich Family*.

    9:00 "The Dark Corridor," by Richard Reich, adapted by Stephen de Baun, for *Philco Television Playhouse*. Director: Gordon Duff. *Cast:* Wesley Addy, Stella Andrew, Jerry Crews, Philippa Bevans, William Whitman, Viola Roache.

19 March 1951— 9:00 "Western Night," by Betty Smith and Robert Finch, for *Lights Out*. *Cast:* Richard Derr, Biff Elliott, William Free, Larry Buchanan, Richard Morningstar, Richard Shankland.

20 March 1951— 9:00 "Eleventh Hour," for *Fireside Theatre*. *Cast:* Hugh O'Brian, Lynne Roberts, John Dunbar.

9:30 "The Hero," by Anne Howard Bailey, for *Armstrong Circle Theatre*. *Cast:* William Tabbert, Kathleen Crowley, Mort Stevens, Harriet McGibbon, Tom Reynolds, Ralph Nelson.

21 March 1951— 9:00 "Of Famous Memory," by E. B. Ginty, for *Kraft Television Theatre*. Producer: Maury Holland. Director: Dick Dunlap. *Cast:* Nancy Marchand, Leslie Nielsen, Mercer McLeod, Berry Kroeger, Lawrence Ryle, Catherine Willard, Patricia Holsley, Victor Matalon, Wallace Acton, Noel Leslie.

10:30 "Conqueror's Isle," for *Stars Over Hollywood*.

22 March 1951—10:00 *Martin Kane, Private Eye*.

23 March 1951— 9:00 *The Big Story*.

24 March 1951— 7:30 *One Man's Family*.

25 March 1951— 7:30 *The Aldrich Family*.

9:00 "Bulletin 120," a story based on a report of the U. S. Public Health Service by Joseph Liss, for *Philco Television Playhouse*. Producer: Fred Coe. Director: Delbert Mann. *Cast:* Stephen Courtleigh, Robert Quarry, Elinor Randel, Daniel Reed, John Randolph, Jack Bittner, Alan Shayne, Eddie Hyans, Leslie Barrett.

26 March 1951— 9:00 "The Power of Brute Force," by A. J. Russell, for *Lights Out*. Producer: Herbert Swope, Jr. Director: Lawrence Schwab, Jr. *Cast:* Tom Drake, Richard Carlyle, Reba Tassell, Scott Moore, Lewis Herbert, Harold Rudd, Fred Hillebrand.

9:30 "Dark Victory," by George Emerson Brewer, adapted by Theodore and Mathilde Ferro, for *Robert Montgomery Presents*. Director: Don Rowe. *Cast:* Dorothy McGuire, John Forsythe, Richard Coogan, Polly Rowles, Helen Carew, Carroll Ashburn, Barbara Townsend, Roberta Balinger, Tyler Carpenter.

27 March 1951— 9:00 "Unwritten Column," for *Fireside Theatre*. *Cast:* Virginia Farmer, Edward Earl.

9:30 "Double Exposure," by John G. Fuller, for *Armstrong Circle Theatre*. *Cast:* Ruth Matteson, Edmon Ryan, Chester Stratton, Dulcy Jordan, Susan Jackson, Francis Compton.

28 March 1951— 9:00 "The Silent Room," by Joe Bates Smith, for *Kraft Television Theatre*. Producer: Stanley Quinn. Director: Dick Dunlap. *Cast:* Meg Mundy, Dan Morgan, Boris Marshalov, Baruch Lumet, Dorothy Raymond, Grania O'Malley, Martin Newman.

10:30 "Old Mother Hubbard," for *Stars Over Hollywood*. *Cast:* Ellen Corby.

29 March 1951—10:00 *Martin Kane, Private Eye*.

30 March 1951— 9:00 *The Big Story*.

31 March 1951— 7:30 *One Man's Family*.

1 April 1951— 7:30 *The Aldrich Family*.

9:00 "Parnussus on Wheels," by Christopher Morley, adapted by Thomas W. Phipps, for *Philco Television Playhouse*. Director: Gordon Duff. *Cast:* Muriel Kirkland, Russell Hardie, William Post, Jr., Una O'Connor, Milton Parsons, Harry Sheppard, Charity Grace, Roy Fant, Martin Greene, Ken Tower, Harold Grau.

2 April 1951— 9:00 "The Mad Dullagham," for *Lights Out*. Producer: Herbert Swope, Jr. Director: Al Tilt. *Cast:* Berry Kroeger, Glenn Langan, Stella Andrew, Doris Rich.

9:30–10:30 "Of Human Bondage," W. Somerset Maugham, adapted by Theodore and Mathilde Ferro, for *Somerset Maugham Theatre* debut. Producer: Martin Ritt. *Cast:* Cloris Leachman, Tom Helmore, Robert H. Harris, John Baragrey, Joan Chandler, Fred Worlock, William Podmore, Betty Sinclair, Clifford Carpenter.

3 April 1951— 9:00 "Gentleman from La Porte," for *Fireside Theatre. Cast:* Eve Miller, Warren Douglas.

9:30 "Moment of Decision," by Turner Bullock, for *Armstrong Circle Theatre.* Producer: Hudson Faussett. Director: Charles Harrell. *Cast:* Bruce Cabot, Tod Griffin, Frank Maxwell, Dorothy Sands, Margaret Hayes, Viola Frayne.

4 April 1951— 9:00 "Yours Truly," by Adelaide Matthews, for *Kraft Television Theatre.* Producer: Maury Holland. Director: Dick Dunlap. *Cast:* Lisa Kirk, Richard Derr, John Randolph, Elizabeth Dillon, Nina Hanson.

10:30 "Pearls from Paris," for *Stars Over Hollywood. Cast:* Raymond Burr, Suszanne Dalbert, Gerald Mohr.

5 April 1951— 8:30–9:00 "The Case of the Careless Junk Man," for *Treasury Men in Action* debut. Producer: Paul Freeman. Director: Dave Pressman. *Cast:* Walter Greaza, Howard Smith, Martin Balsam, William Griffis, Nellie Burt, Charles Mendick, Michael Lewin, Cliff Hall, Todd Russell.

10:00 *Martin Kane, Private Eye.*

6 April 1951— 9:00 *The Big Story.*

7 April 1951— 7:30 *One Man's Family.*

8 April 1951— 7:30 *The Aldrich Family.*

9:00 "Routine Assignment," by David Swift and Tom Seidel, adapted by David Swift, for *Philco Television Playhouse.* Director: Delbert Mann. *Cast:* Billy M. Greene, Frank Maxwell, James Westerfield, Emily Lawrence, Pat Healey, James Van Dyk, Ralph Roberts, Tom Heaphy, Stephen Elliott, Stephen Gray.

9 April 1951— 9:00 "The Crushed Rose," by Edgar Marvin, for *Lights Out. Cast:* John Beal, Barbara Britton, Richard Purdy.

9:30 "Stairway to Heaven," by Michael Powell and Emerie Pressburger, adapted by Alvin Sapinsley, for *Robert Montgomery Presents.* Producers: Robert Montgomery, Norman Felton. Director: Don Rowe. *Cast:* Richard Greene, Jean Gillespie, Bramwell Fletcher, Bob Coote, Francis Compton, Bruce Gordon, Lee Bowman.

10 April 1951— 9:00 "Hot Spot," for *Fireside Theatre. Cast:* Eve Miller, Clark Howatt.

9:30 "Ghost Town," by Frank P. De Felitta, for *Armstrong Circle Theatre.* Director: Garry Simpson. *Cast:* Henry Hull, Melba Rae, Clifford Hall, Paul Crabtree, Stewart MacIntosh, Gene Blakely, Joy Reese, Ruth McDevitt.

11 April 1951— 9:00 "Mrs. Dane's Defense," by Henry Arthur Jones, for *Kraft Television Theatre.* Producer: Stanley Quinn. Director: Dick Dunlap. *Cast:* Cyril Ritchard, Madge Elliott, Faith Brook, Ty Perry, David Orrick, Frances Tennehill.

10:30 "Tales of Jeb Mulcahy," for *Stars Over Hollywood. Cast:* Bruce Cabot.

12 April 1951— 8:30 *Treasury Men in Action.*

10:00 *Martin Kane, Private Eye.*

13 April 1951— 9:00 *The Big Story.*

14 April 1951— 7:30 *One Man's Family.*

15 April 1951— 7:30 *The Aldrich Family.*

9:00 "Hour of Destiny," by Jean Z. Owen, adapted by William Kendall Clarke, for *Philco Television Playhouse.* Director: Gordon Duff. *Cast:* Anne Burr, Dorothy Peterson, Phyllis Love, Richard Kendrick, Harry Bannister, Barbara Joyce, Clorinda Emerson, Dorothy Elder, Beverly Bayne, Charles Carroll, May Cooper, George Smith, Mary Cooper.

16 April 1951— 9:00 "The Witness," by Ernest Kinoy, for *Lights Out. Cast:* Dane Clark, Harry Dorth, Florence Stanley, Dick Sanders, Howard Smith.

9:30 "Theatre," by W. Somerset Maugham, adapted by Irving Gaynor Neiman, *Somerset Maugham Theatre.* Director: Dan Petrie. *Cast:* Judith Anderson, Robert H. Harris, Vicki Cummings, John Baragrey, Michael Wagner, Reba Tassell, Louis Gilbert, Rex Marshall.

17 April 1951— 9:00 "Close Shave," for *Fireside Theatre. Cast:* James Anderson, Ginni Jackson.

9:30 "Honor Student," by Anne Howard Bailey, for *Armstrong Circle Theatre.* Director: Jack Tyler. *Cast:* Donald Buka, Walter Starkey, Jean Gillespie, Raymond Bramley, Art Kohl, Mona Brune, Reginald Mason, James Holland, Nela Chelton, Steven Meyers, Anthony Greg, Blaine Randell.

18 April 1951— 9:00 "Mr. Mergenthwirker's Lobblies," by Nelson Bond and David Kent, for *Kraft Television Theatre.* Producer: Maury Holland. Director: Dick Dunlap. *Cast:* Vaughn Taylor, Henry and Japheth, Vinton Hayworth, Maurice Wilson, Diana Douglas, Philip Robinson, J. Richard Jones, Paul Lipson, Dan Morgan, James Coots, Frank Overton, Jack Ewing.

10:30 "The Kirbys," for *Stars Over Hollywood. Cast:* Ann Rutherford, Cameron Mitchell.

19 April 1951— 8:30 *Treasury Men in Action.*

10:00 *Martin Kane, Private Eye.*

20 April 1951— 9:00 *The Big Story.*

21 April 1951— 7:30 *One Man's Family.*

22 April 1951— 7:30 *The Aldrich Family.*

9:00 "The Birth of the Movies," by H. R. Hays and Bob Arthur, for *Philco Television Playhouse.* Producer: Fred Coe. Director: Delbert Mann. *Cast:* Lillian Gish, Jean Pearson, John Newland, Paul Mann, Brandon Peters, Gordon Peters, Bruce Gordon, Robert Simon, Ben Lackland, Ken Rockefeller, Philip Rhodes.

23 April 1951— 9:00 "The Fouceville Curse," by Hale and Jerry Hackady, for *Lights Out. Cast:* Patrick Knowles, Rosalind Ivan, Alma Lawson, Don Marrison.

9:30 "The Bishop's Wife," by Robert Nathan, adapted by Peter Berry, for *Robert Montgomery Presents.* Director: Don Rowe. *Cast:* Martha Scott, Philip Bourneuf, Richard Derr, Jane Alexander, Olive Blakeney, Eva Condon, Ludwig Roth, Georgia Harvey.

24 April 1951— 9:00 "The Celebrated Mrs. Rowland," for *Fireside Theatre. Cast:* Gertrude Michael, John Warburton.

9:30 "Backstage," by Ira Avery, for *Armstrong Circle Theatre.* Producer: Hudson Faussett. Director: Garry Simpson. *Cast:* William Prince, Patricia Wheel, Jack Arthur, Edwin Jerome, Ann McCrea, Hal Neiman, Lester Lonegan, William De Massena, Carey Leverette.

25 April 1951— 9:00 "Brief Music," by Emmet Lavery, for *Kraft Television Theatre. Cast:* Joyce Van Patten, Pat Crowley, Pat Kirkland, Shirley Standlee, Jane Sutherland, Peggy Nelson, Lynne Lyons.

10:30 "Pretty Boy," for *Stars Over Hollywood. Cast:* Robert Clarice, Lynne Roberts, Raymond Benedict.

26 April 1951— 8:30 *Treasury Men in Action.*

10:00 *Martin Kane, Private Eye.*

27 April 1951— 9:00 *The Big Story.*

28 April 1951— 7:30 *One Man's Family.*

29 April 1951— 7:30 *The Aldrich Family.*

9:00 "Mr. Arcularis," by Conrad Aiken, adapted by Nelson Olmsted, for *Philco*

Television Playhouse. Director: Gordon Duff. *Cast:* Nelson Olmsted, Leora Dana, Edward Andrews, Stuart MacIntosh, Herb Nelson, Joe Bassett.

30 April 1951— 9:00 "Grey Reminder," for *Lights Out. Cast:* John Newland, Beatrice Straight, Helene Dumas.

9:30 "The Moon and Sixpence," by W. Somerset Maugham, adapted by Walter Bernstein, for *Somerset Maugham Theatre.* Producer: Paul Lammers. Director: Dan Petrie. *Cast:* Lee J. Cobb, Peggy Allenby, Romney Brent, Olive Deering, Jay Barney, Bramwell Fletcher, Pat O'Malley, Marcia Marcus, Clark Gordon, Susan Steele, Merl Albertson.

1 May 1951— 9:00 "The Moment of Truth," for *Fireside Theatre.* Edward Norris, Richard Avonde.

9:30 "The Big Rainbow," by David Judson, for *Armstrong Circle Theatre.* Producer: Hudson Faussett. Director: Charles Harrell. *Cast:* Lawrence Fletcher, June Walker, Henry Jones, Jo Ann Paul, Barbara Townsend.

2 May 1951— 9:00 "Brief Candle," by Robert Hare Powell, adapted for *Kraft Television Theatre.* Producer: Maury Holland. *Cast:* Douglas Watson, Mary Howard, Isobel Elsom, Noel Leslie, David Orrick, Graham Velsey, Margaret Burlen.

10:30 "The Second Mrs. Slade," for *Stars Over Hollywood.*

3 May 1951— 8:30 *Treasury Men in Action.*

10:00 *Martin Kane, Private Eye.*

4 May 1951— 9:00 *The Big Story.*

5 May 1951— 7:30 *One Man's Family.*

6 May 1951— 7:30 *The Aldrich Family.*

9:00 "A Secret Island," by Honoré de Balzac, adapted by Paul Peters, for *Philco Television Playhouse.* Producer: Fred Coe. Director: Delbert Mann. *Cast:* Mildred Natwick, Edgar Stehli, Phoebe Mackay, Chris White, Cliff Robertson, Harry Sheppard, Guy Tomajan.

7 May 1951— 9:00 "The Lost Will of Dr. Kent," for *Lights Out.* Director: Albert Tilt. *Cast:* Leslie Nielsen, Pat Englund, Russell Collins, Eva Condon, John Gerstad, Florence Anguish, Marvin Paige.

9:30 "Ladies in Retirement," by Edward Percy and Reginald Denham, adapted by Ellis Marcus, for *Robert Montgomery Presents.* Director: Dan Lounsbury. *Cast:* Lillian Gish, Una O'Connor, Michael McAloney, Cherry Hardy, Betty Sinclair, Ronnie Batten, Ruth McDevitt.

8 May 1951— 9:00 "The Tunnel," for *Fireside Theatre. Cast:* Dickie LeRoy, R. B. Norman.

9:30 "The Open Heart," by Anne Howard Bailey, for *Armstrong Circle Theatre. Cast:* Ivan Simpson, Jonathan Marlowe, Maurice Wells, Humphrey Davis, Gaby Rodgers, Miriam Goldina, Louis Edmonds, Louis Sorin, Sal La Perz, Boris Gregory.

9 May 1951— 9:00 "Till Death Do Us Part," by Leo Tolstoy, translated by Mrs. E. M. Everts, for *Kraft Television Theatre. Cast:* June Walker, Pat Breslin, Charles Summers, Gwen Anderson, John Newland.

10:30 "The Devil You Say," for *Stars Over Hollywood. Cast:* Fred Sherman.

10 May 1951— 8:30 *Treasury Men in Action.*

10:00 *Martin Kane, Private Eye.*

11 May 1951— 9:00 *The Big Story.*

12 May 1951— 7:30 *One Man's Family.*

13 May 1951— 7:30 *The Aldrich Family.*

9:00 "The Visitor," by Carl Randau and Leane Zugsmith, adapted by Kenneth White, for *Philco Television Playhouse*. Director: Delbert Mann. *Cast:* Don Murray, Sylvia Field, Otto Hulett, Romney Brent, Frances Helm, Henry Bernard, Brandon Peters, Anne Ives.

14 May 1951— 9:00 "Dead Man's Coat," for *Lights Outs*. *Cast:* Basil Rathbone, William Post, Jr., Norman Ross, Heywood Hale Braun, Pat Donovan.

9:30 "The Facts of Life," by W. Somerset Maugham, adapted by Theodore and Mathilde Ferro, for *Somerset Maugham Theatre*. *Cast:* Bill Daniels, Jack Lemmon, Veronica Lake, Adelaide Dean, Leslie Barry.

15 May 1951— 9:00 "Hope Chest," for *Fireside Theatre*.

9:30 "Jury Duty," by Turner Bullock, for *Armstrong Circle Theatre*. Producer: Hudson Faussett. Director: Douglas Rodgers. *Cast:* Howard Smith, Paul Ford, Katherine Meskill.

16 May 1951— 9:00 "The Intimate Strangers," by Booth Tarkington, for *Kraft Television Theatre*. Producer: Maury Holland. Liaison: John Rich. *Cast:* Peggy Conklin, Nelson Olmsted, William Lynn, Peter Griffith, Jeanne Flanigan, Isabel Price, Edna Preston.

10:30 "Nor Gloom of Night," for *Stars Over Hollywood*. *Cast:* Buddy Ebsen.

17 May 1951— 8:30 *Treasury Men in Action*.

10:00 *Martin Kane, Private Eye*.

18 May 1951— 9:00 *The Big Story*.

19 May 1951— 7:30 *One Man's Family*.

20 May 1951— 7:30 *The Aldrich Family*.

9:00 "Justice and Mr. Pleznik," by Arthur T. Horman, adapted by Thomas W. Phipps, for *Philco Television Playhouse*. Director: Delbert Mann. *Cast:* Joseph Buloff, Barbara Bulgakov, Ben Lackland, Charles Campbell, Arthur O'Connell, Martin Greene, Leo Penn, Calvin Thomas, Frank Tweddell.

21 May 1951— 9:00 "The Cat's Cradle," by Jerome Barry, adapted by A. J. Russell, for *Lights Out*. Producer: Herbert Swope, Jr. Director: Lawrence Schwab, Jr. *Cast:* Martha Scott, Murvyn Vye, Lorence Kerr, Klock Ryder.

9:30 "The House of the Seven Gables," by Nathaniel Hawthorne, adapted by Gaynor Neiman, for *Robert Montgomery Presents*. *Cast:* Gene Lockhart, June Lockhart, Leslie Nielsen, Richard Purdy, Helen Carew, Daniel Reed.

22 May 1951— 9:00 "Amber Gods," for *Fireside Theatre*.

9:30 "The Vote-Getter," by Cameron Hawley, adapted by Anne Howard Bailey, for *Armstrong Circle Theatre*. Director: Garry Simpson. *Cast:* Arthur Vinton, Muriel Kirkland, Biff Elliott, Patricia Peardon, Cameron Prud'homme, Mary Heath, Palmer Ward, Kaye Lyder, Kay Campbell.

23 May 1951— 9:00 "A Play for Mary," by William McCleery, adapted from his play, for *Kraft Television Theatre*. Producer: Stanley Quinn. *Cast:* Eva Condon, Bramwell Fletcher, Cloris Leachman, James Daly.

10:30 "A Likely Story," for *Stars Over Hollywood*.

24 May 1951— 9:00 *Treasury Men in Action*.

10:00 *Martin Kane, Private Eye*.

25 May 1951— 9:00 *The Big Story*.

26 May 1951— 7:30 *One Man's Family*.

27 May 1951— 7:30 *The Aldrich Family*.

9:00 "The Rescue," by William Burke Miller, adapted by David Shaw, for *Philco Television Playhouse*. Director: Gordon Duff. *Cast:* Sandy Campbell, John

Randolph, James Westerfield, Elliott Sullivan, Dan Morgan, Ben Grauer, Sandy Kenyon, John Drew Devereaux.

28 May 1951— 9:00 "The Pattern," by Ira Levin, for *Lights Out. Cast:* John Forsythe, June Dayton, Dick Sanders, Chris Gampel, Rex Williams, Rita Gam.

9:30 "Cokes and Ale," by W. Somerset Maugham, adapted by DeWitt Bodeen, for *Somerset Maugham Theatre. Cast:* June Havoc, Frederic Tozere, Frank Sundstrom, Earl Hammond, Zamah Cunningham.

29 May 1951— 9:00 *Fireside Theatre.*

9:30 "Over the Fence," by Anne Howard Bailey, for *Armstrong Circle Theatre.* Producer: Hudson Faussett. Director: Ted Post. *Cast:* Barbara Britton, Dick Foran, Nydia Westman.

30 May 1951— 9:00 "Ben Franklin," by Louis Evan Shipman, for *Kraft Television Theatre.* Producer: Maury Holland. *Cast:* Robert Emhardt, Lili Darvas, Olga Baclanova, Ralph Cameron.

10:30 "When the Devil Is Sick," for *Stars Over Hollywood.*

31 May 1951—10:00 *Martin Kane, Private Eye.*

1 June 1951— 9:00 *The Big Story.*

2 June 1951— 7:30 *One Man's Family.*

3 June 1951— 7:30 *The Aldrich Family.*

9:00 "The Adventures of Hiram Holiday," by Paul Gallico, adapted by Alexander Kirkland, for *Philco Television Playhouse.* Director: Delbert Mann. *Cast:* E. G. Marshall, Stella Andrew, Miriam Goldina, Adia Kuznetzoff, Ivan Simpson.

4 June 1951— 9:00 "The Martian Eyes," by Henry Kuttner, adapted by George Lefferts, for *Lights Out.* Producer: Herbert Swope, Jr. Director: Lawrence Schwab, Jr. *Cast:* Burgess Meredith, John Baragrey, David Lewis, Pat O'Malley, Joe Silver.

9:30 "For Love of Mary," by Daniel Taradish, Bernard Feiss, Julian Blaustein, adapted by Gaynor Neiman, for *Robert Montgomery Presents. Cast:* June Lockhart, Vicki Cummings, Viola Roache, John Fletcher, Edith Gresham, Bill Beach.

5 June 1951— 9:00 "The Green Convertible," for *Fireside Theatre.*

9:30 "Lover's Leap," by Ira Avery, for *Armstrong Circle Theatre.* Director: Jack Tyler. *Cast:* Leslie Nielsen, Grace Kelly, Donald Murphy, Alan Abel, Charles Mendick, Larry Buchanan.

6 June 1951— 9:00 "A Seacoast in Bohemia," by Ben Radin. Producer: Stanley Quinn. Liaison: John Rich. *Cast:* Raymond Rizzo, Stuart MacIntosh, Philip Coolidge, Lili Darvas, Biff Elliott, Joyce Van Patten, Dan Morgan, Dorothy Steele, Roger Boxhill.

10:30 "Conqueror's Isle," for *Stars Over Hollywood.*

7 June 1951— 8:30 *Treasury Men in Action.*

10:00 *Martin Kane, Private Eye.*

8 June 1951— 9:00 *The Big Story.*

9 June 1951— 7:30 *One Man's Family.*

10 June 1951— 7:30 *The Aldrich Family.*

9:00 "The Fast Dollar," an original drama by Max Wilk, for *Philco Television Playhouse.* Producer: Fred Coe. Director: Gordon Duff. *Cast:* Pat O'Malley, Judy Parrish, John Harvey, Vaughn Taylor, Leonard Elliot, Roland Wood, Maxine Stuart, Joey Fallon, Bill Poetrude.

11 June 1951— 9:00 "Pit of the Dead," by Wyllis Cooper, for *Lights Out.* Director: William Corrigan. *Cast:* John Dall, Joseph Buloff, William Darriet, Beatrice Kraft.

9:30 "The Narrow Corner," by W. Somerset Maugham, for *Somerset Maugham*

Theatre. Cast: Harry Landers, Harry Mchaffey, Farrell Pelly, Susan Douglas, Treva Trazee, Dennis King, Leslie Linder.

12 June 1951— 9:00 *Fireside Theatre.*

9:30 "The Rookie," by Eli Cantor, for *Armstrong Circle Theatre.* Director: Garry Simpson. *Cast:* Naomi Riordan, Ellen Mahar, Douglas Watson, Eva Condon, Joey Walsh, Leopold Badia, Betty Lou Keim, Lynn Loring.

13 June 1951— 9:00 "Stranglehold," by Channing Pollock, for *Kraft Television Theatre. Cast:* Gene Lyons, Marilyn Monk, Enid Markey, Brook Byron, Don Briggs, Guy Spaull, Ken Walken.

10:30 "Texas Parson," for *Stars Over Hollywood.*

14 June 1951— 8:30 *Treasury Men in Action.*

10:00 *Martin Kane, Private Eye.*

15 June 1951— 9:00 *The Big Story.*

16 June 1951— 7:30 *One Man's Family.*

17 June 1951— 7:30 *The Aldrich Family.*

9:00 "Operation Airlift," by David Swift and George Giroux, adapted by David Swift, for *Philco Television Playhouse.* Director: Delbert Mann. *Cast:* Russell Hardie, Frank Maxwell, David Swift, Lauren Gilbert, John D. Seymour, Paul Lipson, Ernest Borgnine, Mike Kellin, Jack Bittner, Charles Mayer.

18 June 1951— 8:00 "Special Delivery," by Harry W. Junkin, for *Cameo Theatre.* Producer: Albert McCleery. Director: Richard Uhl. *Cast:* June Havoc, Richard McMurray, Charlotte Knight, Carrell Ashburn, Rusty Lane, Bernard Grant, William Kent, Jan Owen, Rosamond Vance.

9:00 "Dead Freight," by A. J. Russell, for *Lights Out.* Producers: Herbert Swope, Jr., Lawrence Schwab, Jr. Director: Albert Tilt. *Cast:* Charles Dingle, Louisa Horton, Rod Steiger, Charles Jordan, John Marriott, Portor Van Zandt.

9:30 "Three O'Clock," adapted by Thomas W. Phipps, for *Robert Montgomery Presents. Cast:* Vaughn Taylor, Olive Deering, Jack Edwards, Gene Reynolds, Sidney Paul, Barbara Townsend, Alan MacAteer, Ella Lithgow, Sandra Ann Wigginton, Anne Ives, Frank Daly, Clark Gordon, Charles Jordan.

19 June 1951— 9:00 "International Incident," for *Fireside Theatre.*

9:30 "Close Harmony," by James Garvin, for *Armstrong Circle Theatre.* Producer: Hudson Faussett. Director: Ted Post. *Cast:* Romney Brent, Madeleine Clive, Jack Sheahan, Henry Calvin, Art Johnson, Byron Halstead, Dorothy Elder, Mason Curry, Kay Campbell, Bill Blivens.

20 June 1951— 9:00 "Only the Heart," by Horton Foote, for *Kraft Television Theatre.* Producer: Stanley Quinn. *Cast:* Dorothy Sands, Isobel Robins, Jack Ewing, Isabel Price, Joseph Anthony.

10:30 "Crew Cut," for *Stars Over Hollywood.*

21 June 1951— 8:30 *Treasury Men in Action.*

10:00 *Martin Kane, Private Eye.*

22 June 1951— 9:00 *The Big Story.*

23 June 1951— 7:30 *One Man's Family.*

24 June 1951— 7:30 *The Aldrich Family.*

9:00 "Dr. Hudson's Secret Journal," by Lloyd C. Douglas, adapted by Joan Crowley, for *Philco Television Playhouse.* Producer: Fred Coe. Director: Gordon Duff. *Cast:* Shepperd Strudwick, Colin Keith Johnston, Barbara Ames, Marilyn Monk, Martin Brooks, Laura Weber, Silvio Minciolli, Blair Davis, Philippa Bevans, Vaughn Taylor.

25 June 1951— 8:00 "Blackout," by Harry W. Junkin, for *Cameo Theatre*. Producer: Albert McCleery. *Cast:* Jeffrey Lynn, Barbara Britton, Harry Hugenot, Robert Bolger, James Little, Paul Lilly, Bob Warren, Ann Anderson.

9:00 "The Passage Beyond," by Doris Halman, for *Lights Out*. Producer: Herbert Swope, Jr. Director: William Corrigan. *Cast:* Ralph Clanton, Monica Lang, Stella Andrew, Byron Russell, Sherry Bennett.

9:30 "The Letter," by W. Somerset Maugham, adapted by Richard Sloane, for *Somerset Maugham Theatre*. *Cast:* Judith Evelyn, Martin Gabel.

10:30 "The Substitute," for *Story Theatre*, filmed dramas shown on WNBT, New York.

26 June 1951— 9:00 "Back to Zero," for *Fireside Theatre*. *Cast:* Bernard Miles, June Rodney.

9:30 "Buckaroo," by Anne Howard Bailey, for *Armstrong Circle Theatre*. Director: Jack Tyler. *Cast:* Lonnie Chapman, Cloris Leachman, Bramwell Fletcher, Jeff Bryant, Roy Fant, Jay Barney.

27 June 1951— 9:00 "Merry Madness," by Sheridan Gibney, for *Kraft Television Theatre*. *Cast:* Cameron Prud'homme, Regina Wallace, Rex O'Malley, Mercer McLeod, Louis Edmonds, Patricia Jenkins, John D. Seymour, Dorothy Rice.

10:30 "The Last Letter," for *Stars Over Hollywood*.

28 June 1951— 8:30 *Treasury Men in Action*.

10:00 *Martin Kane, Private Eye*.

29 June 1951— 9:00 *The Big Story*.

30 June 1951— 7:30 *One Man's Family*.

1 July 1951— 9:00 "The Plot," by William Kendall Clarke, for *Philco Television Playhouse*. *Cast:* Edgar Stehli, Donald Buka, Alfreda Wallace, Helen Dowdy, Dorothy Elder, Elliot Sullivan.

2 July 1951— 8:00 "Betrayal," by Harry W. Junkin, for *Cameo Theatre*. Producer/Director: Albert McCleery. *Cast:* Nina Foch, Philip Reed, Ellen Mahar, Sara Anderson, Jean Hayworth, Madeliene Clive.

9:00 "And Adam Begot," for *Lights Out*. *Cast:* Kent Smith, Philip Bourneuf, Joan Wetmore, Kurt Katch.

9:30 "When We Are Married," by J. B. Priestley, for *Robert Montgomery Presents*. Roddy McDowell, Frederic Tozere, Bramwell Fletcher, Isobel Elsom, Betty Sinclair, Pat O'Malley, Reginald Mason, Patricia Wheel, Margaret Hill.

10:30 "The Celebrated Jumping Frog," for *Story Theatre*.

3 July 1951— 9:00 "Moment of Glory," by George and Gertrude Fass, for *Fireside Theatre*. Producer/Director: Albert McCleery. *Cast:* Joanna Douglas, Vaughn Taylor.

10:30 "Leave It to Mother," by Anne Howard Bailey, for *Armstrong Circle Theatre*. Producer: Hudson Faussett. Director: Ted Post. *Cast:* Enid Markey, Howard Freeman, Cliff Robertson, Fred Barron, Elmer Eahr, Peggy McLean.

4 July 1951— 9:00 "The Adventures of Tom Sawyer," by Samuel L. Clemens, for *Kraft Television Theatre*. Producer: Stanley Quinn. *Cast:* Clifford Sales, Joey Walsh, Susan Harris, Gene Lee, June Walker, Lawrence Ryle, Joe Di Reda, Albert Stauderman, Nancy Malone, Katherine Meskill, Philip Hepburn, John Shellie, Arthur Cassel, Toni Holloran, Lois Holmes.

10:30 *Stars Over Hollywood*.

5 July 1951— 8:30 *Treasury Men in Action*.

10:00 *Martin Kane, Private Eye*.

6 July 1951— 8:30 "Journey Along the River," by Edward Mabley and Joanna Ross, for *The Clock*. Producer: Herbert Swope, Jr. Director: Grey Lockwood. *Cast:* Martha Scott, Lili Darvas, Harold McGee, Sid Cassel.

9:00–9:30 *Door with No Name*, dramas about intrigue in federal agencies, debuts. Producer/Director: Tommy Victor, Walter Selden. *Cast:* Grant Richards, Melville Ruick, Phil Sterling, Adrienne Boyan, Stefan Schnabel.

7 July 1951— 7:00 *Tom Corbett, Space Cadet*, by Ann and Marc Siegel, debuts. Producer: Allen Ducovny. Director: George Gould.

7:30 *One Man's Family.*

8 July 1951— 9:00 "Case History," by Jean Leslie, adapted by Alexander Kirkland, for *Philco Television Playhouse*. Director: Gordon Duff. *Cast:* Jane Seymour, Nydia Westman, Peggy Allenby, Barbara Joyce, Leslie Woods, Robert Pastene, John Boruff, Denise Alexander.

9 July 1951— 8:00 "Avalanche," by Harry W. Junkin, for *Cameo Theatre*. Producer/Director: Albert McCleery. *Cast:* Constance Bennett, Richard Carlson, Martin Kosleck, Elaine Stewart, Rosalind Greene, Jane Murray.

9:00 "The Meddlers," by Manly Wade Wellman, adapted by Douglas Wood Gibson, for *Lights Out*. Producer: Herbert Swope, Jr. Director: Albert Tilt. *Cast:* John Carradine, E. G. Marshall, Dan Morgan, Robert Hullas.

9:30 "The French Governor," by W. Somerset Maugham, adapted by Russell Beggs, for *Somerset Maugham Theatre*. *Cast:* Alfred Drake.

10:30 *Story Theatre*, for WNBT.

10 July 1951— 9:00 "The Vigil," by Ellen and Richard McCracken, for *Fireside Theatre*. Producer/Director: Albert McCleery. *Cast:* Jeff Morrow, Benny DeVries, Katherine Raht, Isabel Price, William S. Rainey, Jane Murray, Alan MacAteer, Lee Marvin, Mildred Dragon, Jonathan Marlowe.

9:30 "Table for Two," by Hamilton Benz, for *Armstrong Circle Theatre*. Director: Garry Simpson. *Cast:* Henry Daniell, Ruth Matteson, Hazel Dawn, Paul Parks, Marian McManus, Woody Morgan, Nell Morgan, George Burton.

11 July 1951— 9:00 "Vienna Dateline," by Morris S. Helitzer, for *Kraft Television Theatre*. Director: Richard Goode. *Cast:* Robert Dale Martin, Mary James, Natalie Core, John D. Seymour, John Stephen, Dan Morgan, Richard and Sandra Wigginton, Gaby Rogers, Louis Edmonds, Victor Chapin, Connie Lembcke.

10:30 "My Nephew Norwell," for *Stars Over Hollywood*.

11:30 *Cinema Playhouse*, for WNBT.

12 July 1951— 8:30 "The Case of the Sweet Tooth," for *Treasury Men in Action*. Producer: Howard Rodman.

13 July 1951— 8:30 "The Hidden Thing," by A. J. Russell, for *The Clock*. Producer: Herbert Swope, Jr. Director: Clark Jones. *Cast:* Robert Sterling, Stefan Schnabel, Frank Tweddell, James Little.

9:30 *Door with No Name.*

14 July 1951— 7:00 *Tom Corbett, Space Cadet.*

7:30 *One Man's Family.*

8:00 "Valley of Terror," a film, for *Double "C" Ranch* on WNBT.

15 July 1951— 9:00 "I Want to March," an original play by H. R. Hays, for *Philco Television Playhouse*. Producer: Fred Coe. Director: Ira Skutch. *Cast:* Katherine Meskill, Sandy Campbell, John Hoyt, Patricia Peardon, Reynolds Evans, Enid Markey, Nina Hanson.

16 July 1951— 8:00 "Deception," by Harry W. Junkin, for *Cameo Theatre*. Producer/

Director: Albert McCleery. *Cast:* Madge Evans, William Post, Jr., William Crane, Philip Faversham, Gregory Robins, Jean Hayworth, John O'Hare.

9:00 "The Devil in Glencairn," by Sir Walter Scott, adapted by Brett Warren, for *Lights Out.* Director: Lawrence Schwab, Jr. *Cast:* Richard Carlson, Halliwell Robes, Jonathan Harris, Thelma Schnee, Tom Poston, Pat O'Malley.

9:30 "The Promise," by W. Somerset Maugham, adapted by David Davison, for *Somerset Maugham Theatre. Cast:* Jack Lemmon, Haila Stoddard, Peggy McCay, Gordon Nelson, Bill Daniels, Harvey Hayes.

10:30 *Story Theatre.*

11:00 *Cinema Playhouse.*

17 July 1951— 9:00 "A Little Night Music," by Raphael Hayes, for *Fireside Theatre. Cast:* Martin Brooks, Louis Sorin, Augusta Ciolli, Allan Shay, Hal Studer, Harold McGee, Ben Yaffee, Don Pardo.

9:30 "Last Chance," by Turner Bullock and Anne Howard Bailey, for *Armstrong Circle Theatre.* Director: Ted Post. *Cast:* Sidney Blackmer, Isobel Elsom, Jack Lemmon, Calvin Thomas, Harold Crane, Kay Campbell, Ernest Chappell.

18 July 1951— 9:00 "Zone Four," by James Fielder Cook, for *Kraft Television Theatre.* Director: Fielder Cook. *Cast:* Richard Kiley, Louisa Horton, Murray Matheson, Roland Winters, Walter Brooke, Grania O'Malley, Ben Cooper, James Van Dyk, Cameron Prud'homme.

10:30 "Sea Baron," for *Stars Over Hollywood.*

11:15 *Cinema Playhouse.*

19 July 1951— 8:30 "The Case of the Formula CDA," by Abram S. Ginnes, for *Treasury Men in Action.*

10:30 *Short Story Theatre,* from Chicago.

20 July 1951— 8:30 "The Lily Pond," by Howard Rodman, for *The Clock.* Director: Grey Lockwood. *Cast:* Kent Smith, Neil Harrison, Frank Thomas, Sr., James McDonald, Carol Olmart, Janet Paul, Liam Bunn, Norman Rose.

9:00 *Door with No Name.*

21 July 1951— 7:00 *Tom Corbett, Space Cadet.*

7:30 *One Man's Family.*

8:00 *Double "C" Ranch.*

10:30 "Through a Dead Man's Eyes," by Cornell Woolrich, adapted by David Shaw, for *Assignment: Man Hunt* debut. Producer: Julian Claman. Director: Dan Petrie. *Cast:* Elliott Sullivan, Adelaide Bean, Ernest Borgnine, Andre Baruch.

22 July 1951— 9:00 "Pretend I'm a Stranger," by Jack Aistrop, adapted by David Shaw, for *Philco Television Playhouse.* Director: Delbert Mann. *Cast:* William Prince, Olive Deering, Henry Beckman, Michael McAloney, Mary Barclay, Marijane Maricle, Florence Robinson, Herbert Armstrong, Peter Von Zerneck.

23 July 1951— 8:00 "Of Unsound Mind," by Harry W. Junkin, for *Cameo Theatre. Cast:* Clare Luce, Philip Reed, Donald Briggs, Scott Tennyson, John Marriott, Tom Gorman, Carey Leverette.

9:00 "Zero Hour," by Ray Bradbury, adapted by George Lefferts, for *Lights Out.* Director: William Corrigan. *Cast:* Denise Alexander, John O'Hare, Richard Wigginton, Sandra Ann Wigginton, Charlie Brill.

9:30 "In Hiding," by W. Somerset Maugham, adapted by Theodore and Mathilde Ferro, for *Somerset Maugham Theatre. Cast:* Nina Foch, John Baragrey, Vicki Cummings.

10:30 *Story Theatre.*

11:00 *Cinema Playhouse.*
24 July 1951— 9:00 "A Jury of Her Peers," by Susan Glaspell, adapted by Frederic Manley, for *Fireside Theatre. Cast:* Jeanette Dowling, Olive Deering, Frank Tweddell, Floyd Buckley, John Hoyt, Gladys Mark.
9:30 "A Beautiful Friendship," by Ruth Woodman, for *Armstrong Circle Theatre.* Producer: Garry Simpson. Director: Jack Tyler. *Cast:* Jerome Cowan, Robert Eckhardt, Bonnie Baken, James Stephens.
25 July 1951— 9:00 "Bright Shadow," by J. B. Priestley, for *Kraft Television Theatre.* Director: Richard Goode. Liasion: Arthur Penn. *Cast:* John Moore, Rhoderick Walker, Richard Aherne, Anita Bolster, Valerie Cardew, Reynolds Evans, Fred Worlock.
10:30 *Stars Over Hollywood,* on local WNBT.
26 July 1951— 8:30 *Treasury Men in Action.*
10:30 *Short Story Theatre,* from Chicago.
27 July 1951— 8:30 "Falling in Love Is Murder," by Thomas W. Phipps, adapted by Thomas W. Phipps and Robert Shackleton, for *The Clock.* Producer: Herbert Swope, Jr. Director: Clark Jones. *Cast:* Alan Marshall, William Crane, Robert Christopher, Susan Shaw.
9:00 *Door with No Name.*
28 July 1951— 7:00 *Tom Corbett, Space Cadet.*
8:00 *Double "C" Ranch.*
10:30 "The Pipes Are Calling," by Dan Sontup, adapted by David Swift, for *Assignment: Man Hunt. Cast:* George Smith, Laurel Shelby, Bob Smith, Russell Arms, Rod Steiger.
29 July 1951— 9:00 "Television Story," by Thomas W. Phipps, adapted by Thomas W. Phipps and Robert W. Shackleton, for *Philco Television Playhouse.* Producer: Fred Coe. Director: Ira Skutch. *Cast:* Gaby Rodgers, Sidney Blackmer, Walter Brooke.
30 July 1951— 8:00 "The Third Time," for *Cameo Theatre. Cast:* Ilona Massey, Lynn Merrill, Rita Shaw, Phil Sterling, Lorence Kerr, Dan Morgan, James Van Dyk.
9:00 "The Fingers," for *Lights Out.* Producer: Herbert Swope, Jr. Director: Albert Tilt. *Cast:* Donald Buka, Susan Douglas, Somer Alberg, Henry Sharp.
9:30 "The Ardent Bigamist," by W. Somerset Maugham, adapted by Russell Beggs, for *Somerset Maugham Theatre. Cast:* Romney Brent.
10:30 *Story Theatre.*
11:00 *Cinema Playhouse.*
31 July 1951— 9:00 "Deliver Us from Evil," by David Swift, for *Fireside Theatre.* Producer/Director: Albert McCleery. *Cast:* Robert Crosier, Franklin Fox, Jason Johnson, Ben Cooper, Harold Grau, Susan Johnson.
9:30 "Mountain Song," by Elizabeth Hume, for *Armstrong Circle Theatre.* Director: Ted Post. *Cast:* James Lipton, Marcia Henderson, Francis Robinson, Frank Tweddell, Edith Sheridan, William Free, Wyrley Birch.
1 August 1951— 9:00 "Hilda McKay," a modern version of Hedda Gabler, by Henrik Ibsen, adapted by Vincent McConnor, for *Kraft Television Theatre. Cast:* Polly Rowles, Robert Pastene, Wendy Drew, John Baragrey, Bruce Gordon.
10:30 *Stars Over Hollywood.*
11:00 *Cinema Playhouse.*
2 August 1951— 8:30 *Treasury Men in Action.*
10:30 *Short Story Theatre.*

3 August 1951— 8:30 "Dream Beach," by Vincent McConnor, for *The Clock.* Director: Grey Lockwood. *Cast:* Jackie Cooper, Ronald Dawson, Hildy Parks, Norma Crane, Harry Clark.

9:00 *Door with No Name.*

4 August 1951— 7:00 *Tom Corbett, Space Cadet.*

8:00 *Double "C" Ranch.*

10:30 "Sentence of Death," by Thomas Walsh, adapted by Max Wilk, for *Assignment: Man Hunt.*

5 August 1951— 9:00 "The Return," by Fred Coe, adapted by Stephen de Baun, for *Philco Television Playhouse.* Director: Delbert Mann. *Cast:* Biff Elliott, Robert Simon, Jill Kraft, Daniel Reed, Alonzo Bosan.

6 August 1951— 8:00 "Strange Identity," by Harry W. Junkin, for *Cameo Theatre.* *Cast:* Jan Miner, Jane Alexander, Ross Martin, Don Biggs, Del Horstmann.

9:00 "The Faceless Man," by George Lefferts, for *Lights Out.* Director: William Corrigan. *Cast:* Gregory Morton, Robert Sterling, Ted Hecht, Louis Sorin, Patricia Peardon.

9:30 "Bewitched," by W. Somerset Maugham, adapted by Kenneth White, for *Somerset Maugham Theatre.* *Cast:* Martha Scott.

10:30 *Story Theatre.* 11:00 *Cinema Playhouse.*

7 August 1951— 9:00 "Agnew Jones and the Giants," by Richard McCracken, for *Fireside Theatre.* *Cast:* Jack Albertson, Maurice Manson, Cliff Edwards, Peter Aureno, Donald Boatz, Judson Rees, Blair Davis.

9:30 "The Mistake," by Anne Howard Bailey, for *Armstrong Circle Theatre.* *Cast:* Frances Reid, Sidney Smith, Felicia Montealegre, Lynn Loring, Maurice Wells, Dorothy Patterson, Kay Campbell.

8 August 1951— 9:00 "Old Doc," for *Kraft Television Theatre.* *Cast:* Vaughn Taylor, Dorothy Sands, John Harvey, Judy Parrish, John Shellie, John Stephen, Natalie Gore, Enid Markey.

10:30 *Stars Over Hollywood.*

11:00 *Cinema Playhouse.*

9 August 1951— 8:30 *Treasury Men in Action.*

10:30 *Short Story Theatre.*

10 August 1951— 8:30 "The Traveler," by Robert Finch, for *The Clock.* Director: Grey Lockwood. *Cast:* Charles Dingle, Biff Elliott, George Forrest, Dulcy Jordan, Harvey Hayes, Joseph Sweeney.

9:00 *Door with No Name.*

11 August 1951— 7:00 *Tom Corbett, Space Cadet.*

8:00 *Double "C" Ranch.*

10:30 "The Trap," by Thomas Walsh, adapted by David Swift, for *Assignment: Man Hunt.* Director: Grey Lockwood. *Cast:* Charles Dingle, Biff Elliott, George Forrest, Dulcy Jordan, Harvey Hayes, Joseph Sweeney.

12 August 1951— 9:00 "Ephraim Tutt's Clean Hands," by Arthur Train, adapted by David Swift, for *Philco Television Playhouse.* Director: Gordon Duff. *Cast:* Hal Currier, Laurence Parvin, Parker Fennelly, Muriel Kirkland, Kevin O'Morrison, Daniel Reed, Elliott Sullivan, Mort Stevens, Bethel Leslie, Roland Wood, Dan Morgan, Harold McGee, Henry Jones, Georgia Harvey.

13 August 1951— 9:00 "The Man from Englewood," by Harry Muheim, for *Lights Out.* Director: William Corrigan. *Cast:* Francis L. Sullivan, Peter Capell, Peggy French, Jack Sheehan, Gordon B. Clarke, Michael Dreyfuss, Tamar Cooper.

9:30 "The Great Man," by W. Somerset Maugham, adapted by Peter Barry, for *Somerset Maugham Theatre. Cast:* Maurice Matheson.

10:30 *Story Theatre.*

11:00 *Cinema Playhouse.*

14 August 1951— 9:00 "Make Believe," for *Fireside Theatre. Cast:* Don Wigginton.

10:00 "The Man in the Bookshop," by William Dudley, *Armstrong Circle Theatre. Cast:* William Prince, Ed Ballentine, Joan Arliss, Audra Lindley, Dwight Marfield, Alexander Campbell, John Winters.

15 August 1951— 9:00 "John Wilkes Booth," by Peter Yates, for *Kraft Television Theatre.* Producer: Stanley Quinn. *Cast:* John Baragrey, Alan Shayne, Oliver Thorndike, Philip Huston, George Roy Hill.

10:30 *Stars Over Hollywood.*

11:00 *Cinema Playhouse.*

16 August 1951— 8:30 *Treasury Men in Action.*

10:30 *Short Story Theatre.*

17 August 1951— 8:30 "Love Is Contraband," by Hamilton Benz, for *The Clock.* Director: Grey Lockwood. *Cast:* Donald Buka, Julie Haydon.

9:00 *Door with No Name.*

18 August 1951— 7:00 *Tom Corbett, Space Cadet.*

8:00 *Double "C" Ranch.*

10:30 Original drama by Abram S. Ginnes, based on materials by Lawrence Diamond, for *Assignment: Man Hunt.* Director: Dan Petrie. *Cast:* Gerry O'Loughlin, Beverly Bayne, David Clark, William Haddock, Beatrice Roth, Frederic Tozere, Tiger Andrews, John McGovern, Russell Arms.

19 August 1951— 9:00 "Come Alive," by William Kendall Clarke, for *Philco Television Playhouse.* Director: Delbert Mann. *Cast:* Valerie Bettis, Lauren Gilbert, Alfreda Wallace.

20 August 1951— 9:00 "Follow Me," by A. J. Russell, for *Lights Out.* Director: William Corrigan. *Cast:* Peter Cookson, Doris Rich, Franklin Fox, Myrtle Tannehill, Dan Morgan.

9:30 "The Yellow Streak," by W. Somerset Maugham, for *Somerset Maugham Theatre. Cast:* Elliott Sullivan.

10:30 *Story Theatre.*

11:00 *Cinema Playhouse.*

21 August 1951— 9:00 "The Lottery," by Shirley Jackson, for *Fireside Theatre. Cast:* Margaret Hayes.

9:30 "Bone of Contention," by Eli Cantor, for *Armstrong Circle Theatre.* Director: Garry Simpson. *Cast:* Coleen Gray, John Morley, Neal Leslie, Richard Derr, John Jacobs, Barbara O'Day.

22 August 1951— 9:00 "Pigs," by Anne Morrison and Patterson McNutt, for *Kraft Television Theatre.* Producer: Maury Holland. *Cast:* Rosemary Rice, William Daniels, Katherine Meskill, Enid Markey, Vaughn Taylor, William Allyn, Harry Sheppard, Alan Woods.

10:30 *Stars Over Hollywood.* 11:00 *Cinema Playhouse.*

23 August 1951— 8:30 *Treasury Men in Action.*

10:30 *Short Story Theatre.*

24 August 1951— 8:30 "Affliction," by Harry W. Junkin, adapted by A. J. Russell, for *The Clock.* Director: Grey Lockwood. *Cast:* Jeffrey Lynn, Jan Owen, Rita Lynn, Eda Heinemann.

9:00 *Door with No Name.*

25 August 1951— 7:00 *Tom Corbett, Space Cadet.*

8:00 *Double "C" Ranch.*

10:30 "Delayed Verdict," by Allan Vaughan Elston, adapted by David Swift, for *Assignment: Man Hunt. Cast:* Timothy Kearse, Paul Langton, Herbert Dillon, Harry Worth, Betty Sinclair, Martin Greene.

26 August 1951— 7:30 *Young Mr. Bobbin,* a domestic comedy, debuts. *Cast:* Jackie Kelk, Jane Seymour, Nydia Westman, Cameron Prud'homme.

9:00 "A Night at the Vulcan," by Nagio Marsh, adapted by Thomas W. Phipps, for *Philco Television Playhouse.* Producer: Fred Coe. Director: Gordon Duff. *Cast:* William Prince, Jerome Cowan, Polly Rowles, Bruce Gordon, Mercer McLeod, Pat Breslin, Stephen Elliott, Elizabeth York, Ralph Clanton, Tony Bickley.

27 August 1951— 8:00 "Heart's Choice," by Raphael Hayes, for *Cameo Theatre.* Producer/Director: Albert McCleery. *Cast:* Tod Andrews, Miriam Goldina, Beverly Whitney, Constance Ford, Vinton Hayworth, Joe Roman, Jack Henderson.

9:00 "Mrs. Manifold," by Stephen Grendon, adapted by Charles Sinclair, for *Lights Out.* Producer: Herbert Swope, Jr. Director: Lawrence Schwab, Jr. *Cast:* Leslie Nielsen, Adelaide Klein, Pat O'Malley.

9:30 "Woman of Fifty," by W. Somerset Maugham, adapted by Russell Beggs, for *Somerset Maugham Theatre. Cast:* Sylvia Field, James Van Dyk, Jack Lemmon, Cynthia Stone.

10:30 *Story Theatre.* 11:00 *Camel Film Theatre,* for WNBT.

28 August 1951— 9:00 "Comes the Day," for *Fireside Theatre. Cast:* Tom Powers, Shiela Bromley.

9:30 "Johnny Pickup," by Doris Halman, for *Armstrong Circle Theatre.* Producer: Hudson Faussett. Director: Ted Post. *Cast:* Arthur Keenan, Anne Jackson, Doug Rutherford, Esther Minciotti, Sandy Sanders.

29 August 1951— 9:00 "Ashes in the Wind," by Mac Shoub, for *Kraft Television Theatre. Cast:* Emily Lawrence, Herbert Rudley.

10:30 "Strange Encounter," for *Stars Over Hollywood.*

11:00 "Gentleman Joe Palooka," for *Camel Film Theatre.*

30 August 1951— 8:30 *Treasury Men in Action.*

10:00 *Martin Kane, Private Eye* is scheduled, but does not return.

31 August 1951— 8:30 "A Right Smart Trick," by Nora Stirling, for *The Clock.* Producer: Herbert Swope, Jr. Director: Clay Yurdin. *Cast:* John Dahl, Noel Leslie, Wynn Gibson.

9:00 *The Big Story* returns.

1 September 1951— 7:00 *Tom Corbett, Space Cadet.*

8:00 *Double "C" Ranch.*

10:30 *Assignment: Man Hunt,* with Helen Warren, Ted Hecht.

2 September 1951— 7:30 *Young Mr. Bobbin.*

9:00 "This Time Next Year," by Fred Coe, for *Philco Television Playhouse.* Producer: Fred Coe. Director: Delbert Mann. *Cast:* Edgar Stehli, Barbara Bolton, Nelson Olmsted, Leona Powers, Hugh Reilly.

3 September 1951— 9:00 "Blackwood Halt," by Gerald Anderson and Warren Parker, for *Lights Out.* Director: William Corrigan. *Cast:* Stella Andrew, Frederic Tozere, Oliver Thorndike, James O'Rear, Byron Russell.

9:30 "Appearances and Reality," by W. Somerset Maugham, adapted by Theodore and Mathilde Ferro, for *Somerset Maugham Theatre. Cast:* Joseph Schildkraut.

10:30 *Story Theatre.*

11:00 *Camel Film Theatre.*

4 September 1951— 9:00 "Second Chance," for *Fireside Theatre. Cast:* Anthony Caruso, Robert Einer.

9:30 "By the Book," by Don Ettlinger, for *Armstrong Circle Theatre. Cast:* Beverly Whitney, Alan Bunce, Audrey Christie, Ernest Graves, Barbara White, Roy Allen, Emil Coleman, Betty O'Leary.

5 September 1951— 9:00 "The Easy Mark," for *Kraft Television Theatre. Cast:* Gage Clark, David Orrick, Roland Winters, Dan Morgan, Frances Waller, Jack Lemmon, Logan Field, Luis Van Rooster, Elizabeth Eustis, Ruth McDevitt.

6 September 1951— 8:30 *Treasury Men in Action.*

10:00 *Martin Kane, Private Eye.*

7 September 1951— 8:30 *The Clock* is replaced.

9:00 *The Big Story.*

9:30 *The Aldrich Family.*

8 September 1951—10:30 *Assignment: Man Hunt* is replaced.

9 September 1951— 7:30 *Young Mr. Bobbin.*

9:00 "Woman of Intrigue," by Arthur Kurlan, for *Philco Television Playhouse.* Producer: Fred Coe. Director: Gordon Duff. *Cast:* Madeleine Carroll, Philip Friend, Murray Matheson, Anthony Dawson.

10 September 1951— 9:00 "Prophet of Darkness," for *Lights Out. Cast:* Sidney Blackmer, Romola Robb, Stuart Maclintoch, Frank Daly.

9:30 "Bubbles," by Wilbur Daniel Steele, adapted by Thomas W. Phipps, for *Robert Montgomery Presents* return. *Cast:* Richard Derr, Denise Alexander, Pat O'Malley.

10:30 "Train Murder," for *Boston Blackie* debut on local WNBT.

11:00 "Kidnapped," for *Camel Movie Hour* on WNBT.

11 September 1951— 9:00 "Homer Takes a Bride," for *Fireside Theatre. Cast:* Robert North, Evelyn Eaton.

9:30 "Sleight of Hand," by John G. Fuller and James Garvin, for *Armstrong Circle Theatre. Cast:* Richard Kollnar, Hildy Parks, Rolfe Sedan, Herschell Bentley.

12 September 1951— 9:00 "The Tale of the Wolf," by Ferenc Molnar, for *Kraft Television Theatre.* Producer: Stanley Quinn. *Cast:* Katherine Bard, Donald Curtis, Joe Anthony.

13 September 1951— 8:30 *Treasury Men in Action.*

10:00 *Martin Kane, Private Eye.*

14 September 1951— 9:00 *The Big Story.*

9:30 *The Aldrich Family.*

16 September 1951— 7:30 *Young Mr. Bobbin.*

9:00 "The Wayward Season," by David Shaw, for *Philco Television Playhouse.* Director: Delbert Mann. *Cast:* Kent Smith, Carol Goodner, Peggy McCay, Margaret Wycherly, Bethel Leslie, Ruth McDevitt, Bill Shumate, Ralph Longley.

17 September 1951— 9:00 "To See Ourselves," by A. J. Russell, for *Lights Out.* Producer: Herbert Swope, Jr. Director: William Corrigan. *Cast:* Cathy O'Donnell, Mercer McLeod, Henry Bernard, Vaughn Taylor.

9:30 "The Mother," by W. Somerset Maugham, adapted by Kenneth White, for *Somerset Maugham Theatre. Cast:* Mildred Natwick, William Redfield.

10:30 *Boston Blackie.*

18 September 1951— 9:00 "Solitaire," for *Fireside Theatre. Cast:* Gertrude Michael, Margaret Field.

9:30 "Flame Out," by Roger Caris, for *Armstrong Circle Theatre.* Producer: Hudson Faussett. Director: Garry Simpson. *Cast:* Leslie Nielsen, Anne Marno, Cameron Prud'homme, Stephen Christian, Robert Burns, Stewart Brown, Robert Nielsen, Pauline Robinson.

19 September 1951— 9:00 "The Wren," by Booth Tarkington, for *Kraft Television Theatre.* Producer: Maury Holland. *Cast:* Pat Browning, Alan Shayne, Howard Wierum, Janet DeGore.

11:00 *Camel Film Theatre.*

20 September 1951— 8:30 *Treasury Men in Action.*

10:00 *Martin Kane, Private Eye.*

21 September 1951— 9:00 *The Big Story.*

9:30 *The Aldrich Family.*

22 September 1951— 7:30 *One Man's Family* returns.

23 September 1951— 5:00 *The Gabby Hayes Show,* by Jerome Coopersmith and Horton Foote, was a children's drama. Producer/Director: Vincent J. Donehue. Stage Manager: Arthur Penn. *Cast:* Gabby Hayes, Mabel Paige, Anne Jackson, Malcolm Keen, Leslie Linder. [Not listed hereafter.]

7:30 *Young Mr. Bobbin.*

9:00 "The Spur," by Ardyth Kennelly, adapted by Joseph Liss, for *Philco Television Playhouse.* Director: Gordon Duff. *Cast:* Alfred Ryder, Wesley Addy, Everett Chambers, Margery Maude.

24 September 1951— 9:00 "Rappaccini's Daughter," by Nathaniel Hawthorne, adapted by Hal C. Hackady, for *Lights Out.* Director: Lawrence Schwab, Jr. *Cast:* Rudolph Watson, Miriam Goldina, Eli Wallach, Hope Miller, Edwin Jerome.

9:30 "I Am Still Alive," by Edward Hope, adapted by Denis Green, for *Robert Montgomery Presents.* Director: Ellis Sard. *Cast:* Donald Woods, Audra Lindley, Jack Hartley, Gerald Smithson, Carol Thomas, Judy Parrish, John Harvey, Jock McGraw, Morgan Beatty, John McGovern.

10:30 *Boston Blackie.*

11:30 *Camel Film Theatre.*

25 September 1951— 8:00 *The Kate Smith Evening Hour,* a variety series that includes dramas, debuts.

9:00 "White Violet," for *Fireside Theatre. Cast:* Eve Miller, Jim Davis.

9:30 "Danny's Tune," by Frank P. DeFelitta, for *Armstrong Circle Theatre.* Producer: Hudson Faussett. Director: Ted Post. *Cast:* George Hall, June Walker, Mary Kay Stearns, Rodney McLennon, Fred Hillebrand.

26 September 1951— 9:00 "The Climax," by Jacques Duval, for *Kraft Television Theatre.* Producer: Stanley Quinn. Liaison: John Rich. *Cast:* Jack Arthur, Olive Deering, Oliver Thorndike.

11:00 *Camel Film Theatre.*

27 September 1951— 8:30 *Treasury Men in Action.*

10:00 *Martin Kane, Private Eye.*

28 September 1951— 9:00 *The Big Story.*

9:30 *The Aldrich Family.*

29 September 1951— 7:30 *One Man's Family.*

30 September 1951— 7:30 *Young Mr. Bobbin.*

9:00 "Byline for Murder," by Andrew Garve, adapted by Walter Bernstein, for

Philco Television Playhouse. Producer: Fred Coe. Director: Delbert Mann. *Cast:* Hugh Reilly, Barbara Joyce, E. G. Marshall, Robert H. Harris, Mardette Edwards, Harry Hess, Vinton Hayworth, Bud Powell, Pat Malone, Vince Harding.

1 October 1951— 9:00 "Will-o'-the-Wisp," by Doris Halman, for *Lights Out.* Director: William Corrigan. *Cast:* Robert Stack, Pat Browning, Ruth White, Lou Anna Gardner, Harry Worth.

9:30 "Grace," by W. Somerset Maugham, adapted by Martha Wilkerson, for *Somerset Maugham Theatre. Cast:* Betty Field, Russell Hardie, Peter Capell.

10:30 *Boston Blackie.*

11:30 *Camel Movie Hour* was Monday. *Camel Film Theatre* was Wednesday on WNBT.

2 October 1951— 9:00 "The Birds Are Walking," for *Fireside Theatre. Cast:* Edward Norris, Jimmy Smith.

9:30 "The Runaway Heart," by Doris Halman, for *Armstrong Circle Theatre.* Director: Garry Simpson. *Cast:* John Newland, Judith Evelyn, Mary Orr, Bunny Lewbel.

3 October 1951— 8:00 *The Kate Smith Evening Hour.*

9:00 "Irish Eyes," by Edward E. Rose, for *Kraft Television Theatre. Cast:* Dick Foran, Sally Chamberlin, Melville Cooper, Eva Condon, Chester Stratton, Andrea Wallace, Biff McGuire, Pat O'Malley, Paul Langton, Chris White.

11:00 *Camel Film Theatre.*

4 October 1951— 8:30 *Treasury Men in Action.*

10:00 *Martin Kane, Private Eye.*

10:30 *Foreign Intrigue,* dramas on film.

5 October 1951— 9:00 *The Big Story.*

9:30 *The Aldrich Family.*

6 October 1951— 7:30 *One Man's Family.*

7 October 1951— 7:30 *Young Mr. Bobbin.*

9:00 "Requiem for Model 'A'," an original drama by David Swift, for *Philco Television Playhouse.* Producer: Fred Coe. Director: Gordon Duff. *Cast:* Carl Frank, Dorothy Elder, Jonathan Marlowe, Michael Lewin, Harvey Fine, Rod Steiger, Gerry O'Loughlin, Guy Thomajan, Fred Stewart.

8 October 1951— 9:00 "Dark Image," by John McGreevey, for *Lights Out.* Director: Lawrence Schwab, Jr. *Cast:* Donald Woods, Ann Shepherd, Beatrice Knight, Leni Stengel.

9:30 "To Walk the Night," by William Sloane, adapted by Irving Gaynor Neiman, for *Robert Montgomery Presents.* Director: Ellis Sard. *Cast:* Geraldine Fitzgerald, John Baragrey, Don Briggs, Matt Briggs, Alan MacAteer, William Jackson, Frank Rowan, Chuck Callahan.

10:30 *Boston Blackie.*

11:00 *Camel Movie Hour.*

9 October 1951— 9:00 "Doctor Mac," for *Fireside Theatre. Cast:* Tom Powers, Emory Parnell.

9:30 "The Commandant's Clock," by William Welch, for *Armstrong Circle Theatre.* Director: Ted Post. *Cast:* Ben Cooper, Richard Cleary, Melville Ruick, Woody Morgan, Arthur Hutt, Donald Harris, Philip Rodd, Andy Mulligan.

10 October 1951— 8:00 "Power of the Press," by Thomas Corley and William Roerick, for *The Kate Smith Evening Hour.* RT: 8:16–8:24. Producer: Ted Collins. Director: Albert McCleery. *Cast:* Lew Ayres, Madge Evans, John Harvey.

9:00 "Seen But Not Heard," by Marie Baumer and Martin Berkeley, for *Kraft Television Theatre.* Producer: Stanley Quinn. *Cast:* Jean Gillespie, Eleanor Wilson, Lawrence Fletcher.

11:00 *Camel Film Theatre.*

11 October 1951—8:30 *Treasury Men in Action.*

10:00 *Martin Kane, Private Eye.*

10:30 *Foreign Intrigue.*

12 October 1951—9:00 *The Big Story.*

9:30 *The Aldrich Family.*

13 October 1951—7:30 *One Man's Family.*

14 October 1951—7:30 *Young Mr. Bobbin.*

9:00 "October Story," an original drama by David Swift, for *Goodyear Television Playhouse* debut. It alternates with *Philco Television Playhouse.* Producer: Fred Coe. Director: Delbert Mann. *Cast:* Julie Harris, Leslie Nielsen, Jane Rose, William Lynn, Florence Halop, Jackie Schelle, Maurice Burke, Jeanne Shepherd, Edith Heiser.

15 October 1951—9:00 "I, Spy," by Gerry Morrison, for *Lights Out.* Director: William Corrigan. *Cast:* Dorothy Stickney, Henry Hull, Alfreda Wallace, Dale Engel.

9:30 "Masquerade," by W. Somerset Maugham, for *Somerset Maugham Theatre.* *Cast:* Bonita Granville, Scott McKay, Paula Lawrence.

10:30 *Boston Blackie.*

11:00 *Camel Movie Hour.*

16 October 1951—9:00 "Treasures of the Heart," for *Fireside Theatre.* *Cast:* William Fawcett, Douglas Dick, Garry Lee Jackson.

9:30 "Lost and Found," by Muffet Peter, for *Armstrong Circle Theatre.* Director: Garry Simpson. *Cast:* Cara Williams, Chester Stratton, Lex Richards, Ann Thomas, Seth Arnold, Frank Mullen, Ann Stillings, Lionel Ames, Inez Juarez, Anne Williams, James Reese, Joseph Leon, Maurice Gosfield, Bodie Wulf.

17 October 1951—8:00 *The Kate Smith Evening Hour.*

9:00 "Moon Over Mulberry Street," by Nicholas Cosentino, for *Kraft Television Theatre.* Producer: Maury Holland. *Cast:* William Edmunds, Tiger Andrews, Dolores Sutton.

11:00 *Camel Film Theatre.*

18 October 1951—8:30 *Treasury Men in Action.*

10:00 *Martin Kane, Private Eye.*

10:30 *Foreign Intrigue.*

19 October 1951—9:00 *The Big Story.*

9:30 *The Aldrich Family.*

20 October 1951—7:30 *One Man's Family.*

21 October 1951—7:30 *Young Mr. Bobbin.*

9:00 "Marcia Akers," by William Kendall Clarke, for *Philco Television Playhouse.* Producer: Fred Coe. Director: Gordon Duff. *Cast:* Olive Deering, James Daly, Kendall Clark, James Gregory, Russell Collins, Maxine Stuart, Francis Compton, Michael Keith, Kathleen Comegys, Frances Williams.

22 October 1951—9:00 "The Deal," by James Blumgarten, for *Lights Out.* Director: Lawrence Schwab, Jr. *Cast:* Anne Marno, Martin Gabel, Joseph Wiseman, Jack Clay, Jack Delmonte, Harvey Hayes, Gladys Klark, Mary Gilden, Mary Leader, Ralph Paul.

9:30 "I Wouldn't Be in Your Shoes," for *Robert Montgomery Presents. Cast:* Katherine Squire, Vaughn Taylor, Raymond Bramley, Jack Arthur, Jim Millhollin, Harry Townes, George Kluge, Grania O'Malley, Bobby Nick.

10:00 *Boston Blackie.*

11:00 *Camel Movie Hour.*

23 October 1951— 9:00 "Torture," for *Fireside Theatre. Cast:* Ken Harvey, Dabbs Greer, Garry Lee Jackson.

9:30 "The Long View," by Kay Arthur, for *Armstrong Circle Theatre.* Director: Ted Post. *Cast:* Thomas Mitchell, Mona Bruns, Biff McGuire, David Orrick, John D. Seymour, Leland Harris, Joe Allen, Jr., James Broderick.

24 October 1951— 8:00 *The Kate Smith Evening Hour.*

9:00 "Intolerance," for *Kraft Television Theatre. Cast:* Margaret Phillips, Alfreda Wallace, John Stephen, Bramwell Fletcher.

11:00 *Camel Film Theatre.*

25 October 1951— 8:30 *Treasury Men in Action.*

10:00 *Martin Kane, Private Eye.*

10:30 *Foreign Intrigue.*

26 October 1951— 9:00 *The Big Story.*

9:30 *The Aldrich Family.*

27 October 1951— 7:30 *One Man's Family.*

28 October 1951— 7:30 *Young Mr. Bobbin.*

9:00 "The Copper," by David Swift, for *Goodyear Television Playhouse.* Producer: Fred Coe. Director: Delbert Mann. *Cast:* Wally Cox, Salem Ludwig, Mike Kellin, Ernest Borgnine, Brandon Peters, Pat Carroll, David White, Thomas Heaphy, Paul Lilly, Robert Dale Martin, Jonathan Marlowe.

29 October 1951— 9:00 "The Veil," by Raphael Hayes, for *Lights Out.* Producer: Herbert Swope, Jr. Director: William Corrigan. *Cast:* Lee J. Cobb, Arlene Francis, Melba Rae, Lenard Barry, Fred Hillebrand, Josephine Woods, Frank Daly.

9:30 "The Fall of Edward Bernard," by W. Somerset Maugham, for *Somerset Maugham Theatre. Cast:* Richard Greene.

10:30 *Boston Blackie.*

11:00 *Camel Movie Hour.*

30 October 1951— 9:00 "Dress Party," for *Fireside Theatre. Cast:* Robert North.

9:30 "Night Song," by Anne Howard Bailey, for *Armstrong Circle Theatre. Cast:* Geraldine Fitzgerald, Donald Woods, Dorothy Peterson, Francis Compton, Tina Teal, James Van Dyk, Kay Campbell, Joseph Ripley.

31 October 1951— 8:00 "Ethel and Albert" by Peg Lynch, for *The Kate Smith Evening Hour.* Director: Greg Garrison. *Cast:* Peg Lynch, Alan Bunce.

9:00 "Hour of Crisis," by Eric Hatch, for *Kraft Television Theatre. Cast:* Cliff Hall, Roy Fant, Hazel Dawn, Robert Paige, Lex Richards, Edith Gresham, Kathleen Comegys, Margaret Alworthy, Peter Boyne.

11:00 *Camel Film Theatre.*

1 November 1951— 8:30 *Treasury Men in Action.*

10:00 *Martin Kane, Private Eye.*

10:30 *Foreign Intrigue.*

2 November 1951— 9:00 *The Big Story.*

9:30 *The Aldrich Family.*

3 November 1951— 7:30 *One Man's Family.*

4 November 1951— 3:00 "House in the Garden," Episode 1 of *Fair Meadows, U.S.A.,* a family serial, debuts. Producer: Maury Holland. Director: Richard Goode. *Cast:* Howard St. John, Ruth Matheson. [Not listed hereafter.]

7:30 *Young Mr. Bobbin.*

9:00 "The Education of a Fullback," by David Shaw, for *Philco Television Playhouse.* Director: Gordon Duff. *Cast:* Joseph Buloff, Vinton Hayworth, Dorothy Malone, Logan Field, Richard S. Bishop, Donald McKee, Jane Rose, Walter Black.

5 November 1951— 9:00 "The Chamber of Gloom," by A. J. Russell, for *Lights Out.* Director: William Corrigan. *Cast:* Geraldine Brooks, Arnold Moss, Harold McGee, Bruce Gordon, Paul Marlin, Paul Gray, Earl Dawson.

9:30 "An Inspector Calls," by J. B. Priestley, adapted by Denis Green, for *Robert Montgomery Presents. Cast:* Herbert Marshall, Frederic Tozere, John Newland, Faith Brook, Isobel Elsom, Bill Daniels, Sara Marshall, Jennifer Raine.

10:30 *Boston Blackie.*

11:00 *Camel Movie Hour.*

6 November 1951— 9:00 "Big Night in Boonetown," for *Fireside Theatre. Cast:* John Mitchum.

9:30 "Fog Station," by Roger Garis, for *Armstrong Circle Theatre.* Producer: Hudson Faussett. Director: Ted Post. *Cast:* William Eythe, Constance Ford, Bob Patten, Frank Felton, Kenneth Boles, Merrill Joels.

7 November 1951— 8:00 "Ethel and Albert," for *The Kate Smith Evening Hour.*

9:00 "Justice," by John Galsworthy, for *Kraft Television Theatre. Cast:* Alan Shayne, Fred Stewart, Malcolm Keen, Ellen Martin, David Cole, Peter Pagan, E. G. Marshall, Noel Leslie, John Moore, Leslie Barrie, Gerald Savoy, Basil Howes, Roger Plowden.

11:00 *Camel Film Theatre.*

8 November 1951— 8:30 *Treasury Men in Action.*

10:00 *Martin Kane, Private Eye.*

10:30 *Foreign Intrigue.*

9 November 1951— 9:00 *The Big Story.*

9:30 *The Aldrich Family.*

10 November 1951— 7:30 *One Man's Family.*

11 November 1951— 7:30 *Young Mr. Bobbin.*

9:00 "Flight to Freedom," by Geoffrey Kean, adapted by Stephen de Baun, for *Goodyear Television Playhouse.* Director: Delbert Mann. *Cast:* Bramwell Fletcher, Laurence Hugo, Robert H. Harris, Theo Goetz, Rita Lynn, Barbara Ames, Peter Von Zerneck, Martin Brandt, Lotte Stavisky, Dehl Berti.

12 November 1951— 9:00 "Beast in the Garden," by Vincent McConnor, for *Lights Out.* Director: Grey Lockwood. *Cast:* Margaret Phillips, John Marivale, J. W. Austin, Betty Sinclair, Harry Hugenot.

9:30 "Before the Party," by W. Somerset Maugham, adapted by Kenneth White, for *Somerset Maugham Theatre. Cast:* Geraldine Fitzgerald.

10:30 *Boston Blackie.*

11:00 *Camel Movie Hour.*

13 November 1951— 9:00 "Seven Graces," for *Fireside Theatre. Cast:* Jim Davis, Jessie Cavitt.

9:30 "Day Dreams," by Michelle Cousins, for *Armstrong Circle Theatre. Cast:* Beatrice Pearson, Herbert Evers, Dorothy Sands, Marlo Dwyer, Nell Walls, Bob Burland, Dennis McCarthy, Earl Simmons, Anita Wevy, Mary Gilden, Neil Frizell.

14 November 1951— 8:00 "Trio by Lamplight," by Paul Tripp, for *The Kate Smith*

Evening Hour. Director: Albert McCleery. *Cast:* Dolores del Rio, John O'Hara, Margaret Hayes. "Ethel and Albert" shown also.

9:00 "Never Be the Same," by Peter Martin, for *Kraft Television Theatre.* Producer: Maury Holland. *Cast:* Chris White, Nydia Westman, Howard Freeman, Jean Adair, Joey Walsh, Dan Morgan, Rick Jason, Michael Mann, James Lee, Bram Nossen, Edith King, Reginald Mason.

11:00 *Camel Film Theatre.*

15 November 1951— 8:30 *Treasury Men in Action.*

10:00 *Martin Kane, Private Eye.*

10:30 *Foreign Intrigue.*

16 November 1951— 9:00 *The Big Story.*

9:30 *The Aldrich Family.*

17 November 1951— 7:30 *One Man's Family.*

11:15–12:53 "Drums," for *Saturday Nite Playhouse,* a film series on local WNBT. *Cast:* Sabu.

18 November 1951— 7:30 *Young Mr. Bobbin.*

9:00 "A Little Night Music," by Mary Jane Ward, adapted by David Swift, for *Philco Television Playhouse.* Director: Gordon Duff. *Cast:* Paul McGrath, Neva Patterson, Amelia Corley, Katherine Meskill, Frances Williams, David McKay, Peter Brandon, Anthony Dawson, Maxine Stuart.

19 November 1951— 9:00 "Friday, the Nineteenth," by Elizabeth S. Holding, adapted by Milton Subotsky and Phyllis Coe, for *Lights Out.* Director: William Corrigan. *Cast:* Eddie Albert, Audra Lindley, Louise Buckley, Zolma Taima, Joan Taylor.

9:30 "The Kimballs," by Mitchell Wilson, adapted by Agnes Eckhardt, for *Robert Montgomery Presents. Cast:* Boris Karloff, Vanessa Brown.

10:30 *Boston Blackie.*

11:00 *Camel Movie Hour.*

20 November 1951— 9:00 "Handcuffs," for *Fireside Theatre. Cast:* Dorothy Comingore.

9:30 "The Oldster," by Eric Arthur, for *Armstrong Circle Theatre. Cast:* Henry Hull, Josephine DeWit, Allen Nourge, Butch Cavell, Neil Harrison, Val Gould, Joe Bernard, Charles Martin.

21 November 1951— 8:00 "Beginner's Luck," by Ernest Lehman, adapted by Jesse Sandler, for *The Kate Smith Evening Hour.* Director: Albert McCleery. *Cast:* Ann Sheridan.

9:00 "Dear Brutus," by James M. Barrie, for *Kraft Television Theatre.* Producer: Stanley Quinn. *Cast:* Jean Gillespie, Richard Fraser, Tom McElhaney, Donald Curtis, Kathleen Comegys, Joseph Anthony, Faith Brook, Thomas Heaphy, Joan Wetmore, Elizabeth Johnson, Joanne Trout.

11:00 *Camel Film Theatre.*

22 November 1951— 9:00 *Treasury Men in Action.*

10:00 *Martin Kane, Private Eye.*

10:30 *Foreign Intrigue.*

23 November 1951— 9:00 *The Big Story.*

9:30 *The Aldrich Family.*

24 November 1951— 7:30 *One Man's Family.*

11:15 *Saturday Nite Playhouse.*

25 November 1951— 7:30 *Young Mr. Bobbin.*

9:00 "The Eleventh Ward," by H. R. Hays, for *Goodyear Television Playhouse.*

Director: Delbert Mann. *Cast:* Margaret Phillips, Jeanne Bolan, Daniel Reed, Richard Abbott, Louis Lytton, Addison Richards, Harry Sheppard, George Smith.

26 November 1951— 9:00 "The Far-Off Island," by Robert Esson, for *Lights Out.* Director: Grey Lockwood. *Cast:* Richard Greene, Lenka Peterson, Gregory Morton.

9:30 "Home and Beauty," by W. Somerset Maugham, adapted by Theodore and Mathilde Ferro for *Somerset Maugham Theatre. Cast:* Constance Bennett.

10:30 *Boston Blackie.*

11:00 *Eleventh Hour Theatre,* as film series on WNBT.

27 November 1951— 9:00 "Not a Bit Like Jason," for *Fireside Theatre. Cast:* Lynne Roberts, Tom Cook, John Sutton, Gloria Marshall.

9:30 "Brand from the Burning," by Doris Halman, for *Armstrong Circle Theatre.* Director: Garry Simpson. *Cast:* Thomas Coley, Grace Kelly, Morton Stevens, Lester Lonergan, Patsy Flicker, Blanche Lytell, Arita Webb, Amelia Barleon, Fred Baron, Sam Buffinton, Carol Reed, Helen Falvey, William Haddock, John McKee, Chris Barberry, Doreen Lane, Charles Lee Saari, Nancy Ann Brandt.

28 November 1951— 8:00 "Anne of a Thousand Days," by Maxwell Anderson, for *The Kate Smith Evening Hour. Cast:* Rex Harrison, Lilli Palmer, Winfield Hoeny, Pat Malone, Natalie Core, Tom Walsh.

9:00 "The Fair Haired Boy," by Loren Singer, for *Kraft Television Theatre.* Producer: Maury Holland. *Cast:* Dick Foran, Richard Carlyle, Noel Leslie, Nelson Olmsted, James Westerfield, Leslie Barrett, Richard Bishop, Frances Helm.

11:00 *Eleventh Hour Theatre.*

29 November 1951— 8:30 *Treasury Men in Action.*

10:00 *Martin Kane, Private Eye.*

10:30 *Foreign Intrigue.*

11:00 *Eleventh Hour Playhouse* (aka *Theatre*).

30 November 1951— 9:00 *The Big Story.*

9:30 *The Aldrich Family.*

11:00 *Eleventh Hour Playhouse.*

1 December 1951— 7:30 *One Man's Family.*

11:15 *Saturday Nite Playhouse.*

2 December 1951— 7:30 *Young Mr. Bobbin.*

9:00 "Incident at Golden's Creek," by William Kendall Clarke, for *Philco Television Playhouse.* Director: Gordon Duff. *Cast:* James Gregory, Valentina Latimore, Leora Thatcher, Dorothy Sands, Fred Stewart, Philip Coolidge, Michael Gorrin, Boris Marshalov, Gene Steiner, Paul Ford.

3 December 1951— 9:00 "The Silent Supper," by Bruce Brighton, for *Lights Out.* Director: William Corrigan. *Cast:* Vanessa Brown, Paul Valentine, Andrew Duggan, Charlotte Knight, Nance Robbins.

9:30 "Top Secret," for *Robert Montgomery Presents. Cast:* Robert Montgomery, Elizabeth Montgomery (debut), James Van Dyk, John D. Seymour, Margaret Phillips, Edward Harvey, Robert McQuade, Reese Taylor, Joseph Holland.

10:30 *Boston Blackie.*

11:00 *Eleventh Hour Theatre.*

4 December 1951— 9:00 "The Squeeze," for *Fireside Theatre. Cast:* Clancy Cooper, William Lester.

9:30 "Key Witness," by Jerome Ross, for *Armstrong Circle Theatre.* Producer: Hudson Faussett. Director: Ted Post. *Cast:* Kent Smith, Barnard Hughes, John McGovern, Patricia Remick, Paul Parks.

11:00 *Eleventh Hour Theatre.*

5 December 1951— 8:00 "Ethel and Albert," for *The Kate Smith Evening Hour.*

9:00 "Loyalties," by John Galsworthy, adapted by A. J. Herbert, for *Kraft Television Theatre. Cast:* Philip Friend, Lloyd Bochner, Toby Robins.

11:00 *Eleventh Hour Theatre.*

6 December 1951— 8:30 *Treasury Men in Action.*

10:00 *Martin Kane, Private Eye.*

10:30 *Foreign Intrigue.*

11:00 *Eleventh Hour Playhouse.*

7 December 1951— 9:00 *The Big Story.*

9:30 *The Aldrich Family.*

11:00 *Eleventh Hour Playhouse.*

8 December 1951— 7:30 *One Man's Family.*

11:15 *Saturday Nite Playhouse.*

9 December 1951— 7:30 *Young Mr. Bobbin.*

9:00 "Money to Burn," by Walter Black and William Mendrick, for *Goodyear Television Playhouse.* Producer: Fred Coe. Director: Delbert Mann. *Cast:* Dan Morgan, Fred Stewart, Leona Powers, Pat Breslin, Ken Walken, Bob Patten, Bert Conway, David White, Mike Kellin, Billy M. Greene, Alice Pearce, Walter Block, Ed Nannery, Louis Lytton.

10 December 1951— 9:00 "The Angry Birds," by A. J. Russell, for *Lights Out.* Producer: Herbert Swope, Jr. Director: Grey Lockwood. *Cast:* John Forsythe, Constance Dowling, Vaughn Taylor, J. S. Martin, James Winslow.

9:30 "Smith Serves," by W. Somerset Maugham, adapted by Russell Beggs, for *Somerset Maugham Theatre. Cast:* Eddie Albert, Joan Bennett.

10:30 *Boston Blackie.*

11:00 *Eleventh Hour Theatre.*

11 December 1951— 9:00 "A Question of Wills," for *Fireside Theatre. Cast:* Maura Murphy, Tom Powers.

9:30 "Marionettes," for *Armstrong Circle Theatre.* Producer: Hudson Faussett. Director: Garry Simpson. *Cast:* Beatrice Pearson, Henry Jones, Joey Walsh, Fred Hillebrand, Bil Baird & Marionettes, Sal Mineo, Sarina Mineo, Malcolm Broderick, G. Vincent Van Lynn.

11:00 *Eleventh Hour Theatre.*

12 December 1951— 8:00 "Ethel and Albert," for *The Kate Smith Evening Hour.*

9:00 "The Golden State," by Samuel Spewack, for *Kraft Television Theatre. Cast:* Jane Rose, Pat O'Malley, Edgar Stehli, Noel Leslie, Logan Ramsey, Gene Lyons, Dorothy Malone, George Roy Hill.

13 December 1951— 8:30 *Treasury Men in Action.*

10:00 *Martin Kane, Private Eye.*

10:30 *Foreign Intrigue.*

11:00 *Eleventh Hour Playhouse.*

14 December 1951— 9:00 *The Big Story.*

9:30 *The Aldrich Family.*

11:00 *Eleventh Hour Playhouse.*

15 December 1951— 7:30 *One Man's Family.*

11:15 *Saturday Nite Playhouse.*

16 December 1951— 7:30 *Young Mr. Bobbin.*

9:00 "Perspective," adapted by H. R. Hays, for *Philco Television Playhouse.* Director: Gordon Duff. *Cast:* Everett Sloane, Augusta Dabney, Cyril Ritchard, Lauren Gilbert, Whit Bissell, Martin Kosleck, Charles Andre, Theo Goetz.

17 December 1951— 9:00 "Perchance to Dream," by Robert Kalvar, for *Lights Out.* Director: William Corrigan. *Cast:* William Eythe, David White, Lou Anna Gardney, Logan Ramsey, Alice Ghostly.

9:30 "Christmas Gift," for *Robert Montgomery Presents. Cast:* Jean Pierre Aumont, Donald Briggs, William Murphy, Margaret Draper, Nina Varela, Sid Cassel, Denise Alexander, Jane Alexander, Tommy Holloran, Judy Parrish.

10:30 *Boston Blackie.*

11:00 *Eleventh Hour Playhouse.*

18 December 1951— 9:00 "Black Savannah," for *Fireside Theatre. Cast:* Joan Leslie, Lester Mathews.

9:30 "Disaster," by Elizabeth Hume, for *Armstrong Circle Theatre. Cast:* Jack Lambert, Gene Reynolds, Robert Weber, Bruno Wick, Ellen Davey, Jason Johnson, Salem Barry, James Gildersleeve.

11:00 *Eleventh Hour Theatre.*

19 December 1951— 8:00 "The Small One," for *The Kate Smith Evening Hour. Cast:* Kate Smith.

9:00 "Incident on Fifth Avenue," by Gerry Morrison, for *Kraft Television Theatre. Cast:* Robert McQuade, Peter Bayne, Joseph Sweeney, Roland Winters, Rex O'Malley, Hildy Parks.

11:00 *Eleventh Hour Theatre.*

20 December 1951— 8:30 *Treasury Men in Action.*

10:00 *Martin Kane, Private Eye.*

10:30 *Foreign Intrigue.*

11:00 *Eleventh Hour Playhouse.*

21 December 1951— 9:00 *The Big Story.*

9:30 *The Aldrich Family.*

11:00 *Eleventh Hour Playhouse.*

22 December 1951— 7:30 *One Man's Family.*

11:15 *Saturday Nite Playhouse.*

23 December 1951— 7:30 *Young Mr. Bobbin.*

9:00 "I Was Stalin's Prisoner," by Robert Vogeler, for *Goodyear Television Playhouse.* Director: Delbert Mann. *Cast:* Edmon Ryan, Constance Reed, Norman Rose, Victor Varconi, Ben Grauer, John Cameron Swayze.

24 December 1951— 9:00 "This Way to Heaven," by Douglass Parkhirst, for *Lights Out.* Director: Grey Lockwood. *Cast:* Burgess Meredith, Kathleen Comegys, Beverly Dennis, Robert Webber.

9:30 "Amahl and the Night Visitors," by Gian-Carlo Menotti, "the world premiere of the first opera written especially for television," and Hallmark Cards. Producer: Kirk Browning. Director: Gian Carlo Menotti.

25 December 1951— 9:00 "A Christmas Carol," by Charles Dickens, adapted by David Swift, for *Fireside Theatre.* Producer: Fred Coe/Gordon Duff. Director: Leonard Hole. *Cast:* Ralph Richardson, Alan Napier, Norman Barrs, Malcolm Keen, Robert Hay-Smith, Richard Wigginton, Mary Lou Deering, Melville Cooper, Robin Craven, Pat Malone, Betty Sinclair, Mabel Taylor, Judson Rees.

9:30 "Enter Rosalind," by Ruth Woodman, for *Armstrong Circle Theatre.* Director: George Simpson. *Cast:* Enid Markey, Dolores Sutton, Ben Cooper, Mary

Linn Beller, Vinton Hayworth, Lee Remick, Sean Downey, Inez Juarez, Dulcie Cooper, Kathryn Lang, Bruce Reynolds, Leo Arnold, Jr., Edwin Bruce.

11:00 *Eleventh Hour Theatre.*

26 December 1951— 8:00 "Reflected Glory," by Jesse Sandler, for *The Kate Smith Evening Hour.* Director: Albert McCleery. *Cast:* Olga San Juan, Edmond O'Brien, Julie Bennett, Jack Albertson.

9:00 "The Nantucket Legend," by George Lefferts, for *Kraft Television Theatre.* *Cast:* Vaughn Taylor, Brook Byron.

10:30 "Two for a Penny," by Carol Warner Gluck, for *Cavalier Theatre.* Director: Robert Champlain. *Cast:* Carl Reiner, Helen Gillette.

11:00 *Eleventh Hour Theatre.*

27 December 1951— 8:30 *Treasury Men in Action.*

10:00 *Martin Kane, Private Eye.*

10:30 *Foreign Intrigue.*

11:00 *Eleventh Hour Playhouse.*

28 December 1951— 9:00 *The Big Story.*

9:30 *The Aldrich Family.*

11:00 *Eleventh Hour Playhouse.*

29 December 1951— 7:30 *One Man's Family.*

11:15 *Saturday Nite Playhouse.*

30 December 1951— 7:30 *Young Mr. Bobbin.*

9:00 "The Sisters," by Robert Alan Arthur, for *Philco Television Playhouse.* Producer: Fred Coe. Director: Gordon Duff. *Cast:* Leslie Nielsen, Natalie Schafer, Dorothy Peterson, Grace Kelly, Philippa Bevans, Lloyd Richards, John C. Becher, Viola Roche.

31 December 1951— 9:00 "Of Time and Third Avenue," by William Welch, for *Lights Out.* Producer: Herbert Swope, Jr. Director: Grey Lockwood. *Cast:* Henry Daniell, Biff Elliott, Bethel Leslie, Edward Gargan, Beatrice Pons.

9:30 "The Class of '67," a special New Year's Eve docudrama from a New York hospital, for *Robert Montgomery Presents. Cast:* Robert Montgomery.

10:30 *Boston Blackie.*

11:55 New Year's Eve Festivities.

Principal source: W2XBS *Television Master Programs*; WNBT *Television Master Programs*, 1946–1951.

Selected Bibliography

Appleyard, Rollo. *Pioneers of Electrical Communications.* London: Macmillan, 1930.

Archer, Gleason L. *Big Business and Radio.* New York: American Historical Society, 1938. Reprinted by Arno Press, 1971.

Arlen, Michael J. *The Camera Age: Essays on Television.* New York: Farrar Strauss Giroux, 1976. These essays originally appeared in *The New Yorker.*

The Atlantic Monthly. An important source for an occasional perspective on television drama.

Barnouw, Erik. *Handbook of Radio Production.* Boston: Houghton Mifflin, 1949.

_____. *A Tower of Babel: A History of Broadcasting in the United States to 1933.* New York: Oxford University Press, 1966.

_____. *The Golden Web: A History of Broadcasting in the United States, 1933–1953.* New York: Oxford University Press, 1968.

The Billboard. This weekly trade publication is a major source of entertainment news and television reviews, 1928–1948.

Biography, a series on the Arts and Entertainment (A&E) cable network. A fine resource for the lives of producers, directors, and actors in television and film.

Bluem, A William. *Documentary in American Television.* New York: Hastings House, 1965.

Blum, Daniel. *A Pictorial History of Television.* Philadelphia: Chilton, 1959.

Briggs, Asa A. *The Golden Age of Wireless: The History of Broadcasting in the United Kingdom.* London: Oxford University Press, 1965. Covers the period 1926–1939.

BBC Handbook. London: British Broadcasting Corporation Broadcasting House, 1955.

British Broadcasting Corporation. *Television Programmes as Broadcast* (26 August 1936–1 September 1939; 7 June 1946–1 January 1953). London: British Broadcasting Corporation. This official program log includes titles, dates, time, cast lists, and music credits. These early volumes are in the BBC Written Archives Centre, Caversham Park, Reading, England.

Britton, Florence. *Best Television Plays 1957.* New York: Ballantine Books, 1957. Includes "Snapfinger Creek."

Broadcasting. The weekly trade periodical contains news and occasional features.

Brooks, Tim, and Earle Marsh. *The Complete Directory of Prime Time Network TV Shows, 1946–Present.* New York: Ballantine Books, 1995; 2000. An indispensable source.

Brown, Les. *Encyclopedia of Television.* New York: Times Books, 1977.

Buxton, Frank, and Bill Owen. *The Big Broadcast: 1920–1950.* New York: Viking Press, 1972; Lanham, Maryland: Scarecrow Press, 1996. A principal source for radio program descriptions and cast lists.

Campbell, Robert. *The Golden Years of Broadcasting: A Celebration of the First 50 Years of Radio and Television on NBC.* New York: Charles Scribner's Sons, 1976. Provides brief narratives on "Weekly Drama," "Soap Operas and Quiz Shows," and "Dramatic Specials." Well illustrated.

Cantor, Muriel G., and Suzanne Pingree. *The Soap Opera.* Beverly Hills, California: Sage Publications, 1983. Includes a case study of *The Guiding Light*, 1948–1982.

The Catholic World. A significant conservative perspective often questioning family values in television dramas.

Chaikin, Judy. *Legacy of the Hollywood Blacklist.* A documentary film. Los Angeles: One Step Productions/KCET, 1987.

CBS Production Handbook. New York: Columbia Broadcasting System, 15 September 1933.

CBS Program Book. New York: Columbia Broadcasting System, 1938–1942, 1944–1945. This monthly publication is especially useful for the mid–1940s.

CBS Sponsored and Sustaining Programs. New York: Columbia Broadcasting System, 1947. Published monthly.

"CBS Television Inaugural Broadcast," 21 July 1931. Script. New York: CBS Reference Library.

CBS Television Master Control Log. New York: Columbia Broadcasting System, 1931–1933, 1940–1941. This official list of programs, in the archives, provides dates, times, program titles, and names of engineers.

CBS Television Operations Master Control Log, 1946–1952. New York: Columbia Broadcasting System. In the archives.

CBS "W2XAB Birthday Program," 21 July 1932. Script. New York: CBS Reference Library.

Cerf, Bennett, and Van H. Cartmell, eds. *Thirty Famous One-Act Plays.* New York: Random House, 1943. Includes "The Valiant," "The Monkey's Paw," "Hello, Out There," "A Game of Chess," and other often televised dramas.

Chamberlain, A. B. "CBS Grand Central Television Studios." New York: CBS General Engineering Department Publications, July 1948.

Chapman, E. H. *Wireless To-Day.* London: Oxford University Press, 1936.

Chase, Francis Jr. *Sound and Fury: An Informal History of Broadcasting.* New York: Harper, 1942.

Chayefsky, Paddy. *Television Plays.* New York: Simon and Schuster, 1955. Opinions and motivations are discussed for six of his plays, including "Marty."

Chester, Giraud, Garnet R. Garrison, and Edgar E. Willis. *Television and Radio.* Englewood Cliffs, New Jersey: Prentice-Hall, 1971.

Chicago Daily News. Helpful for Chicago dramas.

Crosby, John. *Out of the Blue: A Book About Radio and Television.* New York: Harper and Brothers, 1942.

Dunlap, Orrin E., Jr. *The Future of Television.* New York: Harper and Brothers, 1942.

_____. *Radio and Television Almanac.* New York: Harper, 1951.

_____. *Radio's 100 Men of Science: Biographical Narratives of Pathfinders in Electronics and Television.* New York: Harper, 1944.

Dunning, John. *Tune in Yesterday: The Ultimate Encyclopedia of Old Time Radio, 1925–1976.* Englewood Cliffs, New Jersey: Prentice-Hall, 1976.

Dupuy, Judy. *Television Show Business.* Schenectady, New York: General Electric, 1945. A principal source of information about General Electric's dramas and other programs during the early 1940s.

Eddy, William C. *Television: The Eyes of Tomorrow.* New York: Prentice-Hall, 1945.

Edmondson, Madeliene, and David Rounds. *From Mary Noble to Mary Hartman: The Complete Soap Opera Book.* New York: Stein and Day, 1976.

Emery, Walter B. *National and International Systems of Broadcasting: Their History Operation and Control.* East Lansing: Michigan State University Press, 1969

Emmens, Carol A. *An Album of Television.* New York: Franklin Watts, 1980. Contains many photographs, including those of "The Queen's Messenger."

Fidell, Estelle. *Play Index, 1953–1960.* New York: H. W. Wilson, 1963.

Foote, Horton. *Harrison, Texas.* New York: Harcourt, Brace, 1956. Eight television plays written and produced in 1953 and 1954, including "A Trip to Bountiful."

_____. *Three Plays.* New York: Harcourt, Brace & World, 1962. Includes "Old Man," "Tomorrow," "Roots on a Parched Ground."

Gianakos, Larry James. *Television Drama Series Programming: A Comprehensive Chronicle.* Volume I (1947–59). Metuchen, New Jersey: Scarecrow, 1980; Volumes II–VI (1959–1986). Lanham, Maryland: Scarecrow, 1999. A primary reference that lists individually the dramas in most anthologies.

Gish, Lillian, with Ann Pinchot. *The Movies, Mr. Griffith, and Me.* New Jersey: Prentice-Hall, 1969.

Glut, Donald F., and Jim Harmon. *The Great Television Heroes.* New York: Doubleday, 1975.

Golden, Cipe Pineles, Kurt Weihs, and Robert Strunsky. *The Visual Craft of William Golden.* New York: George Braziller, 1962. Golden created the CBS Eye and other promotional materials during the 1950s.

Greenfield, Jeff. *Television: The First Fifty Years.* New York: Harry N. Abrams, 1977. A useful overview of television history, especially drama after the mid-1940s.

Griffith, Francis, J., and Joseph Mersand, eds. *One-Act Plays for Today.* New York: Globe, 1945.

Griffith, Richard, and Arthur Meyer. *The Movies: The Sixty-Year Story of the World of Hollywood and Its Effect on America, from Pre-Nickelodeon Days to the Present.* New York: Simon and Schuster, 1957. Many photographs.

Halliwell's Filmgoers Companion. New York: Charles Scribner's Sons, 1984.

Hailey, Arthur. *Close-Up on Writing for Television.* Garden City, New York: Doubleday, 1960. Includes six plays.

Harmon, Jim. *The Great Radio Heroes.* Garden City, New York: Doubleday, 1967. Has script excerpts.

Harris, Jay S., ed. *TV Guide: The First 25 Years.* New York: Simon and Schuster, 1978.

Hartnoll, Phyllis, ed. *The Oxford Companion to the Theatre.* Oxford, England: Oxford University Press, 1990.

Hatcher, Harlan, ed. *Modern Dramas.* New York: Harcourt, Brace, 1948.

Hawes, William. *American Television Drama: The Experimental Years.* Tuscaloosa: The University of Alabama Press, 1986. Covers television drama's origins in 1928 to 1946 and includes a list of all CBS, NBC, and relevant BBC dramas.

_____. *The Performer in Mass Media.* New York: Hastings House, 1976.

_____. *Public Television America's First Station*. Santa Fe, New Mexico: Sunstone Press, 1996. A history of KUHT(TV), Houston, Texas.

_____. *Television Performing. News and Information*. Boston, Massachusetts: Focal Press, 1991. Spanish, 1993; Chinese, 1999.

Head, Sydney W. *Broadcasting in America*. Boston, Massachusetts: Houghton Mifflin, 1972. Revised by other authors, 1998.

Heath, Eric. *Writing for Television*. Los Angeles: Research Publishing Company, 1950.

Houseman, John. *Run-through: A Memoir*. New York: Simon and Schuster, 1972. Discusses "The War of the Worlds" and *Playhouse 90*.

Hughes, Langston, and Milton Meltzer. *Black Magic: A Pictorial History of the Negro in American Entertainment*. Englewood Cliffs, New Jersey: Prentice-Hall, 1968. Few actors are listed for television; a radio chapter is included.

Husing, Ted. *Ten Years Before the Mike*. New York: Farrar and Rinehart, 1935.

Hutchinson, Thomas H. *Here Is Television: Your Window to the World*. New York: Hastings, 1950.

Journal of Broadcasting. This scholarly quarterly, which has been published since the mid-1950s, contains a few articles on drama.

Julian, Joseph. *This Was Radio: A Personal Memoir*. New York: Viking Press, 1975. Comments on 1930s–1940s radio and the McCarthy era.

Katz, Ephraim. *The Film Encyclopedia*. New York: Harper Perennial, 1994. The best and most extensive collection of brief biographies of those in film and television.

Kaufman, William I., ed. *The Best Television Plays of the Year*. New York: Merlin Press, 1950. In three volumes, completed 1954. Includes scripts from live anthologies, especially "Battleship Bismarck" for *Studio One*.

_____. *Best Television Plays 1957*. New York: Harcourt, Brace, 1957. Six plays including "Lee at Gettysburg" and "Requiem for a Heavyweight."

Kemper, Stanley. *Television Encyclopedia*. New York: Fairchild, 1948.

Knight, Arthur. *The Liveliest Art*. New York: Mentor, 1957. Includes a chapter on "The Challenge of Television."

Krampner, Jon. *The Man in the Shadows: Fred Coe and the Golden Age of Television*. New Brunswick, New Jersey: Rutgers University Press, 1998.

LaGuardia, Robert. *From Ma Perkins to Mary Hartman: The Illustrated History of Soap Operas*. New York: Ballantine, 1977.

Landry, Robert J. *This Fascinating Radio Business*. Indianapolis: Bobbs-Merrill, 1946.

Lass, A. H., Earle L. McGill, and Donald Axelrod, eds. *Plays from Radio*. Cambridge, Massachusetts: Houghton Mifflin, 1948.

Laurie, Joe Jr. *Vaudeville: From the Honky-Tonks to the Palace*. New York: Henry Holt, 1953.

Lichty, Lawrence, and Malachi C. Topping. *American Broadcasting: A Source Book on the History of Radio and Television*. New York: Hastings House, 1975. Primarily discusses radio drama; "Hollywood in the Television Age."

Life. This pictorial magazine has a few fine articles, 1948–1958.

Limbacher, James L., ed. *Haven't I Seen You Somewhere Before?: Remakes, Sequels, and Series in Motion Pictures and Television, 1896–1978*. Ann Arbor, Michigan: Pierian Press, c. 1980.

Lohr, Lenox R. *Television Broadcasting*. New York: McGraw-Hill, 1940.

Lowther, James B. *Dramatic Scenes from Athens to Broadway*. New York: Longmans, Green, 1937.

Lyons, Eugene. *David Sarnoff: A Biography*. New York: Harper and Row, 1966.

MacDonald, J. Fred. *Blacks and White TV: Afro-Americans in Television since 1948*. Chicago: Nelson-Hall, 1983.

Maltin, Leonard. *Movie and Video Guide 1995*. New York: Plume, 1994.

Mann, Delbert. "Remembering." A 1,200-page unpublished manuscript detailing his professional life. Los Angeles Directors Guild of America. Published as *Looking Back … at Live Television and Other Matters*, 1998.

Marill, Alvin H. *Movies Made for Television: The Telefeature and the Mini-Series 1964–1986*. New York: New York Zoetrope, 1987.

Mast, Gerald, and Bruce F. Kawin. *A Short History of the Movies*. A fine history from the director's perspective. Boston: Allyn and Bacon, 2000.

Matelski, Marilyn J. *The Soap Opera Evolution: America's Enduring Romance with Daytime Drama*. Jefferson, North Carolina: McFarland, 1988.

Meyers, Richard. *Super TV Stars*. New York: Drake, 1977. Discusses history of current primetime series. Illustrated.

Metz, Robert. *CBS: Reflections in a Bloodshot Eye*. Chicago: Playboy Press, 1975.

Michael, Paul, and James R. Parish, eds. *The Emmy Awards: A Pictorial History*. New York: Crown, 1970.

_____. *The American Movies Reference Book. The Sound Era*. Englewood Cliffs, New Jersey: Prentice-Hall, 1957. Lists actors' credits and picture credits. Illustrated.

Miller, Lee. *The Great Cowboy Stars of Movies & Television*. New Rochelle, New York: Arlington House, 1979. Part Two: "New Breed of Cowboy TV-Movie Star, 1950–1979." Brief biographies, credits. Photographs.

Millerson, Gerald. *The Technique of Television Production*. Boston: Focal Press, 1985. Perhaps the most widely distributed production book in the world, one of several books by a BBC-TV expert.

Miner, Worthington C. "A Report for the Columbia Broadcasting System on Twelve Years of Television." Typescript, c. 1942. This 500-page report provides complex details on many subjects regarding early CBS history, including dramas.

_____. "Look Back in Wonder." Typescript, c. 1980. An autobiography written with the assistance of Franklin J. Schaffner. Most of the material is included in *Worthington Miner Interviewed by Franklin J. Schaffner*. Metuchen, New Jersey: Scarecrow, 1985.

Mosel, Tad. *Other People's Houses*. New York: Simon and Schuster, 1956. Includes six plays with insightful comments.

The Museum of Television and Radio, New York. Formerly the Museum of Broadcasting. The museum archives post–1946 radio and television programs for research and public viewing. It has an audiotape of "Susan and God" (1938).

Nadel, Norman. *A Pictorial History of the Theatre Guild*. New York: Crown Publishers, 1969. Chapter VIII: "The Theatre Guild on Radio and Television" discusses United States Steel's *Theatre Guild on the Air*.

"NBC Television Code to Commercial Production Procedure." New York: National Broadcasting Company, 1946.

Newcomb, Horace, ed. *Television: The Critical View*. New York: Oxford University Press, 1987. A collection of previously published viewpoints by leading writers.

The New Republic. An important critical source for trends and drama reviews during the 1950s.

Newsweek. This magazine provides context, perspectives, and reviews of television dramas.

The New York Public Library. The Performing Arts Research Center at Lincoln Center has numerous original scripts, documents, and photographs.

The New York Times. A valuable source of articles, some reviews, and important commentary.

The New Yorker. Especially valuable for the insights of its television critics and reviewers during the 1950s.

Nickelodeon, cable television. Telecasts syndicated television series from the 1950s.

O'Meara, Carroll. *Television Program Production.* New York: Ronald Press, 1955. An NBC-TV veteran discusses production in detail.

"operation backstage. Staging Services Handbook of the NBC Television Network Operations Department." New York: The National Broadcasting Company, 1951.

Opotowsky, Stan. *TV: The Big Picture.* New York: E. P. Dutton, 1961. Chapter 9: "The Angry Young Men" discusses television writers.

Paley, William S. *As It Happened: A Memoir.* Garden City, New York: Doubleday, 1979. Details chronologically CBS programming events.

Parish, James Robert. *Actors' Television Credits, 1950–1972.* Metuchen, New Jersey: Scarecrow, 1973; 1948–1988. Lanham, Maryland: Scarecrow, Volume I (Actors), 1989 & Volume II (Actresses), 1990.

Perry, Jeb H. *Variety Obits: An Index to Obituaries in Variety, 1905–1978.* Metuchen, New Jersey: Scarecrow, 1980.

Phillips, David C., John M. Grogan, and Earl H. Ryan. *An Introduction to Radio and Television.* New York: Ronald Press, 1954. Includes excerpts from radio and television dramas, especially *The Plainclothes Man.*

Porterfield, John, and Kay Reynolds, eds. *We Present Television.* New York: W. W. Norton, 1940. A collection of articles written by prominent participants in television.

The Quarterly of Film Radio and Television. Berkeley and Los Angeles: University of California Press. Some scholarly articles on 1950s television dramas.

Quinlan, Sterling. *Inside ABC: American Broadcasting Company's Rise to Power.* New York: Hastings House, 1979. Contains a few references to ABC dramas.

Radio Annual. This trade directory published statistics and provided an annual review of radio from 1937 to 1964, includes some 1940s television information.

Radio News. Some of the articles deal with 1930s television.

"A Remembrance of 'Pappy,' Fred Coe 1914–1979." A booklet published by Delbert Mann, c. 1980. Includes comments from Coe's colleagues and friends, and photographs.

Roberts, Edward Barry. *Television Writing and Selling.* Boston: The Writer, 1960. Excerpts from *Armstrong Circle Theatre* and *Robert Montgomery Presents.*

Robertson, Patrick. *The Book of Firsts.* New York: Bramhall House, 1974. Includes a section on international firsts in television.

Rose, Reginald. *Six Television Plays.* New York: Simon and Schuster, 1956. Includes "Twelve Angry Men," "Crime in the Streets," and commentaries.

Ross, Gordon. *Television Jubilee. The Story of 25 Years of BBC Television.* London: W. H. Allen, 1961. Photographs.

Rothel, David. *Who Was That Masked Man? The Story of the Lone Ranger.* South Brunswick and New York: A. S. Barnes, 1976. A history of the Lone Ranger with the first radio script and many photographs.

Sarnoff, David. *The Wisdom of Sarnoff and the World of RCA*. Beverly Hills, California: Wisdom Books, 1978. A general history with comments.

The Saturday Review of Literature/The Saturday Review. Very helpful insights, some background, and drama reviews.

Seldes, Gilbert. *The Great Audience*. New York: Viking Press, 1951. Includes "Pandora's Box: Television."

Serling, Rod. *Patterns*. New York: Bantam Books, 1958. Includes four plays and commentary.

Settel, Irving, ed. *Top TV Shows of the Year, 1954–1955*. New York: Hastings House, 1955. Includes scripts and comments about Kraft and Goodyear theaters.

Settel, Irving. *A Pictorial History of Radio*. New York: Gossett and Dunlap, 1967.

Settel, Irving, and William Lass. *A Pictorial History of Television*. New York: Gossett and Dunlap, 1969. Mentions "Susan and God."

Settel, Trudy and Irving Settel. *The Best of Armstrong Circle Theatre*. New York: Citadel Press, 1959. Includes three dramas.

Sharp, Harold S., and Marjorie Z. Sharp. *Index to Characters in the Performing Arts, Part IV: Radio and Television*. Metuchen, New Jersey: Scarecrow, 1973.

Shapiro, Mitchell E. *Television Network Prime-Time Programming, 1948–1988*. Jefferson, North Carolina: McFarland, 1989. Lists programs and schedules.

Shayon, Robert Lewis. *Open to Criticism*. Boston: Beacon Press, 1971.

Shulman, Arthur, and Roger Youman. *How Sweet It Was: Television — A Pictorial Commentary*. New York: Shorecrest, 1966. Chapter VI includes fine photographs of anthologies; VII & VIII are about detective shows and Westerns.

_____. *The Television Years*. New York: Popular Library, 1973. Year-to-year photographs of television programs.

Skutch, Ira. *The Days of Live. Television's Golden Age as Seen by 21 Directors Guild of America Members*. Lanham, Maryland: Scarecrow, 1998

Slater, Robert. *This ... Is CBS: A Chronicle of 60 Years*. Englewood Cliffs, New Jersey: Prentice-Hall, 1988.

Sobel, Bernard, ed. *The Theatre Handbook and Digest of Plays*. New York: Crown, 1950.

Standards of Practice for American Broadcasters, effective July 1, 1948. Washington, D.C.: The National Association of Broadcasters, 1948.

Stasheff, Edward, and Rudy Bretz. *The Television Program. Its Writing, Direction and Production*. New York: A. A. Wyn, Incorporated, 1951. Illustrations and drawings show 1940s techniques, including the "Bretzbox."

Stedman, Raymond. *The Serials: Suspense and Drama by Installment*. Norman: University of Oklahoma Press, 1971.

Sterling, Christopher H., and John M. Kittross. *Stay Tuned: A Concise History of American Broadcasting*. Belmont, California: Wadsworth, 1978.

Televiser. This magazine published excellent articles and reviews of 1940s dramas.

Television. This magazine is an indispensable source for information and drama reviews from 1944 to 1968.

Television Factbook. A major data source and directory since it began publication in 1945.

Television Quarterly. The Journal of the National Academy of Television Arts and Sciences. A noteworthy issue was "Television's Silver Anniversary: A Retrospective View," Fall 1972.

Terrace, Vincent. *The Complete Encyclopedia of Television Programs*. Vol. (A–K); Vol. II (L–Z). South Brunswick and New York: A. S. Barnes, 1976; 1980.

_____. *Television Specials: 3,201 Entertainment Spectaculars, 1939 through 1993.* Jefferson, North Carolina: McFarland, 1995.

_____. *Experimental Television, Test Films, Pilots and Trial Series, 1925 through 1995: Seven Decades of Small Screen Almosts.* Jefferson, North Carolina: McFarland, 1997.

Theatre Arts Monthly. Occasional fine articles from the 1930s to the 1960s described television dramas.

"This Is CBS Television City." Hollywood, California: CBS Press Information, November 1952.

Thomey, Ted. *The Glorious Decade.* New York: Ace Books, 1971. Impressions of 1950s anthologies and series dramas.

Time. This weekly magazine had many articles and reviews in almost every issue from 1947 to 1959.

"20th Anniversary of CBS Television: An Account of the Pioneering and Progress of CBS-TV since July 21, 1931." New York: CBS Press Information, 10 July 1951.

Udelson, Joseph H. *The Great Television Race: A History of the American Television Industry, 1925–1941.* Tuscaloosa: The University of Alabama Press, 1982. Details television's early business development.

Variety. A major source of news, features, and reviews after 1938.

Vidal, Gore. *Best Television Plays.* New York: Ballantine, 1956. Eight dramas, including "Man on the Mountain Top."

_____. *Visit to a Small Planet.* Boston: Little, Brown, 1956.

Wade, Robert J. *Designing for Television: The Arts and Crafts in Television Production.* New York: Pellegrini and Cudahay, 1952. Contains photographs and designs of many experimental-period productions.

Whelan, Kenneth. *How the Golden Age of Television Turned My Hair to Silver: The Mad Memories of an Ex-Television Director.* New York: Wacker, 1973. Chapter 9: "The Seven-Day Wonders or the Dramatic Show Director and His Woes."

Wilk, Max. *The Golden Age of Television: Notes from the Survivors.* New York: Delacorte, 1976. Chapters on *Ford Television, Studio One, Mama, Suspense, The Web, Danger,* and *Philco Television Playhouse.*

Williams, Tennessee. *Tennessee Williams: Memoirs.* Garden City, New York: Doubleday, 1983.

Winick, Charles. *Taste and the Censor in Television.* New York: Fund for the Republic, 1959. A summary of current views.

WNBT Television Master Programs. New York: National Broadcasting Company, 1941–1952. This master log lists programs, casts, some scripts and set designs, and comments. Preserved on microfilm at NBC and RCA.

W2XBS Television Master Programs. New York: National Broadcasting Company, 1936–1941. This master log lists programs, casts, some scripts and set designs, and comments. The typed original master program materials have been destroyed, but most of the pertinent information is on microfilm at NBC and RCA.

Wright, Basil. *The Long View: An International History of Cinema.* Great Britain: Paladin, 1976. A unique perspective by one of the great documentary filmmakers.

The Writer/The Writer's Market. A magazine and annual publication that provides useful articles, series summaries, and market updates for script writers.

Wylie, Max. *Radio and Television Writing*. New York: Rinehart, 1958. Includes excerpts from several radio shows.

Yoakem, Lola Goelet. *TV and Screen Writing*. Berkeley and Los Angeles: University of California Press, 1958. Members of the Writers Guild of America discuss programs.

Index